# THE AMERICAN ALPINE JOURNAL 1999

*Steve House on the first ascent of* The Gift (That Keeps on Giving), *Mt. Bradley, Alaska.*
MARK F. TWIGHT

COVER: *The unclimbed Hainablak East Tower and "Cat's Ears Spire" on front, with Uli Biaho (and portrait of the artist) on back, Pakistan Karakoram.* KENNAN HARVEY

*Rich Prohaska at Camp II on the first ascent of the Lauchlan Ridge, Mt. King George, Canada.*
JIA CONDON

ABOVE: *Steph Davis on pitch 22, Inshallah, Shipton Spire.* KENNAN HARVEY

LEFT: *Dean Potter on the first completely mad ascent of the Regular Route, Half Dome.* HEINZ ZAK

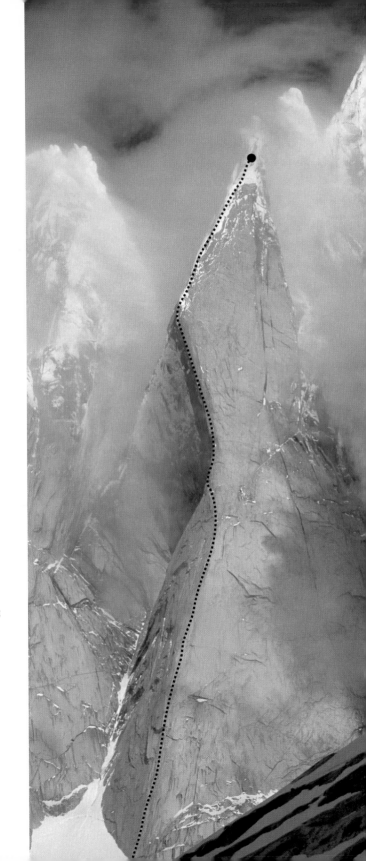

# THE AMERICAN
# ALPINE JOURNAL

710 Tenth Street, Suite 140
Golden, Colorado 80401
Telephone: (303) 384 0110
Fax: (303) 384 0111
E-mail address:
aaj@americanalpineclub.org

PHOTO: *The northwest
arête of the west pillar
of Punta Herron,
Argentine Patagonia,
showing* La Giocanda.
ERMANNO SALVATERRA

ISSN 0065-6925

ISBN 0-930410-84-X

©1999

The American Alpine Club.

# THE AMERICAN ALPINE JOURNAL

## VOLUME 41      1999      ISSUE 73

## CONTENTS

---

The American Alpine Journal artists:
Mike Clelland • Gardner Heaton
David Horowitz • John Svenson
Clay Wadman

# THE AMERICAN ALPINE JOURNAL

Christian Beckwith, *Editor*

**Advisory Board**
John E. (Jed) Williamson, *Managing Editor*; Michael Kennedy, Steven Swenson

**Editorial Assistants**
Paul Horton, Steve (Crusher) Bartlett

**Associate Editors**
Geoff Tabin, M.D., *Mountain Medicine;* Brent Bishop & Chris Naumann, *The Mountain Environment*;
David Stevenson, *Reviews;* Frederick O. Johnson, *Club Activities*;
David Harrah & Angus Thuermer, Jr., *In Memoriam*

**Translators**
Aude Iung-Lancrey, Susanne Schenck & John Mudd, *French*;
Yuri Kolomiets, Natasha Lagovskaya & Heather Williamson, *Russian*;
Emanuele Pellizari, *Italian*; Margaret Thompson & Robyn Fulwiler, *Spanish*; Christiane Leitinger, *German*

**Indexer**
Jessica Kany

**Regional Contacts**
Charlie Sassara, *Wrangell-St. Elias*; Joe Josephson, *Canadian Rockies*; Steve Schneider, *Yosemite*;
Alan Bartlett, *Sierra Nevada*; Yossi Brain, *Bolivia*; Evelio Echevarría, *South America*;
Hernan Jofre, *Chilean Patagonia*; Rolando Garibotti, *Argentine Patagonia*; Damien Gildea, *Antarctica;*
Bill Ruthven, *United Kingdom*; Jean-Marc Clerc, *France;* Franci Savenc, *Slovenia*; Vladimir Linek,
*Slovakia*; Vladimir Shataev, *C.I.S.*; Vladimir Kopylov, *C.I.S.*; Harish Kapadia, *India*; Elizabeth Hawley,
*Nepal*; Asem Mustafa Awan, *Pakistan;* Sasaki Kazuyuki, *Japan*

**With additional thanks to**
Richard Abendroth, Carrie Asby, Irene Beardsley, Michelle Bevier, Billy Beckwith, John Brecher, Dave
Briggs, Antonella Cicogna, Otto Chkhetiani, Nick Clinch, Jia Condon, Liana Darenskaya, Bernard
Domenech, Forest Dramis, Yuri Ermachek, Charlie Fowler, Antonella Giocomini, Lindsay Griffin, Renny
Jackson, Latham Jenkins, Hans & Nancy Johnstone, David Keaton, Erwan Le Lann, Sam Lightner, Jr.,
Charlie Mace, Dan Mazur, Jim McCarthy, Chris McNamara, Eliza Moran, Greg Mortenson, Alison Osius,
Phil Powers, Kath Pyke, Robert Plucenik, Mark Richey, Galen Rowell, Marcello Sanguineti, Christian
Santelices, Filip Silhan, Ashley Simpson, Margaret Thompson, Jon Turk, Mark Twight, Alexander Volegov,
Clay Wadman, Ed Webster, Rick Wilcox, Ken Wilson, Annette Yuan


# FRIENDS OF THE
# AMERICAN ALPINE JOURNAL

The following provided financial support for Volume 41 of The American Alpine Journal:

Yvon Chouinard
Ann Carter
Vern and Marion Read
New York Section of the AAC
The North Face
Peter McGann, M.D.
Gregory Miller

The H. Adams Carter Endowment Fund
for The American Alpine Journal

# THE AMERICAN ALPINE CLUB

## OFFICIALS FOR THE YEAR 1999
*Directors ex-officio

# Preface

The discerning reader will note that relatively little information on 8000-meter peaks is recorded in the 1999 volume. This is not indicative of a fall-off in the amount of activity on the world's highest mountains; as with other disciplines of climbing, the numbers of people on the 8000ers have gone up in the last few years, apparently increased, of all things, by the 1996 Everest tragedy and the ensuing media attention on mountaineering at the highest altitudes. Rather, the majority of ascents on 8000-meter peaks in 1998 were via normal routes, and they were largely comprised of commercial expeditions. There were exceptions, of course: witness Masafumi Todaka's solitary adventures on Everest's north face in the post-monsoon and the Russian attempt on the Lhotse massif's middle summit, the world's highest unclimbed point. But it seems clear that activity on the big peaks is shifting. Strong Himalayan climbers are trying to climb all 14 8000ers or are availing themselves of the opportunity to guide. The testpieces of a generation ago are becoming today's normal routes as more and more "regular" climbers venture to the high Himalaya for 8000-meter experiences of their own. For now, at least, the focus on exploratory climbing up high seems to have ebbed.

Other areas, meanwhile, are receiving more attention. This is part of climbing's evolution: there are always ebbs and flows as different aspects of climbing develop at different times. The 1950s and '60s saw the first ascents of the 8000-meter peaks, the Golden Age of Yosemite developed free and aid climbing techniques that were then exported to rock climbs in remote corners of the world, and in the '70s and '80s the aesthetic, bold "magic lines" were ticked on the highest mountains. Now, climbing's edge is being pushed on the lower peaks by pioneers fully aware of where such climbing might lead them—and later, the rest of us—in the years to come.

Alex and Thomas Huber were at the forefront again in 1998, heightening the free climbing buzz in Yosemite with their 30-pitch, 5.13c *El Niño*, a route established four months after Alex topped out on the 8201-meter Cho Oyu. Steve House continued his alpine tour de force in Alaska and Canada with ascents on Mt. Bradley, King Peak, and in the Canadian Rockies, and as we go to press he travels with a predominantly American team to try a new route on Gasherbrum IV. Kennan Harvey, Steph Davis and Seth Shaw took their talents to Shipton Spire, where their brilliant vision of onsighting a new free route resulted in the 36-pitch *Inshallah*—only ten feet of which was aid. Yasushi Yamanoi's futuristic climbing was again on display with his solo ascent of the east face of Kasum Kanguru, a trekking peak in Nepal. In Pakistan's Hushe region, no less than six teams were active on granite spires that literally lay at the feet of mountains coveted by past generations. Climbers from Rampikino Maspes to Marko Prezelj are calling such climbing today's modern alpinism: with no objectives, no permits, no information at all, you just go, see, and climb—to which we might add, at quite high standards.

Climbing's insatiable curiosity obviously has not abated. From Kyrgyzstan to Africa, new areas continue to be "discovered" as climbers wander farther afield in search of untouched ground. Most of the new terrain consists primarily of rock climbing objectives (Andringitra National Park in Madagascar, the Mt. Trinidad area near Cochamo, Chile, Mexico's El Gigante). This will continue to be the case in the years to come, as it is simply more likely to discover rock walls than it is to find high but overlooked mountains. That being said, politi-

in countries such as Tadjikistan and Afghanistan are saving fine new peaks for future generations. China continues to yield treasures, mainly to Japanese expeditions but also to veteran explorers like Chris Bonington. That other British lion, Doug Scott, gave proof that more remain waiting when he plucked the first ascent of Drohmo, a gem at the base of Kangchenjunga. Fred Beckey was in Canada, Alaska, and China in the last few years, ever searching, ever discovering. Will the passion of climbing's elders never abate?

We hope so. It is precisely this passion that served us in 1998, as access to our climbing areas came under heavier attack than at any time in our history. Who led the defense? "Lifers," long-term climbers who have climbed year after year and are now giving back to climbing in its time of need, that's who. They included people like Alison Osius and Michael Kennedy, who brought their experience and love of climbing to our political arms as they  became the presidents of The American Alpine Club and The Access Fund respectively. Tom Frost continued his amazing fight to save Camp 4. Nick Clinch, Jim McCarthy and Lou Reichardt were all deeply involved in the battles that seemed to come at us without relent. Just as climbing evolves in its different arenas at different times, so, too, do many climbers evolve within the boundaries of their love for climbing, adapting to changing bodies and outlooks to stay involved. It was impressive, and inspirational, and with many of our older climbers leading the way, the American climbing community galvanized as never before. While access issues were the most pressing development in American climbing in 1998, climbers working effectively together to address these issues was arguably the most interesting.

What are the new challenges teaching us as a community? Wherever you go in the American climbing scene today, you are almost certain to hear sentiments indicative of a growing self-consciousness as a user group, and one that understands its obligations at that. Our ever-greater numbers bring growing opportunities to turn one's love of climbing into a viable livelihood, be it guiding the Himalayan giants, writing and photographing for the periodicals, or making a livelihood from climbing businesses. Concomitant with the new opportunities are responsibilities to the welfare of climbing itself. There is a certain danger of undermining climbing's long-term well-being in exchange for individual gain, but the best among us—climbers like this volume's contributors Chris McNamara, Greg Mortenson, and Geoff Tabin—are showing that we can give something back to the land, the crags, and the people we influence. This gives hope that our future will be one of a strong stewardship of our wild places, balanced as we are and as we need to be between an appreciation of the deepest returns from their use and a wise and reasonable approach to how they should be administered. And if we can continue to impart that to the generations to come, our future will be one that honors the deepest and best motives for our climbing.

For all the attention given the matter over the years, very little consensus has been achieved on what exactly the point of climbing *is* beyond the enjoyment we derive from it as individuals. So we might do well here to borrow a line from the 1999 British Mountaineering Council's Winter Climbing Meet: have fun, but try not to mess up the place.

CHRISTIAN BECKWITH

# Access and the Politics of Climbing

## A long-simmering stew

by Michael Kennedy, *President, The Access Fund*

When the history of climbing in the United States in the last two decades of the 20th century is written, 1998 will likely go down as a watershed year, not so much for technical breakthroughs in the mountains or brilliant performances on the crags, but for the fact that this was the year when a long-simmering stew of issues finally came to the forefront of the American climber's consciousness. Loosely categorized under the rubric of "access," these questions of where we climb and the methods we employ will continue to haunt our "sport" (although I hesitate to use that term) for many years to come.

In June, the Forest Service banned the use of fixed anchors in all Wilderness areas under its jurisdiction, arguing that pins, nuts, slings, and bolts left in place by climbers are "installations" similar in character to roads, dams, landing strips, and radio towers. In September, the National Park Service released a climbing management plan for City of Rocks National Reserve, Idaho, that made permanent (after a five-year moratorium) the outright closure of the Twin Sisters to climbing and all other use because it lies within the "historic viewshed" of the California Trail. Meanwhile, the Texas Parks and Wildlife Department imposed such draconian restrictions on climbing at Hueco Tanks that this state park, once the world's preeminent winter bouldering area, was virtually abandoned by climbers.

1998 was also the year in which American climbers rose to the challenge more than ever before in fighting these and many other climbing-related battles. Although it didn't involve closing down an area or restricting climbing, the fight to preserve Camp 4 in Yosemite, initiated and financed entirely by climbers, was a powerful example of activism that put the National Park Service and other federal land management agencies on notice that climbers were a force to be reckoned with. Similarly, within a few months of the announcement of the fixed-anchor ban, a coalition of climbing organizations and outdoor industry notables had galvanized the efforts of mainstream environmental groups, local and national politicians, and hundreds of individual climbers, and convinced the Forest Service to rescind its system-wide fixed anchor ban, at least temporarily. (It is important to note that fixed anchors are still prohibited in the Sawtooth Wilderness, Idaho, an action that sets a troubling precedent.) The Forest Service also initiated a "negotiated rulemaking" process in which climbers, the agency, environmental groups, and other interested parties will (theoretically) come up with a consensus-based plan for managing fixed anchors in Wilderness. (As of mid-May, this group had yet to meet.) In November, the Access Fund, acting on behalf of nine individual climbers, filed a lawsuit against the National Park Service demanding that the Twin Sisters closure be lifted. Unfortunately, ongoing attempts to ease the restrictions at Hueco Tanks have so far produced less encouraging results. All these issues are still to be resolved, but at the very least we've gotten the agencies' attention and let them know that climbers won't take such actions lying down.

Make no mistake about it, though: closures and restrictions like those mentioned above, as well as the increasing number of user fees and permits aimed at climbers and the emergence of solitude as a guiding principle in Wilderness management, herald the dawn of an era in which climbing is in grave danger of being marginalized and perhaps even regulated out of existence. As our numbers have grown, so too have our physical and social impacts and our visibility as a user group. There are powerful and often subtle forces at work, both within our community and outside it, that have transformed, and continue to transform, not just how we act as climbers but how we think about climbing. The climbing world five or ten or 20 years hence will be vastly different from the one we inhabit right now, as will be our relationships with land managers, fellow climbers, and other users of public lands. Whether the changes we've already seen and the ones bearing down on us are good or bad depends on your point of view, but the direction these changes take is still up to us.

For much of this century, climbers have operated at the fringes of American culture. Climbing was something you did when you were young and restless. You learned the ropes from other climbers, much as an apprentice learns from a master, and toiled in obscurity at your craft. It was a harmless enough diversion that would eventually give way to the adult pursuit of work, marriage, mortgages, and children. Those who shunned such norms in favor of a lifetime of road trips (Fred Beckey comes to mind) or who were brilliant and driven enough to advance the standards of the day (Royal Robbins, Jim Bridwell) were lionized by a small and relatively close-knit climbing community. To society at large, though, climbers were seen as vagabonds in pursuit of an incomprehensible and vaguely foolish Holy Grail— if they were noticed at all.

In large measure, too, climbers were paid scant attention by land managers and others concerned with the stewardship of our public lands. When I started climbing in 1970, you had to have a doctor's note for some climbs (like Denali), or comply with silly rules involving helmets and climbing a particular route to prove your expertise (at Devil's Tower), but we were largely beneath land managers' radar screens. No one outside the climbing tribe had much to do with telling you when or where or how to climb, what type of or how much gear you could use. Inexorably grounded in the tradition of exploration, the rules of climbing, though often as strict and unforgiving as the rock itself, were codified and enforced by climbers alone. This state of benign neglect was a perfect fit for an activity like climbing, especially when our numbers were small and our impacts, both social and physical, could be either ignored or simply went unnoticed.

Starting in the 1980s, though, something curious happened: climbing became popular. Better equipment and clothing made traditional climbing and mountaineering less risky and more comfortable, enhancing their innate attractiveness. By emphasizing the gymnastic and reducing risks still further, sport climbing helped open climbing to the masses, with climbing gyms providing a convenient entry point. Power drills made it feasible to climb on numerous previously unattractive cliffs. Information about climbing became readily and quickly available via magazines, guidebooks, videos, and web sites. Climbing schools and guide services, once rare, became nearly ubiquitous, offering an efficient path to the mastery of once-arcane techniques. The climbing and outdoor industries grew in size and clout. The media shone its bright spotlight on our world, and climbing became an icon of the newly legitimate pursuit of adventure in the American cultural landscape. To be a climber today means you no longer have to answer a question like, "How do you get the rope up there?" You're more likely to be asked how you feel about guiding on Everest, or whether the X-Games portrays what climbing is really all about. In short, climbing in 1999 is hip, sexy, and, dare I say it, even respectable.

Of course, much of this is a gross oversimplification. American climbing has always had its upright citizens and its renegades, its visionaries and its derelicts, and society's view of our activities has never been quite so black-and-white as I've portrayed here. An aura of danger and mystery has always surrounded climbing, and pundits have historically been quick to point out the essential irresponsibility of our activity and the unreasonable burden it places on public resources. This is most obvious when it comes to the issue of safety: witness the outcry in 1992 when 11 climbers were killed in a single season on Denali, and the relative ease with which the current $150-per-person "registration fee" was imposed a few years later. (Tellingly, the National Park Service originally proposed a $500 "rescue fee" for Denali climbers, but backed off because of concerns over liability and the "duty to rescue" implied by such a fee. Many, myself included, view the current fee as a thinly-disguised effort to charge a targeted group—climbers—for rescues without actually saying so.)

Increasingly, though, it is the physical and social impacts of climbing that have become the targets of criticism. Anyone who has been around longer than a few years can attest to the fact that today any popular climbing area is more crowded, more frequently, than ever before. This reflects simple math. The number of climbers in the United States has probably tripled since 1985. That's my own conservative, seat-of-the-pants estimate, based on the fact that the circulation of *Climbing* magazine grew more than three-fold between 1987 and 1997. Assuming, for argument's sake, that one in ten climbers buys *Climbing*, you end up with 500,000 climbers in the United States right now versus maybe 150,000 in 1985. I suspect that most manufacturers, retailers, guidebook publishers, climbing schools, and land managers would peg the numbers much higher.

The pace at which new climbing areas and new routes in existing areas are discovered and developed has also increased dramatically—just look at the guidebook section in your local shop or in Chessler's mail-order catalogue. But really good climbing resources are still relatively rare. New mountains don't suddenly arise from the forest, and while climbers are ingenious and persistent in their quest for new rock and ice to explore, very few places offer the combination of quality, ambience, and accessibility that even an average climbing area requires. Well-known crags and mountains that are adequately documented in guidebooks and convenient to major population centers or worthy as destinations in their own right have inevitably borne the brunt of an increasing climbing population.

Whatever the actual number of new climbers, new routes, and new areas, we've seen a lot of growth in a relatively short period of time. And with that growth comes all the impacts associated with greater use: eroded trails, human waste, vegetation loss on and around the cliffs, trash, and conflicts with other user groups, to name only the most obvious. With very few exceptions, climbing resources lie on public lands that we share with many other people. Human-powered activities like hiking, backcountry skiing, mountain biking, backpacking, and kayaking create their own unique needs and impacts, and they've all become more popular. Ditto with ski areas and windshield tourism, snowmobiling and dirt biking, horseback riding and bird watching. There aren't only more climbers, there are more people, period, using and sometimes abusing our state and national parks and forests. We all think we're special, and we're all competing for our share of a limited pie.

It should come as no surprise, then, that decisions about where and how we climb are no longer being made by climbers alone. Indeed, climbing policy has become subject to the same bureaucratic inertia and compromise, the same power struggles between competing interests, and the same quasi-backroom deals to which so much else in our culture is beholden. In short, it's politics as usual.

That's not to say there is some grand, anti-climbing plan being hatched in the labyrinthine halls of the Forest Service, or that a secret cabal of rabid environmentalists at the Department of Interior is out to "get" climbers. In the past ten years we've come under ever-greater scrutiny from land managers, environmental groups, and a public concerned with the fate of our wild lands, but however gratifying conspiracy theories might be, the truth is far more complex.

Climbers have unquestionably found themselves at odds with the small but influential faction within the land management and environmental communities that regards virtually all human use as detrimental to resource and/or historic values. This viewpoint bolsters the argument that fixed anchors are illegal under the Wilderness Act (since any resource impact, however inconsequential, is suspect), and reinforces the closure of Twin Sisters for historic preservation reasons (this despite that agency's own study concluding that climbers had no significant impact on the historic value of the formation). For these zealots, the only way to save public lands is to eliminate impacts entirely. One way to do that is by simply keeping people out, which has largely been the effect of the Hueco Tanks climbing management plan. The recent attempt by the Forest Service to severely limit the number of climbers on Mount Hood, Oregon, by defining solitude as the critical Wilderness value worthy of protection is yet another indication that the arch-preservationist faction is one we'll be battling for the foreseeable future.

Other more subtle factors, though, have had far greater influence on climbing's fate. Chief among these is the simple fact that land management agencies are bureaucracies, and it is the nature of any bureaucracy to perpetuate itself. One way to do this is by favoring activities that serve large constituencies, because wide popular support invariably leads to continued political and economic sustenance. If these activities are economically beneficial to the surrounding communities, or the agency itself, all the better. Land managers also pay the closest attention to those who speak the most forcefully for their interests. As the old adage goes, "The squeaky wheel gets the grease."

Climbers have faced new restrictions in the recent past—and we'll face even more in the future—mostly because our numbers, while growing, are still relatively small. Climbers' economic impacts are poorly documented, but are certainly dwarfed by those of hikers, bikers, skiers, horseback riders, and windshield tourists. While much of what drives climbing policy today is based on an inaccurate picture of what climbers actually do, the true impacts, costs, and management requirements of climbing are rarely viewed in comparison with those of other user groups. The sense that climbing is a dangerous and frivolous activity undoubtedly makes many people less than sympathetic to our needs. (That's one reason there's been no public uproar about the Denali fee.) We have often compounded these political and economic disadvantages by our infighting and our reluctance to band together to protect our common interests.

This at least partly explains why the Forest Service tried to ban the use of fixed anchors in Wilderness, and why the restrictions on climbing in Hueco Tanks, Texas, are now so severe. In both cases, climbing was seen as an easy target. (You can imagine the outcry if backcountry camping or horseback riding were prohibited outright in national forest Wilderness, or if you had to have a ranger accompany your car-camping group at a Colorado state park.) The Forest Service has discovered, to its chagrin, that climbers aren't as powerless and politically naïve as they appear, but this is no cause for celebration. We still have a long and difficult road ahead on the fixed anchor issue, and the outcome is far from certain. And the prospects at Hueco, dismal as they may be right now, should only cause us to redouble our efforts there.

It's far easier to prohibit or limit an activity than to manage it effectively, which brings up another key attribute of a bureaucracy: the need to exert control over its domain. For a land manager, that first means having the authority to define what visitors do, and when, where, how, and sometimes even why they do it. It then means being able to come up with black-and-white rules to keep people in line. Bureaucrats tend to look for a common norm they can build these rules around, which helps explain why land managers have a hard time understanding, for example, the need for new routes. If a given crag already has ten routes, what need is there for another? Why not just climb an already existing route? Why climb a mountain two or three times by different routes if you can get the same view from the top by going up the easiest way? Climbers and their actions don't fit into neat little boxes, and that makes the bureaucratic mind very uncomfortable. Combine all this with the fact that the staff, equipment, and budget resources to promulgate and enforce these rules are almost always in short supply, and it becomes clear why the land manager tends to favor simple and inexpensive management prescriptions. His job is going to be a lot easier if his "customers" don't stray too far from the beaten path, as climbers are wont to do.

In many ways, then, the ideal visitor to our national parks and forests seems destined to become the windshield tourist who drives in, snaps a photo at the scenic overlook, buys a few trinkets at the visitors' center, and leaves—that is, someone who abides by the rules and does what he's told. That's hardly the picture of the archetypal climber, which begs the question: How do we avoid a future of ever-increasing regulation in response to our ever-greater numbers, thereby preserving the freedom that is at the heart and soul of climbing?

We can start by recognizing that climbers have a legitimate interest in how public lands are managed and further, that no one is going to represent our concerns unless we do so ourselves. That means we have to join and support organizations like the Access Fund, the American Alpine Club, and the many local and regional groups that are working hard to ensure climbers' continued freedom. It also means meeting with land managers, writing to your political representatives, and encouraging fellow climbers to participate in the minutiae of climbing management. Only by working together can we stay one step ahead of those who would unjustly limit our use of public lands.

We must also become more cognizant of the impacts associated with climbing and more assertive in mitigating or preventing them. That means volunteering for trail work and chalk clean-ups, picking up trash, and generally being good stewards of our wild lands. It means treating other users with respect; at the very least, we can lower the volume on our boom boxes, tone down our tantrums, and otherwise recognize that the hikers and birdwatchers and families around us have just as much right to be there as we do. We'll also have to be amenable to reasonable restrictions on climbing based on objective criteria and political reality. I may not like the "voluntary" closure of Devils Tower in June each year, or the fixed-anchor restrictions in the new Joshua Tree Backcountry and Wilderness Management Plan, but I'll support both because the alternatives are far worse.

Contrary to climbing's maverick culture and history, it will be critically important for us to reinforce our ability to police our own actions. Management prescriptions that preserve the core values of climbing will only work if climbers can control their worst impulses. Elite climbers, guides, shop owners, manufacturers, writers, photographers, editors, and publishers all bear a huge responsibility in this arena. We'll have to become less selfish and more community-oriented. We'll have to take a critical look at our sometimes-excessive use of fixed anchors, our willingness to aggressively garden and clean routes, and all the other less-than-savory practices in which climbers engage. We can no longer ignore the "dark side" of climbing, nor should we. At times, that's going to mean criticizing climbers whose actions harm the collective good. Climbers are simply going to have to grow up.

All this isn't going to be easy. Climbers are by nature independent, even unruly. All climbing involves variables—weather and conditions, the specific architecture of the crag or mountain, the emotions and physiology of the climbers themselves—that can't be quantified and are difficult if not impossible to regulate in a traditional bureaucratic manner. Climbing demands a high level of initiative, vision, ingenuity, and risk. It obliges us to engage in an intimate relationship with the natural world and to clearly recognize and accept our own mortality as an integral part of that association. The freedom to make our own choices and the concomitant responsibility to accept the consequences of our actions are central to the ethos of climbing and deeply ingrained in our history, mythology, and practice—indeed, they are inseparable from the meaning of climbing itself. If we continue to cultivate a climbing community that is politically active, engaged, and informed, we will, I hope, be able to say the same thing five or ten or 20 years from now.

John Svenson

# 8000 Meters and More

## Working out the moves on the routes of the new millennium

by Alexander Huber, *Germany*

As we climb into the next millennium, we might ask ourselves, where is our sport going? The end of the 20th century gives us a welcome opportunity to discuss the question, but I doubt that the answer will be found easily. It's hard to predict where climbing is going because it depends on each individual and the evolution of his or her personal style. For example, if I look at how my own mountaineering has evolved, I bet nobody could have predicted its direction.

In the early 1990s, sport climbing was my special interest, and I put 100% of my energy into it. The result was the first ascent of several routes that marked the upper end of the scale. After my first 9a (5.14d) in 1992, I managed to establish four more routes at the 8c+/9a grade over the next two years, but none of these routes was harder than the first.

To be "state of the art" in sport climbing for years is very hard work for your mind as well as your body. After years of consistent training, it's difficult to maintain motivation for goals that are more or less repetitions of things you've already achieved. Such feelings are poisonous for a climber's motivation. Thus, after ten years climbing and mountaineering in the Alps, I found myself searching for a new way—a search that, in 1995, led me out of Europe for the first time.

As a climbing mecca, Yosemite was at the top of my hit list and the first stop on the journey. The Valley is the birthplace of free climbing and, furthermore, of big wall climbing in America. The combination of these two disciplines was precisely what I was looking for when I made the free ascent of the *Salathé* in 1995.

The next stop was Asia, or more precisely, Pakistan, for "El Cap on top of Denali:" the west face of Latok II. In 1995, my attempt on the face failed due to bad weather, but in 1997, I came back with my brother Thomas, Toni Gutsch and the well-known American, Conrad Anker. After working consistently above 6000 meters for nearly two weeks on a vertical big wall, we topped out at the 7108-meter summit plateau.

Big wall climbing had never been transferred to peaks higher than the Great Trango Tower. With the ascent of the west face of Latok II, we pushed the limits, but it won't be the end of the evolution. Bagging 8000ers, sport climbing, big wall climbing on El Capitan: after a breathtaking start, the evolution of these disciplines has consistently plateaued. The same is not true for all-around mountaineering. It is just at the start of mixing the disciplines of sport climbing, mixed climbing, big walling and high-altitude alpinism together. The ascent of the west face of Latok II was simply a landmark along the path that will lead climbing into the next millennium: the combination of different disciplines at their highest levels.

A glance down the path reveals that big wall climbing will be transferred to higher altitudes and to the highest mountains of the world in the future. It's one of climbing's most interesting objectives—and, of course, a great challenge for me, too.

But, without taking too high a risk, you cannot ascend your first 8000er with a big wall; it is helpful and sensible to initially get experience with the magic 8000 meters on a normal

*Georg Simair and Alex Huber (right) high on Cho Oyu. What will the new millennium bring for world climbing?* HORST FANKHAUSER

route. For this reason, I focused on Cho Oyu via the Tichy route from the Tibet side. Cho Oyu is regarded as an easy 8000er, and, in fact, the technical difficulties are not greater than on the classic normal routes of 4000ers in the Alps. Nevertheless, for me, having never been higher than Latok II, the sixth highest mountain was a necessary experience. During the ascent I could feel that, even given the absence of technical difficulties, climbing at high altitude is a dangerous game that requires a high amount of good sense.

On May 18, at 12 noon, eight hours after starting from Camp II at 7000 meters, I was atop Cho Oyu with the German Barbara Hirschbichler and Austrians Georg Simair and Horst Fankhauser. The latter saw his first ascent of an 8000er at the age of 55, 27 years after surviving a bivouac under open skies at 8000 meters during Reinhold Messner's tragic 1972 Manaslu south face expedition. Five days later, I was back in Berchtesgaden, my home in the very south of Germany. And with good reason. Each day at high altitude lowers the body's resources, and I just didn't want to lose too much power to too long a stay at Cho Oyu's 5800-meter base camp.

Generally, free climbing and high altitude mountaineering are very contrary. Free climbing is a sport that requires mainly explosive power, while one needs a lot of endurance to be successful at high altitude. Climbing an 8000er causes a horrendous drop in explosive power, and to return to one's previous level in free climbing requires a high amount of discipline.

Of course, with the ascent of Cho Oyu I took a big gamble of not getting back into shape quickly enough for the next goal: a free ascent of one of the major big wall routes on El Capitan. But, on the other hand, it was a great challenge to make a free ascent on the famous *North American Wall* four months after being atop an 8000er.

On September 3, I was back in the Valley, this time with my brother Thomas as partner. Our first stop was the famous El Cap Meadows. Through binoculars we inspected the possibility of a free line on the southeast face, the "right side" of El Capitan. Crazy!

The *North American Wall* had seen several free attempts in recent years, but none could find climbable features on the lower section. Then, in 1997, Conrad Anker, Kevin Thaw and others established *Continental Drift*, and in so doing found that the lower pitches, with some variations, could possibly go free. Armed with this information, Thomas and I started at the top of Footstool, a prominent 50-meter rock tower leaning against the base of El Capitan's southeast face. And, indeed, we found in *Continental Drift* a freeable solution to the lowest third of the southeast face. Three pitches were hard (5.13b, 5.13a, 5.13c), then some easier pitches led us to the Calaveras Ledges and a traverse on low-angle terrain to the original route of the *North American Wall*. Free climbing two more quite easy pitches brought us to the Big Sur, the best bivy on the entire face.

The following pendulums over an ocean of golden granite looked very hard. After the first pendulum went free at 5.13a, we came to a halt. Three rivets lead through a section of blank granite to the second pendulum. There was no chance for free climbing the original route. We inspected the entire area around the pendulums, wasting hours in the hope of finding a free solution we had not yet discovered. No way! At least three meters of blank granite remained at all the solutions. The second pendulum became the crux of our motivation. No way!

When Ray Jardine tried to free the *Nose*, he had the exact same problem. He solved it by hammering his own solution into the granite. Seven meters of blank granite received chopped holds, which were then called the "Jardine Traverse." Even today this remains the only possibility for a "free variation" to the King Swing of the *Nose*. But on the *North American Wall* we accepted the second pendulum as a natural barrier and tried to make the best of it.

Eight meters below and a bit to the left of the no-hands rest we were on, there was another no-hands rest, from which a shallow corner arches to the left to the beginning of the "Endurance Corner." For these unfreeable eight meters I had an idea, which I called the "Man-Powered Rappel." The belayer has a slack backup to the belay and hangs with his hands on the no-hands-rest ledge. One climber down climbs from the ledge. Two meters below, his weight comes onto the rope, which is fixed to the belayer's harness. A short, four-meter rappel down to a small ledge. . . the climber unweights the rope, and the belayer can relax for a short moment. . . again the rope is weighted, and another four-meter rappel brings the climber to the belay at the next no-hands rest.

Of course, the Man-Powered Rappel cannot be referred to as having been redpointed, but it follows free climbing's guidelines: movement over rock using just the natural surface. It was an acceptable solution for us.

After having gained access to the Black Dihedral, the way to the top was open. Just one really hard pitch remained: the "Black Cave." The roof of the Black Cave looked hard and weird. A single two-centimeter sawed-off angle is the only protection for a long cross-through in an incredibly airy position. This would normally be the place for a bolt, but we didn't want to drill on an existing route. Thus, the Black Cave gained its special scary touch.

After having found the free solution, our plan was then to redpoint the entire route as a team, which is the traditional style of free climbing a multi-pitch route in the Alps. It means that each pitch has to be free climbed by both of us without falls. If the leader has redpointed a pitch, it's just half the game; only if the follower has climbed the pitch free and without falls as well has the pitch been redpointed as a team.

LEFT: *Alex Huber in the "Galapagos," pitch 5 (5.13c), El Niño.* HEINZ ZAK

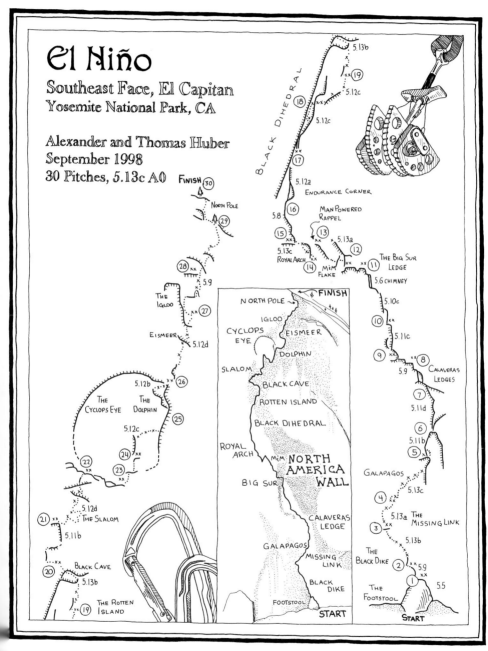

# El Niño

Southeast Face, El Capitan
Yosemite National Park, CA

Alexander and Thomas Huber
September 1998
30 Pitches, 5.13c A0

*The Huber brothers on pitch 34 (5.10d) of* Free Rider. HEINZ ZAK

It took us three days to free the route, with both of us climbing all the pitches without any falls. The right side of El Capitan now had 30 pitches of free climbing at 5.13c, plus the Man-Powered Rappel. In fact, this free climb is not an independent route, but a combination of existing routes (*New Jersey Turnpike, Continental Drift, Heavy Metal and Tinker Toys, North American Wall* and *Sea of Dreams*) and new variations that are never more than six meters away from existing routes and which cannot be called independent. Nevertheless, the route gained a name, just to emphasize that it is not the *North American Wall* that has been freed, but a particular combination of existing routes and variations. In naming the route we followed the suggestion of Conrad Anker and Kevin Thaw, which gave the project the working name *El Niño*.

It could have been enough for 1998 to have such a route under our belts, but I still had other plans. During my attempts at free climbing the *Salathé* in 1995, I made the first ascent of the *Free Rider*, which is now the easiest free climb on El Capitan. Belaying myself with a Grigri, I solo free climbed a four-pitch variation to the headwall of the *Salathé*—a first-class option to free climb El Capitan in a day. Heinz Zak, though, was tired after belaying me on my redpoint ascent of the *Salathé*, and I couldn't find any belayers for the project. Since it would have been an easy prize, the only people who knew about it—Mark Chapman, Heinz Zak and Jeff Achey—were sworn to secrecy, and I had to wait until 1998 for a one-day ascent of the route.

The days became very short in October, and a redpoint ascent by a single person naturally requires less time than one by a team, but I couldn't find anyone willing to belay and jumar the whole day. After a first attempt with Dean Potter, which we abandoned due to slowness, I decided at last, but not least, to climb the route with Thomas. Because of the lack of daylight in October, we started at 3:31 a.m. and climbed the entire *Freeblast* in the dark. Fifteen hours and 25 minutes after starting, having redpointed all 37 pitches, we topped out just as darkness came to Yosemite Valley.

We had free climbed El Capitan in a day—37 pitches with difficulties up to 5.12d! *Free Rider* offers very typical granite climbing with 60 meters of chimneys, 100 meters of offwidth, 100 meters of layback, 100 meters of "no-feature" slabs and more than 100 meters of finger-, hand- and fist-sized cracks. The 5.12 pitches don't require any special granite techniques, but, despite modest difficulties, many meters of pure crack climbing and much desperately "good" offwidth require advanced crack climbing skills. For example, the two offwidth pitches between The Ear and El Cap Spire demonstrate mercilessly to every inexperienced offwidth climber who tries them that there are 5.10d pitches that refuse to be on-sighted.

Thomas and I spent another day in the Valley. The sun set on our trip one last time, bathing the huge walls of Yosemite in the magnificent light we love so much. It's the right time to leave a place—it's the right time to leave Yosemite!

Where is it all going next? Well, I think that I won't ascend another trade route on an 8000er again. Bagging an 8000er via a trade route is still very sustaining and great, but when you are together with so many other climbers, you can't feel the exposure of these magnificent mountains. The real challenge awaits us where nobody else is going. Therefore, I hope that the next trip will be one to an impressive place with good friends and the great exposure of climbing at the cutting edge.

SUMMARY OF STATISTICS

AREA: El Capitan, Yosemite Valley, California

NEW ROUTES: *El Niño* (VI, 5.13c, 30 pitches), a free climb that links parts of established routes with some new variations on the southeast face of El Capitan, September 4-19, Alexander and Thomas Huber; first redpoint ascent, September 23-25, 1998, Alexander and Thomas Huber. *Free Rider* (VI, 5.12d, 37 pitches), a four-pitch variation to the *Free Salathé*, May, 1995, Alexander Huber, solo; first redpoint ascent and first one-day-ascent: October 13, 1998, in 15 hours 25 minutes, Alexander and Thomas Huber

# Zion Solo

## Bridging the gap between work and life

by Amanda Tarr

I emerged, coughing, from a confused sleep. Rolling off the old itchy sofa cushions on the floor of my office, I oriented on my computer's blinking light, crawled to my desk, killed the screen saver and turned on a full-spectrum grow light, my best approximation of a sunrise at three in the afternoon.

With a strict deadline approaching, I'd slipped into this-less-than-ideal schedule for the final push. Through my more difficult university classes, and on into my career as a senior software engineer at a video game company in Boulder, Colorado, I had discovered that my peak mental hours are between 2 a.m. and 6 a.m. I'd been working double time on that schedule for the better part of two weeks, fueling myself with greasy Chinese takeout and the bitter food-service quality coffee that the company keeps in constant supply. It was the final day of work before the product demo would be burned onto a gold CD for the annual trade show. Soon, my colleagues would be flying over the patchwork quilt of the American Midwest on course toward Atlanta, Georgia. The trade show promised to be a mélange of flashing lights, skinny pale-faced teens, and scantily clad "booth bimbos" hired to make video games seem glamorous. I was gladly trading this experience for a trip to Zion National Park, where I hoped to finish a solo first ascent I'd abandoned between Christmas and New Year's. I'd spent the intervening five months contriving elaborate excuses for my failure, and I needed the opportunity to return and free myself from my self-imposed obligation. I proceeded mechanically through the final polishing of our software and, with dawn approaching, guided my truck through the nearly deserted streets of town.

By mid-morning, I cleared the tunnel leading into Zion Canyon. The panorama was awe-inspiring, and my breathing stuttered as it has every time I've broken out of the relative darkness of the narrow passage through the cliff onto the steep slope of the canyon wall. Prior to my first big wall solo, the *Moonlight Buttress*, I was paralyzed with fear at first sight of the walls; I had nearly decided to go backpacking instead. While my respect for the high places has remained unchanged over the years, they have become more familiar to me. The fear has been replaced with a feeling of anticipation and nervousness, much the same as one feels when they step off a plane from a faraway destination into the arms of a loved one whom they haven't seen in months: a warm familiarity is there, but mixed with it is the nagging worry that things may have changed, never to be rediscovered.

The traffic in the canyon was stop-and-go, differing from rush hour on the Colorado Front Range only by the scenery and the percentage of RVs. Not wanting the spell to be broken, I turned up the music and looked at the walls, the budding trees, the river still swollen with spring runoff, anything to remove myself from the similarities to my stressful career-oriented life back home. It was Memorial Day weekend, and I waited for two hours for a bivy permit as the hordes scrambled to get wilderness permits when they discovered that the drive-in campground was full. The campsites closest to the highways filled first, and there was heated competition for the last remaining spots. Finally, I obtained uncontested permission to sleep on the sandstone wall overlooking Emerald Pools.

*Amanda Tarr at home in Boulder, Colorado.* PETE TAKEDA

I packed the first of my loads and started up the trail. Ahead of me, a nearly continuous line of tourists meandered up the trail. They stopped repeatedly, oblivious to me staggering behind with a load that I could barely balance. After an "Excuse me," the most polite phrase I could muster, the dawning of recognition for what I'd said seemed to spread across their shiny, sweat-streaked faces with the speed of a glacier creeping down an alpine valley.

At long last, I was able to strike up the hill, left with only my own scent and the smell of the earth that each of my steps released as I struggled up the soft dirt slope. I dropped my cargo and returned to the trailhead as quickly as possible. I wanted to get my second load up to the base of the wall with time to examine the route with binoculars before the sun left the canyon, taking with it the contrasting light by which I could pick out corners, cracks, and other features.

Looking through the binos, I was suddenly washed with doubt. I desperately wanted someone to talk to, even for a moment, about my uncertainty. I'd never done a first ascent alone, and the consequences of a mistake seemed enormous. There would be no hope of immediate rescue; the top of the cliff was an extremely forbidding slab, and the only access would come from climbing up the vertical wall below. In addition, I was concerned with my descent options. Rappelling would probably be as arduous as climbing up the wall: the buttress was overhanging for at least half of the route, and the features on the vertical or slabby sections traversed too much to facilitate an easy retreat. I needed a familiar face to reassure me, but in the midst of the biggest crowd I had ever seen in Zion, I felt completely and horribly alone.

Desire to get off the ground had me nearly running with my third and final load up the trail to the base of the route the next morning. I quickly set to preparing myself for a solo aid pitch, methodically stacking the ropes, setting an anchor for upward pull, and putting myself

on belay with a clove hitch through two locking carabiners on my harness. The sun line had already crept most of the way down Lady Mountain before I set off on the string of birdbeaks that carried me into the vertical world. A cool breeze blew up from the vicinity of the natural spring below. During the previous winter, the only sound breaking the silence had been the periodic crashes and tinkles of ice falling from the overhang above the Emerald Pools. Now the wind carried murmurs of conversation and the megaphone of a tour bus droning on with various trivia and an inaccurate description of big wall climbing.

I'd completed the first two pitches on my previous attempt, and without the uncertainty of the unknown and the hassle of drilling bolt anchors, I moved with relative self-assuredness. The beak seam led to an awkward squeeze chimney capped with a roof. As I struggled and thrutched my way up through the confining walls, I cursed myself for not leaving the pitch fixed the previous winter. I'd decided against it, because I was afraid that the tourists might notice my rope if the sun struck the wall at just the right angle. With access problems proliferating due to the increasing popularity of adventure sports, our actions can no longer go unnoticed. A rope left in laziness so that I might avoid 200 feet of climbing later on could negatively impact our collective climbing opportunities for years to come.

While exhausting, hauling my bag presented none of the usual complications. I've accustomed myself to the sinking feeling that comes when the haulbag catches under a roof or in a tight chimney. Solo climbers are well acquainted with having to repeatedly rappel down to the bag, free it, and jumar up to resume hauling. It becomes part of the game, just like having to rappel and clean every pitch after the lead, but I find myself fervently hoping during each haul that the bag will reach the belay unhindered.

Good fortune spared me any unwanted difficulties, and I took the opportunity to set up my bivy early. As I lay on my ledge, soaking up the late afternoon sun and rehydrating, I reflected on my life over the last couple of years. There was a clean line that split my experiences between those in the working world and those in the climbing world. The characters I played in each half of my life seemed to be entirely different people. One was driven by security, intellectual achievement, and the desire for the finer things in life. The other wanted only to climb at her limits, travel the world, and absorb the fullness of life gained by living on the edge. Spanning the vast gap between the two, I noted only my relationships with the people I love and a need to achieve.

The next couple of days flew by as I lost myself in the task of climbing upward. Dry air filled my lungs and blew across my face as the sun cooked my shoulders. My lips grew parched and cracked, and my fingers became chapped from the constant work with rough rock and dry nylon ropes. Unlike most desert climbs, the features on the route were delightfully varied, from a parallel crack through a stunning roof to more devious feature systems splitting the otherwise sheer sandstone face. The end of every pitch brought me remarkably to a reasonable ledge. It became a game of wondering when my luck for finding belay stances would run out and I'd be stuck monkeying around on hanging belays.

I had debated whether to set completely or nearly completely natural anchors on the route. While it was a feasible option for me climbing alone, I opted for drilling two-bolt anchors after every pitch. I believe that, at least in an accessible locale such as Zion, new routing is as much a service as an adventure. While I am a proponent of the notion that the character of the pitch may be as difficult or as dangerous as the first ascensionist desires, I also believe in setting anchors that will not only work for me, but also be safe for three heavier people and their corresponding gear.

LEFT: Leaving Llamaland *on Emerald Star Mountain.* PAUL HORTON

When I awoke on my third morning on the wall, the wind was howling fiercely, but I decided to leave my ledge set up anyway in the event I needed to make a hasty retreat to the belay. I set out, placing cams in horrid flaring cracks, praising the designers of modern climbing gear when they miraculously bit into what looked to be impossible placements. Following the flare, a series of beak seams shot off in a traversing line to the left. Placements were found by searching out miniscule plants (usually amounting to a single hair-width stalk) that protruded from the crack. They were my only hope of finding a break in the calcified seam.

The seams gave way to small edges on the face, and as I was on my fourth tenuous hook in a row my portaledge below began to beat violently against the rock. Seconds later the wind gust slammed into me, and it was all I could do to maintain balance. A small edge under my right foot bore a bit of my weight, and when it fractured off, my foot plummeted a couple of inches into my aider step. I wobbled and the hook teetered. I could sense my pupils dilating with adrenaline, and all the world snapped into focus around the tiny square centimeter of soft sandstone supporting my weight. A million thoughts slammed into my head at once. I knew from drilling the belay anchors that the rock was universally permeated under a quarter-inch shell of dry rock. Immediately I thought down to the single solid cam placement between me and the belay. Shaken by my precipitous teetering, I imagined that there was no way the cam could hold in the water-weakened sandstone. I froze with fear. I wanted to reach for my drill. A bolt would change the pitch forever, but I would be able to move on in relative self assurance. I waffled between giving into my fear and continuing on.

Ultimately, I believe it was laziness rather than bravery that allowed me to move on without placing the bolt. The thought of standing high on the hook and drilling was too much for my aching back, and I managed to do as I should and sort out a series of hook moves and shallow beaks to take me to the next substantial feature. It was a flared and hollow crack formed from the convergence of two semi-detached flakes, but in relative terms it was far more confidence-inspiring than the climbing below. I quickly moved up it to drill the only hanging belay on the route.

Finally getting the bivy set up offered minimal relief. My kidneys ached, and blinking my eyes felt like rubbing fine-grained sandpaper over their surfaces. My thumbs and the first three fingers of both my hands were going numb, the onset of carpal tunnel syndrome. I wanted off. Night was no respite; I was tossed about as if I were sleeping in the back of a pickup truck as it sped down an unimproved dirt road. The wind had returned, perhaps perturbed that it hadn't knocked me off the route earlier in the day. I closed the rainfly over my ledge to keep my face from being pelted with any more flying sand, and finally dozed off during a lull in the storm.

Shortly thereafter, I was awakened. The cramped quarters of my sleeping bag had caused me to roll over on my already injured wrists, cutting off further the nerves and tendons that run through the carpal tunnel. I swallowed an emergency painkiller from my medical kit and curled into a small ball. Comforted by my own closeness, I dropped off into an otherwise uninterrupted sleep.

In the morning, it took 15 minutes of concentration to close my hands into loose fists. The connection between my brain and the mechanical motion of my digits was temporarily severed, and I had no perception of their orientation without looking directly at them. Once I fell into the rhythm of climbing, however, full mobility returned and the lingering feelings from the night faded away. I began traversing left, coming closer to the exit chimney I believed would take me off the route. I pendulumed to unprotected, slabby free climbing, but the chimney eluded me, and I only managed a pitch of climbing. The next morning I repeated the staring contest with my fingers, silently pleading with them to function so that I could get to the top.

The final pitch was mostly free, and quite good climbing, terminating with some gymnastic but easy moves up overhanging huecos in the shiny black desert varnish.

Finally, I pulled onto the summit slab and attempted to let out a little whoop, my mood being only slightly damaged when I managed a pathetic croak instead. The only flat spot within a quarter mile in either direction was 400 feet away, so I quickly shuttled my gear over, looking forward to taking off my harness for the first time in days. I spent the afternoon leaning against a lone tree, reading through a mindless fantasy novel that I remember nothing about.

Throughout the climb, I'd been afflicted with a pervasive nervousness about the descent. The summit slabs resemble Boulder's Flatirons, but covered with manzanita, sand, and loose rock. I scurried back and forth, fixing a line to insubstantial shrubs and an occasional tree in order to give myself a measure of security as I lurched across with my overfilled haulbag. After half a day of toiling, I reached the end of the slabs and began drilling 60-meter rappels down the face. I worked with stern concentration; a stuck rappel in the middle of the blank face would have left me hanging like a forgotten wind chime in the door of an abandoned building, my only recourse being a jumar back up on whatever unknown blockage had stopped the rope. Finally, I came within striking distance of the ground, and I was able to truly relax for the first time since I had begun days before.

Later that evening, I relaxed on the tailgate of my truck, nursing a beer as I chatted with friends I'd run into in the parking lot. I felt disconnected, and my thoughts wandered to the days ahead. I would soon have to return to work, to exchange the feeling of empowerment and freedom of a solo climb for days in front of the computer screen. I used to hope that, through creating a fantasy world in a video game, I might enable someone else to temporarily leave behind their personal world of stress and obligations. I don't doubt that this is possible, and I'd like to think that this same belief is what drives many people in the entertainment industry to push themselves to succeed. Unfortunately, I always have a hard time coming back, as if I can only pursue this ideal with half my heart.

In the slang of many online video game players, a llama is someone who appears lost and not at home with their virtual surroundings. The term is somewhat derogatory, and in a sense it's often how I feel about myself as I try to fit into the career-oriented life. When I was on the wall, I felt at times lonely and tired, afraid and timid, but I never once felt that I didn't belong there. So I gave the climb a name that may be a bit of a mouthful, but certainly expresses what it meant to me: *Leaving Llamaland.*

SUMMARY OF STATISTICS

AREA: Zion National Park, Utah

NEW ROUTE: *Leaving Llamaland* (V+ 5.7 A2+, 1,000') on Emerald Star Mountain (two buttresses right of the route *Emerald Star Majesticus*), May 30-June 3, 1998, Amanda Tarr, solo

# Baffin's Still-Untapped Potential

## A bird's eye view of the future

by Mark Synnott

*Greg Child on pitch 11 (A3+) of* Rum, Sodomy and the Lash *on "Great Sail Peak." The melting snowfields on top have Jared Ogden and John Catto hiding beneath the portaledge—the sunnier it was, the wetter the climb. This was the first major wall climb to take place in the Stewart Valley.*

MARK SYNNOTT

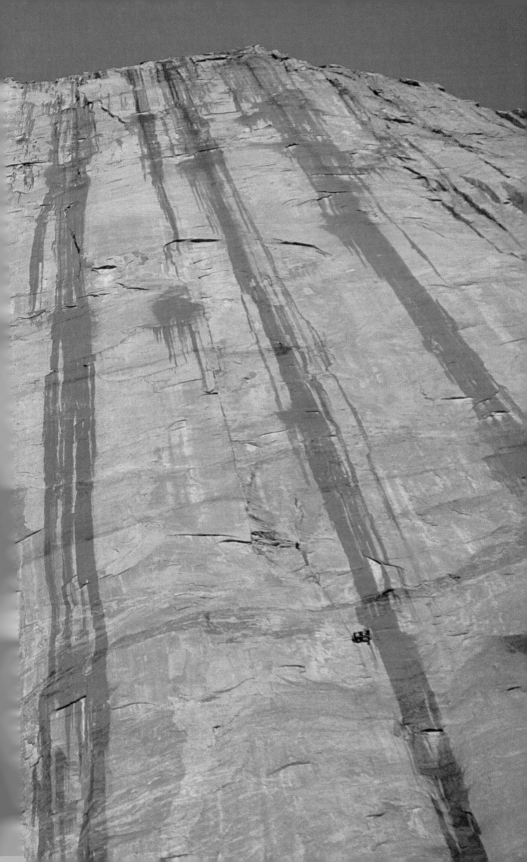

Though climbing has been going on in Baffin Island since at least 1934, and in earnest since the early 1970s, it wasn't until 1994 that the world was formally introduced to the vast untapped climbing potential on the island's east coast. Eugene Fisher, a photographer who visited the area and documented many of the most impressive formations, published photo essays of his discoveries in both *Climbing* magazine and *The American Alpine Journal*. He also published similar material in magazines around the world. In the 1995 *AAJ*, he inspired a generation of big wall climbers when he wrote: "…on the east coast of the world's fifth largest island are a series of 26 fjords, some 18 to 70 miles in length, that contain some of the tallest vertical rock walls on earth, walls that exceed even the fabled faces of Mount Thor and Asgard. . . . Yosemite Valley would count as a minor side fjord if it were located along this vertiginous coast."

I first read these words in the Yosemite Lodge cafeteria in the company of fellow Camp 4 grovellers. We were dumb-struck. The article boasted five El Capitans and two Great Trangos in one fjord, and practically no one had climbed there. Surely, this had to be a wild exaggeration. Maybe. . . but Fisher did back up his claims with some impressive photos, and when I called him, he gave me a detailed and convincing explanation of the triangulation method he used to determine the heights of the walls.

Five years later, after three expeditions to the east coast of Baffin Island and an aerial reconnaissance of my own, I can say without hesitation that Fisher was not exaggerating in the least. This pristine arctic wilderness contains what is likely the highest concentration of big walls in the world, and most of them are still virgin.

Several expeditions have visited the Sam Ford Fjord since these articles were published, and approximately ten major new wall routes have established. The new route activity has finally put the east coast on the map, and it has also brought to light several previous ascents in the area that had fallen into obscurity. At the time of Fisher's first article, a comprehensive climbing history to the fjords didn't exist, but in the intervening years a fair amount of information has been unearthed from back issues of the Canadian and American alpine journals. Apparently, the fjords have a richer climbing history than I first suspected.

On my first expedition to the area in 1995, we knew of only one group that had actually climbed in the Sam Ford Fjord. In 1992, Americans Conrad Anker and Jon Turk used sea kayaks to approach and climb two Grade V first ascents in Sam Ford Fjord. Several years later, when my partners and I climbed new routes on the Turret and Polar Sun Spire, we were surprised and somewhat disappointed to find vintage bolts just below the summits. Only later did we find out that these peaks had been bagged in 1986 by a Swiss team that included the late big wall climbing legend, Xaver Bongard. Nearby Broad Peak, which we also thought to be unclimbed, had been ascended by a team from Washington State University in 1978. The Walker Citadel was climbed in 1977. As it turned out, most of the most compelling formations had already been summited by the time we arrived. True, none of these routes had been major big wall extravaganzas, but they were still long, serious climbs in an area that may have been kept quiet intentionally.

Among those who had long held an interest in Baffin's eastern frontier was the National Geographic Society, but it wasn't until 1998 that they decided to launch their own expedition to this big wall mecca. The trip was the brainchild of Greg Child, and since I was one of the few people who had actually climbed in the area, I was lucky enough to get invited, along with Jared Ogden, Alex Lowe, Gordon Wiltsie, and John Catto. The best part of the expedition was that we had to do an aerial reconnaissance of the entire length of Baffin Island in order to choose our objective. This was truly my dream come true.

In April, 1998, our team flew to Iqaluit and chartered a Twin Otter in the hopes of finding a wall that rivaled the Polar Sun Spire. We spent the first day flying around Auyuittuq National Park, where clear skies offered phenomenal perspectives of Mt. Thor, Mt. Asgard, and many

*This ca. 3,500-foot, northwest-facing wall lies directly adjacent to "Great Sail Peak" in the Stewart Valley. A climb on this wall will be, according to the author, a* Sea of Dreams *type of climb, linking very incipient cracks. He also reported seeing car-sized boulders rip down the side of this face.*

FOLLOWING PHOTOS.
PAGE 36: *The unclimbed 1,800-foot headwall on the north face of Broad Peak.*
PAGE 37: *Future objectives on Baffin's east coast. The author saw so many formations on the team's recon, he couldn't remember where these were located—perhaps "in or near the North Arm, a fjord just north of Quernbitter."* ALL PHOTOS: MARK SYNNOTT

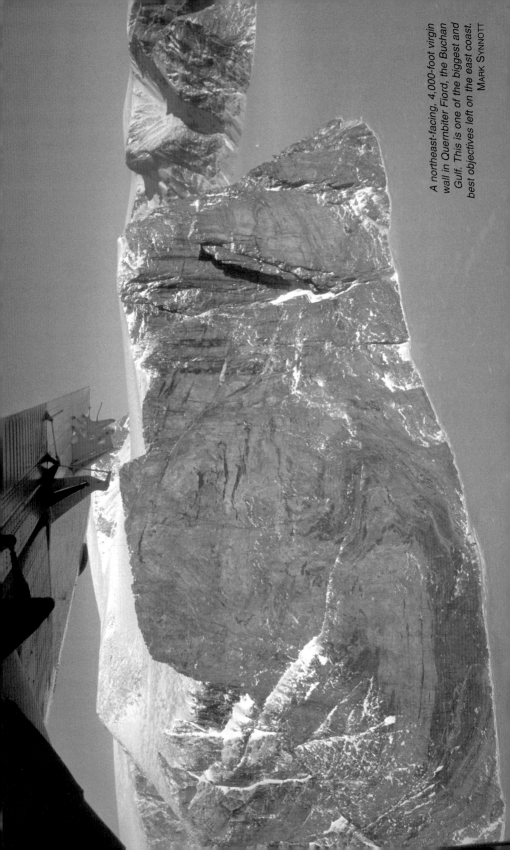

A northeast-facing, 4,000-foot virgin wall in Quernbiter Fiord, the Buchan Gulf. This is one of the biggest and best objectives left on the east coast. MARK SYNNOTT

*Ca. 2,000-foot walls on the north-west side of Scott Island. Teams were active here in Spring, 1999.*
RUSS MITROVICH

other impressive formations. Continuing further up the coast beyond the boundary of the national park, we found stacks of uncharted cliffs in the fjords south of Clyde River, particularly in the Itirbilung and Inugsuin Fjords. The next day we continued into the Sam Ford Fjord, along the way passing Eglington Tower, a free-standing 4,000-footer.

After examining the Walker Arm of Sam Ford, which didn't contain anything too appealing once past the Walker Citadel, we continued exploring the fjords between Sam Ford and the village of Pond Inlet. We were particularly interested in the remote Quernbiter Fjord, which had been recommended by Fisher as an area where we might find a 4,000+ foot cliff. We did find a huge wall in Quernbiter, but unfortunately it was a bit too broken up for our tastes. Still, it was one of the most worthy objectives we saw on our flight. Overall, the potential in the fjords north of Gibbs was not quite as good as I had always hoped. There are dozens of good objectives hidden back in the nooks and crannies, but it was clear that the best concentration of walls is to be found in the area surrounding Sam Ford Fjord. We decided that the very best unclimbed wall in Baffin Island was located in the Stewart Valley, between Sam Ford and Gibbs Fjord. We chose a striking 3,800-foot cliff that we called "Great Sail Peak," in reference to a nearby formation labeled Sail Peak on our map, as our objective.

We wondered, at the time, who had named this mountain, but it wasn't until just recently that we learned of other expeditions that had previously visited the Stewart Valley. In 1977, a Canadian group established a base camp in Stewart Valley and made 19 first ascents in the area. Like most of the early expeditions to the east coast, they concentrated on peak bagging, not on ascending the monolithic walls themselves. Their report contained a reference to climbing what appears to be Sail Peak, but their maps and written description didn't contain enough detail for me to say for sure. They did mention leaving a summit register, which we didn't find when we were on top.

Realistically, most of the best lines in Sam Ford Fjord have been ticked off at this point, but there are still a few exceptions. Eglington Tower (located just outside Sam Ford near Revoir Pass) has still not been climbed by a big-wall route (it was first climbed on August 21, 1934, by Britons Sir John Hanham and T.G. Longstaff, and also climbed in winter by K.W. Barke), nor has the Tugalik Wall, an escarpment several miles long and up to 4,000 feet high. Polar Sun Spire, which is, according to our recon, the biggest wall in Baffin, still has only one route. Closer to the mouth of the fjord, the 4,000+ foot Chinese Wall, attempted unsuccessfully in 1997, is also still virgin. The 2,000-foot Ship's Prow of Scott Island, located at the mouth of Gibbs and Clark Fjords, makes up for its relative lack of height by overhanging continuously in a clean sweep of gneiss that rises directly from the open ocean (Americans are planning an attempt for the spring of 1999). Stewart Valley contains several 2,000-foot walls, in addition to a formation of proportions similar to Sail Peak (it will likely also see an attempt in 1999 by a British team). Gibbs Fjord, where there are several appealing formations well over 3,000 feet in height, has yet to see a single ascent that I am aware of. To the best of my knowledge, no walls in Gibbs have even been named.

Believe it or not, we are starting to run out of 4,000-footers on the east coast, but there are still countless lesser walls, especially in the 2,000-foot range. As Eugene Fisher wrote in his *AAJ* article, "…what confounds the first-time visitor's senses are the miles of 'smaller' cliffs, literally thousands of buttresses and arêtes that are grade V and VI." Contrary to what some people predicted when the east coast began to gain notoriety in the world climbing press, however, the area will most likely never be overcrowded. The unique logistical problem of dealing with ice-packed fjords, coupled with the extreme cold, has so far kept the traffic down to a couple of expeditions per season. It will be decades, perhaps centuries, before Baffin's fjords are even close to climbed out. It is also important to understand that, by and large, the Inuit are com-

*The ca. 2,000-foot, entirely overhanging Ship's Prow on Scott Island, soloed in Spring, 1999, by Mike Libecki.* RUSS MITROVICH

mitted to developing this area to its full potential. In remote arctic villages like Clyde River and Pangnirtung, adventure-tourism and guiding are really the only means by which the Inuit can hope to develop a self-sustaining economy.

Many people have also asked me about the free climbing potential on Baffin's east coast. Unfortunately, it is not great. Because the rock in Baffin—a granitic gneiss—is so young geologically, it has not had the time to fracture into continuous crack systems common in places like Yosemite, Patagonia, and the Baltoro. This translates into huge walls with only limited climbing potential, and that being predominantly hard aid. The lack of deep, continuous cracks, combined with the cold weather, will seriously limit the amount of hard free climbing that can be accomplished in the fjords.

For me, the fact that this will never be an easy place to visit is something that accounts for a large measure of its appeal. For those who do make the effort, chances are good they'll have the entire coast to themselves, or at least their own fjord. It's nice to know, in a day and age when other big wall destinations are becoming over-run, that there is still a place where you can commit yourself to total self-reliance. There's only one point on which I think Eugene Fisher missed the mark: Yosemite Valley would not be a minor side valley on this coast. The more we search for untapped walls around the world, the more we have to appreciate what we have in our own backyard.

# Alone on Mt. Thor

## The second ascent of *Midgard Serpent*

by D. Jason "Singer" Smith

"When there's only one in the crew, everybody gets to be captain." – "Big Wall Pro: Flavio d'Bongo," from *The Complete Book of Big Wall Climbing,* by Chongo.

I turned my head as the first crack sounded, and watched, dumbfounded with awe and reverence, as a 200-foot block separated from the face and plummeted toward the earth. Exploding upon impact, it started a rock slide that would continue for just shy of a mile down the slabs and talus that had been a daily chore for me for the previous eight days. The block, about 40 to 60 feet in diameter, added up to 15 feet of talus at some spots and tossed house-sized boulders like a child kicking at mere gravel. The ensuing dust cloud was quickly forgotten to the howling winds in the valley below. I was still marooned here, alone, hauling a fleet of four haulbags to the sixth pitch of *Midgard Serpent* on Mt. Thor in Baffin Island. Witnessing this powerful force of nature inspired but two thoughts in my head: this is the dumbest idea that I have ever had; and, do I still have enough rope to bail?

My plan to solo a remote big wall was sparked after climbing El Capitan solo over Christmas, 1997. Finishing a moderately difficult 16-pitch route in three days, I was left wanting something bigger. Logistically, Thor, with its relatively short approach, the lack of glacial cover both at the base and summit, and an overhanging headwall that would keep rockfall to a minimum, was the most feasible project for a solo ascent.

Chris McNamara and I had traveled to the Weasel Valley that summer intent on climbing Mt. Turnweather. As rookies on the big-wall scene, we had to rely on our neophyte instincts to tell us that the constant deluge of waterfalls and avalanches on the lower 1,000 feet of our chosen face might make the climbing more tenuous than we had reckoned. In an attempt to salvage our trip, we began carrying all of our gear to Mt. Thor, where we hoped to climb *Midgard Serpent*, a route established over 15 days in 1995 by Brad Jarrett and John Rzeczycki. We arrived at the base two weeks before Chris was scheduled to begin school in New Jersey. Plagued by low food rations, we climbed just two pitches before heading down. I vowed to return to Thor and finish the project.

Pangnirtung, July 15, 1998. The air temperatures was 70°F—warmer than anybody could remember. In the evening, just before high tide, I departed with my local outfitter, Joavee, for the two-hour boat ride up the fjord to Overlord Peak. Once there, I would begin shuttling my loads up the Weasel Valley to Mt. Thor, 20 miles beyond. My plan was to get my bags the ten miles to Windy Lake and set up a base camp. From there, I would take one load per day the remaining distance to the wall. I had planned ahead by shipping 255 pounds of my supplies to Joavee in April; he had snowmobiled the provisions to the

LEFT: *The 3,600-foot west face of Mt. Thor, showing* Midgard Serpent *(VI 5.9 A5).* JASON SMITH

lake, saving me a few days of walking. From the lake, I would carry about 400 pounds of food and climbing gear the remaining ten miles to the base of the wall.

The nearly 24-hour daylight was beneficial for carrying loads, allowing me to run on what my partners know as "Singer Days:" periods that usually begin around noon, but then extend for 12 hours beyond. After two such days I arrived at the lake, physically spent and suffering slightly from food deprivation. Finding my supplies stashed in an emergency shelter, I was delighted to indulge in a meal of macaroni and cheese, along with white chocolate and Kool Aid—all items of untold value after a taxing day of humping loads across the Arctic Circle.

When I awoke, the wall was visible for the first time. I spent the day talking with some passing backpackers and organizing my copious amounts of gear. By the next morning, I had discovered how Windy Lake had come by its name. Each evening, as the sun went behind the surrounding peaks, the temperature would quickly drop. Stout gales would soon roll in, continuing to howl throughout the night.

I then began the first of what would be seven trips to the wall. I would eventually loathe every step. The first mile to the wall was on the standard trekking path, a well-traveled solid walking surface. At a bridge, the standard route crosses the Weasel River, but the trek to Thor continues up the untracked side of the water. Eight miles of rolling tundra are followed by the most imposing talus field I can imagine. Tundra is a most disagreeable surface for hiking, best likened to walking on a wet down-feather bed. With every step, I sank to the ankles while the ground oozed like a sponge, burning my slight legs in minutes, even on level ground.

The excitement didn't really start, however, until I arrived at the talus field. Every trip up this granite staircase of torture was an immensely frightening and fatiguing experience. Thinking it stable, I would step to a desk-sized (or larger) boulder, only to have it, and a ten-foot circumference of rock around it, slide several feet down the slope, with me quivering in the center. Luckily, much of the talus could be circumnavigated by walking up several slabs, but my trips up the field still took between two and four hours.

It was wonderful to finally arrive at the project. Conditions for climbing couldn't have been better: with no wind and flawless white granite to absorb the sun's rays, it was approaching a sweltering 80°. Looking up, however, I felt a strange sensation. The route loomed above as a delicate passage through mostly blank rock. I was somewhere between terrified and psyched.

*On the eighth trip to the base of the wall.* Jason Smith

In his book, *Big Wall Climbing*, Doug Scott called Mt. Thor "exceedingly bare of features." A Spanish team proved this in 1997 by climbing a route on the right side of the face with 260 holes. I felt that a new route on Thor would debauch the rock just for the sake of doing something "new." Also, my emaciated arms hurt at the mere thought of hand-drilling 20 belays. The low 115-hole count of *Midgard Serpent*, as well as the caliber of the first ascensionists, meant that both difficult and quality climbing were assured.

For the next ten days, I carried gear to the wall, taking one day off for rest. The good news was that the weather was holding remarkably well, with temperatures on most days stretching into the 60s. Unfortunately, it would not continue. I awoke on the day of my last trip up the slope to see black thunderclouds rolling over the ridge to the west. The temperature had dropped into the 30s and would remain there for the next three weeks. After fixing two pitches, I carried up two loads of water and went to sleep. It would be my last night on the ground for two weeks.

When I awoke the next morning, the weather had definitely changed for the worse. Although I was mostly protected by the steep angle of the wall, it was snowing lightly, and ice continued to fall from above. I packed up my four haulbags, including 48 liters of water, and clipped everything into my haul line. I reasoned that a single 3:1 haul, while taking more time, would be more energy efficient than two hauls and the inevitable rope cluster that would accompany such a system.

The first 230-foot haul ended up taking three grueling hours to complete. Utterly exhausted by the effort of hauling the load and then leading the next two overhanging pitches, my journal entry that night was kept simple: "I think that the people who think I'm simply stupid for coming here are right. I now think wall climbing is ridiculous. I feel like shit tonight."

Two days later, while hauling my convoy, the huge block to my right crashed to the ground. I stared, motionless, for ten minutes before resuming my work. The previous day I had spent over eight hours hauling two pitches. After watching this spectacle of nature, I realized that I had to do something to move more quickly. I docked the load at the belay, then dug into my bags and trundled 20 liters of my water, effectively committing myself even more to the climb.

I took my first fall the following day. Hooking through a maze of nearly flawless rock, I came to a small flake. I didn't really think that it would take body weight, but, unable to see anything else, and unwilling to drill on an established route, I used it anyway. While getting into my top steps, the feature peeled away from the rock, sending me careening 40 feet back down. I stopped with my head and arm resting comfortably on a small ledge.

My bigger worry, however, was that my right hand had been burned by the rope during the flight. While it was nothing that you'd get sent home from school over, I did lose some motion in two fingers, which really ruined my day. I taped the two injured fingers together, finished the lead, hauled, and crashed into deep sleep.

By the next morning, I had lost much of my psyche. I woke at 10:30 a.m., dreading the steep, arching, knifeblade corner above after my near-mishap of the previous afternoon. A neuro-linguistic programming book that I had brought along kept me entertained in the comfort of my sleeping bag with a steaming cup of tea. I even contemplated taking the entire day off. In the last paragraph, the author explained that he liked to finish his seminars by telling people:

> At any moment that you find yourself hesitating or if at any moment you find yourself putting off until tomorrow something that you could do today, then all you need to do is glance over your left shoulder and there will be a fleeting shadow. That shadow

*Cleaning pitch 9.* JASON SMITH

represents your death, and at any moment it might step forward, place its hand on your shoulder and take you. So that the act that you are presently engaged in might be your very last act and therefore fully representative of you as your last act on this planet. When you hesitate, you are acting as though you are immortal.

Ten minutes later, I was hammering away at a tied-off knifeblade. Two hours later, I wa teetering sideways for a long reach off a delicate bird beak. I think I only whimpered when stopped to look at the piece and knew I was going for another flight. While mid-reach to cli my previous piece, I sailed for another 40 feet of fun.

I've always maintained that free climbing will be the crux of any big wall, and this on proved to be no different. The 13th pitch was a 100-foot direct traverse across the mos unpleasant ledge system that I hope to ever see. Loose, dirty 5.9X climbing offered n protection and demanded strenuous hauling. I was forced to stretch a rope between the tw belays and partly haul, partly walk the haul bags across the span.

As usual with soloing traverses, cleaning the pitch was as much of a thrill as the lead. Th ledge became twice as unpleasant when I noticed that there were several haulbags abandone farther down the ledge. They were Go Abe's, the solo Japanese climber who had perished o the wall the year before. The clouds that were quickly filling the valley below magnified th ominous feeling. Within an hour, the temperature had dropped significantly, visibility wa less than 50 feet, and it had started to snow.

*August 5, 1998.* 10:35 a.m. It is now really time to get off this wall. Last night I jolted awake and thought I was hearing more rockfall. While fumbling for my camera,

I realized that the sound was my watch alarm, beeping. When I tried to turn it off, I remembered that it was always set for 10:30 a.m. It was now only 3:17 a.m. Then I didn't hear it anymore. Haven't seen people in almost two weeks.

*August 5, 1998.* 8:30 p.m. Bivied at top of 14. It snowed all day. Way rad expando flake. Six pitches to go. My head is starting to feel nuked. I was hearing that fucking watch beep all day long, but not really. I took it off and almost hucked it, but decided I need it. My CD player quit working tonight as well. Junk.

I still can't figure out how 12 a.m. can be the hour after 11 p.m. Shouldn't 12 a.m. follow 11 a.m.?

Over the course of the next few days, my psyche and the weather both deteriorated at exponential rates. I found the climbing up the headwall to be not only steep, but very sustained as well. My two-pitch days were becoming difficult to keep up, especially with the now-daily snowstorms. The nature of the climbing had become very much like modern El Cap routes: particularly frightening.

No matter how much I climb, I am always learning new things about the sport, the gear, and the rock. Sometimes it seems like the simplest details are the ones that, when overlooked, can be the most terrifying. For instance: when rope soloing, clipping wire rivet hangers for an upward pull can result in a fall much farther than necessary; and, Grigris and icy ropes were not meant to be friends and should never be introduced to each other. Re-learning both of these lessons had me feeling strong summit fever.

*Atop pitch 13, 2,500 feet up on Hrungnir Ledge on the seventh night on the wall.* JASON SMITH

A laborious corner, a small flake, some free climbing, and I suddenly found myself looking down the east slopes of Mt. Thor. I hadn't walked in 13 days. I stumbled over the summit ridge, untied, and jogged and jumped around the boulders. Suddenly it seemed as if all of my woes on the wall—cold, food, water, wind, snow, rockfall—had been trivial. Being constantly connected to 400 pounds of gear for two weeks had become a psychological weight on my shoulders. Even though I was still miles from shelter, just being untied from the ropes felt like a new life.

In many ways, I was ecstatic that such an experience was close to being over; in others, I felt that I wanted it to go on. I wanted something more. In some warped sense, I wanted an epic; I wanted to get really worked.

I quickly rapped back to the last belay and cleaned the pitch. Just as I finished the last haul, it began to snow intensely. Feeling that a summit bivy would not be much like a slumber party, I quickly packed up my four haulbags and dragged them to a ledge that overhung the face. I attached my drogue parachute and sent the load back to the base.

M y only beta for getting down from the summit was, "Oh yeah, there's this talus and these fixed ropes that. . . . Well, you'll find 'em."

As the blizzard increased, I moved cautiously down the talus. I reached an impassable cliff band, then walked back and forth searching for the ropes through the snow. I finally spotted the anchor, but simultaneously realized that I had inadvertently left my rappel device in the snow at the summit. Fortunately, I had enough carabiners to build a brake, though it would leave me short if I had to rig an anchor.

Halfway down the 200-meter rope was an ice-coated, two-foot core shot. I bounced to get the frayed cord through my device, my eyes glued to the spot until I was safely off the rope. Some more scrambling led into an obvious gully system. Arriving at an 80-foot cliff, I scanned the area for the ropes that had been at all previous and similar areas. There were none. There was also no place to rig any decent anchor. I retraced some of my path back up the slope, but found that the cliff was the only way down. I was now faced with down climbing a low-angle, flaring off-width.

Since I had descended out of the snowstorm and into a drainage gully, the fissure was flowing with a refreshing cascade of ice water. I crawled into the crack and tried to repeat semi-controlled slides to get down. I would slowly squirm down until I was unable to hang on, at which point I would find a chockstone below me and let go, paddling at the rock to stay in the gaping maw. Twice I was able to latch onto chockstones; once I was able to throw in an arm bar.

Soon enough, I was cruising the level ground below. Some time later I stopped to rest on a rock. I awoke to my watch beeping several hours later—1:38 a.m. I groggily pulled out my bivy gear, climbed in, and slept for another 12 hours.

The next day I returned to my base camp at Windy Lake. After resting for two days, I returned to the wall for my gear. For the next week, all the work I did seemed surreal. The lack of real objective dangers combined with the desire to return home forced me to put strong physical demands on myself: I walked up to 35 miles per day to get my gear back to Overlord.

One week later, I had a seat on the morning flight out of Pangnirtung. Fading into sleep, watching the desolate landscape pass below, I was startled by my watch alarm beeping out a wake-up call. As I pulled back my sleeve to inspect the scratched face, I was relieved to see that it was 10:30 a.m., sharp.

SUMMARY OF STATISTICS

AREA: Auyuittuq National Park, Baffin Island, Canada

FIRST SOLO ASCENT: *Midgard Serpent* (VI 5.9 A5, 3,600') on the west face of Mt. Thor, July-August, 1998, D. Jason "Singer" Smith, solo

# The Southwest Face of King Peak

## Personal evolution on an overlooked gem

by Joe Josephson


A profound form of love. This is how a long-time friend once described obsession. Ten years ago I used her words as a kinder, more acceptable justification for doing whatever the hell I wanted. In my impetuous youth, I really had no idea what that was. But I did know one thing. For the better part of a decade I desperately wanted to climb a new route on King Peak in the St. Elias Range of the Yukon Territories, Canada.

My taste for King Peak began in 1989 while on my first big mountain trip: the Trench Route on Mount Logan (19,540'). At 16,971 feet, King Peak is dwarfed by its neighbor, Logan, but nonetheless it is the ninth highest peak in North America. The north face rises in Eiger-like proportions in one dramatic 5,000-foot sweep. The south ridge falls from the summit with Peruvianesque flutings and ends with several tendrils submerged deep in the Seward Icefield. From an eastern or western vantage point, references to Nepal's Pumori are not uncommon.

In this age of trophy climbing, one would imagine a mountain like King Peak to be world-famous and climbed often, yet it remains unique in every sense of the word. When Steve House and I arrived at the base on May 31, 1998, only five parties had stood atop King Peak via four different routes. Of those, only one was alpine style and within the last 30 years.

When it comes to trophies, chasing numbers and focusing solely on achievement, I carry my share of guilt. In terms of climbing King Peak, I found myself wanting to climb the coldest, steepest and, more importantly, the most recognizable feature of the mountain. The austere, unclimbed north face of King Peak became a drive that, although not constant, was nonetheless obsessive.

In the early 1990s, I had made several narrow-minded attempts to organize an expedition to the north face. It was Canadian pioneer Chic Scott who first alerted me to what he called "a route of the 21st Century" on the southwest face of the mountain. In 1995, while attempting to guide Logan, Troy Kirwan, Barry Blanchard and I skied over from base camp with this carrot of information for a look.

The southwest face rises close to 7,500 vertical feet from the Quintino Sella Glacier. The first 4,000 feet is a sweeping 50- to 60-degree ice face which narrows into a small but passable icefall. The upper half of the face is all rock save for a splitter gully that rises to meet the west ridge. The first 500 feet of the gully, with mixed climbing, is clearly the crux, after which the route slants left and becomes a more straight-forward ice couloir.

The line is not visionary. It's obvious. Anyone with a compulsion toward new routes, alpine mixed climbs or just direct lines on big mountains would feel drawn. But in my mind I continued to defer to the hallowed ground of the north wall. The southwest face would be

the "warm up"—the consolation prize. Unfortunately, due to horrific weather, Barry, Troy and I barely got off Logan alive. We hardly saw King Peak, let alone attempted a route.

In the years after our stalled trip, my vision of climbing King Peak evolved from doing one particular route for all the wrong reasons to doing a great route for a few of the right ones. As I mentioned, the southwest face route didn't take a visionary to figure out. But perhaps vision lies in style, and it definitely is found in the relationships required to succeed. Alpinism is all about relationships—with the range, the mountain, the weather, the conditions, yourself, your life, your friends, your lovers, and your climbing partners, if any. None of these take precedence over another. Intimate respect and heed is placed simultaneously on all these factors.

The vision of climbing the north face dimmed. Not to be mistaken, King Peak remained very much in my consciousness. Steve and I were both intrigued by the north wall, just as we would be with any spectacular feature. But by the time we arrived on the Quintino Sella Glacier, there was no longer any desire, latent or otherwise, to climb it.

Instead, we had a simpler objective: the southwest face. We also had an important attitude: a willingness to fail. We wanted to make a continuous ascent of the route by beginning around midnight and climbing the ice face and the crux gully. Then, after 14-16 hours of climbing, we would stop for several hours during the heat of the day to eat, brew up and nap. Once we started getting cold, we'd tag the summit and descend the east ridge to our camp at King Col. We would carry no sleeping bags or tents. Our only bivouac gear would be a single shovel blade and an extra coat each. We would either climb the southwest face in this style, or not at all.

W ithin days of our arrival, we had moved a small camp to King Col, where we joined the critical mass of guided Logan parties. Over the next few days, in the name of acclimatization, we socialized, putzed about, did a little skiing and enjoyed our time together. One fine day we hiked up to the base of the east ridge of King Peak. From this vantage it became obvious the ridge is much steeper and icier than we had anticipated. To down climb it after a long and tiring ascent would be very dangerous, so we quickly decided to descend the 1952 West Ridge/North Face route instead. We moved our cached skis to a spot in the Trench at about 12,000 feet directly below the north face.

On June 7, we moved back to Base Camp to wait for the weather. On June 10, we laid around all evening and, after just falling into a nervous sleep, awoke at midnight on my 31st birthday.

Those individuals who have done a lot of alpine starts with me know I can be frustratingly schizophrenic. One morning I'll be outwardly talkative and hardly containable; the next, I'll stay buried somewhere inside myself and mumble barely a word. I've learned that, for me, both can be equally stimulating, but Steve had yet to understand this. He thought I wasn't psyched. In the hour it took to get ready, Steve had to deal with his own preparation while feeling like he had to motivate me. It turned into a classic case of polar responding. His attempt to motivate me simply plunged me deeper into my introverted side, which accelerated his own excitement.

If I'm feeling lazy or scared, I'll often just want to wallow there like a moose in deep snow until I figure out my feelings. Beginning climbers talk about developing a head so they can get over their reticence. I've worked hard to go the other way. In my tenure of alpine climbing, I've learned to listen to my "spidey senses." But perhaps the most important thing I've learned in my years of climbing is that intuition isn't infallible. I've been lucky. With that hard-earned knowledge I've gotten slower, more cautious, and less likely to go for it. I call it "Retro-Head."

At times I noticed myself getting annoyed at Steve's seemingly endless drive. In moments of impatience, I would want to shout, "Why can't you just calm down!" But this internal dialogue would be quickly replaced with, "Get a grip, JoJo. You know it's not him."

I know few people in this world who are less competitive or have a better understanding about their own mortality than Steve. My irritation was simply my own uncertainty about my feelings, laziness, and fear. Perhaps that is why Steve and I had connected and become friends and climbing partners. Unbeknownst to him, Steve had exposed a weakness and forced me to face it.

We left the tent at 1 a.m. It was a three-hour ski from Base Camp to the bottom of the face. By the time we got there, Steve realized that, in the frenetic pace he set for himself at the tent, he had forgotten one of two water bottles and his extra fleece jacket. Because we barely had anything in the first place, it was a noticeable oversight. I was a little surprised Steve would forget such things and simultaneously felt disappointment and perhaps a little hope: disappointment that we might not get to try what we had planned, and hopeful that perhaps we'd get to ski back to the certainty of base camp. Steve was just pissed. I gave him an extra hat I had planned to leave at the skis and figured we could manage.

Once we got above the bergschrund, we took the rope off and continued up the 4,000-foot ice face we later termed the "Great Sweep." Upon arriving near the base of the crux gully a little less than five hours later, Mount St. Elias was enveloped in cloud. Within minutes, the top 3,000 feet of King Peak disappeared in a large lenticular cloud. We started down together yet alone. Rappelling would have taken too long and been exposed to objective hazards with anchors too timely and difficult to make. These facts weren't up for discussion.

*Steve House with 30 pounds of courage in front of the ca. 7,500-foot southwest face of King Peak.* JOE JOSEPHSON

We barely spoke the entire way down. To ease the monotony, we'd alternate grabbing the top of the ax in piolet panne, holding the shaft just under the head. At times we'd be forced to swing both tools into the steeper, icier sections, but we generally avoided that as much as possible. We'd look for anything resembling deeper snow or softer névé where we could stand without front-pointing or cocking our ankles like the head of a curious dog. I would hone in on the next outcrop or ice feature to break the descent into manageable portions, only to find that I didn't want to look down too often lest I notice how painfully slow we were in reaching those chosen yardsticks. And looking down was only marginally better than looking up at the seracs that threatened the bottom half of the Great Sweep.

Getting off took over six hours of tedious crabbing. At no point could we turn around and face out. Flopped at the base in utter exhaustion and frustration, we agreed it was perhaps the worst thing either of us had ever done in the mountains.

We spent a few days recovering and socializing with new friends in Base Camp. A closer look at the crux gully and time in camp allowed us to rethink our packs. Among other things, we took out our 6-mm rappel line. This left us with one 9.1-mm 60-meter rope, seven ice screws, four cams, six pitons, six stoppers, a shovel blade, a MSR stove, pot, two freeze-dried dinners, tea, about 20 GU packets a piece, a down coat and extra pair of gloves and mitts each. Our packs weighed about 30 pounds combined, including the rope and rack.

Not often have I gone onto a 7,500-foot alpine face with one rope. Yet we knew the rope wouldn't be uncoiled before the crux gully, and once we got over that it would probably be easier to go over the top than retreat. The concept was simple. We were unwilling to down climb the ice face again due to objective danger and the sincere belief that we had burned a few lucky stars the first time.

Understandably, we were nervous about committing to the route without very stable weather. For days, there had been some fog and unstructured, high cirrus clouds streaming above, but the weather remained stable, with about 14 hours out of every 36 being perfect. The entire time we were in Base Camp the altimeter moved very little, if at all.

Our pickup date was June 21. By the 17th, everyone else on the mountain was gone. We were beginning to believe we wouldn't do King Peak. But the weather refused to change, so in the first hours of the 18th we left Base Camp for the second and last time.

Skiing toward the face, the frozen texture of the glacier reminded me fondly of the rumpled white flannel sheets I used as a child. There was none of my moody trepidation, and none of Steve's frantic packing nor forgotten crucial pieces. We knew more about the route and the conditions, we knew greatly more about each other, and we knew more about what we were there to do. The Great Sweep was under us quickly and we arrived at our previous high point by 9:30 a.m. Going a little higher, we found a rock anchor on the right and started belaying.

The first pitch was a nice moderate ice pitch with some thin ice. The second pitch climbed a short bulge to an easier gully that led to a prominent collection of icicles pouring off a thumb of rock to the left. The surrounding rock was proving to be some of the most bizarre, twisted, cooked rock I've seen. Decent rock protection was sporadic at best.

It was Steve's lead. The pitch would clearly be the crux—and it was beautiful, with good, hard mixed climbing to the right of the thumb of icicles. At first I felt a brief twinge of disappointment that it wasn't my lead, but I learned long ago not to argue if my partner draws the short straw and/or wants to do the hard pitch. I'll get my share naturally enough.

From the belay, Steve went into the gully and climbed up a vertical ice pillar in the back of the corner to the right of the icicles. After about ten meters, the angle eased. At this point the prominent icicles were level with and out in space directly behind Steve. Fifteen meters of hard mixed climbing with very little gear led to an invisible stance on the ice above the icicles.

*House getting into the thick of things on* Call of the Wild, *with the crux icicles looming above.*
JOE JOSEPHSON

The rope stopped. For 40 minutes I heard nothing except the occasional jiggle of the rope. Clumps of crusty ice shot over the lip, the bigger ones trying to smash my hands and shoulders, the smaller pieces searching a way into the back of my collar. Steve managed to get four pieces of gear: a slung horn (the best piece), a knifeblade behind a flake, a second (worse) piton and two equalized, tied-off, stubby ice screws. For the last half hour I had been watching the sun come around the face. My thoughts were preoccupied with its arrival—that is, I was looking forward to its heat but praying we'd finish the pitch before it hit.

"Okay," Steve said, breaking the stillness. "I'm going for it."

With Steve's call the sun disappeared, and my only thoughts went up the rope, into my partner and whatever he was dealing with. In all my alpine climbing experiences, it is exactly moments like this that are the most hopeful, the most dreadful, the most intense, the craziest, and the most savory. I concentrated on my belay, adjusting the rope so as not to give unwanted tension and ready to feed it out if he needed slack for a desperate clip. But the desperate clip never came. The rope fed upward at a steady rate and I heard nothing save the pattering of hard snow crystals and the occasional ice chunk bowling down the gully. When I was hit by a pillow of spindrift Steve had knocked down and then heard a telltale hoot, I knew he had reached easier ground.

Upon following the pitch, I seriously wondered if I would have attempted it. Above Steve's gear there was but one narrow strip in the rotten smattering that took good tool placements. This strip was on the right side of an overhanging groove that pushed me backward onto a pillar of unconsolidated ice that resembled wax drippings more than an icicle. This also leaned, forcing me into gymnastic body positions reminiscent of cragging close to the car. Yet the entire 20 meters of this overhanging section was covered in a tapestry of useless crusted snow that is typical of and really only found on alpine routes and for which no roadside waterfall route could ever prepare you.

I was proud of Steve's lead, and thankful it was his. Ten years ago it would have been my focus as well. Today, it was merely a pain in the ass. But it dawned on me that I was at the point I'd evolved to in the last ten years: in the middle of an adventure with an incredibly talented partner and awesome friend, knowing that every aspect of our route and the trip were equally important and valuable.

After a brief, relieved break at Steve's belay, we continued up, sharing the work and the hopefulness. The entire upper face was about 50 degrees and, although it had a lot of rocks sticking out, pure ice. We climbed roped up, placing ice screws and the occasional rock piece between us as we moved together. After nine rope lengths we moved left onto a broad ice slope that, in another four rope lengths, gave easy access to the west ridge. All told, it had taken 13 hours to reach the west ridge from where we left the skis.

We dug small platforms out of the wind on the north side of the ridge and sat down to eat, brew and attempt a nap. We had hoped to stop earlier in the day but had found absolutely no ledges anywhere and no snow to dig into. Cornices had threatened the bottom part of the upper gully. All day high cirrus had been building, yet St. Elias remained clear. We thought little of it, as it was no different than the preceding days' patterns.

Around 9 p.m., the clouds got thicker, blocking the warming sun. Caps formed over St. Elias and Logan, and darker rain clouds could be seen lower in the Chitna Valley. Our hydrating nap in the sun turned into a few hours of shivering and choking on indigestible freeze-dried munge. With nothing better to do, we packed up and nervously headed for the summit.

LEFT: *House starting the WI6X crux pitch, 4,500 feet into the route.* JOE JOSEPHSON

The first pitch from the ledge wandered out across snow slopes to the bottom of a small, broken rock step. A mixed step left put Steve in a shallow snow gully, which he followed to a good belay off a slung horn just below the summit ridge. A short easy section led to the main ridge. We then moved together across the ridge, first on the south side and then, several pitches before the summit, on the exposed north side. We stayed well back from either edge and some ten meters below the true summit for fear of cornices.

All-in-all, it was a disappointing summit. Despite appearances from below, the top was non-distinct and the 11:30 p.m. twilit gloom was ominous. The clouds were thickening and the top 1,500 feet of Logan were already gone.

We returned to the summit rock step, where we made a short rappel off the slung horn (our only rappel on the entire descent). As soon as we got back to the ledge and repacked, the weather really turned. We continued to down climb the ridge by moving together and threading the rope around snow pinnacles, staying on opposite sides of the ridge and only occasionally placing ice screws. We anticipated rappelling the obviously rocky sections we had scoped from the Trench. In the heavy snow and twilight darkness, however, we found not a single rock anchor worth weighting. After battling this peak, I doubt they would be found even under brilliant blue sky and unlimited time to look. On King Peak, they don't exist. With some effort we were able to find our way around the rock sections by down climbing and traversing through bad snow on the north side of the ridge. It was a white-out pretty much the entire way down and we were frightfully dehydrated, but by then we were so wet that if we stopped we'd get too cold. Our only food, GU packets, stuck to our mouths like half-and-half on a hot day.

The trickiest part of the descent was finding the start of the ramp that leads back below the north face. Steve led out on a likely looking snow bench. I wasn't convinced, but lacking a definitive alternative, I went with his judgment. It was too high, leaving us stranded somewhere on the north face with eerie shadows of seracs and omnipresent voids invisible through the whiteout. We returned through deep snow back to the ridge, taking some two hours.

I was pissed. How could he be so impatient? Somewhere inside, though, I knew my anger was nothing but my own fatigue and frustration. I didn't know any more about the descent than he did.

Later on, Steve lowered me down an ice section when I just couldn't take it any more, and then down climbed it himself. The unspoken give-and-take; the shallow desire to say "told you so," immediately followed by unrequested assistance just when you need it most; two people allowing each other to feel whatever it is they feel. This is what alpine climbing is all about. These relationships are only spawned out of intimacy—out of a profound form of love.

A big bergschrund guards the top of the ramp. After several belayed probes and more time and energy than either one of us cared to expend, we found an easy way across. The visibility cleared quite a bit, and the route across the ramp proved to be easy. We spent 40 minutes under very big and active seracs. It's amazing how dread can motivate. It was the best we felt all day as we virtually sprinted to the relative safety of the Trench.

When we got to the skis, I asked Steve if our initial attempt on the face was still the most hateful thing he had done in the mountains.

"No," he said with a smile.

A quick ski on perfect snow brought us down to Base Camp, 35 hours after leaving. I am a survival skier in the best sense of the word and frequently use the phrase "hating life" when describing my ski experiences. Yet halfway to base it dawned on me that I had been skating down the freeze-thaw surface of the glacier. I was even practicing alpine turns on the steeper parts. At that moment, in the King Trench with Steve gliding down somewhere behind me, I was glad to be alive. It became obvious to me why King Peak has been climbed only six times.

SUMMARY OF STATISTICS

AREA: St. Elias Mountains, Canada

NEW ROUTE: *Call of the Wild* (VI WI6, 7,500') on the southwest face of King Peak, June 18-19, 1998, Joe Josephson and Steve House

# El Gigante

## The first ascent of Mexico's biggest wall

by Cecilia Buil, *Spain*
*translated by Robyn Fulwiler and Margaret Thompson*

In 1996, geologist Carlos Lazcano, together with the Caving and Exploration Group of Cuauhtemoc City (GEECC), rappeled the enormous northwest face of El Gigante ("The Giant"). Known up until then as El Cerro Del Coronel ("the Colonel's Mountain"), it became classified as the biggest wall in Mexico.

Two years later, Lazcano headed up a project (in which the government of Chihuahua participated) to find climbers to attempt El Gigante's first ascent. Carlos García and I had climbed together the previous year in Yosemite. We had money that La Peña Guara, my climbing club in Huesca, Spain, had donated toward a new route on a big wall in Baja California. The information we had about the Baja wall was very distorted, and suddenly we found ourselves in a strange situation. With everything ready, we found that we lacked the most important thing: the wall.

In search of a wall to climb, we spoke to Lazcano. He put us in contact with the many people who would come to assist us in the first ascent of El Gigante. D. Fernando Dominguez welcomed us at the San Lorenzo Ranch, where we stayed in a cabin while in Basaseachic Waterfall National Park, location of El Gigante. Anibal and his nephew work at the ranch, maintaining the camping area and cabins. Anibal became the chauffeur of the 4x4 that would transport us during our efforts. He planned to call us via radio every three days from the overlook on the other side of the canyon. D. Santiago, together with another four local guides, transported 300 kilos of food and equipment for us down into the canyon. The GEECC, among whom were Victor, Salvador, and Mario, would rappel the last meters of the wall to supply us with food or water in an emergency. All of Chihuahua followed the event with great interest, informed by nosy journalists, who, in their eagerness for sensationalism, caused a misunderstanding that provoked the strange outcome of this story.

The closer we got to the edge, the more we realized how deep the Candamena Canyon was. El Gigante showed its head at first, then little by little began to reveal its body. Then, before our astonished eyes, an impressive wall with an enormous waterfall rose on the left. A river at the base of the wall squeezed itself between reddish rocks that marked the boundary between the sparsely inhabited area up above and the one at the bottom of the canyon. Our nervousness grew as we contemplated the wall. Should we climb to the left? Were there any cracks? What if the binoculars were useless? We studied the northwest face (few features; no ledges), envisioning a direct line that passed through a roof about two-thirds of the way up. The next day, as we went down the trail the porters had recently cleared with machetes, we discussed whether the wall in front of us was indeed El Gigante.

LEFT: *The 1,000-meter west face of El Gigante in Basaseachic Waterfall National Park, Chihuahua, Mexico.* CECILIA BUIL

*Carlos García cleans one of the lower-angled pitches of* Simuchi. CECILIA BUIL

Just before we reached the river, we began to see El Gigante's profile, vertical, imposing, and even bigger than the one we had seen while descending. There was rock everywhere, enormous and virgin.

We found a small level area between some poplars and huge-leafed plants to set up our tents. The river was very close. It grew wider downstream where we had to cross it to reach the wall. Over the next few days, we worked to build a make-shift bridge, clear the trail and transport gear, water, and food to the base of the climb, all the while observing the wall up close.

At night, one could hear rocks bouncing off the boulders in the riverbed. The plants that dared grow too close to the wall looked as if they had been chopped by machetes. We passed along the base as little as possible.

We carried a lot of equipment—among other things, 45 liters of water, food for two weeks, two static and two 11-millimeter dynamic ropes. Carlos climbed the first pitch, a dirty and disagreeable ramp, casually, without roping up, then left it fixed. The next day we climbed to the first belay stance, a sloping dirt shelf. Carlos moved up above dubious protection toward enormous blocks above the belay. I gave myself slack so I could belay a few meters to the right. As I did, I lost Carlos from sight. Suddenly, he was flying. He stopped, suspended above me.

"The block moved and I fell!" he said. "I'm going back to try it again."

Following the blocks, a well-defined crack rose until it met a smooth rock face. It was getting late; we returned to camp. The ambience of the surrounding night was awesome.

The sudden crash of rocks falling from El Gigante into the enormous riverbed boulders broke the monotonous rhythm of the river. The porters kept a fire burning all night, which served as protection against the cold and the small creatures that inhabit the canyon. The next day we went back to finish the pitch.

I hooked to the right a few meters. The face didn't have any cracks, but there were some tiny pockets in the rock covered with yellow and gray lichen. I hadn't found any gear after a couple of hook moves, so I decided to place a bolt. The rock was so hard that although I worked diligently, after 15 minutes I had only managed to drill a centimeter-deep hole and decided to use it to bathook.

The climbing was fickle, obliging me to advance with caution. The last piece of protection was many meters diagonally below, and my moves became very careful. An hour later I found myself hanging from a RP, 15 meters of hooking behind me, putting in a rivet out of desperation. We had graduated from the most dangerous pitch (A4) of the route.

Carlos led the third pitch (A3+) with RURPs, blades and hooks, and I took over on the fourth (A3), which, although it had a section of loose rock, was followed by a right-arching roof. At least I could get in some cams for gear. The following day, we jugged the 100-meter fixed ropes, bringing up the haulbags and organizing everything so that we could live on the wall for the next two weeks.

The sky clouded over, and it began to rain. We had nothing to eat, so we decided to travel back down the canyon toward the Basaseachic Waterfall. As we arrived at Base Camp, the rain turned to snow.

We walked up to San Lorenzo Ranch, where we recuperated by gorging and not raising a finger.

Five days later, we descended, accompanied by a guide and his two sons, who carried our tent and other equipment. We said good-bye to them and to the river.

"Buen viaje!" they said.

As they retreated a hummingbird appeared, making us smile.

Carlos completed the fifth pitch, a face with small, hidden cracks. While I was breaking down the belay, a rock fell, hitting me on the arm. The haulbag had knocked off a good one. From here on in, we started climbing only when the second reached the belay. We were learning. Our respect for El Gigante increased, and our fear of the deadly rocks kept us alert.

On our second night on the wall, El Gigante's salutation was emphatic: we awoke from our bivy to the creaking of what we imagined was a huge block falling from the roofs to our left. The clamor of it crashing down the lower slabs was followed by the impact of many rocks crashing against the talus at the base. We were speechless. We understood it to be both a greeting and a warning: we needed to find overhangs in order to sleep protected.

The days flew by. The climbing was difficult. Every three days we spoke by radio to Anibal or Santiago, who remained on the overlook across the canyon from El Gigante. The entire city of Chihuahua was following our climb with much interest.

Anibal watched over us like a guardian angel, and we awaited his words impatiently. A series of fortuitous signs came every day, compelling us to continue. We were gradually advancing with the days of the month. Whenever our psych ebbed, we would continually find various natural belays. Perfect timing. . . . But El Gigante wouldn't let us see very high, hiding its summit with roofs until pitch 16. It kept working us over, keeping us scared each and every day.

Sections of compact rock that we could only climb with peckers, RURPs and natural hooking were followed by sections of overhanging exfoliated rock that we had to bathook. The features creaked as we moved over them. When I was forced to drill holes for bathooking on the lower pitches, I drilled them too small. On pitch 7, the hole sheared out as I was moving from one hook to another. Fortunately, I didn't fall, but I did learn how to make proper holes.

After eight days, we were at the point of no return. We had to pass the roofs above us to the right via a disappearing crack. The rock was very sharp. At this point, it would have been very difficult to go down.

On pitch 13, during the night, we counted the holes we had drilled. We thought that after the roof we would have to carry the drill as dead weight, since we didn't expect to have to use it any further.

As we lay in our sleeping bags, we talked about our chances. It was Tuesday, April 13, and the climb was turning out to be very difficult.

The hummingbird returned to see us. "This hummingbird has brought us good luck," said Carlos. "Did you know that the hummingbird was the sacred bird of the Aztecs—the messenger of the gods?"

We decided to call the route Simuchi—"Hummingbird" in Tarahumara, the local language—out of gratitude to the original inhabitants of the region, who had shared their treasure with us and who allowed us to live in its midst for awhile.

On pitch 14, as I was putting in a rivet, I fell, penduluming to the right ten meters upside-down with the drill still in my hand. Suddenly, I could see a dihedral to my left. Half-stunned, I yelled, "I've seen it! We have to go to the left! But I've hit my knee and my head. Can you continue?"

"Of course," replied Carlos. "Come on down." He corrected our direction, advancing toward the left.

The next day we saw that the sheath and some of the rope's core had been cut during the fall. Once again we had to stop and think. The section we were crossing had sections of decomposing rock that formed sharp, inverted flakes, and cracks had become scarce. The climb continued to be difficult. Twelve days on, and we still couldn't see the summit.

Carlos led the rotten dihedral. I couldn't see him. All I could see were flakes of all sizes as they exploded below to the right. Everything sounded hollow. Hanging from this anchor so many meters from the ground was no fun, and it was even less so to haul the bags from one anchor to the next. They got caught in the flakes, but came free with a yank. Pessimism invaded us, and we felt like slitting each other's throats. But we had no options: we could only proceed, blindly. There was no possibility of descent.

In the afternoon we arrived at the Hope Bivouac. It had a tiny shelf on which we could cook. At last we saw the shoulder where the route exited just below the summit, as well as an easier way to it.

On Saturday morning we spoke with Anibal.

"Hi, how is it going? Over."

"Well. How much more do we have? Is this the summit? Over."

"You have 400 meters left. Over."

"That can't be. We've already climbed 750 meters. We're going to try to finish it without assistance. In any case, warn Search and Rescue to stay alert. We have water and food for at least two days. Over."

"Listen, Cecilia, there are some reporters here who would like to ask you something."

I grudgingly explained the situation one finds oneself in after having spent 13 days on a wall. That day we put up three more pitches.

*Carlos García on steep ground on* Simuchi. CECILIA BUIL

The next day we were front-page news in the *Chihuahua Daily.* "TRAPPED ON THE GIANT: They've gone two days without food or water. They cannot go up or down and they're 500 meters from the summit after two weeks." Our families were anxious. Meanwhile, we climbed quickly between wide cracks and free sections, though we knew only small amounts of water and food remained for the meters to come.

We came to the only large ledge on the route, which we called the San Lorenzo Ranch. It was steeply angled, but we could walk around on it and didn't need to clip in our gear. On the morning of April 21, as we were observing an offwidth that turned into a funnel higher up, rocks began to fall. We immediately turned on the radio.

"Hello. Is anyone there? Who is above us? Over."

"Victor and Mario are there," said Anibal. "They're coming down. Over and out."

We couldn't understand what was going on above us. Victor, a caver and doctor, appeared from above, with a concerned look on his face.

"How are you? Better than we had thought, I see—they told us that you had gone two days without water, but obviously that is not the case. I brought two Cokes. Do you want them before you come up?"

"Thanks for coming, Victor, but we don't want to leave. Did you bring food and water?" we asked.

"Sorry, no, but I thought I was going to have to take you off the wall in a bad state. I haven't brought anything," he responded.

"It's just that we're tired and we've now been here for 15 days. How much do we have left?"

"You still have quite a bit to go. It would be better for you to come up. Your families are about to have heart attacks. It would be best if you spoke with them. Everyone is alarmed—it would amaze you," he answered.

I didn't know whether to laugh or to cry. If we did have much more to go, I would abandon the climb, even though after so much effort I didn't want to leave the route uncompleted.

We didn't have an alternative. I began to jumar. After 50 meters I saw the shoulder. We had only three pitches left. On the one hand I was content, but on the other I was infuriated with the gutless journalist who had created such a mess.

"Get psyched," I yelled to Carlos. "There's nothing left."

There were many people on the shoulder. It was incredible, this organized display. The following day we went to recuperate at the village of Basaseachic. We spoke with our families, then returned to spend the night on the shoulder. It took us one day plus the next morning to finish the route. On the last day, the hummingbird was nowhere to be seen.

While climbing the last short and easy pitch, the wind blew in gusts, forcing me to pause. Gray clouds appeared to the northwest while mountain-dwelling parrots flew over the top. We climbed to the summit and contemplated the canyon one last time as nature made us feel her force. We understood. Thank you, Gigante.


SUMMARY OF STATISTICS

AREA: Basaseachic Waterfall National Park, Chihuahua, Mexico

FIRST ASCENT: *Simuchi* (VI 6c A4, 1000m) on the northwest face of El Gigante, April 5-25, 1998, Carlos García Ayala (Mexico) and Cecilia Buil (Spain)

# The Central Tower of Paine

## A singular education

by Steve Schneider

*The South, Central, and North Towers of Paine and Paineta (with Steve Schneider bouldering at ABC in foreground).* CHRISTIAN SANTELICES

My first view of Patagonia was from 30,000 feet. My partner, Jim Surette, and I jostled for window space in the jetliner. Below us, Cerro Torre and her satellite summits stood in full magnificence, stunning fingers of granite, sheer for thousands of feet on all sides, rising up out of the pampas like some huge beckoning hand. We could just imagine a pair of climbers down below us, gunning it for the summit, having the climb of a lifetime. Of course I had read about these mountains and the heroic feats of legendary climbers such as Maestri, Bridwell, Donini—but it was one thing to read about these peaks, and an altogether different experience to see them in their natural splendor and feel their raw power. With a last fleeting glimpse of the 5,000-foot south face of Cerro Torre, my world of Yosemite's walls was shattered. My education in the big mountains was about to begin.

Jimmy and I never came close to sending Cerro Torre, although it was unbelievably exciting just to set foot on that slender spire. On our first attempt we got blown out at the base of the hard climbing. Our bodies were actually lifted off the belays by enormous updrafts as we tried to communicate life-and-death decisions by yelling into each other's ears. By the

*Steve Schneider on pitch 10 (A3+) during a wet snowstorm, one month into the route.* CHRISTIAN SANTELICES

time we got down, I had re-injured a nagging wrist problem that relegated me to "trekker" status. It was probably not the worst luck, since I was now free to explore the park while the other climbers were shut down over the next two months from climbing anything worthwhile by unusually bad weather, even for Patagonia.

Near the end of that 1996-'97 season, I found myself climbing again, this time in the Paine region, 100 miles south of Cerro Torre. I hooked up with Ted Bonetti, a friend of a friend's friend, to make the second ascent of a route called *Caveman*, a fantastic-looking line up a striking 1,500-foot buttress in the seldom-visited French Valley. On top, a stiff wind and darkness arrived simultaneously, and we readied an emergency bivouac. Suddenly, I was spooning a guy I barely knew. As if that weren't exciting enough, the ensuing descent, complete with wicked Patagonian winds that made me feel like I was a kite, had me begging for more. I vowed to return.

The next year, my luck was better: I was present for an unheard-of 20-day clear spell. The highlight of the trip was climbing the west face of the Central Tower of Paine via the unrepeated Italian route, with Andreas Zegers, another guy I barely knew. As it turned out, this Santiago-based climber is Chile's most accomplished big wall climber, with 20 different routes on El Capitan under his belt. We cranked the route in under 23 hours, having a great time climbing through the night on wild offwidth cracks. This was the adventure I was craving, and the chance to use my Yosemite expertise to good measure.

But something was still missing. It was the unknown excitement of making a first ascent, the boldly-go-where-no-man-has-gone-before type of stuff. Which is why I found myself in Chilean Patagonia for a third straight year.

A rriving in Punta Arenas on January 24, 1999, I begin to prepare for a major first ascent up the center of the east face of the Central Tower of Paine. This 1200-meter face already had seven routes on it, but there appeared to be a couple of natural lines left. My partner for the climb was Christian Santilices, who had come to Paine five years previously with fellow Americans Brad Jarret and Chris Breemer and, by opening up the grand 1200-meter East Face of Escudo, basically climbed the hardest route in the Paine. The trio had climbed alpine style for 20 days, with Brad Jarret leading half of the climb—the hard half, up to A4+. I continually looked up to Christian for his experience and perseverance on this monumental climb.

For my own part, besides my two years' experience in Patagonia, I had climbed El Capitan 55 times, including two first ascents, three solos, and eight speed records. But this venture was by far the biggest climb I had ever attempted. We chose to emulate the Escudo climb by climbing alpine style (which had never been done on this wall), pulling our ropes up behind us as we made a series of camps up the face. As a party of two, we were also the smallest party to attempt the wall.

For the next four weeks, with the help of some porters, we established our first camp 400 meters up the wall, the last 150 meters of which shared ground with the 1992 British *El Regalo de Mwoma* route. The British route traversed right from our camp to ascend a "kilometer-high knifeblade crack." Although the initial 400 meters of our line had been mostly slabby free climbing, the climbing that now loomed above was vertical for the next 600 meters. Our line paralleled the British route 100 feet to the right, but it appeared much fainter, with two distinct blank sections between thin-looking cracks. This perhaps explained why it had been left unclimbed.

On February 25, in dubious weather, we committed to the face, moving into Camp I and pulling our fixed ropes as we ascended. We had 16 days of food, 30 liters of water, and, we hoped, enough fuel to cook and melt snow for water.

In the first seven days on the wall, during which the weather was typical Patagonia with snow and high winds every day, we only fixed three-and-a-half pitches. Over the course of the week, I noticed an increasing agitation in Christian, who began expressing a huge feeling of homesickness. Twice he relinquished leads to me that he felt were too hard for himself, and I could tell it bothered him to not be putting in an equal contribution. Still, I greedily snatched them up. The climbing was continually challenging and totally natural: each pitch consisted predominantly of peckers, beaks, knifeblades, and lost arrows—and no rivets. For 1,000 feet, the crack rarely exceeded an eighth of an inch in width, and blank sections were linked via challenging tension traverses. My spirit soared with the beauty of the climb and the experience of living on this remote wall.

On our seventh day on the wall, while waiting out a snowstorm, things came to a head as Christian announced his decision to return to the ground. There was no discussing his decision; the finality in his voice represented a man who had made up his mind. To his credit, it seemed he had willed himself to continue the last couple of days more to honor his commitment to climbing the wall with me than for any desire to make the climb. While perturbed by the turn of events, I had to respect Christian's decision to descend. What remained was the question of what I would now do.

We talked out different options. I still wished to continue. We probably had enough rope to descend to the ground and yet remain fixed to our highpoint. We could descend together, and maybe I could recruit another partner in town to come back up the wall. I could just quit, possibly to return the next year. Or I could just suck up the slack and solo the wall, an outlandish proposition considering nobody had ever soloed a wall this big in Paine, let alone a first ascent. If I chose to go on, it would be the biggest decision in my life (or death). With no other climbers in the valley, a rescue seemed a slim possibility, and a solo ascent seemed just plain dangerous.

*Steve Schneider hanging loose on pitch 12 (A4).* CHRISTIAN SANTELICES

I probably should have bailed with Christian. It certainly would have saved some grief with my family back home. But something in my heart stirred. The thought of turning back made me sick. I realized that I wanted the summit, and I wanted it like nothing I had ever wanted before.

That night, I announced my decision to Christian to continue on alone. He acted surprised about my choice to continue, seemed guilty to be leaving me in a precarious situation, and was visibly stressed about my safety. But Christian's suggestion to come with him next year, when he was more psyched, fell on deaf ears. If I respected his decision to descend, he was equally bound to respect my decision to keep going.

On the morning of the eighth day, Christian and I embraced and went our separate ways. We kept in radio contact for a few hours, and then I was alone.

I began a steady routine of waking up at 7 a.m., having coffee and oatmeal, and then climbing until 8 or 9 at night. Occasionally I would be forced to take a rest day as the incredible effort took a serious toll on my body. I was plagued by leg cramps, general fatigue, and a flare-up of carpal tunnel syndrome that caused stinging pain and numbness in my hands.

On day 11, I set up Camp II 700 meters above the glacier. While Camp I, situated above a large ramp, had been protected from the full brunt of the wind, Camp II was set up on a hanging stance without a hint of a corner to shelter my portaledge. My whole justification for continuing on the wall was the premise that I always had a secure camp to retreat to and make myself relatively comfortable in during the worst conditions. Even with my portaledge now tied down on the outside corners in two different directions, though, I realized that I was hanging my ass way, way out there.

Above Camp II, the crack opened up, allowing for more cam placements and faster progress. The weather had improved to where it was only snowing one or two hours a day. However, it began to get increasingly windy at night. During my 14th night on the wall, the wind absolutely rocked my little hovel. The fly vibrated madly at a huge crescendo all night long. The inside corners of my ledge, which had no tie downs, bounced me up and down continuously. I held on through the night as successive updrafts tried to unleash my ledge from its anchors. Outside, a full Patagonian tempest was in progress, and my premise of feeling safe as long as I had my nice little secure portaledge lost all of its validity as the word "survival" surfaced to mind.

Around 6 a.m., the wind died down. My precious camp remained intact. I rested for four hours, too utterly wrecked to contemplate climbing.

But one detail gnawed at my attempts at sleep. A strategy flaw as serious as the weather now put my ascent in jeopardy. I was quickly running out of fuel. Down to my last canister, my days on the wall were numbered. I had no idea when this last canister would run out, leaving me with no water and short-circuiting my climb.

I had six ropes with which to fix pitches above Camp II. Four were already fixed, and I would have liked to fix two more before making a summit push. But with my fuel supply at a critical level, I made a decision to strike for the summit then and there, even though I was still weary from the previous night's epic.

*Looking down on the exposed Camp II, 2,200 feet up the wall.* STEVE SCHNEIDER

I left Camp II just after noon, summit bound. I climbed one more pitch in daylight, and then continued through the night up such memorable rope lengths as "Starry, Starry, Night," named for obvious reasons, and "The British Are Coming," where the British route traversed mine. Most of the climbing was A1 and A2, although ice-filled cracks slowed my progress. It was 6 a.m. when I arrived at the first of two snowfields that signified a lower-angle section 500 feet below the summit ridge. Not wanting to crampon up in the darkness, I waited for dawn. At 7:30 a.m., the sun came up, bright and warm. A weather check revealed a beautiful day. All systems were go. I marveled at my luck and prepared for the final assault.

In the middle of the next lead, in between placing two ice screws, I glanced up to notice a condor cruising the air currents above. It was my first sighting of one of these majestic birds since I had started the climb. In contrast to my clunky, labored progress, the bird soared in silent, effortless flight. It began a slow circle, and I saw its wings dip, as if in acknowledgment of my presence and our shared solitude. I bent down to the task at hand, and my next glance upward revealed a birdless sky, and a renewed enthusiasm for my escapade.

The next few pitches went quickly as I punched though the second snowfield, stemmed up a verglass-covered chimney, and hit the complex summit ridge of the Central Tower of Paine. I faced a false summit gendarme with the summit just beyond. It took five minutes of gazing to spy a tricky mantle that gained access to an easy traverse of the gendarme. Untying from the rope, I soloed the last few moves to the true summit.

Complex emotions of triumph, pride, joy, amazement, confidence, and completeness each took turns engulfing me in their exquisite flavors. An after-taste of anxiety permeated the experience as the realization of how totally extended I was hit home. I lingered for perhaps 15 minutes, snapping a few photos and admiring the views, then began the descent to my high camp, almost 600 meters below. Although dehydrated and haggard, the descent went well, and I crawled into my portaledge at about 8 p.m., 32 hours after leaving.

It took me two more days to complete the descent. I ran out of fuel at the last minute, and developed a minor case of frostbite on my big toes due to my shoes being too tight, which I have to say was a rookie mistake. I'll probably lose my toenails, but nothing else. I was on the wall for 18 days, 11 of which were solo.

I named the route *Golazo,* after the popular South American cheer of good sportsmanship (it is, as well, my favorite chocolate bar in Chile). I returned to America on March 24, exactly two months after going to South America. I just might take a break from climbing down there next year—although Cerro Torre still looms on the horizon.

SUMMARY OF STATISTICS

AREA: Paine National Park, Chile

NEW ROUTE: *Golazo* (VI 5.10 A4+, 1200m) on the east face of the Central Tower of Paine, February 22-March 11, 1999, Steve Schneider, solo (Christian Santelices to pitch 12)

LEFT: *The Central Tower of Paine. Routes are as follows. A: American (Kearney-Knight, 1981-'82. B: Whale of the Winds (Lazkano-Tamayo-Brand-Hayward-de la Cruz, 1992). C: Insumisioa (Melero-Saez, 1995). D: Via Magico Este (Giarolli-Orlandi-Salvaterra, 1986). E: Riders on the Storm (Batz-Dittrich-Arnold-Güllich-Albert, 1990-91). F: El Regalo de Mwoma (Pritchard-Yates-Craine-Smith, 1992). G: Golazo (Schneider, 1999). H: South African (Scott-Smithers, 1974). I: Una Fina Línea de Locura (Calvo-Luro-Plaza; Benedetti-Lloyd-Luro, 1993).* STEVE SCHNEIDER

# Welcome to Patagonia

## A primer for wild walls and wilder weather

by Charlie Fowler

*The welcoming committee.* CHARLIE FOWLER

November 28, 1997. I'm in Kathmandu, crippled by a 1,500-foot tumble down a mountain in west Tibet. Anatoli Boukreev, on his way to Annapurna, takes me to the airport and wheels me to the plane. I can't walk, but I dream of climbing again. We talk about climbing Shishapangma next fall, shake on it and I fly home. Exactly one year later, to the day, I'm flying south to Patagonia with Steph Davis.

It is a difficult year in between. By spring I can walk, sort of. Easy bouldering and lay-backing cracks at Indian Creek. In June I travel to Zion and do a couple of little big walls. By summer I can wear rock shoes again and go sport climbing. In the fall I go back to Indian Creek, jamming this time. The Himalaya will have to wait, though. The next step will be Patagonia.

I know the Fitz Roy area well, after several seasons there; returning will be a good test. In 1977, Mike Munger and I traveled to Patagonia on my first trip abroad. Jim Donini, like us a Boulder resident at the time, had recently done Torre Egger. He convinced us to go.

I trained hard and practiced aid climbing fast, like my hero, Kor. But Donini said, "Train to free climb well so you don't have to aid." I did not fully understand then the implications of climbing fast in Patagonia, but I took his advice.

Mike and I had intended to do a route on the west face of Fitz Roy, then unclimbed. Upon arriving we quickly realized that project was beyond our abilities. We opted for the nearby Super Caneleta, which had been climbed twice.

The weather, we discovered, is not as bad as people say—it's worse. You're always waiting, then more waiting. Even when climbing, you're just waiting for the weather to get really bad. You're always moving, too. There are few rest days, as you're preparing for when the weather does get good. You do a lot of walking. Welcome to Patagonia.

After three weeks of waiting and preparation, our turn came. On January 23, 1978, we stood on top of Fitz Roy in a gathering storm.

I wanted to return to Patagonia soon after that, but other projects and the lure of travel and adventure took me to other places—the Alps, Peru, the Himalaya. When I did return, the place had changed. There's now a bridge across the Rio Fitz Roy, and a town on the other side, El Chalten. Busloads of tourists come. In the high season, hundreds of tourists hike to the base camps every day. But some things never change—it's easy to blame the weather, but the climbs are still big and hard. Success is elusive, if reaching summits is your measure of success.

Steph and I arrive in El Chalten November 29 and establish base camp at Rio Blanco the next day. Two years before, we had spent almost three months in Patagonia, attempting several climbs and summitting a few. This time, Steph is only planning on spending three weeks, hoping to get lucky. Our goal is to climb the North Pillar of Fitz Roy.

On my first trip to Patagonia there were only a handful of climbers around. By chance, I met an Italian, Renato Casarotto, who was with a large expedition attempting this climb. They didn't make it. Like all successful Patagonia climbers, Renato was not put off by failure, nor intimidated by the tremendous amount of time and hard work required. He returned the following season and soloed the climb.

On December 4, in improving weather, we dig a snowcave at Paso Superior. We are not ready to commit to a multi-day project like Fitz Roy, but we are anxious to climb. We pack up that evening, wake up early and climb the regular route on Guillaumet. By Patagonia standards it's short and easy, hence very popular. A classic nonetheless. Glacier, snow, ice, mixed, then rock and more snow—my first summit since Tibet.

We turn our attention to Casarotto's route. The bergschrund guarding the climb is impassable, so we fix a rock pitch around it.

"Only 5,000 feet to go," Steph quips.

This proves to be our highpoint. As her time runs out, frustration increases. Pretty soon we're out of time for Fitz Roy. We approach the east pillar of Mermoz, a climb we can do in a day, but we bail—bad snow. Steph has had enough, and we pull our gear down from Paso Superior.

There are two types of climbers that come to Patagonia: those who visit once and never come back, and those, like myself, who return often. Each season a crowd of regulars congregate at Campo Bridwell and Rio Blanco base camps. Just as Steph is pulling out, two of the regulars, Kurt Albert and Bernd Arnold, arrive.

The two Germans come armed with a gas-powered Hilti and a pile of fixed ropes and bolts. Their goal: the east pillar of Mermoz. This wall already sports two routes, but the finest line, the "Red Pillar," remains uncompleted. Attempted by several parties in alpine style, it was nearly completed by Americans Kennan Harvey and Topher Donahue in 1994. Over the course of the next month, Kurt and Bernd make their way up the wall, placing bolt belay anchors every 30 meters and an average of three bolts per pitch next to perfect cracks. The season before they established *Condorito* on St. Exupery in the same style, and a few years before that, the monumental *Royal Flush* on Fitz Roy's east pillar.

"We put in three bolts every pitch, whether it needed them or not," Kurt told me of *Royal Flush*. He also told me it was the best climb he'd ever done. One can argue about their tactics, but you can't argue about the quality of the routes they open. I'd seen *Royal Flush*; it looks like one of the best climbs on the planet. In a few weeks, Nate Martin is going to meet me in El Chalten for an attempt on this line. We hope to do all 47 pitches free, in alpine style.

For now, I'm without a partner, but highly motivated. I go back up to Paso Superior with Kurt and Bernd. While they chip away at their project, I contemplate climbing Mermoz as well. On December 21, I leave my snowcave with a 100-meter rope and small rack. I drop through Paso Guillaumet to the west side of the range, then down over the west ridge of Guillaumet, from where I traverse to the west face of Mermoz and its original line of ascent. I leave my mountain boots, axes and crampons at the base. Climbing in rock shoes, I wander up.

Not only do I lack a partner, I lack a topo, too. Looking for the easiest way, I wander a lot and make some route-finding errors, but eventually find myself on top. The summit of Fitz Roy is in a cloud, and a massive storm spills off the ice cap, signalling the end of a three-day spell of good weather.

Days later, I move base camp to Campo Bridwell. Donini is there, with his wife and son. Warren, Russ and Sean are there, to do a big aid climb. First timers, they fail to even get to the base of the climb.

"Welcome to Patagonia," I say.

Toni Ponholzer is there, his eighth season down, to attempt the Egger route on Cerro Torre. Miles Smart, Trym Saeland and I head up the Torre Valley for Cerro Stanhardt. In perfect weather and by the light of a full moon we head for *Exocet*, the classic ice climb. But in the middle of the night it's a waterfall. Still too warm.

New Year's Day. Perfect weather again, so I trudge back up to Paso Superior, alone. Next morning I head back to Guillaumet, this time to do the left French Gully. When I arrive it looks dry and quite hard, so I start a line to its left. After some easy mixed, I break out the rope and self-belay four pitches of sporty ice and mixed that lead to the summit snowfield. From the top, I go down the route Steph and I had climbed.

Nate arrives, and so does a long spell of good weather (of course we don't know this). We hike up the Torre Valley to do a "warm-up." We leave high camp at 5 a.m. I punch a trail up a steep snowfield to the base of St. Exupery's north face.

Nate, breathless, asks, "Don't you ever get tired?"

Yes, I think to myself, when I follow you.

I lead the first five rope-stretching pitches. Starting left of the Kearney/Harrington route, we join the big ramp on that line after two and a half pitches. Nate takes over the lead as we exit the ramp to attack the north face directly. Five more 60-meter pitches, mostly hand and finger cracks, take us to the summit ridge. The climbing is superb and we are elated. I lead two more mixed pitches to the top. Too bad I left my boots and crampons at the base—it's terrifying in rock shoes.

We rappel the east ridge to a big ledge system. It's getting dark, the wind is whipping our ropes around and snow flurries fill the air. I suggest we wait it out till morning. After a while shivering on the ledge, Nate offers, "I've never done an unplanned bivy before."

Welcome to Patagonia.

*Steph Davis near Paso Superior. Behind can be seen Fitz Roy (left) and Mermoz (right).*
CHARLIE FOWLER

Days later, the weather is still good. Kurt and Bernd have finished their route on Mermoz, naming it *Vela y Viento*. Kurt, weary from hauling all that fixed line, says, "Maybe next time I'll do a route alpine style."

Nate and I head back to Paso Superior for a go at *Royal Flush*. Ironically, all the good weather is melting everything; Royal Flush is too wet to free climb. We go to Poincenot instead. The classic Whillans route is unusually dry. We do the ramp, now thin ice, at night. The mixed pitches above are all rock. We linger for almost an hour on top, watching a Swiss couple repeat *Vela y Viento*.

*Royal Flush* is drying out, but the good spell comes to an end nine days after it started. Then two Austrians, Heinz Zak and Peter Janschek, come to climb *Royal Flush* as well. We become fast friends. Unlike Nate and I, their plan is to fix the first 14 pitches, then blast to the top, resorting to "French free" for speed. Heinz is skeptical about our free attempt. "Everything must be perfect," he says of that.

After more weeks of waiting, I begin to think Heinz may be right. I reckon we need at least three days of reasonable weather. It doesn't look like that's going to happen. We get a haulbag and gear up the first few pitches. The Austrians fix four more. Nate's time is almost

up; on the last possible day, we go.

"We either do it or get royally flushed," I joke.

Nate leads three pitches above our highpoint. We descend to a stance and bivy on the wall. The climbing is awesome and we are psyched. We wake up the next day to wind and snow. We're outta there. As we drag our haulbag across the glacier, the wind whips up to a ferocious intensity. Lying flat on the glacier, terrified we'll be swept off, we can barely hang on. They don't call it La Escoba de Dios (the Broom of God) for nothing.

Back at the pass, we rest and dry out. The weather improves, but we only have one more day. The next morning is a go. Heinz and Peter head for *Royal Flush*, Nate and I head for *Vela y Viento*. It's only 16 pitches; we figure we can do it in a day.

I lead the first few pitches, but as the difficulties increase I let Nate take over. Kurt and Bernd, who had not freed the line, told us, "There's a lot of 5.12." I am climbing well, all things considered, but I struggle to follow Nate as he on-sights every hard pitch.

It turns out to be a blustery day, and we fight the cold as much as the rock. The climbing is excellent, but hard to enjoy with numb hands. At the top of pitch 11, a hex marks the spot Topher and Kennan bailed. Another pitch up an ice-filled crack and we're on the north ridge. Kurt and Bernd went left from here, reaching the summit four pitches later. Nate and I go right, onto easier ground. We arrive at the summit just at dark. Rappelling all night is a slow, tedious process. We are back at Paso Superior 28 hours after we left.

Nate takes off. Five weeks in Patagonia is not enough time. Heinz and Peter manage 37 pitches up *Royal Flush* before wind and snow shut them down. A great effort, but they are disappointed, having missed the summit. I have another week in Patagonia. The weather slowly deteriorates and I'm reduced to bouldering at El Chalten.

At the end, an Argentine climber is stranded at Paso Superior with a badly broken foot. Heinz and Peter go up to help with the rescue. Just below the pass, the wind sweeps Peter off and he breaks his leg. I visit the two broken climbers, side-by-side in the hospital, then help Heinz wheel Peter to the airport.

"I'll be back," says Peter.

I know.

SUMMARY OF STATISTICS

AREA: Argentine Patagonia

ASCENTS: Right French Couloir (TD-, 5.9 60° ice mixed, 400m) on Guillaumet, December 5, 1998, Charlie Fowler and Steph Davis; Argentinian Route (TD, 5.10-, 500m) on the west face/north ridge of Aguja Mermoz, December 21, 1998, Charlie Fowler, solo; variation to the Pippo Fraison (line to the left of the French Gully) (TD, 80° ice, mixed, 300m) on Guillaumet, January 2, 1999, Charlie Fowler, solo; *Bienvenidos a Patagonia* (5.11b, mixed, 700m) on the north face of St. Exupery, January 10, 1999, Nathan Martin and Charlie Fowler; the Whillans route (5.8 mixed, ca. 650m) on Poincenot, January 21, Charlie Fowler and Nathan Martin; *Vela y Viento* (5.12 A0, 500m) (with new variant) on Mermoz, February 10, 1999, Charlie Fowler and Nathan Martin

LEFT: *Nate Martin on* Royal Flush *(VI 5.12, ca. 1300 meters), east pillar of Fitz Roy. The route was established by Kurt Albert, Bernd Arnold, Jorg Gershel and Lutz Richter in 1995 with three-bolt anchors at every belay and an average of three bolts per pitch. The haul bag and fixed ropes are from an Austrian team.* CHARLIE FOWLER

# Shipton Spire

## Free as can be in the Pakistan Karakoram

by Steph Davis

The glacier below is so gothically crenulated and gnarled it makes my brain hurt. It's like a wedding cake that got dropped on the floor. A friend told me that this part of the world looks like it has not been cooked yet—raw and huge. Hanging off Shipton on a portaledge, looking down, I see she's absolutely right.

Almost as soon as I'd committed to going to Pakistan, I started trying to talk myself out of it. The summer of 1998 was incredibly volatile, and the politics added an entirely new dimension to the hazards of climbing in Pakistan. Just before I bought my ticket, Pakistan and India seemed on the brink of nuclear war, and President Clinton jumped in and sanctioned both of them. My mother called every other day to alert me to recent hijackings, kidnappings, and anti-American sentiment, and to remind me of how stupid it is to put yourself in such danger when there are plenty of other rocks to climb in places where they don't hate Americans. I was incredibly frustrated; I'd always wanted to go to Pakistan, and now, though I had a Shipton-Tilman grant, strong partners, and a potential objective, I was actually considering canceling the whole thing. Luckily my partners Kennan Harvey and Seth Shaw were unwavering in their commitment. I couldn't stand the thought of not going and then hearing that everything turned out fine, so after much agonizing and no real decision-making, I bought my ticket. It would just be one more element of the adventure.

Once in Pakistan, we found that the many people who had been scared off by the politics kept the dollar rising and the locals rabid for our business. The Ministry and Police in Islamabad gave us no trouble at all. We were filthy rich and even the taxi drivers and shopkeepers served us like royalty. If it weren't for the spray-painted "Down with U.S.A." signs on rock walls along the Karakoram Highway and rumors of U.S. aircraft over Iran, we would have felt foolish for even having questioned the safety of this trip.

Still, as the days went on, I realized that I had no resources for understanding anything about the Pakistani culture or its mindset. I could interpret daily events however I liked, but there was no guarantee that anything I saw indicated either safety or danger for us as Americans. Getting onto the Baltoro Glacier and into the mountains was a relief in one way, but, although we were out of the cities and potential political danger, we would still be committed to re-emerging a month or so later into a totally unknown situation. We could step off the Baltoro into a culture that demanded instant assassination of all Americans, or we could find ourselves just as welcomed as we'd been thus far. There was no way of knowing.

We also didn't know exactly where Shipton Spire base camp *was*. We'd seen photos of Shipton, and talked about the area with Greg Child and Jared Ogden (who'd made the first and second ascents), so we knew it was just beyond the Trango Towers. However, none of our porters or cook/guides had been there. Ultimately, with the aid of a poster photo taken from the top of Nameless and a little head scratching, we found the meadow we'd heard so much about.

We'd received the grant to climb a new route on a sub-6000 meter peak in the Shipton area, and there were a few excellent candidates. I was strongly interested in the "Cat's Ears"* and Hainablak East Tower, conveniently located side-by-side just across from Shipton's base camp meadow. Both are unclimbed and, like Shipton, both are just barely under 6000 meters. Though each has good lines in steep granite, they would require a couple of thousand feet of approach work and would therefore yield less actual technical rock climbing than Shipton. In that sense, they are rather like Nameless Tower. Still, they virtually beg to be climbed.

Although the Cat's Ears appealed to me, Shipton has a good southeast face with a more convenient approach and offers over 4,300 feet of vertical granite coming almost right out of the glacier—nearly twice as much vertical rock as Nameless Tower. The peak had seen only two ascents, both of which required considerable aid. Kennan immediately made it clear that he wanted to not only do the third ascent of Shipton, but also try a continuous free attempt on a new line. Seth and I thought that sounded like a nice idea, but mostly just wanted to get up the proud sail of granite. Altitude was an issue; we'd start climbing at over 15,000 feet and summit at 19,700, which is pretty high to be doing hard free climbing. Moreover, extra days spent redpointing hard pitches could blow our chance to summit at all. Kennan was completely enthusiastic and determined, but this ambition was huge. We'd have to decide on our style later. For now, one thing was sure: we all wanted to climb Shipton.

We spent our first few days carrying loads to the base and squinting through a spotting scope from the base camp meadow, searching for continuous crack systems that could be not just climbable, but freeable as well. Knowing the center of Shipton was dangerous, we picked a line toward the right that seemed safe from rockfall. It looked like the best, most continuous line, until through the scope Kennan saw a white haulbag hanging partway up. With horror, we realized that we'd been seriously considering the route on which the Japanese soloist Ryuji Taniguchi had died in 1996.

The next day, as I picked a line through the crevasses on the glacier, I stumbled across Ryuji's shredded pink portaledge. All of my doubts returned with a vengeance. I'd been so busy worrying about the politics before the trip that I hadn't really had time to meditate about just how dangerous it is to climb in the Karakoram. The same unbelievably clear weather that had us all galvanized was also setting off countless tons of rock, snow, ice and mud around the glacier. I had to be brutally honest with myself: I was feeling edgy. Again. Still.

I'm never sure how superstitious to be when climbing, or what to take as a "sign." Certainly there had been more than enough warning in the form of political unrest to make me feel like a deserving fool if anything went wrong on this trip. Rather than burdening Kennan or Seth with my doubts, I spent the hours trudging to and from the base of Shipton analyzing them internally. Was I just nervous because this trip was bigger and more objectively hazardous than anything I'd done before? Was I paranoid because one of my best friends had just been paralyzed in a climbing accident? Or was I trying to ignore warning signs? If this were a horror movie would the whole audience be shouting, "Run, you stupid bimbo!!!"? As I watched Kennan walk through the meadow after a ferry, I felt a shot of fear at either dying myself or losing him on this trip. But Shipton stood in full view of my tent, proud and constant, exerting an invisible and irresistible pull, refusing to take "no" or "I'm scared" for an answer.

---

*This formation appears to be unnamed on the maps in the Polish book *Western Baltoro Mustagh* by Jan Kielkowski. Hainablak East Tower sits to its immediate south (see cover). Most of the prominent formations around the Hainablak glaciers are designated variations on the Hainablak name. For further explanation of the names of the formations around the Hainablak glaciers, see footnote by Greg Mortenson in Climbs and Expeditions.

We chose a new line through the M-shaped fang-like roofs just left of the first ascent route. It shared the same start up the Footstool, a "small" 1,000-foot pillar pasted to the bottom of Shipton, then moved left into more continuous crack systems. I felt good about this route. It seemed out of the zone of rockfall, as far as you can get from the ominous white haulbag, and we all agreed it had free potential if we chose to try.

To free or not to free. . . . As daft as it seemed to stroll up to a huge peak at altitude with the hope of finding an independent free line, it wasn't a new idea. In 1988, Kurt Albert, Wolfgang Güllich and Hartmut Munchenback freed the Slovenian route on Nameless Tower the year after it had gone up on aid. Looking to increase the challenge, Albert returned the next year with Güllich, Christof Stiegler, and Milan Sykora to attempt a brand new free route to the left of the Slovenian line. They were foiled by a pendulum and a section of A2, but *Eternal Flame* was perhaps the first route in the Himalaya ever attempted as an on-sight free ascent.

Such an approach is a gamble, especially if you move capsule-style without ropes fixed to the ground. On a remote, high-altitude wall, you can only carry a limited amount of food, water, and energy. You could spend days freeing a pitch only to find unavoidable aid higher on the route, and one storm can kill your chances of finishing at all.

Although daunting, the idea of trying a new free route on Shipton was seductive. As Kennan pointed out, it had already been climbed "anything goes" twice. Trying something really new and out there had a certain appeal. We'd done our work at the spotting scope, and we liked our line. It was time to go up and see what happened.

By the time we had fixed lines, hauled gear, and launched onto the wall, we were almost 1,500 feet up, and we still hadn't completely decided if this was a free attempt or just a push up Shipton. So far the climbing hadn't been hard enough to force the decision, but now, at 16,500 feet, we were getting into the high-quality vertical rock.

I felt nervous racking up for my first "real" pitch. A seeping crack turned into a steep offwidth, with ten feet of moss leading into the wideness. I got wet and pumped climbing to the vegetation, then hung and gardened furiously for half an hour. Panting, muddy, and altitude-worked, I looked into the overhanging #5 Camalot crack above and started to French free. By the time I set the anchor, I felt bedraggled, more like I'd survived the pitch than climbed it. It was time for a decision: consider the line fixed and keep moving, or go back and free it.

So far I'd been noncommittal about freeing. With three haulbags, two portaledges, full aid and ice gear, a barrel of water, and countless assorted other stuff, all trying to go up a new route on a giant Himalayan wall, this whole enterprise seemed like challenge enough. But Kennan's enthusiasm was rubbing off; after all, I *am* a free climber. The weather showed no signs of turning bad, and I was starting to feel sure that we could get up Shipton. So why not up the ante and try to free it? Suddenly I was equally committed, as was Seth. The uncertainty of success had just increased exponentially, but we were all of one mind about the goal.

To compensate for the altitude and the environment, we decided to "aidpoint" the harder pitches: the leader would start in free climbing mode, then switch to aid if necessary. With the cracks cleaned and the gear in place, we could go back down and free the pitch. I normally disdain preplaced gear since it makes the climbing easier, but the altitude was making things harder, so it seemed to be a toss-up—and really, the only reasonable thing to do up here.

On the next pitch, Kennan followed the crack until it ran out. We needed to get over left and rejoin the systems that led to the fang roofs. Heads and bathooks got him to the end of the rope—where things did not look freeable.

"I don't know, Kennan," I said.

*Two bathook moves to a rivet later, Kennan Harvey steps into hard climbing on one of the climb's crux pitches.* STEPH DAVIS

*Harvey with industrial-strength Pakistani toilet paper on pitch 22.*
STEPH DAVIS

We decided to move our camp up, but leave the rope hanging and see how the next few pitches looked. We found them to be much more plausible, so Kennan was back in the hot seat

"It's up to you, man," Seth said. "It's your pitch. If you're really psyched, we should go back down for it."

The next morning, Kennan pendulumed back and forth on the end of a 60-meter rope searching for face holds and trying moves from his jumars. He pieced together a sporty sequence through hard face climbing, but there was no getting around a single, ten-foot section of blank granite near the end of the pitch. Mainly to entertain ourselves, Seth and I held an ethics committee from the portaledges while Kennan hand-drilled a few bolts below

"Kennan! We decided you should chip it! Just kidding!"

"No, you should put anchors with really long slings in the blank spot! Just kidding!"

After displaying admirable restraint in ignoring the peanut gallery, Kennan ended up climbing dynamic 5.12, jumping into an aider for two bathook moves to a rivet, then jumping right back into hard free climbing mode to finish the pitch.

We were all inspired by Kennan's effort, and now truly committed to trying to free Shipton. Of course we were disappointed that our free attempt was foiled halfway up the wall, but we were still doing a new route on a high-altitude peak. We were there to climb as much as we could, and ten impossible feet weren't going to slow us down to aid mode. We hadn't been stopped by lack of ability, and the blank section was so short that we actually felt pretty lucky. If we could climb the rest of the route free, it wouldn't bother us a bit. In fact the ten feet of aid were almost a statement of ethical purity; after all, there are various known ways of dispensing with ten impossible feet in the mountains. So no way were a couple of bathook moves on a 4,300-foot free route going to dissuade us from our mission—but those fang roofs still loomed ahead like massive question marks.

For the next few days we ignored them, accepting total uncertainty and focusing on climbing the clean, beautiful pitches in front of us. Twice we got down to our last quarts of water, only to be saved by small runnels on the route. Food supplies became scanty—we would eventually finish the route with two cans of sardines. We looked into the bolt bag one day and realized we'd only brought 18 bolts and a handful of hangers; fortunately, we would end up placing just eight. The only thing I could really count on was Seth's evening update about new uses for his toothbrush (nail cleaning, pot scrubbing), and his insistence that every desperate pitch he freed was merely 11a. Clearly we'd have to name the route for our cook' favorite comment: "Inshallah," God willing. If we ever got off this thing.

On our seventh day, we reached the fangs. The lower roofs formed giant, steep dihedral against the face. Seth shouted down things like "Yosemite granite! Yeahhhhh!" as he pulled hard-looking moves toward the first roof—11a, no doubt.

Steep laybacks, fingerlocks, and stems allowed us to sneak around the roofs, and I could almost smell easy ground above. Seth aidpointed the final corner, running it out above RPs tied-off knifeblades, and a pecker, and allowed that it might be 11+. It was starting to look like we could do this thing—until we reached the final roof crack.

We aided through water and slime, then retreated back to the portaledges to ponder the problem. Ten feet of blank granite in the middle of a 5.12 pitch was one thing; having to aid an entire pitch just because it was wet was quite another. I started to get depressed. Luckily, though we were slim on food, water and bolts, we had a mega-surplus of ultra-absorbent Pakistani toilet paper. We woke before dawn, jugged to the roof before the water really cut loose with icemelt from above, and wiped and sutured the mess into a free-climbable state. Our whoops of victory dwindled off as we realized that the next pitch, a flaring, mossy groove that was running like a water spout, was even wetter and harder. And we were almost out of toilet paper!

# Inshallah (VII 5.12 A1)

*F.A. Steph Davis, Kennan Harvey, Seth Shaw*

hole count: 8

**Baltese Falcon**  ‒ ‒ ‒ ‒ ‒ ‒
(VII  5.11 A.4)

**Ship of Fools**  • • • • • • • • • •
(VII  5.11 A.2  WI 6)

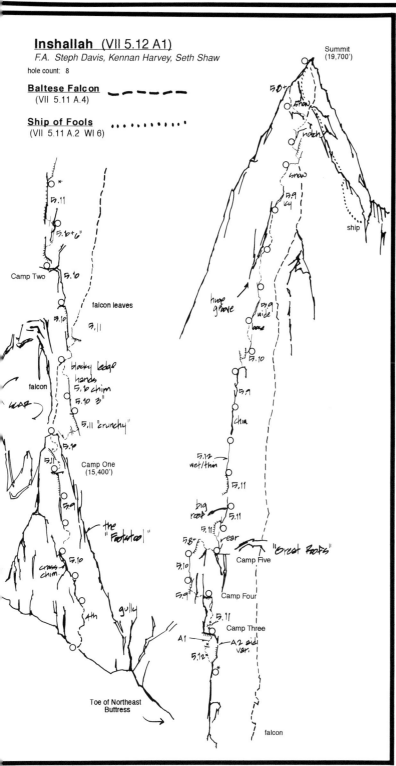

Summit
(19,700')

Camp Two

falcon leaves

blocky ledge
hands
5.10 chim
5.10 3"

5.11 "crunchy"

falcon

Camp One
(15,400')

the
"Footstool"

cross
chim.

Toe of Northeast
Buttress

5.0+

snow

notch

snow

5.9
k4

ship

huge
groove

5.9
wide

5.10

5.9

chim

5.12
wet/thin

5.11

big
roof

5.11

5.8+

5.10

ear

"Great Roofs"

Camp Five

5.9

Camp Four

5.11

Camp Three

A1

A2 aid
var.

5.12+

falcon

**Inshallah (VII 5.12 A1)**
*F.A. Steph Davis, Kennan Harvey, Seth Shaw*

Shipton Spire

*Seth Shaw, Steph Davis and Kennan Harvey below the east face of Shipton Spire after the climb.*
KENNAN HARVEY

Kennan cleaned for an hour, bravely sacrificing his hat and socks, and with a huge amount of willpower brought down the final, slimy crux pitch on his third try. We'd finally reached the promised land of continuous, low-angle cracks that led to the summit gully. Now, unless a big storm came in, we were truly in there.

On July 25, 12 days into our push, we woke at 3 a.m., jugged our lines, and blasted up the final 1,500-foot gully. Expecting difficult mixed or ice climbing near the top, we'd lugged three pairs of crampons and two ice tools up the entire wall, but found only easy rock all day instead. A final pitch of low-angle rock, and just a little snow wallowing, led to Shipton's summit. I sat on the summit at 19,700 feet, having climbed 2,500 feet that day, feeling happy but altitude-hammered. I was ready to get back to the green meadow and well-stocked kitchen tent.

For the next two days, we rapped on nut anchors and talked about food, wishing for such unobtainable delicacies as chocolate cake and donuts. Much to our amazement and delight, our beloved cook Ghulam had sent two porters and a ziplock full of, yes, fresh donuts, to meet us at the base of Shipton. Inshallah!

The final slog across the glacier to base camp was a festive event, since we knew we weren't going to have to make the trip again to carry back loads and the porters knew they were going to get historic tips. Ghulam greeted us with tears of joy, embraces for Kennan and Seth, a handshake for me, and more food. We were chowing hard in the meadow on July 28, having spent a total of 14 days on Shipton.

For the next week, I lounged in the sunny meadow trying to sort my thoughts about our route. I felt a bit dazed, and not quite sure what had hit me. It felt almost too fast, too smooth, if that can be possible. So much for foreshadowing.

Hainablak East Tower and the "Cat's Ears" sat enticingly across the glacier, but they would have to wait for someone else. Shipton stood just as proudly, but the magnetic attraction had been severed; I was freed, even more completely than the route. Our climb had reminded me that bringing an open perspective to a project can significantly affect the style and difficulty of the ascent, and that the "best style" is the one that leaves you the most content. It's all in the eyes, the mind and the heart.

SUMMARY OF STATISTICS

AREA: Pakistan Karakoram

NEW ROUTE: *Inshallah* (VII 5.12 A1, 4,300 feet) on the southeast face of Shipton Spire (a.k.a. Hainablak Central Tower, 19,700 feet), July 13-27, Steph Davis, Kennan Harvey, Seth Shaw

# Modern Alpinism in the Karakoram

## Collecting climbing's overlooked jewels

by Luca "Rampikino" Maspes, *Italy*

*Moonrise over K6, Fathi Brakk and Parhat Brakk, Charakusa Valley, Pakistan. Recent expeditions have foregone traditional objectives like K6 in favor of lower rock pillars.* GALEN ROWELL

There are many kilometers between Alaska and Pakistan, but in the month of July, the two places were extremely close together, almost connected in the sphere of my dreams. I had to make a decision where to go, and the airlines didn't allow me much time to sort out my doubts. On June 29, I boarded a plane with the conviction of having made the right choice: I was going close to my childhood dreams, close to the highest mountains in the world. No longer did I dream of K2 or Everest, however, but of raising the flag of what the weekend warrior calls "modern alpinism:" no permits, no specific projects, no information at all.

Three days later, after the normal routine of approaching the mountains, we reach the Chamonix of the Karakoram, the capital of alpinism: dusty Skardu. With me are the Karakoram veteran and my partner from Patagonian adventures Maurizio Giordani, Natale Villa, and the very young Mattia Locatelli. We are in good hands. Two of the most famous alpine guides in Pakistan, Little Karim and Rozi Ali, advise us to forget our objective, Amin Brakk. As an alternative, they suggest an area "like the Trango Towers." Ali's finger stops a little beneath the words "Charakusa Glacier," and all of a sudden my eyes start to shine. On the somewhat rough map I can almost imagine a dream-like granite, and for some minutes I am able to forget the torment of the previous week that ate away at my stomach.

After three jeep transfers and almost 20 near-miss landslides, we arrive at Hushe, a chaotic village with hidden roads that end at the foot of mountains. Karim receives us in his home, and while he's trying to make us comfortable, I begin to ask him a thousand questions about where we're going and whether we'll find the Eldorado of rock that yesterday I was convinced I'd found.

The morning light that follows is accompanied by a ringing of voices. I wake up excited to begin my first day with the porters and thus celebrate the end of the motorized travel. Three days of easy approach—a piece of cake when compared to the steep approaches of my central Alps—and suddenly, in less than an hour, dozens of towers and pillars leap out at us with an unprecedented violence. From porter to porter, in an English ever more contorted, we succeed in understanding a bit more. We recognize Beatrice, climbed the previous year by a British expedition, but either my English gets totally lost, or the porters only know one word, for everything else is called unclimbed. To some climbers this word means danger; to me it means paradise.

Maurizio is the first one to move from base camp, and he decides to extend his "walk" for a good number of hours, climbing an unclimbed peak. In the meantime, he decides what will come the following day. He has found our target.

We start at dawn with our guide and a porter to get closer to a splendid rock tower that sits sublimely at the top of a long couloir. Its name is Cobra Peak, or at least that's what Little Karim calls it. Without delay, I start to climb at over 5000 meters on solid granite while Natale belays and Maurizio films us with our new digital camcorder. Mattia, meanwhile, waits for us in the couloir below.

I climb a bit slowly, still affected by the lack of acclimatization and the Pakistani cigarettes. I'm already smiling, though, at the idea that in a few hours we will touch the fabulous summit of this unclimbed peak. Optimistic? Well, there aren't any clouds to talk about, and even less wind. . . . A third of the route for each of us, with difficulties enough for this altitude.

The final slabs are pure joy for Natale, who finally screams at us that there's nothing left to climb. He plays a cruel joke on me, yelling down that he has found a Coca Cola can. Maurizio closes his eyes, keeping the joke that Natale has dreamed about for a year. I climb the last four meters in a state of delusion and desperation. Summit. But I see the 5400-meter smile on Natale's face: no cans of Coke in sight for thousands of kilometers. Two days after our arrival, the nightmare of not climbing enough and not having a "good expedition" is already gone, the first route and the first summit already under our belts.

It has been 36 hours since the first adventure on the wall, and only now do I realize I'm not in Patagonia. A damned hot sun, ever-free from clouds, torments us while we look for the next target. We get to the base of Fathi Brakk, the huge granite tower that attracts Maurizio. "Let's take the bivouac gear," he says. "I don't think we'll manage it in a day." Good words from a man who has climbed for 25 years. We leave base camp the following morning and after four hours of approach, we "walk" an extra two up a steep icy couloir before deciding to leave all unnecessary gear—sleeping bags, stove, food, heavy clothing—and go for it. Take it in a day, or leave it.

We then start a race against time that will stop brusquely at half-height on the wall with two pitches of shattered rock. Delicate climbing is mandatory for Natale and Maurizio. They are occupied with a mix of aid and free climbing that is literally terrifying. The terrain kicks back a little, which allows us to speed up, but the afternoon advances. We watch each others' faces, hoping to not have to be the first to utter the painful words, "Let's turn back." Instead, another hour goes by before our heroes declare, "A mountain like this is worth the suffering of an open bivouac." Now at least I know what we'll be up against!

Twelve, 13, 14 pitches, and the summit never arrives. We bid the sun farewell 60 meters from the top. This time I got it right, I tell myself as I hole up in my Gore-Tex suit, noting the slightly preoccupied look on Maurizio's face as he zips into his light fleece. Three cigarettes for me, while Natale fixes his gaze on the tiny dot of light 1000 meters below where Mattia is undoubtedly organizing his dinner. We await the dawn.

After nine hours, our open bivouac above 5400 meters is starting to get annoying, and damn cold. But when Masherbrum is illuminated by the sun, we yell, "Let's finish this route!"

The torture is over. I get up like a Ferrari racing car and sort out every kind of cam, nut and pin for the summit pitches. With my body still trying to wake up, I set out up the final pitch. It's always when you expect easy and warm rock that you get overhanging, cold and difficult pitches—and indeed, that's what I find: the hardest pitch of the route.

I arrange the belay, and with a yell I wake up Natale, who is finally getting sun. A final dozen meters and Fathi Brakk (or "Charakusa Tower," as we will later baptize it) is entirely beneath our feet. There's nothing more to say, nothing more to climb. We can only go down.

We rappel for the entire day without knowing where we will wind up, dreaming of Italian chapati, "K2" cigarettes and Pakistani tea, then drag the ropes (or the ropes drag us) down the glacier, collecting the heavy haulbag that proved to be useless along the way. When we get to base camp, I simply crash on the floor of my tent and sleep very deeply, dreaming of new mountains. I wake up one morning, realizing it has been two days since the climb. Oh, Patagonia, how I enjoyed all those days of bad weather during which I couldn't do anything other than rest!

We've been here one week, and already the expedition could end, and we would return triumphant to our Alps with two new lines on unclimbed peaks. Maurizio actually does leave; he must go back to his business in Italy. For a few days, thank God, the weather turns bad, so I can rest more and, in the meantime, look forward to my classic annual solo blitz.

The Dog's Knob awaits me, but on the morning of the designated day, I stare at Mattia, who is supposed to help me on the approach. My selfishness abates. I simply can't help but say, "Would you like to climb with me?" Mattia is like a rocket: two minutes and 23 seconds later, he's finished packing, harness and climbing shoes included. One thousand meters higher, I remind Mattia what a "boy" of his age is getting on his 17th birthday with a new route in the Karakoram. The only bad part of the day is a storm that forces us down, but not before we have joined a line established previously by the first ascensionists of this marvelous tower of granite.

Ten more days, and ten more days of rock. We attempt a pillar on K7 and on our return to base camp we see new faces. They are Americans Conrad Anker, Peter Croft and Galen Rowell. They too are collecting new lines in this universe of virgin peaks. The one with the biggest pack of all—a pack loaded with more than just film—seems to be Galen. We agree to go with him to a vertical wall half a kilometer high that boasts more than a thousand dihedrals and cracks. Decidedly inspiring.

"He likes cracks, this Yosemite veteran, don't you think, Natale?" I ask. Only two days to go before our return to Italy, and we're ready to tie in afresh with this Italian-American alliance.

RIGHT: *Fathi Brakk.* GALEN ROWELL

*Natale Villa on Iqbal's Wall.* GALEN ROWELL

We don't need to look for an obvious line. The first dihedral is good. Sun, t-shirts, more than 100 photos from one of the best photographers on the planet and a ton of jams: the Pakistan dream unfolds with each pitch, each more difficult and each better, accompanied by the best rock we've seen on the trip. Even the last pitch appears to have been placed there on purpose: it is the hardest and the most beautiful of all.

"OK, Luca, good pitch. 5.11a, I think. I'm very tired. . . . Now to the summit?" asks Galen.

"But we're already on the summit, Galen. Look! Here there's no top, just a very long ridge." The exhaustion of the conquering photographer seems to have all but disappeared, and our companion abandons the rope and gear as he goes searching for the true summit. I look at Natale and snort, glance at the deteriorating weather and get worried. We can't leave Galen alone (or at least we can't leave him alone on the summit), so we begin our pursuit of this Californian who appears mad about the top. A toy train of alpinists runs after each other without ropes up and down tiny towers along the ridge.

At a certain point, having discovered for the umpteenth time he is not on the highest tower, Galen announces in defeat, "Finish. This is not the summit."

"OK, Galen," we say. "Let's go down. Tonight will be the last dinner at base camp. They've prepared Italian food for us, we can bet on that."

Suddenly, the expedition of dreams is over. . . .

SUMMARY OF STATISTICS

AREA: Charakusa Area (K7 Base Camp), Pakistan Karakoram

NEW ROUTES: The Northeast Couloir (IV 5.8) of "Gemelli Peaks" (ca. 5000m), July 6, Maurizio Giordani; the East Spur (V 5.10a A1, 450m) of Cobra Peak (ca. 5400m), July 7, Maurizio Giordani, Luca Maspes, Natale Villa; the West-Northwest Face (V+ 5.10d A3 mixed, 900m) of "Charakusa Tower" (Fathi Brakk, ca. 5600m), July 10-11, Maurizio Giordani, Luca Maspes, Natale Villa; the South Face (V 5.10b, 250m) of the Dog's Knob (ca. 5400m) (new route that finishes on the English Route, without summit), July 17, Luca Maspes, Mattia Locatelli; Italian-American Route (V 5.11a, 450m) on "Iqbal's Wall" (ca. 5000m), Luca Maspes, Galen Rowell, Natale Villa

# Pilgrimage on Bhagirathi

## At the mercy of the mountain gods

by Yuri Koshelenko, *Russia*
*translated by Natasha Lagovskaya and Liana Darenskaya*

On October 14, 1998, at high noon, just 20 steps away from the summit, Igor Potankin and I were peacefully enjoying the magic of our surroundings. Behind the ridge the wind was blowing hard, but here, on the gentle slopes, it was nice. Dark blue-black clouds peeked out from behind Kedarnath. Along the horizon, the wind was rolling in and out of the herds of clouds. In the background two people stood beneath the summit, thinking that the miracle they had dreamed about had happened. There had been times when they had not believed that it would ever come to pass.

After our comrades, Volodia Kachkov and Andrey Lukin, caught up with us, the four of us summited the snowy top of Bhagirathi III. The vista of the surrounding ridges and the rushing clouds brought a quiet joy, but the instinct of the mountaineer would not allow us to relax. There was a descent ahead of us, and our inner compass told us it would be a difficult and dangerous one.

The main idea of "The Russian Project: The Big Walls" was to ascend the greatest faces of the world via new routes—if possible, by very hard routes. Such ascents were to be performed by one team. In 1995, Alexander Odintsov and Igor Barihin established a route up the center of the east face of Peak 4810(m) in the Pamir-Alai. In 1996, on Ak-Su North in the Pamir-Alai, Alexander Ruchkin and Alexander Odintsov put up a new route in the center of the north face. In 1997 in Norway on the Troll Wall, the project successfully completed two ascents: on July 25, Alexander Ruchkin and I put up the Russian Route, while on August 8, Alexander Odintsov and Igor Potankin established the Baltika route.

Our Bhagirathi team had an addition: Andrei Lukin and Vladimir ("Volodia") Kachkov from Saint Petersburg were with us. With this bigger team (which also included our high-altitude cameraman, Ivan Samoilenko), we had bigger plans for 1998. We aimed to perform three first ascents with three independent teams on the west face of Bhagirathi III.

But the original plans began to be revised from the very beginning. My partner on the ascent of the Troll Wall, Alexander Ruchkin from Omsk, had to back out of the project at the very last moment due to his financial situation. Fortunately, another pair, Alexander Odintsov and Igor Potankin, generously accepted me onto their team. So, upon our arrival in Delhi on August 17, our expedition was as follows: Alexander Odintsov was the leader of the project; Igor Potankin and I were in the first group; Andrei Lukin and Volodia Kachkov were in the second group, and Ivan Samoilenko was our cameraman. Based on these teams, we planned two ascents.

In addition to the climbing core of the expedition, there were seven more people, including a doctor, a second camera man and a few others. Some of them had climbing experience, but mostly they joined the team to travel and experience life in Base Camp. The liaison officer appointed by the IMF became the fourteenth member of the expedition. He had a portentous name: Monogar, which sounded like Monogarov, the name of a very famous mountaineer from the Ukraine in the times of the former Soviet Union. We took such a coincidence as a good sign.

After loading all of the expedition baggage, our big team headed out to central Uttar-Pradesh in the Garhwal Himalaya. From the holy town of Haridwar at the delta of the river Ganges, our journey followed the river. On August 23, after all the ordinary adventures, our expedition reached the small town of Uttarkashi in the very center of Garhwal. Here we met with the Sirdar, Mr. Bisht. From then on, all progress depended on his organizational skills and promptness.

It had been raining in the evenings and at night, which meant that the road to Gangotri was possibly blocked. On August 25, we bought some more food and our expedition was expanded by 50 porters, a kitchen-boy and a cook. Now we looked like a little army.

The day was wonderful in all respects. The road to Gangotri was in perfect shape. All of the obstructions had been cleared and leveled, and the higher the road went, the better it became. Little by little we started to notice the high altitude foliage, the first signs of which had already been apparent in Uttarkashi, and the Himalayan cedars, so slender and beautiful. Right in the middle of the journey there was a wonderful place with thermal hot springs called Gangnani. Finally, we were in Gangotri, a place for pilgrimages and mountaineering expeditions. There were groups of porters and swamis in their orange clothes. There were stones polished by water, the thunder of the waterfall, splashing holy water, yoga, and ashrams scattered all over the slopes.

On August 26, our expedition started out on the trail that leads to one of Hinduism's most holy places: Gaumukh, where the Bhagirathi River comes out of the glacier. We followed the pilgrims' road, touching stones that had pictures of Shiva's trident and holy texts, inhaling the high-altitude *prana*, enjoying the serenity of this enchanting land and making quick stops at the local tea-houses for our physical thirst. After a night at the hotel Bhujbas, we continued, washed by the heavens. Soon, the rain grew tired, and we confronted the magnificent sight of the great river being born.

Though Gaumukh is the final destination for pilgrims, our way continued beyond, along a glacial moraine where there are no trails. Thanks to the modest, hard-working porters, whose strength, patience and humility one can endlessly admire, the foremost part of our expedition had already reached Base Camp in Nandanvan.

Between August 28 and September 2, we worked on establishing Base Camp. A reconnaissance was also made on the northern and eastern slopes of Bhagirathi III to find the safest route for descent. The weather stabilized, and during the next few days we carried loads to the wall and made a final decision on two routes on the west face.

Volodia and Andrei planned to climb the western ridge to the left of *Impossible Star*. Alexander, Igor, and I planned to concentrate our efforts on the center of the wall. Our line was to start at the bergschrund, then go straight to the huge protrusion in the lower half of the wall that we named "the Paunch." From here the line was to go along its left edge via an overhanging inner corner. The next reference point was a roof in the shape of a "7" that we called "the Poker." From here the line continued to the black schist criss-crossed by multi-colored bands that comprises the upper quarter of the wall, then up to an area of roofs and overhangs where two prominent features resemble eyes. These we called the "Left" and "Right Eyes;" we planned to climb through the "Left Eye," then, in the upper part of the schist band, exit left onto the western ridge.

Igor and I fixed almost all of the icy approach slopes in six pitches on September 6. Technically it was not very difficult, but falling rocks from above, particularly after 3 p.m.,

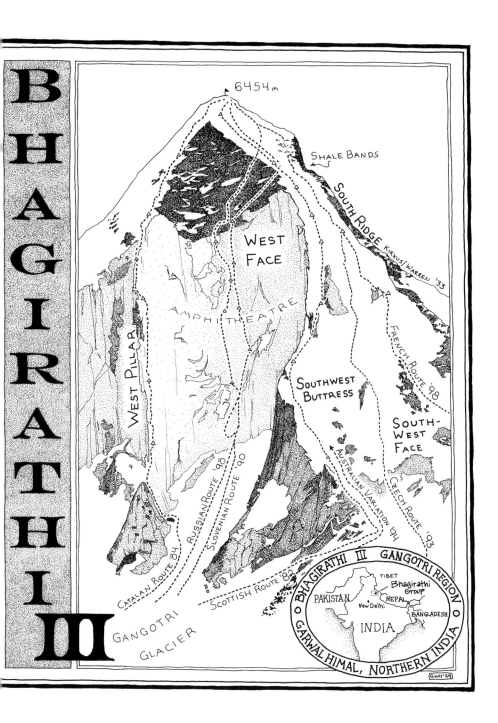

*Igor Potankin moving delicately in the opening pitches of the Paunch.* YURI KOSHELENKO

made it dangerous. The weather deteriorated on September 7. On September 8, Igor, Alexander, and I managed to establish ourselves on the wall above the bergschrund before the avalanches came down. In two days the approach slopes were completely covered with snow. Volodia and Andrei, meanwhile, were preparing part of their route to the left of *Impossible Star.*

The following two and a half weeks changed our plans once again. Uncertainty, bitterness and disappointment were added to our existing problems. We were under the impression that, for some unknown reason, the mountain did not want to welcome us. The monsoon returned. It started to snow, and it began to look as if winter was arriving. We tried to use any sort of break in the weather to advance, but almost all of our attempts ended up with digging out our ropes and equipment from beneath the snow. It was a Sisyphean struggle. We dug trenches that were many meters long and of a man's height. One avalanche swept all of the right side away, compressing the last 50 to 70 meters of the fixed ropes one-and-a-half to two meters beneath the snow. To compound matters, Alexander was experiencing persistent abdominal pains.

September 21. Igor and I finally managed to climb 90 meters of very dangerous ground. We had to crawl along an unstable ice pitch without any decent protection while pieces of ice fell from above. Avalanches threatened to pendulum us 25 to 30 meters. Meanwhile, Andrei and Volodia, who had fixed part of their route and brought their loads up, were ready to start out.

September 22. Lines from the diary: "It is snowing. Wet snow. It looks like it is not going to stop soon. Can it be true that Ivan was right when he said that the first week of good weather would be the only week granted us—that it was an abnormally rainy year, and very soon autumn would change to winter? Maybe we won't reach the summit. There is not much time left.

"Alexander was diagnosed by the doctor with appendicitis."

The permit gave us until September 30. Our chances to summit were melting much faster than the snow in Nandanvan. Facing such a critical situation, we made a decision to unite into one team and climb via one route in any kind of weather. We chose the central route because of the overhanging left ridge of the Paunch, which would cover us en route to the center of the wall. The most important problem here was to find a safe bivouac on the wall.

September 26. Igor and I dug trenches once again.

September 27. "Under fire," we managed to make it to the beginning of the paunch. On the way we fixed four more ropes. Volodia and Andrei used those days to take all of the equipment from their route and move it to the base of the center of the wall.

September 29. Igor and I started out. Alexander climbed with us to cache equipment. He was planning to summit after the doctor performed an operation. If everything went right, the next day he and the cameraman, Ivan Samoilenko, would join us.

The next day, Volodia and Andrei managed to climb about 40 meters through a bunch of small icy overhangs that served as the entrance to the main inner corner at the left edge of the Paunch.

We had just started the climb and it was nearly time to finish. Almost all of the route still lay ahead, but it felt as if we had already ploughed through several mountains. We were burned out, both physically and psychologically. The frozen relief that awaited us looked insidious—but we were determined to climb. So we did.

September 30. Igor led. For the first time since we began on the wall, I found myself in the role of the frozen one, belaying. The night was nasty. In the morning it was 7°C in the tent. The features of the corner did not provoke any joy, either. Obviously, it was a fresh rock scar, and there were still a lot of "live" rocks and blocks. The decent segments for climbing were to the right on the severely overhanging wall of the Paunch. That day we managed 75 or 80 meters and descended to the bivouac in darkness, where we met Alexander and Ivan.

Volodia and Andrei took the lead the next day. They needed to climb a difficult section that led up to a roof, and, if they could, to start on the tiered roofs that were a prominent feature and one of the key parts of the route. It never stopped snowing. The only thing that made it possible to work in such conditions was the overhanging relief. The wall was in winter condition. We were moving up at a catastrophically slow speed. What was next? Would our provisions and fuel be enough for six people? Two things that kept us moving were our determination and our belief in miracles.

October 2. Alexander and I started out to prepare the route. The weather was the same. Working as a leader is the best cure for despondency. We had to make it through the multi-

*Igor Potankin, October 2, Camp I.* Yuri Koshelenko

layered roofs, a key part of the route. It would be all shattered moving blocks. The climbing was very risky, and took a lot of courage. After we made it through the roofs, we arrived at a relatively flat section. As soon as we did, we were transformed into snowmen. In such conditions, we did not manage to finish fixing the second rope.

October 3. Igor and Andrei climbed out onto the shelf in the upper part of the Paunch and made it another 15 meters. The next day was the first clear day since the beginning of the climb. On this day I worked with Volodia. From Igor's final skyhook I pendulumed to the right under an overhang. The rocks were covered by a lot of snow. Very often we had to use skyhooks. There were a lot of unstable points. In some places we had to climb on snow that had been blown onto the rough places of the wall. At one point I felt the snow sliding away beneath my feet. I was flying down. Ivan, who was shooting at that moment, was hit by a huge piece of névé.

The fixed ropes were taking too much time. It took us a whole hour just to jumar through the multi-layered roofs. We had already spent six days working, but we were still in the center of the wall—and it looked like the major difficulties were still ahead.

That day was a decisive one for Alexander. On October 5, he and Ivan went down so that the rest of us would be able to continue the climb. Igor and I began relocating the bivouac to the shelf on top of the paunch. Volodia and Andrei worked on up ahead. Everything fell into place. We were getting used to the thought that we would have to live on this mountain for another week or more. The psychological strain slowly disappeared into the vastness of the wall. We were getting a positive charge. We were ready to accept any experience, be it victory or loss.

October 6. We climbed with eight fixed and three dynamic ropes. Vladimir, after climbing some of the extreme parts free in his rock shoes, severely froze his toes. Because Igor and I had not managed to move all our gear from the first bivouac, we did not take the lead. In the evening we learned that the others had lost the burner from their gas stove, which meant that now there was only one stove for two groups.

October 7. Andrei had begun a difficult and labor-consuming section the day before on which Igor now worked. The overhanging rock threw us off. Igor began bathooking, going from one plate to another via thin cracks and flakes. It was extreme aid in severe cold. The sun appeared only after 3 p.m.

October 8. I finished climbing the pitch that Igor had started. There were some loose pitons that pulled out easily before I moved into a good cam-sized crack. The wall was severely overhanging, and we came out a little more than a meter beyond the last point of aid. Because of our limited number of big cams, I had to leapfrog, which lessened the protection.

Above was the Poker roof. Approaching it was very dangerous. First we would have to climb a flake so loose we referred to it as a "swinging feather," then along "live" blocks that had detached from the wall. Molecules of thin air were the only glue holding them on. We made the roof using a homemade pecker, and I placed two cams in the broken rock. Neither one could hold its own weight. But that was not all. In the corner some of the pitons hardly stayed in; the last one started to come out as I weighted it. I barely escaped a fall.

As for Andrei and Volodia, they were busy moving the bivouac.

October 9. Volodia and Andrei led, climbing a vertical section with some free climbing. Igor rested, while I cleaned the route. After I hit one of the pins under the roof with the hammer, a huge plate I had climbed the day before detached. My mind stopped, and I broke into a cold sweat. But in the evening we had good news: the others had made it to the schist bands.

October 10. Ivan told us via radio that Alexander had left for the historical motherland. It seemed that his disease had been so serious that, even though he was a fighter by nature (in 1994, while participating in the Russian Alpine Championships in the Karavshin region, he had climbed Peak Slesova with a broken leg sustained from a previous climb on peak Asan-Usen), he could no longer tolerate the pain.

Igor led while I belayed. He decided to climb to the right. The black schist looked very rapacious. Roofs looked like opened drawers from Salvador Dali paintings. I could see very well how easily the schist plates break. There was almost no protection except for bolts.

There Igor stopped, took off his climbing shoe and waved his bare foot in the air. It was a wonder that he did not get any ice on his foot. The cold was arctic. Everything was very serious. My hands tensed, awaiting a fall. The oppressive and gloomy atmosphere did not disappear even when the sun showed up. We managed 75-80 meters that day. The character of the movement was a long traverse to the right under huge schist plates.

October 11. It was my turn to play roulette with this terrain. I have never seen anything like it: a belt of damaged black schist with yellow dissemination. Roofs and overhangs looked like noses, eyebrows or bellies, as if all the formations were devouring one another. Everything around looked rotten and rusted as if it had been splashed by gastric acid. The term "rock" could hardly be used. In many places it was just frozen sand covered by some sort of oxides. The pins could not be hammered in; they had to be dug into the sand. The schist roofs stratified under the weight of our bodies. It was a motley, overhanging country. We climbed via aid, and only from the center of gravity. We managed to establish an anchor on the solid light rock using a 12-mm bolt as one of the pieces. The climbing robbed us to the last thread. All of my equipment was put to work, even extra carabiners. My eyes watered, burned by the salt. I managed to climb only 25 to 30 meters.

Andrei and Volodia prepared the fourth camp at the base of the band.

October 12. Volodia and Andrei were ahead while Igor and I cleaned the route. The entire time we had been aiming for the huge angled inner corner that cut through the right side of the black band. It looked like the only exit from the wall. From beneath, this corner is bordered by piles of black and light roofs; from above, it is capped by a heavily overhanging wall. The only features we could see were stratified "scales."

October 13. At last, Volodia and Andrei reached the edge of the wall, while Igor and I moved camp. The terrain was all black schist covered with snow and decorated by icicles. We climbed almost all of it free. We had some problems with the protection. The leader climbed in crampons.

October 14. We started out at 8:30 a.m. from the fifth bivouac. We climbed the fixed ropes and icy slopes, and reached the most tempting place in the world at 12:30 p.m. We saw the summit right in front of us. At last, the mountain had made it possible.

In the morning, though, storm clouds reached the ridge and the walls of Bhagirathi, and now we were not just watching, but living through the battle. We started to descend with two portaledges and our haulbags. It was not possible to take all of our equipment; we had to leave some ropes on the most difficult parts of the route. In the second half of the day, it snowed very hard.

October 16. The weather did not change for the better. We spent the night full of apocalyptic feelings at Camp II on the shelf atop the Paunch. Toward morning a serious storm moved in. I was leading in our descent, preparing the route. I could feel the constant grip with which the mountain held us. There was no room for even a miniscule mistake. After we emerged from the shelter of the Paunch, we found ourselves open to the mountain's threatening elements. The wind swung us as if we were flags. The portaledges floated above our heads, reminding us of a kite. But the biggest danger was still below on the lower part of the wall. While waiting for my friends at the anchors, I counted ten avalanches rushing through the station with a dry hiss. So far, we had been lucky. None of those white predators carried rocks or pieces of ice.

After we jumped off the wall, we found ourselves in the most vulnerable situation. The 400-meter slope was too steep for four exhausted climbers to walk down, especially with all those bags and portaledges. The other side of the slope was not steep enough to allow the equipment to slide down under its own weight. We had to fix the ropes and use them. So far, all the avalanches had fallen around us, but we could not hope for the same on the lower part of the slope. After we made it through more than half the slope, we tied the last three dynamic ropes together and fixed the upper part of it to an ice ax. Volodia and I rolled down, kicking the bags in front. Igor and Andrei were at the station when the One That We Had Been So Afraid Of finally got us. Under the mass of snow, the rope stretched out so hard it looked like a guitar string. Fortunately, it did not last a long time. When we dug ourselves out, we automatically dropped the bags; we realized that any delay might be fatal.

Our tiny yellow tent covered to its top with snow greeted us at ABC in solemn solitude. After plunging through the dry snow between the rocks of the moraine, and after we, finally, had reached safety, we hugged and congratulated each other on the successful completion of the climb.

We did not know that our joy was premature. We were dreaming about getting to Base Camp on time for breakfast. We got all of our things ready. After we ate what was left from the local fauna's scavenging, we headed out toward Base Camp. Our group moved along a surface reminiscent of a marine archipelago. We had to swim through the drifts that separated morainal islands. The wind became stronger, and by the time we reached the lateral moraine, it turned into a hurricane. The wind was suffocating us, filling our lungs, making it impossible to exhale. It was on the watch for us at the most dangerous places of the moraine ridge. It played with us, trying to throw us off the slope, then at the last minute eased its grip. Feeling "aerated" to the point where we felt crystals of ice in our lungs, we finally reached a "green" slope. We had hoped that it would get easier from here, and indeed it was a little bit too tight for the wind, but the snow did not relent. Some of us were swimming on our backs,

*Thirty-four pitches up, Igor Potankin works the route into the schist band.* YURI KOSHELENKO

*Vladimir Kachkov coming off the Poker on the descent.* YURI KOSHELENKO

while others were rolling from one side to another. It seemed that the slope was endless. We stopped somersaulting where the slope became flatter.

From here we hoped to walk straight on the surfaces of the dried-out lakes. It has been a day of endless delusions. We made our way through snow that came up to our waists. Finally, somebody looked at his watch. It was already 2 p.m., and there was not too much light left. When Vladimir, freeing himself from one more snow trap, got on all fours and crawled, others followed his example. The holy mountain was testing us to the last. It wanted us to leave it as Tibetan pilgrims do, prostrating ourselves on the ground with each step. The purification with the fresh snow lasted until 10 p.m., when our weak light was seen by somebody at Base Camp. We took the light that had been lit in response as the highest reward, as joy and deliverance.

SUMMARY OF STATISTICS

AREA: Garhwal Himalaya, India

NEW ROUTE: The Russian Route (VI 5.11 A4, 1110m) on the west face of Bhagirathi III (6454m), September 6-October 17, 1998, Igor Potankin, Yuri Koshelenko, Andrei Lukin, Vladimir Kachkov

PERSONNEL: Alexander Odintsov, leader, Igor Potankin, Yuri Koshelenko, Andrei Lukin, Vladimir Kachkov, Ivan Samoilenko, Ludmilla Krestina (expedition doctor), Alexander Kuznetsov (Base Camp manager)

# Russian Style on Changabang

## A convergence of cultures in the Garhwal Himalaya

by Carlos Buhler

In the spring of 1981, I received a letter from Dane Burns. It contained a variety of xeroxed photos from different magazines and journals showing the southern aspects of one of the most alluring and beautiful mountains I'd ever seen. The mountain was called Changabang. Lines and arrows pointed out both established routes and new possibilities on exciting and wild terrain. Scribbled in along the edge of the photo of Changabang's southwest face were Dane's emphatic thoughts:

"Now does this look like fun climbing at 21,000 feet? .... It sounds hard, but really neat!" Of a line between two arrows, he wrote, "What do you think? I'll get a loan if need be, sell my car or my body. . . . But, let's go!"

I don't remember exactly when I heard the name Changabang for the first time. It was after the 1974 first ascent (led by Christian Bonington with his characteristic entourage of Britain's most accomplished mountaineers) and well before I knew how to launch an expedition to the Himalaya. By the time Dane wrote me, Changabang was embedded in my consciousness. Like a cruel joke, the Indian government decided to close down all climbing on peaks within the Nanda Devi Sanctuary the very next year. Changabang was now closed to climbers indefinitely. It would stay off-limits for the next 15 years.

In 1996, the Indian Mountaineering Foundation made a partial concession to the Sanctuary closure. Those peaks whose flanks fell to the outside of the line would be re-opened for climbing, but only by routes on the outward-facing walls. The Sanctuary boundary ran directly over the summits of Changabang and Kalanka, and their north faces were now open via the Bagini Glacier. But who had been on the Bagini Glacier? As far as I was concerned, the north faces of the two mountains were complete unknowns.

After a repeat of the original route in 1980, Michael Rheinbergers wrote, "On the Nanda Devi, or southern side, the face (of Changabang) seemed to average about 50 degrees, somewhat steeper in places. . . . To the north, the face fell away at a fearsome angle. . . ."

Then, in the summer of 1996, Julie-Ann Clyma and her husband, Roger Payne (General Secretary of the British Mountaineering Council), led the first attempt on Changabang's huge, cold, and impressive north face. The British, it seemed, were always one step ahead when it came to knowing what was out there to climb. Unfortunately for them, they experienced atrocious weather, but still managed to climb high up the steep, iced-up slabs and corners of the immense buttress that protrudes from the left side of the face. More importantly (for me, anyway), they came back with amazing stories and stunning photographs.

Having climbed K2's North Ridge with a very strong Russian team that same year, I was tempted to explore the smaller, and less known, mountains of Asia the next. But the reality for my Russian friends was that only a known 8000er could attract the Russian sponsorship

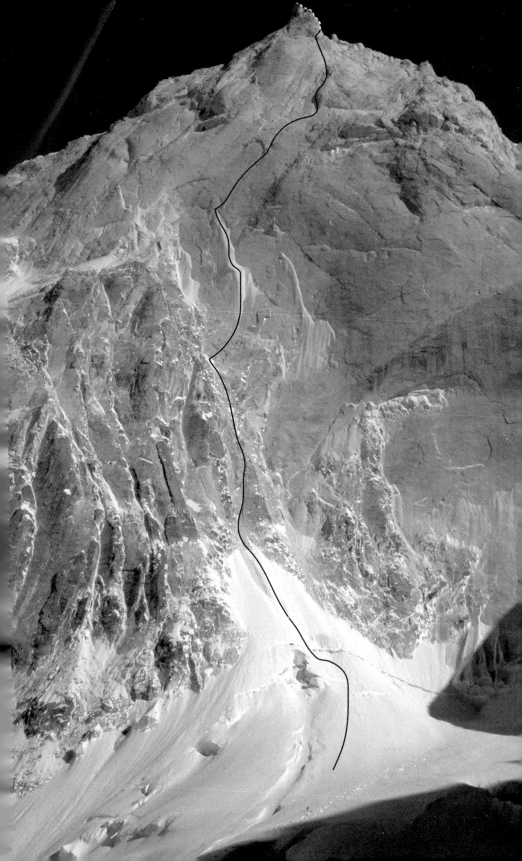

dollars that would make an expedition possible for them in 1997. Though I mentioned Changabang among other objectives, our choice became the Diamir Flank of Nanga Parbat, in Pakistan, which we agreed to in September 1996, just after our ascent of K2.

Nevertheless, when I returned from China to Pakistan in order to catch my flight to London, I ran into Steve Sustad and Simon Yates in Islamabad. Steve spoke to me then about the north face of Changabang. He was part of a team that would be going back with Roger and Julie-Ann to attempt the unclimbed face again in 1997. According to him, there just might be an extra place on the team. I was supremely interested. Though I kept hoping as long as I could, eventually a team of six British climbers was formed. There would be no place for me.

After our success on Nanga Parbat, the Russians were ready to gamble for sponsorship. Knowing that new routes were waiting on many smaller peaks, their curiosity was ripe for original ideas. When I brought up Changabang again, they were ready to try raising money for it. We wanted something out of the ordinary, something new, and something technical. Beneath the north face of Rakaposhi, in the village of Hussainabad (the home of our Pakistani cook, Ali Madat), our decision was made. We would attempt to climb this infamous north face of Changabang. In reality, I still knew very little about it. I had yet to even see a photograph from that side.

On my way home from Nanga Parbat, I stopped and phoned Steve Sustad during my overnight in London. While systematically dropping a small fortune in change into a public telephone at my B&B near the airport, I heard the tale of their epic first ascent and tragedy on the north face. I was riveted to the phone as I listened to Steve recount the climb. It was a remarkable story. When he was done, I asked him, solemnly, whether there were any possible lines to the right of their route.

"Yes, most definitely, but they will be full-on big wall climbs," he said. He warned me that they would require the whole gamut of big wall artillery. When I put down the telephone, I was sobered but intrigued. Big wall it would be.

Our team consisted of five individuals: four Russians (Ivan Dusharin, Andrei Mariev, Pavel "Pasha" Chabaline and Andrei Volkov) and one American (me). As leader of the expedition, my chief role after dreaming up the objective was to get as much of the bureaucratic red tape out of the way as I could and maneuver the team, in one organized heap, to the foot of the mountain.

Base Camp was established on April 24. The pastoral meadow was still hidden beneath three feet of winter snow. The five-hour, ten-kilometer approach from there to the foot of the face quickly convinced us to hire a couple of Indian porters, Govinda and Nanda Sing. The terrain above Base Camp was even more deeply covered. The job of ferrying 25 days of rations and gear to the base of the wall was enormous, but it paled in comparison to the thought of lugging it up the wall itself. Unfortunately, we couldn't employ any enthusiastic Indian porters for that job; we would have to do it ourselves.

As Govinda and Nanda Sing laid their loads down a half mile from the 5,200-foot sheer granite wall, they gazed up at the golden-colored granite ribboned by vertical streaks of blue ice. They must have thought we were completely out of our minds. What an amazing mountain wall of vertical rock and ice! Bordering the face on the left was the ridge followed by the first ascent team in 1974. On the right side of the face rose the rounded ridge from the Bagini Col. These two ridges met at an apex, the summit, centered above the middle of the face. On the lower left of the face, a huge buttress protruded from the wall. The British chose a route on the left side of this buttress in their 1997 ascent. We considered the right side of the buttress for our purposes since we wished to ascend the center of the smooth upper wall. More than a dozen corner systems offered possible routes up the initial 2,000 feet. But above this, there were far fewer options. The smooth upper half of the wall was bisected by three lines of weakness that rose diagonally from left to right. It seemed clear that we had to choose one of these three systems and ride it to its junction with some cracks that angled back left toward the apex of the face.

We spent several days watching and listening to the mountain. Once our initial route choice was made, we knew we'd be committed to that line for the duration of our climb. Though stonefall would be an issue, we agreed to a corner system on the extreme right edge of the buttress where it joined the main part of the face. It formed an iced up corner system of cracks and slabs that would give us the easiest access to our upper wall.

I was sure from the outset that my team was a talented group of individuals. But could we play music together? That had been the question before we began. Though Changabang had been on my mind for two decades, once I brought these men into the picture, I knew the project was no longer my own. It belonged to a larger set of minds. Our most difficult task revolved around coming to grips with the differences in strategy developed by two separate ideologies over the past 50 years. As one might imagine, I, the one American, was at a significant disadvantage when it came to convincing the four Russians that Yosemite methods were appropriate. Whereas Westerners believe in rotating the jobs of climbing a big wall on a mountain rather evenly throughout the effort, the Russians thought that each person should take a fixed position, or task, and stay with it for a long stretch, or even for the duration of the climb. This "collective" style of climbing clashed with my Western style of self-discovery, which they interpreted as individualism. Though we all believed in the concept of teamwork, we drew very different conclusions on how best to obtain it.

I attempted to persuade the group to rotate the many responsibilities of the climb evenly between us. I was not as worried about attaining the summit as I was about having everyone come away from the climb with a feeling of satisfaction and fulfillment. However, the Russians took a different view. They knew that the enjoyment and personal satisfaction from climbing could be had in their home mountains, those closer to Russia and much less costly to reach. On Changabang, they felt they had a job to do. It was their belief that addressing the task at hand (i.e., establishing a direct new route on Changabang's north face) took precedence over any personal goals they might have had before coming on the expedition. In the end, I was unable to convince them of my viewpoint. In order for the climb to be a team success, someone had to compromise. My rational course of action was to adjust my outlook and allow these people to perform using the methods with which they were most efficient. Following this, I then resolved to support and contribute to our venture in every way.

We agreed to a capsule style, which offered the protection and safety of three consecutive camps on the wall installed in one continuous push. With eight 50-meter lengths of static rope, three 60-meter lead ropes and two 55-meter 7-mm lines to leave on the long traverses, we were neither going very heavy nor very light.

On May 6, a severe storm moved into the area. Our reconnoitering and initial fixing of the lower four ice pitches came to a halt. Sitting out the storm at our advanced camp was not relaxing. We knew that huge avalanches poured off the Bagini Col. Would they threaten us with their enormous runouts? Under the cover of clouds and darkness, I could occasionally hear the muffled running of the avalanches. How close were they coming? Unwilling to dig out our gear and relocate our tents in the storm's eye, we tried to shut our minds to the possibility that we might be covered. We could only cajole ourselves into remembering that, during the good weather, the wall below the Bagini Col behind camp had seemed to pose no threat at all. How differently things felt beneath three feet of new snow! I was kicking myself for not insisting that we put our two tents another 100 to 200 meters from the headwall.

*Hauling loads to the second bivy camp on the wall.* CARLOS BUHLER

By May 8, we realized nothing could be gained by waiting in advance Base Camp at the foot of the face for conditions to stabilize. That evening, the skies cleared. But it was clearly going to take several days before things settled down. With no desire to descend the next morning in the heat of the sun, we left ABC at about 8 p.m. It was now clear and cold, with bright moonlight. Over 40 inches of snow had accumulated. To our amazement, our upright grade seven haul bags were completely hidden by fresh powder. What normally took us two-and-a-half hours to descend cost us eight hours in deep snow. It was an exhausting night. Bad weather returned for another day on the 9th. About the same time, I became sick with bronchitis.

On the 10th it cleared again, and the snow started to settle. On May 12, the four Russians went back up to ABC while I remained in B.C. nursing my bronchitis. Once on the mountain, the Russians began doing the grunt work of digging out the gear in the bergschrund from under two meters of new snow, and fixing the next six pitches of mixed ice and rock. On May 15, I made my way to the base of the wall with Govinda and Nanda Sing.

Although our original plans had centered around only four people on the wall, after lugging loads to the foot of the face, it felt unthinkable to expect that now one of us wouldn't begin the climb. Volkov and Dusharin had invited Mariev to participate on the expedition on the understanding that he might not have a place in the actual climb. But having been together on K2 and Nanga Parbat, the four of us were well acquainted. Pasha Chabaline was actually the "invited outsider" from the city of Kirov, yet his big wall experience eclipsed ours. Unlike the four of us, big walls were his focus in climbing.

When the Russians insisted they could easily manage three people in one of the two-person portaledges, the decision was made. Pasha explained that it would be no different than what they

*Pavel Chabaline leading the second pitch above CII while Andrei Volkov belays.* CARLOS BUHLER

were all too familiar with at home in their tiny apartments. Besides, he explained, in a portaledge this size, he had slept as many as five people, with heads all toward the wall and legs extending outward! Who could argue with that?

Our first long day on the face consisted of hauling and dragging all our personal gear and food up the ten fixed pitches to our first hanging bivouac. We brought all the fixed lines up behind us and established our first hanging camp by night fall. For me, it was one of the three or four most exhausting days of the climb.

The next day, Pasha and Andrei went out in front. Ivan, Andrei M. and I began organizing the hundreds of kilos of gear, fuel, and food. We separated items into bags of what we would need over the next five or six days and what we could haul up the fixed ropes for the future. Water was melted; meals were prepared; ropes untangled, dried and coiled; single 3/8" bolt belay anchors were drilled and backed up. It felt like a construction project to me. Judging by the amount of flammable liquid we carried, I figured we had enough fuel for a month. Then I realized it was 110 proof spirit for drinking, not burning! Ah, but I was getting used to these differences.

We worked like this over the next ten days. The two long days (May 19 and 24) of moving our camps were the worst of all. On those days we adopted the practice of carrying a 15-kilo rucksack on our backs and clipping a 20- to 25-kilo haulbag to the leg loops of our harnesses with long slings. In this way (or so the idea went) we would only have to elevate the remaining four 35-kilo haulbags using the standard pulley system. Well, yes. But it didn't make ascending ropes much fun. Especially that one, thin, fraying, 9-mm fixed rope we'd brought along!

The aid climbing on the face became one long psychological endurance effort. On the morning of May 27 we had our ropes fixed to a point within a few hundred feet of the top of the wall. Pasha and Andrei went out to complete the last pitches as Ivan, Mariev and I prepared to follow up behind them for an attempt to reach the summit. We should have known that the last pitches would take twice as long as anticipated—everything else had as well. Although Pasha and Andrei managed to complete the wall and fix our three climbing ropes to the col between the two horns, we ran out of daylight before we could attempt the knife-edge ridge to the top. It was necessary to rappel back down to the portaledges and endure another night in the intense cold.

The next morning our luck seemed to run out. It began to snow at 5 a.m. We waited in our sleeping bags as the hours ticked by. The desire to complete the climb to the summit and be done with it was overpowering. We were all near the breaking point, both physically and psychologically. It is hard to say exactly how much longer we might have lasted—perhaps two or three more days—but we were all aware that our mental limit was near. An accident would be so quick and sudden that our minds would hardly register until after it had occurred. We were losing our ability to concentrate and stay focused.

At 9 a.m., the skies began to clear. No storm. It had only been a squall. By 10 a.m. we were re-ascending the fixed lines to the ridge. Our energy was rekindled by the hope that at last, today, we would reach the top and be able to begin our long-awaited descent. It was electrifying. So much energy began to pour from our tired bodies that I wondered if I would have any in reserve for the dangerous rappel down the wall.

Few summits I have been on are as airy and exposed as the top of Changabang. We followed a rising knife-edge ridge out of the col and up along its lower-angled west side. In minutes we were standing on the apex. It was breathtaking. Nanda Devi was visible in a swirl of clouds off to the southeast. I thought about my friend Ad Carter, who together with his teammates in 1936 had made the impressive first ascent. The forbidden Sanctuary lay in tranquillity at our feet in the deep valley below. Dunagiri, a peak I had heard so much about from Dick Renshaw, sat majestically to the west.

We were in no hurry now. We took in our surroundings calmly. Off toward Tibet, the peaks hung like paintings, forming a backdrop only the imagination could surpass.

Hugs and more hugs. Then, photos, and out came the flags. For a few moments we were free from the burden of the wall. It occurred to me that it was the first time I had been able to stand on something in two weeks. But it was too brief. Quickly the feeling faded and we were forced back to the task. Rappels began, back into the world of the vertical cold north face, on to the retrieval of our ropes and gear. It was almost a cruel joke. We knew much work lay ahead of us in the next two days.

After 21 days of working and living on a mile-high face of ice and granite, we reached the bottom of the wall and made our way back to Base Camp. It had been a very rough road. I had been forced to let go of preconceived ideas on how we would attain the summit. Most of all, I had needed to let go of my ego. If I had not released my grip on my original vision, I would have left the expedition. I continually had to remind myself to ease up on my need for control and allow the Russians to "create" in their own way. Only then was I able to lead the project and contribute significantly to the attainment of our goal. In hindsight, the uneven

*Ivan Dusharin and Andrei Volkov coming up out of the saddle between Changabang's twin horns. The normal route ascends the ridge coming up from the right.* CARLOS BUHLER

distribution between Russians and American had probably been a good thing: had it been a more balanced team, we might never have been able to find a compromise.

Perhaps the most amazing thing about the climb was the fact that we finished the expedition as better friends than when we had begun. Along the way, there arose enough disputes, stemming from cultural gaps and differences in climbing philosophy, to fill a small book. My reward at the end, however, was the honor of working together with a talented team of individuals to establish one of the most ambitious and difficult big wall routes in the Himalaya.

SUMMARY OF STATISTICS

AREA: Garhwal Himalaya, India

NEW ROUTE: *The Lightning Route* (VII 5.9 A4 WI4, 5,200 feet) on the north face of Changabang (6864m), April 16-June 6, 1998, Carlos Buhler (U.S.), Andrei Volkov, Andrei Mareiv, Ivan Dusharin, Pavel Chabaline (Russia)

# Kasum Kanguru's East Face

## Solitary adventures on a never-ending story

by Yasushi Yamanoi, *Japan*
*translated by Eiichi Fukushima*

*Preparation at Base Camp beneath the west face of Mera Peak, which Yamanoi attempted six years earlier.*
YASUSHI YAMANOI COLLECTION

Kasum Kanguru, at 6370 meters and with all the approaches to its summit consisting of steep snow and rock faces, might not be a suitable target for a peak bagger. However, considering the lack of red tape involved in climbing it, the mountain is a great objective as a test of one's technical climbing ability. Although there are several routes on the peak already, the steep east and west faces had yet to be climbed. I thought of climbing the west face at first, but changed my mind upon hearing about the difficult approach and the supposed poor quality of the rock. The east face serves as a backdrop for those climbing Mera Peak, but is probably not given much thought as a climbing objective.

Much effort was expended in collecting photos and other relevant material before leaving Japan. Quite by chance, I discovered that Daisuke Nakagaki, with whom I climbed the southwest face of Pakistan's Bublimotin in 1995, had been collecting many photos of the east face of Kasum Kanguru from a big wall climber's point of view. Those photos showed that there are indeed cracks in the center of the 1500-meter wall, but the preponderance of reddish rock hinted of danger. If it were to be climbed, I would have to use a portaledge.

The right side did not look as steep as the center and the rock looked to be more solid; however, I could not identify as many cracks as I did in the center of the wall. It might be climbable in 30 to 40 hours, but I wanted to solo it, regardless of the particular route.

Many friends have criticized my penchant for soloing, but it really suits my temperament. I do not like to compete and, at the same time, I like to make my own decisions. Furthermore, soloing is not as dangerous for me as people make it out to be. Finally, solo climbing in a remote location leads to a better understanding of one's self and of nature.

For me, solo climbing has resulted in many vivid memories that would not have been possible to experience otherwise. One such experience was camping on the desolate tundra of Baffin Island in 1988 as I waited to climb the west face of Thor in the eternal light of Arctic summer. The feeling of isolation while soloing the 1400-meter wall and the wild and natural view from the summit far exceeds what can be felt on El Capitan. Two winters later, climbing Patagonia's Fitz Roy in the worst weather imaginable on earth taught me courage to face nature alone. Soloing in the Himalaya bestowed on me even more. A rapid free solo of a mixed route in winter on Ama Dablam's west face, where there is no big wall climbing, made me feel like I was a ballet dancer on a mountain; it also taught me to quickly assess a mountain's weaknesses. My southwest face ascent of Cho Oyu in 1994 was an experience akin to climbing to outer space. The view of Everest's north face from the deserted summit gave me a serenity that made me consider staying there for the rest of my life. Two years later, though I failed in an attempt on Makalu's west face, I satisfied my dream of opening an aesthetic route on a steep wall on a high mountain. So, I wondered if Kasum Kanguru's east face could be added to my list of successful wall ascents. I also wondered if I could recover some of the confidence I might have lost on Makalu.

The shock that greeted me upon my arrival in Lukla was the high cost of porter's fees to make the carry to Kasum Kanguru's Base Camp. According to the locals, five porters had died in an avalanche at a 4500-meter pass, which apparently justified the quantum jump in their fees. Even though I had worked as a porter on Japan's Mt. Fuji and so understood their feelings, the high cost still hurt: the economic downturn in the Japanese economy had filtered down to us climbers as well. Nevertheless, the caravan went smoothly, and I walked apart from friends and the porters part of the way to absorb the ambiance of the Himalaya.

Base Camp was set up on April 14, 1998, at 4600 meters, where occasional crumbling seracs impressed upon me the scale of Himalayan mountains. I stayed healthy at Base Camp, thanks to daily vitamins. In contrast, the weather, possibly because of El Niño, displayed an unwelcome pattern of snow every afternoon. This put a premium on a strong motivation to succeed, without which there would be no chance of success.

I studied the wall, adapting to altitude during the inclement weather, and ultimately reached 5700 meters on the classic southeast face. In the meantime, I decided to put the route on the east face, though I eventually moved it farther to the right for safety reasons. On such big walls, the originally chosen line often turns out to be impossible or unwise.

I started out for the east face on my birthday, April 21, immediately after a snowfall. As always with a solo trip, there was no need to accommodate anyone else's schedule. I had only to watch the sun, make the necessary preparations, and head for the summit. I took two ice axes, crampons, the indispensable helmet, five rock pitons, six ice screws, four nuts, 80 meters of six-mm rope, bivy sack, camera, spare gloves and socks, and some food. I already knew that the 1200-meter wall had 600 meters of mixed climbing above the first 600 meters of rock and that it would be dangerous for a slow climber.

I felt the usual tension as I rounded the moraine and headed for the start of the rock. Leaving the ski poles behind, I windmilled my arms, put away the gloves, and started climbing. The 5.9 start required finger strength and left me wishing for some chalk. The rock was dry, but, with no good cracks, the climbing required the utmost concentration. Luckily, the few steep sections were all quite short, though I still needed to climb them without the pack, which I hauled up after with the rope. It became clear that good technique is the overriding requirement for climbs like this, and that physical strength is needed only to execute the technique.

I needed to hurry because of the danger of rockfall when the sun came up. I was especially worried about the V-shaped wall leading up to the central plateau, where numerous bits of rock and ice fell. Its exit was a chimney that required strenuous moves as I stemmed on rock while searching for suitable ice in the cracks for my axe.

The upper mixed portion consisted of rock slabs and steep ice with seracs threatening any access to the ridge. In order to minimize danger, I climbed the uppermost part in the evening,

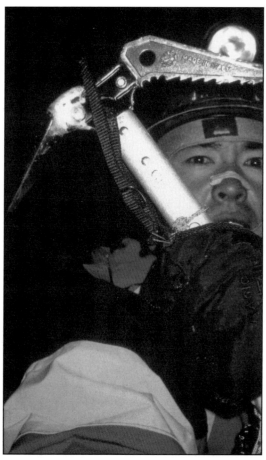

*Self-portrait, 2 a.m., on the summit of Kasum Kanguru (6370m), 22 hours and 1200 meters after leaving Base Camp. It would be 13 more hours before Yamanoi returned to Base.* YASUSHI YAMANOI

but it soon became difficult to pick out suitable lines in the new moon. Climbing in the dark restricts one's vision to only the area illuminated by headlamp; although the steepness may be exaggerated by the limited view, it is easy to concentrate on just the immediate problem.

I entered a steep couloir and looked up to see a huge serac that seemed to be waiting to fall on me. I thought about climbing faster to avoid the danger, but the snow was just too soft to allow that. Cautiously, I gained height little-by-little, occasionally being able to glance back at Peak 43, but then I hit the blue ice in the last section of the couloir, where tension seemed to restrict my field of vision.

I was breathing hard now, especially since I was still carrying the unused climbing rope. Most disappointing was the fact that when I thought I had arrived at where I could escape out of the couloir onto the ridge, nothing but seracs hung above me. I had to rappel from an ice screw, then traverse to the next couloir to the right.

The final climb to the summit was not particularly dramatic, but the intense cold, the hint of light in the sky, and occasional lightning over Mera were enough to emphasize the insignificance of my existence. After caching unnecessary gear, I arrived at the summit at 2 a.m., 22 hours after leaving Base Camp. I spent only one or two minutes on top taking pictures before starting down through a fantasy panorama of snow-covered peaks. I felt satisfied, even though I could see higher mountains.

After the euphoria of reaching the summit, I had to work up my adrenaline in order to concentrate on the long descent. The initial rappels from a bollard and then an ice screw were followed by difficult down climbing, all the while battling tangled ropes and telling myself to stay in control. When I reached the lower rock section, the sun began to soften the consolidated snow, increasing the objective danger. This, coupled with the realization that I was running out of pitons, caused me to risk moving toward Peak 43, where I rapidly down climbed a line amidst falling rocks. I was nearly exhausted, but I couldn't rest until I was out of danger. I finally stopped on a green hill below the moraine to enjoy a chocolate and rest.

Amidst the beauty of flowers and grass on this rocky knoll, I admired the view (unconsciously looking for routes and holds at the same time) of the west face of Mera, which I had

*After the climb.* Never-Ending Story *(VI 5.9 AI4, 1200m) takes a line above Yamanoi's head to the upper snow-and-ice slopes, then moves left to the summit.* YASUSHI YAMANOI COLLECTION

challenged six years earlier. It was not until I returned to Base Camp, 35 hours after the start, that I uttered the words, "I did it."

As I think back on it now, even though it sounds pretty good to hear the words, "the first ascent of the east face of Kasum Kanguru," it was not an especially wonderful line. It was a technical challenge, all right, but at the expense of objective danger that would keep me from recommending it as a good climb. It was simply a route that reaffirmed my ability to challenge a big wall. I think I have overcome my sense of failure on Makalu and would consider a bigger climb in the Himalaya next year. I have now done ten Himalayan climbs in eight successive years, but alpine-style climbing, with its constant sense of discovery, affords no chance to rest. There are always other mountain ranges and climbs that pass through my consciousness: *Sea of Dreams*, *Grand Illusion*, Cerro Torre, etc., etc....

Rats—I wish I had unlimited funds and physical strength....

SUMMARY OF STATISTICS

AREA: Nepal Himalaya

NEW ROUTE: *Never-Ending Story* (VI 5.9 AI4, 1200m) on the east face of Kasum Kanguru (6370m), April 21-22, 1998, Yasushi Yamanoi, solo

# Tang Kongma and Drohmo

## Building a bigger window

by Doug Scott, *United Kingdom*

To climb new routes, alpine style, up high, it is necessary to have experience and strength. How quickly the pursuit is taken up depends on one's window of opportunity. Inevitably, strength will diminish to the point where the burden of food and equipment cannot be carried or carried fast enough. For most regular Himalayan climbers, this window lasts for 15 to 20 years. As Shakespeare commented upon opportunity, "Which taken at the flood leads on to fortune/Omitted, all the voyage of life/Is found in shallows and in miseries." There will only be regret if those vital years were spent doing what others had done 40 years earlier and probably with a better acceptance of a far greater commitment.

This is often the case with those chasing the 8000-meter summits as they are caught up in the tyranny of numbers. The main gain when men, setting off in isolation and going for it with a self-contained team of one or two friends, and mountains meet is the experience of the aftermath once you are back down safe, and before habitual routines are resumed. In those delicious moments you find a clear head and returning strength, you are self aware and have greater understanding, are more tolerant, objective and enthused for life back home. The trick, of course, is to keep it going for as long as possible, and to retain it as a useful reference point when all seems lost again.

Last autumn, only a few new routes were climbed in Nepal, and yet at the same time 28 expeditions were "climbing" (mostly jumaring fixed ropes) on Ama Dablam. What kind of aftermath awaited those climbers when they descended to the distraction of so many others, the space between their thoughts completely full with the stress of exiting out of the Lukla airfield?

There are other good reasons for climbing new routes, especially mixed rock, snow and ice routes. There is the intrinsic interest to be found in the judgments and decisions that have to be made en route: where the route should go, where to belay, whether to bivouac the night, whether to turn back or go on in the face of uncertain weather, avalanche potential, serac collapse, rock fall. All these uncertainties focus you right there, stopping the mind from wandering onto useless trivia for days on end.

It is easy to get hooked on alpine-style climbing, but hard to get off. Well past my window of opportunity, I launched a trip to Drohmo in the spring of 1998. Not all the various ingredients for a good and safe climb were in place, so the attempt was abandoned at the start of the climb before I could know how it would turn out or how I would cope.

I had to find out. More to the point, I simply yearned to lose and then to surpass myself in the process of discovery. In September, Roger Mear and I returned to northeast Nepal and set out to climb Tang Kongma and the south rib of Drohmo.

We arrived at the yak pasture of Lhonak (4800m) on September 19 after a short two-day walk from the heli-pad at Ghunsa. We were accompanied by yaks and porters carrying 23 loads. Our three old friends, Shera Zangbu, Nawang Kasang and Janak Tamang, walked in

*A view from high on Kangchenjunga, showing A: Ramtang Peak, B: Wedge Peak, D: Tang Kongma, and D: Drohmo. The route up Drohmo is marked.* Doug Scott

from the road head at Basantapur and were with us to help out at base camp and up to the foot of our mountain.

On September 22, we scrambled up the grass and scree to Pt. 6019 (as indicated on the Swiss Janak Himal map), from where we had useful views of Tang Kongma's (6215m) west ridge and a possible way up the mountain. On September 25, accompanied by Shera Zangbu and Nawang Kasang, we established "Rock Camp" (5200m) in a little grassy hollow below a 40-meter vertical rock face that can be seen from halfway down the Lhonak-Pang Pema path. It is just left of the central glacier moraine on the south side of Drohmo. The day after, the four of us set off from Rock Camp at 6 a.m. for the northeast ridge of Tang Kongma, knowing the route would give us good views of Drohmo.

We traversed around the intervening spur to the glacier valley that drains the east side of Tang Kongma. After some difficulties descending the steep and loose valley side, we gained the boulder-strewn valley floor. Half an hour's walk later, we put on crampons and ascended the east glacier of Tang Kongma. We roped up on meeting deep fresh snow where the glacier leveled out and zig-zagged around crevasses to reach the base of the northeast ridge at the col overlooking Broken Glacier to the north. The snow on the ridge was stable and we made good progress on two ropes. Roger and I climbed up the crest of the ridge and our two Sherpa friends climbed up a subsidiary crest 100 meters left. We came together after three hours at a six-meter ice step where we took a belay. Roger led up to belay on an ice stake, which we left for the return. By 1 p.m., Roger and I joined Shera and Nawang on the rocky summit where they had already built three large cairns. There was no sign of any one else having been here, though we knew that the Swiss had made the first ascent via the Northeast Ridge in 1949. We descended the same way, facing out, and arrived back at Rock Camp 12 hours after setting off.

Rain and snow fell continuously from September 27 to
October 2, but that gave us a
well-needed rest and time to
savor our first climb. We
walked up to Rock Camp on
October 1, taking in a diversion to Pang Pema to check
out the progress of a British
Kangchenjunga expedition.

On October 3, with the
help of Shera and Nawang,
we established ourselves at
the head of the south glacier at
a point below the steep snow
slopes leading up to the south
rib of Drohmo. The next day,
with low cloud and snow flurries blowing around, Roger
and I decided to fix our four
ropes up the deep avalanche-
prone snow to the base of the
rib. Six months earlier, with
Lindsay Griffin and Skip
Novak, the various factors
necessary for a good climb—
fitness, experience and weather—had not been in place. But
now everything was right.

On October 5, we began
our climb, ascending the
ropes and taking the last two
with us for what we hoped

*Roger Mear on the south rib.* DOUG SCOTT

would be a four-day push to the top. As there were only two of us, the food, fuel, cooking gear,
rock and ice climbing equipment and the MacIntyre bivouac tent weighed in heavy, as did the
commitment to this prominent and elegant feature of the mountain.

Roger scrambled up loose mixed ground and disappeared over to the left of the ridge line.
Two hours later all the rope was out. Muffled shouts indicated I should move up to his traverse
line—at which point we had an altercation. I had expected to go more or less directly up a line
of weakness on the crest of the buttress and not cross three steep ribs with soft snow gullies in
between that plunged down to the glacier, now a thousand feet below. Roger brought the ensuing long-range debate neatly to a close by suggesting that we should perhaps give up the climb!
With that, I shouldered my rucksack and set off to traverse the 60 meters of atrocious snow and
to connect again with Roger. My beaming partner was well pleased with himself for having led
such a difficult pitch. He was also pleased, as was I, that the climb could now continue. We both
really needed this one. Already I was finding that the hard pitch had stretched my mind and

LEFT: *Drohmo, with the south rib in the center of the fluted face.* DOUG SCOTT

*Roger Mear on day 3.* DOUG SCOTT

body, dusting away the cob-webs that had accumulated, it having been some time since I had climbed hard pitches in the Himalaya. The next three pitches went more or less straight up over steep red and rough granite (V) and into snow gullies (IV). The last pitch of the day brought me to a ledge and snow cone (6207m) suitable for dig-ging out a tent platform. Roger came up in the gloom as the Everest group was bathed in orange light 75 miles away.

That next frosty morning, under a cloudless sky, we set off up the buttress, climbing more snowed-up rock to a belay point from where we could traverse right for 80 meters to a belay on loose blocks. The sun was now shining over Tent Peak right onto our route, making the next two pitches of snow-covered steep ice (IV) a worrying lead for Roger. Eventually I led on through, angling up left back to the crest of the buttress, placing runners on flakes of granite that poked out of the snow and ice. We were now above the prominent rock bands that are an obvious feature of the lower third of our route.

Roger led the next four pitches up the snow arête to the left of the great overhung bulge of ice we dubbed "the cauliflower." Sound belays were hard to find under all the monsoon snow. It usually entailed considerable digging to find rock or good ice. We had intended to sleep on the gentle slopes above the cauliflower, but after a 20-meter probe, Roger returned while the sun sank down beyond Everest and the full moon came up over Kangchenjunga. We settled into our tent, pitched inside an icy grotto.

Another bright and frosty morning helped us make good progress up the steep snow arête, then up a vertical and difficult band of rock (V). By midday, we were walking over the top of the cauliflower to the base of the right-hand of two summit snow and ice ribs. The sun was blasting down, inducing lethargy, so we put the tent up and took the early afternoon off in favor of a brew and a snooze. Thus refreshed, we fixed our two ropes up steep ice and rock steps before descending to our third bivouac.

On October 8, we left our tent and set off up the ropes with light sacks. It was such a relief to be liberated from our burden and to make good time up the ropes. The end of our route was now in sight. There is usually a sting in the tail, and here it was mushy snow and more dubious belays. The last two pitches were unprotected apart from me sitting in huge bucket steps dug out of the arête. Even after digging down six feet, the ice axes just disappeared into the unconsolidated snow. The snow was particularly soft on the west side of our rib and for some reason, never as pleasant as the northeast ridge of Tang Kongma.

At 2:30 p.m., I joined Roger at the top of the south rib of Drohmo. We were now on the long summit ridge of the mountain where clouds had been gathering, blown up by strong southerly winds. To the north we caught glimpses of the rounded peaks below Jannak and the Tibetan plateau beyond. The chances of climbing Drohmo from the north looked bleak, if not impossible, as so much soft snow lay above overhung ice cliffs.

We climbed up and along the summit ridge to the west and called it a day at 3 p.m. on top of a corniced peak overhanging the north face. We registered 6855 meters on the altimeter. According to the latest map of Nepal produced by the Finns last year, the highest summit of Drohmo is at least half a mile away and, at 6881 meters, 26 meters higher than where we were. Although we could not see it through the clouds, we must assume it to be a fact, as the latest calculations should be the most trustworthy. We were well satisfied with the 28 pitches we had climbed from the glacier up the south pillar of our mountain. We down climbed and abseiled back to our last bivouac and next day reached the glacier after a total of 25 abseils. Nawang and Shera came up the next day to share our obvious delight and to help us remove our two fixed ropes and move the glacier camp down to Base Camp.

Roger, fit and faster from two months' guiding in the Alps, and more youthful than I, had led the majority of the route. To compensate, I had carried a bit more and took on the chores of cooking; but still I wish now I had led my share of the climb. I also feel uneasy that we had fixed those first four pitches, which took away a little of the commitment. These are just personal regrets that every climber must have when he does not lead when he could and fixes rope when his courage fails him. Still, the overall impressions of being up there with Roger remain good ones.

It was not a big thing in itself to spend those four days checking out a way up the south rib of Drohmo and putting the rest of life to one side while we engaged rock and ice and a lot of monsoon snow and were carried along by that urge for clarity that comes from (near) total commitment to this simple self-imposed task. We took every pitch as it came, not knowing how we would do it, but finding a way and a sense of well-being after each difficulty was passed. So it had done the trick, lifted my spirits as it always does when on a new route with just one or two other good friends and where the outcome remains uncertain to the end.

SUMMARY OF STATISTICS

AREA: Nepal Himalaya

FIRST ASCENT: The northeast ridge of Tang Kongma (6215m), September 26, Shera Zangbu, Nawang Kasang, Janak Tamang, Roger Mear, Doug Scott; the south rib of Drohmo (6881m) to the south summit (6855m), October 4-9, Roger Mear and Doug Scott

PERSONNEL: Shera Zangbu, Nawang Kasang, Janak Tamang, Roger Mear, Doug Scott

# Ak-Su in Winter

## Where the Russians get their ya-yas

by Pavel Chabaline and Igor Nefyodov, *Russia*
*translated by Yuri Kolomiets*

The Laylak Ak-Su in the Pamir-Alai mountain range is a paradise for alpinists. An entire constellation of grandiose granite peaks juts from a narrow 20-kilometer strip of the Turkestan ridge. Every summer, outstanding mountain climbers gather there. On the area's menu, there are rock formations for every taste. The north face Ak-Su North Peak is a delicacy for the gourmet: over 1500 meters of irreproachable granite. To feel the grandeur and power of this mountain, one needs to come to its base—or, even better, experience it on any of the 13 established routes. Until the winter season of 1998-'99, however, no one had succeeded in going to the top of Ak-Su in winter.

This winter saw the first two winter ascents of the peak's north face, which had been attempted many times in previous years. The first team to reach the top was a group comprised of Pavel Chabaline (Kirov), Alexander Abramov (Moscow), and Ilyas Tukhvatullin (Tashkent, Uzbekistan). Together with a support group of two, the team flew into the area on December 6. Their ascent of the 1860-meter *Cold Corner* route (6A), which has an average angle of 76 degrees, began on December 8. After four days of preparation, the team started up the route, which they climbed in capsule-style. Forty-five pitches were ascended over ten days. The team reached the top of the wall on the night of December 21-22. After a cold night on top, they began their descent. The weather had been unstable during the ascent, with snowfall every three days. They sustained no frostbite or injuries despite night-time temperatures that reached -20°C and hurricane-force winds encountered on the ridge.

The second team was comprised of two men from Ekaterinburg, Mikhail Pershin and Igor Nefyodov. On December 13, after two days spent fixing ropes, they started climbing the 1988 Chaplinsky route (6B). This very steep face route is about 1860 meters long. The two spent six of their 19 days on the route waiting for good weather. They made the top of the wall late on December 31 in a complete whiteout with terrible winds and reached the summit in time for the new year. Figuring in the time they spent waiting for good weather, their total climbing time was about 13 days—rather good time for climbing this route, even in summer. Four rappels into the descent on January 1, they were stopped again by a terrible storm that forced them to wait another two days for "reasonably bad weather" before continuing down.

Both teams boasted climbers who had attempted the wall in previous winters. Pavel Chabaline is Mr. Ak-Su. He has made nine ascents of the wall, including a number of new routes. In 1995, he made an attempt on the wall in winter, climbing for a week before being forced to descend. Last summer, he took his skills to the Indian Himalaya, where he led every wall pitch of the 1998 Russian-American route on Changabang's north face. Mikhail Pershin and Igor Nefyodov and a small group of their mates had made a go of Ak-Su's north face via

LEFT: *Ilyas Tukhvatullin (left) and Alexander Abramov with the object of their affection, the north face of Ak-Su North Peak, Laylak Ak-Su region, Kyrgyzstan.* PAVEL CHABALINE

the *Severe Beauty* route in February, 1998. Low clouds and steady snowfall enveloped the mountain during their attempt. The wall is like a huge funnel, picking up snow all along the face and sloughing it off in dust-like avalanches onto mountaineers' heads. Snow percolates through the finest holes of clothing, clogging eyes and ears and noses. Having managed only several rope lengths, Pershin and Nefyodov's team had to give up. But one might say that it served as a kind of reconnaissance.

After preliminary work on their respective routes, both teams began climbing a day apart. What follows is the story of their climbs.

PAVEL CHABALINE

On December 21, 1998, at 6 p.m. local time, we stood on the top of Ak-Su Peak, Alexander "Sasha" Abramov for the first time, Ilyas Tukhvatullin for the fifth, me for the ninth time via the north face of my favorite mountain. One feature set this ascent apart from a long line of similar climbs. It was the first winter ascent of this wall.

The Laylak Valley is like a magnet for me, and every year I long to go there. Each climber has his or her own road, dreams and plans. It so happened that my climbing life since the early 1990s was closely connected with this mountain. But for all the most beautiful routes done, the new lines conceived and followed, there remained one dream: the wall in winter.

Three years ago, we had a go at it. After a week of struggle with bad weather and circumstances, we had to go down. I said then, "Now I know how to do it, but I do not know who else will." Besides our attempt, another four had been made, all abortive. Nonetheless, the right moment came at last.

Even though the days are at their shortest, the best month for this climb is December with its more stable weather and minimal probability of prolonged snowfall. We planned to climb capsule style, working from various portaledge camps for several days on end while we fixed the next 300 to 400 meters of the route and hauled loads. The idea was to live there as long as necessary, be it two weeks, three weeks, a month. . . .

We were very lucky. The entire ascent, including fixing ropes and rappelling the route, took 16 days. We left our surplus petrol and food at our last bivouac, one rope length beneath the summit ridge. If necessary, we could have stayed there quite comfortably for another 16 days, and a bit more without comfort.

The main difference between winter and summer climbs is that in winter daylight is twice as short, you are twice as slow and you carry twice as much petrol and food. All in all, everything goes very slowly. The only advantage is an abundance of ice that does not melt. Conversely, the ice is very hard. I cannot imagine climbing on Ak-Su's north face with any kind of ice tools, no matter how curved. Only ice sky hooks ("ice fifis") work. In winter there is no point even to try without ice hooks. In fact, we made our entire ascent of the wall with either aid or ice hooks. Protection was arranged by means of a shorter version ice screw made especially for winter ice by the Ural company Alvo-Titan. Ordinary screws are too long for the shallow ice runnels. We had to sharpen the hooks two to three times a day, because the entire time the climbing was mixed and we were constantly changing from rock to ice and the other way around.

We took spare crampons and hooks, as we did not know how this bloody ironmongery would behave in such cold. We had a spare primus as well, plus a gas stove to heat the primus, plus a gas lamp, all put into different bags so we would not be stranded without cooking uten-

RIGHT: *Pavel Chabaline on pitch 4 (A2) of the* Cold Corner *route on the first winter ascent of the north face of Ak-Su North Peak. The 900-meter Admiralteets is to his right.* ALEXANDER ABRAMOV

sils. We once had a very nasty experience of four stoveless bivouacs—in summer, though.

Yet in general I do not consider technical difficulty to be the main problem on such walls. We had all done some winter "sixes" *(the most difficult grade assigned to a climb in the Russian grading system-Ed.)*; the real problem is to survive and go on climbing without a considerable loss of strength, without losing momentum. Hence in winter you have an approach to such climbs that is, compared to summer ascents, essentially new. In summer you can put four people on a portaledge 1.3 meters by 1.8 meters—rough, but possible. In winter it is possible to fit only three.

Our first attempt at winter climbing on Ak-Su yielded a priceless experience. The main reason for our retreat was that we slowly turned into frozen lumps in our jackets and sleeping bags. The constant temperature difference inside the tent

*Pavel Chabaline (who led the entire route) on the ninth day of ascent. Note ice fifi.* ALEXANDER ABRAMOV

created moisture and hoar-frost on the walls and forced us to descend. This year a company made us special Thinsulate suits that did not imbibe moisture, so our things were always dry. The suits proved to be free of the typical "arctic drawbacks." Loose fitting and not too thick (you could put the hood on over a helmet), they allowed us not just to move, but to climb. Two rectangular sleeping bags, zipped together, formed one collective bag, big, comfortable and, above all, warm and dry. Practically all our middle layers were made of fleece and windstop fabric. The latter is fully windproof, yet breathes. Gloves, mittens and balaclavas made of fleece completed the gentleman's set.

All this gear was "baptized by fire" (by deep frost actually). On December 20, after having ascended the wall proper, we fixed six ropes in an ice gully on the other side of the ridge and ran up against a rock wall 200 meters long. In summer I would not even dream about tackling such a wall, but now all the rotten overhangs were frozen. Besides, the ridge proper was not at all attractive. What stuck in our minds was the last pitch: 15 meters of aid over a cornice, then 30 meters of overhanging rock "feathers" mixed with unstable blocks. I was scared to touch it at all, but had no choice. Hoping to get in a piece of gear, I hit a block with my hammer. I thought a grenade had exploded nearby. Sasha and Ilyas were standing 30 meters below, and there appeared a crack that connected all the way to the ice screws to which they were clipped. The descent of that pitch was so frightful we did not even dare to retrieve the abseil rope: our lives would have been at stake.

On December 21, we reached the top in a hurricane with -30C° temperatures and had to bivouac at 5200 meters. For shelter, we had a sheet of plastic, and for warmth, a gas stove unusable in such wind. You could say that that bivouac was a cold one. We sat it out in our new suits under a boulder, tied to the ropes, and the next day were down to our ledge by lunch. There, we rested and warmed ourselves until morning. The result: nobody got frostbite or fell ill.

Strange as it may sound, the wall proper did not bother us much. The real trouble we expected, and found, on the summit ridge. Quite often in summer there is a hell of wind up there; in winter, it is simply a kilometer-long snow plume accompanied by a jet's roar. In addition, the ridge, with ten pitches plus traverses, pendulums and abseils, is far from being technically easy.

We rappelled our route. When going up, Sasha had placed bolts every 45 meters and marked them with five-meter thin red cords. They helped us greatly on our descent. We placed 26 bolts, and rapped from screws for the last ten abseils. On December 23, we were down once more.


IGOR NEFYODOV

A k-Su again, a long, long way into Kyrgyzstan. The sun had yet to appear, and the wall looked cold and unaffable—the wall we had once before failed to climb. Man comes back to the place where he has failed unwillingly, but we returned to try to gain the summit once more. There were five of us: Mikhail Pershin and I, both from Ekaterinburg, and our mates, Andrey Belkov, cameraman, Andrey Selivanov, doctor, and Evgeny Novoseltsev. Our attempt the previous February had basically been thwarted by the weather. It was therefore decided to try the wall in December. We tested our big wall tactics with an ascent of a 220-meter unfinished monolithic concrete TV tower in Ekaterinburg, then started up Ak-Su on December 13. From that moment on, we could only descend if we gave up the ascent.

The days were short and the sun never hit the wall. The cracks were clogged with solid ice that split off into plates beneath the blows of the hammer. Only with a combination of ice hammer and ice fifi could we climb the difficult sections of verglassed rock.

But all this meant nothing in comparison to the weather. With that, there is nothing you can do but wait. Waiting exhausts the nerves while the stocks dwindle. Taking into account all these factors, we took 20 days' food supply. But even that proved to be not enough. We would spend 19 days on the wall and four more on the descent. Ten days of the 23 would be lost to bad weather.

W e began working, our hearts overflowing with joy and fear, with 40 kilos of iron, four ropes, a portaledge, and one goal for the two of us. We had chosen the Chaplinsky route (Russian Grade 6B, or roughly VI 5.10 A3, ca. 1800m), a rather difficult route, even in summer. Now it was winter, and nobody took us seriously. Pavel Chabaline wished us luck, but he preferred to go up along the *Cold Corner* route.

At the start, everything was all right. The weather was fine. We climbed through the first roof, managing one pitch per day. Ah, winter. But the wonderful feeling didn't leave us: we were finally on the wall.

On our third night in the portaledge, a storm suddenly broke. It snowed heavily, and the walls of our "house" were covered with ice. Sitting in the tent, we sang songs at first, then read the book about hobbits by Tolkien that Belkov had palmed off to us at the last moment, then told each other stories from our military experiences. We had to shake the snow off constantly in order not to be crushed. It was good that we had taken the book. It was not so boring under those conditions.

It came to mind that the book was about us. The same small hole, outings there and back again, and the same thought: "Why the hell did we agree to do all this?"

While reading the book about the hobbit, we noticed that when he was hungry he dreamed about his favorite fried eggs with ham and a cup of coffee in the morning. It made our mouths water. Mikhail promised to cook those very same fried eggs after the descent. At the end of our adventure in the mountains, when we had only broth to eat, I would close my eyes and see that morning paradise and a birthday cake on the table.

The route was choked with ice and snow. Whereas free climbing is possible in summer, in winter it is only aid climbing or climbing with ice fifis. We constantly had to clear cracks to hammer in pitons. On the whole, this made for tense work all day long without relent.

The Chaplinsky Couloir was solid ice. With a blow of the hammer big dinner plates of ice broke off. We had to file our ice fifis and ice screws all the time.

We gained the upper ice slot above the "Cross" in the darkness. Swearing, we pitched our portaledge in the twinkling of an eye. Nothing could be seen, but we were in already.

And extreme conditions again. A Swedish primus stove, which we bought in Moscow, refused to burn normally. What the hell! The primus, adjusted to run on both petrol and gas, clogged up with both fuels the same way. It tried our patience every evening. Each time, as he turned it over in his hands, Mikhail threatened to break the stove into smithereens or crush it with a huge rock just after the descent. "Or maybe," we said, "it would be better to exchange it for a Russian petrol stove?" A desperate thought indeed.

On December 30, having made the north face, we went out on the ridge. It was terribly cold, but we were happy to have done the wall. Only one day remained to the top.

Well, at last, on New Year's Eve, we were there. New Year's, on top of Ak-Su. It had never happened before. We gave thanks to Pavel Chabaline for leaving food for us: meat and lard, soup, chocolate. It really was a New Year's present. It was snowing and the wind was strong. Since we couldn't wait for midnight (we were too hungry), we greeted the new year a bit early. We wished each other the quickest possible descent and said good night. The next day, we would need to start going down.

January 1. The weather was not too good but we decided to descend regardless. We hoped to rush through the raps but couldn't. The descent along the snow cornices and the awful knife-edge of the ridge didn't make us happy. We couldn't get through it with our loads, so we decided to

RIGHT: *Ak-Su North Peak, showing routes on the north face. 1: Troschinenko/Original North Wall Route (6A, 1982); 2: Kavunenko/Left Pillar (6A, 1984); 3: Moshnicov's Split (6B, 1984); 4: Vedernikov/Right Buttress (6A, 1986); 5: Popov/Central North Wall (6B, 1986); 6: Pershin Variation, Right Buttress (6B+, 1988); 7: Moshnicov's Split, Kostenko Variation ("Cold Corner," 6A, 1988); 8: Central North Wall, Chaplinski Variation (6B, 1988); 9: Central North Wall, Chabaline Variation ("The Nose," 6B, 1994); 10: Right Buttress Direct, Klenov Variation (6B, 1996); 11: Ruchkin/Direct North Wall (6B, 1997); 12: Klenov/Direct North Wall (6B, 1996). Chabaline, Abramov and Tukhavatullin climbed (3) to (1); Pershin and Nefyodov climbed (5) to (8).* TOPO BY CLAY WADMAN

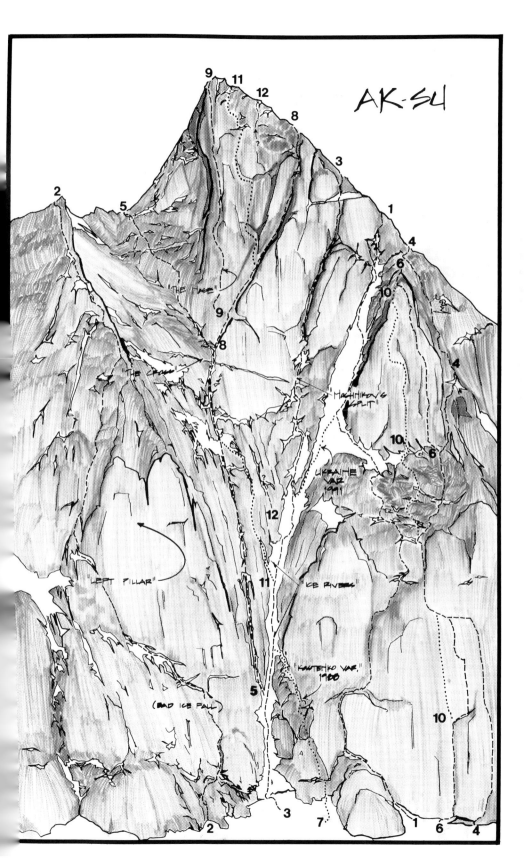

rappel directly from the buttress to the cirque. I thought, "Nobody has ever done it this way."

It was cloudy, snowing heavily and there was a strong wind and poor visibility. We succeeded in rapping only three pitches before we decided not to try any more. We found a postage-stamp spot of snow and dug in.

Two days passed. It seemed that it was beyond our powers. We were running short on food.

If we're going, we thought, let's go. We tied two ropes together with our haulbags beneath us and rapped down. We went through snow, down the wall, dropping, dropping. By then, we were doing it automatically. It was getting dark. Finally, Mikhail's joyful cry: "The ground!" I still had about 30 meters to go. I threaded a rope but it stuck somewhere in the darkness. I no longer gave a damn about it, and, having left the end of the rope on the wall, I fell.

That was all. Deep snow under our feet. It wasn't home yet, but at least we were on the ground.

The ascent had been most difficult in bad weather, when we had to spend time in the tent and it was impossible to say how much longer the weather would continue. The rivers of spindrift that forced us to dig out our tent streamed into the tent while we were outside. We had no problem with fuel, but it was hard with provisions. When we were down to just tea, we would go on dreaming or telling stories (about military service, mainly), but deep in our souls we felt like a cat on hot bricks. On the whole, we hadn't been able to move six days out of 19 because of bad weather. Six days of captivity. It was no less difficult than working on the wall.

And there was also the lack of sunshine, the terrible cold, the hauling of loads, the work of the climbing itself, and the way leading us ever so slowly up to the ridge and then, at last, to the summit. The summit of our dreams. But all in all, life had continued, even under those extreme conditions. Our will never broke and we didn't bore each other to death. Our resolution and sense of humor never left us in our singular controversy with the mountain. Now one may say that the problem of climbing the north face of Ak-Su North Peak in winter has been solved.

Of course we were glad to have made our contribution to the answer. Our victory had been no easy matter, and thus there was a bit of sadness. We left a piece of our souls behind. After descending from Everest on the first Soviet ascent of the mountain, Edward Myslovsky said, "There was a dream, and it came true. Now you need to find a new one." I agree that a person must always have a dream. For now, exhaustion won't let us think about anything else. But summer will come and bring new prospects, new ascents, new meetings with old friends, and new Everests that we will find impossible to turn down.

SUMMARY OF STATISTICS

AREA: The Laylak Ak-Su Region of the Pamir Alai, Kyrgyzstan

FIRST WINTER ASCENTS: The *Cold Corner* route (6A, 1860m) on the north face of Ak-Su North Peak (5217m), December 12-23, Pavel Chabaline, Alexander Abramov, Ilyas Tukhvatullin; the Chaplinsky route (6B, 1860m), December 13-January 4, Igor Nefyodov and Mikhail Pershin

PERSONNEL: Pavel Chabaline, Alexander Abramov, Ilyas Tukhavatullin; Nefyodov and Mikhail Pershin, Andrey Belkov, Andrey Selivanov, Evgeny Novoseltsev

# Alum Kuh

## A climbing appointment with the Islamic Republic of Iran

by Kath Pyke, *United Kingdom*


It's strange how things turn out. I had never really considered Iran to be my top choice of climbing destination, but September, 1998, found myself and three other women venturing cloaked, hooded, and without an unnecessary inch of flesh exposed through the crowds of Tehran airport. We drew curious stares. Our backpacks and haulsack straps contrasted with the somber scene around us, and even their faded hues formed the only point of color in an otherwise predominantly black-and-gray environment. Even at 3 a.m. the airport was in total congestion, largely due to the fact that meeting a relative on a Saturday night is a highly popular family outing.

As we pushed our laden trolleys toward the exit, we couldn't help but notice the covered, draped nature of every female we encountered. Not a spare wisp of hair was visible, although in some cases elegant footwear and a flash of denim hinted at the possibility of Western dress beneath the obligatory hejab*.

My State-side friends had been incredulous at the concept of Western women climbing in a Middle Eastern country, and remarked equally on the political timing of our visit. The United States had recently bombed various Middle Eastern venues in retaliation for Taliban hardliner Bin Ladin's (declared "U.S. Enemy Number 1!" by my local Colorado newspaper) campaigns against the West. Within the week, Iran would mobilize forces and headline its own papers with arguments on whether or not it should declare war on Afghanistan.

As guests of the Iran Mountaineering Federation, we were one of the first Western climbing teams to be invited into Iran since the revolution some two decades earlier. The trip had come about through the British Mountaineering Council International Women's Climbing Meet, held in North Wales some months earlier. Leyla Pope, a climber with dual British/Iranian nationality, had captured our imagination with a report on something largely unknown to the rest of the world: Iranian women's involvement in climbing. We were curious to learn more. Leyla secured an invitation from the Women's Mountaineering Federation and assembled a team. The ensuing group was comprised of Celia Bull, Glenda Huxter, Leyla and me, with a track of first ascents and international expeditions between us.

We had been lured to the country with tales of a "second Yosemite," and our plans were to climb, and possibly attempt a new route, on Iran's highest north wall, Alum Kuh. Alum Kuh, at 15,819 feet, forms part of the Alborz Range in northern Iran. Its 2,000-foot north face is the finest in the country; as we later found out, it also has a reputation of being one of the world's deadliest. In exchange for being hosted by the Federation, we would run a climbing skills workshop for some 20 women climbers selected from Iran's 24 provinces. The focus of our trip was to explore the climbing possibilities, but as the

---

*Hejab is the Iranian term given to appropriate dresswear in the Islamic Republic of Iran (IRI). In post-revolution Iran, the black, all-enveloping "chawdor" (literal translation: tent) has been replaced in urban areas and among the younger generation with the equally acceptable ankle-length "manteau," or coat, usually matched by a white or black headscarf.)

The north face of Alum Kuh, 2,500 feet from glacier to summit. The Amralaiy-Rost route is the prominent, slightly shadowed, slanting line on the left of the main face. The 1936 North Ridge route follows the ridge on the right to the summit. KATH PYKE

*Kath Pyke on an A2 pitch on the Amralaiy-Rost route.*
GLENDA HUXTER

weeks unfolded it became clear that the climbing was merely a backdrop (albeit serious at times) to an insight into a society's culture and values—a Muslim society, no less, that actively supports the participation of both genders in rock climbing, though via a segregated approach.

One of the problems for the aspiring rock climber in Iran is that, following the revolution, there has been neither information written about climbing areas within the country nor climbing information exchanged with the outside world. Coupled with the fact that women need to be escorted and covered at all times, it soon became obvious to our small British team that our options were hardly flexible.

Three days later we had met with our hosts and been transported by bus and jeep to the trailhead. By now we had donned our more appropriate mountain hejab (a robust and shorter manteau with headscarves tied in the least hot variation). Sweating, we toiled with hardware and altitude through cloud inversion to base camp at 14,500 feet. A preliminary glance soon made clear what language barriers and pigeon Farsi (*Farsi is the official language of Iran-Ed.*) had failed to impart: namely, that although Alum Kuh is indeed a steep wall, and one composed of granite, it is hardly the "Second Yosemite" with which we had been lured. No one had mentioned that Alum Kuh was capped by several hundred feet of continually discharging rubble, or that fridge-sized stuff regularly scoured the approach slopes.

The next day (our headscarves by now replaced with equally appropriate, but more functional, balaclavas), a closer look from the glacier reinforced our view that there was not much likelihood of doing anything new. Where potential existed there was significant rockfall, and we only had a certain amount of time. Our teams split. Pope and Bull, along with several extra teams from the Federation, opted for the classic 1936 North Ridge route, a clean(er) and classic alternative to the summit. Huxter and I decided to stick with the north wall proper. We picked an obvious and previously climbed line, but with the added adventure bonus of no route details, let alone indication of grade.

For 15 pitches and 20 hours (the latter due to taking a left when we should have taken a right and descending into the wrong valley), we climbed what turned out to be the 1964

Iranian-German Amralaiy-Rost route, a not-too-demanding V+ 5.9+ with two pitches of A2 (N.B.: Brit aid grade!) and chimney sections complete with thick ice pillars at the back. We carefully climbed around these in the sub-zero temperatures, agreeing that they were better dry than dripping. Not so easy was the 400-foot rubble exit, reminiscent of the more esoteric parts of our own British hero crag, Gogarth.

The climb provided a good alpine route, perhaps made more special by the area's remoteness and the experience of spending an entire week above a cloud inversion generated by the Caspian Sea. Afterward, armed with more knowledge, we wished we'd tried something steeper to the right. However, it was too serious a place to spend too much time; we'd had our own close encounters and were all too aware of the number of people who had come to grief under the aforementioned blocks.

Some days later, we did at last find a source of climbing information at the Rhudbarak home of local guide and village hero, Mr. Nagavi (oh, why didn't the Federation take us there first?!). Nagavi summited Everest last year and is a national figure, though such news rarely makes its way to the States. We sat cross-legged on a lush Persian carpet surrounded by to-die-for sweetcakes made especially tasty after our previous diet of Magi noodles and dehydrated figs. After being plied with somewhat less savory black tea, we were led shoeless into a dim place known as the Visitors' Room.

It gradually dawned on us that to cross that threshold was to step back in time. The room was bare, but the walls were covered with beaming team photos, visitors' books and climbing memorabilia with a singular unifying theme: everything was crumbling, curling, sepia-tinted. The photos showed sideburns and shirts with large pointed collars. In short, everything had halted in 1978. Nothing more than half a page in the visitor book separated the late 1970s entries from the scrawl of two Dutch trekkers who had ventured there this year—half a page

*Press conference in Tehran. From left to right, Glenda Huxter, Celia Bull, head of the Women's Mountaineering Federation Mrs. Rahimzadeh, and two Iranian journalists.* KATH PYKE

*Instructors and climbers warming up at the start of one of the workshop days.* KATH PYKE

representing 20 years of total change in a nation's society, lifestyle and outlook.

We delved into the archives. Records showed that Alum Kuh supports a number of lines, most of which were put up by European teams in the 1960s and '70s. There are also a fair number of aid lines, some of which could undoubtedly now go free—and those aspiring to visit the area and dabble with Alum Kuh's deadly reputation will soon have their chance. Things are changing fast, and the presence of the Dutch trekkers was significant: foreign currency is sorely needed, the dollar is foremost among currencies and tourism is a popular word if not yet a frequent phenomenon. 1998 saw the first map produced for the area in 20 years, and it won't be long before there's a climbing guide in English. Even while we were in the country, the Iranian government began a series of changes that now make it possible for Westerners to visit without visas or special invitations.

Back in Tehran, we attended to the other part of our agenda. Playing out the role of political pawns, we met a roomful of journalists, all female and all clad completely in black. We hoped to overcome the visa barrier and set up an exchange for three Iranian women climbers to attend a climbing course in Europe, but first we had to meet our workshop commitment and step into the role of climbing instructors. The course would cover rope work and climbing skills and was focused on raising the standards of women's guiding to that of their male counterparts.

A week later, ten miles from the outskirts of Tehran, we stood beneath a dripping overhang on a hillside with small crags and outcrops. Our group, mostly under the age of 35, was comprised of some 20 women from a range of backgrounds and household incomes, all of whom were remarkably self-sufficient. We worked with interpreters and our ever-increasing vocabulary of climbing Farsi. There was great curiosity, not least on our part. How would it be to teach climbing and wear harnesses over (or under?) hejab?

*The beginner's group bouldering.* KATH PYKE

As it turned out, there was no such issue. The outer clothing is for mixed company, and with no men around and amid the privacy of the rock outcrops, garments were removed to reveal more functional long pants and loose shirts underneath. The headscarves remained, but by now they were securely wedged under the ubiquitous baseball cap. As the week progressed, even the headscarf was removed in the intimacy of meal times.

We split into three groups to focus on different skill levels and became acquainted with the participants. Shiva Nani, who was training to be a mountain guide, was in the highest skill level group. Though she was accomplished, to achieve that final extra level of tuition required coaching and assessment by internationally accredited instructors and assessors, preferably female. There were no such people in Iran.

I was lucky to take the beginners' group. The majority were in their teens, and highly motivated. One individual astounded us by occasionally breaking off into heart-rending Persian folk songs. Another member of my group similarly stood out. Samaih Asgar was 15 years old and came from the town of Mashad near the Pakistan border. She had traveled by bus for 36 hours to attend the workshop. She was accompanied by her father and 14- and nine-year-old brothers, gentle, courteous folk who camped modestly and discreetly away from the group for the entire week. Between them, they had one steel locking carabiner and an oversized and fraying Whillans harness that went round each of them twice. By the end of the week, the workshop had become a family affair: the boys became an integral part of our group and the father watched over the climbing gear when we descended for overnight accommodation in Darband. We wondered at the progressive attitude shown by Samaih's family in their support for her participation in the skills week.

As the days went by, we realized it was more than just about climbing. Samaih's father is a teacher, and all his children are being rigorously schooled in English. Samaih is bright and ambitious, though in some ways a little pushy. The word precocious springs to mind

She was always the first to want to do anything, sometimes at the expense of others and her own personal safety. One morning, in her eagerness to examine an instructor's belay, she soloed up an outcrop only to get stuck on the descent. Only some careful coaxing saved her from a severe fall. But Samaih is challenging attitudes, and if she is to make headway in modern Iran, she needs such an approach. Climbing facilitates that confidence, and we were not there to check it.

Later in the week we ran a bouldering skills session. For some it was their first experience with the discipline. Not so for 24-year-old Parisa Nobari, who has held the position as Iran's top female indoor competition climber for the past two years. In Iran, climbing competitions are segregated by gender, which allows women to compete without hejab. In mixed company, however, cultural convention dictates that hejab must be worn. For female indoor competition climbers, participation in competitions outside the country is effectively prevented. On this topic, Parisa shrugged and laughed. She was hopeful that one day, constraints would be lifted. Currently, if any Iranian citizen wants to travel outside of Iran, a special visa needs to be obtained, for which large fees are required—something beyond the reach of everyday Iranians. Parisa was less concerned about competing internationally than simply being able to travel freely outside of Iran and meet people from different countries.

The week closed on a high note. It had been a rewarding time of shared experiences and a unique opportunity for Middle Eastern and Western women to meet. In 80°F temperatures, we donned backpacks over hejab and trekked down the hillside and out through the local villages. As we did, we came across a group of men at one of the bouldering areas. They were clad in shorts and vests, their scant clothing the epitome of Western style. Given our sweating and uncomfortable state, the contrast was striking. Shiva, the aspirant guide, smiled wryly and plodded on. To our Western outlook the scene screamed of injustice, but we were not there to judge. The trip had been about insights and opportunities, and it did not seem fitting for minds conditioned in the West to pass judgment on Middle Eastern values after only a few weeks.

Courtesy of a generous invitation, we recuperated from the week's demands in the privacy of a British/Iranian home. Set in the quieter suburbs of Tehran, high walls hid landscaped grounds, and a liberal atmosphere more akin to pre-revolution Iran prevailed. Our hejab lay crumpled by the pool as we swam with many more inches of flesh exposed. Partygoers arrived, sipped illicit gin, and exited in miniskirts beneath the obligatory cloaked streetwear.

In the last few weeks my entire experience had been dominated by clothing and headdress. Free of this aspect for one afternoon, my thoughts returned to our earlier adventures on Alum Kuh. I talked to someone from the Federation about the fragility of the Alum Kuh region and we discussed the new pressures: the encroaching roads, the mining, the less-than-scrupulous muleteers and the piles of batteries and blackened cans smoldering in heaps next to mountain huts. Changing times call for new approaches, and Iran, with its awakening tourism, needs its own resource management plan as much as, if not more than, our Western homelands. My mind raced with possibilities for international agency partnerships, grant funding and just how far the dollar goes in such places.

Tehran airport was on full alert. We left the country amid heightened security, and from a terminal surrounded by sandbags and antitank missiles. As we did, I pondered why I had dragged a haul sack of effectively unused hardware half-way around the world in search of a Second Yosemite. And I wondered why I had put myself through an experience so uncomfortably dominated by what you wear and how this makes you feel. Mountaineering in hejab is undoubtedly hard; on the approaches alone, you dehydrate faster than in more practical clothing. And in my three and a half weeks in Iran I had not had one conversation with a man other than at the private party. But these are the views of a mind conditioned by Western society. Without knowledge of Iranian society, Western preconceptions of Iran are frequently misguided at best. It would take much more than three and half weeks to come to any conclusion on issues of dress and gender segregation.

By working within cultural dictates, and to some extent supported by the efforts of the Women's Mountaineering Federation, Iranian women are freely able to climb. Education, per-capita income and international policy may be the greatest barriers to developing those carefully acquired skills any further.

Back in body-beautiful Boulder, the contrast between our two societies is driven home by one singular item—the sports bra. Culture, religion and 9,000 miles separate whether it is viewed as an under or outer garment. It is almost impossible to venture onto Boulder's rock faces or sidewalks without viewing the omnipresent item. With its sleek line revealing flesh (and sexuality), I am constantly reminded that in other parts of the world, women who climb lead their lives very differently.

SUMMARY OF STATISTICS

AREA: Alborz Range, Iran

ASCENT: The Almralraiy-Rost route (V+ 5.9+ A2, 15 pitches) on the north face of Alum Kuh (15,819'), September, 1998, Kath Pyke and Glenda Huxter

# Mountaineering in Antarctica

## A survey of Continental climbing

by Damien Gildea, *Australia*

Antarctica has been hailed as the mountaineering destination of the 21st century, and not entirely without reason. In addition to containing almost every conceivable type of mountaineering challenge, Antarctica has that other great allure—numerous unclimbed mountains and incredible potential for new routes. With nearly half of the 4000-meter peaks yet to see an ascent, dozens of 3000ers similarly virgin, and many areas still to be trod by humans, the continent holds years of challenges. Big wall routes and technical ice climbs abound on lower peaks, and the ski-mountaineering potential of many areas is well beyond the demand of current adventurers.

Of course, access remains the largest obstacle to mountaineering in Antarctica. Although there is always talk of government-supported tourism, currently the only realistic option is the well-known private air operator Adventure Network International (ANI). ANI can, for a price, provide air access to all the mountain areas in Antarctica—and given the size of Antarctica, the location of some of its major mountain areas and the relative lack of man-made infrastructures for transport and shelter, air access remains the only feasible option at this time.

This article gives a basic overview of past mountaineering in Antarctica, but it also tries to give some indication of future challenges and interesting objectives. Only the major areas in Antarctica are dealt with here, though notable mountaineering has occurred in the Prince Charles Mountains in MacRobertson Land, the Executive Committee Range and Ford Ranges of Marie Byrd Land and the Shackleton Range of West Antarctica.

## ANTARCTIC PENINSULA

Historically, the Peninsula area, including the South Shetlands, South Orkneys and other islands, has been one of the most traveled and climbed mountain regions in Antarctica. Though Argentines, Chileans, Americans and, more recently, Ukrainians have all made a number of worthwhile ascents, almost all of the significant mountaineering done here has been the work of personnel employed by the British Antarctic Survey (BAS), formerly known as the Falkland Islands Dependency Survey. Much of the BAS climbing was done either in the course of surveying, geological work or field training, but the most significant climbing was done unofficially, for recreation—and, due to official aversion to and overt prohibition of recreational mountaineering by base personnel, was almost always unreported. Thus, records of first ascents, even of major peaks, are rare and open to error.

Mountaineering here, as in Victoria Land, benefited from the presence of experienced and keen mountaineers working as safety and field personnel in support of the science programs. In the 1960s, these mountaineers included the Scots John Cunningham, who led the 1964 first ascent of the Peninsula's highest peak, Mt. Jackson (3184m), and Bugs McKeith, who accomplished a huge amount of climbing on smaller Peninsula features at quite a high level of technical difficulty, often solo. In the 1970s, the now well-known British alpinists Rob

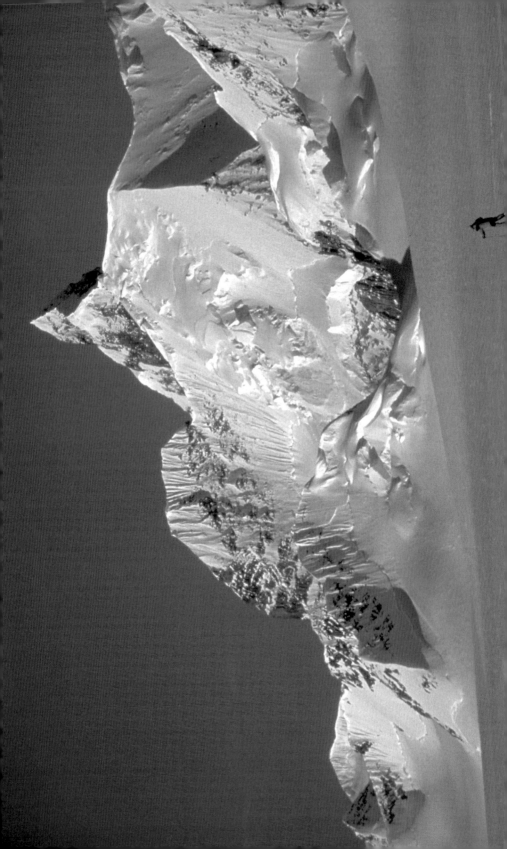

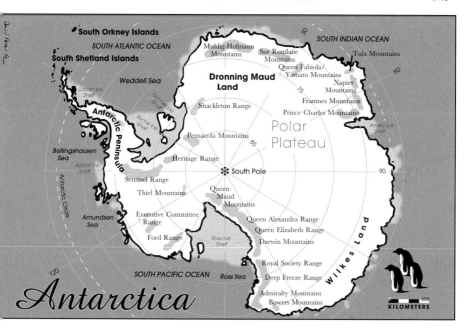

Collister and Roger Mear also traveled the mountains of the Peninsula. Collister was involved in a strong attempt on the difficult Mt. Wilcox (1981m) and in the 1971 ascent of the 1200-meter north face of Blaicklock Island.

In more recent years, the Peninsula has been a popular destination for yacht-based climbers, who have made a number of first ascents and repeat ascents of significant peaks, some by technically difficult routes. A number of such ascents have been reported in this journal and elsewhere, but particularly of note is the 1996 first ascent of Mt. Foster (2100m). This, the highest point of the mountainous Smith Island in the South Shetlands, was a coveted prize that had beaten at least two previous attempts. A Canadian/New Zealand crew on board the yacht *Northanger* made the ascent, one of a number of notable climbs made from this vessel in recent years. It was in attempting to reach Smith Island for climbing in late 1977 that one of the century's most celebrated exploratory mountaineers, H.W. Tilman, along with his crewmates aboard *En Avant*, lost his life at sea.

More recently, in January, 1999, an Australian expedition aboard the yacht *Tiama* accomplished some of the most notable climbing in the region in a number of years. Kieran Lawton, Julie Styles, Geoff Moore, Robyn Clelland, Roland Eberhard and Chris Holly, inspired by a fine photo by Gordon Wiltsie, made the first ascent of Pilcher Peak. The team climbed the south ridge after skiing in with sledges to the glacier on the east side of the peak. However, the peak in this photo is not the true Pilcher Peak, but a sharp peak on a ridge leading up to the plateau that constitutes the spine of the peninsula. The real Pilcher Peak (as indicated on the map) stands out to the north of the plateau and was summited by the entire group on January 16. The other, smaller ridge peak was then christened "Wiltsie's Peak," and was attempted by Styles and Lawton. They climbed for four days in poor visibility on the south

LEFT: *On the Calley Glacier, Danco Coast, Antarctic Peninsula. The pointed peak was mistakenly referred to as "Pilcher Peak" in various captions; it was renamed "Wiltsie's Peak" by the 1999 team that attempted it.* GORDON WILTSIE

ridge but were forced to turn back a mere 50 meters from the summit due to horrendous snow conditions. The party then skied back to Brialmont Cove where they made another three first ascents on peaks, including a rock spire. After leaving Brialmont Cove, the expedition then visited Booth Island, where Styles, Lawton and Eberhard climbed a steep ice couloir on the south-western side of the southernmost peak on Booth Island—almost certainly a new route though possibly not the first ascent of the peak.

As to future objectives, there is a large number of inland peaks, many over 2000 meters, that would require an extended journey by ski for access. In addition to first ascents of less accessible peaks, the future here will undoubtedly see more technical routes added to peaks that have already been climbed. This has already occurred on Mt. Scott (880m), a popular objective above the Lemaire Channel, and there is enormous potential for this type of development on the strikingly featured peaks of Wiencke Island. There are still some attractive unclimbed peaks on Elephant Island, while a ridge on Mt. Parry, Brabant Island has a vertical rise of over 2400 meters—straight out of the sea! It is one of the biggest features of its type in the world, and it is unclimbed.

## SENTINEL RANGE

Here, the continent's highest peaks sweep up from the ice in soaring arêtes, tempting couloirs and gigantic faces of steep rock and ice. With the five highest peaks in Antarctica all of them over 4500 meters (Vinson Massif, 4897m; Mt. Tyree, 4852m; Mt. Shinn, ca 4700m; Mt. Craddock, 4650m; Mt. Gardner, 4587m), it is no wonder that the Sentinel Range has been the focus of most of the continent's private mountaineering over the last 15 years.

Though most of the major peaks were climbed for the first time by the government-supported, Nicholas Clinch-led 1966 American Antarctic Mountaineering Expedition, the majority of climbing activity has, in more recent times, been centered on guided ascents of Vinson Massif, particularly as one of the Seven Summits. At the end of the 1998-'99 season a total of over 300 individuals had reached the summit, with repeat ascents, mainly by guides taking the overall number of ascents to just over 400. Vinson Massif has now been soloed traversed, descended by both ski and paraglider, climbed by a husband-and-wife team climbed without an ice ax and climbed in as little as nine hours from base camp.

Mt. Shinn, Antarctica's third highest mountain, has also proved a popular addition for Vinson climbers, but by far the most significant mountaineering has taken place relatively recently on the other 4000-meter peaks of the range. In late 1997, a large couloir on the rarely traveled eastern side of the range was the route of the third and fourth ascents of Mt. Tyree—first by a strong French party, who were then followed a month later by the renowned American climbers Conrad Anker and Alex Lowe. Both the second and third ascents of this peak were by new routes, the second having been the relatively well-known tour de force of the American Terrence "Mugs" Stump. Stump was actually working for the U.S. government as a Safety Officer for scientists operating in the area, and, though no well-publicized at the time, there was a certain amount of consternation in official circles at his "extracurricular" activities.

In November, 1989, Stump soloed a new route on the intimidating west face of Tyree— over 2500 meters of steep rock and ice climbed on-sight, unroped and in a single push Shortly before this, he had soloed the similarly difficult southwest face of Mt. Gardner, the continent's fifth highest peak, making its third ascent. Arguably a decade ahead of their time these were the biggest, hardest climbs that had ever been done in Antarctica. The fine style in which they were executed was not only a tribute to Stump's alpine abilities, but an important standard by which future ascents in the range could be judged.

*"Pic Gryzka" near Mt. Tyree in the Sentinel Range, first climbed during the 1997-'98 season by a French team. The proposed name commemorates Jean-Marc Gryzka, who was killed during the trip.* P. DE CHOUDENS

The early 1990s saw notable additions to the range by, among others, the well-known American climbers Jay Smith and Robert Anderson. In December, 1994, the Swiss super-alpinist Erhard Loretan, veteran of some of the most outstanding ascents of 8000-meter peaks ever accomplished, soloed the first ascent of Mt. Epperly (4359m), the continent's eighth highest peak. He returned in 1995 to repeat this route for a film, but not before making the first ascent of a less prominent peak of 4360 meters that lies between Mt. Epperly and Mt. Tyree. Loretan ascended this unnamed peak alone via a reasonably difficult couloir on the southwest face. This peak received its second ascent in January, 1998, by Conrad Anker, again solo, by a new route on the southwest face.

January, 1996, saw the celebrated French alpinist Catherine Destivelle and her partner Erik Decamp shun the crowd on Vinson Massif and climb two new routes much further to the north. They began with the first ascent of the attractive smaller peak Mt. Viets (ca. 3700m) by a moderate route on the south face. Two days later, they ascended a 4000-meter-plus peak to the north of Mt. Viets by a much more difficult route on its west face. While posing for the summit photo, Destivelle plunged through a cornice. The fall resulted in a badly broken leg and other injuries. For 15 hours, the pair performed an amazing self-rescue, using a torturous combination of rappelling, down climbing and lowering to reverse the 1500-meter route of ascent, after which Decamp returned Destivelle to their tent, tending her injuries for three days while they waited for suitable weather for an air evacuation by ANI.

The 1997-'98 season saw strong performances from a French Groupe d'Haute Montagne party who made, among other ascents, the first ascent of the fine peak Mt. Shear (4050m) and the striking, unnamed 3950-meter rock pyramid near Mt. Tyree. The French proposed the name of "Pic Gryzka" for this latter peak for one of their party, Jean-Marc Gryzka, who was killed during the trip.

The range also witnessed some fine climbing by Finland's most accomplished Himalayan climber, Veikka Gustafsson, and his compatriot, Patrick Degerman. This pair made the first ascents of both Mt. Bentley (4145m) and Mt. Davis (ca. 3950m), a rapid fourth ascent of Mt. Gardner, and first ascents of two unnamed peaks, one of them ca. 4050 meters, situated between Mt. Anderson and Mt. Bentley. At the base of Mt. Gardner the pair found a food cache left by the 1966 party, which had made the first ascent of the peak.

The recent 1998-'99 season brought some less than perfect weather conditions, leaving many potential Vinson climbers languishing in Punta Arenas, Chile. Nevertheless, Conrad Anker and Dave Hahn managed to make the fifth ascent of Mt. Gardner via the route of first ascent, finding two food caches from the 1966-'67 expedition in the process. Anker also unsuccessfully attempted the west ridge of Mt. Epperly with the well-known American, Jim Donini. It was up to Rodrigo Mujica and his client, Bob Elias, to pioneer some first ascents, which they did, above the Embree Glacier in the northern Sentinel Range. In the last week of November, Mujica and Elias climbed an unnamed 3400-meter

BELOW: *The peaks around the Embree Glacier, visited for the first time in the 1998-'99 season. From the left: the north and northeastern aspects of Mt. Anderson, Mt. Bentley, Mt. Davis, Mt. Hale, and "Natalie Peak."* RODRIGO MUJICA

peak they christened "Natalie Peak" and the next day another unnamed peak of 3200 meters they dubbed "Kristen-Jule Peak." Both ascents involved moderate climbing over mixed ground in high winds and very low temperatures. These two peaks are directly north of Mt. Hale (3595m). Mujica and Elias also made a strong attempt on a sub-peak of the impressive Mt. Todd, turning back only 200 meters from the summit after covering some interesting mixed terrain and steep ice. This adventurous pair were almost certainly the first people to visit the area and certainly the first to do any mountaineering here.

So what remains? The obvious challenges are the unclimbed 4000-meter peaks of the range. There are two, Mt. Anderson (4157m) and Mt. Giovinetto (4090m), neither of which are easy snow hiking. Other high unclimbed peaks here include Mt. Press (3760m) and Mt. Todd at the northern section of the main range and Mt. Morris, closer to the action between Mt. Shear and Mt. Ostenso (4085m). New route objectives include the unclimbed east face of Vinson Massif, an ascent of Mt. Tyree from the south—possibly as part of a "grand traverse" of Vinson Massif, Mt. Shinn, Mt. Epperly, Mt. Tyree and Mt. Gardner—and what is perhaps the grand prize of the range, the unclimbed south face of Mt. Craddock (4650m). This face features in one of the color photos in *The Antarctic Mountaineering Chronology*, but is incorrectly captioned as Mt. Slaughter, a fine, smaller peak that received its long-awaited first ascent in December, 1998, by Guy Cotter of New Zealand and Terry Gardiner of the United States. These possible routes are just the more obvious options, barely taking

into account the eastern side of the range, which, partly due to more difficult access and slightly higher avalanche danger, has seen just a small handful of ascents.

A recent development of some significance in the Sentinel Range—and to a lesser extent in Droning Maud Land—is the climbing of relatively minor peaks and their subsequent naming by the summiters. This has been happening for some time with regard to subpeaks of Vinson Massif, but it has more recently been seen on some of the higher unnamed peaks of the range. Whether some of these peaks even deserve their own name is unclear although there is no set policy as to what actually constitutes a separate "mountain" or "peak." Suffice it to say that some names given are more appropriate than others. There are official policy structures such as those set out by the U.S. Board on Geographic Names whose Advisory Committee on Antarctic Names determines whether a name proposed for a feature becomes officially accepted. Other nations, such as New Zealand and the United Kingdom, have similar structures to name features in their Antarctic territories. While the ethical integrity of most climbers in naming certain peaks cannot be questioned, the chances of such names becoming accepted has, for various reasons, proven slim. Naming peaks after oneself has never been widely respected, and naming features after commercial sponsors or products will ensure rejection by most in the climbing community and will certainly do so amongst the relevant authorities. Antarctic naming policy can be found by contacting the USGS at http://mapping.usgs.gov/www/gnis/antex.html.

The other increasingly pertinent point on nomenclature is the name of Vinson Massif. Regardless of one's personal or otherwise definition of a "massif" or "peak" or "mountain," the name of the highest mountain in Antarctica is Vinson Massif. It is not Mt Vinson, Vinson Peak or any other variation, no matter how well-intended. The proliferation of these erroneous alternatives seems to be not so much a deliberate agenda geared toward changing the existing name, but more the result of either authorial laziness, geographical ignorance or the editorial "dumbing-down" of seemingly foreign or unusual terms for a mass market.

## DRONING MAUD LAND

One only has to look at a selection of Gordon Wiltsie's stunning photos of this region to see that there is the potential for hundreds of major big wall routes. Peaks that have already seen major big-wall routes include Ulvetanna (2931m), Kinntanna (2724m) Rakekniven (2365m), "Rondespiret" (2427m) and Trollslottet. Though a few photographs of these spectacular spires had been published in scientific journals in the past, it was the spectacular 1994 publication, *Queen Maud Land, Antarctica*, by Ivar Erik Tollefsen, that drew the attention of the world's climbers to this area. Tollefsen's expedition, the first private mountaineering expedition to the area, made a total of 36 ascents. These included number of technical big wall routes, though the bulk of the less technical ascents were made during ski traverses.

Quite a large number of ascents have been made on lower and/or easier peaks. Prospective first ascensionists here should bear in mind, however, that many of the less difficult peaks may well have had ascents by scientists any time in the last 50 years. Air access to the region is very good and, thanks to their current logistical support of the South African national Antarctic program, also regular. Aircraft land on a blue-ice runway in the area known as Blue-1, which is in sight of the better-known peaks of the region.

RIGHT: *The 800-meter "Ronde Spire" (Rondespiret), showing the 1996 Norwegian first ascent route.*
IVAR TOLLEFSEN

# TRANSANTARCTIC MOUNTAINS—MAIN SECTION

Since the 1950s, several scientific parties have traveled in these mountains, though relatively few ascents have been made. More recently, U.S. scientists have reached a number of high points by helicopter, but they have not necessarily ventured to the summit of the peak on which they were working. Two of the main summits that have been climbed by scientists include Mt. Markham in 1985 and Mt. Kirkpatrick in 1991. To date, no private mountaineering expedition has entered the main section of the Transantarctics—the Queen Elizabeth Range, the Holland Range and the Queen Alexandra Range.

In stark contrast to Droning Maud Land, some of the highest peaks here are, when seen from certain vantage points, not even distinguishable as peaks. Many are just an area high point on the northern escarpment of the polar plateau. In aerial photographs taken from southern perspectives, they appear as large, flat expanses of bare snow and ice rising to an almost imperceptible summit peak, while from the north they impress as enormous walls of jumbled icefalls, snow fields and rock faces. Many such faces are well over 2000 meters high, though rarely very steep. Access to these faces is often up long, severely crevassed and broken glaciers of a gigantic scale. Some of the lower peaks are better featured, but there are no Antarctic Cerro Torres or Walker Spurs hidden away in these icy realms. The real adventure lies in the potential for traveling over terrain that has never felt a human foot and in reaching the summits of the more than half a dozen unclimbed "4000ers" that remain here. There are some impressive features, however, such as the northwest ridge of Mt. Mackellar (4297m) and the east face of Mt. Miller (4160m); both are unclimbed 4000ers. For mountaineers, access is the issue here. Government logistical support of private mountaineering expeditions is always a possibility for the future, but, realistically, at present the answer is again ANI.

# TRANSANTARCTIC MOUNTAINS—QUEEN MAUD MOUNTAINS

In mountaineering terms, by far the most interesting section of these mountains is the area surrounding the Scott Glacier as it flows from the ice cap down to the Ross Ice Shelf. Correspondingly, this area has also seen considerably more climbing activity than the rest of the Queen Maud Mountains, both by government and private expeditions. Ascents were made in this area as long ago as 1908, by members of Shackleton's party, 1911, by members of Amundsen's party, and 1929, by members of Byrd's party. In the early to mid 1980s, further climbing was undertaken here in the course of scientific work, much of which involved the American alpinist Mugs Stump as he assisted his brother Ed and others in geological work on some of the most interesting peaks of the Scott Glacier area. Highlights included the 1980 first ascent of The Spectre, the most prominent spire of the Organ Pipe Peaks; the second ascents of Mt. Zanuck (2525m) and Mt. Pulitzer (2156m) in 1985; and the first ascents of Mt. Borcik (2780m) and Heinous Peak (ca. 3400m), the latter by a single-push, 20-hour ascent of the very difficult 2500-meter high east face. (Rock samples were collected all the way, of course.)

The highest peaks of the Queen Maud Mountains have seen comparatively little mountaineering activity: no private mountaineering expedition has visited the area, and the only ascents have come from government scientists. One such scientific foray, however, involved one of the 20th century's most impressive but least-known pieces of mountain travel. In January, 1962, the Briton Wally Herbert—later to make his name reaching the North Pole—and three New Zealanders, McGregor, Otway and Pain, used dogsledges to traverse great distances in this area and climb at least 11 major peaks, nine of them over 3000 meters. The

LEFT: *Mt. Andrews (background) and the Organ Pipe Peaks, Transantarctic Mountain Range.*
GORDON WILTSIE

highest of the peaks is Mt. Fridtjof Nansen (4070m), the first 4000-meter peak to be climbed in Antarctica as well as the most southerly 4000-meter peak on the continent. They were the first to retrace Amundsen's route down the Axel Heiberg Glacier as well.

## TRANSANTARCTIC MOUNTAINS—VICTORIA LAND

It is probably in the various ranges of Victoria Land that the greatest amount of climbing on high peaks has been done by government personnel—almost exclusively New Zealanders. Dogsledge traverses of the 1950s and 1960s produced dozens of ascents of high 3000ers and the second Antarctic 4000-meter peak to be climbed: Mt. Lister (4025m), in December, 1962. More recently, helicopter access to areas further away from Scott Base has allowed the tradition of making ascents to continue when possible. This is aided by the fact that the New Zealand program has historically drawn its field staff from experienced mountaineers, many of them guides such as Rob Hall and Gary Ball. A number of big peaks have seen repeat ascents, such as Mt. Lister and Mt. Huggins (3735m) in the Royal Society Range, and, of course, the famous volcano Mt. Erebus (3795m) on Ross Island, which has proven to be a popular outing. Mt. Erebus remains the only major Antarctic peak to have had a winter ascent, by the Briton Roger Mear, in June, 1985. Though records of ascents are by no means comprehensive, this has more to do with the sheer amount of climbing done than any desire to suppress such information.

There are no unclimbed 4000ers left here, but a number of big 3000ers remain unclimbed, as do countless peaks of lesser height. Particularly interesting are the mountains of the Admiralty Range. Attractive objectives here include the possibly virgin Mt. Sabine (3720m), the daunting east face of Mt. Herschel (3335m), which forced a 1967 party led by Sir Edmund Hillary onto a less difficult route for its first ascent, and the attractive big peak of Mt. Black Prince (3406m), climbed once with difficulty, and Mt. Ajax (3770m), which is probably unclimbed. Here, Mt. Minto (4165m) saw its first ascent in February, 1988, by an Australian party who man-hauled their supplies from the coast, having sailed there from Sydney. As for the other big peaks, Mt. Adam (4010m) was climbed by New Zealanders in 1981 and 1991, but Mt. Royalist (3640m) may well be unclimbed. On many subsidiary peaks and ridges, 2000-meter-plus faces sit unclimbed above huge glaciers not always conducive to travel on foot. For those willing to make the effort, this area of Victoria Land would seem to be one of the more promising Antarctic destinations for big, interesting unclimbed terrain that is relatively accessible to private mountaineers.

## SOUTH GEORGIA

The relatively small island of South Georgia holds some disproportionately huge mountaineering objectives and has seen a considerable degree of mountaineering activity both by government scientists and private mountaineering expeditions. Two ranges, the Salvesen Range and the Allardyce Range, constitute the spine of the island. Mt. Paget (2935m) is the highest peak of the latter, and has seen a number of ascents, although significant new route potential exists, particularly on the northern side. South Georgia's fourth-highest peak, Sugartop (2325m), has had at least two ascents, but one of the most impressive ascents in the mountaineering history of the island was the first ascent of the second highest peak on the island, Nordenskjöld Peak (2355m). The Frenchman Christian de Marliave executed this daring ascent solo in early 1988 while based aboard the yacht *Damien II*. The highest unclimbed peak on South Georgia is Mt. Roots (2280m), which has repelled at least five attempts, the highest getting to around 2000 meters. Together

Nordenskjöld Peak and Mt. Roots, when viewed from the north, present an attractive, if somewhat difficult, smorgasbord of unclimbed alpine terrain. At present, most mountaineers will find that access to the island for any useful period of time is by chartered yacht only, an option that does, however, allow the possibility of boat transport between base camps, thereby increasing the choice and accessibility of objectives.

Wherever one climbs in Antarctica, it would do well to keep in mind the less-desirable effects of mountain tourism in other parts of the world and actively work to ensure there is no repeat of those mistakes. Organizations such as the International Association of Antarctic Tour Operators (IAATO) only provide guidelines and monitoring. It is up to individuals who choose to travel adventurously in Antarctica to be responsible for their own safety and environmental impact. Long may it be so.

Selected References

Alberts, F.G., editor. *Geographic Names of the Antarctic, Second Edition.* Reston, VA: USGS/United States Board on Geographic Names, 1995.

Gildea, Damien. *The Antarctic Mountaineering Chronology.* Self-published: Australia, 1998. (e-mail:dageogil@tpgi.com.au)

Stump, E. "The End of the World." In *Climbing* 171, September 15-November 1, 1997, edited by Michael Kennedy, pp. 106-113, 1997.

Tollefsen, Ivar E. *Queen Maud Land, Antarctica* (English language edition). Larvik, Norway: Ostlands-Postens Press, 1994.

Tollefsen, Ivar E. *The Ronde Spire, Antarctica* (English language edition). A.s. Joh Nordahls Tyrkkeri, 1998.

# Madagascar's Big Walls

## The first ascent of Tsaranoro Atsimo

by Erik Svab, *Italy*

*The local villagers of Andringitra National Park, Madagascar, with Tsaranoro Atsimo and Be in the background.* EMANUELLE PELLIZZARI

Have you ever dreamed of a corner of paradise and then, in the realization of the dream, found it to be truly immense? So it befell us for one month in the heart of Madagascar. In the southeastern part of the island, in the Andringitra National Park, there is a valley of high walls of super compact granite. The most impressive of these forms the east face of Mount Tsaranoro, which is two kilometers long and up to 800 meters high. Tsaranoro is composed of three independent summits. On two of these, Tsaranoro Be and Tsaranoro Kely, routes had been put up. The third summit was still virgin.

Our dream began when Marco Sterni and I saw a photo of the granite wall in the Italian magazine *Pareti* on which the boys from Southern Tyrolia had put up *Gondwanaland*, a long (19-pitch) and committing (5.12c) route. From then on, we had only one immutable focus: to see Tsaranoro and to try to climb it in the style we had used for years in our own Dolomites and Julian Alps—ground up, with a high degree of difficulty, and using bolts only where it wasn't possible to get any other gear. A visit with Helmut, who made the first ascent of *Gondwanaland*, confirmed our suspicions: we would be dealing with a stupendous place. It was an adventure not to be missed.

After one year, we were there: the airport in Antananarivo, capital of Madagascar. The stress and exhaustion of our preparations dissolved. It's impossible to cling to the past when you are overwhelmed by an intense present, a different way of life, new rhythms to which you must adapt. My God, what poverty! We were not used to seeing people shoeless and half-naked—but in Madagascar the land gives one everything, hunger is non-existent, and poverty becomes simplicity and wealth.

Seven of us crammed in a Toyota with all our climbing gear, our provisions and more than 15 cases of water. We were wasted, but full of enthusiasm and impatient to see the spacious valley of Andringitra National Park. After a number of kilometers, it became impossible to continue by jeep: we had to get out and go forward on foot, following a roadcut that more closely resembled a path in the savanna. The high grass was of an intense yellow interrupted here and there by enormous boulders of dark granite. We were enraptured by them, moving almost unconsciously for want of familiarizing ourselves with this kind of rock. Though it was barely our first day in the valley, we had dreamed and waited so long that we were impatient to measure ourselves against it, so different a rock from that to which we were accustomed.

We put up our tents under a group of mango trees that soon became our home. Exhausted from three days of travel and trekking, we went to sleep. The next day, anxious to climb to the base of the wall, we left our tents and made our way to the small village of Tanambao. We thought to take leave of the inhabitants quickly, but we immediately discovered an uncommon pride in their eyes. It became clear that we were aliens to them, come to disturb the peace of the place. They didn't understand why we *vazah* (foreigners) wanted to come climb on their mountains. The locals climb what summits they can without ropes, but only to transport the remains of the deceased to inaccessible places. It is, for them, part of a strong tradition of demonstrating respect for ancestors. They couldn't comprehend that we climb only for fun, only for passion. Strange: at home in our Western world, we are often faced with the problem of explaining to others why we climb. Now we had to do so here as well, on an island that has remained the same for 1,000 years and where the people continue to not understand the strange habits of foreigners. We quickly became indebted to our guide, Jean-Calvin, for explaining to the chief that our intentions were good.

At the end of the negotiations, we came to understand that it would be the young man Jojò, son of the village chief, who would show us the way. He walked, almost running, barefoot among the granite stones, to bring us to the base of the wall. Once we arrived, we spent our first day deciding where to begin our route. The possibilities were immense, but the wall that attracted us the most was the steepest wall in the valley, one no one had climbed on before. We watched as lemurs shot up the initial slabs with extreme ease. Nature makes us green with envy when we become aware of the simplicity with which it moves. As far as climbing is concerned, the easiest thing to do would be to transform ourselves into birds. But here we were, and we are only men, with merely the strength of our hands and legs to climb the splendid, terrible wall soaring over us. And now we were to begin the realization of our dream—and now to begin the dance!

Our bodies wanted to move, our hands yearned to caress and then clasp the ideal holds formed by quartz crystals. We began to ascend on a granite eroded and worked like splendid slabs of limestone. It is a rock very different from the granite of Mont Blanc or Yosemite: no dihedrals or cracks, only slabs and bulges. What strange climbing! If you use force you don't rise a centimeter; only agility, together with ever-fluid movement—a search, almost, for an elegance of gesture—will ultimately carry the day.

It appeared that it would be nearly impossible to climb through the middle of the wall. A mixed color somewhere between black and yellow indicated an overhanging section when we scoped it with binos. No cracks and extremely compact rock meant we couldn't use pitons or natural gear for protection. Instead, with the help of a battery-powered drill, we would be forced to place bolts while hanging from hooks.

We had come to Tsaranoro seeking to limit the use of fixed gear as

*Erik Svab on the fifth pitch (7b) of* Never the Same.
ERIK SVAB COLLECTION

much as possible. We wanted to create a route that presented notable mandatory difficulties and that asked of future ascensionists a certain commitment to climb it. This is, in fact, the purpose of modern multi-pitch routes: to unite physical and psychological difficulties to create a difficult and committing climb even for those who repeat it. To aid from bolt to bolt is a game without a purpose, because then the limits don't exist. You can truly climb everywhere. For us, if we aren't in shape to climb something free, we try variations or give up and return when we are better trained. This is how we always establish new lines at home, and it is the same method we wanted to use in Madagascar.

The bolts were spaced at an average of around six meters apart. This was not a sport route, but one that required a certain psychological commitment. Falls might seem normal in today's climbing, but it's difficult to convey the anxiety that gripped us during the climb, the fear that we had to live with and continually overcome. Every fall could mean the end of the dream in that sea of granite. Even on the most difficult pitch, 15-meter falls are possible; elsewhere, one can fall up to 25 meters—or not at all, because it would be too dangerous to slam onto a ledge or angled slab below.

Our fingers were begging for rest, and we had to temper our desire to climb on the wall every day with a need to renew our energies. We alternated climbing days with rest days at

LEFT: *Tsaranoro Atsimo and Be, showing* A: Never the Same, *and* B: Gondwanaland.
EMANUELE PELLIZARI

*Sterni on the first attempt of the crux (8a+) of* Never the Same. ERIK SVAB

base camp, where water gathered in a hole in the paddy field. We fixed a jerry can from a mango tree for a shower; the trees also gave us shade, and a breeze made our rest days very pleasant. Meanwhile, the people from the village surrounded us, observing curiously. Our contact with them will remain with us always, making us remember Madagascar as a place in which we climbed, but above all one in which we came to know a people stupendous in their simplicity.

We continued to advance our route very slowly. Every day we gained precious meters, hoping that the next day we would understand the wall better, hoping that we would be able to climb all the pitches free. We didn't want to put up an aid climb! We are trained for free climbing, and we wanted to find a route straight up through the middle of the overhangs. But each day the pitches became more difficult and it became ever harder to have faith, both in ourselves and in the possibility that the wall would go free. Exhaustion arrived, and our thoughts brought us far away, out of the valley to the beaches and clear water of the sea.

We returned to camp on a Sunday to find a warm welcome. The children of the village sang and danced for more than an hour, and the curiosity and joy we felt in watching them made us forget all our exhaustion. Another day passed by, and we succeeded in climbing a few more difficult meters on what was becoming "our" wall. The next day we would need to rest well, because after that the day of truth awaited us—a day that might be our last. We went to sleep dreaming of the summit.

The much-desired day arrived. But after so many days of intense sun, we found our-selves stopped a few meters from the summit by a powerful tropical hail storm! We sat on the ropes to keep them from soaking, tired as could be from having climbed all day. It was almost as if nature were mocking us, once again demonstrating how small we were before its presence. But after an hour a rainbow announced that, on this day at least, nature was magnanimous. We had permission to rapidly climb the last bit to the top.

The tropical sun returned after the rain and hail, and the change in weather accentuated the contrast. We had a few moments to realize that no one had ever climbed up here before: the summit is flat, and surrounded on all sides by walls that one would have to climb to ascend. There were no signs of humans. We had time to scoop up a small piece of granite to bring to those who had faith in us, to those who stayed at home, and to keep alive the memory of a moment when our hearts gathered up a fragment of the story of alpinism.

We called our route *Never the Same*, because we're convinced that it will never again be possible to climb so beautiful and difficult a route on a wall that marvelous in such a tranquil and uncontaminated place. Two friends from Brescia, Ermanno Francinelli and Mario Cavagnini, were with us as well, and they too were able to achieve their objectives, repeating five established routes, including *Gondwanaland* on Tsaranoro Be. We had experienced a singular and unrepeatable adventure: for us, Tsaranoro Atsimo had the power of revelation, an adventure of being in which every minute fiber of our selves was thankful for its existence.

The peace and serenity of the valley below Tsaranoro will soon be disturbed by other climbers and tourists come from all over the world to see and use this beautiful place. We realize that some of the fault will lie with us. We had hoped to be successful to the maximum, and our definition of success helped limit our devastating impact on the ambiance and the people of the place. Still, we remind all those who have the fortune and opportunity to find themselves in this or similar places in the future that we are only visitors and must comport ourselves with the respect and discretion Nature commands.

SUMMARY OF STATISTICS

AREA: Andringitra National Park, Madagascar

NEW ROUTE: *Never the Same* (V 5.13c/d A0, 13 pitches, 670 meters) on the east face of Tsaranoro Atsimo (South) (2000m), September 11-16, Rolando Larcher, Marco Sterni, Erik Svab (Pitch 8, 5.13c/d, was climbed with one rest on the attempt to redpoint the route. The moves were made, confirming the grade, but the route awaits a redpoint).

# North Africa and the Middle East

## Desert climbing on a larger scale

by Tony Howard, *United Kingdom*


The great Sahara desert, stretching for 2,500 miles across North Africa, has long presented a barrier, a tantalizing mystery and a challenge to European explorers and travelers.
Concealed within the desert, remote mountains provided a refuge for various tribal peoples,
who undoubtedly reached some of the tops on hunting trips. Early travelers and Victorian
adventurers also climbed a few remote summits, but it was not really until the 1930s that
mountaineers and cartographers began to climb and document ascents of North Africa's
numerous and varied peaks, from the frequently snow-capped mountains of the High Atlas in
Morocco and the Simiens in Ethiopia, to the barren volcanic plugs and craters of the Hoggar
and the Tibesti in Algeria and Chad. The great linking theme of these European ascents has
always been adventure and exploration, the essence of the achievement often being as much
in getting there as in the actual climbs.

With the passage of time, the difficulty of access has, in many cases, eased considerably:
good roads now cross Morocco's Atlas mountains, and the Trans-Sahara Highway reached
the oasis of Tamanrasset in the Algerian Hoggar in the early 1980s. Other previously remote
desert mountain areas in Libya, Egypt and the Sudan that had previously been "cara-
vanserais" on ancient trade routes (the mountains being an inevitable source of water for
scattered oases) also gradually became linked to the outside world by improving road or rail
systems over the last century.

In the Middle East, mountain exploration was slower, impeded, perhaps, in places like
Oman and Yemen, by the vagaries of politics in the early half of this century further compounded by tribal and ideological struggles that sometimes lasted into the 1980s. Jordan as
we know it today was not even on the map, while Saudi Arabia continues to be a virtual "no
go" area.

Morocco is both culturally and environmentally colorful. With its snow-capped peaks,
great gorges and mud-brick Berber villages (complete with fruits, nuts and cereals drying on
their flat roofs), it has much of the magic of the Himalaya, especially in its more remote mountain valleys that are only accessible by trekking in. This, together with the bustling bazaars of
its ancient walled cities and their kaleidoscope of snake-charmers, traveling musicians,
dancers, story-tellers, and sizzling food stalls, makes a visit to Morocco's mountains a must.

In the early 1960s, I made my first trip to Morocco with friends from our local north
Manchester "Rimmon Mountaineering Club." The Atlas Mountains extend for about 600
miles, from the verdant Rif Mountains down to the Mediterranean, to the arid Anti-Atlas in
the south, where granite boulders provide problems reminiscent of Joshua Tree. We visited
this area in the winter of 1962-'63, when we were treated to raw cow's brain in olive oil after
seeing the emaciated beast have its throat cut in the dusty village street—a memory that
lingers more vividly than our games on the exfoliating granite!

LEFT: *The 2,000-foot domes of Jebel Kassala (in Sudan, on the Ethiopian border) from the west.* DI TAYLOR

For the mountaineer, the pièce de résistance is a winter ascent of Jebel Toubkal, which, at 4165 meters, is billed as "North Africa's highest mountain." Though none of the routes are particularly difficult, we found the trek in in the early 1960s, coupled with our ascent by a possible new route, a great adventure. Nowadays there are mountain huts and guides, and ascents are commonplace, though this in no way detracts from the panoramic view of the lush land to the west and the great Sahara to the east. For those in search of solitude, other nearby peaks are considerably less frequented and offer more difficult winter ice or long-distance ski tours.

Morocco drew Mick Shaw and me back for more trips in the 1970s, first in November, 1973, when we visited the 1,000-foot cliffs of the Todra Gorge in a side canyon of the great Dades Valley, which divides the High from the Central Atlas. Twenty-five years later, there are more than 200, no doubt excellent and often difficult climbs in the Gorge. Most of the them are bolted, and many would say that Todra is now the best climbing area in North Africa, but, from my point of view, the Gorge lacks the wilderness ambience that is the essence of Morocco's mountains.

There is equally good, more traditional climbing in the remote mountains to the north of Toubkal and Todra, on the limestone walls of Jebel Aioui and the Taghia Canyon in the Central Atlas. This area has also seen considerable climbing development by the French, with routes up to ED sup* and lengths of 1,000 to 2,000 feet. In the late 1970s, we were probably the first (and are maybe even now still the only) Brits to climb there, enjoying the high-mountain location and the excellent climbing on spectacular "Dolomitic" towers.

Also in the 1970s, we moved further afield, following the Mediterranean coast en route from Morocco to Corsica. We sat for three days of incessant rain and mist in Algeria's coastal Grande Kabylie Mountains and were rewarded only by a momentary glimpse of a 600-foot limestone tower rising from dripping vegetation before moving on in search of warmer rock. On our next visit to Algeria, we drove south for over 1,000 miles, following the line of the then-unfinished Trans-Sahara Highway to the oasis of Tamanrasset and the Hoggar Mountains, which rise to about 9,000 feet. After three days of traveling through vast desert dunes and past lonely oases, the towers of the Hoggar are a welcome sight for the climber.

Tamanrasset ("Tam") is the base for explorations, where blue-robed Touareg guides can be hired to visit the surrounding peaks of the Atakor and other nearby mountain areas. Or, like us, you can simply head out on rough tracks to the foot of your chosen volcanic plug. Perhaps the best towers are Iharen and the Tezoulags, with columnar 1,000- to 1,300-foot Devils Tower-like walls and routes up to F6. Most other towers, which rise in confusion throughout the Atakor, have faces up to 1,000 feet high with classic climbs of around F3 - 4, though harder routes exist. Most first ascents were established by French, Italian and Spanish climbers, and a few by the British. There are also numerous opportunities for new routes.

Our winter visit to the Hoggar left us with memories of endless desert vistas and semi-nomadic Touareg passing through on camels. As usual in desert terrain, the rock, on which we teetered high above, left much to be desired, though the cracks and corners were magnificent; overcoming the idiosyncrasies and occasional instability of the rock became a perverse pleasure with its own satisfactions, making topping out on new routes in the often-icy winds that much more rewarding.

Across the desert to the east, the Tafidet area, with virtually no climbs recorded, is even less seldomly visited, while 180 miles to the north of the Atakor is the Tefedest area, dominated by

---

*French grades are in common use throughout the area. TD, ED, etc., refer to the overall seriousness of the climb, taking into account the length, danger, sustained nature of difficulty, problems of retreat, and so on. French rock grades indicate technical difficulty of individual rock pitches. See Appendices at the back of this journal for a complete explanation of grades.

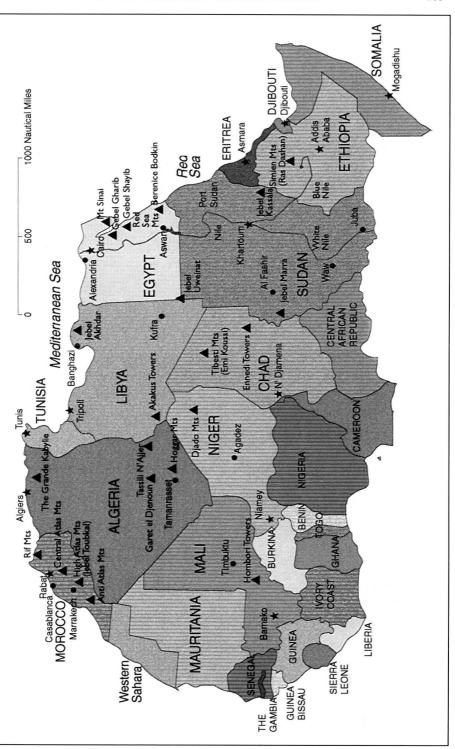

*The 1,300-foot west face of South Tezoulag in the Hoggar Mountains, Algeria.*
HOWARD/TAYLOR COLLECTION

the peak of Garet el Djenoun (2327m). There are some quite long and serious routes here, mostly hard and often using aid, some being 1,500 feet, ED with pitches of 6c. Even more remote, 250 miles to the northeast, is the Tassili N'Ajjer desert plateau, which reaches to the Libyan border and offers a playground of large granite boulders with well-preserved pre-historic inscriptions and paintings dating back 5,000 years.

Sadly, Algeria these days is caught up in an internal struggle for political dominance. It seems, as a consequence, the Hoggar and Tassili will be left to the Touareg and the desert winds for some time to come. No one will be crossing the desert south west from "Tam" to the Hombori Towers near the legendary Timbuktu in Mali, almost 1,000 miles away. Fortunately, however, these impressive peaks towering over the Dogon villages, with routes up to 2,000 feet (mostly in the TD and ED category), have other, easier means of access and attract increasing numbers of climbers.

Back north, and moving east along the Mediterranean coast from Algeria, the small country of Tunisia offers little for the climber, though Di Taylor and I did some bouldering there on the limestone sea cliffs of Cap Bon in the 1980s, and the great Bill Tilman, finding some rare wartime entertainment in 1943, searched almost in vain for rock on the 1180-meter Jebel Zaghouan.

East again is the vast land of Libya. Like Tunisia, it has a great historical past, as shown by the splendid Phoenician, Greek and Roman cities along the coast and in the hills of Jebel Akhdar to the east. The policies of the current Government have not been conducive to tourism, but a serious effort is now being made to encourage visitors. As a consequence, Di and I were invited there as guests of Wings Travel of Libya in 1997. We explored the hills, valleys and small limestone cliffs of Jebel Akhdar, then headed south, across 700 miles of desert. En route, we crossed the edge of the great Ubari Sand Sea with its hidden jewel-like lakes concealed by endless dunes. Our destination was the remote Akakus Mountains in the far southwest.

The bizarre contorted towers rise from huge orange dunes as far as the eye can see. The rock is exfoliating badly but, perched dramatically above large loose cliffs, the highest towers teased us with what looked like good rock (which perhaps it would have to be, to stay up there). Unfortunately, with no maps and limited time, we were unable to find a way up to them. The main attraction of the Akakus for its rare visitors are the fine rock paintings and inscriptions depicting elephants, rhino and other wildlife of 5,000 years ago when this part of Africa was green. Small stone arrowheads from this period are still found on the wind-swept surface of the sand.

South of here, across the Libyan border, are Niger and Chad. There's a good chance we'll be in Niger this winter, having a look at the rarely visited mountains of the Djado Plateau, one of the few parts of north Africa still extremely difficult to access. Reaching the mountains of Chad is no easier. There, the great extinct craters of the Tibesti rise to 3415 meters at Emi Koussi and are home to the hardy and independent Tibbu people. These high, lonely mountains have been intermittently visited by climbers for over 60 years, with a recent 20-year gap due to the political situation.

Again, it is the journey as much as the climbing that attracts the desert mountain enthusiast. One might continue to the almost-unvisited Ennedi Towers out east, toward Sudan, then travel north by the ancient 1,000-mile slave trade route of the Darb el Arabain ("40-day road") to Cairo, following the intermittent camel trail still visible in Egypt's Western Desert. There are no mountains on this side of the Nile, other than the lonely summit of Jebel Uweinat (1893m), which marks the meeting point of Egypt's border with Libya, Chad and the Sudan. East of the Nile, however, North Africa rises to a final barrier of mountains that run almost the full length of Egypt's 600-mile Red Sea coast.

We had a quick trip here in the 1980s, finding harsh, stony deserts concealing some attractive-looking mountains—though, as ever, the exfoliating granite creaked alarmingly underfoot. Sadly, we were refused access to one of our main objectives, the great slender needle of the "Berenice Bodkin" with a huge natural rock arch nearby, both commented on by Murray but unvisited since his time and still unclimbed.

Not far south of "The Bodkin" is the border with Sudan (hence the reason for the closed zone). Mick, Di and I visited this country in 1983, climbing on the 2,000-foot granite domes of Jebel Kassala on the Ethiopian border. The area around the Kassala oasis is the homeland of the Hadendowah and Rashaida and other colorful, swash-buckling tribes who still carry huge swords and spears. Smuggling and brigandry is as much the order of the day as camel-herding and agriculture!

It was a fascinating place to climb, the only initial deterrents being the featureless nature of the domes and the large and numerous Rupell's Vultures(!). Having summited on a 1,500-foot F5 route first climbed by Robin Hodgkin and L.W. Brown of the British Alpine Club in 1939, we were shocked to see people coming in from the Ethiopian desert to the east, the vanguard of refugees from the great drought and famine that was to hit the world news in 1984. It was no place to continue climbing, so we crossed the Sudan to the borders of Chad, 800 miles to the west, in search of other mountains.

The 1980s also found us in Egypt's Sinai Peninsula, the most famous peak of which is Mt. Sinai (or Jebel Gebel Musa, 2285m), where Moses reputedly received the Ten Commandments. Here, despite the creaking granite, the encompassing desert with its semi-nomadic Bedouin people, coupled with its Biblical aura, lends a special ambience to the climbing. Numerous routes have been recorded on the cliffs around the ancient Monastery of St. Catherine's (location of the Burning Bush). There are crack climbs up to 2,000 feet (though most are shorter) and 6c. A few have even been fitted with bolts, which, though they permit otherwise unprotectable climbs to be led, seemed to us anomalous, being in proximity of the monastery.

For Di and I, the late 1980s and '90s were predominantly a time of Middle Eastern exploration, though we did get a chance to wander through the vast and varied land of Ethiopia with its myriad tribal peoples, its ancient cultures and high mountains. The summit of Ras Dashan (4620m) provided us with a seven-day trek, camping and staying in small villages en route with the very hospitable local people, who are poor in wealth but rich in spirit. Though we had no climbing gear with us, it seemed the rock towers to the north and northeast of the Simiens would be worth returning to.

By this time, however, we were immersed in Jordan and Oman. The latter gave us opportunities for a couple of trips as we worked on an Adventure Tourism Report for the government. This found us crossing the vast dunes of the Wahiba Sands, which sweep down to the contrasting blue of the Arabian Sea, or sailing below the high sea cliffs of the remote Musandam Peninsula, which guards the Persian Gulf, or driving and trekking through Oman's many mountains looking for the best rock to climb (much of it was awful, but some of the limestone was excellent).

One of our first routes was on the great wall of Jebel Misht close to the northern edge of the infamous Empty Quarter, where resident climber Alec McDonald and I found a new 1,000-foot TD up its southeast pillar on excellent limestone. The "plum" 3,000-foot south pillar had already been done by French guides some years previously; aid was originally used on its lower vertical section, but it has now been climbed free.

Smaller cliffs in the nearby Jebel Akhdar Massif also provided numerous routes of quality, as did the cliffs of the great gorge of Wadi Dayqah in the mountains of the Eastern Hajar. Both

these areas are accessible from the capital, Muscat, in half a day by off-road vehicle. The mountains of Oman also entertained us in other ways, with descents of splendid canyons such as Wadi Beni Awf with its waterfalls, pools and cavern. On the south side of Jebel Akhdar, we descended the three miles of the Hoti Cave, abseiling and swimming beneath parched limestone peaks to exit by a short dive through a sump—a rather different experience for the desert traveler. Since then, others have been attracted to Oman, climbing routes of "alpine proportions" on Jebel Misht and on the impressive peaks above the black chasm of Beni Awf.

On the Mediterranean Coast, Lebanon (to which we traveled in February, 1999) is positively encouraging visitors. High above Beirut, the Middle East's highest summit, Qornet Es Saouda (3088m), offers both winter skiing and autumn trekking. Below its western slopes, the impressive limestone Qadisha Gorge is beginning to be explored by climbers, and the whole area is riddled with excellent caves. The Qadisha Gorge is about 1,000 feet deep with lots of limestone cliffs, but often broken; the best I saw were about 500 feet and they looked good in a beautiful setting. The magnificent Jeita Grotto is in the foothills. Further south, the forested Shouf Mountains look interesting, but Lebanon's second highest top, Mt. Hermon (2814m), is currently in a closed area on the Syrian border.

For us, however, the major attraction since 1984 has always been Jordan. Our attention was initially drawn to the mountains of Wadi Rum in the south of Jordan by David Lean's film *Lawrence of Arabia.* We then read T. E. Lawrence's masterpiece, *Seven Pillars of Wisdom,* in which he extols the region as "Rumm the magnificent ... vast echoing and god-like." Of his

*"Rumm the magnificent. . . vast echoing and god-like."* Mick Shaw and Alan Baker overlooking
Jebel Khazali and the mountains of Rum, from Jebel Rum. HOWARD/TAYLOR COLLECTION

admiration for the area and the local Huweitat Bedouin, he leaves no one in doubt! Our sub-sequent application for permission to visit Wadi Rum resulted in a request from the Tourism Ministry to assess the area for climbing and adventure tourism, though our researches revealed that only one climb had been so far recorded, in 1949, by Sylvia Branford and Charmian Longstaff with a local Bedouin hunter, Sheikh Hamdan, to the top of Jebel Rum (1754m). (We have since learned that the top had been reached in 1947 by Major Henry-Coombe Tenant of the Welsh Guards and Corporal Lance "Havabash" Butler, Royal Signals, who were accom-panied to the summit plateau by Major St. John Armitage.)

The European ascents, however, pale in significance when it is realized that Thamudic inscriptions indicate this difficult summit was climbed about 2,000 years ago by hunters. The local Bedouin continue this tradition, hunting ibex on these magnificent and complex mountains to this very day. None of their routes can truly be said to be "easy." Certainly all of them are serious undertakings, and some have moves of F5. When you realize that they are traditionally climbed alone and without equipment, you begin to appreciate the daring and commitment of their ascensionists.

On our first visit, Mick, Di and I were accompanied by our old climbing friend Alan Baker. The four of us were immediately made welcome by the local Bedouin, who accepted us into their black goat-hair tents. Though initially suspicious of our reasons for wanting to climb in Wadi Rum, they were obviously proud of their routes; they pointed us toward them, giving only enough information to get us started, and were there to meet us on our return, grinning mischievously if we had been lost in the bizarre maze of these sandstone mountains. We learned to think like Bedouin and discovered a wealth of unique Bedouin climbs, some of them ascending miles of rock to reach remote summits; for their grade, they rank amongst the best rock adventures in the world. Also on this first trip, we were pleased to top out on one of the few summits not climbed by the locals, up a 1,500-foot TD. We also made the first tentative foray onto Jebel Rum's vertical 1,500-foot east face, finding some F6b crack climbing. There was obviously much to do in this 1,000-square-mile area of desert mountains.

Over the following years, we were joined by our friends from France, Wilfried Colonna and Bernard Domenech (whom we had first met in the Morocco's Taghia Canyon in the 1970s). The Remy brothers from Switzerland joined the bonanza, "a new route every day" their mantra. Albert Precht and friends from Austria became annual visitors, and, more than any others, made the big walls their home, climbing with the nonchalance borne of increasing familiarity over 2,000-foot faces formed of rock like melting candles or bracket fungi. Geoff Hornby and team from the U.K. became aficionados, as did others from Spain, France and elsewhere in Europe. Together with our French friends, we concentrated on searching out the classic lines up cracks, pillars and walls, sometimes overlooking the campsite, or, increasingly, out in the more remote parts of the desert. By the 1990s, Rum had become acknowledged as one of the world's best desert climbing areas.

The much-admired climbing ethos of the local Bedouin has largely been preserved so that drilled placements have been kept to a minimum. Only the most-frequented descents have been fitted with abseil chains, as much to clean up the growing confusion of worn slings as to improve the safety. The "golden age" of rock exploration in Rum is now undoubtedly over, though there is still much to be discovered. Most visiting climbers, however, are happy to repeat the best of the 400 climbs described in our guide, *Treks and Climbs in Wadi Rum*, which vary in length from a single pitch through to 2,000 feet and include star routes of all grades up to F7b and ED sup. If that is not enough, there are more in the "new routes" book at the campsite!

The Bedouin continue to play a key role; their encampment in the main valley of Rum has grown to a village of houses. Three of the locals have been trained in rope safety in the U.K. to

*Tony Howard on the* Vanishing Pillar, *Jebel Kharazeh, with Rum village below.*
HOWARD/TAYLOR COLLECTION

help them work as mountain guides. The area is prospering and has been designated a National Park with the inclusion of local people on the committee, a move that we have long supported.

We still return annually to Rum, and its battleship mountains rising from seas of orange sands still offer us opportunities for new climbs. Perhaps more importantly, its scattered Bedouin camps have become our "second home."

Meanwhile, we have discovered there's more to Jordan than meets the eye: the mountains guarding the ancient carved city of Petra, 60 miles from Rum, are providing us with magnificent wilderness treks. The huge canyons descending to the Dead Sea (at 400 meters below sea level, the lowest point on earth) have given us some heart-stopping descents as we abseiled over overhangs and through waterfalls. The forested hills in the north have revealed limestone cliffs hidden below Islamic castles. Climbing possibilities are everywhere. The adventures are endless and, together with the people, will continue to tempt us back.

Guidebooks and relevant information:

Morocco:
> Collomb, Robin G. *Atlas Mountains, Morocco*. West Col: 1980.
> Domenech, Bernard. *Le Maroc: Les Plus Belles Courses et Randonées*. Denoël: 1989.

Algeria:
> Lloste, J.M., and Aulard, C. *Guide des Escalades du Hoggar*. C.A.F.: 1962.
> Fantin, M. *Taureg Tassili Sahara*. Tamari Editori: 1971.
> Agresti, I. and H. "The Hoggar: In the Heart of the Sahara." In *The Alpine Journal*. The Alpine Club: 1974.

Algeria and Chad:
> Fantin, M. *Uomoni e Montagne de Sahara*. Tamari Editori: 1970.

Sinai:
> The Israeli Mountaineering Federation has some photocopied route information.

Oman:
> McDonald, R.A. *Rock Climbing in Oman*. Apex Publishing: 1993.

Jordan:
> Howard, Tony. *Treks and Climbs in Wadi Rum*. Cicerone Press: 1987, 1997.
> Howard, Tony, and Taylor, Di. *Walks and Scrambles in Wadi Rum*. Al Kutba: 1993. Updated (Jordan Distribution Agency): 1998.
> Howard, Tony and Taylor, Di. *Jordan: Walks, Treks, Caves, Climbs and Canyons*. Cicerone Press: 1999.

Mali
> Topos for Hombori Towers may be available from the Club Alpin Francais, 24 Rue de Lumière, Paris. Also, see info in *Rock & Ice* numbers 43 and 45.
> Route descriptions and other information will also be found in the *Annales du Groupe de Haute Montagne* (GHM) and *La Montagne et Alpinisme* (France), *Desnivel* (Spain), and *The* (British) *Alpine Journal*. The 1950s journals of the British Climbers' Club and Cambridge Mountaineering Club have information on The Hoggar.

# After Thin Air

## The legacy of the 1996 Mount Everest tragedy

by Michael Chessler

You already know the names of the mountain and the climbers. Climbing mania like this had never happened before. It started with what was supposed to be a routine guided ascent of the highest peak trod by man. The peak had first been climbed a half century before and the public knew only the names of the first two men to climb it. It came as a surprise to the nation that climbers were risking their lives and the lives of their guides while spending great sums of money to climb this peak. And then a sensational magazine article of the ascent led to a best-selling book. Soon everyone wanted to see and hear the author in person. The lectures seemed to go on forever, the media loved it and the multitude of related books became a publisher's dream come true.

Soon everybody was talking about the famed expedition. Climbers and non-climbers alike debated the ethics and propriety of guided mountaineering. The author was thrust into a position as the leading authority on the subject, and everyone was moved by his book and lectures. He became rich from royalties, and his name will be forever associated with the peak he climbed but once. He is indelibly a part of mountaineering history and literature.

Oh! Did you think I was talking about Jon Krakauer, *Into Thin Air* and Mount Everest? Heavens, no! I was talking about Albert Smith, *The Story of Mont Blanc*, and the Mont Blanc mania of the 1850s! Mountaineering, with its media extravaganzas and celebrities, triumphs and tragedies, rule makers and rule breakers, best-selling books and wannabe rebuttals, has been around since the sport was introduced on Mont Blanc by J. Balmat and Dr. M.G. Paccard on August 8, 1786, and became popular after Albert Smith's lectures from 1852 to 1858.

The public has actually gone into a frenzy over mountaineering many times before. Besides Albert Smith in 1851 and Whymper's Matterhorn climb in 1865, all the British Everest climbs from 1921 to 1953 were vigorously reported in the press and on the lecture circuit. John Noel made the first Everest films in 1922 and 1924, and in 1933 the first aerial movies of the peak were taken. These films saw wide circulation. According to Walt Unsworth, Mallory's great line, "Because it is there," was said to a reporter (undoubtedly looking for a sound bite) after one of his many lectures. The press also had seizures after Annapurna in 1950, the Everest first ascent in 1953, and when the Americans spent an unheard of $250,000 to climb it in 1963. (That was mostly media money, by the way.) John Harlin III noted that CBS did a special on his father's death in 1966, and I remember cutting Eiger and Everest articles out of the *New York Times* in the 1960s. *Life* magazine put Bobby Kennedy's down-jacketed image on its cover when he summited Mount Kennedy. It is therefore hardly surprising that today there are many climbers who regard the whole Krakauer-Everest phenomenon as a non-event, and have not read the book. It has all happened many times before.

Salkeld and Boyle's 1993 bibliography *Climbing Mount Everest* listed 586 books on the mountain and 316 expeditions to climb it. Very few of these have become well known to the general public. The 620th ascent of Everest in 1996 was not expected to be book-worthy, either. While *Into Thin Air* has had the greatest impact on the public's perception of climbing of any book in 50 years, the success of this book is clearly part of a much bigger story, one that reflects the nature of American society. Why did media and the public collapse into frenzy following *Into Thin Air*? Why did this Everest story make the big time when so many others did not?

Because *Into Thin Air* is the perfect story. Its major elements were suspense, adventure, death, money, ego, power, male rivalry, sex and the immortal battle with nature. It had a big media build-up. It had rich Americans risking their lives for no useful purpose, and spending an obscene amount of money doing it. It made us jealous and it made us angry—and the cameras caught it all. What could be a greater rush than climbing the world's highest mountain and coming back to the adulation of friends and strangers? And what could be worse than squandering your money, being involved in a catastrophe, and having to spend the rest of your life explaining your hubris?

We were waiting for the tragedy to happen. We had the lights on and the cameras rolling, and Jon Krakauer just walked right into the picture. Americans love a good tragedy, and we want it on tape for the six o'clock news. Jack Ruby and Rodney King taught us the value of good film footage. There is a straight line from Abraham Zapruder to David Breashears. Today, news events may as well not have happened unless there is a camera recording it, and there were cameras aplenty on Everest on May 10, 1996. Three people were broadcasting the ascent on the Internet, Scott Fischer was making videos, and Rob Hall had a cell phone. Book and magazine contracts had been arranged, TV reports were being broadcast, and the David Breashears' IMAX expedition stumbled onto the greatest story of their lives. Like many reporters today, they became a part of the story. Krakauer himself was on the mountain to report on the issues of guided climbs on Everest for the influential magazine *Outside*. As a top-notch and lucky journalist, he wrote the story he saw. When I asked Krakauer how he felt about what the media did to him and his book, he replied, "I am the media."

At the time of the 1996 disaster, both TV and the print media went berserk. Gay Ellen Roesch, the newly hired librarian at the AAC, spent her first few months on the job fielding interminable media requests for facts, quotes, photos, history, film, but mostly, sound bites. I asked Mike Kennedy of *Climbing* magazine if, as a journalist, he felt like he was dealing with some imbecile cousins when the networks called. He could not give me a reply on the record. David Breashears describes most media interviews as follows. "They have no interest in what I've done. All they have is a keen interest in getting access to an event that riveted the world. They want to reduce the story to cliches."

*Into Thin Air* sold 800,000 hardcover copies plus 1,760,000 copies in paperback. Those are big numbers. It has been translated into 19 languages. *Into Thin Air* was a hardcover, then a large-print book, an abridged cassette, an unabridged cassette, a CD, a mass-market paperback, an illustrated edition, a made-for-TV movie and a trade paperback. There is no other way to do the book.

And of all the climbing books in recent times, *Into Thin Air* was most intensely read! It appealed to both men and women; whole families read the book. It was taught in classrooms. Not an airplane or terminal in America lacked someone engrossed in the book. At every private gathering, people were discussing and arguing the ethics, judgment and sanity of the guides and clients, and the miracle of Beck Weathers.

Simultaneous with *Into Thin Air*'s high ride, the IMAX *Everest* film was filling theater seats across the country. Krakauer's book and the IMAX movie created a whirlwind effect. Once you saw one, you had to see the other. The book had depth, emotion and details, while the film was visually breathtaking. If the IMAX *Everest* film was given a big boost by the success of *Into Thin Air*, in the end the IMAX film may have had a greater impact on the public because many more people saw it than read the book.

In America, we measure success in dollars. Using the dollar figures we know, it is possible to estimate the financial impact of the Everest tragedy. The IMAX movie grossed 60 million dollars, the Krakauer book grossed perhaps 50 million dollars. The other Everest books and movies added perhaps another 50 million dollars. Therefore, the books and films directly related to Everest 1996 may have generated 150 to 250 million dollars in revenue. Now add just the additional revenue earned by tangentially related films and books like *Seven Years in Tibet* and *Endurance*, all the TV shows and magazines sold, the charitable contributions and speaking fees, the trinket sales and publicity tours, the babysitter fees while the parents went out to see Krakauer and Breashears speak. This was a major international media and financial juggernaught that may have generated half a billion dollars in spending. That is why the media loves these tragedies so much.

There were two book and film tours going on in 1997. While Krakauer was playing to packed houses across America, he was being pushed by his publisher to add more cities and interviews. At the same time, David Breashears was hired by National Geographic to promote their book *Everest: Mountain Without Mercy*, written by Broughton Coburn as a tie-in to the IMAX film. The tours attracted crowds so large that some bookshops had to hire auditoriums.

When the IMAX film opened in May 1997, it was a fresh media event. Breashears attended over 20 grand openings and gave live talks to invited audiences of opinion leaders, often as benefits for the American Himalayan Foundation. He flew to Paris, the Netherlands and Japan for IMAX openings there. IMAX has dozens of theaters in Asia and Europe, and Everest was a huge hit in those places, too. He was on TV and radio: Larry King, National Public Radio, Charlie Rose, Tom Snyder and even Conan O'Brien. When *People* magazine designated Breashears as the world's "sexiest explorer," the whole incident was reduced to a new level of farce.

These live presentations by the actual climbers brings us back again to Albert Smith. His live performance of Mont Blanc in London brought the drama of climbing home to everyone in the audience. It does not matter if you have read every book on Everest, seen the films, clicked on the websites. "The most memorable moment is when you shake hands with and speak to the climber himself," says Breashears, whether it is Albert Smith, George Mallory, Krakauer, Breashears or Messner. "Only then does it becomes real for you."

It is not surprising that the success of *Into Thin Air* also created a publishing outwash plain that many are calling a new genre of "true adventure." Practically every major magazine featured the Everest story on its cover. Perhaps 10,000 climbing books have been published over the centuries, but to the experts of Madison Avenue, *Into Thin Air* was the first that mattered. First there was Broughton Coburn's *Everest, Mountain Without Mercy* and Anatoli Boukreev and G. Weston DeWalt's *The Climb*. Soon to follow were Matt Dickinson's *The Death Zone*, Ed Douglas's *Chomolungma Sings the Blues*, Joe Simpson's *Dark Shadows Falling*, Roberto Mantovani's *Everest: History of The Himalayan Giant*, Lene Gammelgard's *Climbing High: A Woman's Account of Climbing Everest*, Mark Pfetzer's *Within Reach: My Everest Story*, Colin Monteath's *Hall and Ball: Kiwi Mountaineers*, Mike Groom's *Sheer Will* and Cathy O'Dowd's *Everest: Free to Decide*. A South African reporter named Ken Vernon has written *Ascent and Dissent*, a more complete version of the South Africans' travails. Tom Hornbein's *Everest: The West Ridge* has seen a considerable resurgence of interest because Krakauer refers to Hornbein as one of his mentors: Borders Books alone ordered 400 copies of Unsworth's *Everest* history, entirely wiping out the publisher's stock. While Krakauer's other book, *Into the Wild*, was already on the best-seller list, the boost from the new book kept the old one selling for another two years. Some books are already collectible. Signed first editions of *Into Thin Air* sell for a mere $75 because there are 110,000 first editions. However, signed copies of Anatoli Boukreev's *The Climb* fetch $500 because he signed only a few before he died on Annapurna. And people want even more: I have been asked if Ed Viesturs is writing a book!

Then there was Caroline Alexander's *The Endurance* and Bill Bryson's *A Walk in The Woods*, both of which made many best-seller lists. Margo Chisolm's *To The Summit*, Ruth Ann Kocour's *Facing the Extreme*, Jim Wickwire's *Addicted to Danger*, Laura Evans' *Climb of My Life*, Jon Waterman's *A Most Hostile Mountain*, Kurt Willis's trilogy *Epic, High*, and *Rough Water*, Wainwright's *Deathful Ridge: A Novel of Everest*, Salkeld's *World Mountaineering* and Poindexter's *To The Summit* also followed. Finally, the most unlikely book to emerge as a best-seller was the 1997 *American Alpine Journal*. Because it had three articles on the 1996 Everest tragedy, the *AAJ* sold out within a year. Someone even asked me if the disaster was covered in *Accidents in North American Mountaineering*.

In addition to all the new titles, there were also many reissues and new covers on mountaineering and polar classics. Krakauer's *Eiger Dreams* got a new publisher and cover. In 1990, David Roberts and Jon Krakauer collaborated on a book called *Iceland*. At the time, the publisher asked Roberts, "Isn't Krakauer a writer too?" Roberts jokingly replied, "No, he's just a climber and photographer who writes if they can't get a real writer." But for a 1998 edition, Krakauer was given higher billing than his mentor Roberts. New paperbacks were also published of Harrer's *The White Spider*, Olsen's *The Climb Up to Hell*, Leamer's *Ascent*, Lansing's *Endurance*, Worsley's *Shackleton's Boat Journey*, Huntford's *Shackleton*, Buhl's *Nanga Parbat Pilgrimage*, Benuzzi's *No Picnic on Mount Kenya*. Houghton Mifflin asked if the time was right to re-issue Jim Curran's *K2: Triumph and Tragedy* with a better cover. It was and they did. Soon to be reprinted are two of the best Everest books of all time: Unsworth's *Everest* and Peter Gillman's *Everest: The Best Writing and Pictures From Seventy Years of Human Endeavour*. Even Sebastian Junger's *The Perfect Storm* is seeing many sequels, all concerning death at sea, another hot topic. And there is tremendous interest in Shackleton's expeditions as well, which is also related to the public's thirst for true adventure and exploration heroes.

Publishers continue to cash in. 1999's harvest of adventure books includes David Breashears' *High Exposure*, Jeff Long's novel *The Descent*, Ed Webster's *Snow on the Kingdom* plus a Vittorio Sella photo book, *Summit: Pioneering Mountaineering Photographer*. Aperture, publisher of the Sella book, said specifically that they hoped it would benefit from the new interest in mountaineering. DeWalt is adding 40,000 words to a new edition of *The Climb*. Dickinson's *Death Zone* is getting a new title, *The Other Side of Everest*. According to Audrey Salkeld, Goran Kropp, the Swedish cyclist and Everest soloist, has written *Odyssey*, Ed Douglas and David Rose have collaborated on a biography of Everest (and K2) summiter Alison Hargreaves, and Matt Dickinson has finished an Everest novel titled *Bivouac*. As for the future of adventure publishing, Krakauer is now advising Random House on a new line of adventure reprints, and Norton has teamed up with *Outside* magazine to do a series of adventure books, starting in the year 2000.

The Internet is the hot new medium, and it, too, had a major impact on *Into Thin Air*, and vice-versa. The expedition in 1996 and the book in 1997 coincided with a surge in Internet activity. Websites were pushing the Everest story, but to raise cash, selling climbing books became the obvious way to go. Thousands of books were sold over the Internet. It seems that now every Himalayan expedition has its own website. Larry Johnson, leader of the 1999

Everest expedition looking for Mallory's remains, remarked that fund raising was certainly easier than if *Into Thin Air* had not happened.

Adventure films were also doing well. IMAX *Everest* was the big hit, and Breashears says that in his opinion Titanic's incredible success stemmed partly from the public's insatiable fascination with man against the elements. *Into Thin Air*'s made-for-TV-version, although derided by climbers, also had a big public impact. *Seven Years in Tibet* and *Kundun* were major Hollywood releases with appeal to climbers, although only the Brad Pitt film was a commercial success. *The Fatal Game* told a story similar to *Into Thin Air* and was a film festival and video hit. Some climbers preferred the video *The Making of Everest IMAX* over the actual IMAX film itself. The 1998 Nova special *Everest: The Death Zone* with Breashears and Viesturs also got approval from the climbing community. Goran Kropp, who summited Everest after everybody else went home, made a humorous film that was popular at film festivals. A trio of videos called *Everest: Mountain of Dreams, Mountain of Doom* has become a mass market best seller. Just received in for spring 1999 is a video by Alan Hobson and Jamie Clark called *Above All Else: The Everest Dream*.

In Hollywood, Universal studios has options on the stories of some of the other Everest 1996 climbers, and Tom Cruise has an option on *Touching the Void*. Jeff Long's *The Descent* has major studio interest. Rumor has it that this fall the director of *Zorro* will start shooting a climbing action thriller called *The Vertical Limit*, based on a fictional ascent of K2.

How many of the above books and films would have been published, or sold as well as they did, if *Into Thin Air* had not been such a blockbuster? Many were undeniably in the works before Krakauer appeared, but *Into Thin Air* definitely was the spark that caused many authors and publishers to act. For example, Boukreev's book was obviously written as a rebuttal to Krakauer's. And it worked; several readers have said they think Boukreev's is the better book with a more factual account of the climb.

Before *Into Thin Air*, the general public had no idea that such dangerous and expensive activities were taking place in the Himalaya. Unlike Messner and Bonington in Europe, no climber's name has ever been a household word in America. Now everybody knows one climber's name: Jon Krakauer. They read him and believed every word he said. Eventually the public got almost as caught up in the nitty-gritty arguments over turn-around times and oxygen use as climbers did. Every climber I asked corroborated that his non-climber friends turned to him for an explanation of what happened. This discussion of detail has an important purpose besides mere curiosity. Climbers are generally meticulous about getting to the "truth." Examining the details is a way of dealing with the trauma of death. As John Harlin III, only ten years old in 1966 when his father plummeted from the Eiger, says of his experience, "I examined the evidence minutely to find out what went wrong on the climb, to assure myself that Dad had not made a mistake."

They say that there is no such thing as bad publicity, and indeed *Into Thin Air* and the IMAX film had the ironic effect of creating a stampede of climbers and trekkers to the Himalaya. Professional guides have said that a routine phone call from a prospective client goes like this:

"I'd like to climb Mount Everest."

"How much climbing have you done?"

"I've never climbed. I just want to climb Mount Everest."

"Our policy is that all climbers be properly prepared. That means we will first teach you how to climb on Mount Rainier. Then you will climb McKinley or Aconcagua to get some altitude experience. If you do well at altitude, we can talk about the Himalaya."

"Hell, I don't want to climb Rainier or McKinley! I can only get a four-week vacation next year! I don't have time for all that!" Click.

Jon Krakauer essentially stopped giving lectures and making public appearances when his book tour ended. He did make a few attempts at public discussion, though. One event was an on-line debate between DeWalt and Krakauer in an e-zine called *Salon* in the summer of 1998. Accusations were hurled, mostly at the deceased guides, but there was also a tasteless insinuation by DeWalt that, as a reporter, Krakauer's presence itself contributed to the tragedy. There was also a juicy rumor going around that one of the Everest climbers had lawyers contacting Krakauer advising him to be careful about what he said in his book about their client. No wonder he has stopped lecturing. Random House still gets ten requests a week for him to speak. When Krakauer does choose to appear, such as at the American Himalayan Foundation's annual dinner in 1998, the clamor for tickets is so great that you'd think John Lennon had returned for a reunion with his old band.

David Rosenthal, the editor and publisher of *Into Thin Air*, says, "At first Jon did not want to write the book, but catharsis was a major reason for doing so." Krakauer happens to be an exceptionally gifted storyteller; his wordcraft has twice turned a good story into a great one. The function of a well-written, timely and well-promoted book is to bring attention to what is ordinary and make it noteworthy. David Rosenthal had the vision to see that potential in Jon Krakauer, and that's the fundamental reason why *Into Thin Air* came to be written.

The subtitle of *Into Thin Air* is *A Personal Account of the Mount Everest Disaster*, and nothing could be more truthful. Krakauer has said that he wished the book had stopped selling a half million copies ago. When Krakauer realized what the American Himalayan Foundation was doing for the indigenous people in the Himalaya, he changed the thrust of his lectures. He offered to personally match dollar-for-dollar any contributions his audiences made to the AHF and has given over $100,000.

If there is to be a beneficial legacy to the lives lost and the aftermath of the climb, it is what the climbers have done themselves. Norbu Tenzing, whose family has produced 11 Everest summiters, says, "This book and film have done more good for the people of Nepal than any single event since the first ascent by my Dad and Hillary in 1953." Another positive result of the Everest tragedy is that some of the proceeds from Anatoli Boukreev's book *The Climb* have been donated to the Kazak Army Sports Club to continue the mountaineering programs that lost their funding after the fall of communism. Linda Wylie, Boukreev's girlfriend, initiated this financial aid in Boukreev's name as something that he certainly would have wanted to do with the unexpected windfall from his book. While there is little more to be learned by debating why Boukreev descended ahead of his clients, or why Rob Hall and Scott Fischer did not turn their clients around at 2 p.m., there is much to be gained by taking some of the money from the sale of three million books, and giving it to people who need it.

Trying to affix blame for the deaths of climbers has happened before. Just look at the controversy surrounding Wiessner's actions on his 1939 K2 expedition. Whymper's 1865 ascent of the Matterhorn caused a controversy that simmered for 50 years. Arnold Lunn writes, "Queen Victoria was deeply shocked, and asked the Lord Chamberlain if something could not be done to stop mountaineering by law." (National Park Service, take note!) Whymper's telling of that tragedy in *Scrambles Amongst The Alps* has a direct parallel to Everest in 1996: a killer peak was climbed at inordinate loss of life, a book was written to huge public acclaim, the author became wealthy from the royalties, and he was nailed by his critics. I predict that in 20 years, should you mention Everest to Jon Krakauer, his reaction will be much the same as Ed Hillary's today: he'll reluctantly say a few words he's said a thousand times before, and politely try to change the subject to something more important and timely. If Jon Krakauer can put *Into Thin Air* behind him, then maybe it's time for the rest of us to do so as well.

So what will be the long-term effects of *Into Thin Air*? If history is a guide, the public will forget about climbing until another tragedy occurs. Jon Krakauer will fade from the public's eye because he wants to. Some climbers will always admire him for his writing and his good works, while others will always feel that Boukreev's version was right. *Into Thin Air* will become one more in a line of classic expedition accounts that stretches back to *Scrambles Amongst the Alps*. The copyright on *Into Thin Air* and IMAX *Everest* will run out in 95 years; I for one look forward to reading the multi-media centenary edition in 2097, with a built-in copy of the IMAX film on mini-DVD to watch in my nursing home. Guided Himalayan climbing will continue, because there will always be those who want to climb mountains and cannot do it any other way. Mount Everest itself will never lose its allure, even though it will have long since become, as Alfred Mummery once said of the Grepon, "an easy day for a lady."

# Mountain Medicine

## A review of High-Altitude Cerebral Edema

by Geoffrey Tabin, M.D.

The week before Jeff Colovis and I went to climb the Black Dike on Cannon Cliff in New Hampshire, he broke four toes in an accident at his construction job. I suggested we delay our ice climb. He replied with an innocent, "Why?"

"Because it will hurt your foot," I said.

"Well, that would be my foot's problem," he shot back. "I want to climb."

After the ascent, I asked Jeff how he was doing. He answered, "Great! My foot hurts, but I had a fine day."

At least somewhere, in even the most reptilian human brain, we are aware of sensations in our bodies. When we are cold, hot, short of breath, or in pain, a signal is sent via our nerves to the brain, which interprets the signals and tells us how we are doing. Things become more difficult, however, when it is the brain itself that is suffering. Often, the brain is unaware of its own difficulties, being either oblivious or too sick to assess its own symptoms. The result can be impaired judgment and the ignoring of serious deficits in function. In mountaineering, this condition is seen in the progression from Acute Mountain Sickness (AMS) into High Altitude Cerebral Edema (HACE).

HACE can progress rapidly from impaired judgment to disorientation, coma, and death. This year's mountaineering medicine review will focus on HACE. We will review what is known about the symptoms of and treatment for HACE and explain new research that is shedding light on the pathophysiology of what is happening in our brains when we go too high too fast.

High Altitude Cerebral Edema has long been considered a severe form of high altitude illness resulting from swelling in and around the brain. The brain is the keeper of consciousness and initiator of commands to all other organs. The human anatomy has protected the brain in a rigid, bony, strong but inflexible vault. Being rigid, the skull allows no room for expansion. Thus, any swelling inside it has the effect of compressing the brain itself.

The brain is nourished continuously with blood from the heart that carries life-sustaining oxygen and glucose. Anything that disturbs the flow affects the brain and will cause rapid loss of consciousness. The brain is only 2% of the body by weight, but utilizes 15% of the body's oxygen. Any decrease in the oxygen flow to the brain has immediate effects.

The brain is also protected internally by a modification to the brain capillary wall called the blood brain barrier. Unlike other capillaries (the small tubes that carry oxygenated blood to tissues), the brain capillary consists of a continuous wall of crescent-shaped endothelial cells that overlap in "tight junctions" to minimize formation of open pores. Surrounding the endothelial cells are additional protective layers: a basement membrane and partial coating of glial cells. Substances leaving the blood plasma must penetrate several membrane layers before entering the extra-cellular brain fluid. Differences in the transport mechanisms and permeability among molecules effectively allow the blood brain barrier to act as a selective filter, allowing oxygen and glucose to reach hungry neurons, but preventing leakage of plasma fluid.

Previously, when high-altitude sojourners experienced such symptoms as headache, dizziness, appetite loss, nausea, and even changing consciousness, it was believed that the physiologic disturbances were neurological in origin. Some experts concluded that hypoxia (low oxygen) interfered with energy production—in particular, production of adenosine triphosphate (ATP) in brain cells. ATP is present in all cell types and permits a finely adjusted use of energy. Without adequate ATP, researchers concluded, brain cells could no longer work properly.

In the last decade, it has become clear that ATP in the brain is not adversely affected by the degree of hypoxia that occurs at high altitude. Unlike the condition that occurs with high-altitude hypoxia, when ATP is depleted, unconsciousness is immediate. Therefore, another mechanism must be responsible for the initiation of Acute Mountain Sickness.

A number of plausible explanations have been proposed. One likely candidate was the brain's "transmission system," which is composed of chemicals called neurotransmitters. It is the effect of hypoxia on neurotransmitters, for example, that causes muddled thinking and slow reaction times at altitudes of about 5500 meters or more. But these symptoms are quite different from those of Mountain Sickness, which include a feeling of listlessness, low energy, lack of appetite, and mild headache.

Another proposed mechanism for the physiology of Acute Mountain Sickness was that hyperventilation by the lungs in an attempt to bring more oxygen into the system leads to blowing off excess $CO_2$, which changes the body's pH in a manner known as respiratory alkalosis. This acid base imbalance can lead to nausea and lack of appetite. A third idea was that increased blood flow to the brain causes pressure and headaches. The brain attempts to keep its oxygen level steady. When there is less oxygen per volume of blood, the brain reacts by redirecting more blood flow to itself, causing an increase in the volume of blood inside the rigid skull, and thus, pressure. This would explain the pounding headache one feels in the temples with each heartbeat with early mountain sickness. Dr. Charlie Houston, the godfather of high-altitude research, believes that "all or most signs and symptoms at altitude, and from many other causes of hypoxia, are fundamentally mediated by the central nervous system, whether it be via the brain or its neurons." If this is correct, then AMS is a mild form of HACE.

Other clues to understanding AMS came from the very sickest climbers, those who developed full-blown High-Altitude Cerebral Edema. Their symptoms pointed to swelling of the brain itself as a likely cause for the more mild AMS as well. Inder Singh, an Indian military physician, described the effects experienced by thousands of Indian soldiers who were rushed from a relatively low altitude to a very high one when the Chinese attacked their border in the Himalaya. Singh measured the pressure of the soldiers' cerebral spinal fluid by doing spinal taps. He found it was higher when the soldiers were severely ill. He also did a biopsy on the brain of a soldier who died of presumed altitude illness that showed marked edema. Since the symptoms of these soldiers with cerebral edema were essentially exaggerated symptoms of AMS, Singh logically assumed AMS to be due to increased intracranial pressure resulting from swelling of the brain.

It is because of Singh's studies as well as autopsies conducted by other researchers on trekkers and climbers who had died as a result of severe brain swelling that the extreme form of AMS came to be known as High-Altitude Cerebral Edema. Still, important questions remain unanswered: What exactly causes cerebral edema? Is it really a physiologic extension of AMS? Why are some susceptible and others not?

Three theories were used to explain the swelling in the brain. The first was the so-called Cytotoxic theory. In cytotoxic edema, lack of oxygen to the brain causes a slowing of an essential oxygen-dependent mechanism that pumps fluid out of cerebral cells. The result is that individual brain cells swell, increasing the volume of tissue in the skull. A second theory was the

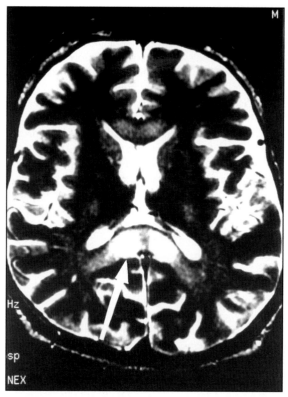

MRI of the brain of a climber with High-Altitude Cerebral Edema. The abnormal collection of water in the posterior corpus callosum is marked with an arrow. The abnormality resolves as the victim recovers. PETER HACKETT, M.D.

Vasogenic theory, which suggests the pathophysiologic cause to be an extravasation of fluid from the blood vessels caused by a leaking of the blood brain barrier. Finally, a combination of both mechanisms plus the increase in cerebral blood flow was deduced to be an overall method of expanding the volume in the skull and placing pressure on the brain.

Until recently, there were no sensitive ways to view the brain inside the skull of a living human or to determine the degree of swelling that might or might not be present. With the advent of computed tomography (CT scanning) and Magnetic Resonance Imaging (MRI), researchers could finally obtain brain images of persons who became ill at high altitudes. Location of the edema in the brain could give clues to its cause, and comparison of brain images across a range of illness could explain the relationship of AMS to HACE. Unfortunately, however, CT and MRI machines are expensive and cumbersome and cannot be taken up on the mountain.

Peter Hackett, M.D., worked from 1981 to 1989 on Denali, frequently treating victims of Acute Mountain Sickness. Several of his patients were evacuated from Denali to a hospital in Anchorage, and Hackett obtained MRI scans of these victims. Hackett's findings show that plasma was leaking from blood vessels and forming pools between brain cells, particularly in an area of the white matter known as the corpus callosum (which consisted of fibers that unite the two cerebral hemispheres). The brain cells themselves did not appear swollen. This exact image had never before been seen in any condition.

With descent, the plasma, which is mostly water, apparently stopped leaking and was reabsorbed into the blood circulation, which explained why the severe symptoms were completely reversible. Hackett and his colleagues studied a total of nine High-Altitude Cerebral Edema victims; the findings were present in seven of them. The paper reporting these findings was published on December 9, 1998, in the *Journal of the American Medical Association* and concludes that the blood brain barrier is indeed the culprit in HACE. There are many hypotheses as to what may cause the brain's blood vessels to leak at high altitudes. Further studies in humans and perhaps animal experiments using species that are susceptible to edema in the white matter may help resolve this question in the next few years.

Other recent research has focused on the role of nitric oxide (NO) as an important factor in hypoxia-reduced capillary leakage. NO is found in the inner lining of blood vessels. Its principal action is to cause relaxation of the muscles surrounding the capillaries, allowing the smaller vessels to dilate. NO also seems to decrease the effectiveness of clot formation in the bloodstream. The effects of decreased oxygen levels in the bloodstream have been postulated to include affecting NO production and thus increasing leaking from blood vessels while at the same time decreasing clotting to stop the extravasation of edema fluid. This research fits well with Dr. Hackett's MRI findings.

Hackett's findings also explain why there is a beneficial effect in the administration of steroids in altitude illness. Dexamethasone may work its effect by decreasing blood brain barrier permeability. Dexamethasone prevents the increase in permeability of cultured endothelial cell monolayers that are subjected to hypoxia. The finding also explains why this edema may resolve very quickly without permanent damage once a person retreats to lower altitude.

Hackett's findings do not exclude an element of intracellular edema as well, but they clearly suggest that vasogenic edema is the major operant factor in the pathophysiology of HACE in the phase that it becomes clinically evident. The reason why certain individuals' blood brain barriers may be more susceptible to leakage than others, and why certain people become more symptomatic than others, still remains a subject for further research. Genetic differences in the response of the blood brain barrier regulation and genetic differences in cerebral vascular leakage under hypoxic conditions are currently under investigation. It may also be that people who do well at high altitude have more room within their skull to accommodate the edematous fluid and do not have the same increase in pressure on the brain. This would support what many lay people have long hypothesized: people who climb frequently to high altitudes must have empty space in their skulls.

A few years ago I was in a panel discussion on high-altitude climbing. I was asked what were the most important attributes for doing hard routes in the Himalaya. My answer was, "A high pain tolerance and a very short memory." The moderator next turned to Simon Parsons, an Australian climber, and asked his opinion. Simon replied, "What was the question?" Perhaps the answer should be a very small brain.

BIBLIOGRAPHY

1. Hackett, P.H., and Roach, R.C. "High-Altitude Medicine." In *Wilderness Medicine*, edited by Auerbach, P.A., 1-37. St. Louis: Mosby, 1995.

2. Hackett, P.H., Yarnell, P.R., Hill, R., Reynard, K., Heit, J., and McCormick, J. "High-Altitude Cerebral Edema Evaluated with Magnetic Resonance Imaging:  Clinical Correlation and Pathophysiology." In *The Journal of American Medical Association* 280, 1920-1925. 1998.

3. Krasney, J.A. "A Neurogenic Basis for Acute Altitude Illness." In *Medicine Science Sport Exercise* 26, 195-208. 1994.

4. Hackett, P.H., and Shlim, D. "The High Life: Health and Sickness at High Altitude." In 1997 *Medical and Health Annual*, edited by Bernstein, E., 24-41. Chicago: Encyclopedia Britannica, 1996.

5. Krasney, J. "Cerebral Hemodynamics and High-Altitude Cerebral Edema". In *Hypoxia: Women at Altitude*, edited by Houston, C., and Coates, G., 254-268. Burlington, Vermont: Queen City Press, 1997.

For a complete bibliography, the most recent abstracts from the International Hypoxia Symposia, and links to mountain medicine web sites, see http://www.hypoxia.net

# The Mountain Environment

## The year in garbage

by Brent Bishop and Chris Naumann

In the United States and around the globe, there is a growing awareness that climbers must take responsibility for their environmental impacts and even clean up after others. Having a "minimum impact" can no longer be the goal; rather, climbers must strive to have a "positive impact." Rock climbers contribute to trail erosion each time they visit the crag, and therefore understand that they should initiate and volunteer for trail maintenance events. Similarly, expeditions should not only pack out their own garbage, but also collect and properly dispose of the trash left behind by previous teams. An integral part of accomplishing this positive-impact is maintaining an open forum to address environmental issues and outline strategies by which climbers can make a difference. "The Mountain Environment" section contributes to this forum by documenting the successful clean-up efforts of individuals and teams.

To further address the environmental issues that concern the American Alpine Club and its members, the Mountain Environment section now includes reports of domestic efforts to restore and sustain the alpine regions in our own backyard. The ethic employed on Denali or at Hueco dictates the attitudes and practices exported with an expedition to the Garhwal or Ak-Su. The standards we set and accomplish in the States establish the foundation for traveling and climbing responsibly abroad. The efforts detailed below distinguish those individuals and teams that truly made a difference in 1998. May their commitment inspire our mountaineering ethic to a higher level at home and overseas.

## INTERNATIONAL CONSERVATION

### MOUNT EVEREST, NEPAL

The Spring 1998 season saw three teams actively pursuing conservation work on Everest using the incentive program that was started in 1994 by the Sagarmatha Environmental Expedition. The Boston Museum of Science Expedition, led by Wally Berg, removed 35 discarded oxygen bottles from the South Col. The "Everest Challenge" team's primary goal, in which they were successful, was to have Tom Whittiker become the first amputee to summit the world's highest mountain. The team's environmental component resulted in the retrieval of 89 bottles of oxygen, in addition to the 59 the expedition brought to the mountain, and 1,000 pounds of garbage from Camp II.

The Everest Environmental Expedition '98 (EEE '98) retrieved 3,200 pounds of general trash, 49 oxygen bottles (in addition to the 110 used by the team), 211 discarded fuel canisters and 546 used batteries. Most significantly, Pasquale Scaturro and Guy Johnson developed the first system to effectively handle fecal material at Base Camp. Ultimately, the system allowed the team to collect and dispose of 535 pounds of human waste.

The toilet system was adopted from river rafting practices that mandate no fecal material be left behind. American Innotek supplied the expedition with seven- and five-gallon buckets that were fitted with rubber seals and industrial leak-proof screw tops. After each use, an organic powder was added to facilitate the biodegrading process (it was later found that the powder was only effective at lower altitudes). The buckets were used as the team's Base Camp latrine and at Camp II in the Western Cwm. The buckets at Base Camp were carried down valley to have the contents composted. The buckets from Camp II were hauled half a mile away, where the contents were disposed of in a crevasse. This system, which was used effectively by 12 team members and countless guests in Base Camp, represents a pragmatic solution to the human waste problem that expeditions have historically failed to address. Considering the simplicity and feasibility of the fecal disposal method, it should become the new paradigm for all expeditions.

# MEXICO

R.J. Secor, the author of *Mexico's Volcanoes: A Climber's Guide*, reports that the Mexican volcanoes, particularly Orizaba, have seen an improvement in environmental conditions over the last five years. This is particularly due to the efforts of El Groupo de Los Cien, the Mexican conservation group that administers the huts and which has provided the funding to hire a ranger on Orizaba, build latrines at the huts, and remove rubbish from the mountains. Although far from perfect, the huts are becoming cleaner due to the efforts of El Groupo de Los Cien.

# ACONCAGUA, ARGENTINA

Aconcagua receives a tremendous amount of traffic, which brings increased pressure on the environment. Those climbers who have been on the standard route and stayed at Plaza de Mulas will remember the dismal state of the camp. The camp has now been cleaned and moved 100 meters above the old camp. The US $120 permit fee goes directly to the funding for rangers and the removal of trash. To further address the problem of trash, park authorities are issuing trash bags with each permit. Climbers must show their permit as well as the used trash bags to a ranger upon completions of the climb. Teams without a permit and filled trash bag face a fine of US $100.

Matthew Nelson and Mike Wilke from Tucson, Arizona, traveled to Aconcagua not only to climb, but also to undertake a clean-up project on the mountain's crowded normal route. The two concentrated their environmental efforts on Camp Canada, Camp Alaska, and Nido de Condores. They cleaned Camp Alaska and Camp Canada thoroughly, but were only able to make "a small dent" at Nido de Condores before a storm halted their efforts. All told, the two collected 220 pounds of garbage in just one day. In addition to their clean-up efforts, Nelson and Wilke raised over $2,000 for Native Seeds/SEARCH and FUNAM, non-profit organizations that support the indigenous people of South America, their traditional communities and sustainable environments. Both climbers plan to organize several more expeditions in the near future.
For more information please contact:
Aconcagua Journey
4500 West Speedway Blvd (Gatehouse)
Tucson, AZ 85745
Tel: 520-770-0668

*Construction of one of the latrines at Paiyu on the Baltoro Glacier, Pakistan Karakoram.*
GREG MORTENSON

# KARAKORAM, PAKISTAN

Greg Mortenson of the Central Asia Institute and Brent Bishop, in conjunction with Nike, continued the trash removal and porter training programs they established in 1997. Mortenson and Bishop's efforts involve the local Balti people in the planning, implementation and evaluation of the projects to insure long-term conservation management. The most significant project of 1998 was the construction of three permanent latrines at the established camps on the Baltoro glacier for use by climbers, trekkers, and porters. The Everest Environmental Project, directed by Bob McConnell, made this project possible with a sizable grant. Thousands of pounds of timber, cement, and other building supplies were carried up the Baltoro glacier to build the latrines. Thanks to the expert local craftsmen, the toilets are so well built that the local military officer asked to store artillery shells in them during the winter!

Mortenson and Bishop coordinated the collection and removal of over 8,000 pounds of tin, glass, plastic and other debris discarded by foreign expeditions and trekking groups. The garbage was carried by porters from the latrine project and several climbing expeditions to Skardu. Porters typically travel back down valley with empty packs after hauling loads up the Baltoro for trekkers and climbers. The Balti porters welcomed the opportunity to supplement their normal salaries with the incentives paid for transporting the garbage.

Continuing the porter training programs that they started in 1997, Mortenson and Bishop conducted several interactive sessions involving over 300 Baltis in the major valleys near K2. Emphasizing the mutual exchange of information and ideas, the porter training curriculum included:

1. Resource conservation considerations, including fuel and firewood management
2. First aid training and safety classes, including crevasse rescue
3. High-altitude disorders and preventative measures
4. Cultural comparisons of the different foreigners visiting the region
5. Discussions on hygiene and sanitation
6. Government regulations and ration allocations

The porters ultimately share this valuable information with others from their villages, benefiting the entire community. In 1999, Mortenson and Bishop plan to remove 10,000 more pounds of garbage and train 1,000 additional porters while continuing the latrine project. For more information, please contact:

Central Asia Institute
617 South Fifth Avenue
Bozeman, MT 59715
Tel 406-585-7841
Email:cai@gomontana.com

# KILIMANJARO, TANZANIA

Kilimanjaro, like other popular peaks around the world, has seen a dramatic increase in adventure tourists and their environmental impact. The campsites and trails to the top of this beautiful mountain have been littered with toilet paper, cigarette filters, and food wrappers. The Kilimanjaro National Park Administration (KINAPA) has made an unprecedented effort to haul trash off the mountain. They have organized regular clean-up crews and have stationed rangers at both Machame and Mweka gates to oversee campsite cleanliness. In addition, 17 toilets have been installed at different high-use areas. Despite these good efforts, KINAPA has been unable to keep up with the ever-increasing pressures.

Last year, Wesley Krause of African Environments, a Tanzanian tour company, received a grant from the Everest Environmental Project (EEP) to undertake the first international clean-up project on Kilimanjaro. Krause, with the support of Mr. Moriana, Senior Warden of the Park, conducted the project from March 26 to April 5, 1999. Park employees had already made considerable progress cleaning up and improving the Marangu route: a new trail from the gate to the summit is nearly complete, and the entire route has seen considerable reclamation. Therefore, all efforts were focused on the Shira, Machame, and the Mweka routes. Over 110 workers, including eight local guide services and members of the Everest Environmental Project, contributed to the clean-up efforts. The Kilimanjaro Park officials provided trucks, tools, and other logistical support. For nearly ten days, workers collected and carried out trash that had accumulated over the years. In addition, countless kilos of garbage were collected and burned on the mountain. The teams were able to remove two abandoned metal huts (weighing more than 1,440 kilograms), one broken toilet from a non-camping area (80 kilograms), and 908 kilograms of non-burnable rubbish.

During seminars held on the mountain, Park officials, guides, porters and volunteers discussed the problems they had seen on the mountain and focused on ways to solve them. The participants proposed that the future areas of focus should include:

1. Promote the incineration of all burnable garbage, and carry out all non-burnable trash
2. Minimize the use of firewood by properly outfitting guides and porters
3. Build more toilets in high-use areas for use by clients, guides and porters
4. Create new trails to reduce environmental impact
5. Request tour operators to educate tourists on environmental issues
6. Coordinate with KINAPA to improve garbage disposal and enforcing regulations
7. Assist local communities with development of recycling programs

The Kilimanjaro Clean-Up Project represents an ongoing effort to promote environmentally sustainable tourism on the mountain through the next millennium. Those who are interested in future Kilimanjaro clean-up efforts should contact:

Wesley Krause
P.O. Box 2125
Arusha, Tanzania
Tel: +255 57 8625/7285
Fax: +255 57 8625/8220
E-mail: Wkrause28@habari.co.tz

To submit information regarding international clean-up projects (planned or completed) please contact:

Brent Bishop
International Conservation Committee
5530 Stucky Road
Bozeman, MT 59715

# DOMESTIC CONSERVATION

# ALASKA

The AAC has jointly sponsored a "wise-use" project with the Mountaineering Club of Alaska (MCA). Ralph Tingey, Steve Davis, and Mark Miraglia, of the AAC Alaska Section, have coordinated the design of trailhead signs to be posted at various locations. The signs are provided to remind climbers (and the public) that many of the areas they enjoy in south-central

Alaska have the potential of being restricted if people aren't more cognizant of how their actions can affect the land owner or other users. The signs list a number of common sense "do's and don'ts" that should result in fewer climber/landowner conflicts, as well as demonstrate to the public that the climbing community is taking a proactive stance in addressing public concerns and land management issues. In addition to an AAC Conservation Committee grant, additional grants have also been received from the MCA and REI, Inc. The signs are currently being made and it is anticipated they will be available for posting in the spring of 1999.

## DENALI

Environmental issues, including trash left on the mountain and the improper disposal of fecal material, are still a large concern on Denali. Denali rangers report that since the climbing rules and regulations were published as booklets and translated into several languages (German, French, Spanish, Japanese, Korean, etc.) for foreign climbers, improvements have been made with trash removal and fecal disposal. However, there is still a small percentage of climbers who do not comply accordingly, and the park has taken steps to address the problem.

After a study last year to track the use and disposal of white fuel cans, changes have been made for the upcoming season. Fuel cans will be marked and signed out. Climbers must return the cans upon the completion of their climb. Teams with unaccounted cans will be fined $150. The same study found that the 11,000-foot camp received more days of use than previously thought. Increased pressure at this camp has resulted in the Park's decision to place semi-permanent toilets at the camp like the ones found at Kahiltna base and the 14,000-foot camp. Climbers who do not dispose of fecal material properly on the mountain will be fined $100.

## NORTHERN ROCKIES

The AAC made initial contacts with the U.S. Forest Service regarding a proposed trail restoration and improvement project in the Lone Peak Cirque area of the Wasatch Range. The AAC determined that the proposed trail restoration work is already included in the USFS Master Plan for the region. According to John Hendrix (USFS), the regional office in Ogden, Utah, has considered this project to be important for many years, but, in light of the difficulties in finding volunteers to work at altitude, has lacked the resources to organize a volunteer trail construction effort. AAC members Robert Price and Doug Colwell will begin the initial scouting efforts in the spring of 1999 with the USFS to better define the project limits and required work. The USFS has reported that they expect to be able to obtain a categorical exclusion from official assessment; however, public notification will be required before work can begin. The Conservation Committee will provide a grant to support printing, mailing, and organizational costs for the volunteer trail work. The regional forest supervisor is expected to supply necessary materials and tools for the volunteers. Work is anticipated to begin on this project sometime in the summer of 1999.

## SOUTH CENTRAL

The AAC sponsored a major trail restoration project at Enchanted Rock State Natural Area in Texas. The trail project addressed erosion and degradation of the hiking and climbing access trails in the Echo Canyon and Motorboat Rock areas of the park. Local Texas climbing organizations from Austin, Dallas, Houston, and San Antonio donated the proceeds from their annual Granite Gripper Climbing Competition to launch the project. The AAC Conservation Committee and the AAC South Central Section also provided a grant of $1,000 for the purchase of trail building materials. Imported trail building material (matching granite stone from nearby quarries) was required due to the Natural Area designation of the park. During the past year, nine separate volunteer trail building workdays were held with approximately 20 to 30 volunteers each day. The groups moved over 100 tons of rock using wheelbarrows and other manual means to build retaining walls along steep slopes in the Motorboat Rock area and backfill behind eroded tree roots. The trails and watercourse drainage along Echo Canyon were also improved. An additional $2,000 was secured from Exxon Corporation through employee-sponsored grants by AAC members Natalie Merrill and Paul Majers. Several Texas climbing clubs provided an additional $1,500 in donations. The money will be utilized in 1999 to purchase additional trail building materials and continue the trail restoration work.

In February, 1999, the AAC, Michael Lewis and Barry Wilson (organizers of the Enchanted Rock project) received the "Texas Trail Boss" award from the Texas Trails Symposium in Grapevine, Texas, in recognition for their hard work and organizational efforts. The Symposium was a three-day event sponsored by the Texas Parks and Wildlife Department, National Park Service and others. The award recognized the significance of the project and the contributions from these two volunteers.

To submit information regarding domestic clean-up projects (planned or completed), please contact:

Mike Lewis
Domestic Conservation Committee
10921 Hollow Ridge
San Antonio, TX 78254

# Climbs and Expeditions, 1998

*The north face of the Grand Teton.* GARDNER HEATON

Accounts from the various climbs and expeditions of the world are listed geographically from north to south and from west to east within the noted countries. In this year's volume, we start with activity previously unreported, misreported or underreported in these pages. We then cover activity in the Contiguous United States and move to Alaska in order for the climbs in the Alaskan Wrangell-St. Elias Mountains to segue into St. Elias climbs in Canada.

Unless noted otherwise, accounts cover activity in the 1998 calendar year (January 1-December 31). First-person accounts from winter 1998-'99 activity and shoulder-season areas (e.g., Patagonia) are included when possible. Climbers returning from the southern hemisphere can help us in future volumes by submitting accounts as soon as they return home. We encourage climbers to submit accounts of other notable activity from the various Greater Ranges to help us maintain complete records.

Appendices at the back of the book list addresses for expedition permits and regulations, conversions of meters to feet, and comparisons and explanations of the various ratings systems.

# PREVIOUSLY UNREPORTED

## CONTIGUOUS UNITED STATES

### UTAH

Canyonlands National Park

*Green River Area, The Warlock, Free Ascent.* This area is outside of Canyonlands National Park but approached via the Horsethief Trail road. In October, 1997, Marco Cornacchione and Bret Ruckman climbed the first free ascent of *Dude, That's Not Funny* on the Warlock, just north of and outside the Park in Hell Roaring Canyon. The crux involved a 5.12a offwidth. With the permission of the first ascensionists, Ruckman and Cornacchione drilled a fixed piton to allow careful removal of the loose blocks at the end of the second pitch and thus make this pitch safer, both for leading and for the hapless belayer underneath.

ERIC BJØRNSTADT

Zion National Park

*Angel's Landing, Swoop Gimp or Be Dust.* Previously unreported is *Swoop Gimp or Be Dust* (VI 5.10 A2+, ten pitches), located right of *Moonlight Buttress* and left of the *Wages of Sin/Forbidden Corner* area. The route was begun by Rick Donnelly and Andy Dannerback and finished by Barry Ward and Alan Humphreys.

ERIC BJØRNSTADT

ARIZONA

*Lost Coyote Tower, Ascent.* Previously unreported is the first ascent of Lost Coyote Tower (II A1 5.8) by Fred Beckey and Dave Pollari. The spire is located eight miles southeast of Rock Point, Arizona.

ERIC BJØRNSTADT

TEXAS

Big Bend National Park

*Boquillas Canyon, Campanile Boquillas.* In January, 1997, I soloed *Campanile Boquillas* (IV 5.10 A2), which ascends a 500-foot limestone tower on the right (Mexican) bank about one mile into the canyon. The route starts in a chimney on the left edge of the face that faces the river and then wanders up the center of the face to the summit with three points of aid. On the same trip, I soloed the *Left Rabbit Ear* (5.9) in the Rabbit Ears Spire from the notch.

JIM BEYER, *unaffiliated*

COLORADO

Rocky Mountain National Park

*Wild Basin Area, Various Ascents.* Bruce Miller and Clay Wadman climbed a new route, *Mil-Wad* (5.12), on Mt. Alice in 1994. Jim Bodenhamer and partner freed the old 5.9 A3 *Central Pillar* at 5.11c in 1997. Also in Wild Basin, Jeff Thornburg and partner climbed a two-pitch 5.12 route on the south face of Chiefshead in 1993. This was the first route established on this sunny face.

KATH PYKE, *United Kingdom*

*Longs Peak, Chasm View Wall.* On Chasm View Wall, in between *Red Wall* and *Directissima, Middle Ground* (5.11) was established by Chip Chase et al in 1996.

KATH PYKE, *United Kingdom*

ALASKA

*Alaska Range, Traverse, and Kahiltna Dome, North Ridge.* In March, 1997, Meg Perdue, Peter Yeomans, Greg Wolfgang and I traveled by dog sled from Denali National Park's north entrance to Wonder Lake with two musher friends who took the dogs back out and left us to complete a 210-mile north-to-south dog sled/ski traverse of the Alaska Range. We made the first recorded ascent of Kahiltna Dome's north ridge (twice) and descended the east ridge onto the Kahiltna to get flown out at the toe of the Kahiltna Glacier. We would have gone to the road, but the snow was a nightmare of mashed potatoes.

MIKE WOOD, *unaffiliated*

*Ned Lewis on the Royal Tower in 1994.* KRISTIAN SIELING

LITTLE SWITZERLAND

*Royal Tower, East Buttress, and The Throne.* In mid-June, 1994, Ned Lewis enticed me onto the Pica Glacier's Royal Tower with a beautiful picture of a 1,500-foot unclimbed rock buttress rising out of a smooth glacier. We spent five days hand-drilling bolts at the belays to the first nine pitches—the only bolts we placed. Unknowingly, we were within three pitches of reaching the top before we decided to descend.

Back on the Pica Glacier in the last week of June, 1997, Doug Munoz and I unloaded our gear from the plane only to spot two climbers on the initial pitches of the route we had flown in to finish. Trying to make the best of it, we headed over to the southeast flank of the Throne, another spectacular Little Switzerland peak just across from the Royal Tower. We skied almost to the pass between the Throne and the Ogres to begin climbing a large tongue of rock. We found fun, steep, 5.10 climbing on rock steps between snow bands. There are endless route combinations and we saw evidence of previous ascents in some areas. By mid-day we were on the summit with an easy descent ahead. When we returned to camp, all we could see of the climbers from earlier that day was a fixed rope on the first pitch of our intended Royal Tower route.

The next morning, a short ski, a mild bergschrund and we were on Royal Tower granite. After a relatively comfortable night on the ledge at the top of pitch six, we saw two climbers quickly scaling the route below us. Throughout the day they continued to gain on us. Finally, Doug and I finished the rock route just a few pitches above them. On the way down we met Mark Price and Craig Short from Bellingham, WA. Two days earlier they had climbed the first few pitches of the route, spotted the bolts, then decided to hit virgin territory on the Throne while the weather was still good. After our quick introduction, Mark and Craig finished the rock route and continued onto the snow above, where they were turned back by scary snow conditions. Doug and I probably climbed eight hours the first day and took about 20 hours to finish the rock face and descend the second day. Mark and Craig made a round trip—includ-

LEFT: *The east buttress of Royal Tower in Little Switzerland, showing* The Chase. KRISTIAN SIELING

ing their snow summit attempt—in about 24 hours. Doug and I saw no evidence of previous passage beside the bolts Ned and I had placed. We called the route *The Chase* (IV 5.10 A2).

KRISTIAN SIELING, *unaffiliated*

# CANADA

## NORTHWEST TERRITORIES

### LOGAN MOUNTAINS

*Vampire Peaks, The Vampire Spire, First Ascent.* During June, 1994, in the Vampire Peaks of the Northwest Territories, Jeff Hollenbaugh and I, accompanied by photographer Greg Epperson, climbed a granite spire that we dubbed the Vampire Spire. Our route, *The Infusion* (IV 5.11 modern A2+), was around 800 feet long on excellent alpine granite. The spire would offer several other excellent lines. We had hoped to do more, but we moved our camp once during the two-week trip, and had a bit of stormy weather as well. As far as I know, some of the mountains in the area had been climbed via mountaineering routes.

MIKE BENGE

### Cirque of the Unclimbables

*Mt. Proboscis, Spanish Variation, Second Ascent.* Over the first two weeks of July, 1997, and as part of the BBC television series "The Face," Nancy Feagin and I made the second ascent of the Spanish Variation to the 1963 route (McCarthy-Kor-Robbins-McCracken) on the Southeast Face of Mt. Proboscis in the Cirque of the Unclimbables. A full account of our trip is contained in *The Face*, published by BBC books and authored by Richard Else and Brian Hall. Note a mistake in the topo on p. 87: pitch 5 (shallow corner and crack) is 5.11c, not 5.10d as printed. Also note that Nancy was able to free the whole route, but due to time constraints associated with making a documentary, was only able to top rope the crux pitch (5.12a). Future aspirants will be pleased to know that we did considerable cleaning in the cracks. We recommend going later in August when it will be as dry as possible (we had immense problems with summit snow melt filling the cracks with cold running water). Overall, an absolutely grand time was had by one and all.

BARRY BLANCHARD, *UIAGM, ACC, CMC*

*Mt. Proboscis, Attempt.* It was reported that Spaniards Eduardo Martinez, Iñaki Fernández and Juan Vallejo attempted a new route on Mt. Proboscis. The trio managed 350 meters in 15 days; the climbing to their high point was A3. (*Desnivel* 146)

RIGHT: *The southeast face of Mt. Proboscis, showing the 1963 route. The Spanish Variation to the 1963 route (indicated with arrow) was (almost!) freed in 1997.* BARRY BLANCHARD

BAFFIN ISLAND

Auyuittuq National Park

*North Tower of Asgard, North Face, Nunavut.* From July 4 to 21, 1996, Txus Lizarraga, Raul Melero, Natxo Barriuso and I (all from Basque Country, Spain) put up the route *Nunavut* (VI 5.8 A4, 800m) on the north face of Asgard's North Tower. (See note in the 1997 *AAJ*, p. 210.) The route is between the Swiss Route and *Hyperborea*. It follows the obvious roof and dihedral in the middle of the wall. The beginning is situated in a flake; to continue, follow the wall until it reaches the roof. After the dihedral, continue up the wall to reach a system of cracks that leads to the summit. We climbed in capsule-style: one camp at the foot of the route and two camps in hammocks on the wall. We rappelled the route. We experienced 17 days of climbing and one of descent. We approached Asgard by helicopter; we returned by walking and rafting to the sea, making a descent of the Weasel River in the process.

MIGUEL BERAZALUCE, *Basque Country, Spain*

NORTH CASCADES

*Slesse Mountain, East Face.* Slesse Mountain (8,002') is a dark fang of granodiorite standing in a spectacular alpine environment. Dave Edgar and I were privileged to make the first ascent of the awesome east face in July, 1997. The route (VI 5.9+ A3+, 23 pitches) begins in the center of the face from the head of a pocket glacier and terminates at a notch just short of Slesse's summit. The climb required nine days, with each bivy requiring a portaledge. Twenty-three belay bolts and 30 rivets were placed. Free climbing shoes and a modern wall rack are required. An impressive moment occurred when we watched the pocket glacier beneath us rip out and run into the valley below. The climb is a little run out in places. There was some big excitement when Dave took a 50-foot tumbler. It was quite the show: a big scream, then yellow-and-red Gore-tex blending together as he bounced off a few ledges. The wild thing was his only pro for the last 30 feet—the piece that stopped him—was a short knifeblade in a diagonal seam that wasn't fully driven. It bent at a 70° angle. Luckily, it held.

SEAN EASTON, *Canada*

GREENLAND

*Tupilak East, New Route.* It was reported that in September, 1997, Kurt Albert, Stefan Glowacz and eight others put up a 700-meter route on the south face of Tupilak East (2264m) in the Tasermiut Fjord area of east Greenland. The 22-pitch route was climbed with maximum difficulties of F7a. Approach was made by kayak. (*Desnivel* 141)

*Ulamertorssuaq, Jacques Cousteau.* It was reported that in 1997, Spanish climbers Miquel Angel Gallego, José Luis Clavel, José Matas and José Seiquer put up *Jacques Cousteau* (F6c A4, 1000m) on the left side of Ulamertorssuaq's west summit. Further details are lacking. (*High Mountain Sports* 195)

# SOUTH AMERICA

## PERU

### CORDILLERA BLANCA

*Caraz II, South Face.* It was reported that, during the summer of 1997, Britons Al Coull, Mark Kendrick and Muir Morton established the *Superduper Couloir* (TD, ice/mixed 80-90°, 500m), a fairly direct central line on the south face of Caraz II (6020m) above the initial complicated icefall. It was the face's second route. (*High Mountain Sports* 189)

*Copa, Various Activity.* It was reported that French climbers were busy on Copa (6173m) in April and May, 1997. Gael Bouquet des Chaux first soloed the Southwest Pillar, a 400-meter rock climb (D+) that ends at P.5300m, in six hours on April 27. He then teamed up with S. Goriatchec and climbed the southwest ridge and south face of Copa on May 3, 1997. The 1300-meter route, which took the men 11 hours to climb and for which they proposed a name of *La Marguerite del l'Adjudant Chef*, finished on the summit ridge at ca. 5900 meters and was graded ED1. Bouquet des Chaux then teamed up with Gilles Grindler to climb a longer, independent line on the southwest pillar. *Top 93* (TD) was 600 meters long and finished on the "top" of P.5300m. Bouquet des Chaux then went on to solo the 400-meter pillar (D+, one section of F6a) right of the normal route's couloir the same day. On May 7, all three climbed the normal route to the main summit of the peak. (*High Mountain Sports* 189)

*Quebrada de Rurec, Via Monttrek.* It was reported that Spanish climbers Eloi Callado and César Pedrocchi established what was perhaps the first wall route in the canyon of the Quebrada de Rurec in the summer of 1997. Over 13 days, the two climbers put up *Via Monttrek* (F6c A4-, 750m). The area is also known as Catedrals de Rurec and described as having "awesome potential" for big rock routes. (*High Mountain Sports* 189)

*Huandoy Sur, Desmaison Route, Second Ascent.* We went to Peru between June and August, 1997, to climb Huandoy Sur's south face. At the start there were four of us on the project: Gerome Blanc-Gras, David Jonglez, Daniel Dulac and me. After 20 days of preparation, during which we fixed three pitches with the teams, Jerome and I continued alone.

We arrived in Huaraz on June 9; the team split on around June 29. The other two thought that climbing the south face would be impossible before their scheduled July 15 return to France. In total, the ascent took more than ten days. The first two days were spent fixing three pitches (we left a static rope fixed on the face and kept food and gear at the top), after which the team split. Then, with a lot of doubt about the outcome, Jerome and I climbed one more pitch in two days, but the weather was not very good. So we descended, returning to Huaraz on July 10 to say good-bye to our friends and get more food. We returned to the face equipped with more food. With the arrival of the full moon, the weather was fairly clear and we climbed for four days, climbing all the aid climbing in three more days and fixing all the static rope we had. When another storm arrived, we went back to Huaraz, using all 500 meters of fixed rope to descend the beautiful overhanging face into the foggy void of the storm. (There was a lot of ambiance in this part of the overhanging wall!)

After ascending the 500 meters of fixed rope (and bringing with us more food), we left the

*The south face of Huandoy Sur, showing A: French route (June 3-27, 1976); B: Italian route (June-July 6, 1976); C: Japanese route (June 24-July 22, 1976).* HENRY KENDALL

fixed ropes behind and continued climbing, bringing with us two 50-meter ropes, going alpine-style with portaledges. It took us four more days to finish the climb of Huandoy and attain the summit; the last part of the wall was less steep, and it was possible to free climb most of it. However, in certain parts it was still necessary to aid. This second part of the south face of Huandoy offers exceptional mixed climbing. In the final part of the wall, we climbed about 200 meters of original ground, using all methods possible and sleeping on our comfortable portaledges. We reached the summit in the afternoon of July 22, our friendship stronger between us.

On the descent, we found a way via the southwest ridge that was full of seracs, and the route finding proved difficult. But finally, we bivouacked near a col, sheltering ourselves beneath a serac, where we put the portaledge. The following day was difficult, but after serious doubts about route finding we arrived at our base camp before nightfall. We were happy to be on flat ground, and to contemplate what we had done.

We left five new bolts; there are a few old Desmaison bolts on the route. It is a wonderful and serious climb.

YANNICK GRAZIANI, *France*

*Yerupajá, South Face, Ascent.* It was reported that in 1997, an Austrian team climbed the south face of Yerupajá (6634m) to the south summit on what may have been a new route. Further details are lacking. (*High Mountain Sports* 189)

*Trapecio, South Face.* It was reported that in 1997, Francois Baroux, Frédéric Bréhé, Pierre Plaze and Christophe Vigne climbed a line on the south face of Trapecio (5653m) that followed the prominent twisting couloir to the left of the Lowe Route to reach the southwest ridge. The climbing above was deemed too dangerous to continue, at which point 11 rappels were made to regain the ground. The climbing encountered was given a grade of TD+. (*High Mountain Sports* 189)

# BOLIVIA

*Condoriri Region, Various Ascents.* While visiting the Condoriri region in July, 1995, I "enchained" two peaks, climbing them back-to-back to make one long route. From our 15,000-foot Base Camp above Lago Condoriri, I first climbed Cerro Condoriri (18,600') by its southwest ridge in two hours six minutes and returned to Base Camp in an hour. Then I climbed Piqueno Alpamayo (17,640') by its southwest ridge in two hours seven minutes and ran back to BC for a total time of six hours 50 minutes for both peaks. These are both quite moderate routes where an ice ax and a ski pole suffice for the climbing.

MARK F. TWIGHT, *Groupe de la Haute Montagne*

*Cordillera Real, Various Ascents.* In June and July, 1996, Scott Backes, Ed Pope, Betty Roberts and I visited the Cordillera Real. We first traveled to the Jhanko Kota region, where we made a quick ascent of Cerro Wila Llojeta (5244m). I then soloed a fourth-class route on the south side of Pt. 5458m. The next day, Backes and I climbed a new five-pitch route up the northeast face of a subsidiary summit of Cerro Wila Lloje (17,400'). The route, *And Justice is Served*, featured two "real" pitches on perfect granite—5.9 and 5.10b respectively—followed by moderate climbing to the summit.

Pope and I then climbed a new four-pitch waterfall route, *Judgment Day* (WI4), on the southwest side of Cerro Waja Apacheta (it does not go to the summit). Rarely getting any sun, the ice was so hard I stripped the hangers off two titanium ice screws.

Pope and Roberts returned to the States, while Backes and I made our way to the east side of the Ancohuma-Illampu Massif. We made Base Camp at Laguna Negra (15,300'). Backes came down with amoebic dysentery so I went soloing, first climbing *Merciful Release*, a new 1,200-foot route (D-) on the northeast face of Viluyo Ancohuma (18,200') that had sustained 45-50° ice, in four-and-a-half hours round-trip from BC. I then climbed Jhankopiti (19,300') by the northeast ridge in an easy afternoon.

The return of Scott's health coincided with three days of snowfall. Despite the weather, on the third day of storm he insisted we move up to a bivouac at 17,000 feet below Illampu and Pico del Norte.

The following day we rested while spindrift ran and a strong high-pressure system moved in. On July 13, we went for it. Backes opted for a fanny pack while I simply stuffed my pockets with a hat, gloves, GU, and a pint and a half of Cytomax. We each carried two ice tools, one collapsible ski pole, the waistbelt to our harness and one carabiner each. We left the bivy at 11 a.m. and stepped onto the summit of Pico del Norte (19,800') at 3:08 p.m. after having simul-soloed a new route we graded TD. The route shares the normal line on the south side to the col between Pico del Norte and Gorro del Hielo; the final 1,400 feet are independent and feature difficult, but reasonable mixed climbing. Short, fierce mixed climbing cruxes were interspersed with sections of 50-55° névé. After reaching the summit, we down climbed the east ridge, raced under the seracs below the Gorro del Hielo and ran back to the bivy, arriving after six hours and 15 minutes on the go.

We named the route *Fuck 'Em, They're all Posers Anyway.* It's our comment on the sport-climbing, alpinist wanna-bes whose paper-thin résumés pretend to confer on them the right to suck the life and spirit out of alpinism, replacing its soul with high number grades and pre-rehearsed routes, "Hot Flashes," power drills and contracts. These climbers might prefer the definition of "alpinism" be expanded to include whatever it is they choose to do, but alpinism is a very specific type of climbing. Alpinism defines mountain climbing reduced to its purest essence. Carrying a minimum of equipment on their backs, climbers move quickly and autonomously in a single push. Alpinism means attempting to climb mountains on the most equitable footing possible, neither applying technology to overcome deficits in skill or courage, nor using permanently damaging tactics, and adhering to this ethos from beginning to end.

MARK F. TWIGHT, *Groupe de la Haute Montagne*

*Chaupi Orco Area, Various Ascents.* A 19-strong German Alpine Club Youth expedition (JDAV), accompanied by Bolivian guide Aldo Riveros, made a number of first ascents and new routes in the Chaupi Orco area from August 14-20, 1995. On the ridge to the northeast of Chaupi Orco (peaks listed left to right as you see them from the glacier below Chaupi Orco): a new route on Hanako (5720m) via the southwest face (max. 60°, 200m); the first ascent of Tunto Potosí (5500m) via the southwest face (max. 70°, 220m; descent was made to the south along the ridge toward Ramatoc, then directly to the glacier from the lowest point on the ridge); a new route on Ramatoc (5550m); the first ascent of Sabe (5600m) via the southwest face (max. 80°, 200m; descent was made along the ridge north to Mato and then directly to the glacier); a new route on Chaupi Orco (6044m, which they named Chaupi Orco Sur and gave a height of 6088m) by going west up and over the ridge running southeast of Chaupi Orco to set up a high camp at 5700 meters and then climbing from the south; and a new route on Chaupi Orco Norte (6000m) via the east face (max. 60°, 500m). The expedition produced a detailed report in German with excellent topo shots.

YOSSI BRAIN, *United Kingdom*

*Northern Apolobamba, Various Ascents.* A German expedition from Forchheim, with Bolivian guide Aldo Riveros, made a number of first ascents in the northern Apolobamba in

1997. They established a base camp at 4600 meters on August 19 to the east of Paso Lusuni, which lies to the north of the Chaupi Orco area. On August 24, the first of two parties set off and climbed Pt. 5400m immediately to the south of Paso Lusuni and continued south to put in a high camp at 5330 meters. The next day, they continued south along the ridge and crossed Pt. 5830 (called Angelicum and first climbed by an Italian expedition in 1958) to reach Chaupi Orco Norte. A second party followed the same route one day later. After establishing a second high camp to the north of base camp at 5200 meters, they climbed Pts. 5150, 5285, 5220, 5350 and 5300 from August 27-31, 1997—all first ascents. These peaks lie on the ridge running north of Paso Lusuni, which marks the Bolivia-Peru border. They then returned to Base Camp and on September 1-2, 1997, climbed Pts. 5500, 5070 and 5050, lying to the south of Base Camp and also first ascents. German members of the expedition were Klaus Köberle, Franz Kraft, Alexandra Langer, Ralf Meßbacher, Matthias Schaffland, Angelika Schmidl, Barbara Schübel, Michael Taumann and Hendrik Wagenseil. They produced an excellent expedition report in German.

YOSSI BRAIN, *United Kingdom*

*Huayna Potosí, East Face.* On August 19, 1997, in a 17-hour round trip, Marcos Barlena (Chile) and Eric Winandy (Belgium) climbed a route to the right of the classic *Vía de los Franceses*, staying below the southeast ridge of Huayna Potosí's Pico Sur. They climbed an ice section (55°) to reach a IV-V rock section that brought them to a 55-60° névé section. A second rock band (IV) brought them to the 50-55° snow ridge to the right (east) of Huayna Potosí's South Peak. Descent was made to the north and then down to the normal route.

The Chilean-Belgian route follows a line below the Bordas-Muñoz route, which joins the southeast ridge in the middle, before the rock section.

YOSSI BRAIN, *United Kingdom*

CONDORIRI GROUP

*Cabeza de Condor, New Route.* In August, 1996, Erik Monasterio (Bolivia/New Zealand) and Jared Ogden (U.S.) climbed a new route on Cabeza de Condor (a.k.a. Condoriri, Gran Condoriri, 5648m). Starting at the easternmost part of the face, the pair climbed directly up (max. 60°) over unstable snow through a series of extremely unstable rock bands that resembled loosely stacked dinner plates.

YOSSI BRAIN, *United Kingdom*

*Huallomen, Clarification.* The new route on Huallomen (a.k.a. Wyoming, ca. 5380m) claimed in good faith by Marcello Sanguineti and Alessandro Bianchi (see 1998 *AAJ*, p. 264) was in fact a variation: Britons Steve Richardson and Angus Ridge climbed the route (IV, max. 80°) July 31, 1997, and wrote a brief description in the Club Andino Boliviano's new routes book. The Italians climbed the route August 18, 1997, and wrote a detailed description. The British route finished direct, while the Italian route finished to the left.

YOSSI BRAIN, *United Kingdom*

SOUTHERN CORDILLERA REAL

*Tiquimani, New Route.* In August, 1997, Spaniard Pere Vilarasau soloed the imposing Tiquimani in an impressive five hours round-trip. The 5519-meter mountain northeast of Huayna Potosí (misnamed Cerro Illampu on the IGM maps) has seen few ascents in recent years due to increasingly thin conditions. From a camp ten minutes from the face, Vilarasau climbed 50° scree to a 100-meter mixed (V 80-90°) section to reach a 50°, then 70-80° section to the col on the ridge. He then followed the ridge to the summit with one abseil before the last 100 meters (III) up to the summit. He descended the same route. The snow and ice were good, but the rock was very poor.

YOSSI BRAIN, *United Kingdom*

# CHILE

CENTRAL ANDES

*Tupungato, South Face.* It was reported that on January 6, 1997, Christiane Herrmann, Olaf Hollik and Frank Kostrovn climbed the south face of Tupungato (ca. 6550m), a popular high volcano in the Central Andes. The line (40-50° snow) may or may not have been new. (*High Mountain Sports* 190)

*Cerro Giobbi and Cerro Centinela, First Ascents.* I decided to take a sabbatical to guide young climbers to unexplored mountain ranges and to give them, in practical terms, some of the climbing forces that drove us in the 1960s.

In January, 1997, we went with the climbers of the Club Alpinista Paulista (Brazil) to southern Chile. The chosen range was located close to an unknown and never-visited fjord 100 miles southeast of Puerto Eden, a village on Wellington Island. Base Camp was destroyed twice by big waves and icebergs coming from a huge icefall half a mile away. Some of us had to sail back to a nearby, more protected shore to fix the damage to the boat's hull made by the ice.

In spite of the weather conditions, we succeeded in climbing, alpine-style, two virgin summits: Cerro Giobbi (1650m), located at 49° 57' 36" S and 73° 49' 27" W, and Cerro Centinela (1450m), located at 49° 57' 22" S and 73° 49' 48" W. Both of them rise straight up from sea level. Centinela was climbed on January 27, 1997, and Giobbi on February 3.

The area is impressive for its climbing potential, weather conditions, glacial activity and difficult access and retreat. We were also able to locate Cerro Gariota (ca. 2600m), a fantastic unclimbed rock and ice pyramid north of Penguin Fjord.

After the climbs, we began to pull out from the area, but were locked in by 15 miles of icepack. After getting ashore and reinforcing the hull with wood, anchor and old tires, we spent two days pushing against the ice to reach the Icy Channel. Sailing north, we arrived at Puerto Eden days later.

CARLOS COMESAÑA, *Brazil*

ARGENTINE PATAGONIA

*Argentine Patagonia, Various Ascents, and Second Ascent of Condorito.* (This account complements the brief notes in last year's volume, pp. 281-2.) On January 29, 1998, Michael Richter and I climbed Guillaumet via the Col de Droite. On February 4, Jack Tigle (Scotland) and I climbed the Aguja de la Silla via the Brecha de los Italianos (normal route, 5.9). The route starts from the same point as the American route on Fitz Roy. On February 8, Jack Tigle and I climbed Poincenot via the Whillans route. Ten other teams climbed this route in February. In February, Jack Tigle and I climbed Fitz Roy via the Franco-Argentine route (5.10.+). The conditions were perfect, so we managed to climb every pitch of the route free. Starting at Paso Superior (high camp) at 2 a.m., we reached the top at 7 p.m. and were back at Paso Superior at 3:30 a.m. the next day. I needed five attempts to reach the top.

On February 18, I climbed Aguja Saint Exupery via *Condorito* with Rainer Treppte. It was the route's second ascent. The route has 101 (!) bolts, including two bolts at every belay. The first eight pitches are perfect, involving steep cracks of every size, then two pitches of free/A1/A2, then four pitches of flakes/cracks.

On February 24, Frank K. (Belgium) and I attempted the Casarotto Pillar on Fitz Roy via the Kearney-Naight route. We made it up to rock pitch 8. After climbing the 400-meter couloir, we slept for two hours. The morning started with clouds and at 11 a.m. the top of Fitz Roy was covered in clouds and storms started again. February 23 was the last good weather day of the season.

JENS RICHTER, *Germany*

# ANTARCTICA

*Antarctic Peninsula, Various Ascents.* It was reported that in February, 1997, Greg Mortimer led an Australian team that made a number of ascents from their boat, *Professor Molchanov*. The team climbed the central peak of Ronge Island; a 600-meter peak on the south side of Seaplane Point in Curtis Bay; and another ca. 600-meter peak, "Mt. Dan Roberts," at the southeastern end of Lemaire Island. No further details are available, though the ascents were believed to be straight-forward. (*High Mountain Sports* 190)

*Mt. Shinn, Northeast Face.* It was reported that Ralph Dujmovits led a four-member team that made the first ascent of the easy northeast face of Mt. Shinn (4557m) in December, 1995. They then climbed the southeast flank (50°) of Mt. Avalanche (3950m), the south ridge (I/II, 50°) of Mt. Jumper (2890m), and the North (2450m) and South (2400m) summits of Mt. Bearskin. (*High Mountain Sports* 190)

# AFRICA

# MALI

*Hombori Tondo, General Overview.* Le Main de Fatima is the best-known feature of the many huge sandstone "mesas" that populate the arid interior of Mali. Much of the development of the five colossal weathered sandstone towers, which rise up to 600 meters from base to summit, has been under the influence of Spaniard Salvador Campillo, who first visited the area in 1978, returned to climb his first route (solo) in 1982, and in 1988 married a local woman from the village of Daari very close to the towers' base. The couple now splits time between Mali during the winter (the climbable months in the area are November to February) and Spain during the summer. Campillo has gained the trust and respect of the indigenous peoples and remains the sole person able to negotiate access to the various cliffs of the area with the village chiefs on whose land they lie. It should be noted that it is customary to bring gifts for the village chiefs in exchange for permission to climb on the formations.

Teams from both France and Spain visited the Hombori Mountains in the winter of 1995-'96 and again in '96-'97, creating a number of new routes. A large group of Spanish climbers in the company of Campillo put up a number of routes in the region of Le Main de Fatima the first winter. On Kaga Tondo, these included *Complicado Burocratico* (F5, 250m), and *Primera Instancia* (7c+, 200m) on the walls immediately right of the big couloir separating the east faces of Kaga Pamari and Kaga Tondo. On Suri Tondo, routes included *Con la Izquierda Cuesta Más* (6c+ A3+, 500m), *Txatxaponk* (6c+, 470m), a route that follows a series of cracks and corners on the east pillar, and *Verga Dura* (6c+, 400m). On the Grimari Dagana Massif, above the village of Grimari Dagana, the towers of the Wambe Ballo are an area of extensive area of rock with potential for great number of new, if somewhat shorter, climbs. Routes established included *Pilla que Vomito* (6b, 220m); *Monica* (5c, 130m); and *Nouvel An* (5c, 130m) on the Bicéphale Tower. (*High Mountain Sports* 184)

*Kaga Tondo, Solucao Suicida.* Various Ascents. It was reported that from June 6-13, three Brazilians (Márcio Bruno, Eliseu Frechou and Sérgio Tartari) put up the 550-meter *Solucao Suicida* on the east face of Kaga Tondo. It is believed that this is the first big climb to be put up in the Hombori Mountains in the middle of the African summer. The ascensionists spent six days on the wall in temperatures up to 50°C, drinking six liters of water per day. (*High Mountain Sports* 184)

*Le Main de Fatima, Various Ascents.* It was reported that the British team of Grant Farquar, Louise Thomas and Mike "Twid" Turner established the 450-meter *Grains of Time* (British E4 5c) on the north face of the north tower of Suri Tondo in January, 1997, over three days. The three climbed a number of established routes in Le Main de Fatima massif during their stay, including three routes on Kaga Tondo—the North Pillar (F5c, 600m) via a Spanish variant up the east face; *Turismo Alternativo* (7b+ A0, 170m) and *Vuelva Usted Mañana* (6a+ A2, 260m) on the south-facing fin that forms the edge of Kaga Tondo; and *Macumba Circus* (7b+, 150m) on Kaga Pamari.

On the Grimari Dagana Massif, Farquar and Ray Wood and Ed Douglas put up the four-pitch *Wild Turkey* (6b, 140m) on the right-hand tower of two towers called The Twins, while Thomas, Turner and Salvador Campillo established *Chicken Head* (6b, 130m) on the left-hand tower. Both routes were the first ascents of the respective formations. (*High Mountain Sports* 184)

# INDIA

## LADAKH

*Kang Yazé, Free Tibet.* It was reported that in the summer of 1997, Pedro Rodriguez and Javier Perandones put up the 1000-meter snow and ice route *Free Tibet* on Kang Yazé (6404m). The initial 200 meters of the route were 45-50°; the final 800 meters averaged 70°. (*Desnivel* 143)

*Meru, Attempt.* It was reported that Nick Bullock, Julian Cartwright, Jamie Fisher and Owain Jones (all U.K.) attempted the east face of the Central Summit (ca. 6500m) of Meru in September, 1997. They were plagued by bad weather, but managed to make two attempts. The first brought them over Scottish 5 terrain to a bivy at the start of the steep granite ridge. They fixed 60 meters of rope up the ridge crest the next day before a storm forced a retreat. Jones opted out of the next attempt, which saw the team regain their bivouac site. One of Cartwright's crampons snapped en route, but they carried on the next day, nearly reaching the second bivy before Cartwright's other crampon snapped as well. Undaunted, Bullock and Cartwright fixed ropes the next day on the granite ridge to the point where it merges into the steep upper fin. From there, they moved across steep snow to an ice corner. The next day, Fisher led a hard ice pitch into the corner before it began to snow. The three bivied at ca. 6150 meters next to the fin. The next morning, Cartwright was moving across the fixed rope to the corner when one of the anchors pulled, sending him for a 12-meter fall. The three then decided to retreat. (*High Mountain Sports* 187)

*Kedar Dome, East Face, The Sunrise Pillar.* It was reported that Polish climbers Janusz Golab and two friends repeated Martin Moran's 1984 route *The Sunrise Pillar* on the east face of Kedar Dome. The team spent five days on the route before topping out on the top of the pillar (5760m) on September 20, 1997. (*High Mountain Sports* 187)

*Srikanta, North Ridge.* It was reported that in September, 1997, an all-woman's team from Uttarkashi climbed Srikanta (6133m), the western-most peak in the Gangotri, via the north ridge. Nari Dhami, Suman Kutiyal, Lata Joshi and Radha Rana summited on September 27 after setting up three camps on the mountain. This was the first time the seldom-visited peak has been climbed since 1984. (*High Mountain Sports* 187)

*Suitilla, Attempt.* It was reported that a five-member team from Bombay attempted the "Peak of Needles," unclimbed Suitilla (6373m), via the southwest face/southwest rib in 1997. The approach took nearly three times as long as normal (14 days) due to bad weather, landslides and porter problems. Base Camp was set up on September 14 on the Yangchar Glacier; ABC was placed below the southern icefall. The team then spent six days pushing a line through the complex, 600-meter face to reach the rib. The high point of 5800 meters on the rib was reached in heavy snow before the expedition was called off. (*High Mountain Sports* 187)

*Gepang Goh, Southeast Flanks.* It was reported that an Indian Army team climbed a new route on Gepang Goh in July, 1997, via its southeast flanks. They gave the peak an altitude of 6088 meters; in the past, it has been given 5870 meters. (*High Mountain Sports* 187)

*Gya, Mistaken Attempt, and Other Ascents.* It was reported that three expeditions attempted this unclimbed peak in 1997. In April, Arum Samant led a three-man team (Anil Chavan and Vinod Bodh) from Bombay that also included High-Altitude Porters Pasang and Prakash Bodh. Base Camp was reached in near-winter conditions before the climbers embarked on a route that Samant, Pasang and Prakash Bodh and Dhanajay Ingalkar had tried in 1996 up the east face of the south-southwest spur. The 1997 team veered right on prominent snow ramps to a col at the foot of the southeast ridge. Gya's final crest looked too difficult, so Pasang and Prakash Bodh and Arum Samant turned right and climbed the previously virgin Gya East (6680m) instead.

The team descended to BC, where members broke into small groups to make the first ascents of Drisa (6275m), Cheama (6230m) and Namkha Ding (5665m).

Yousuf Zaheer, who had tried Gya twice before including its first serious attempt, returned in July to make another attempt on the west pillar, this time with Chaman Singh. They were forced to retreat, then moved north, where they established three camps on the west spur, which leads to the second summit north of Gya. From their third camp, they moved right to the northeast ridge, reaching Gya's subsidiary summit (6520m), which they called Gya North. Time constraints prevented them from continuing on to the main summit.

In August, the Principal of the Himalayan Mountaineering Institute in Darjeeling led an expedition comprising members from seven Asian countries that included many strong Indian climbers. They attempted two lines simultaneously: the west spur and the north ridge. The technical terrain was extensively fixed in achieving the summit, which 32 climbers reached. Problematically, when authorities reviewed photos of the ascent, it was determined that the team had climbed Gyasumpa, a peak very close to where Zaheer's team had placed their Camp III a month earlier. Zaheer and company had navigated the same terrain with relative ease. (*High Mountain Sports* 187)

*Kula, First Ascent.* It was reported that Kula (a.k.a. Chalung, 6546m) was climbed for the first time by a 11-member Japanese expedition led by Tsunso Suziki. The team ascended the northwest ridge; eight climbers reached the summit on July 11, 1997, followed by three more on the 13th and another eight (apparently with some repeat summiters) on the 15th. (*High Mountain Sports* 187)

*Pologongka, First Ascent.* It was reported that Britons Mike Ratty, Richard Law and Trevor Willis, plus their LO, Narindar Chakula, made the first ascent of Pologongka in August, 1997.

*Hainablak East Tower, with the line of attempt indicated (see account on following page).*
THOMAS TIVADAR

Ratty had been granted permission for the peak in 1995 only to have it rescinded at the last minute. In 1997, the team first attempted the south face of Chakula, a day's walk from the road, via its south face, reaching a height of 6000 meters before being turned back by soft snow. The expedition then moved its ABC below Pologongka, from where Law, Ratty and Singh climbed the southwest buttress in a day on August 21 at Alpine F. (*High Mountain Sports* 187)

# PAKISTAN

*Hainablak East Tower, Attempt.* (This account clarifies an inaccurate report from last year's volume; see 1998 *AAJ*, pp. 321-322.) On our three-man, four-week Karakoram big wall expedition, we attempted the unclimbed 1400-meter northeast face of Hainablak East Tower (ca. 5800m). We were very early in the season, and had a lot of bad weather (with only four really nice days). We also ran out of our time. We climbed 21 pitches between June 3 and 21, 1997, in capsule style. The climbing to that point was 5.10 A4. (See photo on preceding page.)

THOMAS TIVADAR, *Germany*

Looking down Hatija *("strong-willed")* at Louise Thomas and Glenda Huxter from 1,800 feet up Beatrice. KATH PYKE

Hushe Region

*Beatrice, Southeast Face.* In last year's volume (p. 327), the two 1997 British routes on Beatrice were reported. We now have the opportunity to show the lines of ascent (see photos, left and right).

*Ghulam Tower, Giorgio Lorenzo.* It was reported that the four-man team of Riccardo Milani, Adriano Selva, Andrea Spandri and Natale Villa made the first ascent of the Ghulam Tower (4720m), a rock spire on the west bank of the Gondokoro Glacier that is more or less opposite Balti and Cholon peaks. The ca. 15-pitch route, *Giorgio Lorenzo* (TD+, 650m), roughly followed the left edge of the face overlooking the glacier; difficulties

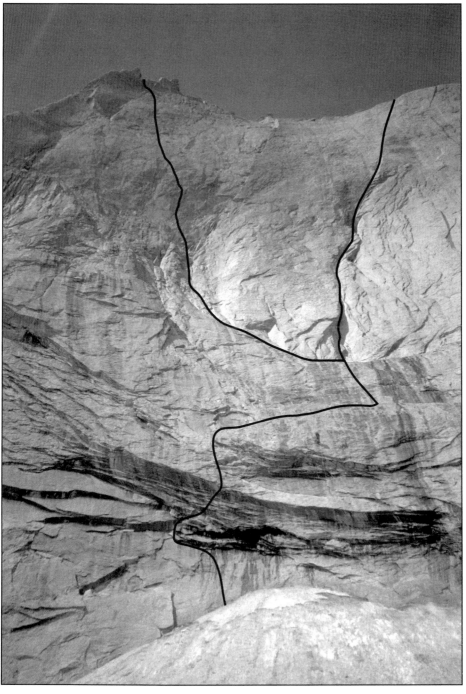

*Beatrice (ca. 5900m) in the Charakusa area, Pakistan Karakoram. The women's route*, Hatija *(VI E3 6a A3+, 20 pitches) is to the left, the men's,* The Excellent Adventure *(VI E3 6a A3+, 20 pitches), to the right.* GRANT FARAQUAR

were reasonable yet sustained (V to VI) on excellent granite. The crux pitch entailed VII climbing and A3 hooking. No bolts were placed on the route. (*High Mountain Sports* 188)

## COMMONWEALTH OF INDEPENDENT STATES

*Khan Tengri, Attempt, Tragedy, and New Route.* It was reported that Yuri Krasnoukhov was attempting the standard route on Khan Tengri in mid-August, 1997, and while climbing from the CIII ice cave to the summit fell down the south flank and died. D. Komarov and V. Shamalo climbed up on August 17 to locate the body via the Southwest Face. They found Krasnoukhov's body, then continued on to the summit via a new route. The crux proved to be steep slabs on the upper part of the route, which was graded 5B. The climb placed third in the Russian championships. (*High Mountain Sports* 188)

## TIBET

### CHOLA SHAN

*Chola Shan Range, Various Ascents.* In July and August, 1997, Joanne Jeske and I traveled widely throughout Kham, the old eastern province of Tibet. With the exception of Minya Konka and vicinity, this region has largely been neglected by climbers, despite the fact that it is one of the most mountainous areas of Asia.

Traveling by local buses, we arrived in the town of Dege in early August. Here we stocked

*The northwest face of Chola Shan I. Solid line indicates ascent route. Dotted line indicates hidden finish to summit and descent.* CHARLIE FOWLER

up on food and fuel, then backtracked eastward along the main highway from Lhasa to Chengdu to the sacred lake of Lhamcoka. This pristine lake is situated below the main peaks of the 100-kilometer-long Chola Shan. The highest peak of the range (6168m) was climbed by a large expedition of Chinese and Japanese mountaineers in 1988 from a base camp at the south end of the lake.

Joanne and I approached differently, hiking up a steep valley about four kilometers to the west of the lake. We established a base camp (5000m) at the toe of a glacier plateau, directly below the second highest peak of the range, Chola Shan II (6119m). Starting in the middle of the night and climbing alone, I made a rapid ascent of this peak, arriving at the summit at sunrise. The route was mostly non-technical; I wandered up the broad glacier and onto the southeast ridge, which was followed to the top. I returned via the same route. This was perhaps the first ascent of the peak. I also got a good look at the northwest face of the highest peak, Chola Shan I, from the top. This was to be my next objective.

After some rest and a recon with Joanne, I again set off alone and at night for Chola Shan I. The bottom third of the route was a 45° snow and ice slope that led to the main business of the route, a wide gully winding to the south face. Conditions were excellent and I made good progress, overcoming sections of 80° ice and wandering a bit to avoid mixed sections. Firm snow on the south face led to the summit, which I reached in the early morning. After leaving a few prayer flags, I descended the north face/ridge, which proved to be more difficult and time-consuming than the climb. It would have been better to just descend the route! Overall, the route was a classic snow and ice outing, of modest scale (800m from glacier to summit) and moderate difficulty. There are many other fine rock and alpine routes in this area.

CHARLIE FOWLER, *unaffiliated*

QIONGLAI SHAN

*Qionglai Range, Various Ascents.* In late August, 1997, I returned to the Siguniang Shan area of the Qionglai Range, on the eastern edge of the Tibetan Plateau. I had previously visited and climbed in this area (see 1996 *AAJ*, p. 310). Accompanied by Joanne Jeske, I hiked up the Changping Valley and revisited a base camp I had used in 1994. Then, I had climbed two of three peaks in a group north of the main Siguniang massif. On this occasion I made a solo ascent of the third peak, via the south ridge, which was mostly rock scrambling. This peak, at about 5700 meters, appears to be the highest of the three. I descended the same way. In the future this whole area should become very popular with climbers, as there are unlimited possibilities for rock and alpine routes on fairly low-altitude peaks, and with very easy access from the city of Chengdu. Indeed, many routes have now been done here.

CHARLIE FOWLER, *unaffiliated*

*Gurla Range, Ascents and Other Activity.* Our team consisted of Tom Simons, Quinn Simons, Soren Peters and myself as guide. Our main objective was Gurla Mondata (7700m), the third-highest peak in Tibet, located in the west near the frontier with India and Nepal.

We flew to Lhasa in early September, 1997, where we spent a week making preparations and sightseeing. We did several hikes to acclimate, including an ascent of the sacred Gephel Ri (17,000+') above Drepung Monastery. In addition, we left Lhasa with a staff of Tibetans

*Tom Simons, Quinn Simons and Soren Peters on the 6900-meter Guna La. Behind them are the north and east aspects of Gurla Mondata, and the 6900-meter peak the team had climbed previously to Gurla Mondata's north. Solid line indicates ascent route; dotted line indicates the fall.* CHARLIE FOWLER

appointed by the Tibet Mountaineering Association: a liaison officer who couldn't wait to get us home, an interpreter who couldn't speak English, and three drivers. We also hired Kwang Tamang, a climber from Nepal, as our cook.

We spent a week on the road from Lhasa to Darchen, the town below Mt. Kailash. Here, the police were less than accommodating. They now charge foreigners a fee to do the sacred walk around the holy mountain, and were turning away poor pilgrims from India and Nepal who could not afford it. In addition, they told us our permit was no good, that we could only spend two days there, that we had to hire yaks and stay in guest houses at hugely inflated rates and generally pay them more money. I refused all of their demands.

While our staff stayed at Darchen, the four of us did the circuit around Mt. Kailash in five days. After crossing the Drolma La (18,600'), we took a detour and climbed a 6000-meter peak immediately east of Mt. Kailash. This peak was just south of another 6000-meter peak I had climbed in 1994 with Paula Quenomoen (1996 *AAJ*, p. 319). Back in Darchen, we met some Swiss climbers who were working in the area. They had climbed several peaks in the area as well. It should be noted that although Tibetans normally climb sacred mountains, there is a strong feeling among Tibetan climbers, pilgrims and even the TMA that people should not climb Mt. Kailash. Climbers, widespread disrespect for local peoples, cultures and environments are often cited as reasons for the ban. In the past, however, the Chinese government has issued permits for Mt. Kailash, and they certainly haven't stopped collecting money from climbers who trash other sacred peaks, such as Mt. Everest.

From Darchen, it was a short drive to the Gurla range. We established Base Camp (4700m) on the banks of the Gurla Chu, just northwest of the main peak. Over the course of several days, the four of us made an Advanced Base Camp at 5700 meters, then a high camp at 6200 meters, directly below Gurla Mondata's north face.

Directly north of Gurla Mondata is another peak; at 6900+ meters, it is certainly one of the highest peaks in west Tibet, yet overshadowed by the massif's bulk to its south. We climbed this peak in three days round-trip from ABC. The first day we climbed gullies on the south face to reach the west ridge, which we climbed to 6300 meters. The next day we continued up the ridge to the summit, then returned to our bivy. On the third day we descended to ABC. It was an easy but exposed route; the main difficulties were breaking trail in crusty snow.

To the northeast of Gurla Mondata is Guna La, an even finer peak, also quite high (6900m). This we did next. From our high camp, we climbed over a pass and down to a huge glacial plateau, which we crossed, then made camp at the base of the peak. Feeling fit and acclimated, we got up in the middle of the night, climbed the southwest ridge to the summit and back to camp in a single push. We had a perfect day on a beautiful route, with some exposure and only moderate difficulties. We also got a good look at Gurla Mondata that enabled us to pick out a route.

We descended to Base Camp for several days of rest. Tom had decided not to join us on this climb, but when we headed back up the hill he came along to high camp with us to carry down gear we wouldn't be taking higher up. Quinn, Soren and I began the climb by crossing the glacier from high camp and heading directly up the great white slope of Gurla Mondata's north face. Wind and snow forced an early bivy under a serac at 6500 meters. The next day was clear, though, and we headed up. Alternating the lead often, we climbed slowly but steadily through the night until the next morning. We rested for a long while, then continued on to a bivy spot at 7500 meters, 100 meters below the summit plateau. Quinn was slowing a bit, so we took a rest day here, with the intention of then blasting to the summit and down the long but easy west ridge, which would dump us at Base Camp. Quinn improved somewhat, but the weather didn't: high winds and blowing snow kept us at camp another day. The wind turned out to be a blessing after all—it blew away a lot of loose snow, and when it died, conditions were better than ever.

Soren led, belaying just below the summit ridge. While he belayed Quinn, I went on ahead toward the top. Unfortunately, Quinn got frostbite on his hands and could not complete the pitch. I descended to Quinn and Soren lowered us both back to our bivy. The next day we began the descent of the route we had just climbed. Descending the route was easier than anticipated, and with Quinn in the lead we made rapid progress.

At about 6800 meters, though, things went wrong—someone fell, then we all fell roped together. We slid down the steep slope, then launched over a giant serac, falling over 300 feet through the air. One thousand five hundred feet after it began, we cratered. Soren and Quinn were dazed but unhurt in the fall, but I wrenched my leg and could barely walk. We bivied in the crater, then the next day Soren led Quinn and me down to the glacier, where we bivied again. The next day they took off for help while I suffered alone. Soren arrived that day at Base Camp; Kwang went up and found Quinn. They arrived at Base Camp late that night. Kwang turned right around the next morning, and with two local yak herders he had recruited, helped me down that day. With Tom now in the lead, Base Camp was quickly dismantled and we hit the road for Kathmandu and home.

CHARLIE FOWLER, *unaffiliated*

# CHINA

## CHINESE TIEN SHAN

*Geregeer Mustagh, First Ascent.* It was reported that in the summer of 1997, a joint Academic Alpine Club of Shizuoka and the Shizuoka University Alpine Club Japanese expedition made the first ascent of Mt. Geregeer Mustagh (5250m) in the Chinese Tien Shan. The team reached Base Camp on August 7 in good weather. Camp I was established at 3260 meters on the right side of the Geregeer Glacier on the 8th; CII was established two days later at 4120 meters higher on the glacier. On August 12, five members left CII at 7:05 a.m., reaching a col between Gareeger Mustagh and Pt. 5129m at 11:35 a.m. From there, Yusuke Sakuraba, Hajime Yoshida, Takashi Sato, Hisakazu Fukazawa and Iiji Hiraki all summited between 12:30 and 1:35 p.m. The team descended from CII to BC on the 14th, and departed for Boltong the next day. (*Sanfaku* 93)

## CHINESE KARAKORAM

*Aghil Mountains, Various Ascents.* New Zealanders John Cocks, Kristen Foley, Tom Davies, John Wild, Dave Ellis, Dominic Hammond and John Nankervis, accompanied by Liaison Officer Jin Ying Jie and cook Gao Zheng, spent five weeks in autumn, 1997, climbing near the Shaksgam River. We left Kashgar on September 3. After crossing the Aghil Pass with camels from Mazardara, we established Base Camp at Durbin Jangal. Two days were spent reconnoitering the Aghil Mountains in the immediate vicinity. Further access for camels to this section of the Aghil proved difficult due to the narrow and steep-sided limestone gorges. Assisted by camels, the team then moved up the Shaksgam to the Southeast Skyang Glacier. For acclimatization, ascents of two non-technical snow peaks at the head of the glacier were made. The first of these (5959m) may have been climbed previously by Kurt Diemberger's party in 1994. The second (6068m) was a first ascent. Attention then shifted to the beautiful virgin peak of 6648 meters on the high ridge dividing the Southeast Skyang and North Gasherbrum glaciers. After recces of possible approaches, a glacier immediately east of the peak and flowing into the Southeast Skyang was ascended to a high camp at 5600 meters. A one-day push was made by all the party; Cocks, Foley and Hammond eventually summited by a route that gained the south spur from a high col immediately north of Pt. 6311m. This involved some technical ice climbing. Wild and Ellis were unsuccessful in an attempt on the same route two days later due to one of the few spells of bad weather encountered. Later, the team relaxed in the beautiful area between the North Gasherbrum and Urdok glaciers with magnificent views of Broad Peak, the Gasherbrum family and other peaks. During this period, Hammond, Cocks, Foley and Nankervis made a first ascent of a ca. 6350-meter peak in the Aghil Mountains, which was accessed from a long narrow rock gully opposite the terminal face of the Gasherbrum Glacier. The expedition then returned to Base Camp, Mazardara via the Aghil Pass and Kashgar for "celebrations" on October 10.

JOHN NANKERVIS, *New Zealand Alpine Club*

# NORTH AMERICA

## CONTIGUOUS UNITED STATES

### WASHINGTON

#### NORTH CASCADES

*Thunder Peak, East Ridge.* Thunder Peak is an 8,800-foot satellite of Mount Logan in the North Cascades. Its 2,000-foot east ridge first caught my eye 15 years ago during a ski ascent of Logan. The ridge features two notches, at 7,500 and 8,000 feet, and rises sharply to the summit. On Labor Day weekend, Silas Wild and I hiked from Fisher Creek to a 5,200-foot lake north of Mount Logan. This is the normal approach to the Banded Glacier. On September 6, from a camp above the lake, we crossed a 7,040-foot col ("Birthday Pass") to reach the base of the route. We scrambled the first few hundred feet of the ridge, then belayed three pitches to the notch at 7,500 feet. While preparing to rappel, we found rope fibers, evidence of a previous climbing party. Since we saw no other artifacts, we don't know whether the earlier party retreated from this point or finished the climb.

We rappelled 80 feet into the notch. The crux of the route was a 5.7 pitch out of the notch. From there to the second notch the climbing was mostly low-end fifth on solid rock with excellent views. The second notch had a short rappel and a rotten gully, but the rock improved above it. We reached the summit in about ten hours from camp (Grade III). The descent back to camp was uneventful until the last few feet of moraine. There Silas was caught and partially buried by a rock avalanche. Miraculously, his only injuries were bruises, a small gash on his leg and a broken wrist. He was able to start hiking the next day, and after another night on the trail, reached Colonial campground early the following morning.

LOWELL SKOOG

#### Pasayten Wilderness

*General Sherman, East Face.* On May 31, Billie Butterfield, Dave LeBlanc, Juan Esteban Lira, Natala Goodman and I climbed an outrigger summit of Sherman Peak at the south edge of the Pasayten Wilderness. General Sherman (7,640') lies due east of Sherman's true summit (8,204') and faces the impressive east wall of Isabella Ridge. The ascent was made via the east slope and face starting at a gravel pit on the Eightmile Creek road, one mile south of the Copper Glance trail head. From the gravel pit, we went due west up through wildflowers, very light understory, and many game trails. At 6,200 feet, we broke out of the forest into light larch and snow. We followed a nice connecting set of steep snow gullies to a 7,580-foot notch just south of the summit at 7,640 feet. From this notch a short scramble (Class 3) took us to the top. We found a cairn on top but no information on who preceeded us to this interesting summit. Five hours up and three down. Recommended for early season.

DON GOODMAN

## OREGON

*Mt. Hood, South Face.* A new route was put up on Mt. Hood in Oregon on September 19. Two separate lines in the same general area were climbed, as my partner, Kendall Dewey, and I elected to climb solo, but within close proximity of one another. From Timberline Lodge we made our way up and across the Palmer Glacier to the base of the Steel Cliffs located on the south face of Mt. Hood. We then ascended a 40-55° mixed couloir leading up the Steel Cliffs toward the base of an obvious buttress. From the buttress, we trended west, following a 40-45° face to the base of a steep mixed couloir that leads directly to the top of an obvious ridge-line. Kendall elected to continue climbing the face, while I made my way through the mixed, 40-60° couloir. After meeting at the top of the ridgeline, we continued along a windblown, rimed ridge to a 30-45° face that led to a short exit couloir, eventually reaching the top of the Wy'east Face and on to the summit. The entire route took 12 hours car-to-car. Due to the length and consistent steepness of the route, parties may elect to bivy. An ideal bivy would be at the top of the ridgeline that leads to the windblown, rimed ridge mentioned above. Cold weather and many freeze-thaws are mandatory for making this route safe.

BLAIR WILLIAMS

## CALIFORNIA

*American Safe Climbing Association, Activity Report.* With a huge lift from the American Alpine Club, the American Safe Climbing Association started off its first year with a bang. During 1998, we reached our goal of replacing 1,000 bolts on popular climbs in Yosemite, Indian Creek, Zion and Calaveras Dome.

The ASCA is a non-profit organization dedicated to making the sport of rock climbing safer by replacing unsafe bolts and anchors and by educating climbers, land managers and the public about climbing and anchor safety. The replacements were made possible through generous contributions from more than 100 climbers, hardware donations from industry leaders and, especially, the $2,000 Lyman Spitzer Award from the AAC. More than a quarter of the ASCA's projects in 1998 were funded by this generous bequest.

In Yosemite, Erik Sloan, Jim Herson and I led the efforts to replace bolts on numerous free and wall routes. Included, among many others, were the bolts on *Salathé, Nose, Mescalito, Sons of Yesterday* and *Serenity Crack.* Of special note were the routes *Lurking Fear, Prow, Zodiac, Shaky Flakes* and *Rambler.* Each received more than 35 replacement bolts, leaving these walls and multi-pitch routes with some of the most bomber anchors in the Valley. They should be solid for decades to come. Many routes were also replaced in Tuolumne Meadows last summer by numerous Search and Rescue team members, chiefly James Selvidge and Greg Barnes. Greg also replaced a number of bolts on Calaveras Dome and Hammer Dome.

Yosemite was the site of the ASCA's first rebolting clinics. About ten climbers learned the art of pulling and placing bolts, and many more will have the opportunity to take a clinic in 1999. If interested in learning to rebolt, e-mail Chris McNamara: <chris@safeclimbing.org>.

It's hard to spend much time on El Cap without feeling the need to do something about the trash that is strewn on the ledges, approaches and summits of popular climbs. In November, Erik Sloan joined me on a mission to rappel *Lurking Fear* and clean up all the trash from summit to base, including manky bolts. We expected to find some weird stuff, but we had no idea that at the end of the day we would have a two-gallon motor oil container, an old portaledge, seven belay seats and a large boom box! We also replaced every remaining quarter-inch bolt and dowel on the route, leaving *Lurking Fear* with the most bomber bolts of any El Cap route.

In April, the ASCA broadened its efforts to Indian Creek, Utah. John Wason led the effort to replace most of the popular climbs on the Super Crack Buttress and Battle of the Bulge Buttress, and in Donnelly Canyon. In addition to replacing terrifying anchor bolts (John pulled one out with his fingers!), unsightly clusters of bleached webbing were removed and replaced with camouflaged chains. The project was funded with money raised by John and Patagonia at the Phoenix Bouldering Contest and with gear donations from Metolius, Petzl and Fixe.

The ASCA also replaced anchors in Zion, Utah, where Jason Stevens organized the replacement of crucial anchors and bolt ladders on the classics *Spaceshot* and *Prodigal Son*.

Leading members of the industry that provided help included Black Diamond, Blue Water, *Climbing* magazine, Fixe Hardware, Hurricane Mountain Works, Kinnaloa, Leeper, Metolius, Misty Mountain, MK Productions, New England Ropes, Patagonia, Petzl, *Rock and Ice*, The North Face and Touchstone Climbing. For this year, our goal is to replace 2,000 bolts in Yosemite, Zion, Indian Creek and the Calaveras area, among others. Anybody willing to help in the effort or wanting to learn more about the ASCA can check out our web site, <www.safeclimbing.org>, or contact us at 1622 Hopkins St./Berkeley, CA 94707. Phone: (510) 558-6919; Fax: (415) 389-8595.

CHRIS MCNAMARA

Yosemite Valley

*Yosemite Valley, Various Activity.* Dean Potter, in outlandishly bold style, made a new solo speed record of the Regular route on Half Dome. Taking only 4:17 (and smashing the old record by 16 hours), Potter free-soloed most of the route, carrying a rarely-used rope on his back most of the way. It was perhaps Potter's fifth time up the route that summer, and he said he had things fairly wired. Indeed, with Venezuelan José Pereyra, he broke the duo record on Half Dome later in the season, coming in at 2:54. Two other records that fell to this pair were the *Salathé* in 7:33 and *Lurking Fear* in 7:15. They also pioneered a new technique to enable the pair to climb together with relative safety. It involved putting the rope through a Ropeman (a tiny jumar), so that if the second fell, he would not pull the leader off—very ingenious. These three records were set during a five-day span in September. The pair also made a new record on *Half Dome Direct* (8:20). Potter also free-soloed Royal Arches in 57 minutes car-to-car.

Alex and Thomas Huber were also in the Valley to do some long free climbing. The pair have each freed the *Salathé Wall*. This time they headed to the east side of El Cap. Working off the Footstool, they freed some existing pitches on *Continental Drift* that were among the hardest yet on El Capitan. This gained them access to the upper *North American Wall*, which they more or less followed to the top. The Black Cave came as another crux at 5.13b, protected by a short sawed-off angle. *El Niño* (5.13c A0) has only 30 feet of aid (a blank section above Big Sur) on the entire route, and took the Hubers only three weeks to complete. Alex also added a variation to the *Free Salathé. Free Rider* avoids the lower 5.13 crux used by

Skinner-Piana in 1988, and avoids the headwall with a detour to *Excalibur* to produce a route that is a mere 5.12d. The pair redpointed the route with both climbers free climbing each pitch in under 16 hours, the fastest free ascent of El Capitan. (For a complete account of the Hubers' efforts, see the article at the beginning of this journal.) *El Niño* was soon repeated by the young British team of Leo Houlding and Patrick Hammond. (See below.)

Local Valley climber Scott Burke, in a monumental effort that required 261 days spread out over three years, became the second person, and first male, to free climb every pitch of the *Nose.* Previously, only Lynn Hill had free climbed the route. While Scott managed to redpoint the second crux pitch (the "Changing Corners" or "Houdini" pitch), he had to be content (for the time being) with a toprope ascent of the Great Roof during a ground-up ascent of the climb in November. On the Great Roof, he decided to take the toprope ascent as good since a storm was reportedly on the way. Scott did not lead every pitch of the *Nose,* but did free every pitch. He plans to return next year to properly lead every hard section. He feels the Great Roof warrants a rating of 5.14a. Although Lynn Hill rated this pitch 5.13, others who have checked out the moves, such as Yuji Hirayama, have offered a 13d/14a rating for those of normal finger stature as well.

Warren Hollinger was responsible for three new El Cap routes over the summer. With Bryan Law, he established *Ned's Excellent Adventure.* (See below.) *Disorderly Conduct* (VI 5.9 A3±), put up with Miles Smart and Bart Groendycke, shares some pitches with *New Dawn* before breaking out left of *Genesis* above Boot Flake. A second ascent was made one month later by Eric George, Brent Ware, with Eric Coomer. Another route, *Nightmare on California Street* (VI 5.10 A4+), was put up by Hollinger and Grant Gardner between *Sea of Dreams* and *Wyoming Sheep Ranch* in July. It featured a 63-hole count. The topo stresses that a 65-meter rope is mandatory.

The *El Cap Girdle Traverse* (VI 5.10 A4) was finally climbed by Chris McNamara and Mark Melvin. McNamara's intimate knowledge of the rock made this oft-tried adventure possible in only five days, with two seperate returns to the ground for a night out at the salad bar. It is 75 pitches long and features some classic climbing on the *Zodiac* and *Salathé.*

On the speed climbing scene, several records were again established. Brian McCray and Miles Smart climbed *Aurora* in 23:55 in an incredibly fast on-sight in August. However, the pair rested on top for half an hour before hauling up their bag, which must be added to their time. (The route's not over till the bags are hauled, the last pitch is hauled, and everyone is on top.) McCray teamed up with his wife, Roxanna Brock, for the fastest female-male time of *Eagle's Way* in 19:06, the third-fastest time overall. Hans Florine, Brian McCray, and Wayne Willoughby made the fastest ascent of the *Bad Seed* to date. They took only 19:12 to dispatch this route, which is the first one-day ascent of El Capitan by a disabled person (Wayne Willoughby suffers from post-polio syndrome).

Venezuelan José Pereyra and Russ Mitrovich climbed the *Zodiac* in 8:40; the previous record was 10:57. The same pair also teamed up with Potter to make the first one-day ascent

RIGHT: *El Capitan, showing routes established in 1998. A:* Girdle Traverse *(McNamara-Melvin); B:* Disorderly Conduct *(Hollinger-Groedycke-Smart); C:* Nightmare on California Street *(approximate)* *(Gardner-Hollinger); D:* El Niño *(Huber-Huber); E:* Continental Drift *(Anker-Thaw, 1997); F:* Heavy Metal and Tinker Toys *(Ayad-Bridwell-Hausoeffer); G:* Ned's Excellent Adventure *(Hollinger-Law).* *Not shown:* Highway to Hell *(Berecz-Tivadar) (near* Iron Hawk, *joins* Atlantic Ocean Wall *near its belay #11).* THOMAS EVANS

of *Mescalito* in 23:28, breaking the existing record by over four hours. Hans Florine and Nancy Feagin became the first male-female team to climb El Capitan (the *Nose*) and Half Dome (Regular Route) in a day, and sixth overall. Willie Benegas (Argentina), Steve Schneider, and Andreas Zegers (Chili) made a record 39:37 ascent of *Excalibur*. The *Reticent Wall* saw several repeats, most notably its first solo by Grant Gardner on only his fifth El Cap route, and also by Wally Barker. Barker, as well as Brian McCray, soloed *Surgeon General*. Chris McNamara made a record 13:13 solo ascent of *Lurking Fear*.

STEVE SCHNEIDER

*El Capitan, El Niño, Second Ascent.* In the meadow, on a clear fresh October afternoon, Patrick "Patch" Hammond and I reclined in our hammocks of smoke and alcohol, eagerly scoping the east buttress of El Capitan with the Huber brothers and their binoculars. I'd spent six week on the Valley floor waiting for this: the moment I became completely focused on one goal, psyched for the thin line of slabs, ledges, corners, and roofs that is *El Niño*.

Based on advice from many Yosemite locals, we decided there would be a storm before the end of October. It was already the last week of the month. In an uncharacteristically rational decision, we concluded we would not go on the wall without synthetic sleeping bags, a haul sack and a portaledge with an expedition fly. (We weren't willing to pay a $15,000 rescue fine.)

That very evening in the bar, Kevin Thaw introduced us to Conrad Anker. Over a pitcher of conversation, they sorted us out all the kit we needed. We covered the beer. Later, Kevin, Conrad, Patch and I, accompanied by Dean Potter and José Pereya, bouldered around Camp 4, where we finalized our "big wall philosophy" and, with the others' help, established our plan of attack for *El Niño*.

Our philosophy, which we developed whilst toying with the Hubers' stagnant, Bavarian sense of humor, and playing with possibilities of jumping problems on the boulders that surrounded us, was simple:

"Big walling is easy! We'll take climbing gear, camping gear (of vertical context) and shit-loads of water."

The plan of attack was no more complicated:

"To the Big Sur big-wall style. Onsight. Ditch stuff. From Big Sur, one push to summit. Onsight."

With an absolute minimum of effort we placed ourselves, fully equipped, on the top of the Footstool at the base of the route. My father happened to be in the Valley at the time. He helped us grunt loads up the talus field, and he too stood with us on our little stool in this, a really special moment of great anticipation and excitement.

First day, first pitch: the climbing's like slate. Balancey, small holds, technical. I'm pulling hard, starting to sketch wildly, my foot slips....

Having described it all a thousand times, the ins and outs of every move on every pitch now seem rather trivial. What is important for the record is: I grabbed a quickdraw on the first pitch (5.13b), narrowly avoiding a 70-foot fall. I sent it first redpoint. I pulled on the first bolt on the second pitch to check and chalk the holds. Sent it first go. I onsighted the rest of the 5.13 pitches, along with all the other pitches (half of which I led), placing all my gear. I sec-onded all of Patch's pitches clean. Patch did not climb all the hard pitches.

Patch and I are both talented slab climbers. After flying success on the first three pitches, we knew only the Black Cave was going to pose any real threat.

By the time we had climbed and hauled the next three pitches, and set up the goddamn portaledge for the first time (it took two hours), it was dark. A really late start, along with another two hours wasted attaching the enigmatic flysheet to the portaledge, meant we only managed two pitches before the skies turned black and the rain began. We huddled in the ledge (conveniently strung in a runoff waterfall) for 25 hours.

A first-light conditions-check revealed the awe-inspiring sight of complete cloud cover in every direction, penetrated for two minutes by the mighty golden pillar of the Nose as it protruded proudly through the abyss.

Two o'clock the next day. Clear skies; unbelievably dry rock, dry ropes and the first snow of the season glistening on the tops. A few good pitches saw us with fixed lines to the Big Sur.

Couldn't face more ledge epics, so Patch took responsibility for the pig and I jumared with the erected portaledge. I felt like a human kite! Another day passed until we finally had 300 feet of 8.2-mm dynamic rope fixed to the Black Cave.

Our plan was that Patch would go up first, load-free, to rest, as he would try the roof first. We thought it would prove difficult, but if we both freed it by noon, we could drop our lines, abandon our camp and go for the top.

What actually happened was that, whilst following Patch up the ropes, a ball-breaking 50 feet of load-bearing, untensioned bouncy jugging, I heard a call: "Chalk bag." No whistling sound, no black image falling—yet no chalk bag. Having disposed of mine earlier on the climb, this posed a serious problem. Hanging there in extreme discomfort, I got really pissed off as I became painfully aware that things were not going according to plan.

I rapped back to camp, filled a stuff sack with chalk, and jugged the line to the Rotten Island. Here we utilized the big wall essential. No, not the stereo, duct tape! With some small wires and imagination we had created "The El Niño." Dips to the elbow and holds three blocks of chalk.

Few words were spoken. I went first.

"Wow, I made it, man! Onsight! Fierce!" was my next explainable thought. Patch yelled his approval. He wasn't fussed about seconding clean. It was 11:30 a.m.

Lines, camp, Conrad's abandoned gear. We had one-and-a-half liters of water, four Snickers, one tin of peaches and one warm jacket. We had to top out that day.

Patch's lead was the easiest pitch of the day: 5.11a. Should've taken half an hour. Ten feet above the belay he was out of sight, and lost. Two and half hours later we were finally at the top of that god-forsaken pitch. I could feel my toes again and I no longer wanted to strangle Patch. So far every pitch had been three star, even the 5.9!

Beautiful timing saw me arrive, thirsty but fit, on top of the final hard pitch. It was virtually dark. For the life of me, I couldn't see a line that would go at 5.10 through the ceilings of looming gray granite above. Maybe the Hubers' "special topo" (they gave us their original) lied. It had once. The "M+M" flake pitch (5.13b) and the "Royal Arches" pitch (5.13c) weren't graded!

"Thank God it's his lead," I thought. Lamps on, a half-hour of frustrated fumbling in anticipation of a very uncomfortable night, and then—

"Eureka!" Patch cried. A line of white tape dots, stuck there by the clinically redpoint-minded Huber brothers, guided us quickly and continuously through the last three pitches.

It's so hard to describe the senses of euphoria, of freeness, of accomplishment, and of horizontal existence that hit us on that final belay. I felt then, as I do now, that we were truly living the good life.

We headed straight for an empty but welcome Burke's camp. As we parted for separate tents, the last thing I remember saying was, "Patch, that was the best route I've ever done!"

"For sure! Thirty three-star routes in one!" he agreed.

"Yeah, and I think we've just made one of the cleanest-ever ascents of El Cap!"

As I lay in my nice dry sleeping bag (courtesy of Burke's camp), I dreamt of my return to the Valley and of the next route to climb free on this beautiful, BIG wall.

*El Niño* was my first wall. The feeling of great exposure, excitement, partnership and fun, combined with the experiences of a big wall, dominate my memories of the climb.

LEO HOULDING, *stoned*

*El Capitan, Free Rider.* On September 21, Peter Janschek and I finished a free ascent of *Free Rider*. We swapped every lead. The leader redpointed every pitch. We did not pre-place any gear. The second also climbed every pitch free: I redpointed every pitch seconding, Peter redpointed every pitch except one hard one and one easy one in which he slipped due to the wet crack. We first climbed the *Freeblast*, and had to wait two days because of bad weather. We then took three days to do the climb because we had terrible weather. The first day we got in a thunderstorm below The Block, so we had to rappel down to El Cap Spire. The next day the storm

hit us below the roof of the *Salathé*, so we had to wait for the next day to continue. Although it took us quite a long time, we still believe that we did a correct free ascent of *Free Rider*.

HEINZ ZAK, *Austria*

*El Capitan, Highway To Hell.* Gabor Berecz and I, both from Munich, spent a few weeks again this year in Yosemite. After making the fifth ascent of *Never Never Land* (VI 5.10a A3-) with bivies, climbing the very dirty *Aquarian Wall* (VI 5.10a A2+) (both original A4) and an onsight 25-hour push on *Zodiac*, we climbed a new route on El Capitan. It takes a good line close to *Iron Hawk*, mostly on real nice natural formations. After seven new pitches (in a row!), it joins *Atlantic Ocean Wall* near its 11th belay. We christened the route *Highway To Hell* and graded it VI 5.9 A5 in our clean new-wave style, which means we try not to use bolts and rivets or any other

*Gabor Berecz on pitch 1 (A5) of* Highway to Hell.
THOMAS TIVADAR

drilled protection on the pitches. Some people from the Valley didn't like our style; they cut our fixed line on the really dangerous first pitch ("The Guillotine," A5). It is a bad tendency if climbers don't respect one another's work and style. And also, foreigners have the right to climb new routes on El Cap, if they can! We, for example, don't like the long rivet ladders on many other new routes, but we would never go there to chop the rivets or to cut a fixed line. There are fewer possibilities but more and more activities and climbers each year. It would be nice (and also necessary) if we all could understand each other. We should at least try. Otherwise we'll ultimately run into a war.

Our friends and wall partners from Philadelphia, Oskar Nadasdi and Enci Szentirmai, made the second ascent of Eric Kohl's *Pressure Cooker* (VI 5.10 A4) in September in five days. They also made the second ascent of *High Plains Dripper* (VI 5.11 A5) this year, but reported that *Pressure* is harder than *High Plains*. The freeclimbing is also harder than 5.10, and scary.

THOMAS TIVADAR, *Germany*


*El Capitan, Heavy Metal and Tinker Toys.* In August, Boulos Ayad, Tyson Hausdoerffer and I managed to establish an 11-pitch new route on the southeast face of El Capitan that we named *Heavy Metal and Tinker Toys* (VI 5.10 PDH). The route joins *Atlantic Ocean* to *New Jersey Turnpike* for 19 total pitches, which we climbed over ten days; 18 belay bolts, 36 machine bolt rivets, and 54 filled holes were used in total.

We used the new Abbreviated Aid Rating System (AARS) to define difficulty on this route. This was done to avoid the commonly misinterpreted, redefined, and generally abused A1 through A5 system. The AARS has only three difficulty ratings: NBD (No Big Deal), NTB (Not Too Bad), and PDH (Pretty Darn Hard). Concomitant when deemed warranted is a danger or serious rating, i.e., WHU (Way Heads Up), or the more concerning DFH (Don't Fall Here).

The new route starts about ten meters right of *Wyoming Sheep Ranch* and *Continental Drift*. Boulos, only 19 years old, led the very serious first pitch, which involved difficult aid climbing with ground fall potential. This pitch crosses the long traverse on the first pitch of the *Drift* about 50 feet above the ground. We fixed a rope, and the next day Tyson led pitch 2, crossing a 35-foot blank section on 5/16" machine bolt rivets placed in shallow 1/4" holes. Caution should be exercised on these rivets during subsequent ascents.

The next three pitches are easy to follow if not generally easy to climb. These pitches are all PDH and except for pitch 3 tend to move right toward the *New Jersey Turnpike* route. Tyson led the sixth pitch, which intersects the *Turnpike* by means of a pendulum. Pitch 7, though not particularly difficult, is somewhat serious and may be hard to see where to go initially. A small pendulum right from the third of three hook moves leads to easy free climbing, also to the right. After 30 or so feet, climb up on thin and sometimes expanding flakes to a three-foot roof formed by a very large flake. There is a single unnecessary bolt here, to mark the belay. Near the end of the next lead move right to a ledge and a two-bolt belay anchor.

The next day, after a super-human hauling effort the day before, Tyson led a long PDH, WHU pitch to a small triangular ledge. Boulos led the next pitch (NTB) to the top of a small pillar only 15 feet left of the *Gulfstream* route. In the finite quest for new territory to climb, I moved down and left to free climb up some large loose flakes before aiding on copperheads to some more very loose flakes that took me back to the *Gulfstream* route, 20 feet below Boston Tea Party ledge. At this juncture our vain hope of establishing a totally separate line dwindled to sad reality. Above we spotted copperhead wires growing from a crack we had proposed to use. At this point we joined the *Atlantic Ocean* for two pitches and then onto the *New Jersey Turnpike* to finish.

JIM BRIDWELL, *unaffiliated*

*El Capitan, Ned's Excellent Adventure.* In the sweltering heat of early August, Warren Hollinger and I established a new line on the southeast face of El Cap. We began three days after I topped out on the Porcelain Wall (see below) and climbed nine new pitches as a variation of *Lost In America* (LIA). I had completed the first two pitches previously, as a separate project, then later realized there were more new features above. We decided to climb the first two pitches of *LIA* to speed things up. From the shared second belay, Warren led up and left through "The Cauliflower," trundled a loose block, then nailed a steep, left-leaning corner to a hanging belay. My next pitch involved more trundling, some expando, hooking, heading, a little nailing, and a few rivets. A difficult pendulum to a hook brought Warren back into *LIA* below its fifth pitch belay. He continued on, free climbing to The Bay of Pigs and stretching the rope its full 60 meters. We climbed the next two pitches of *LIA* and then celebrated the full moon with Old English and tequila. Two more pitches of *LIA* brought us to the tenth belay, just below the Fly or Die. I climbed 20 feet to the traverse, deviated left, then up onto the super-steep headwall via a delicate flake and more heads. Warren's next pitch climbed a small corner, "The Black Thumb," then a rivet ladder, and finished on hooks to a small stance. A large ramp, "The Black Crescent," led me to many hooks, a bit of easy free climbing, and the next belay. Warren then traversed left, popped over an arching roof, and free-climbed to a stance. Another short free pitch led us to the summit, where we enjoyed our last warm beers. We spent seven days on the wall and climbed 14 pitches. The loops on fixed heads were duct taped closed and many of the moves are reachy (we are both 6' 3").

This route is dedicated to the memory of my uncle, Ned Gillette, who was killed in Pakistan at the time of this ascent. His incredible inspiration will never be forgotten.

BRYAN LAW

*Reticent Wall, Solo Ascent.* Tomaž Humar (Slovenia) climbed El Capitan's *Reticent Wall* (VI 5.9 A5, 850m) solo, finishing on October 26 after 15 days on the route. In Slovenia, in the Kamnik Alps, Tomaz has put up several demanding technical routes (A4 and A5). After climbing the *Reticent Wall*, he felt his routes in Slovenia have been graded correctly. He is the first European climber to solo the route, and third overall.

TOMAŽ HUMAR, *Slovenia*

*Porcelain Wall, Sky Is Falling.* In late July, Eric Kohl and I established a new line on the left side of the Porcelain Wall. We named the route *Sky Is Falling* (VI 5.10+ A?, 15 pitches, 73 holes) due to the amount of loose rock regularly shed from the face (our lead line was chopped by rockfall while fixed on the first pitch). Seven loads apiece were carried to the base as the first five pitches were fixed. Eric led the first two, 5.10+ polished slab pitches, runout between stance-drilled quarter-inchers. True to his style, he used recalled Leeper hangers as well as a few rusty relics I'd kept after re-bolting belays on *Zenyata Mendata*. The third and fourth pitches climbed through a recent rock scar (a large section that appeared in my three-year-old photos was now gone) and involved a short section of free climbing and trundling. This led to "The Death Splitter," a beautiful 80-foot blade/arrow crack that separated an enormous slab from the wall. The fifth pitch, "Ron Faucet," had me groveling through running water and a mud-oozing corner that finally sloped onto "The Garden Terrace," a huge overgrown ledge system strewn with loose blocks.

After two days of rest, we hauled our pigs to "The Terrace" and Eric began leading the next pitch, battling bushes and small trees and tossing the occasional loose block. Suddenly, the one-inch cam he was on popped. He went 20 feet, landed on his side on a small shelf, bounced off and continued for another 20 feet until his next piece finally caught. Shocked, I lowered him the remaining ten feet to the ledge and asked if he was all right. He had badly scraped his shoulder, hit his head quite hard and was bleeding. Muttering something about "damn A1 munge," he cleaned himself up, took a hit off the vodka bottle, and to my amazement was back on lead in less than 15 minutes. For the following three days, he became dizzy every time he looked up. Eric now wears a helmet.

A pitch of good nailing and heading brought us to the second ledge system, where we bivied and found signs of Harding's passage: a bed of arranged blocks and a sardine tin. Eric led off the ledge on creaky blades and hooks, then used ball nuts in an expanding corner that made strange popping noises from within. Hooks, heads and beaks brought me to the largest feature of the route, a huge, right-facing A1 corner that arced to a roof, where I belayed. Eric's next pitch, "The Chinette Pitch," traversed right on blades, hooked a flake, then nailed more blades and beaks into a pair of expanding splitters. I then led off the belay on six beaks, a few heads and a hook, then joined Harding's route for 90 feet of frustrating bat hooking, protected by a few manky Z-macs with plumber's tape hangers. From our toe-sized belay stance, Eric traversed left for 80 feet on hooks and rivets, then, after several tries, pendulumed from a blade in an expanding roof to a skating hook. He then pasted heads to the belay. Nineteen rivets, a few circleheads, and many hooks brought me to "Swill Station Zebra," a welcomed narrow ledge. With heads and blades, Eric ascended a tight corner, drilled two rivets, and nailed his way to "The Sky Lab" at belay 14. The final pitch consisted of beautiful beak seams connected by hook traverses, a large ledge, and a perfect bugaboo splitter that continued over the 90° summit edge, providing a natural belay. We spent eight days on the wall, bivied on top, and quickly descended to The Deli the next morning.

BRYAN LAW

*Tenaya Canyon, New Route.* While some Club members are painting their names across the skies above the world's great mountain ranges, others toil in obscurity among the well-worn furrows of our home ranges. Thus my partner Tim Laidman and I happened upon a new route in Yosemite's Tenaya Canyon. We climbed consistently easy to moderate slabs immediately west of Snow Creek and east of the Snow Creek Slabs route described by Roper. This casual cruise allows one to enjoy the delightful music of this creek as it cascades over polished granite and boils through a series of small falls and pools before disappearing into the forested canyon below. This climb offers a variety of possible routes parallel to the creek. In fact, it is not a climb so much as a game, the idea being to climb as close to the creek as possible, where the rock is steeper and smoother, the moves harder and the chance of falling into the swift-moving stream greater. The less bold climb further from the stream, following long cracks and flakes to obtain protection.

The creek has a lower and an upper section divided by a small pool. The upper section is steeper and more interesting, with a section of 5.8 cracks and flakes at the start. At the top of the slabs, the canyon narrows and is overgrown with jungle. Exit left to the Snow Creek trail.

PAUL MINAULT

SIERRA NEVADA

*The south face of Peak 4151 on Mt. Corcoran.* DAVID HARDEN

*Peak 4151, South Face.* Mt. Corcoran consists of four widely separated summits along the Sierra crest. The southernmost peak, a.k.a. Peak 4151, presents a striking sight in the upper reaches of Tuttle Creek's south fork. The south face rises steeply for more than 1,000 feet across the drainage from Mt. Langley. On the Fourth of July, Bart O'Brien and I spent a great day climbing a system of corners and cracks on the right edge of the wall. Starting with a chimney in a large dihedral, the route unfolded with one delightful pitch after another. Most were in the 5.8/5.9 range, with a few harder sections. We cut left about halfway up to avoid an ominous, overhanging offwidth. Higher, we angled back right into more steep cracks and corners. After 11 pitches of crisp, shining rock (IV 5.10a), we scrambled onto the summit ridge.

DAVID HARDEN

*Temple Crag, Backside of Beyond.* Temple Crag has a hidden face. Last October, when the Celestial Arêtes retreated behind snow and ice and shadow, I recalled a sunnier side, and Jim Herrington and I went over Contact Pass to have a look. The south face is half a mile wide with less relief and simpler architecture, but we still wandered over slabs and past shimmering tarns for a couple of hours before the main features settled into focus and we chose a line. Near the right edge of the face, a crack/chimney line runs straight up to the left side of a small tower on the skyline. Beginning 40 feet to its right, we were soon in the system and two pitches up. Above, the crack bulged into an unappetizing chimney, so we again took to the wall on the right. Steep face climbing kept opening upward, cruxing just as it linked to a traverse left back to the chimney, now narrowed to offwidth. Increasingly blocky climbing led straight up two more pitches. By then it was dark and snowing lightly, but the angle broke and an easier pitch went by starlight and headlamp to an excellent summit (six pitches, 5.9+). We named the line for Allan Bard. "You know you are on the backside of beyond when you feel the crisp bite of winter air in your lungs and the sting of wind-driven snow on your face," wrote Allan. Can this be the first new route on Temple Crag in 21 years?

DOUG ROBINSON, *Moving Over Stone*


NEVADA

*Rainbow Wall, The Big Payback.* Tony Sartin, Dave Evans, and I started *The Big Payback* (5.10 A3, 11 pitches) in April, 1997. We climbed four pitches of the route, then came back the following year (1998) to finish, which we did in April. The route follows the most obvious feature on the wall, a left-to-right giant flaring corner system, through a roof, then follows an obvious drainage system to the top of the wall.

The route climbs the first pitch of *Sergeant Slaughter*, traverses directly right for about 100 feet to an anchor (established by Danny Meyers, who had tried this route, a 150-foot straight-in beak seam, three times, reaching three different high points and backing off each time). It climbs through the roof, then up two pitches of good climbing through a mossy flaring drainage to a super big bivy ledge. From there, the route continues through loose blocks through another roof, then ascends two more pitches up more right-leaning funky drainage systems to a notch, then one chimney pitch to the top. It has great flaring chimney pitches, which might be why no one has climbed it. I've climbed most of the routes on the wall and it's as good or better than the rest—good adventure climbing, and super exciting. Bring a modern aid rack, with as many big cams as you can find.

KEVIN DANIELS, *unaffiliated*


*Rainbow Wall, Various Activity.* The Rainbow Wall in Red Rocks, Nevada, is the closest thing to a big wall you will find near Las Vegas. This 1,000-foot sandstone wall is predominantly vertical and well-featured with edges, seams and cracks. Because the approach to this colorful mosaic takes between one and three hours, the wall maintains its pristine character. Although the quality of the climbs is classic, the routes are adventurous by nature and contain sections of brittle, if not loose, sandstone.

The Original Route is an open book in the center of the wall. A popular aid line, the route was controversially equipped with nearly 80 bolts for a free ascent attempt several years ago. Consequently, the bolts were chopped. Dan McQuade replaced only a quarter of the bolts and did the first free ascent of the route, rating it 5.12b (13 pitches of mostly 5.11 and two 5.12s). This route is what originally attracted us to the Rainbow Wall. While we were climbing it, we were struck by the beauty and solitude of the region and the possibilities of free climbing other existing aid lines. Brian McCray climbed the Original Route, flashing all the pitches but two, and getting its second free ascent in April. A month later, Roxanna Brock teamed up with Bobbi Bensman to do the first female free ascent (FFFA) of the route in a day.

After freeing the Original Route, our attention was soon drawn to *Sergeant Slaughter* (A3) on the left side of the wall. The second pitch (the crux, 5.12b) begins in an easy left-facing corner, and shortly turns into an increasingly difficult right-facing corner. The pitch ends 120 feet later as a gaping six-inch layback. The next two pitches follow a flaring crack and chimney, the most notable being the second, the "Bitch Pitch" (5.11+).

A 5.12 face and a 5.11- squeeze chimney were also memorable. Three bolts, drilled by hand, were added to the route to protect the nine-pitch free climb. The bolts were kept off the original aid line. At the end of May, we finished our free ascent. We came back in early June to free it in a day.

Brian had been admiring a long brown dihedral on the right edge of the wall. He initially aided the route solo and equipped it with some bolts necessary for free climbing the route. In mid-June, Roxanna joined Brian for the first free ascent of *Brown Recluse* (5.11). The route contains nine pitches of 5.10 and 5.11 climbing.

ROXANNA BROCK *and* BRIAN MCCRAY

# UTAH

*Wasatch Range, Ski Traverse.* It was reported that Doug Byerly, Jon Allen and Lorne Glick made perhaps the first "high ski traverse" of the Wasatch Range. Starting at the southern end of the range with Mt. Nebo, the trio spent 23 days covering 250 miles, finishing in the Wellsville Range on March 20. In the days prior to their start, they made 11 caches of food and fuel, which allowed them to keep their packs down to 30 pounds apiece. (*Rock and Ice* 86)

## Moab Area

*Ron's Tower, First Ascent.* This tower was climbed by Steve Anderson, Bill Duncan, and Matt Simpson at II 5.8 A2-. The first ascent follows obvious cracks up the south face. All aid is clean. Ron's Tower is reached by a float trip down the Colorado River. The first ascent team put in at Loma, Colorado, and rafted to The Black Rocks area. The tower is up Moore Canyon and the route climbs the most prominent spire in the area by its south face.

ERIC BJØRNSTADT

*Moab Area, Various Ascents.* Kevin Chase, Tom Gilje, and Tait Rees made the first ascent of the lone tower located on the north side of Heat Wave Buttress via the route *Spitting Cobra* (5.12 AO). This is located off State Highway 313, nine miles north of Moab.

In Kane Creek, *Bounce Test* (five pitches, III 5.7) was established by Andy Roberts, Jason Schroeder and Liz Devaney in April. Upper pitches were added by Andy Roberts and Jason Hodgeman. The route is located right of the famous mastodon petrograph high above the Colorado River just beyond Moonflower Canyon. Half a mile south of the Happy Turk in

Kane Creek, Cameron Burns and Jesse Harvey climbed a 200-foot tower named Shelbyville via *Mr. Putterman Goes to Washington* (II 5.9 A1). Approximately eight miles south of Moab is the popular Kens Lake. Just south, a dirt road approaches the Wingate cliffs prominent to the east. In April, Linus Platt, John Rzyczecki and Brad Bond climbed Old Dad Spire, putting up *Old and In The Way* (5.10c A0, 190').

ERIC BJØRNSTADT

*River Road Area, Various Ascents.* Along the River Road (east of Moab), *O'Grady* (5.12+) was climbed in September by Jay Smith and Kitty Calhoun. This route is just right of Lighthouse Tower above Big Bend Recreation Area. In the same area in February, one crack system left of Dolomite Wall, Smith and Calhoun put up *Clearlight* (IV 5.11+R). At Mile Marker 12, *Nuke 'em Rafi* (5.11a A1), was established by Jay Miller and Andy Roberts in June.

In the Richardson Amphitheater area of the River Road, Brad Bond and Alden Strong climbed the East Face (5.9 A2, 200') of the Stinger. Indian Chief Tower up above mile marker 28, named after its distinctive profile, was climbed by a two-pitch 5.7. The first ascent was claimed by the FBI (Fat Bastards International) in March.

ERIC BJØRNSTADT

*Moab Area, Various Ascents.* Sunshine Wall is an exciting Wingate buttress bordering the northern reaches of Salt Valley, just north of the border of Arches National Park. It is reached by a good dirt road that branches east from U.S. 191 approximately five miles south of I-70. To enter Salt Valley, take every major right turn after leaving U.S. 191.

Mike Baker, Leslie Henderson, and Wilson Goodrich first visited the area back in May of 1997 and established several routes. Development of routes from 5.8 up on cracks and faces on good rock has progressed steadily since then, mainly due to the efforts of Mike Baker and various partners, yet the place has the potential for many more routes. It is remote, yet accessible with a two-wheel drive, low-clearance vehicle, and is sure to become a popular climbing destination.

James Garrett, Pete "Big Billy" Keane and Brad England made the first ascent of Tower #143, the largest free-standing spire (at 250') in the main cliff area. The route was named *Burning Shoes* (III 5.9 A2) and was climbed in October. Brad Bond and Steve "Crusher" Bartlett climbed a 200-foot tower a few hundred yards to the east via the two-pitch *Dickfour* (5.9+ and A2+).

ERIC BJØRNSTADT

*The Nuns, Various Activity.* Three new routes were established on The Nuns in Castle Valley. *Bad Habit* (5.11) climbs the east face and was put up by John Catto, Jay Smith, and Mark Hesse. *Holier Than Thou* (5.11c) weaves its way up a dramatic calcite curtain on the north face, and was climbed by Smith and Hesse. The two also put up North Face Right (5.10a).

ERIC BJØRNSTADT

*Lighthouse Tower, Free Ascent.* On October 24, Bill Wright, George Bell, John Prater and Ken Leiden made the first recorded free ascent of the Northeast Face on Lighthouse Tower (III 5.9S). The crux was a crumbly offwidth crack; oversize friends are mandatory. The Northeast Face was the first ascent route of Lighthouse Spire (III 5.8+S A2) and is now its fourth or fifth free route.

GEORGE BELL

Arches National Park

*Hot Wheels Tower, Funny Car.* In the Windows area of Arches National Park, Brad Bond rope-soloed the first ascent of *Funny Car* (5.8 A2+) on the Hot Wheels Tower. Bond: "Linus Platt acted as technical advisor during the ascent." The climb is 100 feet south of Tonka Tower.

ERIC BJØRNSTADT

*The Penguins, New Route.* On the west side of the Penguins, Todd Gordon, Mary Ann Loehr and Margie Floyd established *Petrified Bear's Dick* (5.9 A2) in April.

ERIC BJØRNSTADT

Fisher Towers

*Fisher Towers, Various ascents.* The Minotaur saw a first ascent (IV 5.9+ C2) by Lisa Raleigh and Duane Raleigh in five-and-a-half hours with no pitons and only two bolts. The route begins just right of *Ancient Art* and climbs the formation in seven pitches.

Shawn MacRoe and Chris Van Leuven climbed *Not So Soft* (VI A3+ 5.8), a new line up the northwest face of Cottontail Tower. The route starts 300 feet right of *West Side Story*, and joins *Brer Rabbit* on the big shoulder after five pitches.

In a five-hour, 25-minute solo climb, Brad England, with Phil White in support, made the first ascent of the Finger of Fate Gendarme (5.4 A1) in October.

ERIC BJØRNSTADT

Mystery Towers

*Mystery Towers, Various Ascents.* In March, in the remote Mystery Towers just east of Fisher Towers, Keith Reynolds and Alan Stevenson climbed *The Fortress* (5.8 A3, five pitches) on Kitty Litter Wall. The route ascends the south-facing buttress adjacent to The Citadel, with minimal nailing. Reynolds comments: "The fifth pitch is possibly the worst pitch in the Mystery Towers—loose and crumbling 5.8+ Moenkopi mud cracks." The Reynolds/Stevenson team also made a free ascent of the *Pink Pussycat* (5.10), located up the left drainage beyond The Aliens. It was first climbed nearly 30 years ago by Bill Forrest and Don Briggs and rated 5.9 A3. *Pillar of Hercules* (V A3+ 5.9, 1,000+') was climbed by Duane Raleigh and Tony Wilson in four days with 35 bolts. The route is located between Hydra and Doric Column.

ERIC BJØRNSTADT

Canyonlands National Park

*Monument Basin, Meemohive, Captain Pugwash.* Dave Levine and I visited Monument Basin in April and, after attempting to free the short but steep aid section on the *Meemohive*, found a devious traverse to the right into an easier crack system. This then rejoined the original route below the top pitch, giving a new free rating of 5.10b.

STEVE "CRUSHER" BARTLETT

*Tristin's Tower, Airport Tower, Ascents.* Tristin's Tower in the Lockhart Basin area of Canyonlands was climbed by John Burnham and Bill Duncan. Bret Ruckman and Marco Cornacchione made the first free ascent of Airport Tower via *Wind Shear* (5.12a/b), calling it a five-star route.

ERIC BJØRNSTADT

*Green River Area, Felony Tower.* This area is outside of the Park but approached via the Horsethief Trail road. Jim Bodenhamer, Tom Cosgriff, and Roger Schimmel climbed Felony Tower via *Poncho Couldn't Come* (IV A2 5.11), with Bodenhamer, Schimmel, and Chris Archer working on the lower pitches. They give their Wingate sandstone route a five-star rating. It is located near the end of the buttress at the lower end of the Horsethief Trail switchbacks descending to the Green River.

ERIC BJØRNSTADT

Remote Southern Areas

*Rims Recreation Area, Various Ascents.* Thirty miles south of Moab (via U.S. 191) is the BLM's Rims Recreation Area, a high mesa bordered by Indian Creek (south) and the Colorado River (west). Hatch Wash slices through the mesa, exposing high-quality 300-foot Wingate sandstone walls. In May, Mike Baker soloed *Laughing Thunder* (IV 5.9 A2+) on the wall east of Cogswell Tower, which was dubbed Enchanted Mesa. In September, Baker rope-soloed *Silent Destiny* (5.9), also on Enchanted Mesa.

Mike Baker and Kirby Spangler also climbed *Orient Express* (IV 5.10 A3+) right of *Silent Destiny* and directly in line with the rappel route into the canyon when approaching from the east. On the approach to Rims Recreation Area (a dirt road between mile markers 93 and 94), signs direct one to Looking Glass Rock. Its first ascent was made solo by Mike Baker. *Adventure in Entradaland* (II 5.8 A2) climbs through a hole from inside the arch. Baker: "This is the steepest pitch I've ever climbed. Major pucker factor." In August, Dave Medera and Brett Sutteer ascended Looking Glass Rock by the East Rib (5.7, 290'). Brad Bond soloed a remote tower off the rim of the Recreation Area. Thirty-two miles south of Moab, and west of U.S. 191, lies the Orphan, which is reached from the rim left (south) of Canyonlands Overlook. Bond climbed the tower in two pitches (III 5.9 A2, 180') on June 11.

ERIC BJØRNSTADT

*Indian Creek, Various Activity.* In Indian Creek, there is ever more development, little of which gets reported. Previously unreported is *Sports Page* (5.10), climbed by Steve DeFino and Jonathan McCue. The route is approximately 200 feet down the Newspaper Rock Nature Trail at the #7 marker post. On Reservoir Wall, Jay Smith and Dave Medera established two new routes. *Shattered Faith* (5.11a, 190') climbs a left-facing corner with a couple of roof pulls and is the second corner system left of Steve Hong's *Thank God for Pods. Goddamn* (5.12b/c) ascends a corner to a splitter crack just right of *Thank God for Pods.* In April, on Meat Wall, approximately 100 yards right of *T-Bones Tonight,* Carol Ciliberti, Will Gilmer and James Garrett established *No More Meatloaf* (5.11). The route is 25 feet right of *Camping Under the Influence.* A short chimney with a small roof marks the start of the climb.

ERIC BJØRNSTADT

*Valley of the Gods.* In March, on the Seven Drunken Sailors formation, Mike Baker and Leslie Henderson established *Borracho Grande* (5.9 C2, two pitches, 180').

ERIC BJØRNSTADT

Zion National Park

*Zion, Various Ascents.* A major route was established across from Angels Landing, between Weeping Rock and Touchstone. *Beyond the Pale* (VI A3 5.11a) was begun by Mike Baker and Leslie Henderson and finished by Baker and Chris Ducker. *A Future With No Days* (VI 5.8 A2+) was established by Ben Folsom and Lance Bateman. The route climbs a line between *Angel Hair* and *Empty Pages* on Angels Landing.

ERIC BJØRNSTADT

*The Sentinel, Brown-Eyed Girl.* In late April, a certain Montana boy (who wishes to remain anonymous) and Joel Nolte climbed a new route on the north face of the Sentinel formation, in the Court of the Patriarchs. *Brown-Eyed Girl* (V+ 5.8 A3+) follows thin, bottoming cracks and seams up the left side of the steep, shield-like headwall. Not to be confused with the beautiful but (sadly) bolted crack to its right, our route has holes only for belays and for the crossing of blank terrain.

JOEL NOLTE, *unaffiliated*

*Traverse of West Temple and Towers of the Virgin.* On the spring equinox, Dan Stih and I made a complete traverse of the West Temple and the Towers of the Virgin. The idea materialized while making the first ascents of the towers in the winter of 1997. Dan and I originally climbed Altar of Sacrifice straight on, during a four-day push, fixing ropes and hauling as far as the plateau. Once on the plateau, we climbed each of the towers in succession. The following summer we planned a lightweight alpine-style traverse of the towers, including the West Temple, which would be used as a staging point.

In March, Dan and I climbed the Southwest Ridge of the West Temple (II 5.5) and made five rappels from trees and bushes into the hanging valley between the West Temple and the Sundial. We then made an exposed fourth-class traverse across the east face of the Sundial and behind the towers into Christopher's Valley, where we bivied. On March 20, we climbed the Sundial (5.10+, seven pitches), The Witch Head (5.10, five pitches) and The Broken Tooth (5.10, four pitches). We then climbed the Rotten Tooth from the south via a grotesque route (5.3, three pitches). We climbed the Altar from the west via a prominent gully (5.9), summiting just before dark on the 20th. We then spent the night on top of the Altar's east face, one of the most spectacular of our 75-plus bivies in the park. The following morning we rappelled down the Altar's north face, becoming temporarily stranded in the center of a 200-meter blank vertical wall while drilling hanging rappel stations. In the end, self-preservation sent me prussiking in search of better rock. Twenty meters above, I found stone hard enough to trust three equalized anchors, and after one more station, the descent ended in a hanging valley. We made an unsuccessful attempt on the southeast ridge of the unclimbed Meridian Tower, then spent the rest of the afternoon exploring the valley between the Altar and Meridian Tower, bivying that night in the hanging valley beneath the Altar.

On March 22, we rappelled 460 meters down the gully just left of the east face, using only natural anchors. In all, we rappelled more than 1800 meters and climbed at least that much rock. The only fixed anchors on the entire traverse are on the north face of the Altar.

RON RAIMONDE

*Zion, Enchainment.* It was reported that in April, Mike Pennings and Jeff Hollenbaugh linked the routes *Touchstone Wall, Space Shot, Monkeyfinger Wall* and *Moonlight Buttress* in 18 hours, free climbing through 5.11 and simul-climbing much of the terrain. The pair also made the third ascent of the Anker-Stump route on the far left side of the Streaked Wall, presumably on another day. (*Climbing* 178)

*Mt. Kinesava, Arrakis.* In early October, Dan Gambino and I climbed a new route on the southwest face of Mt. Kinesava. *Arrakis* (V 5.8 A2+) is ten pitches long and took three days to complete. Located about 600 feet left of *King Corner*, the route follows cracks and dihedrals on the last section of clean face before the wall breaks up into corners and arêtes on its left side. This face is plainly visible at sunset. The flat pillar at mid-height offers a superb bivy; the sloping ledge system at three-quarters height is not so superb. Descent was made by rappelling the route (this required the addition of an extra set of anchors to the left of the sixth belay). All belays have at least one bolt; those on the upper half of the route generally have two. All bolts are 3/8" x 3" except for the single 3/8" x 2 1/4" atop the final pitch. Sixty-meter ropes were used, but the route could probably be done with 55-meter ropes. Gear ranged from birdbeaks to large tube chocks. In a fit of genius, the first-ascent party failed to take free-climbing shoes. These would have allowed most of the lower half of the route to go free at 5.11 or less.

JOEL NOLTE, *unaffiliated*

*Emerald Star Mountain, Leaving Llamaland.* From May 30-June 3, Amanda Tarr established the route *Leaving Llamaland* (V+ 5.7 A2+, 1,000') on Emerald Star Mountain, two buttresses right of the route *Emerald Star Majesticus*. A full account of her solo climb appears earlier in this journal.

*The southeast face of West Temple, showing* Back Where
it All Begins. DREW SPAULDING

*West Temple, Back Where it Al*
*Begins.* On April 10, John
Rzyczecki and I started a new
route on the southeast face of the
West Temple. The route, *Back*
*Where it All Begins* (VI 5.11a A3),
follows the obvious diagonal line
up the center of the wall facing
Springdale. We spent 12 days
completing the route, rappelling
on April 22. Eight nights were
spent on the wall. The route
involved 16 60-meter rope-stretching pitches with bolted belays.
Eighty percent of the lower wall
was great free climbing, with little
aid necessary. Almost all of the
last eight pitches required thin aid

DREW SPAULDING, *unaffiliated*

## ARIZONA

*Oak Creek Canyon, Lucifer's*
*Tooth, New Route.* In late
December, Ned Overs and I established a new line on the severely
overhanging east face of Lucifer's
Tooth in Oak Creek Canyon, located just north of Sedona, Arizona.
The 110-meter *Black Sunshine* (IV 5.10 A3) follows a 5.10 and A1 finger crack for the first
pitch to a semi-hanging belay. An A1 splitter crack and some free climbing, followed by a
few rivets and a short pendulum, lead to an overhanging A2 seam, and then to a hanging
belay. From here the line continues up an overhanging A3 crack to a small roof, and higher
to the last hanging belay. Another overhanging A3 nailing pitch finishes (via a few rivets and
5.5 face) to the summit of the spire. The rock is excellent throughout, and all belays have
solid bolts or fixed pins. Lucifer's Tooth is in a spectacular location high in Counterfeiter
Canyon, which contains beautiful sandstone spires and unclimbed Zion-like walls.

RON RAIMONDE

*Boboquivari Peak, Babo Heads.* In January, I soloed *Babo Heads* (IV 5.11a) on the south face
of Boboquivari Peak. The route starts a few hundred feet left of the Southeast Arête and
climbs a line of bolts (placed during someone's failed attempt) to a crack line that leads to the
prominent notch on the Southeast Arête in nine pitches.

JIM BEYER, *unaffiliated*

**COLORADO**

**Colorado National Monument**

*Colorado National Monument, Various Ascents.* Over the Edge Spire was climbed by its west face via *Child's Play* (II 5.8+R) by Jon Burnham and Bill Duncan. The east face was climbed by Mike Colacino, Scott Evens, and Matt Simpson via *One Toke Over the Line* (II 5.10b).

In Rough Canyon, Tabeguache Tower was climbed by Steve Anderson, Bill Duncan, and Matt Simpson. (The Canyon is just east of the Monument.) The route (IV 5.9R A2) ascends a crack system on the east side of the landform.

ERIC BJØRNSTADT

*Western Colorado, Various Ascents.* On August 4, Jesse Harvey, Pat Goodman and I made the first ascent of a yummy 350-foot flake of rotten sandstone, limestone and shale that we dubbed Putterman's Flake. It sits a couple miles north of (the Cameo) Exit 46 on Interstate 70, east of Grand Junction in Debeque Canyon, and is easily viewed from the highway unless you are paying attention to the road. The flake had been eyed by many Colorado climbers for years, and some were under the impression that it lies upon private land. It does not. Some were under the impression it wasn't worth climbing. It was. Our four-pitch route, *The Snows of Puttermanjaro* (III/IV 5.9 A2-), climbs the northern edge of the flake, then proceeds into the weird, cavernous notch between the flake and the canyon wall, then wraps around the outside of the flake, finishing up an overhanging wall, which Harvey (wearing his signature Hawaiian floral print shirt) led in 100°F heat.

Two other towers of note: in late June, Harvey and I climbed the 160-foot Jolly Tower, a beautiful free-standing pinnacle 800 feet west of Liberty Cap, in Colorado National Monument, via *Marital Bliss* (II A2-). And, in early August, Harvey, Jon Butler and I climbed the 250-foot Oompah Tower, just a few hundred feet south of Jolly Tower, via *Ethan Putterman and the Chocolate Factory* (III 5.9 C1).

CAMERON M. BURNS

**Big Dominquez Canyon**

*Thor Canyon, Various Ascents.* Big Dominquez Canyon is located on the Uncompahgre Plateau near Unaweep Canyon southeast of Grand Junction. Thor Tower is the obvious tower at the head of the canyon. Two routes have been established on the tower. *Thor's Hammer* (5.10+), which ascends the west face, was climbed by John Culberson and Mel Thorson. *Spanish Inquisition* (5.11+) was put up on the east face by Culberson, Thorson and Jose Iglesia.

ERIC BJØRNSTADT

**Rocky Mountain National Park**

*Rocky Mountain National Park, Various Ascents.* Tricky to describe what started it, but the 1998 summer season in RMNP saw a frenzy of new route activity the likes of which haven't

*Wisteria Tower, The Palisades, Longs Peak.* Slumgullion takes the crack system on the left side of the tower.
KATH PYKE

been seen for years. For those involved, it meant a mad time of plotting and scheming, chancing the weather and desperately trying to find a suitably motivated partner for some of the projects. Nearly all of the 1998 routes were put up free and onsight, and most followed natural crack lines with no need for bolts or pins. This says a lot about the climbing potential in the Park. In addition, this modern, minimum impact approach is ever more appropriate for the future of climbing in the more remote alpine and tundra areas of our National Parks.

Most of the action can be ascribed to a core group of highly motivated individuals. Way back before the alpine season was even supposed to have started, one of the key figures, a certain Doug Byerly, was spotted at one of those local "in" parties, furtively dropping hints about hidden areas, south faces and early season routes. Doug and his various partners were responsible for 12 new routes, all multi-pitch. (See note by Byerly below.)

In addition to climbs noted below, Arrowhead Peak was the focus of much activity. Ex-pat Brits Andy Donson and Dave Light put up the hardest line on the east face, *Ithaca* (5.12b, five new pitches), in 1997 via overlapping slabs just right of the *Airhead Dihedrals*. This piqued people's interest, and the summer of 1998 saw the addition of four more routes to the right of

*Kath Pyke on the fifth (crux) pitch of* Medusa *on the southeast face of Arrowhead Peak.*
ANDY DONSON

the route (see additional notes below). From left to right, a route by Bernard Gillet and partner attacked the next dihedral system to the right of *Ithaca*, producing a four-pitch 5.11. This was followed by *Medusa* (Donson, with newcomer Brit, Kath Pyke), a five-pitch, 5.11a "J" crack system of real quality status that is the third system to the right of the *Airhead Dihedrals*. Caught in a hair-on-end and carabiner-sparking thunderstorm, the pair named the route after the goddess Medusa, known for the snakes in her hair. On Arrowhead Peak's southwest face, *Independence* (5.10, three pitches), a splitter dihedral, was put up by Pyke and Dylan Taylor. The higher you go on Arrowhead, the better the quality of the rock.

Over on the Longs Peak massif, up and behind the Diamond, the elegantly positioned Palisades was the scene of three new multi-pitch lines, the first new routes here for over two decades. Mark Howe and Joni Dutton found themselves doing a striking line, *Beat the Heat* (5.10d, three pitches), on the central dihedral system of the Great White Tower simply because people were already on the popular Flying Buttress further down the valley. Kath Pyke focused her efforts on the left arête of Wisteria Tower to produce the fine *Slumgullion* (5.11d, three pitches). This is the hardest addition to the Palisades and probably one of the only new routes in RMNP where all the pitches were led by a female. The belayer, Mark Howe, wanted no part of it! Also in the Palisades, *Earth, Wind and Fire* (5.10d, two 60-meter pitches), climbed by Doug Byerly and Kath Pyke, takes the west face of Great White Tower.

KATH PYKE, *United Kingdom*

*Rocky Mountain National Park, Various Ascents.* The summer of 1998 was a productive one for new route activity in Rocky Mountain National Park. At least 20 new routes were established, three quarters for which I was responsible. I kicked the season off with Terry Murphy, finding a fine new line on the southeast face of Dragontail Spire in Tyndal Gorge. The seven-pitch *Dragonslayer* offers varied climbing up to 5.11d. Next, the two of us climbed an excellent four-pitch route, *Ravensong*, on the west face of Notchtop Peak above Ptarmigan Glacier. This route follows obvious cracks to a white roof band that succumbed (after several long falls) at 5.11c. The two of us found a huge unclimbed face a week later in the Andrews Glacier cirque and climbed *Wings of Desire* (5.10d) in seven pitches, finding difficult sections interspersed with frighteningly loose rock. For my next project, I teamed up with Bruce Miller and tackled the dark, compact northeast face of Sharkstooth Peak, also in the Andrew's Glacier area. This promising face turned out to be a haunted house of sundry horrors, including excessively licheny rock and disposable holds, one of which landed squarely on the small of my back as the rain began to fall, heightening the peril of the situation. Needless to say, we persevered on our route, *Decline of Western Civilization*, finding climbing up to 5.10 and wishing to never find ourselves on this chunk of choss again. On the walk out, I spied a line Matt Hobbs had told me about and he and I returned with Sari Nicoll to establish a six-pitch climb, *Heat Wave* (5.11c), that we held in very high esteem. This line climbs the sunny pinnacle on the south face of Mt. Otis, also in the Andrew's Glacier area. With solid rock, four pitches of 5.10, and one acrobatic roof at 5.11, it ranks as one of the best free climbs in the Park at its grade.

Later in the summer, I teamed with up Sari Nicoll again for an exciting, three-pitch variation to the *Flying Buttress* route on Mt. Meeker's south face. *Kiss The Sky* featured a 5.11 hand-to-finger crack through a small roof and some very loose rock that was cleaned up for subsequent ascents. Next on tap was a trip into the Glacier Gorge to the south face of Arrowhead Peak with Kath Pyke. We climbed two excellent three-pitch lines, one, *Goldfinger*, a beautiful 5.11d crack on the golden central buttress, and the other, *Raindance*, a 5.9+ on the slabby left face. I returned a couple of weeks later with Jon Allen to establish another climb, *Refugium*, to the left of *Raindance*, finding excellent rock and intricate climbing up to 5.11. That same day we established a wonderful 5.10d/5.11a, *Dreams of Babylon Burning*, a seven-pitch route up the center of the east face of McHenrys Peak.

After another new route with Kath Pyke on Wisteria Tower (see above), I wrapped the summer season up with a great climb, *Solar Arête*, on Solar Wall above the Loch Vale near Zowie Pinnacle. Jon Allen and I found five pitches of stimulating face climbing through roof bands on a sunny arête, the crux being a stemming dihedral that fell at 5.11b. No bolts or pitons were placed on any of these routes, nor were any taken along. I'm certainly not against use of bolts in the Park, but wish only to see them used tastefully. It is hoped that the huge resource of rock will be respected for future generations to enjoy and cherish.

The 1998 ski mountaineering season in RMNP was somewhat bleak, as there was precious little snow on the steeper aspects. Nonetheless, I managed to repeat some of the classic testpieces established by John Harlin III and Jimmy Katz in the early 1980s. I skied the north face of Longs Peak, twice solo, and the ominous, committing Y Couloir on Mt. Yipsilon, also solo. I then added a few testpieces of my own, including the West Face Couloir of Mummy Peak, the South Couloir of Chuiquita Peak, both alone, and the western-most couloir above Ptarmigan Glacier on Flattop Peak with Jon Allen.

In the Indian Peaks Wilderness, I skied the stunning South Couloir of Shoshoni Peak and the exposed East Face of Apache Peak in a fine solo outing.

DOUG BYERLY

*Longs Peak, Four Pitches, 24 Hours.* In the first week of September, Mic Follari and I completed a new route on the Upper East Face of Longs Peak in Rocky Mountain National Park. Three brilliant pitches of 5.6-5.8 were done to get to Broadway. Pins were noticed along the way; we later learned that this was the 1956 *Glendennings Arête*. After reaching Broadway, it is possible to solo up another 400 feet; a short section of 5.7 is encountered upon leaving Broadway, then it is easy fourth to fifth class scrambling. A prominent right-facing dihedral system to the east was taken after the angle increased. The dihedral yields four pitches of 5.9-5.10 climbing. Descent was made via the Loft between Mount Meeker and Longs Peak. The route was named *Four Pitches, 24 Hours* for humiliating reasons I'd rather not discuss.

MATT HOBBS

*Longs Peak, The Diamond, Left For Dead.* During the first week of August, Shane Wayker and I finished a new route on the far right side of the Diamond, approximately 50 feet to the right of Sunshine. Peter Takeda and I fixed the first four pitches of this route in the fall of 1996. Terrible weather forced us to retreat one pitch from the top. I then returned in the fall of 1997 with Mike Duncan. Once again we were stopped by horrible weather. This year, to increase the likelihood of clear skies, Shane and I hiked in on August 3. There was one drawback to going in during the summer. The runoff from the melting north face would be draining down the route.

We hiked in under stormy skies and bivied under a tarp on Broadway. Unfortunately, we awoke to an inch of fresh hail, but by mid-morning the sun came out and dried things off nicely. As I started up the first pitch (5.7 A1 wet), dark clouds moved in and it started to rain, hail and snow. Shane led the second pitch (5.9 A1) in relative comfort due to the steepness of the wall. We fixed these two pitches and retreated to the tarp.

During the night three inches of snow fell. We slept in, and by 9 a.m. the sun was out and most of the snow was gone. We jugged our lines to the start of the fixed ropes Pete and I had installed on pitches 3 and 4 in 1996. The old lines looked great, so we jugged on lead and placed gear every ten feet or so. (Pitch 3 was A1+; pitch 4, which required some thin nailing, a few beaks and heads, was A3.) By the time we arrived at the start of pitch 5, we were both soaked. The weather was stable, but the north face had started to drain. Luckily, it was my lead. (I would rather climb in a cold shower than belay in one.) Forty feet of tied-off knifeblades, beaking, heading and hooking took me to the base of a large roof (A3+). Easy aid led out right for 15 feet and then up an overhanging chimney and onto the north face. Incredibly, Shane had not gotten hypothermic while belaying for three hours in an icy shower. He cleaned the pitch and we carefully rappelled the route (which we called *Left For Dead*, VI 5.7 A3+, 800'), stripping the fixed ropes as we descended. The tarp was warm and dry!

DAVE SHELDON

*Longs Peak, Lower East Face, Babies 'R' Us. Babies 'R' Us* (III 5.12a) is a five-pitch route on the Lower East Face of Longs Peak that offers steep slab climbing on mostly high quality granite. It starts 250 feet right of the North Chimney, immediately right of a conspicuous black streak, and eventually crosses the black streak several times. Because the black streak is often wet, the best times to do the route are either late May/early June or late August/early September. The first three pitches weave their way up discontinuous weaknesses and when these features end, you can expect some difficult thin edge climbing with bolt protection. The first pitch is 5.11a and requires some route-finding skills at the bottom, but four bolts steer the climber to a nice belay perch. The second very difficult pitch involves a fair bit of 5.11b face work with an improbable 5.12a crux sequence and eventually crosses the black streak. The third short pitch traverses leftward to an arête (5.11a) and reaches a comfortable belay. Pitch four traverses back right across a tenuous face section to reach a welcome crack system (5.9+) that leads to another good belay. The last pitch traverses rightward to avoid easy cracks above, and gains a nice corner. When the corner fades, the route forces the steep wall above, protected by small wired nuts and two bolts (5.11a).

The route took Randy Farris and I seven days to establish over the summers of 1997 and 1998. All bolts were drilled on lead except the last two. Progress was slow, and on some days we would merely place one or two bolts. In the summer the route can stay sunny until around 2 p.m. and is well out of the way of the usual rock fall hazards from the North Chimney and Diamond. We rappelled the route in five rappels; there is one fixed station at each belay.

The name of the route derives from the fact that we both had newborns at home—perfect training for those alpine starts.

BRET RUCKMAN, *unaffiliated*

*Ships Prow, Sarchasm.* As reported in last year's volume, Pat Adams and Jim Redo climbed the three-pitch *Bologna Pony* (5.12c) on Ships Prow. This was one of the hardest climbs in the Park until Tommy Caldwell upped the ante with a 120-foot direct start that weighs in at 5.14a, and is thus one of the hardest climbs in Colorado. Writes Caldwell, "There are more battles to be fought in doing a climb like *Sarchasm.* Its distance from the trailhead (five miles or so) is a big incentive to put forth a strong effort with each attempt. The altitude and the almost certain afternoon storms affected the strategy of the climb and lent an extra measure of urgency each day as the clouds rolled in. Several good climbers have said to me that it will be a long time before *Sarchasm* gets repeated, if ever. I hope this is not the case. The perfect rock and magnificent setting make all the effort more than worthwhile. I will certainly seek similar opportunities."

*Mt. Evans, The Rusty Dagger.* The *Rusty Dagger* was poised over our heads in a dead straight line. It seemed inconceivable to Cameron Tague and me that this compelling and pure feature could have been overlooked, since the rest of the cliff had received considerable attention by the free climber. At that time, the route existed as an aid climb, with ratings around the A2/A3 level. The system kicks off as a shallow right-facing dihedral that slowly tapers away after 100 feet. At the third pitch the dihedral system reappears, switching to face left. The crusty red right wall of the dihedral gradually widens as height is gained, resembling a rusty dagger. Huge unweathered granite blocks were piled at the base of the wall, suggesting that the system hadn't been around too long.

The celebrations started early on August 16 as we smugly congratulated ourselves for reeling in the big one; we even went so far as posturing for the camera à la El Cap Meadows. Oh brother, were we headed for a big fall.

We managed to dispatch the first two pitches, which looked to be the crux of the route, without incident. The granite turned out to be a little crunchy with the occasional huge spine of detached rock along the way. Protection was generally abundant. On a roll, and prematurely flushed with success, we relaxed, as the next pitch looked casual by comparison. Wrong. Although not technically too hard, the red crud proved to be highly unpleasant. Crumbly and unsound in surprising ways, this pitch slowed us down and put a bit of a damper on our victory march. The fourth pitch had a little extra water and attendant mud and vegetables. Some risky detours and imprudent gardening got me past these obstacles and on to a spacious swampy ledge, from which I could survey the final hurdle: the dripping offwidth triple roof stack. Fifty feet of reasonable-looking dihedral led to this. A loud voice in my mind shouted, "Climb this next bit and then let Cameron get the offwidth."

Twenty-five feet up, my plans were scuppered. A sodden layback, featuring green algae the likes of which I hadn't seen since Britain, was just too insecure. With disappointment, I grabbed a cam by my waist, which immediately popped out of its slimy placement and sent me tumbling 20 feet, narrowly missing the swampy ledge. I quickly decided to offer the pitch to Cameron, who proceeded to cruise past my high point. "Nice work—you might as well keep going to the top," I shouted up. To my horror, he fixed a poky belay just below the final pitch, setting me up for the dripping offwidth triple roof stack.

Soaking and cold from the previous pitch, we debated our options. My feeble pleas for a quick escape downward were rejected by a suddenly buoyant Cameron. With frayed nerves, I stemmed my way up the repulsive corner, fully intending to back off at the first slimy cam placement. Unfortunately, the first roof was just manageable in its drenched state and I found myself committed to the pitch. The next roof, however, was a stopper, and, fully expecting to fly again, I hung on a slimy #5 Camalot. To my relief, it held. With renewed confidence in my pro, and only 30 feet of climbing to the top, I resolved to frig my way up through the rest of the pitch. While Cameron slowly froze at the belay, I built up a full head of steam thrashing around in the nose-grinding hanging slot that breaches the final and largest roof. An improbable right-leg knee bar got me past this final obstacle, and 20 easy feet from the top. "It's in the bag," I shouted down. But of course we weren't going to get off that lightly.

As a final retort to our premature celebrations, the top of the cliff decided to drop off with me hanging on to it. Having trusted so many loose flakes throughout the day, I didn't hesitate to yard on the hollow-sounding flake at the top of the route. The fall left me dangling ten feet below the lip of the third roof. I'd taken a smart blow to my left hip, which jolted with pain if I jerked on it. The rope had stripped in the fall, and the core strands were splayed out over the lip of the roof above me. My initial attempts to swing back into the rock were unsuccessful, and after each attempt I would swing back out, cringing, as the core strands grated back and forth over the edge of rock. Third time lucky, I wedged myself back into a slimy cleft below the final roof.

After disposing with the trashed section of the rope, the crux roof had to be re-climbed. My left hip jarred with pain if any weight was applied with the leg bent, but was still effective if used straight. Eventually crawling onto the summit, I fixed the rope for Cameron to jug out on while I lay in an exhausted heap and savored my release. I discovered I could stand on the left leg and even walk. Thus I was able to limp back to the truck unaided.

It later transpired that the femur was split near the head; it would require a screw to fix it. I would like to take this opportunity to thank Cameron for letting me carry my share of the gear back to the parking lot.

Andy Donson, *United Kingdom*

## Wyoming

Grand Teton National Park

*Mount Moran, Various Ascents.* In July, I soloed *South Buttress Drifter* (V 5.10c) on the South Buttress of Mt. Moran. The route weaves through roof bands 150 feet right of the South Buttress

Right. Three days and five nights were spent putting in this classic. Three bolts were placed.

In October, I soloed *Whirl of Hate* (VI 5.10 A4) on the south buttress of Moran. This is the first VI and the first big wall route in the range. Seven days and 14 nights were spent on the route in stormy weather. I was pinned down by a snow and ice storm for four days near the top of the route. The route starts to the right of *Deliverance* and crosses South Buttress Right at the Grand Traverse. I nailed (A4) the huge roof band above and continued up and left against the grain.

JIM BEYER, *unaffiliated*

*Grand Teton, Second Tower, New Route, and Mount Moran, South Face, Various Ascents.* In August, I made roped solo ascents of two new routes in the Tetons. The first was the Central Dihedral (IV 5.10+/ 5.11-) on the south face of the Second Tower. The line follows the large dihedral to the right of the Tower Two Chute. I first attempted the line with Jeff Wilson, but we were stormed off after the first pitch. The second route (IV 5.10X) is located on the south buttress of Mt. Moran between the *Deliverance* and Habeler variations. It starts to the right of *Deliverance*, below the fourth-class step on the second ramp in the large dihedral arcing to the right, and ends near the end of the Grand Traverse pitch on the South Buttress Right route. It takes a standard rack to 4".

In late July, Jim Beyer and I made the second ascent of a route Jim had done earlier that month. The *South Buttress Drifter* is 150 feet right of South Buttress Central and 500 feet left of South Buttress Left. It goes all free with lots of 5.10 and is 12 pitches long.

JOHN KELLY, *unaffiliated*

*Teewinot, Mt. Owen, Grand Teton, Enchainment.* Fellow Exum guide Hans Johnstone and I took advantage of a rare shared day off in August to finally bag three routes we had never been on by enchaining the North Face of Teewinot, the North Ridge of Mt. Owen and the North Face of the Grand Teton. While our goal was to get into the mountains sans the burden of clients and to cover some major new ground, we also set some simple rules. Number one, we couldn't skip any of the technical climbing on a route by traversing in high; we basically had to do the route as described in the guidebook. Number two, the route had to be listed in Leigh Ortenburger and Renny Jackson's guidebook as a prominent north face or north ridge route. Number three, the North Ridge of the Grand was out because we had climbed it. And number four, we had to climb to each peak's summit.

We began the day by headlamp, around 4 a.m., under a display of aurora borealis rare for the region. Dawn was lipping the horizon as we completed the traverse to the north face of Teewinot and began scrambling up the ramp that crosses the face from east to west and accesses the upper, easy slabs of the northwest ridge. A post-cold front chill made the thought of difficult climbing unpleasant, so we basically put it out of our minds for the time being, hoping to simply get a jump on the day and summit Teewinot via the easiest of the routes up its north face. We topped out around 7:15 a.m.

Then we set out for the descent and traverse all the way over to the base of Mt. Owen's north ridge. The challenge was to avoid substantial fields and couloirs of snow left from a wet June, while in the meantime avoiding clobbering one another with endless loose boulders. Perhaps over-estimating our route-finding skills, we had brought one diminutive ice ax between us, of which I carefully maintained possession. At the same time, our footwear consisted of some

*Hans Johnstone bare-handing it across the bottom of the* Run-Don't-Walk Couloir. MARK NEWCOMB

flimsy, sticky rubbered approach shoes (probably the ones worn by Hans in that shoe ad where he's not wearing a helmet). When crossing frozen snow, I chopped steps while Hans pecked his way along my tracks using a sharp rock for added purchase. Finally, we plunged into the 15-foot bergschrund between the rock and the snow, tunneling our way over to the base of the northeast face. A short but steep, grimy and poorly protected pitch accessed a corner of the face, and from there a series of ramps and benches took us up and across the stream draining the face proper, then around the base of the *Crescent Arête* and into the bottom of the *Run-Don't-Walk Couloir*. After crossing the couloir, we ascended a nice pitch of slab climbing bounded by a corner on the left that led to more ramps that finally led to the striking, diagonal slash that marks the North Ridge proper.

From there the route was obvious, leading up through a couple of interesting chimneys to the Yellow Tower, which we tackled via steep cracks on its west side. More wandering up the east side of the ridge, then onto the spine of the ridge itself, led to an awkward 5.9 slot protected by a piton, which is the first place we roped up for the day. Hans, who doesn't understand awkward, took the lead, and soon we were on our way again. At that point we felt slightly behind schedule, so we bent the rules slightly at the very top of the route by climbing the final chimney of the Koven Route rather than stay on the more difficult spine of the ridge all the way to the summit.

Then we traversed along the west side of Owen, rapped into Gunsight Notch, scrambled up and left over steep ground to the east side of the Grandstand and zig-zagged down slabs until we were just above the Teton Glacier. A short rappel off an old bolt left behind during a rescue off the north face years ago brought us to the top of the glacier. From there we traversed across loose and gritty rock to what we thought was the base of the regular North Face route.

Soon the climbing became more difficult than we knew it should be. Others had made the same mistake, so we used bail slings already in place to rap down and left to the correct line.

We maintained our wayward tendencies as we ascended, getting lost no less than four times before knowing for sure we were on route at the unmistakable Guano Chimney. Having wormed up the chimney, and sporting a fresh coat of guano, we wandered up the slabs of the first ledge, scrambled to the second ledge and got off route yet again when Hans led a striking but tricky pitch of climbing to get off the end of the second ledge. Back on route for the Pendulum Pitch, I led across surprisingly dry rock, stepping around just a couple patches of ice. Hans led the final section, topping out in the soft, burnished yellow of evening sun. We summited the Grand at 7:15 p.m., exactly 12 hours from when we had summited Teewinot.

Moving over all-too familiar terrain on the descent, we made it to the developed trail near the Platforms before having to turn on our headlamps, and back to our car by 10 p.m.

MARK NEWCOMB

*Mt. Moran, Northeast Ridge, First Descent.* On May 14, I completed the first descent of Mount Moran's classic northeast ridge, solo and on a snowboard. Hans Johnstone, Rob Haggart and I attempted the route in February but were forced to retreat due to inclement weather and poor visibility. This ridge is the sight of the November 21, 1950 plane crash, and the route was one of the last of the unskied/unsnowboarded classics left in the Tetons, with over 6,000 vertical feet of elevation gain. I skied across Jackson Lake, then skinned halfway up the ridge on 130-cm skis. After the snow became too steep, I abandoned the skis and post-holed up the rest of the ridge to the top of the face. It was a treat to bask in the sun's warmth, overlooking Idaho! I was traveling very light and took only ski poles, leaving crampons and axes at home. The snow had softened during the day slightly and now, at 3 p.m., the sun had left the face, leaving firm snow. I took the basket off one of my poles and had it ready to use for self-arrest if necessary. On the descent I encountered variable snow, from powder to firm sun-baked snow to breakable crust and back to powder again. It was an incredibly enjoyable descent, looking down the ridge with Jackson Lake looming below. I completed the climb and descent in 14 hours car-to-car.

STEPHEN KOCH, *unaffiliated*

WIND RIVER RANGE

*Mt. Sacagawea, Northwest Face.* On September 3, after humping into Titcomb Basin with enough gear for 15 days in the wilderness, my brother Jamie and I established a first ascent on the northwest face of Mt. Sacagawea. The incredible *Dixie Chickens* (5.9R, ten pitches) begins 200 meters to the north of the classic South Summit/West Face rib route pioneered by Fred Beckey in 1969. This shadowed 1,500-foot route is everything you want in an alpine tour: classic hand-jamming and finger-locking, runouts, loose rocks, no crowds and over a two-day walk back to safety. The route is named after Arkansas' desperate quest to have more chickens within its political boundaries than people on the planet.

WILLIAM McREE ANDERSON, IV

*Ambush Peak, East Face, and Other Ascents.* The Wind River Mountains of Wyoming harbor many unclimbed walls and much beautiful scenery. On August 28, Chuck Calef and I established a new route on the ca. 2,000-foot east face of Ambush Peak. The year before we had been turned back due to bad weather. This year we were luckier. We spent a few days "warming up," establishing a few new routes and variations to existing routes, including *McMuffin* (II 5.8R, six pitches) on the left side of the obvious M-dike on Point 12,187, which finishes with the big white dihedral to the gully between Point 12,187 and Point 12,173. We also added a direct start to the Mt. Bonneville traverse, from the southwest.

Having established a direct start of 600 feet of slab climbing (5.8R) to the Grey Ledges last year, this year we solo climbed up via the East Chimney Route and traversed into the Grey Ledges. From this point, the climbing goes straight up (5.6) and trends right (5.9) toward the "Inverted Staircase," the right end of the big roof system dominating the center of the east face. Remarkable features let us cruise through the feared Inverted Staircase for two pitches (5.9) to a big corner. After a third-class traverse on grassy ledges, a diagonal line through a vertical garden of grass and dihedrals (5.8) led to some wet sections and the "Tower" (5.9), a large chimney system ending in a pillar. From the Tower, the route goes straight toward the main summit (5.8), passing some stacked door-sized death flakes, and finishing up an easy chimney. The climb took 12 hours and included 12 long pitches (mostly 50m) above the Grey Ledges. We expected more difficult climbing, but the route follows surprising lines of knobs and good cracks on mostly excellent rock. We called the route *Wish You Were Here* (IV 5.9).

Last summer there were, as far as I know, two other teams attempting the east face of Ambush Peak. One team made an attempt straight up to what I called the Grey Ledges and returned from there. The other team made an attempt to the left of the middle of the east face, angling out toward the south face. In this region an old fixed rope is hanging. We left nothing on the route; no bolts were drilled and no pitons were used.

THOMAS LEITNER, *unaffiliated*

*Mt. Hooker, Northwest Passage.* In mid-September, Ryan Hokanson and I hired two horses to pack our luggage up to Hailey Pass. Our objective was the north face of Mount Hooker, a 2,000-foot vertical expanse of beautiful orange granodiorite. After establishing a base camp among the krumholtz and talus below the wall, we began scouting for a passage through the vertical seas above. The western portion of the face was not visible from our camp, but as we approached it, we found it bathed in late afternoon sun. The prospect of climbing in warm sunshine, in this reputedly frigid place, seemed inviting. We studied the wall for a time and decided on a line. Our proposed route started in a conspicuous corner and roof system that travels up and left through the bottom third of the dead vertical northwest face of Mount Hooker. It actually linked more obvious features than most of the previously established routes, but it also sported a conspicuous blank area. During the next five days of intermittently stormy weather, we were able to fix five pitches of sustained A3 broken by periods of intriguing free climbing. This carried us through the initial corner and roof system, and into the bottom of the blank section, which yielded to 5.9 face climbing. After a day spent "hydrating" by soaking up rainwater at base camp, the clouds ebbed and were replaced by a flood of calm, blue sky.

Time to sail! Jugging and hauling brought us to our bivy with time to spare. From this vantage point, the wall above did not appear so featureless. I left my aiders at the belay and began free climbing. Flakes that had been invisible from the ground provided hearty laybacks and locking jams. Soon I was 200 feet above the portaledge. I had navigated the remainder of our anticipated crux section, yet I had not done a move harder than 5.8! The remainder of our voyage wove its way through a complex passage of vertical crack systems. Pitch after pitch ended with the drill still at the previous belay. In fact, throughout the entire route the only drilling done, aside from several of the belays, was the enhancement of one hook move on the fourth pitch. Just three days after leaving the ground, we found ourselves once again on horizontal land, having completed *The Northwest Passage* (VI 5.9 A3, 12 pitches) over a period of nine days. The summit of Mount Hooker is a vast and fairly level island in the sky. Upon reaching it, a climber may shed the harness and pack it away in the depths of a haul bag, the only remaining problem being to carry said haul bag back to the car.

KIRBY SPANGLER, *unaffiliated*

*Mt. Hooker, Year of the Horse.* Hiring horses and taking the "long way in" from Dickenson Park, Jeff Maus, Kevin Dunkak and I spent 11 of 21 days scouting, fixing and climbing a 13-pitch route on the north face of Mt. Hooker. (This line shares ground with the 1995 Donahue-Harvey route; see topo.) Our line climbs up the large alcoves to the left of the *Third Eye* and to the right of *Red Light District.* On the third night of our seven-day push, we saw what we thought was a dramatic display of the northern lights above Muesembeah Peak. Astronomers have since said that the celestial events we witnessed on August 27 had more to do with a mega star than the northern lights. Whatever it was, it was an awesome sight. The route, *Year of the Horse* (a.k.a. *Northern Lights,* VI 5.10 A3), shared a pitch and a half from a previous attempt, from the high point of which we removed water bottles and rusted cans. We used 19 holes, including one pre-existing.

CLAY WADMAN

MONTANA

Glacier National Park

*Glacier National Park, New Ice and Alpine Routes.* New routes in Glacier National Park often come in flurries, largely because they depend on rare combinations of fair weather and minimal avalanche hazard. Such was the case in 1998, when climbers established several new ice and alpine routes during brief windows at the end of one winter and the start of the next. On April 1, Marc Venery and Blase Reardon climbed *The Bohdi Tree* (IV WI4, 450') in Avalanche Basin. This climb shares a first pitch with *Monument Falls.* The route diverges left at the snow ledge, then ascends a sustained headwall for two pitches. Though the fall was warm and dry, a polar front arrived the week before Christmas, diverting locals from moist-tooling experiments on mossy boulders. Routes formed within days, and climbers established three new routes in Avalanche Basin. On December 20, Kirby Spangler and Marc Venery climbed *Contrarian Investment* (IV WI5, 400') in bitterly cold temperatures. The route is the leftmost

RIGHT: *Mt. Hooker. A:* Red Light District *(IV 5.12-, Toula-Lleuben, 1992). B.* Brain Larceny *(V 5.12R, Donahue-Harvey, 1994). C.* Northern Lights *(VI 5.10 A3, Wadman-Maus-Dunkak, 1998). D:* Third Eye *(VI 5.10 A4, Quinlan-Middendorf, 1993). E.* Boissonneault-Larson *(VI 5.10+ A4, 1979). F.* Sendero Luminoso *(VI 5.10 A4, Quinlan, 1980s). G.* Shady Lady *(VI 5.11 A4, Dockery-Bradshaw, 1978). H.* Original Route *(VI 5.9 A4, Robbins-McCracken-Raymond, 1964). I.* Northwest Passage *(VI 5.9 A3, Hokanson-Spangler, 1998). 10.* Free variation. NORM LARSON

of three drips on Bubba's Moonshine Wall, and like the remaining two routes, rewards a long, dangerous approach with an airy, fantastic position. Two days later, Spangler and Venery returned with Ryan Hokanson. The trio climbed *The Fountainhead* (IV WI4, 275'), a steep pillar below and left of *Monument Falls*. Spangler and Hokanson rested another day, then followed Kelly Cordes up *Treehugger* (III WI4, 200'). This route is located 300-400 feet above the outlet of the lake, in an amphitheater on the lower reaches of Bearhat Mountain.

BLASE REARDON, *unaffiliated*

*North Face of Mt. Edwards, Ascent.* Chris Trimble and I hiked in to an igloo constructed at Lower Snyder Lake late in the evening on April 2. At 7 a.m. the next morning, we were looking up at the north face of Mt. Edwards immediately above Upper Snyder Lake. The vertical gain from the lake to the summit is 3,500 feet, with the lower third being a rock band. Chris and I had climbed *Baby Semmler* on this wall previously, but our goal this trip was to continue on the upper two-thirds of the mountain to the summit.

We climbed *Six Pack of Beer and Nothing to Do*, a 1,400-foot WI4 done previously by Kalispell locals, reaching the top of this climb at 4 p.m. We slogged on to intersect the north ridge at around 7,700 feet. Despite the early hour, we elected to bivy here because of the pleasantness of the evening and the spectacular position of this bivy spot, surrounded by the peaks of Glacier National Park.

In the morning we continued for three hours of steep snowy climbing on the north ridge of Mt. Edwards with an occasional excavated rock move to the summit. We descended the east ridge toward Comeau Pass, then down the small ice climb below the pass between Mt. Edwards and the Little Matterhorn. Firm snow conditions at the time made this route safe, feasible, and enjoyable. The route (V WI4 5.8) is very good ice/alpine route, but is not recommended in summer or during periods of high avalanche danger.

JIM EARL

# ALASKA

*Thorn Peak, East Face, 100 Years of Solitude.* During late July, 1992, I traversed the Gakona Range from the range's high peak (mislabeled on most maps) of Gakona over to Thorn Peak (Peak 9200'). My main memory of the climb was banging in a ringing angle piton, taking a peek down the east face of Thorn through the mist and then blindly rappelling down the south face.

February, 1995. Convincing neophyte climber Rick Studley to attempt a winter ascent of the unclimbed and unseen east face of the Thorn was easy. Skiing 40 miles up a frozen river covered with a foot and a half of water was not. Five miles from the road and two days into the slog from hell, we turned around.

February, 1996. Ian McRae didn't want to ski 40 miles to climb a face I had no photos of. When we got a grant to fly in, he bit the hook. After taking all our money, our pilot landed us a week from our objective. Ian and I proceeded to spend the next 17 days in -50°F weather hating life, digging snowcaves, and trying to stay warm. By the time we got to the base of the face, we were complete-

LEFT: *Ian McRae at the base of the east face of Thorn Peak during the 1996 attempt.*
JEFF APPLE BENOWITZ

*Rick Studley on* 100 Years of Solitude, *east face of Mt. Thorn.* JEFF APPLE BENOWITZ

ly spent. Climbing 3,000 feet of technical ground at those temperatures was not going to happen.

April, 1997. Photos in hand, I thought it would be easy to get a partner for the obvious gem of a line. Landing in a Super Cub at the base of the face alone, I knew I needed to work on my salesmanship. Climbing half the face and finding the crux rock band devoid of ice and me devoid of aid gear left me nowhere to go but down and out. Skiing the 40 miles to the road was a chore—then one of my skis broke in half. Let's just say I had an adventure.

Early March, 1998. Rick Studley, an old man by now in the climbing world of Fairbanks, was once again easy to convince to try the still-unclimbed east face of the Thorn. With a paved snowmobile trail leading two-thirds of the way in, the ski took only three days. When we reached the base of the rock band, it was obvious that March was the month. Thin but climbable ice headed straight up for 800 feet. After fixing our one rope and a few aiders on the crux two pitches (WI5 5.5), we dug a cave and holed up for the -30F° night. The next day the sun was strong. We ate ramen, then swung leads up thin, but plastic ice. Soon the ice was behind us and two pitches of scary snow tunneling brought us onto an arête near the summit. Rick ran up the snow and rock arête and belayed from a place I had reached six years ago. Descending the highly corniced north ridge and than down a 2,000-foot snow gully quickly brought us back to our skis at the base of the climb. Skiing out in a marathon two days was uneventful.

The route was named *100 Years of Solitude* for the only book I had to read on my solo attempt and because it will probably be 100 years before this hidden gem gets climbed again.

JEFF APPLE BENOWITZ, *unaffiliated*

## ALASKA RANGE

*Denali National Park, Mountaineering Statistics.* Most weather forecasters will attribute the strange 1998 climbing season facts to El Niño: the Park saw a 100% success rate this past year for winter ascents of Mt. McKinley, and a 36% success rate during the peak climbing season. The three mountaineers who made it to the top of North America's highest peak in winter (see "Climbs and Expeditions: Alaska," in the 1998 *AAJ*) thanked El Niño's warmer winter temperatures for their successful summit, while the majority of McKinley's peak season climbers cursed its unseasonably snowy and windy weather.

During the regular climbing season (from April to July this year), only 420 climbers reached the summit of Mt. McKinley. This represents the lowest success rate in the past ten years. For almost a century the average success rate has been about 50%. Climbers faced some harsh conditions this spring and were forced to wait out many severe storms. The low summit success rate was disappointing for climbers, but there was also a fairly low number of fatalities this past season. For the most part, climbers were staying put during the inclement weather and not taking unnecessary risks.

The longer an expedition stayed on the mountain, the greater their chance for a successful summit bid. The average time spent on the mountain for all expeditions was 17 days. For a successful summit team, the average length of stay was 21 days.

## TOTAL CLIMBERS BY ROUTE

| MT. MCKINLEY | Attempts | Summits |
|---|---|---|
| American Direct | 2 | 2 |
| Cassin Ridge | 2 | 0 |
| East Face | 1 | 0 |
| Muldrow Glacier | 27 | 19 |
| Muldrow Glacier Traverse | 13 | 6 |
| Orient Express | 5 | 0 |
| South Buttress | 1 | 0 |
| West Buttress | 1,027 | 366 |
| West Buttress Traverse | 4 | 2 |
| West Rib | 20 | 3 |
| Upper West Rib | 28 | 4 |
| | | |
| TOTAL | 1,166 | 420 |

| MT. FORAKER | Attempts | Summits |
|---|---|---|
| Sultana | 7 | 0 |
| Talkeetna Ridge | 2 | 0 |
| Viper Ridge | 2 | 0 |
| | | |
| TOTAL | 11 | 0 |

| MT. HUNTER | Attempts |
|---|---|
| Southwest Ridge | 6 |
| West Ridge | 11 |
| Moonflower | 12 |
| Wall of Shadows | 2 |

Climbers on Mt. Hunter are not required to register with the National Park Service, so statistics are not complete. However, reports indicate that none of the attempts on the mountain were successful.

DENALI NATIONAL PARK REPORTS

*Denali, Youngest climber to Reach the Summit.* Korean climber Kim Young Sik celebrated his 12th birthday two days before he summited via the West Buttress route on June 27.

DENALI NATIONAL PARK REPORTS

*Denali, First Double Amputee to Summit.* Korean climber Kim Hong Bin became the first double amputee to summit Denali, which he did via the West Buttress route. Bin had lost both hands to frostbite on a 1991 Denali accident.

DENALI NATIONAL PARK REPORTS

*Mt. Hunter, Northeast Buttress, North Couloir.* Scott DeCapio and I landed on the Kahiltna Glacier's Southeast Fork in mid-May with aspirations to try the *Moonflower* on Mt. Hunter's north buttress. However, the complete absence of high-pressure days failed to elicit the requisite melt-freeze cycles for ice formation on the route. Thus we spent our time wandering aimlessly about the glacier on skis, exploring crevasse fields and cragging on the stable ice seracs at the base of Mt. Francis's east face. One day in late May we decided to head toward a route we had heard of just beyond Hunter's north buttress. In low visibility, we skied to where we guessed the route to be, then sat on our packs and waited for a view. Through a brief clearing emerged a tapering couloir that snaked up the left side of the triangular peak immediately past the North Buttress Couloir and icefall. This peak (*not* the Kahiltna Queen, which is farther northeast) has been called the Northeast Buttress of Mt. Hunter, and is a spur peak off the flanks of Hunter. We crossed the bergschrund and climbed pitch after pitch of old gray ice, with the couloir steepening to 70° as it narrowed toward the obvious crux pitch 1,500 feet up the route. The crux proved to be very difficult thin manky ice and dry-tooling up to 95° with terrible protection. I suspect this pitch is filled with ice and considerably easier in more typical years (when enough sun results in melt-freeze ice). Five hundred more feet of 50-70° ice led to the summit ridge. On the last pitch, ice fall split a large gash in my forehead and eye, causing additional excitement and worry. However, my eyesight returned and the bleeding slowed, so we elected to continue to the summit of the buttress via another 500 feet of easy snow and ice. We rappelled the 2,500-foot route in a storm, being pummeled by constant spindrift avalanches. At Kahiltna base, 21 hours after leaving, we ate, drank, cared for my eye, and called Paul Roderick of T.A.T. for a flight to the comforts of Talkeetna.

KELLY CORDES, *unaffiliated*

## Ruth Gorge

*Mt. Bradley, South Face, The Gift (That Keeps On Giving).* Taking advantage of weather patterns allegedly caused by El Niño, and assurances by Park Ranger Darryl Miller that the winter in the Alaska Range had been "extremely mild," Jonny Blitz, Steve House and I flew onto the Ruth Glacier on February 28. The first few nights at our 4,400-foot base camp were quite cold (-25 to -30°F), but temperatures moderated thereafter. The camp received approximately ten hours of daylight, increasing by seven minutes per day, and just five hours of sunlight, as the sun rose from behind the Hut Tower and disappeared behind Mt. Wake.

After some reconnaissance and ski touring, we chose a line on Mt. Bradley. Our first attempt ended in retreat. Ice conditions were not ideal: much of what we counted on being ice was thin ice over powder snow or simply frothy snow plastered on the rock. I made a false start on pitch two before backing off and traversing around the offending difficulties. Jonny ran out of rope and ice and eventually, after spending a lot of time searching for anchors, had to belay off his tools. Steve made two attempts on pitch four before finally hanging his pack

*Steve House on pitch 11 of* The Gift (That Keeps on Giving). MARK F. TWIGHT

on a screw and leading through without it. Unfortunately, these mistakes ate up the daylight and after deciding no one was psyched to lead the sixth pitch, and with no way to aid climb around it, we retreated.

On March 7, we attempted the line again. The sixth pitch, dubbed the "Super Third Eye Opener," though quite dangerous, wasn't as difficult as expected and led us out of the initial dead-end gully. We climbed ten pitches the first day, fixing a rope and bivouacking at the bottom of the ninth pitch. Climbing through the headwall on day two was hard enough that we only managed four pitches before another bivy. The most striking pitch on the route, pitch 14, "The Super Giant Waterfall of Love," was led by House. Steep, bottomless snow led to moderate mixed climbing into a cave behind a free-hanging icicle. House pulled on to the icicle

*The south face of Mt. Bradley, showing* The Gift (That Keeps on Giving). MARK F. TWIGHT

and made three moves before it snapped off above his tools. He rode it down, ripping the first piece of gear before simultaneously hitting the snow slope and being stopped by a good cam. After a rest, he climbed back into the cave, onto the remaining ice, and through to a steep, but thin pillar. The pitch was very sustained, with dubious protection for 35 meters to a semi-hanging belay below a huge chockstone and snow mushroom—a true two-and-a-half hour lead.

On day three, we opted to leave the bivy gear behind and go as fast as we could for the top or to where difficulty stopped us—"fast" being a relative term, as the 15th pitch (A3) took Blitz three hours to lead. The "Super Three-Hour Pitch" involved aiding off ice tools used as hooks, tied-off knifeblades, real hooks and a lot of back-cleaning (the rack was too small for the type of climbing encountered). The gully opened up above it and we made good progress to a dead-end below another massive chockstone. Two difficult mixed pitches got us past it on the right, and led to more moderate snow. As darkness fell, we confronted yet another chockstone, but managed to sneak through "The Glory Hole" behind it on 90° ice. At 8 p.m. we reached the col at 8,700 feet. Four hundred feet of easy snow separated us from the summit, but true to my nature, we started rappelling, reaching our bivy at 1:30 a.m. We arrived at Base Camp on March 10 after a leisurely descent the next afternoon.

*The Gift (That Keeps On Giving)* follows a huge gully system west of *The Pearl*, a difficult rock route put up by Andy Orgler on the most obvious pillar dominating the south face. *The Gift...* is 3,200 feet high, and 23 (60m) pitches if you use the rope all the way. Thirteen of these pitches are "hard." The technical ratings are 5.9 A3 WI6 XX. Our grade, a Texas "two star," is as ambiguous as any other alpine grade and means absolutely nothing.

MARK F. TWIGHT, *Groupe de la Haute Montagne*

*Mt. Huntington, West Face, Attempt.* After flying over 1,200 miles of seamless clouds, Brad Grohusky and I were assured that the rumors of a particularly wet season in Alaska were true. The clouds looked just as permanent from below as the Talkeetna Shuttle Service van drove us to the end of the road. Four wet days later, we were still waiting for the weather to clear from the narrow entrance to the Tokositna Glacier. In a magnanimous gesture, our pilot, Jay Hudson, turned around from another flight destination when he saw a window in the weather, and at 10 p.m. on June 13 we moved into our Base Camp on the upper Tokositna Glacier.

Our objective was a new route on the west face of Mt. Huntington that consists of about half rock wall and half mixed climbing. After scoping out the wall and assessing the sizeable avalanche hazard (a result of heavy recent snows), we decided to set our immediate goal as getting up the wall, at which point we would re-evaluate the snow-choked upper sections. On June 14, we hastily packed the haul bag and then broke trail to the base of the wall, thus beginning our daily commute.

The rock was excellent Alaskan granite, although it was even more compact than we'd reckoned from the ground. We soon fell into a routine of getting to the base of the wall before the morning sun made the bergschrund too soft to ascend easily and then alternating days on the lead. Thankfully, the route is well situated and steep enough that any rock/ice fall was off to the sides. This allowed the leader to concentrate on the thin (A3) nailing that comprised the majority of each pitch. At night, the belayer would handle all of the camp chores and we would crawl into our sleeping bags after a typically long Alaskan day.

*Brad Grohusky on pitch 4 (A3) of an attempt on the west face of Mt. Huntington.* ROD WILLARD

After five days, during which we had climbed about half of the wall, we declared a rest day. A bit of sunning in t-shirts was quickly replaced by an afternoon storm and our efforts to keep the runway firmly packed. On June 20, another large low-pressure system, coupled with work commitments, forced an early exit for me. Luckily, John Lohuis had arrived in Talkeetna early and was able to fly in with Hudson that evening and make the partner exchange a simple one. The weather returned to its wettest, forcing Grohusky and Lohuis to spend more time in the tents than on the wall. Upward progress continued when possible, with the seam system opening up to allow some clean aid. A decision had to be made before the Tokositna Glacier became too crevassed to allow a plane landing: keep going and risk having to leave all of the fixed line on the wall, or leave a clean route and return another day. From Brad's high point he could see easier ground ahead leading to the mixed section above. "I shed a tear realizing that the route goes, but that we were out of time," wrote Brad later. The pair stripped the route, waited out another storm and then cleaned out camp and winged it back to Talkeetna. Having learned many lessons and tasted the endless possibilities of the Alaska Range, we cannot wait to return.

ROD WILLARD

*Mt. Russell, North Ridge.* On March 2-7, Colby Coombs, Caitlin Palmer, Meg Perdue and I flew to Mt. Russell in the Alaska Range. Colby, Meg and I made the sixth ascent of Mt. Russell, the fourth ascent of the North Ridge, and the second ascent in winter; Meg is the first woman recorded to have summitted Mt. Russell. It is a beautiful alpine route in a remote edge of the Alaska Range. The North Ridge route offers a safe and very aesthetic line to an awesome summit that is way off the beaten path, with many climbable peaks surrounding the upper Yentna glacier.

MIKE WOOD, *unaffiliated*

KICHATNA SPIRES

*Mt. Nevermore, East Face, The Call of the Raven.* In June, Mike Houston (a.k.a. Mausen) and brothers Doug and Jed Workman flew to the Tatina Glacier and spent 40 days in Alaska's Kichatna Spires, making the first ascent of the east face of Mt. Nevermore. We had planned on scoping a route on the fly-in, but were unable to due to shitty weather; we were blessed when Mike Pennings and Jeff Hollenbaugh (who had been unsuccessfully awaiting a break in the weather to try the face themselves) handed us a photo of the unclimbed 2,500-foot face. Ferrying loads from the Tatina Glacier to the Monolith Glacier took almost nine days due to constant bad weather. Five days were then spent fixing 800 feet of rope from the ground. A camp was established on the wall, from where we climbed capsule style, fixing another 600 feet of rope to our next camp. In total, the climb, *The Call of the Raven* (VI A2+ 5.9), took 13 days, from June 16-July 25, with eight days being spent on the wall.

The lower half of the wall entailed lots of bathooks and thin nailing (A2+? . . . sure). Though the cracks opened up high on the route, the weather prevented much free climbing. After completing the wall itself, we continued on a fifth-class ridge toward the summit, eventually turning around about a quarter mile from the actual peak of Nevermore due to rain, lack of food, and 24 hours to make it back to the landing zone for our scheduled pick-up. The weather ranged from 60°F and sunny to 30°F and raining to 20°F and heavy snow. Sunny skies after heavy snows created an abundance of slush avalanches, which spit from high on the wall, keeping us mildly entertained. The adventure was the Workmans' first trip to Alaska and Mausen's first grade VI.

DOUG WORKMAN, *unaffiliated*

*The east face of Mount Nevermore. An excellent photo of the east face of this peak is found in the 1998 AAJ, p. 91.*
DOUG WORKMAN

CHUGACH RANGE

*Monument Peak and Mt. Awesome, Ascents.* In March, Willy Peabody and I climbed Monument Peak at the head of the Monument Glacier in the Chugach Range via the north ridge. We then made the second ascent of Mt. Awesome via the south face.

MIKE WOOD, *unaffiliated*

*Mt. Fairweather, Winter Ascent.* On February 15, Nancy Juergens and I were landed in the foam of heavy surf approximately three miles south of Cape Fairweather. At low tide on the following day, our partners, Jeff Carter and Josephine Warden, joined us, and we began shuttling our 480 pounds of supplies through wonderful old growth rain forest. During the first week, we based out of a camp in the woods only two miles from the beach. Traveling with skis on our backs through devil's club, route-finding challenges and even mosquitoes combined to prevent rapid progress. The second week found us on the glacier—for one camp. We were forced into the vegetation again by an ice fall below firn line. Leaving the brush behind at our third camp, we settled into a routine of: one full carry the first day; move camp the next; on the third, two people retrieved the final load while two scouted ahead with light loads to determine the route. By the end of the third week, we had bypassed two major ice falls by traversing the hillsides on the east margin of the Fairweather Glacier and had our seventh camp at 4,300 feet, the standard Base Camp for the route.

Only a week of food and fuel remained to attempt the route. Our strategy during the planning phase of this climb was to allow many days to move up the mountain slowly, but this was no longer feasible. Following a day of rest at Base Camp, we broke trail up 3,000 feet of the route. On the next day, we moved into a cave camp at the 8,000-foot level. The ensuing day was one of scouting and rest. Jeff and Josephine decided that they would not continue up in order to give the expedition the best chance of success. On the 23rd day of the trip, Nancy and I moved into a cave near the 12,000-foot level with a couple of extra days of food and fuel to support our summit bid. Two days of wind and snow confined us to the entertainment of a Tom Clancy novel and the joys of a temperamental stove. With a "let's see how far we can get" attitude, we departed high camp at 8 a.m. on March 12. Our enthusiasm was dispirited by ominous black clouds building in the southern sky. As we cramponed up 45° wind-scoured slopes, traversed corniced ridges and avoided crevasses, we constantly watched the clouds to the south and kept tabs on each other's energy levels. Summiting at 3 p.m., we were thrilled that the clouds remained high, allowing us to see St. Elias and Logan to the north and Glacier Bay to the south. The alpenglow that enveloped us as the sun set between the clouds and the horizon lit up St. Elias like a beacon and was a highlight of the trip. The nerve-wracking after-dark return to high camp heightened our appreciation of our accomplishment.

The following morning we embarked on our exciting 7,700-foot descent back to Base Camp. A speedy 2,000-foot glissade aided in getting us back to the 4,300-foot camp by sunset. Our partners welcomed us with hot drinks and homemade pizza. Work commitments dictated that we be in Talkeetna mid-month, so we regretfully decided to get picked up at base camp at 4,300 feet, thereby foregoing our adventure back to the sea. A couple of fixed ropes on the rocky section of the ridge were the only sign of previous visitation that we saw, which lent to the overall sense of satisfaction and accomplishment that we all feel about our expedition.

JOE REICHERT

Wrangell-St. Elias Range

*Mt. Leeper, Ascent.* On May 13, Art Weiner and I were flown into the upper Yahtse Glacier at around 4,700 feet by Paul Claus of Ultima Thule Outfitters. As we flew in, Paul mentioned that in 1993, he had landed in his Super Cub high in a bowl on the north side of Mt. Leeper (9,603'). But Art and I were here to try to be the first to climb this peak, which is only 15 miles or so from the Gulf of Alaska. The Yahtse Glacier flows southeast from Barkley Ridge and into Icy Bay, so this region is constantly threatened by storms and high winds and receives an unusually high amount of precipitation.

We immediately moved up the glacier to around 5,600 feet and set up our first camp under Leeper's north face. The next day we skied through the icefall and established high camp at around 6,700 feet on the northwest ridge. We were southeast of the rocky pyramid of Pt.7072'. On May 15, we skied up the northwest ridge to around 9,100 feet, where we were forced to kick off our skis. A huge serac that splits the ridge and separates it from the summit forced us to the left. From here we kicked steps up the ridge and walked onto the summit in the early afternoon. Throughout our climb we were hit by increasing winds, which forced an abbreviated stay on the summit. We hurried down safely back to camp before a storm closed in behind us. Six of the next seven days were spent in the tent due to high winds, snow and whiteout conditions. We did get two brief stretches that allowed us to get back to our landing area and food cache, where we were picked up only one day later than scheduled on the 23rd. This may have been the first ascent of Mt. Leeper, but only time will tell.

DANNY W. KOST

*Peak 8933', Ascent.* On April 23, six of us (Mimi Bourquin, Paul Claus, Ruedi Homberger, Cristine Legnet, Reto Reutsch, and myself) flew from Ultima Thule Lodge to an unnamed glacier to the north and east of P8933' at around 6,700 feet. We skied down to around 6,200 feet at the base of the icefall, which flows north from the summit. We skied up through the icefall and reached the summit by early afternoon, enjoying the views from the summit during a break in the unusually stormy spring this part of Alaska had been experiencing. The others enjoyed the skiing down through the icefall while I slowly skied my way back to the bottom as best I could.

On the way back we stopped and skied up the northwest side of Table Mountain (8640'). This peak was first climbed in 1913 by a boundary survey party, which did a number of first ascents in the area and got high on Mt. St. Elias as well before weather turned them around.

DANNY W. KOST

*Peak 10,522', Ascent.* On May 29, Kelly Bay of Wrangell Mountain Air flew me into the upper Chisana Glacier at around 8,300 feet on the southeast side of this mountain. I was climbing alone since I had been unable to locate a climbing partner. In early April, I had been in this same area with Howard Mozen to attempt Peak 10,522' and others, but we were unsuccessful due to high winds and snow.

I immediately donned skis and headed up toward the 9,200-foot col due east of the summit. Here I kicked off the skis and donned crampons. I followed this eastern ridge, which was fairly easy until a couple of hundred feet from the summit, where a large serac was separating from the summit block. There was a large crevasse that skirted the whole summit block with an overhanging ice wall on the uphill side. I crossed the crevasse on the far right and stayed on the ridge crest around the serac wall. This offered some nice 40-60° climbing on snow and ice for 60 feet or so with 3,000 feet of exposure down the northeast face. Above this it was an easy walk to the summit. I first saw this peak from the summit of the Presidents Chair in 1993. Peak 10,522' resembles Mt. Deborah of the Alaska Range and I had referred to it as "Little Deborah" since that initial sighting. I believe this was the first ascent of the peak.

DANNY W. KOST

*Mt. Bona, St. Elias Mountains.* On May 27, Paul Claus flew AAC members Steve Malmberg, George Rodway, Dan Vogt, and I to 10,500 feet on the upper Klutlan Glacier, just south of the Bona-Churchill plateau, to attempt Mt. Bona (16,421'). Our original plan was to place two camps at 12,700 feet and 14,300 feet respectively. Due to one week of bad weather and six to eight feet of new snow, we began to run out of time and made the decision to place just one camp at 12,700 feet and go for the top in one long day. George Rodway remained in Base Camp nursing a gallbladder infection with painkillers and antibiotics. On June 1, the weather cleared up temporarily, and we began the move up to occupy Camp I. Lenticular clouds soon moved in and it snowed several feet the next day. Finally, June 3 dawned clear and calm and we climbed via the knife-edge summit ridge of Churchill's Chin (14,916'), reaching the summit of Mt. Bona at about 3 p.m. All three of us fell into hidden crevasses on the east summit ridge. We returned to Camp I and descended to Base Camp in a whiteout the next day. We were flown out on June 6. We encountered two other teams on the mountain, a party of three Germans and a two-person American team. Both parties bailed off the mountain early due to the horrendous weather.

DAVE PAISLEY

# CANADA

## ST. ELIAS RANGE

*Peak 11,700', Southwest Ridge.* After an injury in our party halted our attempt at the standard King Trench route on Mt. Logan, Morgan Lakey and I turned our frustrations to a pyramidal rock and snow peak five kilometers northwest of the standard Base Camp on the Quitino Sella Glacier. The top 100 meters of the peak is just visible over a ridge to the immediate west of Base Camp. With three days' food, we skied over to the south face and examined a series of interesting rock ridges and couloirs. The most inviting ran continuously from the foot to the summit on the southeast face but started avalanching when we arrived. We selected a long couloir that gained the southwest ridge about mid-way up, then waded, ploughed and scrambled up to the ridge. The southwest ridge was hard-packed snow with gently undulating cornices that made for excellent climbing. On June 8, after five-and-a-half hours from our camp at the foot of the mountain, Lakey and I topped out in a nearly total whiteout, which spoiled what should have been a tremendous view of Mt. Logan. The summit was recognized by key rocks we had noted from below and the fact that it was downhill in all directions. Upon return to the Logan Base Camp, discussions with Paul Claus, climber/pilot for Ultima Thule, indicated that he may have climbed the same peak by possibly the same ridge a few years earlier. Although the maps suggest an elevation of about 11,700+ feet, the local pilots distrust the figures, believing it to be higher.

JEB SCHENCK, *unaffiliated*

*"Mt. Swanson," Northwest Face.* During the end of April and beginning of May, Jim Earl and I ventured to a little-explored area in the St. Elias Range referred to as the Fourth of July Cirque. This area is on the Hawkins Glacier at the base of the southwest and west faces of University Peak; to the north are the incredible south walls of the Thwaharpes Celeno and Ocypete peaks as well as a handful of unclimbed prizes.

On our second day in the area, we set our sights on the north face of "Little Ama Dablam," so named by Paul Claus, who made the first ascent of this 10,000-footer. After the first pitch of beautiful Alaskan ice (up to 85°), we began simul-climbing the middle 60° slopes. After approximately 600 feet of climbing, my crampon broke and we were forced to retreat and one-leg it back to camp.

This small mishap was the cause of great festering in our camp while, during blue-bird days, we waited for Paul to retrieve our spare pair of crampons from his house. This occurred eight days later. The weather had changed, and light snow held us in camp the entire time.

As soon as we were resupplied with fresh 'poons, we set our sights on another objective, "Mt. Swanson" (named in memory of our friend who perished in a helicopter accident in January, 1997). This 10,800-foot peak features a stunning 5,000-foot northeast face that

The 5,000-foot northeast face of "Mt. Swanson" (10,800'), showing line of ascent. JIM EARL

drained into the Hawkins Glacier at our feet. Leaving at 4:30 a.m. on April 29, we skied to the base, then climbed up the initial 1,000-foot snow ramp and avalanche runnel to the route's short crux: 100 feet of mixed 5.8 (M4) and thin smears of ice. The crux deposited us onto the 2,000-foot, 70° snow gully that leads to a 140-foot ice gully with bullet-proof ice (60-85°), including some thin technical sections. A short traverse put us into deep snow on 60° ice. After much work and "chunneling" for two more pitches, I was able to top out on the cor- niced east ridge, 600 feet away from and 200 feet below the summit, in deteriorating weath- er. I immediately down climbed back to Jim. After a short brew up of hot liquids, we descend- ed our route through poor weather and heavy spindrift back to Base Camp, arriving at 6 a.m. on the 30th after 26 continuous hours of climbing.

The next two days passed easily, despite the weather. We were content to sleep and eat. Unfortunately, the weather remained poor for an additional five days, which cut short the big- ger plan of exploring the flanks of University Peak. On May 6, Paul swooped in through a hole in the weather and returned us to civilization.

BRENDAN CUSICK

*Mt. McArthur, South Face, Fred Said Buttress.* It was reported that in mid-June, Canadians Rick Clements, Chris Kettles, and Troy Jungen, under the watchful eye of Fred Beckey, spent three days climbing the *Fred Said Buttress* on the last prominent unclimbed buttress on the south face of Mt. McArthur (14,243'). The three climbed snow and ice couloirs to the right of the buttress down low to avoid bad rock on the lower portion of the route; higher, they encoun- tered good rock and exposed pitches as they followed the buttress directly to the summit. It was the sixth ascent of the mountain; all six have been made by new routes. (*Climbing* 180)

Kluane National Park Reserve

*Mountaineering Summary and Statistics, 1998.* This year there were 42 expeditions com- prising 163 people within the icefields of Kluane. This is a slight increase in numbers from last year. The maximum number of climbers in a single season was 186 people in 1992.

There were 24 expeditions and 105 people on Mt. Logan this year, representing 64% of the people in the icefields. The King Trench route, on the west side of the mountain, saw 13 expe- ditions and 70 people; the East Ridge had 11 expeditions and 35 people. No significant attempts were made on other routes on Mt. Logan. Once again, large crevasses on the King Trench route above 15,000 feet created some route-finding challenges, but apparently not as troublesome as in 1997. A solo traverse was accomplished this year of Mt. Logan from the East Ridge to the King Trench by Martin Minarek, a tenacious Czech climber.

Other mountains that were attempted included Mt. Kennedy, Mt. Hubbard, Pinnacle Peak, Mt. Wood, McArthur Peak, Mt. Queen Mary, Mt. King George, Mt. Lucania, Mt. Macauley, Mt. Steele and Mt. Walsh. An interesting high-line traverse was accomplished from Mt. Wood to Mt. Steele, taking in Mt. Macauly, by a group of five in August (see below).

The weather during the first half of the season, from mid-April to early June, was rather bad. High winds and consistent precipitation aggravated most expeditions during this time. The usual period of clear, stable weather that settles into the Icefield ranges during the late spring was kept out by a series of low-pressure systems from the Gulf of Alaska. Many groups reported extended tent-bound stays.

There were two significant search-and-rescue operations this year. One climber became disoriented on attempting to exit the icefields via the Kaskawulsh Glacier and Slims Valley. A two-day helicopter search located him, unhurt but heading away from his intended destination. Two climbers on the King Trench route were reported overdue and probably out of food and fuel by their aircraft pilot. Five days after their expected completion date, the weather cleared up enough for a helicopter search of the area. The pair were located at 16,500 feet on the route. Food, fuel and a radio was dropped to them and they managed to descend without any further assistance. One of the climbers sustained a substantial frostbite injury to his hands during their day to the summit. He subsequently was treated in an Anchorage hospital and lost tissue from several fingers.

Anyone interested in climbing within Kluane should contact: Mountaineering Warden, Kluane National Park Reserve, Box 5495, Haines Junction, Yukon, Canada Y0B 1L0, or call (867) 634-7279, or fax (867) 634-7277, and ask for a mountaineering registration package.

ANDREW LAWRENCE, *Park Warden*

*Mt. Wood to Mt. Macauley to Mt. Steele, High Traverse.* On July 28, John Millar, David Persson and I flew in to the Trapridge Glacier, where we met Alun Hubbard and Dave Hildes, who were finishing up glaciology fieldwork. In the next five days, we made three camps on the east face of Mt. Wood (4840m) at 3000, 3900, and 4200 meters, and summited in fine weather on August 3. Highlights of the climb included spectacular icefalls at the 3200- and 3700-meter levels that required complicated route finding. From camp in the Wood/Macauley col, we climbed the straight-forward northeast ridge of Mt. Macauley (4690m) to the summit and continued to the col between it and "Southeast Macauley." On August 5, we made the first ascent of what was perhaps the highest unclimbed peak in Canada, "Southeast Macauley" (4420m; GR 268818), via its mellow northwest ridge, and then made a gliding descent of its equally casual southeast ridge. Up until this point in the traverse, most of the terrain was broad ridge or face and well suited for skiing.

After a storm day, we continued along the ridge, which was becoming narrower and heavily corniced. On August 7, we summited the previously unclimbed "Northwest Steele" (4220m; GR 323787). Over the next two days, we made slow but important progress over heavily corniced, exposed ridge, which included a somewhat rotten 20-meter knife-edge ridge section. Next, we descended from "Northwest Steele" into the notch separating it from Mt. Steele. This descent was a cautious wade through 40° waist-deep snow at the top of a 1200-meter avalanchey slope in order to avoid ice cliffs.

The notch was undoubtedly the crux of the traverse, as it was riddled with heavily corniced knife-edge ridges separated by platforms. One cornice was too precarious to cross, so we were forced to drop down onto the southwest side of the ridge via a 100-meter 55° snowslope, traverse a very unstable, 50° bowl, and then re-ascend to the ridge crest via a 100-meter 75° ice slope covered in 30 centimeters of rotten snow and ice. Following the ice pitch, we reluctantly set up camp in the exposed notch. The next day, we tackled the last major technical difficulty in the notch, a set of three massive cornices (dubbed "the cobras"), the first of which was a severe knife-edge ridge capped with two rotten cornices, one on top of the other. While leading across it, David broke through many times.

*A windy day at 4000 meters on the north ridge of Mt. Steele.* DAVE HILDES

Finally, we arrived at our main objective, the unclimbed north ridge of Mt. Steele (5073m). Except for one dangerous cornice at 3840 meters, the north ridge was just a snow slog. An extremely windy day forced us to stop early and camp in the shelter of a crevasse at 4220 meters. On August 13, we summited Mt. Steele in superb weather, having completed the first traverse from Mt. Wood to Mt. Steele. We called the traverse *Millar's High Life* (Alaskan Grade 6, WI3). After descending the southeast ridge of Steele, we flew out of the St. Elias to Kluane Lake on August 15.

According to Wallis (1992 *CAJ*, pp. 4-19), "Southeast Macauley" would have become the highest unclimbed peak in Canada once Atlantic Peak was climbed in 1995. However, according to Wallis (1998 *AAJ*, pp. 230-231), "South Slaggard" (4370m; GR 220786) was the highest unclimbed peak in Canada when he climbed it in July 1997. Various reliable sources have confirmed that our ascent of "Southeast Macauley" was the first. I invite Mr. Wallis to clarify this apparent discrepancy.

JEREMY FRIMER, *Varsity Outdoor Club (UBC)*

*Mts. Hubbard, Kennedy, South Kennedy, and Alverstone, Various Activity.* On June 22, Kurt Gloyer of Gulf Air Taxi flew Douglas Bonoff, Doug Zimmerman, and I to the 2580-meter level on the Cathedral Glacier in Kluane National Park from Yakutat. Two days were spent hauling loads to approximately 3300 meters. On June 26, we established a camp at 3880 meters on the Cathedral Glacier between Mt. Alverstone and Hubbard. On June 27, we attempted the east face of Alverstone but were unsuccessful due to poor snow conditions.

The next day, at 1:30 a.m., we departed camp for an ascent of Mt. Hubbard via the north face/icefall. Easy climbing led around seracs until we were able to gain the east shoulder at

4200 meters. We summited Hubbard (4505m) in cold, clear conditions at 5:30 a.m. That afternoon we descended to our 3300-meter camp for a day off.

The following day (June 29) we established a camp at 3450 meters on Mt. Kennedy. With favorable conditions, we decided to attempt the unclimbed South Kennedy (3656m) along its north ridge. Easy climbing led to a final steep pitch of snow. The summit of South Kennedy was very exposed and too small for one climber, let alone three. As a result, the final pitch was climbed and down climbed, thus allowing each of us to summit. On June 30, we climbed the west ridge (normal route) of Mt. Kennedy (4238m) in clear conditions.

Clear skies and a lack of new snow made early day travel easy. Late-day snow conditions deteriorated significantly, keeping us in camp as we observed the cascade of serac avalanches. Route-finding options on the Cathedral Glacier were limited. Establishing the camp at 3300 meters required several hauling systems for the sleds.

Conditions for our two-week stay on the Cathedral Glacier were exceptional. The weather was perfect. On July 2, we descended to 2580 meters and were able to contact Gulf Air for a July 3 pickup. The Fourth of July was spent in Yakutat celebrating. Doug Zimmerman placed seventh in the Bay to Breakers 10K race on the Fourth of July. Doug Bonoff and Bob walked the course.

ROBERT M. PLUCENIK

*Mt. Alverstone, West Face, Pugilist at Rest and The Wilford Couloir.* In May, Barry Blanchard and I set out to climb the west face of Mt. Alverstone. After flying in with Gulf Air to the Hubbard Glacier, we set up Base Camp. A few days later (approximately May 10), we started up Alverstone. The climbing turned out to be a little less technical than we'd hoped for. We established a bivy approximately 2,500 feet up the climb. The next day we followed a gully system up to the summit ridge, where we encountered a whiteout. We pushed a few hundred feet more along the summit ridge, then turned back in poor conditions. We had climbed the face, but had not continued to the summit.

A week later, we set out for a rock pillar on a ridge line that comes off the northwest side of Alverstone. The pillar looks somewhat like the Gervasutti Pillar in France. We started up the obvious main corner/buttress system and found excellent rock and mixed conditions. At mid-height, we bivied. The next day, we started with hard rock and mixed ground, then the terrain turned more mixed than ice. At the summit, weather conditions worsened and we descended in high winds to an open bivy at the base of the climb. We called the route *Pugilist at Rest* (5.10 A3 M5, 3,000').

A week later, we went back to this same formation, which we called "Point Blanchard," and climbed the couloir just to the left of our previous climb. This line was a bit easier but had excellent Grade V water ice in it. We managed this climb, the *Wilford Couloir* (5.9 M4 WI5, 2,700') in one push. Generally, the rock was good in this area.

MARK WILFORD, *unaffiliated*

*King Peak, Call of the Wild.* From June 18-19, Joe Josephson and Steve House made the first ascent of *Call of the Wild* (VI WI6, 7,500') on the southwest face of King Peak. A full account of their fast and light ascent appears earlier in this journal.

*Barry Blanchard in the* Wilford Couloir, *"Point Blanchard," Mt. Alverstone.* MARK WILFORD

*"Point Blanchard" on Mt. Alverstone. The longest arête is the location of* Pugilist at Rest; *the* Wilford Couloir *is the couloir just to the left.* MARK WILFORD

*Mt. Logan, South Face Attempt, and Mt. King George, Lauchlan Ridge.* John Chilton, Rich Prohaska and I went to the St. Elias Mountains with the help of the John Lauchlan Award to climb the south face of Mt. Logan. We drove to Kluane Lake and waited for 11 days before the weather allowed us to fly into the mountains. We made three attempts during this time.

Our plan was to climb the east ridge to acclimatize and to leave a fuel and food stash at the top of the south face. We made an ABC at the base of the east ridge and waited another five storm days. We decided to go back to Base Camp and eat Base Camp food and waited another six days, one of which was spent retrieving ABC.

Twenty-three days into the trip, we decided to pull the plug on the south face. Our new goal was the unclimbed west ridge of King George, some 30 kilometers away. We spent three days climbing the Lauchlan Ridge (5.9 WI3, 6,000'), and then down climbing the south ridge. Two days later, we flew out to Kluane Lake.

JIA CONDON, *Canada*

*Mt. King George. The 6,000-foot Lauchlan (west) Ridge is the prominent ridge running bottom right to top left.* JIA CONDON

NORTHWEST TERRITORIES

LOGAN MOUNTAINS

*The south faces of the Vampire Spire, The Canine, and The Fortress in the Logan Mountains.*
HARRISON SHULL

*Vampire Peaks, Various Ascents.* On July 17, John Young, David Coleman, Cogie Reed, Harrison Shull, and I were dropped off in the Vampire Peaks for 27 days. The Vampire Peaks lie roughly 15 miles away from the Cirque of the Unclimbables in the southwestern corner of the Northwest Territories. Our main objective was to climb an unnamed massif via a virgin 2,000-foot-plus wall dubbed "The Phoenix." After spending the first day scouting out our line, we fixed the first two pitches. The line that we chose took a direct path up the prow of the buttress on beautiful crack systems the entire way. Harrison, John and I then committed

*Matt Childers and Cogie Reed on* Cornerstone *(IV 5.10 A2+), The Fortress, Vampire Peaks.*
HARRISON SHULL

o the wall with four days of supplies and gear. After waking the next morning to rockfall hitting the portaledge fly, we began our steady progress up the wall. The climbing was predominately moderate aid with some good free climbing mixed in. Our line proved to be every bit as beautiful as it had appeared from the ground. When the prow that we were following ended, we climbed a long chimney pitch followed by a fourth-class gully to a false summit. climbed the last 200-foot pitch via a system of broken cracks and ledges to the top. We summited on our fifth day on the wall and were greeted with good weather. We called our route of first ascent *Freebird* (VI 5.9 A2+).

While we were on the Phoenix, Cogie and David were starting a route on a feature directly across from us dubbed the Golden Buttress. Cogie, David, John, and I all summited several days later via *Golden Wing* (III 5.10 A2+).

After completing our objectives in the first valley, we moved camp up to the previously described Vampire Spires. We spent the next three days humping loads up talus slopes and bushwhacking through willow thickets. The Vampire Spires are composed of three distinct spires (The Fortress, The Canine, and the Vampire Spire) that sit in the head of the valley we were camped in. The Vampire Spire was climbed by a party in 1994 (see account by Mike Benge on p. 194), but the Fortress and the Canine remained untouched.

After spending a day bouldering and sorting gear under blue skies, Cogie and I set off to attempt the Fortress. Once again we were blessed with a straight-forward and striking line up the center of the feature. Clean dihedrals and splitter cracks gained us about 600 feet to a spacious ledge for our first bivy. We made good progress the first day and were hopeful of our summit chances the next. Cogie gave me a good scare the next day by taking an ugly 15-foot edge fall when the rock exploded around a stopper he was on. A couple of hours beforehand, ohn ended his trip by spraining his ankle while taking a big fall attempting a line to the right of ours with David. After topping out on the buttress late that afternoon, we then picked our way through false summits and rotten gullies until we finally ran out of rock to climb. We rappelled back down to our portaledges as a storm was coming in and settled into sleeping bags with the satisfaction of having accomplished one of our goals. We called our route *Cornerstone* (IV 5.10 A2+).

With only a few days left until our pick-up, Cogie and I decided to try the last unclimbed spire, The Canine. The rock on the Canine proved to be much looser than anything we had previously tried. The climbing demanded our full attention. After a couple of short falls, a stopper that busted my chin open, and a 40-foot head-first fall, we were definitely taking our situation seriously. We were finally forced to retreat about 100 feet from the summit due to impending blizzard conditions, a bizarre, criss-crossing dihedral crack system that lay ahead, and a pickup date within two days' time. In retrospect, our line will go using a variety of angles.

MATT CHILDERS

## BRITISH COLUMBIA

### COAST MOUNTAINS

*Waddington Range, Various Activity.* This was an interesting year, with a long, dry, hot introduction to the season putting the glaciers into very difficult conditions for travel, but shaping up the mountains (especially the rock lines) better than in most summers. A lot of activity was

recorded, most of it focused on peaks other than "The Wadd," which was climbed on
twice—the Bravo Icefall was not in friendly shape!

The year started with an incredibly adventurous outing when Frenchman Lionel Daud
and his friends (his brother Damien, George Jougeau, and Swiss big-wall specialist Jean
Michel Zweiacker) spent three weeks ferrying 300 kilos of gear on foot and skis into th
range to attempt a new route on Combatant Mountain. Lionel and Damien eventually climbe
a snow/ice approach plus six difficult mixed and rock pitches (to 6c A1) left of *Skywalk* o
the southwest pillar. Four days of storm forced retreat from a portaledge bivy well short o
the summit, although a nut in a crack was passed on the last pitch, so the route may hav
joined *Walk on the Wild Side*.

Jim Haberl and Keith Reid made the first repeat (with minor variations) of the very fir
*Risse Route* (IV 5.8 ice to 50°, 700m) on the south face of the Northwest Peak of Waddingto
in June, which is usually a washout month.

Ben Gilmore and Kevin Mahoney flew into the Waddington-Combatant Col early in Jul
(again, earlier than is typical), and made the second ascent of the complete North Couloir (I
5.6 A1, ice to 65°, 1500m) of Mt. Hickson over two days as a warm-up. They followed th
with a new two-pitch 5.10a direct start to *Skywalk*, and topped off their visit with a steep ne
rock route (*Solo Blue*, IV 5.6 A3, six 60m pitches) on the west face of the Middle Buttress o
Combatant. Ben completed this route on his own because of a tendon injury suffered by Kevi

The "old-timers" from Seattle (Glen Cannon, Dave Knudson, Mike Martin, Peter Ren
Mickey Schurr, and Jon Wellner, with youngster Chris Fast) visited the Sunrise Glacie
Numerous first repeats were made, and several first ascents. Of particular note were th
climbs made on the small rock peaks between Cataract, Isolation, and Malemute glacier
attractive and seldom-visited destinations, and the first ascent of d'Artagnan Spire in the Fou
Guardsmen.

A large group from Seattle (five members) and Germany (three members) spent the la
week of July and first week of August in the range, accomplishing several significant climb
and establishing new records for intra-group angst. Bruno Boll, Daniel Hamann, and Forre
Murphy made the second complete ascent of the South Buttress (VI 5.10 A1, 1600m) o
Tiedemann in five days round-trip. Dan Aylward and Forrest then climbed the long-admire
North Rib (IV 5.10, 800m) of Marcus in a day and a half round-trip, while Bruno and Danie
blitzed the neighboring North Face (IV 5.6, 900m) of Merlon in only 17 hours round-tri
Unfortunately, the rock on Merlon was dangerously poor, and this impressive face earned
"Not Recommended." Later in the trip, numerous climbs on the Upper Tellot Glacier wei
done, with perhaps the finest being a new line (5.10d, three pitches) by Bruno and Daniel o
the superb east face of Dragonback.

Doug Clark and Keith Pankow attempted the South Buttress of Tiedemann a week or s
after the above party had made their ascent, reaching the base of the final 13-pitch upper pi
lar after three days. Here a storm moved in, pinning the two in their bags for a very unplea
ant day before they were able to force a retreat. Bad weather is always a factor to consider i
the Coast Mountains, even in the finest summer.

Michael Down and Graeme Taylor were on the Upper Tellot Glacier twice during the sun
mer. On the first trip, in August, they climbed the impressive Northwest Buttress (IV 5.
500m) of Mt. Shand, which unfortunately finished with a couple of extremely precariou
dangerously loose pitches. This was followed by several other smaller day-climbs, includir

the pleasant North Face (II, ice to 55°, steeper at the 'schrund, minor mixed, three 55m pitches) of Dragonback and the excellent Southeast Pillar (II 5.10+, three pitches) of Mt. McCormick. The later trip, in early September, netted the Northeast Face Direct (III 5.9 A2, nine pitches) on the impressive prong of Stiletto Needle.

The redoubtable Fred Beckey revisited the range for the umpteenth time, accompanied by Kai Hirvonen, Lorne Glick, and Witt Richardson. The latter three made a very fine new route, climbing the oft-admired, occasionally attempted Southwest Face (V 5.10 A2, nine 60m pitches) of Stiletto Peak in two days. Numerous other shorter routes on the fine granite of the Upper Tellot Glacier peaks followed, including the first free ascent of the south face (II 5.11a, three pitches) of Tellot Spire.

DON SERL, *Canada*

CANADIAN ROCKIES

*Mt. Quadra, Gimme Shelter.* In March, Alain Massin and Steve Pratt managed the second ascent of *Gimme Shelter* on Mt. Quadra. First climbed over two days in 1983 by Kevin Doyle and Tim Friesen with exceptionally thin ice for seven pitches, it was easily the hardest ice climb in the world at the time. The last few seasons, it has been forming as a fat pillar of straight-forward water ice. Despite the WI 5+/6 conditions, the seracs at the top of the route have become very unstable, with several close calls keeping most suitors away. The significance of this long-awaited second ascent is somewhat diminished due to the relatively easy conditions of the route and the fact that repeating the route is now simply a matter of being willing to brave the obscene serac hazard.

One of greatest and most sought-after alpine water ice routes in the world, *Slipstream*, in the Columbia Icefields, also has a disintegrating serac barrier. Until recently, the serac atop this 3,000-foot route has been relatively mild, but a large blue hole has appeared directly over the route and is now regularly discharging down the climb.

Other hanging glaciers in the Rockies are in various states of disrepair. Numerous alpine routes are now decidedly unsafe. The North Glacier of Deltaform, *Photofinish* on Andromeda, the *Hourglass Route* on the north face of Athabasca, the Elzinga/Miller on the north face of Cromwell and, most disturbingly, the glacier atop the Lowe Route on the north face of Mt. Alberta have become or are quickly becoming a toss of the dice.

JOE JOSEPHSON, *Calgary Mountain Club*

*North Face of the Saskatchewan Mountain Massif, The Silver Lining.* On April 5, Barry Blanchard, Steve House and I left the Big Bend parking lot on the Icefields Parkway and skied several kilometers toward the toe of the Saskatchewan Glacier. Our objective was the first steep chimney cutting through the 2,000-foot wall on the left side of the valley. The approach was made up a wind-blown slope to the base (about two hours from the car). The first pitch was the crux, requiring difficult dry tooling to spotty ice above a large roof. Due to unprotectable, detached ice, the next pitch followed a tricky rock corner to a cave on the left, followed by an exposed dry tooling traverse back to the ice. These pitches do not always form and in better times may be straight-forward ice. The next seven pitches followed classic alpine mixed and ice terrain up the gully. Highlights include a wild mixed section coming

out of a large cave on pitch 8 and a difficult overhang on pitch 10. Pitch 11 avoids the obvious, bomb-bay chimney by traversing left to reach an easy gully that leads to the summit
slopes. We walked off avalanche-prone slopes in the bowl to the west. The route is 14 200-
foot rope lengths and was climbed in 12 belayed pitches. Most belays were off pitons, and
none are fixed. We left two in-situ pins near the top. The route, *The Silver Lining* (IV 5.9
WI6R or so), was climbed in 19 hours car-to-car.

JOE JOSEPHSON, *Calgary Mountain Club*

*Mt. Babel, East Face, Free Ascent.* In August, John Culberson and I made the first American
ascent of the East Face of Mt. Babel in the Canadian Rockies. This grade IV limestone wall
has seen few ascents overall, and fewer yet as a free route. It was first climbed with aid sections by Bobby Greenwood in 1969. It was freed in 1992 by John Marshall at 5.11b, also the
style in which we climbed it.

The mountain hovers over Consolation Valley, a short hike from Moraine Lake. The route
is steep enough that a rock gently lobbed from the top hits the talus without a bounce on the
way down. The rock is reasonable limestone with good protection at the hard parts.

DAVID TURNER

BAFFIN ISLAND

Auyuittuq National Park

*Cumberland Peninsula, Ski Mountaineering Expedition.* The objective of our Baffin Island
ski mountaineering expedition was to make a self-sufficient 20-day journey in the
Cumberland Peninsula mountains, climbing suitable peaks en route with standard alpine ski
mountaineering gear. Between April 16 and May 6, the seven-member expedition (Danny
Baillie, Rodney Franklin, John Kentish, Ian McKirdy, Graham Rowe, Charles Turner, and I)
completed an exploratory journey through the mountains of the Cumberland Peninsula, to the
east of the Weasel Valley and to the north of Kingnait Fjord. The Expedition was entirely
self-sufficient from the point of drop-off by skidoo, with the supplies and equipment being
pulled and carried with a combination of rucksack and specially adapted children's sledge.
After a few days around Mt. Asgard, the team moved southeast out of the Auyuittuq National
Park into a very dramatic area of large glaciers and steep rock walls. A fairly circuitous travel of some 150 kilometers was made back to a pick-up at the head of Pangnirtung Fjord.
Fourteen peaks were climbed en route. Most summits involved a combination of ascent by
ski and foot, generally via the easier-looking ridges. The climbing never exceeded alpine PD+
in technical difficulty. Where possible, we attempted peaks suitable for ski ascent and
descent. Climbs had to be accomplished relatively quickly in order to let the journey proceed.
Of the peaks climbed, four had names and a further four appeared to have had previous
ascents (i.e., cairned and/or recorded ascent). No mention has been found of the remaining
six, but even so we would hesitate to claim any first ascents. It is highly likely, though, that
many of the ascents were "firsts" in the ski-mountaineering sense. The southwest face of
Valhalla Mountain was skied by two members from just below summit rocks to the glacier
base, a vertical descent of some 500 meters with an average angle of 40° (max. 45°).

The full list of ascents is as below (together with an approximate alpine grade):

| Date | Peak | Grid | Height | Party | Grade |
|---|---|---|---|---|---|
| April 18 | West Summit of Adluk Peak | | | | |
| | | LU941971 | 1820m | DW, CT, IM, RF, D13 | F |
| April 18 | Unnamed Peak | LU962988 | 1850m | GR, JK | F |
| April 21 | Unnamed Peak | MU178895 | 1920m | DW, CT, GR, IM, RF, DB | F |
| April 22 | Qilaut Mountain | MU243802 | 2150m | DW, CT, RF, DB | PD+ |
| April 25 | Valhalla Mountain | MU290832 | 1720m | DW, CT, GR, IM, RF, DB | PD+ |
| April 26 | Unnamed Peak | MU315812 | 1660m | DW, CT, GR, IM, RF, DB | F |
| April 27 | Unnamed Peak | MU243745 | 1900m | DW, CT, GR, IM, RF, DB | F |
| April 27 | Unnamed Peak (Cairned) | | | | |
| | | MU232756 | 1680m | DW, DB | PD |
| May 2 | Unnamed Peak | MU056758 | 1780m | DW, CT, GR, RF, DB | PD |
| May 2 | Unnamed Subsidiary Peak | | | | |
| | | MU068750 | 1820m | DW, CT, GR, IM, RF, DB | F |
| May 3 | Unnamed Peak (Cairned) | | | | |
| | | LU008694 | 1820m | DW, RF, DB | PD |
| May 3 | Unnamed Peak | MU014682 | 1550m | DW, DB | F |
| May 4 | Takuniakvik Peak | LU994705 | 1830m | DW, GR, RF, DB | PD+ |
| May 4 | Summit Ridge of Unnamed Peak | | | | |
| | | MU010674 | 1650m | DW, DB | F |

The weather was generally high pressure with clear skies and little wind. Daytime temperatures ranged from -10°C to -15°C with nighttime lows of -30°C. Travel was restricted on three out of 20 days. Snow cover was good, but of dubious quality, with approximately 30 centimeters of windpack layers overlaying one meter of depth hoar. It was apparently a high snowfall year for the area. John Kentish broke a back molar tooth in half on day four and, in some pain, decided to retreat alone down the Weasel Valley to get treatment.

DAVID WILLIAMS, *United Kingdom*

*Mt. Thor, Midgard Serpent, Solo Ascent.* In July and August, the young big wall climber Jason "Singer" Smith made a solo second ascent of *Midgard Serpent* (VI 5.9 A5, 3,600') on the west face of Mt. Thor. An account of his climb appears earlier in this journal.

*Summit Lake Area, Various Ascents.* Six of us from the Banff area converged on Summit Lake during the first two weeks of May. We only had time for a short trip, so were banking on a lucky weather window. People seemed to think that going before the sea ice breaks yields less humidity in the air and therefore better weather. A suspicious theory at best, but we were clinging to it.

Our arrival at Summit Lake seemed to be timed perfectly: a north wind brought the clear skies we wanted, but unfortunately was accompanied by -20C° temperatures. At this point, the prospects for even going ski touring were looking rather grim and we resigned ourselves to be happy with even one summit. On the first day, Marc Ledwidge, Rob Orvig and Larry

Stanier climbed the Swiss Route to the top of Mt. Asgard. At the same time, Tom Fayle, Mark Klassen and I climbed an unnamed and possibly unclimbed peak just to the southwest of Asgard itself. Our unnamed peak climbed a big snow face to a ridge, had three pitches of fifth class, and then followed a sharp ridge to a summit. This was a great cold-weather route, as it wasn't too hard to keep moving.

Two days later, Tom, Mark and I climbed another new route on the southwest face of Asgard's north tower. We named our route *Polar Thievery* after an incident that occurred with some snowmobilers at Summit Lake. Approaching as for the Swiss Route, our climb then cuts across snow and rock slabs to the very right-hand edge of the southwest face somewhere near the *Bilfrost Buttress* (though we never did locate this route). *Polar Thievery* takes a crack system that starts directly below and finishes in the large obvious corner on the upper right side of this face. We did eight pitches of awesome crack climbing on perfect granite up to 5.11a, but in drier conditions one should expect two or three more pitches.

After a rest and a ski tour to scope out another project, we split into three teams of two. Mark and Rob climbed the north face of Bilbo Peak, Larry and Tom climbed the Scott/Hennick Route on Asgard in 44 hours from Summit Lake, and Marc and I climbed the south ridge of the big unnamed peak to the northwest of Northumbria, directly north from *Tinfoil Ridge*. The route was ten pitches of good stone up to 5.10a, and we called it *First Air* after a startling commercial flight that buzzed us on the summit.

We all reunited back at the head of the Fjord to be picked up on skidoo 12 days after we arrived. As we rode the machine out in the wet and stormy weather, I couldn't help but laugh and think that very occasionally, some weather folklore can actually come true.

GRANT STATHAM, *Canada*

*Mt. Asgard, Mt. Overlord, Mt. Turnweather, Ascents.* To travel north of the Arctic Circle, journey five days amid otherworldy landscapes to the base of a 4,000-foot granite monolith, then ascend an unending system of solid cracks to the summit in the company of good friends: this is a wondrous thing for a climber, and a great gift of life. Over our 43-hour round trip on the northeast buttress of Asgard's North Tower, the arctic sun never set on Rich Prohaska, Jia Condon and I while we established *Line of Credit* (5.10 A1, 4,000'). We placed no bolts and three pins and climbed 23 pitches with the use of a 60-meter rope.

On Mt. Overlord, we climbed the Central West Buttress (5.10 A1, 4,000'), the prominent diagonal buttress leading to the center of the west face. Old fixed lines were discovered on the lower portion of the climb without evidence of passage higher up*. The climb took 36 hours round-trip from the Overlord shelter; descent was made via the glacier and valley directly north of Mt. Overlord. Excellent views of the tide rolling in and out over many kilometers of the Pangnirtung Fjord were visible.

After ferrying loads the 12 kilometers to the north face of Mt. Turnweather, Jia Condon and Rich Prohaska chose a prominent feature right of the center of the face. We spent eight nights climbing *Dry-Line* (VI 5.10 A2+, 3,000'), getting precipitation on virtually every day, and being pinned by a snow storm for a day during the descent. We found the rock quality to be mostly good. The climbing was mostly easy aid with a little hard (for us) free climbing. We

RIGHT: *The northeast buttress of Mt. Asgard, showing* Line of Credit. SEAN EASTON

*The Inugsuin Pinnacles, with "Nuksuklorolu Tower" (showing* Welcome, Nunavut*) on the right.*
MANRICO DELL' AGNOLA

bolted most of the belays and rappelled the route.

SEAN EASTON, *with* RICH PROHASKA, *Canada*

*This climb appears to share much ground with the 1975 British (Ken Rawlinson and Steve Blake) route (see *AAJ* 1976, p. 468).

*Mt. Asgard, Scott Route, and Various Beta.* In early August, Jeff Bowman and I climbed the 1974 Scott Route on the southeast buttress of Mt. Asgard with two bivouacs (owing to a 4 p.m. start). Because of the relative popularity of this route, we thought we'd pass along a few observations. A March, 1998, article in *Climbing* magazine claims the Scott Route is 40 pitches; 24 is closer to the mark (note: don't bother with a 60m rope). Much worse, the route line drawn onto the Asgard photo is dangerously wrong. Instead of climbing the giant corner between the two lower buttresses (a feature nicknamed the "Death Gully" by 1970s climbers), ascend slabs to left-facing corners near the center of the southeast buttress. The first eight or so pitches (5.8) have fixed double-piton belays every 150 feet that would allow rapid retreat if the weather turns sour. The mid-section is about eight pitches of fourth-class rubble. The final eight pitches offer glorious climbing (at last!) and are generally 5.8 to 5.9 with spots of 5.10 that would be easily aidable. We didn't attempt to free the chimney (reputedly 5.11), in part because of a tempting line of aid bolts at its edge. These self-driven bolts must have been placed in a hurry; only about half an inch of each two-inch bolt actually penetrates the rock.

In other news, Japanese climbers helicoptered onto the King's Parade Glacier for new aid routes on the west face of Friga (see below), but the park superintendent says he will no longer permit helicopter landings in the park. If you have more money than time, consider having your food and gear snowmobiled to Summit Lake the February before your climb. We didn't do this, but we did leave our climbing gear there to be picked up the following winter, thus saving ourselves double carries on the hike out. The 65-pound pack cost $136 for the snowmobile pickup and $238 for air cargo transport to Oregon. Make arrangements through Joavee Alivaktuk in Pangnirtung, phone and fax: 867-473-8721.

JOHN HARLIN III, *Hood River Crag Rats*

*Mt. Frigga I and Mt. Frigga II, Ascents.* Minoru Nagosi and seven other people, all from Hiroshima, Japan, ascended Mt. Frigga in Auyuittuq National Park in Baffin Island. They climbed on the west faces of Mt. Frigga I and Mt. Frigga II. On the west face of Mt. Frigga I, three of them climbed 11 pitches (VI A3+) capsule-style from July 17 to August 13. They were forced to rappel because of a storm. From their rappel point, they were 300 feet from the top. On Mt. Frigga II, four members of the team climbed 16 pitches (VI 5.10c A2) from July 18 to August 8.

KAZUYUKI SASAKI, *Editor, Run Out*

Inugsuin Fjord

*Nuksuklorolu, The Belluno Spur, and Other Ascents.* Two Italian expeditions explored less-known parts of Baffin Island in 1997 and 1998, tallying a number of ascents. In 1997, one

*The Belluno Spur.* White Man's Wind *takes the spur's crest.* MANRICO DELL' AGNOLA

woman and five men (Antonella Giacomini, Manrico Dell'Agnola Giuliano De Marchi, Michele Gasperin, Alessandro de Guelmi and Simone Gorelli) traveled by foot between the town of Clyde River and Ayr Lake, the headwaters of the Kogalu River, climbing five peaks en route that may or may not have been virgin. In August, 1998, Antonella Giacomini, Manrico Dell'Agnola Giuliano De Marchi, Simone Gorelli, Giambattista Calloni, Luigi Da Canal, Luca Spanò, Luigi Zampieri and Alex Gordon (cameraman) returned with the intent to climb in Sam Ford Fjord. When difficulties with the approach scuttled their plans, they turned their attentions to Inugsuin Fjord, where they made nine ascents, including *Welcome, Nunavat* (VI 5.11 A1, 800m) on "Nuksuklorolu Tower" (1350m) in the Inugsuin Pinnacles, and *White Man's Wind* (V 5.10 A0, 1000m) on the "Belluno Spur." (Spanò and Calloni put up a variation to this with sections of 5.8+ A0.) The name *Welcome, Nunavat* was chosen in recognition of the new Canadian province of Nunavat, while the Belluno Spur was named for Belluno, the capital of Dolomites, from which five of the eight climbers hail.

Sam Ford Fjord

*Great Cross Pillar, South Face, Non-Conceptual Time.* Three days of rough travel brought my partner, Sean "Stanley" Leary, and I to the Great Cross Pillar in Sam Ford Fjord. We said goodbye to our Inuit friends and guides, then busied ourselves establishing a base camp in a wind-sheltered alcove west of our line. For three days we fixed through blustery weather; on the fourth we committed to the vertical world. After a week on the wall, life became routine.

As the days passed by, we watched springtime take effect on the world below us. We couldn't help but wonder how much more time we had before it was no longer safe to travel. We

*Great Cross Pillar, showing* Non-Conceptual Time. AIMÉE AUCOIN

climbed onward, ascending a pitch, perhaps two each day, pushing to finish before summer left us stranded. When we had three, sometimes four ropes fixed, we'd haul our five bags and set up a new camp. Our favorite camp was our last one, high on the headwall. It had a luxurious ledge five feet long and two feet wide. With 12 days of fatigue catching up, and a terrific castle to relax in, we found it all the more difficult to motivate for the arduous work of climbing upward.

We spent the next two days fixing three pitches, and, without knowing exactly how close we were, decided it was time to make a summit push. We set out after seven hours of rest, jugging our lines in blue skies and mild temperatures. To our excitement, one aid pitch and two mellow free pitches later we were at the top of the technical summit. After a mile of ridge climbing and hiking, we were as high as one could climb on the Great Cross Pillar.

Resting at Base Camp, we waited patiently for the Inuit to arrive, which they did, and not a day too soon. We took off across the melting expanse of sea ice, navigating through gaping crevasses and talus fields made of ice. Twenty hours into the journey, I peered over at Stanley, perched peacefully on a mountain of foam and caribou fur in the back of the sled. His calm, peaceful grin caused a wave of excitement to wash over me. We had accomplished what we came to do: *Non-Conceptual Time* (VI 5.11 A3+, 2,800', 20 pitches, 15 days), the third route on Great Cross Pillar.

AIMÉE AUCOIN

*Walker Citadel, The Mahayana Wall.* On May 9, Russel Mitrovich, Mike Libecki, and Josh Helling arrived in the small village of Clyde River, Baffin Island. The next day was spent traveling 60 miles across the frozen Arctic Ocean on snowmobile. The highly inspired expedition team pulled more than 600 pounds of food and equipment behind them. By May 12, they had already established Base Camp, and began climbing the 4,200-foot north face of the Walker Citadel.

The climb began with moderate aid and some mixed snow and ice. After fixing 550 feet of rope, the team hauled their seven haul bags under a large granite ceiling. This rock shelter became Camp I as they committed to a capsule-style ascent. They fixed two more steep aid pitches and one scary free climbing pitch. On May 17, a strong Arctic storm blew in, trapping them in their three-man portaledge for the next six days. The winds blew harshly as snow and ice encased their vertical world. With ropes frozen useless, the team was caged under their stormfly like prisoners. Soon the wall could hold no more snow and large avalanches crashed down the massive cliff. The first large avalanche to bombard them ripped their zippered nylon doors down to fill their portaledge with heavy snow. Hearts beating strongly, they endured more than one dozen similar events.

On May 23, they were finally able to climb in poor, but tolerable weather. The next 1,000 vertical feet were spent aid climbing through snow- and ice-filled cracks. On June 1, Russel, Mike, and Josh crawled onto a large snow-covered ledge to establish Camp IV under another large ceiling of rock. The tactics of such natural shelters would prove to save their lives repeatedly as rock, snow, and ice fell regularly from above. The rock quality was mostly good granite until pitch 17. The next 700 feet consisted of a red, rotten, decomposed gneiss. Difficulties were encountered not only in getting reliable protection, but also in finding secure anchor sites. With extremely heavy loads, the team managed to safely haul their bags with the help of a 600-foot static rope. Soon enough, the upper north-facing headwall became steeply overhanging and solid.

Beautiful corners led into a sky-scraping abyss. Blessed with mostly moderate but cold weather, they climbed consistently upward. At about 3,700 feet above the frozen sea ice, the late spring temperatures began to warm. Sky-blue meltwater flooded the once-white surface below. The three dedicated young men knew that sea ice break-up would soon be near. Fixing only one long pitch above Camp IV, they then made a lengthy push toward the summit. On June 13, Russel Mitrovich, Mike Libecki, and Josh Helling stood on top of the towering Walker Citadel, having established *The Mahayana Wall* (VII 5.10 A4).

The next three days were spent repacking haul bags and rappeling down the 4,200-foot Arctic wall. After 36 nightless days of focused climbing, the team was finally back to the watery base of the looming cliff. A dream once questioned possible was now entered forever into their lives.

JOSH HELLING


*The Fin, Nanuq.* From August 27 to September 7, Natxo Barriuso, Txus Lizarraga, Raul Melero and I, all from Basque Country, made the first ascent of The Fin in Sam Ford Fjord via the route *Nanuq* (VI 5.10 A3, 600m) on the wall's west-northwest face. We had attempt-

LEFT: *The 4,200-foot north face of the Walker Citadel.* JOSH HELLING

ed the first three pitches in 1995. The first third of the route was aid climbing that wandered up the compact and overhanging wall, traversing along various roofs that forced us to attack the pitches from the side.

The second part is an obvious dihedral that continues to the summit. It featured beautiful granite climbing with chimneys and offwidths. The last pitches we climbed were iced up. The route featured almost 700 meters of climbing on 600 meters of wall.

We climbed capsule style, with only one camp on the wall before the dihedral. Six days were spent fixing the first part and seven were spent in hammocks. We reached the summit on September 7, then rapped the route. We approached the mouth of the fjord in canoes, with local guides from Clyde River.

MIGUEL BERAZALUCE, *Basque Country, Spain*

Stewart Valley

*"Great Sail Peak," Northwest Face, Rum, Sodomy, and the Lash.* On May 18, I flew to the arctic village of Clyde River, Baffin Island, with Greg Child, Alex Lowe, Jared Ogden and David Hamlin. In Clyde, we met Gordon Wiltsie and John Catto, who had arrived early to do some filming with our Inuit outfitters. Our expedition, sponsored by the National Geographic Society and The North Face, had the intention of documenting the first ascent of Baffin Island's most northerly big wall. Gordon Wiltsie was on assignment to shoot stills for *National Geographic* magazine, as was videographer John Catto for the Explorer television series. David Hamlin, a producer for Explorer, would accompany us to Base Camp and then return home with the Inuit after dropping us off.

The real boon of this expedition was an aerial reconnaissance of the entire length of Baffin Island we did in order to choose our objective. We decided that the very best unclimbed wall in Baffin Island was located in the Stewart Valley, between Sam Ford and Gibbs Fjord. We chose a striking 3,800-foot cliff (ca. 5,300') as our objective.

On previous expeditions, it had taken less than 12 hours to reach Sam Ford by skidoo from Clyde River. This time around, hampered by stormy weather, it took us nine days to reach the Stewart Valley. This valley is probably an old fjord that once connected Sam Ford Fjord and Gibbs Fjord. Glacial moraine now blocks both ends of the valley, forming a narrow lake about ten miles long. We had realized from the start that getting our gear-laden komatiks across these land bridges onto the lake was going to be the crux of the approach. Using three interconnected skidoos to generate maximum horsepower, our Inuit guides skillfully ferried one komatik at a time through the boulderfield below Stewart Lake. It was a sobering exercise because we knew that once the snow melted, the Inuit would no longer be able to access this valley.

We chose a suitable sight for Base Camp under "Great Sail Peak," then bid farewell to David Hamlin and the guides from Qullikkut. Frustrated and antsy from the nine-day approach, we immediately began ferrying loads up 2,000 feet of loose slabs to the base of the wall. It took a week of three and four carries a day to get all our gear—23 haul bags' worth—packed up and ready to go. The first 1,700 feet of the wall, which was broken up and loose, led to a gigantic ledge, football fields wide, that traversed the entire length of the cliff. Above this was a vertical 2,000-foot headwall—the cleanest piece of rock I have seen in Baffin.

On the lower section of the wall we chose the steepest possible line to minimize objective

*Walls of the Stewart Valley. The 3,800-foot northwest face of "Great Sail Peak" is to the right, with Rum, Sodomy and the Lash marked.* MARK SYNNOTT

hazard and also to make hauling easier. Another week of brute manual labor enabled us to fix the choss wall and haul our 23 bags onto the big ledge. From the ledge camp, Greg, Jared, Alex and I began fixing pitches that followed a thin seam on the Half Dome-like headwall. The crack was continuous, yet thin enough that we made most of our progress with copperheads, hooks and tied-off pins. We fixed six long pitches to a point directly beneath the only roof of the route, the sight of our first and only hanging portaledge camp. With a 1,000-foot static line, we took turns hauling five bags at a time up to the bivy. It was a spectacular position, looming above Alex's A4+ pitch, "The Trade Winds." Eventually we secured our 23 haul bags between the three portaledges.

Splitting the roof directly above camp, a tiny copperhead seam shot through the impeccable Baffin gneiss. The crack was as splitter as the *Shield*'s "Triple Cracks" or anything on *Sunkist*. Greg Child did us proud and led the whole thing without placing a single rivet. I cleaned the pitch and found that Greg had placed about 100 feet of small copperheads in a row. We all agreed it was darn close to A5. All told, on this section of the climb there were

seven pitches back-to-back of solid new-wave A4 or harder. What's really scary, though, is that we actually had to relead some of these pitches for the camera. The problem was that we couldn't shoot video and stills at the same time (due to conflicts with motor drives and flashes), so some pitches actually got led three times. All of this ate up lot of time, especially because the weather was quite often lousy.

After fixing for another week above the hanging camp, our three-ring, six-person circus finally topped out on June 25, 17 days since leaving the ground, having completed the route *Rum, Sodomy, and the Lash* (VI 5.10 A4+). We managed to summit on the most beautiful day of the expedition, allowing us ample time to enjoy the magnificent panorama. To our east and west, we could clearly make out the tops of the tallest peaks in Sam Ford and Gibbs Fjord. To the south and north, we could see out onto the Barnes Ice Cap and also across the vertiginous Arctic Ocean. On the way down, we spent three days at our hanging camp waiting out bad weather in hopes of doing more filming. The weather proved entirely uncooperative, so we eventually bailed, sending down some of the cargo by express mail.

In Base Camp, all of the snow had completely melted and we realized once and for all that the Inuit would never make it in to pick us up. It also wasn't realistic for us to ferry all our gear ten miles to the mouth of Sam Ford Fjord. Luckily, a helicopter was in the area doing land claim surveys, and the pilot agreed to pick us up for roughly the same fee we would have paid the outfitter. Checking out "Great Sail Peak" and the other still-virgin formations of Stewart Valley from the chopper window was a fitting end to my third expedition to Baffin Island.

MARK SYNNOTT

*Baffin Island, A Glimpse into the Future.* Prolific big waller Mark Synnott has made three trips to Baffin Island, including last year's (see above) on which he made an aerial reconnaissance of potential objectives. An overview of some of what the future might hold for the island appears as an article earlier in this journal.

# ELLESMERE ISLAND

*Ellesmere Island, Barbeau Peak and Various Ascents.* In June, an expedition to Ellesmere Island made a rare ascent of Barbeau Peak, highest point in the Canadian Arctic, and cleared up some confusion concerning its location. The eight-man party was composed of Dan Bennett, Jack Bennett, Tom Budlong, Tony Daffern, Pete Ford, Dave Rotheroe, Bill Salter, and Greg Slayden.

The best topographic maps do not clearly indicate the location of the peak. Hattersley-Smith, a member of the first ascent party in 1967, gives its location as 81° 55' N, 75° 1' W. However, Errington, leader of the second ascent party, locates Barbeau Peak as the one at 81° 53' N, 75° 17' W, over three miles to the southwest (see *AAJ* 1982, p. 176, sketch map).

Our party flew by chartered Twin Otter from Resolute to the North Ellesmere Icecap and established their first camp at 81° 57' 44" N, 75° 30' 40" W on June 14. Conditions during the week on the icecap were ideal: temperatures of about 30 to 40°F, perfectly clear, soft snow, and no major crevasses. From camp, Daffern, Ford and Slayden set off for what appeared to

LEFT: *Jared Ogden on pitch 16,* Rum, Sodomy and the Lash, *with Gordon Wiltsie belaying.*
MARK SYNNOTT

be the highest peak in the range. After gaining the col to the west of the peak, they attempted the west ridge, but turned back near the summit when it became steep and icy. After retreating to the col and making a ski traverse across the northwest face to the broad north ridge, they easily climbed to the snowy, knife-edge summit, which they reached on the morning of June 15. This peak was clearly the highest in the vicinity, and sighting using levels in the perfectly clear, calm conditions confirmed this judgment.

Several hours later, Bennett, Bennett, Budlong, Rotheroe, and Salter also climbed to the summit of Barbeau Peak via the north ridge. They, too, sighted using levels and could find no other higher summit within view. Also, they discovered a register in the rocks of the pinnacled south ridge, just below the summit, with notes from both the 1967 first ascent and Errington's 1982 second ascent. So the location of Barbeau Peak, confirmed by two separate GPS readings, is 81° 54' 49.8" N, 75° 00' 41.0" W. This means that Errington's sketch map in the 1982 *AAJ* is incorrect: Barbeau is "Peak I", not "Peak K".

After Barbeau Peak, the party turned its attention to other peaks while traveling down the Air Force Glacier. These peaks were possibly unclimbed; there are no records of any ascents, but all are technically easy and not particularly remote. On June 17, D. Bennett, Daffern, Ford, and Slayden climbed a prominent 6,400-foot sub-peak at 81° 55' 36" N, 76° 32' 4" W. Then, on June 18, Bennett, Bennett, Daffern, Ford, Salter, and Slayden climbed a 5,500-foot peak at 81° 50' 22" N, 76° 49' 22" W. This very prominent knife-edge summit was given the provisional name of "Highpointers Peak," since five in the party are members of the Highpointers Hiking Club.

On June 21, the expedition exited the Air Force Glacier and then continued down the tundra of the Air Force River valley to the Tanquary Fjord ranger station and airstrip, where they were picked up on June 28.

GREG SLAYDEN

# GREENLAND

Roosevelt Fjeld

Johannes V. Jensen Land

*"Avanarsuasua*\*," *Exploration.* The 1998 Euro-American North Greenland Expedition returned for the third time in a series of expeditions (1995, Schmitt, Deuel; 1996, Schmitt, Skafte) to further the exploration of this northernmost peninsula of the world. This expedition, like those before it, had a broad focus that included archeology, paleobotany, oceanography, ornithology and mountaineering. A valiant attempt by Ko deKorte and Hans Stopler to cross the peninsula from Friggs Fjord to Bliss Bugt through the Bennedict Range was successful. Ascents of the northernmost mountains of the peninsula, Greenland and the world were also successful. On July 16, a group of eight climbers (Mara Boland, Peter Skafte, Craig Deutche, Bill VanMoorhem, Detlief Stremke, Roger Brown, Ole Jorgen Hammeken and Dennis Schmitt) proceeded west along the coast from Kap Jessup to the base of a mountain at the northeastern extremity of Sands Fjord. We ascended the four-kilometer east ridge across the ice shoulder to a summit of three rock teeth (Kiguti Pingasut) at 900+ meters. Ole

Jorgen flew the Greenland flag at this place, which we called "Hammeken Point." Deutche, Hammeken and Schmitt followed the ridge another kilometer and a half to its highest summit (Ikiorti) at 1000 meters. We placed a cairn here. By all standards this peak and the three teeth must be reckoned as the most northerly summits in the world. Extreme high winds were to buffet our final descent.

In the weeks to follow, an observation was made (Skafte, Boland, Brown) of the northernmost archeological site in the world. This could prove that the Independence I migration occurred. A number of climbs in the Sifs Trench were also accomplished. The second ascent of the highest peak (1700m) in the Birgit Koch Tinde was made from the north. We found a cairn from the 1969 British Joint Services Expedition on this summit.

West of the lower Sifs Lake is a pass at 600 meters. A camp was established at the small, unmapped lake here. The south ridge of Peak 1310 was climbed from this camp and a cairn placed on its summit.

DENNIS SCHMITT

*Inuit for "Most Northerly." This proposed appellation for the northern-most peninsula of J.V. Jensen Land was submitted by the expedition to Greenland Domestic Authority in 1998 and is pending approval.

*Akuliarusinguaq Peninsula and Sanderson's Hope, Tilman-Style.* Reverend Bob Shepton (Skipper and leader), Brian Newham (Mate), Danuska Rycerz, Steve Marshall and Annie Wilson left Britain on June 18 and sailed to the west coast of Greenland in a 33-foot sailing boat, *Dodo's Delight.* The aim of the expedition was to ascend (preferably unclimbed) mountains from the boat as Eric Tilman had done in the past. The Atlantic crossing (Castlebay to Nuuk), a testing introduction to two of the climbers who had never sailed before, included two gales, a storm off Cape Farewell, winds that reached 55-60 knots, and a 90° knockdown in which we were picked up and projected down a steep fronted wave just as conditions were beginning to moderate. We suffered some damage to the hull, but were able to proceed to Nuuk, where the boat was lifted out at the Boat Club from July 4-16 for repairs to the hull. On July 24-25, we moved up to Akuliarusinguaq Peninsula (71°N 52°W), where we made a quick recce of the southern end via Nugatsiauptunua Fjord. We then moved around to the northern end via Ingia Fjord and anchored close in at the side of the Puartldarsivik Inlet, where the glacial river disgorges in an alluvial fan. It was big, desolate, deserted, glacially shattered country, with peaks that were arguably bigger, though not as high, as those on the east coast.

The boat acted as Base Camp; for some more remote peaks an Advanced Base was established up the glacial river glens. The routes on Sandersorfs Hope were climbed directly from the boat (the only way of reaching them). Ten summits on Akuliarusinguaq were climbed, five or possibly six of which were over 2000 meters, and one on Qeqertarssuaq to the south.

Among other ascents in the Akuliarusinguaq Peninsula, on July 31, Danuska and Bob climbed "The Old Man" (ca. 1800m). Some "discussion" was had at the top regarding whether it was justifiable to climb the final 100-meter rock stack on such loose rock. Different philosophies ensued from old (bold and foolish) and young (wanting to live longer). After suitable Polish protestations, the dear lady, in typically kind fashion, then found a line that might go—

*Reverend Bob Shepton on the summit of Pt. 2060—near midnight. Karat Isfjord and the three peninsulas can be seen in the background.* DANUSKA RYCERZ

and proceeded to lead all five pitches to the top! The ascent and descent took 31 hours of continuous effort. There wasn't any darkness, but it still was too much for an old man.

To our knowledge, five of the ascents were firsts, including the highest in the area—the four in the north and Sorte Pyramide on Qeqertarssuaq. We discovered afterward that an Italian expedition had visited the southern part of the peninsula in 1969, and had previously climbed the peaks there. So our ascents in the southern part represent second ascents and the first British, and three of the peaks were in fact climbed by new routes: Pt. 2060 by its west ridge, and Pts. 1941 and 1990 (the one just to the north) by their northeast ridges. Also, it was the first time the summits on the high northwest plateau, including the Italians' subsidiary peak (which we had not bothered to count), had been ascended on skis. And of course this was the first time any of these mountains had been climbed from a sailing boat.

Two new snow and ice routes were established on the big headland of Sanderson's Hope. These were the first two routes, we believe (apart from walking to the top by an easy way), to be put on this famous navigational landmark named by John Davis on his 1587 voyage as he took his offing from Greenland to try and discover the Northwest Passage.

We hope we did enough to honor the memory of that extraordinary character and exceptional explorer Bill Tilman. This was, after all, the 21st anniversary of his sad loss at sea.

Names and heights in mountain areas are taken from Saga maps.

REVEREND BOB SHEPTON, *United Kingdom*

Northeast Greenland

*Petermanns Bjerg, Ascents.* On June 11, Paul Walker landed a climbing party on an unnamed glacier beneath the unclimbed north face of Petermanns Bjerg (2933m) at 73°N in Fraenkels Land. The group established Base Camp and began their assault on as many new peaks in the area as time and conditions would allow. Characteristic of northeast Greenland, superb weather persisted for three weeks, and a total of 35 ascents were made, of which 30 are believed to be first ascents of previously unclimbed summits. The fifth ascent of Petermanns Bjerg was made via the south ridge on June 15 and was followed by ascents of Lille Petermanns Bjerg (2675m), Kalifbjerg (2632m), Kerberus (2564m), Trappebjerg (2520m), the twin peaks of Baselfjeld (2668m and 2585m), and Gog (2651m). The earlier expeditions of 1929, 1951, 1977 and 1985 had all sailed into the fjords and trekked for several days to reach Petermanns Bjerg. Consequently, time was always short and very little else in the region had ever been climbed. As a result, the group had the enviable pleasure of climbing many of the fine peaks of significance in the region. Climbing conditions were excellent, due both to the stability of the snow and ice at this latitude and the settled weather and 24-hour daylight. One of the most notable ascents was a 600-meter rock climb by Phil Cann and expedition doctor Rod Lindenbaum, who made the first ascent of the northwest face of Kerberus during a 20-hour climb.

JAMES GREGSON, *Alpine Club*

*Shackletons Bjerg, Various Ascents.* On July 1, Nigel Edwards brought in a group of seven climbers that included the Greenland expedition veteran Derek Fordham. A total of ten ascents, of which seven are believed to be firsts, were made during their stay. Flying in on the Twin Otter arriving to pick up Paul Walker's group (see below), they made a sixth ascent of Petermanns Bjerg via the south ridge, along with repeat ascents of peaks climbed by Walker's group, before embarking on a multi-day ski tour to the fringes of the icecap to the west. From here, the husband-and-wife team of Duncan and Tessa Wardley made several ascents of new peaks (ca. 2150-2350m) while Edwards, Fordham and the remaining members of the team, Sean Crane, Dr. Roos Allsop and Dr. Dave Seddon, skied on for a further day to Shackletons Bjerg (2808m), which had been climbed once previously, by John Haller's 1953 expedition. This posed a suitable objective to end the expedition; however, strong winds forced their retreat.

Meanwhile, at Constable Point airstrip, two further expeditions were busy preparing to visit the region. On July 17, the Twin Otter flew seven members of the Derby Mountain Rescue Team, led by Steve Hilditch, directly to a Base Camp beneath the southeast face of Shackletons Bjerg. The plane then diverted off to the west to collect Edward's group from the icecap, leaving Edwards behind to join an incoming expedition that included his wife Nicky and that arrived in the area the following day. Five members of the DMRT group then reached the summit of Shackletons Bjerg on July 20 via a new route on the southeast face/southwest ridge, thus claiming its second ascent. A further 20 ascents of peaks and tops in the region were made by the group, the majority of them firsts, including Guldtinderne (2470m) and Hamlet Bjerg (2410m).

JAMES GREGSON, *Alpine Club*

*Shackletons Bjerg Area, Goodenoughs Land, Various Ascents.* Attracted by the existence of many virgin peaks in an area reputed to have long periods of stable fine weather, I went for a fifth visit to Greenland, joining 13 others: Nigel Edwards, Nicola Gibbs, John Burton, Diane Burton, Alan Law, Matt Sutcliffe, David Jehan, Stephanie McDearmaid, Keith Partridge, Andrea Partridge, Steven Ripley, Paul Walker, and Sandy Gregson.

On July 17, we flew from Iceland into the airstrip at Constable Point (Nerlerit Inaat), where we met Paul Walker and all our previously freighted gear. The next day, Paul flew his final Tangent group of 14 members to an area on the edge of the icecap (2060m, N 72° 54' 44", W 29° 11' 39") in two groups at the site of the lone Nigel Edwards (see above). We had aerial photographs for this area, but no published map is available. Earlier research indicated visits by a 1953 expedition, plus the visit by the British group of which Edwards was a part.

In the course of four or five days, 17 summits were reached by team members. These included a continuous traverse of the ridges linking Venus (2390m), Uranus (2450m), and Pluto (2460m); four summits on Simons Island Peak (main top: 2410m) on the very edge of the Inland Ice; Trio (2400m), and Peeping Peak (2450m); Middle Peak (2310m), End Peak (2320m), and Wart Peak (2310m). Most of these ascents were on mixed ground with poor-quality rock. We opted to climb during the night-time hours—in a true "midnight sun" latitude—to try to find better snow conditions.

On July 25 we packed up for a move over to the foot of Shackletons Bjerg for a new camp at ca. 1840 meters. This trek, taking over eight hours, moved us about 16 kilometers east from our drop-off point.

In the late evening of July 26, Sandy and I skied up to the snow shoulder at the foot of the southwest ridge of Shackletons Bjerg and climbed and photographed our way along the very attractive and increasingly exposed arête to the summit. While we were on this fine summit, most of our friends were observing us from another top across the glacier. After climbing back down the arête, we enjoyed a very rapid ski back to camp. On July 27, the others went to repeat our climb on Shackletons Bjerg in equally pleasant midnight sunshine, while Sandy and I made a ski ascent and descent of Pulk Peak (2325m) from where we could watch their tiny figures on the skyline ridge.

In the evening of July 28, six of the team moved off to the southeast to make a third camp at the head of the Passage Glacier. Sandy and I skied up the glacier below Shackletons Bjerg to climb to the summit of an attractive mountain we called Echo Pond Peak (2530m) after the sound effects we experienced in an enclosed meltwater bay ringed by low cliffs at the bottom of its west ridge. During the night of July 29, the remaining eight of us packed up and followed the tracks the others had made over the 15 kilometers to camp above the Passage Glacier (2080m) at N 72° 49' 59", W 28° 29' 47". There were a number of good-looking peaks accessible from this camp.

Over the next few nights, in various combinations of rope-teams, a further 20 summits were reached. Among the best climbs were the Orions Belt traverse, linking the three peaks of Nevis (2275m), Link Peak (2290m), and Snow Queen (2420m) over a mix of fine airy rock and snow arêtes (this was climbed by most expedition members on successive nights), plus the traverse of the five Molars (highest: 2285m) on Toothed Ridge by Sandy and myself.

On August 4, a group of seven from Derby Mountain Rescue Team (England) made a rendezvous with our camp, as they were to share in our fly-out arrangement. This group had operated in an area to the east of Shackletons Bjerg, making a number of first ascents, includ-

*Looking north from Echo Pond Peak to Petermann's Bjerg.* JIM GREGSON

ing a new route on that peak.

Early on August 5, a helicopter buzzed into our camp to ferry us to an area of quasi-level tundra by the head of Kjerulfs Fjord, where a wheeled Twin Otter chartered from Air Iceland could land (the ski-plane not being available to us on this date). The Twin Otter came in to make an amazingly short landing on the bumpy unprepared tundra, and transferred us in batches out eastward to the airstrip at Mestersvig. From there, we left by charter flight back to Iceland, rounding off another successful trip. Of the 40 summits reached, 20 were first ascents.

JAMES GREGSON, *Alpine Club*

*Rignys Bjerg Mountains, Various Ascents.* Lying 130 kilometers east-northeast of the Watkins mountains, the Rignys Bjerg ranges have, until 1998, eluded all mountaineering expeditions on the grounds of cost and complex logistics. Covering an area of over 5,000 square kilometers at 69°N, they contain hundreds upon hundreds of unclimbed peaks up to 3000 meters that stretch along the east coast of Greenland from the fjord regions right through to the fringes of the great Greenland icesheet. Rarely are areas such as this to be found anywhere in the world outside of Antarctica. However, on June 11, with air reconnaissance of the mountain ranges and subsequent landing site having taken place the day before, a Twin Otter was positioned at Constable Point to fly two small and independent expeditions led by Mark Bailey and John Hulse to an area into which no mountaineering expedition had ever penetrated. Comprising two separate groups of three and four members respectively, these teams climbed a total of 28 new peaks within a three-week period in a variety of climbing combinations. Very good weather prevailed for the majority of the duration except for one major snowfall and subsequent four-day period of unsettled weather.

JAMES GREGSON, *Alpine Club*

*Western Staunings Alps, Various Activity.* Team members Colwyn Jones (Joint Expedition Coordinator), Stephen Reid (Joint Expedition Coordinator), John Bickerdike, Brian Shackleton, Jonathan Preston, Colin Read, John Peden, and Chris Ravey left Glasgow May 2. The expedition was landed by ski-equipped Twin Otter on the Sefstroms Glacier (1210m) in the Western Staunings Alps on May 6. The landing was two days later than planned due to bad weather affecting visibility on the proposed landing site.

On May 7, Jones, Bickerdike, Reid and Preston attempted the northernmost of two unclimbed ca. 2700-meter peaks (mentioned on p. 83 of Donald Bennet's guide, *Staunings Alps*. West Col: 1972) between Attilaborgen and Trinity via the left-hand of two obvious couloirs on the east flank of the mountain. A ridge was gained, but further climbing was thwarted by a mixture of hard blue ice, loose rock and general exhaustion. During the ascent and descent, exploration and observation were made of the glacier features giving access to this face. They named several of these features. The main glacier was called the "Essemmceebrae Glacier" while the northerly branch was called the "McKenzie Glacier." A view was obtained into the intriguing "Inner Sanctum," a glacier basin between Trinity and the Helmspids flanked by rock pillars and guarded by vast crevasses that extended completely across the entrance.

Meanwhile, Shackleton, Read, Peden and Ravey attempted an unclimbed snow peak, one of two unclimbed mountains lying in the area between Sussex, Magog and Cantabrigia on the Cantabrae. Access was via a couloir left of a hanging glacier on the northwest face. This led to a snow ridge where Shackleton and Read turned back. Ravey and Peden carried on and reached the summit via a short but difficult rock slab (V) in the early hours of the morning. The peak has been named "Hecla" (2400m) and graded PD.

On May 9, Reid, Preston, Bickerdike and Jones climbed the highest of four unclimbed peaks (the northerly of the two marked on Bennet's map) on the dividing ridge between the Upper Sefstroms and Grantabrae glaciers. The ascent was made by linking a series of couloirs and ice fields with occasional mixed climbing on the southwest face. This led to a short easy rock section and a spectacular summit block. The peak was called "Tillyrie" (2415m) and the route graded AD.

Meanwhile, Peden, Ravey, Shackleton and Read made the first ascent of the unclimbed rock spire south of Emmanuel (pictured in Bennet, illustration 5). This peak is particularly spectacular when viewed from the Upper Sefstroms, where it is seen to have a large hole or "window" directly through it just below the summit. The spire was gained via a long couloir on the southwest face between it and Emmanuel; seven pitches of rock (up to IV) led to the top. The peak was named "Tupilaq" (2450m) and the route graded TD. This team did not return to Base Camp until 11 a.m. the following morning, having summited at 1 a.m. During the descent, Brian Shackleton sustained a minor facial injury when a loose block was dislodged by an abseil rope. This was treated successfully by Colwyn Jones.

On May 10, Bickerdike and Reid made the first ascent of a small but prominent unclimbed southerly outlier of Kapelle. The route was via an easy couloir and snow fields to its east and the peak was called "Rabsontinde" (F, 1640m).

On May 11, Preston, Reid, Bickerdike and Jones climbed the second highest of the four unclimbed peaks (the southerly of the two marked on Bennet's map) on the dividing ridge between the Upper Sefstroms and Grantabrae glaciers via a broad couloir (which they named the Coltart Couloir) lying between the mountain and the headwall of the Sefstroms Glacier. This led to a snow ridge, and a short rock pitch (V) led to the summit. The peak was named "Coltart" (2395m) and graded PD+.

May 13 dawned clearer and Peden and Ravey tackled an unclimbed snow peak southeast of "Coltart." This was climbed via the Coltart Couloir and a snow ridge. The slightly higher rickety rock spire to the west was not attempted. Descent was via the south ridge and the Sefstroms Glacier Headwall. This peak of 2350 meters has been named "Seanearbheinn." It was graded PD+.

At the same time, Read and Shackleton attempted a group of three rock spires lying to the northwest of Tillyrie via a couloir on the southwest face. Intense cold and ice-glazed rock forced a retreat just short of the summit. Meanwhile, Preston, Bickerdike and Reid made a reconnaissance of the unclimbed south face of Sussex, a spectacular 800-meter-plus sheer rock wall. This would make a superb target for a future expedition.

By the evening the weather was worsening and a storm put paid to all further climbing aspirations. On May 15 we began an arduous and difficult journey back to Mesters Vig, which was reached at 1:30 a.m. on the 21st. The party was flown to Iceland the same day.

STEPHEN REID, *United Kingdom*


*Watkins Mountains, Various Ascents.* A seven-member expedition left Iceland on May 24 and was landed in the Watkins Mountains by Twin Otter ski plane. Following a day's ski touring to Base Camp, all seven members made the 20th ascent of Gunnbjorns Fjeld (3693m), the highest peak in the Arctic, by the south ridge on May 28 in perfect weather. Indeed, the weather remained perfect for the whole duration of the expedition, allowing fourth ascents of Dome (3682m) and Cone (3669m), the second and third highest peaks, on June 1 and 2 respectively. (These peaks were first seen by Gino Watkin's 1930 Arctic Air Route Expedition and later named by Alistair Allen's 1971 expedition.) Late in the evening of June 4, the team came across the Dane Hans Christian Florian, who had recently arrived at Gunnbjornsfjeld Base Camp with an Austrian team following a mammoth three-week ski tour from Scoresbysund. Florian's group made a successful 21st ascent of the peak and fifth ascents of Dome and Cone. The group then skied off to a further Base Camp on the more easterly Woolley glacier. From here the group split, allowing John Starbuck, Lyle Closs and John Gluckmann to continue on for a further day's travel to the head of the Woolley Glacier. They then succeeded in making the third ascents of the fourth and fifth highest peaks in the Arctic, Mound (3609m) and Peak 3547m, on June 6 and 7, first named and climbed by Jim Lowther's 1988 expedition. (These peaks were climbed by Florian-Muller-Grossman in 1996 and incorrectly claimed as firsts.) Paul Walker (leader), Phil Cann and expedition doctor Rupert Bourne made what is believed to be a first ascent of P.2848m via a side glacier that runs parallel to, and on the northern edge of, the Woolley Glacier.

On June 10, the group was flown out to the small airstrip at Constable Point in northeast Greenland. This allowed them to pass over range upon range of unclimbed peaks in the Rignys Bjerg and Blosseville Coast region in order to carry out air reconnaissance and identify the proposed glacier landing strip for the two imminent British Rignys Bjerg expeditions (see above).

JAMES GREGSON, *Alpine Club*


SCHWEIZERLAND


*Schweizerland Mountains, Various Activity.* A seven-member team was flown to the Tasiilaq Mountain Hut (built in 1996 and run by Hans Christian Florian) in the Schweizerland mountain region of east Greenland by helicopter in March. The three-week expedition was very much an exploratory one. Temperatures were more comfortable than expected and rarely fell to below

-20°C. The expedition made a number of easy ascents before skiing out to the coast to be collected by helicopter at the small Inuit settlement of Kummuit. Guaranteed winter conditions
prevail well into May in this area and thus offer good opportunities for late spring expeditions.

JAMES GREGSON, *Alpine Club*

*"The Fox Jaw," Molar Tooth, Lovin' All the Right Places.* In mid to late summer, Mike Libecki
and I flew via Iceland to Kulusik Island and the full-service village of Tasiilaq before getting helicoptered into the Schweizerland mountains of east Greenland. We were located ca. 30 kilometers from the nearest Inuit village of Kummuit on the Arctic Circle and a three- to four-hour hike
from the Tasiilaq Mountain Hut. We spent 23 days in the area exploring and climbing.

Due to time limitations and a heavy year of sea ice, we chartered the helicopter to drop us in
the valley below walls I had seen the previous year. Upon landing, we were struck with the
beauty and enormous potential of climbing in the area, which we named "The Fox Jaw" for an
arctic fox that marked our food cache and the fact that the walls look like a row of teeth. We
used the name Fox Jaw because after extensive research and air reconnaissance and studies of
Saga maps we were not able to find any names of history or previous ascents. The name is
meant strictly to help with location and identification. Other walls in the Jaw are the "Baby,"
"Cavity Ridge" and "the Fang." We decided to climb one of the walls that we called "the
Molar." Over nine days (July 30-August 7), we fixed four 60-meter pitches, spent four days
waiting out rain and snow storms in the portaledge, then free climbed the last two-and-a-half
pitches to the summit. Our route, *Lovin' All the Right Places* (V 5.10 A2+) was, like most of the
walls in the area, 1,400 feet long. We placed one bolt and six rivets plus bolts at the belays. The
rock was very solid and clean granite with great potential for free climbs. Views from the summit allowed us to see many walls on the other side that rivaled and surpassed those on ours.

The "Fox Jaw" peaks in the Schweizerland mountains. MIKE LIBECKI

We descended our route. It took us four days to ferry our loads the nine miles out to the fjord for a boat pick-up.

DAVE BRIGGS

*Lemon Mountains, Various Ascents.* The Cumbria East Greenland Expedition members (Steve Brailey, Pete Dawson, Jeff Haslam, Chris Cookson, Ian Cousins, Colin Dulson, Gwyn Lewis, Dave Wilson, and Keith Miller) flew from Glasgow to Iceland and then by ski plane to Greenland, landing on a glacier in the southern area of the Lemon Mountains on July 18. Despite unusually unsettled weather, the team completed a number of first ascents in the area around Base Camp (960m; 31° 52' W, 68° 25.5' N) over the next two and a half weeks. There were a total of 12 days when it rained at some time, on two occasions for over 36 hours. Glacier conditions were also generally poor. A number of expedition members fell through snow bridges into crevasses while exploring and climbing around Base Camp, and also on the trek out.

New peaks and routes climbed were: Thunder Road (31° 30' W, 68° 26' N), Dome de Jenel (31° 58' W, 68° 24.6' N), Isobelar (31° 54' W, 68° 25.8' N), Laurenar (31° 48' W, 68° 23.9' N), the South Summit of Mjeslen (31° 47' W, 68° 27' N) via the southwest ridge, Eljam (31° 50' W, 68° 23.6' N) by two different routes, Lilevat (31° 46' W, 68° 24' N), and Icon Peak (32° 01' W, 68° 25.5' N). There were also two unsuccessful attempts on Crystal Peak (31° 52' W, 68° 26.2' N).

On August 4, the team journeyed for six days out to the coastal airstrip at Sodalen. During the latter part of this trek, two members revisited part of the area explored in their 1994 expedition. They were interested and alarmed to note many examples of considerable glacial retreat.

STEVE BRAILEY, *Cockermouth Mountain Rescue Team*

*Redekammen, climbed by Wilkenson and Bartlett, in the south of Kangerlluqsuaq Fjord on the east coast of Greenland (see account on following page).* BRIAN DAVISON

*Kangerlluqsuaq Fjord, Various Ascents.* On July 12, eight of us (Phil Bartlett, Dave Wilkinson, Helen Geddes, John Hudson, Graham Robinson, Ken Findlay, Pete Nelson and Brian Davison) were dropped by ski Twin Otter to the south of Kangerlluqsuaq Fjord (68° north) on the east side of Greenland for five weeks. Kangerlluqsuaq Fjord (Inuit for Big Fjord) is located about half way (200 miles) between Ammermaslik (now called Tasiilaq) and Scorsby Sound, two settlements on the east coast. Chris Bonington and Bartlett made trips to the Lemon Mountains on the north side of the fjord; we were the first to climb on the south side. Base Camp was a couple of miles north of Redekammen, at 2555 meters the highest peak in the area. There were some impressive rock walls as well as snow peaks. No climbing had been done in the area, the last people to visit being geologists as part of Gino Watkin's trips in the 1930s.

A total of 36 ascents were made in the area. Dave and Phil climbed Redekammen and members of the group climbed three other named peaks in the area: Kangerlluqsaq Tinde (2260m), Hovedvejs Nenatakker (1800m) and Fangetarnet (1610m). On August 16, we were collected by plane. I was home in the U.K. less than 24 hours later—a great way to do things.

BRIAN DAVISON, *United Kingdom*

*Ulamertorssuaq, Moby Dick, First Free Ascent.* One week after our departure from Copenhagen, Dusan Beranek, Ivan Doskocil and I from Slovakia reached Base Camp below Ulamertorssuaq. Also present were expeditions from Great Britain, Switzerland, the U.S. and Iceland. Our goal was to free the route *Moby Dick* (9/9+ A2, 31 pitches, 1100m). The American team (Todd Skinner, Paul Piana, Bobby Model et al) had fixed ropes on *Moby Dick* and we did not know whether to climb it or not. We asked and learned that they would move their ropes to the right. Our route would be free.

We planned to climb the route in six days. The long days in Greenland are perfect for climbing. We started our climb on July 11 at 4 p.m., climbing eight pitches (3, 2, 6+, 6+, 6+ 7-, 8-, 7-). At 10 p.m. we rappelled and slept near the face. The climbing, partly dihedrals and slabs, was nice but not perfect. On July 12 we started at 9 a.m. and climbed until dusk (11:30 p.m.), when we reached the "Black Heart," a ledge 400 meters above the ground. The climbing was a bit harder and nicer: 5+, 5, 8-, 8-, 7+, 7+, 8-. There were some bolts on the slabs but mostly it was necessary to place gear. On pitch 8 there is a blind bolt four meters above the belay. Don't clip this bolt: *Moby Dick* traverses to the left. The same on the tenth pitch in the dihedral: there is a blind bolt to the left, but it is better to follow the dihedral.

The weather on July 13 was perfect too. We wanted to climb the 17th pitch, the hardest one apart from the technical pitch near the top that prevented the original ascensionists from freeing the route. After eight hours of rehearsing, Dusan Beranek finally freed this pitch at 9+ (he had clipped the first two bolts, come down, then freed it, yo-yo). It is very nice slab climbing with tiny edges—bouldery with long reaches. We climbed only four pitches that day: 6+ 9+, 8/8+, plus the 19th pitch, on which we placed protection for our next attempt. The weather changed the next day. The American team had fixed ropes close to our route and we asked them if we could use their ropes for jumaring back up. When they said yes, we decided to rappel. We descended in heavy rain to wait for the next good weather.

Two days later we were again on the Black Heart ledge, ready to finish our route. The next pitches were strenuous, but beautiful—cracks, cracks and more cracks, plus a lot of air. Above the 19th pitch, Dusan led the harder pitches, and Ivan Doskocil, 24, on his first big wall, climbed the easier ones. The pitches went as follows: 9-, 9-, 7, 8+, 9-, 8, 8, 8-, 8-, 7. On July 18, we decided to climb as high as the 29th pitch by dusk and finish our route at night.

We reached a small ledge just below the aid pitch at 11 p.m. but were not able to continue because we could not see the bolt ladder or where to go. The night was terrible. We were very tired after three days of hard climbing. On July 29 at 4 a.m. we decided to continue. Dusan was destroyed, so the next pitches were up to Ivan and me. Ivan climbed the A2 pitch and at 10 a.m. we were on top of Ulamertorssuaq. We had not freed pitches 24 (8), 25 (8), or 29 (A2).

The next morning we saw cirrus clouds again. This time the weather was bad for a week. We waited in ABC with the American climbers and the team from Iceland (Jokull Bergmann, Stefan Smarason, Gudmund Tomasson and an American fighter pilot, Joe Weinberger) who wanted to climb a new route to the right of *Südtiroler Profil.* (They descended after about 20 pitches, saying that the Austrian climbers were crazy because there were a lot of hard pitches up to 7c+, poorly protected with home-made hangers and ten-meter runouts.) Denis Burdet, Olivier Schaller, and Regis Dubois from Switzerland were also there. During their stay, they put up two first ascents: one, *Dalphin Safe* (8 A0, nine pitches) on July 7 on a pyramidal tower left of Ulamertossuaq, and another, *Pet Gaz* (8- A1, 500m), from July 15-16, on a wall behind Ulamertorssuaq (Honey Buttress) where the British team (Tony Pennings et al; see below) also made a first ascent.

On the morning of July 26 the weather was quite good. We jumared 700 meters, but by noon it had started to snow and we had to rappel down. We had booked the speedboat for July 30, so our last day for climbing was July 28. On July 28 we woke at 5 a.m. and started jumaring at 8:30. We jumared 500 meters in 80 minutes. We lost 90 minutes when we found that the American fixed ropes were torn up in an awful offwidth corner crack. We had left almost all of our gear on the wall but by chance we had five cams with us. We climbed this pitch and finally at 1 p.m. we traversed to *Moby Dick.*

We quickly freed pitches 24 and 25, both graded 8. The weather was good but very cold. Bobby Model appeared on our fixed ropes, wanting to take pictures of our efforts to free the 29th pitch. At 7:30 p.m. we reached the small ledge just below the A2 pitch. During our descent on July 19 we had added two more bolts to this pitch for free climbing. Dusan tried some moves and clipped some gear. At 8:45 he said he was ready, then climbed like a magician. At 21:15 he clipped into the belay. After 700 meters of jumaring and 300 meters of hard climbing spread out over 12 hours in cold weather, he had freed the aid pitch at 9+ on his first attempt.

I wanted to try it too, but I recognized that it was too late and we had four more hours ahead of us of rappelling and stripping all of our gear from the wall. But I am not sad; we were a brilliant team. We were on the ground by 1:30 a.m.

VLADIMIR LINEK, *Jamesak, Slovakia*

*Nalumasortoq, New Route.* It was reported that a Swiss party was believed to have climbed a direct route on the right-hand pillar of Nalumasortoq, cutting through the left-facing diagonal corner system attempted in 1996 by a British team and completed by a (possibly Swiss) team in 1997. The pillar lies immediately left of the 1975 original route on the south face. The same Swiss team is also believed to have climbed a shorter route near the pillars ascended by Penning et al (see below) at British HVS E1. Further details are lacking. (*High Mountain Sports* 195)

*Ulamertorssuaq, War and Poetry.* Our team (Jeff Bechtel, Steve Bechtel, Mike Lilygren,

*Paul Piana on pitch 23,* War and Poetry, *Ulamertorssuaq.* BOBBY MODEL

Peter Mallamo, Bobby Model, Paul Piana, and Todd Skinner) left Lander, Wyoming, on July 1, driving two days to Ottawa, Canada, in a Suburban loaded with hundreds of pounds of food, gear, and climbers. We flew from Ottawa to Nuuk, Greenland, and eventually to the small village of Nanortalik. From here, we hired the boat Nanortalik Colo to deliver us up the Tasermiut Fjord to our objective.

After being dropped off at the shore, the team shuttled loads for several days to our Base Camp on the grassy bench below the wall. We began with the objective of free climbing the route *Moby Dick*, but quickly abandoned it in favor of a more aesthetic line to its right.

Mike and I took turns leading for the majority of the first part of the wall. The route followed incipient cracks and flakes with long stretches of sustained slab climbing in between. At about the 1800-meter level, we established a bivouac at "The Dark Heart," a long and narrow ledge.

The route's crux pitches, both mid-range 5.12, led from the ledge into a gigantic right-facing corner. We followed the corner for several more pitches to a sloping ledge and second bivouac. Higher, with Paul and Todd in the lead, we traversed right out of the ever-widening corner to find the single most spectacular crack any of us had ever seen. "The Bowstring Crack" consisted of 300 feet of hand and finger jams leading to a small alcove. Above, the cracks eased up in difficulty. The last five pitches followed straight-in cracks to the summit.

Our team fixed anchors on the route, *War and Poetry* (VI 5.12c), allowing for safe and quick descent for all parties climbing on the tower. Additionally, we removed hundreds of feet of old static line from the wall and gave it to the boatmen in Nanortalik.

In all, the climb took just over five weeks. Much of the time was spent waiting out rain storms and hauling our mass of equipment around Greenland. We are quite pleased with the route, with all members of the team agreeing that this was one of the very best routes any of us has ever done.

STEVE BECHTEL, *unaffiliated*

LEFT: *Ulamertorssuaq. A:* Jacques Cousteau *(Gallego-Clavel-Matas-Seiquer, 1997). B:* Magic Romblon *(Agier-Payrau-Vigier, 1977). C:* Moby Dick *(Albert-Gargitter-Glowacz-Götz-Langen-Masterson, 1994). D:* War and Poetry *(Bechtel-Bechtel-Lilygren-Mallamo-Model-Piana-Skinner, 1998). Missing:* Geneva Diedre *(Dalphin-Piola-Probst-Wiestlibach, 1983) (between D and E). E: Quadrophenia (Cavagnetto-Motto-Piola-Ravaschietto, 1995). F:* Südtiroler Profil *(Hainz-Obrist, 1996). G:* L'Inespérée *(Daudet-Robert, 1996). All lines are approximate except for* Moby Dick.
PETER MALLAMO

*A:* The James Hopkins Trust. *B:* Honey Buttress. *C: Half Dome, showing* Les Temps sont Durs
*(Castella-Lehner-Truffer-Zambetti, 1998).* TONY PENNING

*James Hopkins Trust and Honey Buttress, Ascents.* I first went out to Greenland in 1996 with
Silvo Karo (Slovenia) and Jerry Gore (U.K.). We climbed a route on the left-hand pillar o
Nalumasortoq and, on the third or fourth day of our climb, while the other two battled it ou
above me, I gazed out over the fantastic scenery of unclimbed rock pillars and walls, plan
ning my next visit.

1998, and I was back in Greenland with two of my favorite people: Bob Honey, who ha
planned our journey from the U.K. via Iceland and who was going to act as Base Camp man
ager, and my climbing companion, Ian Parsons.

The first climb we went for was on a wonderful, alpine-looking pillar that I been dreaming
about for two years. I had promised a local children's charity, the James Hopkins Trust, tha
I would name the climb for them if we were successful.

We spent a night at the top of a long easy ramp at the foot of the pillar and, after a goo
night's sleep, we followed a series of cracks, grooves and corners that eventually led to th
summit. The route was about 2,000 feet and because of the almost continuous daylight w
were able to get up and back down to the top of the ramp in 21 hours. Overall, we though
the grade to be British E4 5c (5.11b/c).

After a week of bad weather, we were able to move back up for our second objective. Ou
first choice was on the north face of a mountain that we had christened Half Dome, but du
to the weather the face was running with water. This was not a problem and we turned ou
sights on another unclimbed pillar to the south of our previous climb. The climbing wa
almost identical in every way, including the grade but about 200 feet less in height. We calle
this climb *Honey Buttress* after our good friend waiting patiently back at Base Camp for us

There is still a tremendous amount to climb in this area, from big-wall style to easy alpine and everything in between. It still feels remote, and with care, it will remain unspoiled. Whether you travel by helicopter or boat, it's expensive getting to the area once you arrive in Greenland, so it's best to book in advance. Some parties have been known to lose a week sorting out their transport once they have arrived in Greenland.

TONY PENNING, *Alpine Climbing Group*

*Nalumasortoq, Central Tower, Vertical Dream.* It was reported that Christian Dalphin, A. Castella, R. Lehner, A. Truffer and N. Zambetti climbed a mostly new line on the Central Tower of Nalumasortoq in June. *Vertical Dream* begins by sharing six pitches with *Cheese Finger at 3 O'Clock*, a route Dalphin helped create in 1996. These pitches were almost freed in their entirety at F6c and 7a; one section of A2 remains on the second part of pitch three. Where *Cheese Finger* moves right to the beginning of the big dihedral, *Vertical Dream* climbs left in a crack system left of the crest of the pillar. The climbing went at A1, A2 and 6a, but the climbers think it could all be freed at 7b or 7c.

The team then climbed the 15-pitch, 500-meter *Temps Sont Durs* on the slabby east-northeast face of Half Dome. The climb, which begins 80 meters to the left of the sheer north face, went all free at 6c. (*High Mountain Sports* 197)

# MEXICO

*El Potrero Chico, Overview.* The First Annual Potrero Chico Clean-Up and Trail Day in El Potrero Chico, Mexico, took place on New Year's Day. A small turnout of 30 climbers helped remove two truckloads of trash from the base of *Space Boyz*, a popular spot for the locals to hang out, drink beer, and watch the crazy gringos.

David Hume had a productive trip to the Potrero, quickly ticking many classic lines. He did the second ascent of *Time for Living* (13a), on-sighting all six pitches, on-sighted *Devil's Cabana Boy* (13a, five pitches) and sent the *Mothership Connection* (13a, two pitches) second try. At the nearby area Culo de Gato, Hume also did the first ascent of an open project named *Snake Belly* (13d), one of the hardest lines in Mexico. Also at the Culo, Guadalajaran climber Andres Mueller sent *Avenida de Pina* (13d), the hardest ascent by a Mexican climber.

This winter, about 30 new routes graced the walls of the Potrero, many of them in the moderate range. Kurt Smith, Elaina Arenz, and Andres Mueller developed the wall Avenida de la Revolucion, with six lines ranging from 11- to 12+. Magic Ed and Rodman bolted the dihedrals left of the Surf Bowls, which yielded seven routes in the 5.9 to 5.11+ range, including trad, bolted cracks, and face climbs. A group of Italians also contributed several routes on the Mileski Wall and in the Virgin Canyon from 5.9 to 5.12.

Highlights from last year's season included the 20-pitch project *Mi Regalo Favorito* on the Outrage Wall. This line took two months to bolt ground-up by Kurt Smith and Jeb Vetters. The pair spent 21 nights living on the wall to push this line up the left side of the Outrage Wall and up to the summit of Cerro San Miguel. A serious finger injury sidelined Kurt this winter and he hopes to complete this monster project in time for the new millennium. Later that same season, Magic Ed and Dane Bass put up the mega-long *Black Cat Bone* (5.10+) to the right of *Space Boyz*. This nine-pitch line sports mixed jungle climbing and a classic roof for the crux. Last winter also saw the largest development of single pitch lines from 5.8 to 5.12 with 40 new routes in three months.

KURT SMITH, *unaffiliated*

*Cerro El Gavilan, Spanish Harlem.* It was reported that Albino Pon and Rodman and Marcus Garcia put up the 11-pitch *Spanish Harlem* (a.k.a. *The Prow*, 5.11+ A1) over 13 days on Cerro El Gavilan near El Portrero Chico. The route was established ground-up and is mostly naturally protected. (*Rock and Ice* 86)

*El Gigante, Simuchi.* In the Basaseachic Waterfall National Park, Chihuahua, Carlos García Ayala (Mexico) and Cecilia Buil (Spain) made the first ascent of *Simuchi* ("*The Hummingbird,*" VI 6c A4, 1000m) on the northwest face of El Gigante from April 5-25. A complete account of their climb appears earlier in this journal.

# SOUTH AMERICA

## VENEZUELA

*Roraïma Tepui, El Mundo Perdido.* Tony Arbones (Spain) and I established the route *El Mundo Perdido* (VI 7b+ A2, 480m) on the southwest face of Roraïma Tepui in February in Venezuela. The expedition lasted two weeks—one for trekking and another of climbing. The route wanders up a 460-meter sandstone face that overhangs all the way. We established the route from the ground up. The high level of the climb was the result of a mistake: we wanted to put up a sport route with hard free climbing and good bolts, but after our powerdrill broke, the route turned into a traditional-style route with natural protection.

The route's 17 pitches went as follows: 6a, 6b+, 6c+, 7a+, 7a, 7a, 5+, 7a+, 6b+, 7a+, 7a, 7b+, 7a+, then three meters of aid on hooks, then 7b, 7a, 7a+, 7a+, 6c. All the pitches were freed except pitch 12, which was not linked up, and pitch 14, which includes a short section of aid. We swapped leads, and left nine 10-mm bolts (on pitches 3 and 4) and some 20 pegs.

We also found 17 hand-drilled 8-mm bolts without hangers. Once back in Europe, we learned the bolts were from an aid route that met our climb in places. *Gorilas de la Niebla* ("*Gorillas in the Mist,*" VI A4) was put up over 11 days by Xabier Izagirre and Raul Alava at the end of 1996. While on the wall, we didn't even knew that the hangers were those of a finished route, as climbers from Caracas had told us no one had climbed this main wall of Roraïma. When we found the first hangers on pitch 6, we didn't follow their path but only tried to reach the top by the most logical way for us. On some pitches we found several more hangers, on others, none. It appears that we followed a line close to *Gorillas*, but didn't free climb their route.

JEAN-MINH TRINH-THIEU, *France*

# ECUADOR

*Cotopaxi, Northeast Face, New Route.* From February 28 to March 1, Gaspard Naverette, Jurg U Umlaut and Gabriel Llano climbed a new route on the northeast face of Cotopaxi (5897m). From the refuge, the three traversed eastward around the mountain for three hours, crossing three ridges to reach camp. They then headed up, summiting after seven hours, having picked their way through innumerable crevasses, some of which had to be descended into and then climbed out of. Said Llano: "It's a different mountain from that side—you never see Yanasacha (the landmark rock outcrop on the north face to the left of the normal route)."

YOSSI BRAIN, *United Kingdom*

*Chimborazo, North Ridge of Veintimilla Summit.* On December 20-22, Byron Sykes and I, with support from Jens Larsen and Jorge Davila, climbed the striking line of the prominent north ridge of the Veintimilla summit (20,561') of Chimborazo. By 3 p.m. on December 20, we had completed crossing the "paramo" of the approach, a distance of just a few miles from the Ambato-Guaranda road. From there, three hours of hiking and loose scree scrambling led us to a bivy site at the toe of the north ridge (ca. 16,000'), just short of the snowline.

From our bivy we climbed up a short ridge that led to the prominent rock walls guarding the difficulties. These walls are a lower eastern extension of Las Murallas Rojas (the red walls). Traversing westerly on snowslopes to a notch between a large rock pillar and the rock wall on our left then allowed us a view directly up several pitches of ice, which proved the key to the route. Rockfall was constant, and it was obvious that the gully had been scoured by collapses of the Reiss Icecliff, which hangs 1,000 feet above the route on the right. We were able to scramble along rock and black ice on the left side of the gully for about three pitches to the final rock band. Sound darker rock, followed by a band of very friable frozen mud, led for 80 feet to a belay perch. We then quickly climbed back left toward the ridge crest and away from the danger of the Icecliff. An uncomfortable but dramatic bivy site was located beneath the last rocks of the route at 18,900 feet, protecting us from the hail. We started quickly on December 22, but soon encountered calf- to thigh-deep rotten snow on steepening slopes. For fear of being avalanched off our route, we began a long traverse west toward the standard route, reaching it after three hours of motivated snowplowing and crevasse crossings.

The Veintimilla summit lay 1,200 feet above us, but due to the lateness of the hour, and satisfied with our climbing, we simply opted for the descent.

ALEX VAN STEEN

# PERU

## CORDILLERA BLANCA

*Pisco West, East Face, Canadian Non-Direct.* In May, Chris Geisler and I established the route *Canadian Non-Direct* (5.9 WI 4+ 90°, 400m) on the east face of Pisco West (5752m) in 12 hours. (*This face was climbed in 1977 by John Bouchard and Marie Meunier directly to the summit via the "easiest line." The ascent was not reported at the time.—Ed.*) The ascent featured mixed climbing to the left-hand edge of the snowfield in the center of the east face. We then traversed the snowfield to its right edge. Mixed climbing amongst strange snow clumps was followed to the base of the summit snow cap. One pitch of vertical snow took us to the summit. Descent was made via the standard route.

SEAN EASTON, *Canada*

*Chopicalqui, North Face, Mirton Novice Extreme.* On July 20, Pavle Kozjek (Slovenia) climbed *Mirton Novice Extreme* (TD/ED, 5+ 90°, ca. 800m) on the north face of Chopicalqui (6354 m). (*According to Brian Sharman's* Climbs of the Cordillera Blanca of Peru, *there are two existing routes on the northwest face; there is not a true north face to this mountain, so it is assumed the ascent took place on the northwest face.—Ed.*) Kozjek's first attempt (July 13-14) was unsuccessful. A day spent reconnoitering a route through the broken north glacier left him too tired to begin the climb the next morning. On July 19, Kozjek started at the Portachuelo Pass and crossed the less dangerous glacier below the northwest ridge. The next day he started at 4:30 a.m. and began up the center of the north face. The weather was cold and cloudy, ideal for climbing the face, where ice and stone falls are the main danger. Although the face seemed to be almost completely dry (rock only), there was more than 50% ice climbing. He climbed the ramp to the right, reached the buttress and followed it to the top of Chopicalqui Norte (6050m), avoiding the overhanging seracs below the top with a 100-meter traverse to the right. The rock was poor in the middle of the route. He descended the same route, with some rappels.

The climb (ascent and descent), which was undertaken with no rucksack, took about nine hours. It seems to be the best and safest way to climb the big Andean walls, which are often exposed to stone and ice fall.

PAVLE KOZJEK, *Planinska zveza Slovenije*

*Artesonraju, Southeast Face, and Tocllaraju, Northwest Ridge, Descents.* In May and June Ptor Spricenieks, John Griber, Jason Schutz, Kris Erickson and I teamed up with film-makers Rob DesLauriers and Frederick Jacobi and local guide Koky Castaneda to ski and snowboard two wild lines on Tocllaraju (6034m) and Artesonraju (6020m).

During the last week of May, we acclimatized by ferrying loads to our upper Base Camp at the foot of the Tocllaraju glacier (5000m), taking rest days to boulder some excellent problems in the valley below. After six days, we felt ready to attempt a descent of Tocllaraju's northwest ridge from the summit. On May 28, we all headed up the lower glacier below the west face. Our group quickly became spread out and at 5800 meters, Kris and I continued alone to the summit. As we climbed, we realized that the "snow," a bad mix of ice and unconsolidated faceted crystals, was not what we were looking for at 6000 meters on a 65° slope. After summiting, we skied an exhilarating knife-edge ridge with wild exposure, then rappelled 60 meters across a bergschrund to more moderate slopes below. After a couple of hundred meters, we met the rest of the group for some mellow corn skiing to the top of a lower head wall. This proved to be the crux of the descent. The snow was rippled and icy, and the pitch neared 60°. One by one, we made sketchy turns down to the lower glacier. The rest of the descent was super fun gliding on perfect sun-cooked snow.

The 1000-meter southeast face of Artesonraju, which had never been snowboarded, was the real focus of the trip. In the first week of June, we ventured into the Parón Valley. The

*Artesonraju, with the southeast face in shadow, from Base Camp in the Parón Valley.*
KRISTOFFER ERICKSON

conditions on the southeast face were not what we had hoped for. This was an unusually dry season in the Cordillera Blanca and as a result, the snowpack in the mountains was thin and the glaciers broken. According to one local hostel owner we talked to, glaciers have been receding as much as ten meters a year over the last decade.

On June 12, we headed across dry glaciers to the base of Artesonraju. The southeast face was firm and scary wind-scoured sastrugi snow. Booting up it proved to be easy, but coming down was a different story. At 5800 meters, the face became extremely steep—close to 60°. By the time we summited, the weather had deteriorated, making it difficult to assess the descent route. Ptor volunteered to check out the skiing on belay, cutting turns while Jason belayed him from a pair of skis he had driven in the snow. Everyone made their way safely through the initial you-fall, you-see-God slot. We were in constant radio communication with Koky and Freddy, who were filming from Pyramide. They relayed crucial information about the location of huge seracs below us, which were difficult for us to spot in the swirling clouds. Skiing was dicey. It was possible to find little pockets of wind-blown snow, but between these were stretches of difficult turns where it was hard to get an edge to bite. A final hop across the bergschrund at the bottom marked the end of a successful expedition.

HANS SAARI, *unaffiliated*

*Cordillera Blanca, Various Ascents, and Observations on Glaciation.* From July 20 until August 20, Jimmy Surette and I climbed in the Cordillera Blanca and found conditions utterly unlike anything we expected. For years the glaciers have been receding in the equatorial regions, but the last two years have been exceptionally dry in Peru, accelerating the deterio-

*Jim Surette, with one of the Pukajirka peaks appearing through the clouds.* TOPHER DONAHUE

ration of ice features at an alarming rate. First we found much rock exposed on the previously icy south (shadowed) face of Chacraraju. A recent snowstorm completed our jinx and caused high avalanche hazard. We then hiked to the Pisco/Huandoy area and found faces that have been climbed on ice melted to the unstable earth beneath. Rockslides were more common than avalanches. A line of blue water ice gave us a safe route on the 1,500-foot south face of Pisco. We were happy to climb, but the deterioration of the once-stellar alpine area weighed heavily on our spirits.

We moved to the Santa Cruz Valley to try the awesome granite-and-ice plumb of Taulliraju. We found established routes utterly dry or with just a veneer of slush bonded lightly to the rock. The less steep northeast ridge looked like the least of many evils, and we found some of the wildest ice features we'd ever seen. From a bivy atop an ice face, we tried for the summit in a day, but turned around when navigating the steep ridge guarded by every conceivable ice goblin proved too time consuming.

With enough time for one more thing, we tried Rinrijirca, a peak called "easy" in the guidebook. The book suggested two to three hours for the ascent; it took us 12, and we encountered overhanging ice where climbers once walked on a snow ridge.

TOPHER DONAHUE, *unaffiliated*

*La Esfinge, East Face, Free Ascent.* Ralph Ferrara and John Reyner freed the 1985 route on the east face of La Esfinge on August 14-15. They had attempted the route in June, managing four pitches. It is possibly the second free ascent of the route; Julio Fernández, Guillermo Mejía and David Rodríguez made what was perhaps the first, fixing four pitches, then climb-g the route on October 2-3, 1997. Fernández led the more difficult pitches (up to 5.11c), and s companions jumared. J. Boyer and A. Bozzy may have climbed that route free in July, )95, but further details are lacking.

ANTONIO GÓMEZ BOHÓRQUEZ, *Spain*

ORDILLERA DE HUAROCHIRI

*evado Pariacacca Norte, Traverse.* The twin Nevados Tuyujuto or Pariacacca (5756m and 701m) belong to the Cordillera de Huarochiri (locally also called Pariacacca), some 100 lometers east of Lima. Gonzalo Menacho and I reached the area of Lake Huaylacancha 250m) by car, where we camped in order to acclimatize. We then climbed above 2mbladera Lake and placed a camp near the ice. On May 20, we ascended Pariacacca II orte (5701m) by its north ridge, following a few variants up a rocky rib. We then descend- l by the south ridge, having accomplished the traverse of this peak.

ALBERTO MURGUÍA, *Lima, Peru*

ORDILLERA RAURA AND CORDILLERA DE LA VIUDA

*ordillera Raura and Cordillera de la Viuda, First Ascents.* The Peruvian climber Alberto urguía and I traveled by bus to Mina Raura, located northeast of Lima and surrounded by ck and ice peaks. The employees of the mine gave us ample hospitality. We first attempted evado Pichuycocha (5215m), but were defeated by the glassy ice left by droughts. As a mpensation, on June 16 we made the second ascent of Cerro Puyhuancocha (5062m), a ng rock ridge situated between two icefalls, south of Pichuycocha. We found a surveyor's irn on the summit.

I also made two forays into the Cordillera de la Viuda in the Lima hinterland, making four st ascents. I first explored the Antajacha and Cunchupata valleys, which were devastated droughts, and then moved to the Curicocha basin, where I camped by a water trickle. On ay 2, I climbed Peak 5000m, which I named Cerro Calcuchima. On the 27th, I climbed ak 5050m, which was baptized Cerro Quizquez (both names represent historic Inca gener- s). The same day I traversed the three summits of Cerro Carhuac Loma (5150m). In a sec- d trip I travelled to the north end of La Viuda. From the big Chuchún Lake, I toured sev- al basins and explored some peaks. On June 29, under threatening skies, I climbed Cerro uluscocha (5000m) and then returned to Lima.

EVELIO ECHEVARRÍA

OLIVIA

*livian Climbing, Overview.* It was a dry year. The Bolivian government introduced drink- ; laws, which meant bars had to shut at 2 a.m. except for Saturdays and Sundays, when they ut at 3 a.m. There was also some weather, or rather a lack thereof: El Niño meant the 1997- 3 Bolivian wet season was the driest and hottest in ten years, so by the time the 1998 climb- ; season arrived there was very little snow around and most of that got burnt off, leaving vasses wide open and unbridged.

A more unpleasant effect was the creation of nieve penitentes, especially on eastern slope Climbers had to weave through them with their ropes getting caught all over the place. The were also a number of short periods of bad weather during what is normally extremely stab and good weather through the austral winter (June to September).

Liam O'Brien published a new improved second edition of his *A New Map of th Cordillera Real*, the only map to cover the whole of the cordillera and the only map to cove the section running southeast from Cocoyo (access for Ancohuma from the east) to Jankh Laya, which is still unmapped at 1:50,000. Mapping in Bolivia faces a slightly uncertai future after the decision by the U.S. State Department-funded National Imaging and Mappir Agency (formally the Defense Mapping Agency and before that the InterAmerican Geodes Survey) to close their La Paz office. The office helped the Bolivian Instituto Geográfic Militar produce maps, training local personnel and supervising mapping in the country, whic is still not completely covered by 1:50,000 sheets.

YOSSI BRAIN, *United Kingdo*

CORDILLERA REAL

*Pico Gotico, West Face, New Route.* On August 26-27, Erik and Grigota Monasterio estal lished the highest pure rock route done in Bolivia. From a high camp at 5250 meters, one how west-southwest of Laguna Glaciar (5038m) on the moraine directly below the west face Pico Gotico (Pico Gotico is marked Pt. 5750 on the DAV Illampu map), they fixed the fir three pitches, including the crux third pitch (F6c/A2), a sustained 50-meter, four-centimet crack with featureless walls on either side and a series of overhangs which were aided. Th next day they jugged the fixed lines, then climbed another seven pitches to summit two hou after the agreed turn-around time and rappelled back down in the dark. They reached the bc tom of the route at 8 p.m. They encountered difficult end-of-season conditions, cloudy, co and windy with temperatures never much above freezing. It began snowing half an hour aft they completed the route.

YOSSI BRAIN, *United Kingdo*

*Tres Marias group and Chachacomani, Various Ascents.* Britons Phil Amos and Ada Thomas spent three weeks in this area of the central Cordillera Real. The Tres Marias is triple-peaked ridge east of the distinctive Chachacomani (6074m), a.k.a. "Chisel Peak." Apa from some poorly documented expeditions organized by the American Alpine Institute, no lot has been done in the area in recent years. On July 16, Amos and Thomas made the four ascent of the West Ridge (AD) of an unnamed peak (ca. 5500m), the northernmost of the Ti Marias. The route was 500 meters with rock up to 60°; the last 30 meters was ice up to 4( They then continued to Wampa (ca. 5550m), the middle of the Tres Marias, by walking alo the snow ridge linking the two summits, then descending to Base Camp via the col betwe the Tres Marias and Chachacomani. The pair got avalanched in dry snow and went 50 mete before managing to stop.

On July 19, they climbed a new route (TD, 12 pitches, 700m) on the south face of Co Rico (ca. 5600m), the southernmost peak of the Tres Marias. They descended to the nor east and then to the col between Coco Rico and Pico Elena to the south. They then continu to the big col between Wampa and Coco Rico and down to Base Camp. On July 21, they made the second ascent of the West Face (AD+, 400m) of Wampa (ca. 5550m). On July 23-24, they climbed a new route on the southeast ridge of Chachacomani (6074m), starting from the col on the normal route up to Chachacomani's distinctive south face. They climbed three rock and ice pinnacles at up to 60°, crossed what looks like a snow dome from below, and then descended to a col at ca. 5750 meters, where they camped. This section of the route is believed to be a first ascent. The next day they continued by climbing Chachacomani's Southeast Buttress (D). This route was described in the 1990 *AAJ* (p. 194) as rock at 5.7; the Brits found it to be 5.6. It took them seven hours to climb the 250 meters to reach the summit of Chachacomani. They then traversed Chachacomani's summit ridge and descended a ridge off the west end of the ridge, rapping five times en route.

The two mention that the Achapampa area is not depicted on the 1962 Reading map as it appears on the ground. Negruni as marked is Warawarani; Rumca as marked is Chajowara. (Amos and Thomas plan to produce an updated map of the area.)

YOSSI BRAIN, *United Kingdom*


*Chearoco, Southeast Face.* Our expedition consisted of Mary Stigge, Jean Aschenbrenner, Wesley Berg and Jack Zuzack as members and Doug Solfermoser and myself as co-leaders. The objective was to climb Chearoco (6127m), the large peak to the southeast of Ancohuma. We approached from the west following the Kellihuani River. Despite many past reports of problems in this area, we found the locals to be very friendly and helpful. We chose the South Face route on Chearoco. This route turned out to be a grade more difficult than we were expecting due to glacial recession, the same problem seen in Peru. We made two attempts, the first coming within 100 feet of the summit and the second succeeding, putting Doug, Wes, Jack and myself on the summit on July 20. Research from past *AAJ* reports and other sources indicate that this may have been the second ascent of this route.

MARK SCOTT-NASH


*Cordillera Real and the Cordillera de la Quimsa Cruz, Various Ascents.* On June 1, the Salt Lake-based team of Ben Folsom, Steven Su, and Andy Gresh arrived in La Paz, Bolivia, intending to do lightweight ascents in the Cordillera Real and the Cordillera de la Quimsa Cruz. After several days in La Paz, the entire team, along with several friends from Salt Lake City, departed on June 7 for the town of Sorata, hoping to make an ascent of Ancohuma via the normal route (Laguna Glaciar) for acclimatization purposes. The attempt over June 9 to 13 was unsuccessful due to sickness, heinous penitentes, and underestimation of the route's length.

On June 18, I arrived in La Paz and joined up with Ben and Steve. After two days of organization/acclimatization in La Paz, Steve and I departed for the 6080-meter Huayna Potosí, which we climbed on June 23 in three hours via the normal route. This year the summit ridge was rather exposed. On June 27, Ben, Steve, Andy, and I left La Paz for the Condoriri group. After a day of rest, Ben, Steve, and I departed Base Camp at 5 a.m. and headed for Ala Oeste (the "left wing" of Condoriri). Andy remained in camp due to a twisted knee and a persistent head-cold.

We were at the 'schrund at 11 a.m. and after a short bit of shenanigans were established on the face. We simul-climbed the entire 650 meters, which was a variation of the Mesili route

*Ben Folsom pointing out* Red Storm Rising *on Ala Oeste.* BART PAULL

on the face. The line follows ice runnels in the central part of the wall up to a large serac about half-way up the face, then cuts slightly left. The conditions varied and we passed sections of styrofoam, brittle ice, plate ice, crappy ice, etc.—the full Andean experience.

We topped out at 3 p.m. in a rather intense hail storm and immediately began the descent via ten 60-meter rappels. The majority of our anchors were good V-threads drilled in runnels of ice. We were back to Base Camp and coca tea at 10:30 p.m. The day's catch: *Red Storm Rising* (D 70°, 650m).

Other routes climbed by the team were: Illampu, via the direct normal route, July 6, Ben, Steve, Andy, and me; Pico Norte, via its 900-meter east face couloir, on July 18, Pat, Eric, Steve (it should be noted that the normal route on Pico Norte has basically ceased to exist; it is an unsavory rappel descent at best due to glacial recession); the technically easy 5540-meter Viluyo, on July 17, Ben and me; the French route on Huayna Potosí, July 25-27, Danika Gilbert and Steve; Illimani (6640m), on July 26, Ben.

It is sad to see how much recession has taken place in Bolivia over the past couple of years. Routes on Illampu, Condoriri, Tiquimani, and other peaks are now very dangerous or impossible due to lack of adequate snow/ice coverage.

I thank the American Alpine Club for the support given to me. Without your help this trip would not have been possible. ¡Gracías por los recuerdos! Uastata sita!

BART PAULL*
*Recipient of a 1998 AAC Mountaineering Fellowship Fund Grant

*Cordillera de Quimza Cruz, Los Cuernos del Diablo.* On April 11, Pete Grosset (UK) and I climbed a new route on Los Cuernos del Diablo (5271m). The route consisted of six pitches (250 meters) on solid granite and followed a straight line directly up to below the northeast horn. It finished on the upper two pitches of the original "Classic" route of the 1987 Bolivian-German expedition. The overall grade of the route was 5.10b, with excellent protection following connecting cracks.

DAKIN COOK

CORDILLERA APOLOBAMBA

*Cordillera Apolobamba, Overview.* After an unprecedented amount of activity in the area in 1997, 1998 saw three commercial expeditions and perhaps only four significant climbing trips to the Apolobamba. Conditions were good early in the season, but nieve penitentes developed in June, presenting familiar time-consuming problems.

YOSSI BRAIN, *United Kingdom*

*Chaupi Orco Norte to Chaupi Orco, Traverse.* On May 26, British La Paz residents Yossi Brain and Pete Grosset, together with visiting Brits Glen Wilks and John Mudway, climbed Chaupi Orco Norte (6000m) in the northern Apolobamba, believing it to be Chaupi Orco (6044m), the highest mountain in the range. However, when they stood on the summit it was obvious that there was a higher mountain lying to the south on the other side of four peaks. After climbing the first two intervening peaks (Pts. 5960 and 5920m), Mudway and Wilks decided to return via the ascent route, while Brain and Grosset continued with the remains of one bar of chocolate and one liter of water each. They climbed the next two peaks (Pts. 5870 and 5860m) to reach the big col to the north of Chaupi Orco. From the col, they climbed more or less direct to the southwest ridge and then followed it over a series of false summits to top out around 4:30 p.m. From Chaupi Orco, they descended north back to the col between Chaupi Orco and Pt. 5860 meters and then headed down. The descent was a nightmare, and they returned to camp at 9:30 p.m. after 17 hours on the hill. Brain was so dehydrated that the next day when he slipped over on ice and badly cut his wrist, the blood just oozed out like red oatmeal and didn't drip.

Technically the route could be graded at AD+, as long as one remembers the whole day was spent over 5200 meters (most of it between 5800 and 6000m) and there does not appear to be an easy way off if you are unable to finish the route. It was the probable second ascent of the four intervening peaks. The first Chaupi Orco-Chaupi Orco Norte traverse was done by a German expedition from Munich in 1969. They took three days, but mention only three intervening peaks.

Yossi Brain, *United Kingdom*

*The Names of Chaupi Orco, Clarification.* There has been consistent confusion on the names of Chaupi Orco since the second ascent in 1958. The Germans Werner Karl, Hans Richter and Hans Wimmer climbed Chaupi Orco in 1957 and gave it a height of 6044 meters. Their expedition was the first climbing expedition to visit the Apolobamba. In 1958, an Italian expedition (Giancarlo Frigieri, Pietro Magni, Umberto Mellano, Romano Merendi, Andrea Oggioni, Gianluigi Sterna and Camillo Zamboni) climbed the main peak to the north of what the Germans had named Chaupi Orco. Following advice from locals, they called *this* Chaupi Orco and gave it a height of 6100 meters, as it appeared to them higher than the southern peak. They then climbed the peak the Germans had called Chaupi Orco and, following advice from the head of the Peruvian village of Trapiche, named it Salluyo, but maintained the same height of 6044 meters.

The British Imperial College 1959 expedition produced an excellent map (published in the *Geographical Journal*, December, 1960). While they didn't climb in the Chaupi Orco area, their map listed Chaupi Orco as 6044 meters and Chaupi Orco Norte as 6000 meters. They placed Chaupi Orco Norte at the point where the ridge running north of Chaupi Orco meets the ridge lying to the east. This is actually Angelicum, first climbed by the Italians in 1958.

In 1961, the Hitotsubashi Japanese expedition reverted to the German names and heights and made the third ascent of Chaupi Orco (6044m), the second ascent of Salluyo, which they gave a height of 5808 meters (this corresponds to the peak the Italians named Pico Jorge Chavez, a name apparently given them by locals) and second ascent of Chaupi Orco Norte (6000m).

The Ober-Fränkische Anden-Expedition 1968 maintained the German position with Chaupi Orco (6044m) and Chaupi Orco Norte (6000m). The 1969 *Alpine Journal* report of the 1968 Hofmann German expedition (p. 271) states, "Chaupi Orco, 19,830ft [6044m], and its northern neighbour, so far unnamed, measured at exactly 6000m." Chaupi Orco's "northern neighbour" is, in reality, a lot more than 44 meters lower; presumably, it refers to Chaupi Orco Norte, which the Imperial College expedition map had so named in 1960.

The 1970 *Alpine Journal* and the 1970 *American Alpine Journal* (pp. 32-37) reported that the Munich Andean expedition traversed from Chaupi Orco (6044m) to Chaupi Orco Norte

(6000m). Then the 1973 *American Alpine Journal* (p. 401) states that, according to Mario Fantin and the 1958 Italian expedition, Chaupi Orco should be Salluyo, Chaupi Orco Norte should be Chaupi Orco, and the Italian Chaupi Orco is higher than Salluyo. The *Alpine Journal* repeated this position in 1974 in more detail, stating, "the Italian climbers Mario Fantin and Camillo Zamboni revealed that there is only one Chaupi Orco peak, corresponding to the one previously known as Chaupi Orco Norte (6000m), to which an estimated height of 6100m has been given. The mountain hitherto known as Chaupi Orco (which retains its height of 6044m) should receive, according to the Italians, the name of Nevado de Salluyo." This is a straight restatement of the Italian 1958 position without any additional information. However, the Campese Italian expedition in 1980 produced a good map of the area in *La Rivista del Club Alpino Italiano* (Sept./Oct. 1982) showing Chaupi Orco Norte (6000m) and, to the south, Chaupi Orco (6044m). They also gave a height for Salluyo as 5808 meters, the same as that given by the Imperial College map in 1960.

The best map currently available of the area was drawn up by Paul Hudson in 1993 based on the Royal Geographic Society Boundary Commission review of 1911-'13 and the collected wisdom of all expedition reports since then. Hudson maintains the German convention, Chaupi Orco (6044m) and Chaupi Orco Norte (6000m), and repeated the 1960 Imperial College map mistake on the placing of Norte.

In *Mountaineering in the Andes, Second Edition* (1994), p. 110, Jill Neate, referring to the German expedition of 1957, restates the Italian position: "Salluyo (then called Chaupi Orco);" and then on p. 112, "Chaupi Orco (Chaupi Orco Norte) 6100m 1-1958 [Italians]. . . . Salluyo (Chaupi Orco) 6044m 1-1957 [Germans]. . . ."

The name Chaupi Orco in Quechua means "Middle Peak." However, it is unclear from what direction it is the middle peak—perhaps the Peruvian side.

To summarize, ignoring the change of height to 6088 meters recently declared by the Germans (JDAV 1995, which called Chaupi Orco "Chaupi Orco Sur," and DAV 1997, which also came up with a new height for Chaupi Orco Norte of 6030m) and a Russian map that gives a height of 5920m for Chaupi Orco, there are two conventions on the naming of Chaupi Orco: the German of 1957 and the Italian of 1958. Since then, these two positions have been restated by expeditions to the area without any new information. The Apolobamba has never been properly surveyed beyond the work done by the Imperial College expedition of 1959, and there are no 1:50,000 topographical sheets for the area. The Italian convention is based on the belief that Chaupi Orco Norte is higher than Chaupi Orco. It certainly appears that this is the case when you are on the glacier below the peaks on the Bolivian side, when Norte is the far more obvious of the two peaks. However, having climbed Norte myself believing it to be Chaupi Orco and stood on top of it in perfect visibility and looked south and seen another higher mountain and then climbed that, I believe that the German convention is correct and that Chaupi Orco is higher than Chaupi Orco Norte.

Anyone feel like going and measuring Chaupi Orco and Chaupi Orco Norte properly? (With thanks to Marcello Sanguineti for help and investigation of Italian expedition reports.)

YOSSI BRAIN, *United Kingdom*

*Cuchillo, New Route.* In July, Jeff Newsom and Chris Gardei (U.S.) gained Cuchillo's (5655m) west ridge via the fourth snow and ice gully from the east (60-65°). The pair were forced down off the ridge on to the other side of the mountain. They then climbed west-fac-ing scree slopes to join Cuchillo's north ridge and moved up to a subsidiary hollow ice sum-mit to the west of the main summit. The pair went through an ice tunnel and then continued along the ridge to summit Cuchillo in the dark on July 11. They said of their climb, "Overall we would grade the route a D, only because there were a few sections that were 70-80°. However, they were very short and in some cases could probably be avoided. The ice tunnel was about 20 meters long and we were forced down from the ridge because it was jumbled and very slow going. It would have involved some crumbly rock and rappelling, which we certainly couldn't have done in a day." They descended the east ridge.

Yossi Brain, United Kingdom

*Sunchuli Valley Area, New Routes.* Italians Marcello Sanguineti (Club Alpino Italiano Chiavari) and Alessandro Bianchi (CAI-ULE Genova) returned to Bolivia for the second year running to climb three hard new routes in the southern Apolobamba, a.k.a. Puyo Puyo or Pupuya. The southernmost part of the Pupuya Range was discovered by Germans in 1957, who saw these mountains from the top of Huelancalloc, but didn't climb them. The first to climb there were the Japanese in 1961 and 1965. Since many of the routes opened before 1998 are normal routes, there is in Puyo Puyo potential for direct routes on previously unclimbed walls.

After 300 kilometers and 12 hours in a jeep from La Paz, the pair established Base Camp just south of Paso Sunchuli (4700m). On August 14, they climbed a new route on the east face (D, 400m) of Cavayani (5700m), for the peak's fourth ascent. They descended the southeast ridge (F, 400m) and then the east slope to rejoin the approach route. On August 16, they climbed the normal route (east side and northeast ridge) on Cuchillo (5665m) to check out the ridge running west toward Cavayani and descent routes from Pt. 5550m, which they climbed five days later. A second new route (ED1-, 700m) on August 19 was put up on the southwest face of Corohuari (5668m); this was the hardest route yet recorded in the Apolobamba and the third ascent of the mountain. The pair climbed the hardest part of the route through seracs at up to 90° to reach a broken plateau, then up on 55-60° slopes to the beginning of a rock wall. They then traversed left on ice (70°, then 60°), to rejoin the snow and, after 100 meters at 60°, reached a col. After 200 meters of 70-75° snow, they finished along the west ridge. The descent was to the north, followed by a traverse northwest below the ridge and then up to a col between Sunchuli (a.k.a. Cuchillo II, 5450m) and Pt. 5400m and then down the northwest slope.

On August 21, they made the second ascent of Pt. 5550m via a new route (TD, 350m) up the previously unclimbed south face. The route went to the left of an obvious serac to reach the bergschrund, crossing it in one pitch (max. 85°). They then followed a snow gully (55-60°) to below a big serac. They traversed to the left of the serac, then climbed three pitches (max. 70°) to reach the summit. The pair down climbed the north side of the mountain rather than abseil to avoid stone and ice fall once the face was in the sun.

They observed a remarkable glacier recession in the Apolobamba, which was confirmed by miners who work in the region. Also because of the very dry season, many glaciers presented a great quantity of big penitentes (particularly on Cavayani, Cuchillo, and the north side of Pt. 5550m). The extremely dry season also caused many walls to present more difficulties than they offer in normal years.

Marcello Sanguineti, Club Alpino Italiano

*Hichukhota Area, Various Ascents.* A French expedition spent seven days in the Hichukhota area and made the following ascents: Wila Llojeta (5244m), August 27; Jankho Huyo (5512m), August 28; Jishka Pata (5508m), August 30; the southeast ridge of Wila Lloje (5596m), August 31; and the southeast ridge of Warawarani (5604m), September 1. The expedition was made up of Florence Barrault, François-Xavier Grillon, Olivier Guidet and Gregoire Volluet. No further information was available.

YOSSI BRAIN, *United Kingdom*

*Condoriri Group, Overview.* The dry conditions meant that Cabeza de Condor (5648m) was devoid of snow and the few teams that attempted it reported extremely dangerous conditions (the peak is made of rotten loose rock). The popular Pequeño Alpamayo (5370m) was very icy and the descent to it from the minor peak of Tarija proved to be a loose-rock nightmare.

YOSSI BRAIN, *United Kingdom*

*Ala Derecha, Possible New Route.* On August 7, Erik and Grigota Monasterio (Bolivia-New Zealand) climbed the ice face to the right of Ala Derecha and to the left of the rock band, west of the small but distinctive pyramidal snow peak marked Cerro Illampu on the IGM map (a.k.a. Techo de Paja, Diente). The possible new route was 400 meters long; the last three pitches to the col were 60-80° (D) on excellent ice. They then followed the ridge right to the base of the rock, from where it was 30 meters to the summit (F4). Descent was made via seven rappels, the first five of which were off ice bollards due to the very poor rock.

YOSSI BRAIN, *United Kingdom*

*Huayna Potosí, West Face.* The increasingly popular 1000-meter West Face of Huayna Potosí (6088m) had very few ascents this year due to poor conditions. Spaniard Pere Vilarasau and Andorran Frank Van Herreweghe climbed the American Route (later named *Vía de Lyons* by French climbers unaware of the previous ascent) on July 7 in 11 hours. They reported IV+/V rock to access the face, which was covered in black ice the whole way up with sections up to 75°. Normally, the route is no more than 55-65°.

YOSSI BRAIN, *United Kingdom*

*Milluni Valley, Various Ascents.* Slovenian Branko Ivanek, a La Paz resident and guide, made a number of probable first ascents of icefalls in the Milluni Valley, south of Huayna Potosí. On July 23, with Bolivian guide Marco Soria, he climbed an 80-meter icefall on Pico Milluni in five-and-a-half hours. Starting at 4940 meters, the route, which they called *Amistad*, was two pitches (UIAA IV, max. 90°) on ice five to ten centimeters thick. To the right of *Amistad* are two other icefall routes, *Branco Blues* (III/5) and *Bolivian Journeys* (III/4+), climbed by Neil Brodie (U.K.) and Patrick Berthet (France) on June 13.

YOSSI BRAIN, *United Kingdom*

*Illimani Group, Traverse.* British La Paz residents Yossi Brain and Peter Grosset teamed up with visiting Italians Alessandro Bianchi (Club Alpino Italiano-ULE Genova) and Marcello

Sanguineti (CAI Chiavari) to attempt the full five-peak traverse of Illimani (6439m) in August. The three-peak traverse of Picos Norte, Central and Sur is climbed on a reasonably regular basis starting from camp on the west side of the mountain. The five-peak traverse from north to south or vice versa has been attempted a number of times but there are only records of two completions, both south to north: Anton and Ria Putz (Germany) in 1979, and B. Francou, J.-E. Sicart, P. Wagnon (French), in 1997. Parties often get frostbite while spending several days above 6000 meters.

On August 25, the four climbers were driven to 4450 meters on the north side of Illimani below Mina Aguila, where the road marked on the Deutschen Alpenverein map runs out. A hike up-valley brought them to a long gully and then to a bivy among the rocks at 5400 meters, northwest of the first significant peak on the north ridge of Illimani.

On August 26, the team moved straight on to the glacier through nieve penitente ice spikes to join the north ridge at 5700 meters. They crossed two minor peaks before climbing the so-called (see below) Pico del Indio (6109m). They then climbed a 60° face to join the *Vía Khoyu Khoya* route on Pt. 6175m, which has a spectacular overhanging cornice clearly visible from Illimani's normal west face route approach and climb. They crossed Pt. 6175m and camped on the other side at 6150 meters at 4 p.m. Most of August 27 was spent in clouds, including the enjoyable technical finish to Pico Norte (6403m), a series of moves up to 70°. They then had to descend the long and exposed south ridge, which was in a bad condition, in wind and clouds. The clouds cleared just before sunset. They got off the ridge by down climbing the east side to reach a flat area to camp at 6170 meters at 10 p.m. On August 28, they rejoined the ridge, followed it down to the col between Picos Norte and Central and then spent the rest of the day climbing up the eastern side of the ridge to Pico Central (6362m). This was mainly walking but with some 60° climbing to reach the ridge proper, 150 meters below the summit. They topped out at 4 p.m. and descended to camp at 6260 meters in the broad col between Picos Central and Sur.

On August 29, they climbed Pico Sur (6439m), summiting by 8 a.m. After breakfast back at camp, they headed south, saw a peak (Pt. 6301m) that stands alone beyond the end of the ridge coming down from the southeast off Pico Central, and climbed it. They then dropped down to the base of the last of the five major peaks, Pico Layca Khollu (6159m), and climbed it, finishing on some beautiful névé and then dropping down through penitentes to get below 6000 meters for the first time in three days. It was then a tiring descent through deep snow up to their knees to the end of the glacier, where a series of down climbs and one rap brought them to the scree slopes by 6 p.m., where Brain and Grosset recovered the body of a Spanish climber from the previous year. They reached abandoned mine buildings and a possible camp at 7:30 p.m., one hour after sunset, but Grosset made the call for the forced march out to Cohoni to catch the 2 a.m. bus. Brain and Grosset reached Cohoni at 1:30 a.m., just in time to jump on the bus as it was pulling out of Cohoni square. The others missed the bus, slept in the square and had to wait for the telephone office to open at 8 a.m. the next day before ringing La Paz for a jeep to come and pick them up.

YOSSI BRAIN, *United Kingdom*

*The line of the British-Italian traverse of the Illimani peaks.* COURTESY MARCELLO SANGUINETI

*Illimani Peak Names.* By far the best map of Illimani is *Cordillera Real Süd Illimani*, published by the Deutschen Alpenverein in 1990. It contains far more information than the *Bolivian Instituto Geográfico Militar* maps and has relief shading. It is also accurate. (N.B.: When the then-head of the U.S. Defense Mapping Agency in La Paz, Liam O' Brien, climbed Illimani to verify its height with modern instruments, he came out with a height of 6439 meters for Illimani's highest peak, compared to the DAV figure of 6368 meters.) From the DAV map, starting in the north, the first of the five peaks is marked as Pico del Indio (6109m). Next is Pico Norte (a.k.a. Pico de Paris, 6403m), then Pico Central (6362m), Pico Sur (6438m) and finally Pico Layca Khollu (6159m). The *Bolivian Instituto Geográfico Militar* map uses the same peak names.

It should be noted that Pico Norte is not Pico de Paris. Pico de Paris was thus named by Frenchman Charles Wiener on May 19, 1877. Wiener did not climb Pico Norte, which was climbed for the first time in 1950 when Hans Ertl and Gert Schröder got up it by what was then the hardest route in Bolivia.

Wiener got to the base of Illimani by following the Río La Paz, which cuts through the Andes immediately south of Illimani and divides the Cordillera Real from the Cordillera Quimsa Cruz. He started from the southeast from what was then the hacienda of Cotaña and is now a village. If he had climbed Pico Norte, he would have crossed Pico Sur on the way and thereby have made the first ascent of Illimani's highest peak.

Pico de Paris was renamed Pico del Indio by Martin Conway, the first person to summit Illimani's highest peak, Pico Sur (September 9, 1898). While on the subsidiary peak of Pico de Paris, Conway found a piece of goat hair rope and took this as proof of a legend that a shepherd climbed up into the eternal snows, never to return. (Conway appears to have overlooked the possibility that Wiener's party might have left the piece of rope.) Conway then named the peak Pico del Indio in honor of the legendary shepherd.

If Conway had climbed the as-marked Pico del Indio on his way to Pico Sur, he would have made the first traverse of the entire mountain. In his account of the climb, there is no mention of successive nights above 6000 meters, high narrow exposed ridges or any of the rest of what makes a good climbing tale.

Wiener's account of his expedition was published in 1880 as *Perou et Bolivie*; a Spanish translation was published in 1993. His account lacks any significant detail, and it is not possible to tell what he climbed. His given coordinates for the peak climbed are from Paris and not from Greenwich, England, making it difficult to establish what he climbed. However, he clearly states that he climbed the most southeastern of Illimani's peaks, that it was next to the highest peak and that it had an altitude of 6131 meters. Following the DAV map, these facts would make Wiener's peak Pico Layca Khollu (6159m).

Further clarification: Hans Ertl, in the 1953 *Mountain World* (p. 149), writes: "In 1877, Pico dell Indio, southern outpost of the Illimani, was climbed by Wiener. . . . In 1898, Conway crossed the Pico dell Indio. . . and made the first ascent of the south summit of Illimani."

Further confusion: in an article by C.R.P. Vandeleur in the 1955 *Alpine Journal* (p. 172), he quotes Conway as being aware that Wiener had made a considerable ascent on the same side of Illimani as himself, but he could not work out what peak Wiener had climbed. A footnote, presumably written by the *AJ* editor, says that Wiener climbed the Central and lowest summit of Illimani. However, 1) according to the DAV map, Pico del Indio (6109m) is the lowest of the five major peaks, followed by Layca Khollu (6159m), Central (6362m), Norte

(6403m) and Sur (6368m); 2) if you got up Pico Central, it would be about 45 minutes to cross the basin and climb Pico Sur.

Further clarification: Evelio Echevarría states in a footnote in the 1978 *American Alpine Journal* (p. 577) that Wiener got to a summit (6131m) on the south side and named it Pic (sic) de Paris, and that Conway traversed this peak in 1898 on his way to the summit and renamed it Pico del Indio. He also states that Norte was first climbed in 1950 by Ertl and Schröder and Pico Central by Bolivians in the 1950s.

There is sufficient proof to argue that the DAV and IGM map names are wrong. I think there is enough evidence to suggest that the as-marked Pico Layca Khollu is in fact Wiener's Pico de Paris and Conway's Pico del Indio.

YOSSI BRAIN, *United Kingdom*

CORDILLERA QUIMSA CRUZ

*Cordillera Quimsa Cruz, Note on Activity.* Please note: the only way to know what has been climbed in the Quimsa Cruz is if climbers use grid references to identify the peaks. There is more confusion over peak names in the Quimsa Cruz than in any other part of Bolivia. Climbers tend to make up their own names for peaks and routes, which makes it very difficult to find out what has been done.

YOSSI BRAIN, *United Kingdom*

*Quimsa Cruz, Various Ascents.* The 1998 Scottish Bolivian Expedition (Tony Barton, leader; Ken Marsden, Tom Wiggins, Tony Hill, Russel Weedon, Dougie Bayne and John Miller) touched down at El Alto on June 7. After ascents in the Condoriri group (Tarija, 5250m; Jancopiti, 5875m), part of the team left. The remaining members turned our attention south of the Cordillera Real to the little-visited Quimsa Cruz, a compact range of mountains some 50 kilometers long with a high point of Cerro Gigante (5748m). Its central and southern parts are glaciated, while in the north, apart from a few minor glaciers, it consists of a wonderful array of rocky peaks and spires up to 5350 meters. Armed with a full set of maps, we arranged 4x4 transportation and after seven hours arrived at Viloco, a large and somewhat unsightly mining town. It is worth remembering that but for the mines there would be no road. A simple three-hour walk took us to a campsite. The next seven days featured excellent weather and we were able to climb several routes, four of which we believe to be first ascents, and all on impeccable rock. Ascents included: the west ridge of Cerro Torrini (5100m; GR 587 420), July 1, Barton and Wiggans, solo. The east ridge (V-, 200m, five pitches) of Cerro Taruca Umaña (4852m; GR 572 403), July 2, Barton, Wiggins and Marsden. The south ridge (III+, 155m, three pitches) of Pt. 4905m (GR 577 410), July 3, Barton, Wiggins and Marsden. The east face (IV, 195m, six pitches) of Pt. 4685m (GR 591 393), July 5, Wiggins and Barton. The east ridge/north face (V, 240m, seven pitches) of Grosse Mauer (5080m, GR 599 387), July 6, Barton and Wiggins. The north ridge of Pt. 5060m (GR 591 399), July 6, Marsden, solo. Grid references refer to the IGM Viloco 1:50,000 sheet.

Considerable potential remains and with all the peaks so close to hand it is a pleasant area in which to climb.

ANTHONY BARTON, *United Kingdom*

*Northern Quimsa Cruz, Various Ascents.* Frank Van Herreweghe (Andorra) and Marc Gavalda put up two rock routes on minor peaks way to the left of the Obelisco and Halcon peaks: *Kawsachun Coca* (6b A1, 160m) on June 10, and *Uk amaki* (6b, 215m) on June 12. On the north face of Cuernos de Diablo (5270m), they put up a new variation (F6b, eight pitches) to the classic North Face route on July 23. The pair reported superb climbing on clean granidiorite with excellent protection. There is an aluminium box left by the 1987 German expedition on the summit for registering ascents. The pair were the 11th to write in the book. On July 25, they put up a new route on the first tower left (from Base Camp) of the obvious flat-topped tower southeast of Pico Halcon. The pair followed a finger-to-fist crack in the middle of the tower, reaching a corner crack after one pitch. They then climbed one full pitch up the corner crack until it became too wide to jam or protect, at which point they veered right for 50 meters. The final pitch brought them to a platform from where they bouldered to the summit. They reported no signs of previous ascents and graded the climb F6b, very mossy.

YOSSI BRAIN, *United Kingdom*

*Cordillera Quimsa Cruz, Various Ascents.* It was reported that Spaniards Óscar Acín, Javier Pina and Miguel-Angelo Zaragoza made a number of first ascents in the Cordillera Quimsa Cruz. They first climbed *Directa Inti* (IV/3) on the 500-meter south face of Nevado Piroja (5400m). Next, they put up *Vía de Rationes y Hombres* (IV/4) on the 400-meter south face of Vola Collo (5200m), a direct route that climbed mixed ground (80°) to the upper snow face (max. 65°) to the top. Descent was made by rappelling the route. They then climbed *Vía Aragonese* (IV/4) on the 500-meter south face of Nevado San Luis (5600m). The route trends slightly to the right, passing to the right of the large serac band half-way up the face and left of two rock barriers higher up. The crux was the exit pitch onto the summit ridge. (*Desnivel* 141)

CORDILLERA OCCIDENTAL

*Cordillera Occidental, Overview.* Snow conditions were extremely poor in the Cordillera Occidental. Bolivia's highest mountain, the extinct volcano Sajama (6549m), is normally a snow plod, but the 1998 season saw very few non-guided or guided groups summiting due to the length of time needed to climb a 40-meter, 60° ice gully to reach a huge and time-consuming penitente field with spikes up to 1.8 meters high. Parinacota (6330m) was completely clear of snow on the east (normal route) side, leaving a massive amount of decidedly unpleasant-looking volcanic scree. Teams were failing on the Chilean (western) side of the mountain due to the length of time needed to get through the penitentes. No peaks south of Parinacota had any snow at all.

YOSSI BRAIN, *United Kingdom*

CORDILLERA SUD LÍPEZ

*Cordillera Sud Lipez, Overview.* The Cordillera Sud Lípez lies to the east of the southern part of the Cordillera Occidental and runs down to the Bolivia-Chile-Argentina border. Major peaks include Cerro Lípez, Morurco (5681m), Uturuncu (6008m), and Zapeleri (5656m), which sits exactly on the point where the borders of Bolivia, Chile and Argentina meet. The peaks are volcanic, technically easy and normally snow-covered, but in 1998 no snow was seen anywhere in the area, leaving huge piles of scree to climb. The first recorded climbing in the area was by the Frenchman G. Courty before 1903, which left the intriguing reference in Jill Neate's *Mountaineering in the Andes*, "Nuevo Mundo, 6020m, location uncertain." Further exploration in the area was done by German geologist Frederic Ahlfeld, who emigrated to Bolivia in 1924. Ahlfeld began exploring the region in 1945 and climbed a number of peaks, including Uturuncu and Bonete (5695m).

In 1962, in a letter to Andean historian Evelio Echevarría, Ahlfeld stated that Nuevo Mundo, at ca. 5850 meters, was the highest peak in the Cordillera Sud Lipez and suggested that it was one of the two Cerro Lípez peaks. The Bolivian IGM map has a Nuevo Mundo lying immediately south of Cerro Lípez. However, in his book *Geografía Física de Bolivia*, published in 1969, Ahlfeld has a drawing of a Nuevo Mundo (5438m) and a description of its location far to the north of the Cerro Lípez group.

La Paz residents Toto Aramayo (Bolivia), Yossi Brain (U.K.) and Dakin Cook (U.S.) decided to go and look for Nuevo Mundo. After ten days and 2700 kilometers in a long-wheelbased Toyota Land Cruiser, they found Ahlfeld's Nuevo Mundo (5438m), failed on Cerro Lípez due to appallingly loose rock, and managed to climb Uturuncu (6008m) on October 8. They were greatly helped by the existence of a sulphur mining road to 5770 meters, which left them a 45-minute stroll to the summit.

Uturuncu would appear to be a good contender for Courty's Nuevo Mundo and, once you've got to it, certainly deserves the epithet, until now applied to Huayna Potosí in the Cordillera Real, as "the easiest 6000er in the world."

YOSSI BRAIN, *United Kingdom*

# CHILE

*Chile, Various Activity.* In the last two southern summers (December through March), I accompanied local mountaineers in repeat climbs in central Chile. However, on the four first ascents I was able to make in that period, I had no companions. On December 16, 1997, I climbed Cerro Pastén (4357m) in the upper Yeso valley east of Santiago, and Cerro Parrera (4569m). The latter peak is situated in the sources of the Navarro Creek, Aconcagua Province. In both ascents, I was harassed by very strong winds. In the following Chilean summer, I climbed P. 4121m, situated at the head of the Arroyo Blanco Creek and south of the Nieves Negras Pass, on December 31, 1998. I named it Alto del Arroyo Blanco (High Peak of the White Creek). Its southern ridge, which I used, had unstable rock and was quite exposed. On January 14, 1999, I ascended the fine red rock pyramid of Cerro Gastón (4024m), also situated in the upper Yeso valley of the Santiago hinterland.

EVELIO ECHEVARRÍA

*Cochamo, Various Ascents.* It was reported that British and American climbers have begun developing an area of granite big walls in the Patagonian Andes east of Puerto Montt in a valley 15 miles from the town of Cochamo. Briton Crispin Waddy discovered the area in 1997, cutting a machete swath throught the dense jungle to the 2,000-foot west face of Mt. Trinidad, where he, his girlfriend Nell, and Noel Craine attempted a route only to have the attempt cut short by forest fire. Accompanying them was Simon Nadin, who, with a partner, made the first ascent of the mountain via the north ridge. In 1998, Waddy, Craine and Nadin returned with a number of climbers. Steve Quinlan and Nathan Martin (U.S.) put up *Welcome to the Jungle* (5.11 A3), a corner system on the left side of the wall. Waddy, Craine and Dave Kendall climbed the wall's central prow to create *The Ides of March* (5.11 A3+), while Nadin and Grant Farquhar put up a 21-pitch 5.12 A2+ route on an overhanging crack system to the right. (*Climber*, June 1998)

*Towers of Brujo, Clandestino.* From February 5-19, Toni Arbonés, Nicolas Meyer and I established *Clandestino* (ABO 7c+ A0, 400m), a free route in the Towers of Brujo in the Central Cordillera. There is no map of this part of Chile, and as far as I know our tower has no name. The area is regarded as a replica of Patagonia—but with sun. Indeed, in summer (February), the weather conditions are remarkably stable. It is not the least important advantage in the Towers of Brujo, the bases of which are at around 3300 meters, and surrounded by hanging glaciers and seracs on the northeast face of Brujo Falso. We carried a total of 250 kilos of gear and supplies to this very isolated area to put up a route reminiscent of Michel Piola's routes in Chamonix.

The 13-pitch *Clandestino* (ten pitches of which are F7; the hardest is 7c+) is the fourth route in this difficult-to-access area. Waldo Farias, a Chilean andinist, was responsible for the first route, *Reflexion Vertical* (A1/6a), on a 300-meter tower. He made several attempts on the area's largest tower (400 meters), but was put off by the particularly long and difficult approach, and a granite that is similar to Yosemite but the cracks of which are closed. In 1998, a team that included Jens Richter and John Brewer made the first ascent of the tower via an elegant dihedral (6c/A2+). *Clandestino* takes the vertical pillar on the right-hand side of the dihedral.

We established the route ground-up in seven days of climbing, sometimes lowering down to sleep at Base Camp, other times sleeping on the wall. The very sheer granitic face offers only one ledge of two square meters up to the fourth pitch, making the use of portaledge essential. The approach from Base Camp to the wall is composed of a walk up on unstable moraine, and then a three-hour "stroll" on a glacier with lots of crevasses. Certain pitches were opened on-sight on natural gear, while others were put up with aid. Since our intent was to establish a free climb, each aid pitch was revisited, and in some places retrobolted in order to be redpointed. We freed all but two ten-meter sections, both of which were bolted to go at A0, and pitch 10, which was climbed with one rest. The in-situ equipment (about 60 bolts) is designed for free climbing repetitions of the route; only additional cams are necessary to repeat the route. Bolting was done using an electric power-drill, the batteries of which were charged by solar panel.

The concept of establishing free climbing routes with more thought for the repetition than the establishment was initiated in Chamonix by Michel Piola, whose 1980s mega classic *Le Voyage Selon Gulliver* began the current focus on hard alpine free climbs in the Alps. We exported the idea to the Andes with *Clandestino*. Right now, the mountaineers and climbers of South America do not seem receptive to such an idea; the geography of the Andean summits makes for mountaineers who are not often rock experts, while the local rock climbers are mainly into gym or typical sport climbing. If mountaineers and rock climbers are good in their respective pursuits, the challenge will be for one or the other to reach the main tower of Brujo and climb it.

JEAN-MINH TRINH-THIEU, *France*

# ARGENTINA

## CORDILLERA DE LA TOTORA

*Ascents in the Cordillera de la Totora.* This big but little-known range in San Juan has many unclimbed peaks. There were some ascents in the late 1970s, including the highest peak, Cerro de la Totora (5770m). Some years ago, a Spanish team climbed some minor summits.

In October, Nèstor Pèrez, Mauricio Bianchi, Bernardo Heredia and I were joined by veteran Josè Luis Fonrouge. We reached the abandoned mine of La Alumbrera and continued with our vehicle along a precarious track. Next day we continued walking the Rio de la Alumbrera and the Arroyo (Creek) Pedrazal. The rocky creek was the natural access to the heart of the range. We camped at 3000 meters. The next camp (3800m) was erected by a huge erratic block near the glacier of Las Totoras. Finally we continued via a moraine to a camp (4100m) in a cirque at the range's border. We left early on October 15. Pèrez, Heredia and I went to a 5180-meter unclimbed pyramidal peak. We climbed a snow line on the north face, then followed an unstable ridge. Pèrez gave up only 80 meters short of the top. Heredia and I stood on the previously unclimbed summit at 5 p.m. with an excellent view toward Mercedario, Aconcagua and other mountains. The other group ascended the long northeast ridge of Cerro Piramide (5593m), reaching its untrodden summit at 4:30 p.m. This was perhaps the highest unclimbed peak of the region. They descended directly via snow gullies. On October 16, we descended to our vehicle.

MARCELO SCANU, *Buenos Aires, Argentina*

*Cerro Campanario, Attempt.* In January, Diego Iglesias, Diego Socolinsky and Gabriel Brenta attempted Cerro Campanario (ca. 5400m), a rock spire they had tried in 1992 via *Yellow Pipi*, a difficult route first climbed in 1986. On their latest attempt, Camp II was established at 3700 meters, the last place with water. The next camp was at the base of the glacier. They discovered a dihedral in the southeast pillar, which they reached after climbing the glacier and a couloir (55°). They climbed seven pitches (6a A2) but were turned back two easy rope lengths short of the summit by the lateness of the hour and the fact that they did not have bivy gear.

MARCELO SCANU, *Buenos Aires, Argentina*

## CENTRAL ANDES

*Aconcagua, General Overview.* The tallest peak in the Western Hemisphere had a tough season. The normal routes up the 22,832-foot peak are non-technical, and easy access to high altitude has proved increasingly deadly in recent years as more people have attempted the mountain and the weather has worsened. In the 1998 season, the mighty El Niño pelted Aconcagua with high winds, rain and snow, and as many as 15 climbers were killed. Unlike the heavily publicized Everest tragedy, these climbers died one to three at a time over a three-month stretch, and thus went virtually unnoticed by the public.

I worked as a guide on the Polish Glacier side of the mountain and was amazed at what I saw and heard. Teams were pinned in Camps I and II for a week or more by poor weather. Four bodies were stacked in Camp II. A German climber in his late teens lay frozen near the summit on the Polish Direct. (He had been feeling tired and was encouraged by his partners to take a nap and catch up when he felt better.) Three Brazilians were avalanched off the technical and massive South Face, and an American froze to death while climbing alone in a storm on the Normal Route.

The official number of deaths could not be attained, because the Argentine permit office feared the impact on tourism. I was more-or-less escorted out once the officials learned of my request for information. However, rangers in Base Camp gave an unofficial estimate of 13 to 15 killed. Although all guides agreed the weather was worse then they had ever seen on Aconcagua, unsound decisions to push for the summit are behind most of the deaths.

KENT McCLANNAN, *unaffiliated*


*Walther Penck, Ojos del Salado Region.* Walther Penck, near Ojos del Salado, is one of the world's highest volcanoes. In February, a group led by Jaime Surez climbed a sub-summit: Volcan de los Arianos (6562m). This was perhaps the first ascent of this summit.

MARCELO SCANU, *Buenos Aires, Argentina*


*Ojos del Salado Area, Various Ascents and Observations.* From February to March, I was in northern Chile and Argentina in the area south of Ojos del Salado with a group of seven, all from Germany: Martin Blumenstock, Fritz Felber, Michael Fuchs, Werner Geys, Alexander Hartlein, Bernd Tarnosky, and Manfred Unterholzner. Five of us (Blumenstock, Fuchs, Hartlein, Tarnosky, and me) climbed Veladero (6436m), a peak near Bonete Chico. We found only a pick ax on the summit, which had probably been left by Johan Reinhard in 1985 or 1986. Two days later, we tried to climb Bonete Chico (6759m) but failed to reach the summit due to a heavy storm. In Jagüe we met Sr. Urriche, who made the first ascent of Bonete Chico with Cicchitti in 1970. In 1954, Cicchitti climbed Pissis, but he thought he had climbed Bonete Grande. He wrote of a mountain with four or five very high summits and he saw a very high mountain south of the mountain he climbed. This means he was on Pissis and what he saw was Bonete Chico. Walther Penck, who said he had climbed Bonete in 1913, most likely reached the summit of a nameless mountain (6222m) about eight kilometers north of Bonete Chico. He came from the east along the Rio de la Tamberia. A sketch in his book, *Puna de Atacama*, shows the route to a summit north of what is now called Bonete Chico.

Later Felber, Fuchs, Geys, and Tarnosky climbed Ojos del Salado (6885m) while Blumenstock, Hartlein, Unterholzner and I reached the summit of Tres Cruces South (6749m), where we found a broken ski-pole, a note of Greg Horne's (1995)—and an old box with Paryski and Osiecki's calling card from November 26, 1937! So they didn't climb the central peak on this day as is written in Jill Neate's *A Survey of Andean Ascents, Second Edition.*

ALEXANDER VON GOTZ, *Deutschen Alpenverein*


# TIERRA DEL FUEGO

*Monte Sarmiento, Attempt.* Nelson Bareta and Nativo Fransen of Brazil, and Eduardo Lopez, Mariano Sebesta, and Walter Rossini of Argentina departed December 14 from Puerto Bahía Mansa with the goal of repeating the 1995 route on Monte Sarmiento. During their 29 days waiting for an opportunity to climb, they saw the mountain twice. They made their first cache at approximately 600 meters in heavy rains. Three days later they made their second carry in the rain. On the 11th day, they saw the west summit for the first time for some two hours. On the 14th day, the rain stopped for some eight to ten hours. In the hopes of good weather, they climbed to Camp I the next day and slept there for the first time. They were able to see the east summit for one hour and the west summit for two hours. On the 16th day, it began to rain again. They remained in Camp I. On the 17th day at noon they went down to Base Camp, taking advantage of a break in the weather to reprovision Camp I. When they went down, the mountain cleared and for the first time they saw it in all its grandeur. This lasted two hours. On the 22nd day, they climbed to Camp I again. The next day they climbed up in bad weather and reached 1000-1100 meters, but a snow storm left them without visibility and forced them to go down. On the 26th night, they saw clear skies for the first time. When they woke at 2 a.m., however, the mountain was not visibile. It was their last day before they would have to catch their boat. Until this moment, it had been raining every day. Unexpectedly, the mountain cleared at 7 a.m., and the team began up. They found the 1995 route very changed, which forced them to try a new route on the west face. Conscious of the avalanche danger and the late hour, they nonetheless continued. Once above 1000-1100 meters, they crossed the west ridge and continued climbing with the hope of reaching the 1995 route. Two-thirds of the way up the mountain, in strong winds, they observed that avalanches had already fallen from the east summit toward the Lovisato Glacier. They decided to go down. Once in Camp I, as they prepared for the descent, they heard a considerable avalanche above the west face, followed by a dozen more avalanches.

The team carried out ten bags of garbage that they collected from the beach. They wondered how so much garbage could be found in such a remote place. The expedition members believe it is possible to reach the south ridge of the peak by the Mauri-Mafei route. Regarding the west summit, there don't seem to be too many options between the 1995 route and the west face, both being very prone to avalanches.

FACUNDO JOSÉ, *Club Andino Bariloche*

CHILEAN PATAGONIA

*Chilean Patagonia, Overview.* The weather in Chilean Patagonia was terrible from November to February. March was very good from the first to the 16th. Climbing activity in Paine National Park was down in general—perhaps 50% less than in the last three years.

HERNAN JOFRE, *Amerindia Concept, Chile*

*Escudo, Southwest Face, First Winter Ascent.* On August 7-8, Italians Marco Balla Longa, Marco Birolin, and Mario Curnis climbed the Southwest Face of Escudo in the Valle del Silencio. It was the first winter ascent of this route.

HERNAN JOFRE, *Amerindia Concept, Chile*

*Aleta del Tiburon, East Face.* From January 15 to 25, in the Valle del Frances, Esteban Chacon (Chile) and Hubert van Ham (Dutch) established *Game Over, Man!* and *Pa' la Casa* ("Go Home") on the east face of Aleta del Tiburon. The following notes are from Hubert's report. "On January 16, we climbed nine pitches on the south ridge until being blocked by a steep and compact section just under the first (lower) summit. The grade of this route is about 5.7/5.8, with a very nice seventh pitch through a crack. We named the route *Game Over, Man!* The second route was climbed on January 20, a perfect day with no wind. Leaving Campamento Britanico at 4 a.m., we walked around the west face until arriving at steepening slabs above a glacier. From this point the two summits can be seen (and seem really close). Not having crampons, we did four traversing pitches toward the northeast above the glacier to arrive at the starting point. We started climbing this traverse, which had good rock but little protection, at 7:30 a.m. The next 12 pitches went straight to the summit. The first of these was especially beautiful on slabs with fine cracks. The last four pitches to the summit are steeper on better rock, though still with little protection. A very nice line then leads straight to the top. We arrived on the summit at 2:30 p.m. We rappelled the west face from 3 p.m. to 9:30 p.m. and arrived at Campamento Britanico at 12:30 a.m. We named the route *Pa' la Casa* (5.8, 16 pitches)."

HERNAN JOFRE, *Amerindia Concept, Chile*

*Escudo, North Face, Bukowski Route.* Our original goal was the striking north pillar of Escudo. In 30 days, Jack Lewis and I managed only seven pitches on the pillar because of continual bad weather. High winds cut through one of our fixed ropes and damaged a second fixed rope. On February 21, 1999, we abandoned the north pillar with the hopes of getting one climbing day in before we had to leave.

On March 1, we climbed a new route in 14 hours round-trip on the north face of Cerro Escudo. Our route ascended 200 feet of low-angle rock slabs at the base of the north face to a large ledge. This ledge was followed up and left on scree and snow to the base of an ice couloir, which we called the *Bukowski Couloir*. This was climbed for 1,000 feet to the northeast ridge. A 60-foot rock pitch (5.10a A0) put us on easy ground. Scree and snow climbing up the ridge took us to the upper ice slopes. Ice climbing over and around black sedimentary rock towers on the upper ridge took us to the summit. We are sure the *Bukowski Couloir* (IV 5.10a AI2) is the easiest route up Cerro Escudo. The upper mountain was socked in, but winds were light with occasional snow showers.

TOM BAUMAN

*Cuerno Principal, South Face, Attempt.* From January 24 to February 2, 1999, Corrado Pipolo and Mauro Florit (Italy) climbed four new pitches (510d A1) on the south face of Cuerno Principal in the Valle del Frances before poor weather conditions forced them to go down.

HERNAN JOFRE, *Amerindia Concept, Chile*

*Cerro Mascara, The Magic Carpet Ride.* During the months of January and February, 1999, Conny Amelunxen and I completed the first ascent of the 800-meter east face of The Mummer (Cerro Mascara) in the Bader Valley of Torres del Paine in Chile. This major Patagonian prize had been attempted at least three times previously with no success.

RIGHT: *Conny Amelunxen on the approach to the east face of La Mascara (a.k.a. The Mummer) in the Bader Valley, with* The Magic Carpet Ride *marked.* SEAN ISAAC

We arrived in Chile on January 7. After sorting out permits and buying food in Puerto Natales, we left for Torres del Paine National Park to arrange horses to carry the majority of our equipment to Campo Welsh, 45 minutes shy of Base Camp. The next two weeks involved humping all of our gear from there to Base Camp and eventually onto an advanced high camp at the edge of the glacier an hour from the face. In between carries, we managed to fix the first four pitches. With two weeks of hard work (and one rest day) behind us, we committed to the face capsule-style on January 27 in typical unsettled Patagonian weather, armed with three haul bags full of the necessities required to live on a wall for two weeks.

The route primarily involved direct aid with very little free climbing. Due to the difficulty and our long pitches, we operated on a pitch-a-day speed until we neared the top, where more free climbing opportunities presented themselves. The wall took 14 days to climb and descend; however, four of these were stuck in our portaledge as continuous storms caused serious slough avalanches and dangerous ice bombardments. Spontaneous rock fall occurred frequently to our right in the scooped face, but our pillar was somewhat protected. It was the wind that caused the most anxiety, as it threatened to shred our portaledge fly and cut our ropes. The cold temperatures that we experienced wreaked havoc on our bodies: our finger-tips cracked painfully, our feet suffered from trenchfoot and we were always wet and cold at night due to the constant decline of our sleeping bags as they became more and more soaked from the endless condensation and puddles in the portaledge.

On February 6, we switched plastic boots for cold, tight rock shoes and cruised the last five pitches to a point three meters below the actual summit. These last moves we left unclimbed because they involved a 45° slab carpeted in a layer of thick, black lichen, which was surprising, since there had been no vegetation on the entire route until the summit ridge. Now that we were on the ridge, exposed to the 100-kilometer-per-hour westerly winds blowing off the ice cap, the final moves seemed too sketchy, so we called it good and began the rappels back to our portaledge. That night, yet another snow storm blew in, keeping us trapped in our hanging tent for two days before we could safely descend the rest of the route to the ground.

We named our route *La Alfombra Magica* (*"The Magic Carpet Ride,"* VI 5.10 A3+) after one particularly scary episode on the wall in which the tie-down that secured the bottom of the portaledge came undone, causing us to hover and bounce violently in the air for what seemed like an eternity. Of the route's 17 pitches, only one was particularly loose, with the rest ascending beautiful straight-in cracks and perfect corners on solid granite. We rapped the route off bomber anchors: piton/nut anchors higher on the mountain, then mainly two-bolt (3/8") stations. This was the third new route on the mountain after Dave Cheesemond/Phil Dawson's first ascent in 1976 and John Merriam/Jonathon Copp's one-day ascent of *Duncan's Dihedral* last year. Acres of unclimbed granite remain on The Mummer as well as on the other equally impressive formations of this rarely explored valley.

SEAN ISAAC, *Canada*

Supported by a Canadian Himalayan Foundation grant

*Valle Bader, Note on Naming.* There has been some confusion in the past few years regarding the naming of two distinct valleys within the Torres del Paine National Park, both of which have been called Pingo ("wild horse") Valley. The original valley to carry this name is at the southern end of the Park and separates the Grey Glaciar from the Tyndall Glaciar and the southern reaches of the Patagonian Ice Cap. This valley has been called Pingo Valley since its days as ranch land before the region became a park. It took its name from escaped horses that enjoyed its verdant green pastures in summer.

The other valley in question, and the more important one for climbers, is situated between the Ascensio and French valleys. This valley's walls are made up of the Cuernos and the granite spires La Mascara, La Hoja and La Espada (the Mask, Blade and Sword respectively) on the southwest side, Fortaleza (the Fortress) on the northwest end and Almirante Nieto (Admiral Nieto) on the northeast.

Gino Buscaini and Silvia Metzeltin, long-time Patagonian explorers, list this valley as the "Pingo Valley" in their 1990 book *Patagonien*. They copied their map from a map produced by Billboudry in 1959. There are, I speculate, two ways that the valley could have originally received the name "Pingo." Explorers could have been told by locals that the valley was "a pingo valley," meaning that the valley was a place that wild, escaped horses would frequent. The other possibility is that it was named for the small glacial lake in the valley, which can be termed a "pingo" by geologists. In any case, the park service never recognized the name (there is reason to believe they were never given copies of Buscaini or Billboudry's work).

In the 1995-'96 season, two Chilean climbers, Christian Oberli and Sven Bruchfeld, made the first ascent of *Bohemian Rapsody* on La Hoja in this "Pingo Valley." Theirs was the second ascent of a tower within the valley. (The first ascent, *Fist Full of Dollars* on Cuerno Norte, reported in the 1996 *AAJ*, p. 227, was referred to as having been achieved in the "Pingo Valley.") When Oberli and Bruchfeld approached the park service about climbing there, the only name they could find was from Buscaini's book. Problematically, the park service did not want to call the valley Pingo (nor were they aware that it had been named that elsewhere) because it would be confused with the other, larger Pingo Valley and Pingo Lake and Glacier to the west. Oberli and Bruchfeld, having no other information to go on, used the name "Pingo" when they wrote up their subsequent account in the AAJ and other publications (see 1997 *AAJ*, p. 265, and 1998 *AAJ*, pp. 267-8).

In 1997, I spoke with the owner of the Hosteria Las Torres, Jose Antonio Kusanovich. His family has owned the access corridor to the Ascensio Valley and the valley in question for close to 20 years. He told me that the name of the valley was changed due to confusion and that the name "Bader" was the name of the original owner of the Estancia Cerro Paine, which is what the Kusanovich family now owns. To honor the original owner and to quell confusion, the valley was officially named Bader and placed on all park maps in 1998.

It is important to remember that this park is still evolving. It became a national park in 1959 and its uniqueness was fully recognized in 1978 when Torres del Paine was declared an international biosphere reserve by UNESCO. When I first came to the Park in 1994, the official park maps had many misplaced names of peaks and camps. Over the subsequent years, names have been clarified and their places on the map confirmed. CONAF, the Chilean park service, is also still in a state of evolution and is very underfunded. Because of this, the park rangers do not get out into the field as much as they should and need our assistance in helping the park evolve.

Climbers have the opportunity to greatly impact the policies, negatively or positively, that the park imposes on climbing. In the past, world-class climbing expeditions from a variety of nations have left fixed ropes and trash at base camps and on walls. This past season, Steve Schneider and I brought down approximately 200 pounds of trash and fixed rope left by Spanish

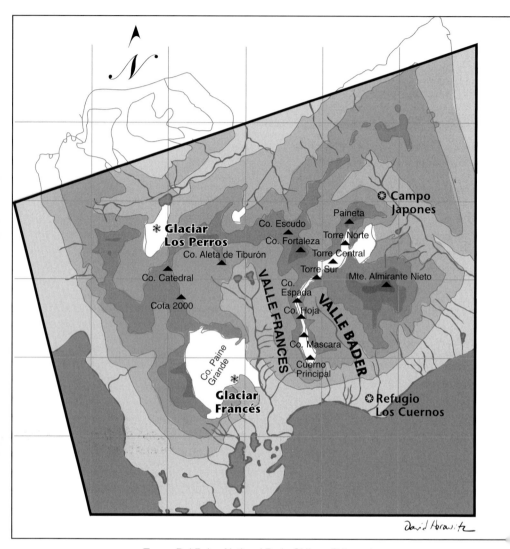

Torres Del Paine National Park, Chilean Patagonia.

and Italian expeditions on the Central Tower. To avoid over-regulation, it is extremely important that we climb with as little impact as possible. Report your ascents, treat CONAF and the
local people with the respect they deserve and set a good example for those that follow.

CHRISTIAN SANTELICES

*Central Tower of Paine, East Face, Golazo.* In February, Steve Schneider and Christian
Santileces began a new line on the 4,000-foot east face of the Central Tower of Paine.
Over four weeks, they fixed nine pitches in between the British route and German route;

pitches 6 through 8 shared the British line, which had decayed fixed ropes on the first 400 meters, presumably from a Spanish expedition. Camp I shared the British Camp I, which was littered with old batteries, leftover rope, and four haulbags containing blue containers. These were all removed during the course of their climb.

On February 22, they moved onto the wall, pulling their ropes up behind them. After a terrible week of weather, they had only climbed three-and-a-half pitches. These turned out to be the crux. On the morning of the eighth day, Santelices descended to the ground, taking three ropes with him. Schneider continued on solo for 11 more days, eventually summiting on March 12. He took three days to descend the entire route, leaving only 50 meters of rope behind that he was unable to retrieve from a rappel. *Golazo* (VI 5.10 A4+) is the eighth route to breach the east face of the Central Tower. Over the course of 25 pitches, no rivets were placed. Most anchors have two bolts.

Writes Schneider, "I ask anybody that climbs in Patagonia to clean all trash from their expeditions, including all fixed rope. Nothing should be left on a climb except rappel anchors. This place is a paradise of adventure and beauty. Let's keep the wilderness clean so that others that follow may enjoy their climbs in the purest manner." A full account of his climb appears earlier in this journal.

STEVE SCHNEIDER

ARGENTINE PATAGONIA

*Cerro Torre, Attempt.* During the good-weather period in early January, Toni Ponholzer and a man named Franz (Austria) climbed to within four pitches of the northwest shoulder via a line Ponholzer had attempted previously on the east, northwest and north faces of Cerro Torre with Tommy Bonapace and Gerold Dünser. With no fixed ropes, they started from the base at first light and arrived at the Col of Conquest at 3 p.m. the same day. Theirs is the highest point anyone has ever been able to reach via the claimed Maestri-Egger line. They reported very difficult climbing in the upper portion of the route. This was the finest bit of climbing done in the area this season.

ROLANDO GARIBOTTI, *Club Andino Bariloche, Argentina*

*Cerro Torre, Attempt.* On my latest experience in Patagonia, Maurizio Giarolli and I made an attempt on a new route on Cerro Torre via the northeast pillar and the center of the north face. Unfortunately, bad weather only allowed us to put up a difficult but secure variation along the lower part of the northeast pillar as far as the 1959 Egger-Maestri traverse, halfway up the Torre. We made several attempts in November, then, from December 4-9, managed 520 meters (11 pitches) at up to ED 5.10 A1/2. Conditions were not good and cracks were choked with snow. In normal conditions it would be possible to climb all the aid sections free. Then, in extreme and dangerous conditions, we continued 150 meters halfway along the Egger-Maestri 1959 traverse and then, with another three rope lengths, to part-way up the north face under a continual bombardment of fragments from the ice mushrooms.

ELIO ORLANDI, *Italy*

*The profile of the Col of Conquest, seen from pitch 16, the north face of Cerro Torre. In front can be seen the south face of Torre Egger and in the background the fog on the Continental Icecap and a storm that would soon reach the climbers.* ELIO ORLANDI

*The Northwest Arête of the West Pillar of Punta Herron, La Gioconda.* The weather was always bad, even when we humped loads to Paso Marconi. On October 12, we decided to leave for the Circle of the Altares. The weather was beautiful, but after only two hours of walking we were in a storm. Since we had no desire to turn back, we kept going. It would be a long day on the Continental Icecap; the sled sank into the snow, the wind never stopped, we got lost in the snow many times. After 16 hours, we arrived at the red knife-edge arête.

The weather didn't look like it was going to get better, and after a week shut up in a snow cave we decided to attack the wall regardless. We also didn't have a lot of time left. Thus we began our trials and tribulations. One day we were able to climb 60 meters, another day only 20, then another 40, and every time we returned to the snow cave. Every time we were cold—very! When we descended from the wall it was always dark and the following day we would pass the hours trying to dry the gear out with a gas stove. By then we didn't have any more rope to fix (it hadn't even been in our plans to fix the wall). Our two static lines, the haul line and the 11-mm lead line were stretched out almost 300 meters on the route.

It was already November and we hoped that with the full moon the good weather would begin. And so it did! On November 4, we jugged the lines on the northwest arête of Punta Herron and in the evening bivied in the portaledge beneath the enormous overhangs. On November 5, the weather was beautiful and thus, with the last light of the day, we were almost out of the 250-meter overhanging face. But during the night the weather changed for the worse again. It snowed and the wind began to blow. Continue or give up? The greatest desire was for a warm bed, or for a beach on the Maldives, or a five-star hotel; instead, the most perverted part of our minds pushed us to climb another brief section in the tempest. Then, another bivy in our humid tent. Sometimes you can't understand what makes you go on. That day we overcame the last four pitches that brought us to the summit of the Pillar of Punta Herron, to the exact point where the route *Gracias a la Vida* arrives.

My idea was to climb to the summit of Punta Herron; Mauro wanted only to get as far as this. I would like... him, no! But I didn't insist. Even I was sick to death of this. I had had enough. There would be another 60-70 meters of rock, then the mushroom, a bivy, nothing to drink, nothing to eat, no sleeping bags, and we were already very cold....

We descended to the portaledge. The last night... the last day on the wall... the snowcave again... paradise.

We had climbed *La Gioconda* (ED, ca. 800m) on the northwest arête of the west pillar of Punta Herron from October 10-November 17, 1998. We were on the wall continuously from November 4-8. The climb was established in good part via aid, primarily because of the conditions of the cracks and the weather. In ten days of climbing, we had only two days of good weather.

*Mauro Giovanazzi on the northwest arête of the west pillar of Punta Herron.*
ERMANNO SALVATERRA

ERMANNO SALVATERRA, *Italy*

*Cerro Stanhardt, Leonardo Da Vinci.* On the west face of Cerro Stanhardt, Frenchmen David Autheman and Antoine Noury attempted a new route to the summit of a pillar attached to the face, which they named "Punta Shanti." They reached a point 50 meters below the top of Punta Shanti, and rated their efforts to that point at 5+/A2+, ED. Their 500-meter attempt, which they called *Leonardo Da Vinci,* was climbed over a three-week period with extensive use of fixed ropes. The summit of Punta Shanti is some 500 meters lower than the summit of Stanhardt itself. It is unclear whether their original intentions were to climb the whole face or just to the summit of this secondary pillar. The route was climbed between November 13 and December 15.

ROLANDO GARIBOTTI, *Club Andino Bariloche, Argentina*


*Cerro Fitz Roy, Royal Flush.* In February, 1999, Peter Janschek and I did the third ascent of *Royal Flush* on Fitz Roy. After fixing six pitches, we stayed three days on the wall. Kurt Albert and Bernd Arnold, who put up *Royal Flush,* ended their route on the Swiss Edge, which is the top of a pillar right on the arête between the east and the north faces of Fitz Roy. On the Swiss Edge, *Royal Flush* meets up with *El Corazon.* Albert and Arnold did not climb higher than the Swiss Edge, so we had climbed all 34 pitches of *Royal Flush.* When continuing on *El Corazon* to the top, we only managed to climb two-and-a-half more pitches before a strong storm hit us 150 meters below the summit and forced us to abseil.

HEINZ ZAK, *Austria*


*Cerro Fitz Roy, Attempt.* Americans John Catto and Pete Gallagher attempted to climb a new route between the Cassarotto and *Devil's Dihedral* routes. Fixing ropes, they climbed nine pitches, but gave when they were confronted with continuous thin cracks that required very technical aid climbing. Mark Hesse (U.S.) also took part on a few of these attempts.

ROLANDO GARIBOTTI, *Club Andino Bariloche, Argentina*


*Cerro Fitz Roy, West Face, Ensueño.* Silvo Karo (Slovenia) and I arrived in Chaltén in the very last days of January with the obvious intention of doing some climbing, but also hoping for a lot of bad weather so we could enjoy the peaceful and calm life that the Patagonian forest provides. After a short excursion to the base of Cerro Pier Giorgio, we turned our sights to the west side of Cerro Fitz Roy. We did not have to wait long before the weather gave us an opportunity to use all the equipment we had brought with us. At 6 a.m. on February 11, we crossed *Supercanaleta*'s bergschrund and immediately took a right turn onto the golden rock of *Ensueño,* first climbed by Andrea Sarchi, Mauro Giradi and Lorenzo Nadali (I) in 1995 over a five-day good-weather period (see *AAJ* 1996, pp. 11-18). We climbed in blocks and did some simul-climbing as well. By 4 p.m. we had free climbed all 37 pitches of this route, with the leader redpointing all pitches. The first ascent party had graded this route at 5.12 A1, but we thought a 5.11c rating was more accurate. We found the rock to be not as solid as expected in sections, and the climbing to be at times difficult, with long runouts and very tricky gear. The last few pitches were climbed in snowy and windy conditions. Upon reaching the *Supercanaleta* on its very last section around 4 p.m., we continued for a couple more pitches, but upon arriving at the Gendarme Ridge some four to five pitches from the easy ground leading to the summit near where the American route joins the route, we were forced to retreat due to the rain/snow and strong winds. We were somewhat disappointed not to have reached the summit, but after many hours of rappelling in cold and wet conditions we were both quite sure that we had made the right decision. We were back in our camp in the Sitting Man Ridge by 1 a.m., in time for yet another big pot full of polenta. During the remaining two weeks we stayed in the area, the weather was never good enough for climbing, but we had a great time walking, reading, eating and hanging out with many good friends from Chaltén.

ROLANDO GARIBOTTI, *Club Andino Bariloche, Argentina*

*Aguja Mermoz, Vela y Viento.* Kurt Albert and Bernd Arnold (G) climbed a new route on the east buttress of Aguja Mermoz that they named *Vela y Viento* (5.12 b/c ED, 500m). They finished on January 9, after several weeks of attempts with the use of fixed ropes. This line was previously attempted in 1993 by Topher Donahue and Kennan Harvey (U.S.), who climbed to within 20 meters of the summit ridge but were forced to retreat due to a very iced-up chimney. The route features well-bolted anchors and bolts next to cracks (Harvey and Donahue had climbed much of the same line without placing bolts or using fixed ropes).

ROLANDO GARIBOTTI, *Club Andino Bariloche, Argentina*

*Aguja St. Exupery, West Face, Attempt.* Greg Crouch and J. Jay Brooks (U.S.) attempted to climb a new route on the west face of Aguja St. Exupery to the right of *Chiaro di Luna*, but despite many valiant attempts in less than ideal weather, they were forced to give up the idea after having climbed some nine pitches. Their best attempt took place February 12.

ROLANDO GARIBOTTI, *Club Andino Bariloche, Argentina*

*Argentine Patagonia, Various Activity.* As we had the preceding season, we arrived at Chaltén at the beginning of October with a head full of ideas. But "el tiempo" did not give us the same luck. Nevertheless, we had a very good time in this beautiful range.

From November 7 to 19, we climbed the Volcan Lautaro (3380m) in the middle of the Ice Cap, which we reached in five days via Paso Marconi. We skied up two-thirds of the way to a cirque between the south and southeast ridges, then continued via an easy walk with crampons to the south summit. From there, it was a short walk down and across the crater to reach the top among incredible rime formations. We were super surprised to discover the volcano to be active—islands of hot rock and gas in an arctic ambiance! We then had a very good ski down.

On December 5, we attempted Cerro Pier Giorgio in alpine style via the *Greenpeace* route. We twice reached a point a third of the way up the face on the best granite we have ever seen. After a really hanging bivy (due to strong wind), we changed our minds about continuing. N.B.: After the first pitch, do not follow the old fixed rope. It leads too far to the right—the wrong direction.

On December 12, we climbed the east face of Val Biois via the Gabarrou-Marsigny-Vimal goullote, an unbelievable ice line, finding wet snow and wet ice conditions.

We also climbed Fitz Roy via the classic Franco-Argentine route during a limited good weather window on December 8. We reached the summit around 6 p.m. and rappeled in a storm. It was a high experience for us. We were forced to make a light bivy at the base of the route because of storm. Hasta luego, Patagonia!

LAURENCE MONNOYEUR and BRUNO SOURZAC, France

*Argentine Patagonia, Various Activity.* We stayed in Patagonia from December 2, 1998, to February 16, 1999. In this time we climbed the following peaks: Cerro Solo, December 8; Aguja Guillaumet, *Via Amy,* December 20, in seven hours from Paso Superior and back, on our second attempt; Fitz Roy, Franco-Argentine Route, January 10, 1999, in 19 hours from Paso Superior and back, on our third attempt (we descended in a storm); Poincenot, via the Whillans Route, on January 14, in about 12 hours from Paso Superior and back, on our third attempt; Mermoz, via *Vela y Viento,* the new route by Kurt Albert and Bernd Arnold on the Red Pillar, on January 16 on our first attempt, a wonderful climb and an excellent line. We also made two attempts to the Shoulder/Ice Cave of Cerro Torre between January 27-February 10.

The weather conditions this season was very unstable, so we are really glad that we were able to climb so many peaks without any accidents. We enjoyed our stay and will come back soon.

ANDY MAAG and ILONA BLEULER, Switzerland

*Argentine Patagonia, Various Activity.* Charlie Fowler (U.S.) was in the area from late November until mid-February. With various partners, he climbed the following. Right French Couloir (TD-5.9 60° ice mixed, 400m) on Guillaumet, December 5, 1998, with Steph Davis; the Argentinian Route (TD, 5.10-, 500m) on the west face/north ridge of Aguja Mermoz, December 21, 1998, solo; a variation to the Pippo Frasson (line to the left of the French Gully, TD, 300m, 80° ice, mixed) on Guillaumet, January 2, 1999, solo; *Bienvenidos a Patagonia* (5.11b, mixed, 550 meters) on the north face of St. Exupery, January 10, 1999, with Nathan Martin; the Whillans Route (5.8 mixed, ca. 650m) on Poincenot, January 21, with Nathan Martin, in January, 1999 with Nathan Martin; *Vela y Viento* (5.12 A0, 500 meters, third ascent, with new variant) or Mermoz, February 10, 1999, with Nathan Martin. A full account of his productive stay appears earlier in this journal.

*Argentine Patagonia, Attempts and Ascents.* My objective was to attempt the unclimbed west face of Torre Egger with two French climbers, David Autheman and Antoine Noury, and a Norwegian climber, Trym Saeland. When Trym and I arrived at Base Camp, David and Antoine were already there. They had used two days of good weather to start fixing a route on a sub-pillar of Cerro Stanhardt (see description of their efforts above). This took the west face of Torre Egger out of our plans, because they had used a number of bolts on fixing the sub-pillar. With the bolts we had left, we felt Torre Egger's west face would be impossible.

After another four weeks of waiting out bad weather, Trym and I decided to attempt the route *Todo o Nada* (5.9 A1 WI5X) on El Mocho during a marginal weather day. The formation was sheltered and low enough that we were able to summit. The climbing was scary because it had been warm and we were often on vertical snow, not ice.

After climbing El Mocho, Trym and I attempted a continuous push on Cerro Torre that was stopped in the middle of the night as bad weather moved in. We descended to our advanced

*St. Exupery, with the north face, location of* Bienvenidos a Patagonia, *in shadow.* CHARLIE FOWLER

ase camp of the Norwegian Bivy the next morning and rested all day and night. With the ext day came a half day of good weather, which allowed us to reach pitch 12 of the *Compressor Route* on Cerro Torre. By that time we were in a very bad storm and ended up aving to bivy without bivy gear when our rappel ropes got stuck. I made one failed attempt t *Exocet* on Cerro Stanhardt with Charlie Fowler during another too-brief half-day spell of ood weather. On January 10, 1999, I began my return journey to Seattle. Trym Saeland stayed on and was rewarded with an ascent of the *Compressor Route* on Cerro Torre with Warren Hollinger and Russ Mitrovich.

My sincere thanks to the Mountaineering Fellowship Fund Grant Committee for the grant that helped finance this trip to Argentine Patagonia.

MILES SMART

*South Patagonia Ice Cap, Traverse Attempt.* From December 5, 1998-January 5, 1999 Karl Feaux, Rob Weber, Bart Matthews and Kyle Bohnenstiehl (leader), attempted a par- tial traverse of the South Patagonia Ice Cap. This remote area, also known as the Campo de Hielo Sur or the Hielo Patagonia Sur (HPI), is the largest icecap outside the polar regions and the third largest ice mass in the world. Stretching nearly 325 kilometers in length and averaging 35 kilometers wide, the Ice Cap contains 48 distinct glacial outflows and covers an area of 13,000 square kilometers, which includes 15 distinct mountain ranges, at least one active volcano (Cerro Lautaro) and numerous unclimbed peaks near 3000 meters. After a five-hour boat trip from Tortel onboard the *San Juan*, we landed at Don Juan Nahuel's cabin near the Glacier Jorge Montt at the northern terminus of the Ice Cap with 700 pounds of equipment. According to Chilean authorities, our expedition was the first American team to go up this route. Camp II was established on the glacier at 500 meters after a difficult approach through rivers and thick brush that followed Eric Shipton's 1962 route (*AAJ*, 1962). We were disappointed by the dryer-than-normal winter and were unable to ski until Camp V, which we reached after ferrying loads for 12 days across difficult crevasses that would normally have been snow bridges. 1998, like 1997 was an especially bad year for ascending onto the Campo de Hielo. We gained the alti plano at Camp VIII and, after abandoning our principle objective, Cerro Lautaro (3380m) we aimed to climb Cerro Wonni (2498m). Strong winds and heavy snow trapped us at Camp IX for three days, and we were forced to return to the boat landing, as we were out of time.

The Glacier Jorge Montt is actively retreating, making this approach route onto the Ice Cap very time-consuming and difficult. Previous parties attempting the traverse encoun tered significant difficulty navigating, especially during foul weather. We used GPS, RADARSAT and LANDSAT data for navigation; all were useful to us, particularly dur ing storms. Users of Iridium phones, take note: fuses in the 12-volt charger can burn out and accounts cannot be re-established over the phone. Complete details of our trip can be found at www.nagis.com

Note: In the 1997 *AAJ* (p. 256), the Arved Fuchs expedition, which made the longest unsupported north-south traverse yet, mistakenly noted that they had made the first cross ing of the "Mayo Fall" on foot. In 1994, Americans John Schutt and Mark Houston crossed this difficult section under their own power (1995 *AAJ*, p. 207).

KYLE BOHNENSTIEHL

*Southern Ice Cap, Integral Crossing.* From November 1, 1998, to January 30, 1999, four Chileans (Pablo Besser, Rodrigo Fica, Mauricio Rojas, Jose Montt) made the first integral crossing of the Southern Ice Cap. Further information is lacking.

HERNAN JOFRE, *Amerindia Concept, Chile*

CLIMBS AND EXPEDITIONS: ANTARCTICA

# ANTARCTICA

*Antarctica, Overview of Mountaineering Objectives.* In an article that appears earlier in this journal, Antarctic climbing chronologist Damien Gildea offers up an overview of mountaineering objectives that updates and complements the excellent article "Mountaineering in Antarctica" in the 1985 *AAJ* (pp. 142-153).

## ANTARCTIC PENINSULA

*Antarctic Peninsula, Various Activity.* In January, 1999, an Australian expedition aboard the yacht *Tiama* accomplished some of the most notable climbing in the Antarctic Peninsula in a number of years. Kieran Lawton, Julie Styles, Geoff Moore, Robyn Cleland, Roland Eberhard and Chris Holly made the first ascent of Pilcher Peak, climbing the south ridge after skiing in with sledges to the glacier on the east side of the peak. They had been inspired by a fine photo by Gordon Wiltsie that has appeared in a number of publications. However, the peak in this photo is not the true Pilcher Peak, but a sharp peak on a ridge leading up to the plateau that constitutes the spine of the peninsula. The real Pilcher Peak (as indicated on the map) stands out to the north of the plateau and was summited by all the group on January 16. The other smaller ridge peak was then christened "Wiltsie's Peak" and was attempted by Styles and Lawton. They climbed for four days in poor visibility on the south ridge but were forced to turn back a mere 50 meters from the summit due to horrendous snow conditions. The party then skied back to Brialmont Cove where they made another three first ascents on peaks, including a rock spire, of altitudes up to ca.1800 meters. After leaving Brialmont Cove, the expedition visited Booth Island, where Styles, Lawton and Eberhard climbed a steep ice couloir on the southwestern side of the southernmost peak on the island—almost certainly a new route, though possibly not the first ascent of the peak.

DAMIEN GILDEA, *Australia*

*Renard Tower, Hart am Wind.* It was reported that Stefan Glowacz, Hoger Heuber, Kurt Albert, Jürgen Knappe, Hans Martin Götz and Gerhard Hiedorn established *Hart am Wind* (5.12c, 800m) on the Renard Tower. The 17-pitch was climbed over three days; anchors are bolted, while the rest of the climb relies on natural protection. Further details are lacking. (*Rock and Ice* 93)

## DRONNING MAUD LAND

*Rondespiret and Other Ascents.* In the 1997 *AAJ*, p. 268, an account may be found of the Norwegian expedition that successfully made the first ascent of the 800-meter Rondespiret (The Ronde Spire, 2427m) via the northeast face (Norwegian Grade 6+ A3+, 21 pitches) from December 23, 1996-January 8, 1997, by Aslak Aastorp, Robert Caspersen, Håkon Stover and Ivar Tollefsen. Also climbed on the same trip were Grushaugen (1673m), on December 27, 1996, by Tina Jørgensen; Vetlehaugen (1363m), on December 30, by Vebjørn Sand; Krakken (1446m), on December 30, by Tina

Jørgensen; Niesene (1390m), on January 1, 1997, by Tina Jørgensen; Shiraishi (1930m), on January 2, by Tina Jørgensen; Bautaen (Norwegian Grade 5 A3, four pitches, 1639m), on January 12, by Aslak Aastorp, Robert Caspersen, Tina Jørgensen, Håkon Staver, and Ivar Tollefsen; and Cap Gemini (6+ A2, three pitches, 1782m), by Aslak Aastorp, Robert Casperson, and Ivar Tollefsen, on January 14. We are now able to publish a photo that shows Rondespiret and other peaks in the area.

ELLSWORTH MOUNTAINS

SENTINEL RANGE

*Embree Glacier, First Exploration and Various Ascents.* Bob Elias, Kurt Cox and I flew from Punta Arenas to Patriot Hills on November 13, 1998. We were forced to wait for one week by bad weather before we could fly to our objective, the Embree Glacier, so in the meantime we climbed an ice face on Patriot Hills' north face. This route was to the right of Patriot Hills' much easier normal route, which we used for our descent. Ours was a fun 50° ice route; we did about ten pitches to the summit, from where we had a spectacular view of Mt. Simmons. Jim Donini soloed the route alongside us, finishing before we did. (It is uncertain whether this line had been climbed previously.)

Two days later my clients and I set out to climb Mt. Simmons (1590m), joined this time by Donini and Elizabeth Sodergren. My clients and I got about 150 meters from the top, but did not continue to the summit due to miserable cold weather and high winds. Jim and Elizabeth continued to the summit. The route was the most obvious and easiest line on Mt. Simmons' northwest face.

On November 21, my client Robert Elias and I landed on the Embree Glacier at 78° 04' 17" S, 86° 02' 16" W, at an altitude of 2200 meters. We were, to the best of our knowledge, the first people to set foot on this glacier. We set up Base Camp on a beautiful windless day. We had spectacular views of the surrounding peaks, which according to our research were all unclimbed and mostly unnamed. The most spectacular peaks were Mt. Todd, Mt. Press, Mt. Bentley, and indisputably the tremendous north face of Mt. Anderson.

On November 22, we did our first exploratory climb in fierce winds and temperatures of -40°F. We climbed the peak immediately north of Mt. Hale (78° 04' S 86° 9' W) via the northeast ridge. We "named" the unnamed peak "Natalie Peak," a beautiful 3400-meter summit (all names are tentative pending approval by the U.S. Board on Geographic Names). The climbing was moderate, involving mainly snow and ice climbing at the beginning and middle sections. The upper section was mixed climbing, and very challenging because of high winds and brutally cold temperatures.

On November 24, we climbed a second unclimbed peak north of Natalie Peak via its northeast ridge and named it "Kristen-Jule Peak" (ca. 3200m). It involved fun moderate mixed climbing with an interesting ridge. On November 26, we attempted to climb Mt. Little Todd, a sub-summit of the impressive Mt. Todd (3600m, 78° 03' S 85° 56' W), via the west ridge, finding great mixed climbing and several 60° ice pitches. We reached a

RIGHT: *The Rondespiret is the slender needle in the center of the photo. The peaks to either side are unclimbed.* IVAR TOLLEFSEN COLLECTION

point about 200 meters short of the summit in deteriorating weather.

On November 27, Conrad Anker, Jim Donini and Mike MacDowell joined our Base Camp, armed with a Twin Otter full of equipment, gourmet food, great wine and great spirits. The weather got worse the next day and never improved. The area is excellent, and there are more first ascents to be done. I feel like we barely touched its potential.

RODRIGO MUJICA, *unaffiliated*

*Mt. Slaughter, First Ascent.* It was reported that Guy Cotter and Terry Gardiner made the first ascent of Mt. Slaughter (ca. 3600m) south of the Vinson Massif. The two sled-hauled for a day, then spent another day reaching the base of Mt. Slaughter's north face. Cotter led 11 70-meter pitches over 50-60° ice in a thin gully that divides two buttresses to the right of the summit. A few more pitches brought the men to the top. (*Rock and Ice* 91)

*Antarctica, Various Ascents.* The weather in interior Antarctic during the austral summer of 1998-'99 can best be described as chaotic. Frequent moist storms brought an abnormal amount of snow to this very dry part of the planet. The complications were directly felt by Vinson climbers, many of whom were unable to fly onto the continent. Delays of 21 days were the norm. On December 1, Dave Hahn and I climbed the West Couloir on Gardner. This is the classic route established by the Nick Clinch-Pete Scheoning team of 1966-'67. We discovered remnants of that expedition, including old hemp rope, pitons and a cache of chocolate at the last camp. The chocolate was still edible. With this summit, I have climbed six of the highest summits in the Sentinel Range (Gardner, Tyree, Loretan [a.k.a. "Kindness"], Shinn, Vinson and Craddock). Epperly is still waiting. I lost my psyche as I heard about Dan Osman's death the day I was to head out of camp. I sat around and drank scotch instead. . . .

Jim Donini and I tried the west ridge of Epperly but turned back half-way up. It is perhaps the longest ridge above the glacial trim line in the Sentinels, and has lots of gendarmes. On December 28, I climbed the west ridge proper on Vinson Massif. This is the right-hand skyline as seen from Base Camp. I think it is a different route than what the Slovenians climbed in 1996, though it is hard to figure out. The route involved 2000 meters in elevation gain, rock up to 5.6 and alpine névé. A most enjoyable route. Total time round-trip was 18.5 hours. I had to walk down so it wasn't that fast.

I skied the prominent fin north of the north ice stream on the west face. The run had a section of 40°. Dave Hahn and I would like to re-route the normal route up this fin, as it is less exposed to objective hazards than the current route up the icefall between CII and CIII. My time was two minutes slower than last year, but I stopped to visit en route and who really gives, as Vonnegut says, "a flying fuck at a rolling donut."

Dave's Vinson Massif total is now 14.

CONRAD ANKER

# EUROPE

## NORWAY

*Spitsberen, Various Activity.* Spitsberen is a group of islands north of Norway (78°N); Longyearbien is the capital. They were originally discovered in the 17th century and used as a base on a number of attempts on the North Pole by Nansen and others. Although not technically Norwegian territory, the islands are "looked after" by Norway. They are a major polar bear breeding ground, so you have to travel everywhere with a rifle. The highest hills (ca. 1700m) are in the north of the main island, Svalbard, which is where most people visit. Despite their northerly latitude, the islands lose all snow apart from their glaciers and ice caps during the summer months due to the warming influence of the Gulf Stream; in summer, travel is more difficult as the land becomes unfrozen tundra. There is a lot of very loose sedimentary rock, making climbing very unpleasant in summer.

Last March and April, I traveled to Spitsberen to do some glaciology, which involved blowing up bits of glacier, driving around on the skidoos and seeing the polar bears. We had some cold temperatures (-33°C) and got a couple of sessions to go climbing. We did Mount Aspelin via a snow plod up the east ridge and down the northeast ridge, which was straightforward, though it was good to get out at midnight on April 11 after a days' work. It was a bit of a problem mountaineering with a rifle over one shoulder. Mount Aspelin is the highest point in the south of the island, so it gave some good views. Everything is still snow-covered this time of the year, which offered good skidooing and travel on the sea ice.

On April 19, we had finished all the science, so Andy Smith and I did a brilliant ten-kilometer ridge on the north side of the Ragna Mariebreen Glacier. The traverse included four peaks: Framnuten (817m), Tverregga (925m), Gimlingen (975m), and Thoretinden (1081m). Climbing (up to IV) was necessary to get up or off all of the peaks, and Gimlingen was particularly difficult and dangerous with a narrow ridge as the summit (which I stood astride). I think it was the first ascent of most of the peaks; it certainly was for Gimlingen. I've since heard that Thoretinden was ascended up snow slopes from the north about 12 years ago around Easter time. We then descended to a col at the end of the ridge and skied 15 kilometers back to the camp. The rock was appallingly loose and some of the ridge was thin, but it was one of the best days I had had in the mountains for years and the ski back really ended it well.

BRIAN DAVISON, *United Kingdom*

*Troll Wall, Rock Fall.* It was reported that the 1300-meter Troll Wall on the north face of Trollryggen (1742m) experienced a series of rockfalls beginning in September. The first came from high on the face in an area known as the Gray Wall; the fall strafed the lower sections of the Swedish, Spanish and Rimmon routes. All routes in the vicinity of the wall were seriously affected. A month later a far greater rockfall occurred down low on the wall between the Rimmon Route and the 1986 route *Death to All*. The fall registered 2.0 on the Richter Scale at recording stations in Norway and Sweden. (*High Mountain Sports* 197)

*Lofoten Islands, Vagakallen, Freya.* It was reported that in July, the German couple Daniela and Robert Jasper established a 30-pitch, 800-meter route, *Freya* (F7c A3+), on Vagakallen (942m).

The route takes the front face of the mountain's most prominent feature, the north face of the Storpillaren ("The Great Pillar"). The couple on-sighted or redpointed in the first attempt all but four of the pitches. Most of the route went free, but the middle section had several aid pitches, the crux of which went at new-wave A3+. The Jaspers climbed capsule-style with portaledges to a terrace at two-thirds height, from where they finished in one long day. They descended to the ground, then climbed the route again for a television crew. *(High Mountain Sports* 197)

# MIDDLE EAST

# IRAN

*Alum Kuh, Ascents, and Insights into Iranian Climbing.* In September, Leyla Pope, a Briton with dual British/Iranian nationality, organized an expedition to Iran to explore the climbing of Alum Kuh. As guests of the Iran Mountaineering Federation, the three women that joined her—Kath Pyke, Glenda Huxter and Celia Bull—comprised one of the first Western climbing teams to be invited into Iran since the revolution some two decades earlier. The four women spent a number of days in the Alum Kuh area, during which time Pyke and Huxter climbed the 1964 Iranian-German Amralaiy-Rost route, and Bull and Pope, along with several extra teams from the Federation, climbed the classic 1936 North Ridge route. In exchange for being hosted by the Iranian Mountaineering Federation, the Britons ran a climbing skills workshop for some 20 women climbers selected from Iran's 24 provinces. Pyke's insights on the trip appear in an article earlier in this journal.

*Minaret Peak, Ascent.* On May 5, Al Read, Jean Weiss (U.S.), Abbas Jafari (Iran) and I left the Iran Mountaineering Federation's hut at the village of Rudbarak in the foothills of the Alam Kooh (also transliterated as Alum Kuh; see above) range of Alborz mountains in north Iran. We headed up the Hezar Chal Valley, skirting around the west to the south side of Mt. Alam Kooh (16,200'), the second-highest peak in Iran. We had to change our original plan of going to the famous north face and ridge. The El Niño spring had deposited unusual amounts of snow on the high north glacier, and our mule drivers couldn't take our camp to the north face.

Hezar Chal Valley turned out to be a great choice. Ali, our local cook, said that the last time a foreign group visited this side had been in 1981, when a Polish film crew spent a week there. Alone in this vast cirque, we established our Base Camp at 11,500 feet in the center of the valley. We climbed a very enjoyable new alpine route (III 5.0) on the south face of Minaret Peak (13,770'). This peak bore a striking similarity to Wyoming's Grand Teton. Our route started on a shallow snow gully on the left edge of the steep south face. A few pitches higher, where the gully divided, we climbed left to a short rock section. Delicate climbing on not-very-solid rock led to the extreme left buttress of the face. Another steep gully above was climbed directly to a shoulder just below the summit. On the summit, as sign of hospitality to the American guests of Iran, Jafari suggested the peak be renamed the "Exum Minaret" in honor of the Exum Mountain Guides in the Grand Teton National Park, Wyoming. We spent two more days at the camp, during which Jafari and I climbed a rounded 12,500-foot peak. The next day, Read, Jafari and I climbed the circuitous south face of Alam Kooh (third and fourth class).

HOOMAN APRIN, *unaffiliated*

# AFRICA

*Africa, Far-Flung Explorations.* Briton Tony Howard, who, with his partner, Di Taylor, has been exploring north Africa and the Middle East from a climber's perspective since the 1960s, shares some of his tales and insights in an article that appears earlier in this journal.

## MOROCCO

*Morocco, Overview.* During 1998, whilst working in Morocco, I took the opportunity to explore the enigmatic pleasures of the Atlas Mountains. Morocco is accessible and user-friendly for the tourist, but remains a niche destination as far as mountaineers are concerned. It can, however, be a highly worthwhile niche destination. Attractions include vast areas of undiscovered rock in the more remote areas, and the possibility of substantial snowfall transforming the summits into a wilderness ski-touring playground.

Inevitably, popular attention is drawn to the highest summit, Toubkal (4167m). From an alpine climbing perspective this massif is disappointing, since the normal routes are fairly trivial. There are some good long rock and ice climbs, however, such as on the north face of Tazarhart (3980m), and the area lends itself to ski touring. It has been well documented.

Of greater interest from the exploratory viewpoint are the cliffs hidden in some of the Atlas valleys. The awe-inspiring Todra Gorge has been well-publicized abroad and is consequently something of a honeypot for visiting rock climbers. The climbing has been developed substantially during the 1990s and there are now many bolted areas with mostly one- or two-pitch routes. Classic middle-grade routes the length of the 250-meter Pilier de Couchant in the main gorge have also been disfigured. The bolts happily occupy the majority of visiting climbers, leaving the vast remaining acreage of quality red limestone for the exploratory climber.

In 1998, I climbed routes at British VS in the main gorge right of the Pilier de Couchant and on the ramp just left of the Hotel Yasmina. In the nearby Dades Valley, the largest cliffs mostly lie below the road in a narrow river gorge. Huge areas of continuous climbing can only be approached by multiple abseil or by wading the river. Given that the rock is also rather loose, routes here would be serious undertakings. This area is probably untouched. Beyond, the small upper gorge cut through by the road has shorter but attractive cliffs. However, my attempt at a route on the west side led to much falling rock that threatened the gawping tourists below and eventually ended in a retreat in the face of a loose overlap.

Lower down the valley, some distinctive rock formations known as the "doigts des singes" (monkey fingers) are clearly seen from the road. Some of these are reputed to have been climbed on, but close inspection reveals them to be rather gritty, with no cracks for gear.

Climbing of an altogether better quality is to be found in the remote area on the northern fringes of the Central High Atlas centered on the village of Zawit Ahansal. This has been described as the best rock climbing in Morocco and likened to the Dolomites (such comparisons should be treated with caution). The access route, via Ait-Mohammed, includes over 50 kilometers of rough unsurfaced road and traverses the Tizi-n-Ilissi at 2650 meters. On the

*The Todra Gorge as seen from* Family Entertainment *near the Pilier de Couchant.* PAULL KNOTT

north side of Aroudan (3359m), there are three kilometers of crags up to 800 meters in height. The nearby area just south of Taghia is equally impressive. A number of routes, up to ED VI A3, are described in *Le Maroc: Les Plus Belles Courses et Randonees*, by Bernard Domenech. Considerable further potential almost certainly exists.

Further east, new route potential exists on an extensive and somewhat more accessible 300-meter crag on the north side of Irhil ou Abbari, near Sidi Yahia ou Youssef in the Jbel Masker range. Here, too, French climbers were active in earlier decades.

The limestone escarpments and wooded hills of the Middle Atlas offer little at this scale, but do have the allure of frequent rock outcrops with no visiting climbers. Unfortunately, most of the crags turn out to be of poor quality. Exceptions include single-pitch routes in the Foum Kheneg Gorge on the Azrou-Midelt road near Timahdite, and limestone bouldering off the Ifrane-Dayet Hachlaf road. The former yields a wealth of well-protected natural lines best approached outside the nesting season. Also worth investigating are sizeable steep limestone crags near the Sources de l'Oum-er-Rbia and the possibility of short ice climbs near the summit of Jbel Tichchoukt.

Other ranges worthy of investigation include the granite of the Anti Atlas near Tafraoute, visited by British climbers since the early 1990s, and the rocky summits of the Eastern end of the Jbel Sahro massif. In Morocco in general much potential remains, especially for those with the time to invest in penetrating well beyond the reach of the tarmac road.

PAULL KNOTT, *United Kingdom*

# MALI

*Hombori Mountains, Various Ascents.* It was reported that a number of climbs went up on or near Le Main de Fatima in the winter of 1997-'98. On the Grimari Dagana Massif, on December 13, B. Regien and C. Dumont d'Ayot put up *Vendredi XII* (6a, 250m) on the north pillar of Wambe Ballo. Salvador Campillo and B. Marnette established *Soleil Noir* (TD/TDsup, 160m) on the east summit of the Ciseaux de Grimari on January 28. On Taganagategue in the Boni-Loro Massif, Campillo and Marnette put up the 180-meter *Khili-Khili* (6a A1). In the Bani-Kani area on the Fifth Tower of the North Dyoude Massif, Campillo and Marnette put up a 220-meter TDinf. route via its northwest spur.

*The Hand of Fatima, Harmattan Rodeo.* For many years, my regular gang of climbing partners—Todd Skinner, Bobby Model, Andy deKlerk, Ed February, Scott Milton, Bill Hatcher and Peter Mallamo—and I were intrigued by photos we had seen in Spanish magazines of Le Main de Fatima ("The Hand of Fatima"), a lovely grouping of giant pinnacles resembling the hand of the prophet Mohammed's favorite daughter that rises from a parched landscape of massive quartzite towers and walls in Mali. From mid-December to mid-January, 1997-'98, we found ourselves living below and on these beautiful towers. To ensure we were choosing the finest climbing objective, we spent two days hiking around many of the area rock formations. The team unanimously agreed upon the region's most outstanding challenge: a new route up a severely overhanging outside corner of a 1,400-foot spire called Kaga Pamari, the little finger of Fatima's hand.

Day after day was spent climbing a little higher. Each night, we would rappel fixed ropes to try to converse with local tribesmen visiting our Base Camp. Sobered by the need to redpoint numerous formidable pitches in a limited time, we held council while dangling from anchors halfway up the spire. Scott, Todd and I thought we might have bitten off more than we could chew, but the quartzite-wise South Africans, Ed and Andy, just smiled. Taking South African confidence as counsel, we decided to risk glorious failure trying to accomplish a resplendent goal rather than settle for success on a lesser objective. We continued to work our way up the spire and our quartzite savvy strengthened. After ten days, we began our final push, a free climb from bottom to top.

Ed led the first pitch. Climbing all day, we arrived beneath a giant roof 750 feet above the base. We suspended our portaledge camp under this roof, which conspired with a weather front and the natural *venturi* effect caused by the chimney between the two towers to nearly blow us off the planet. The Harmattan is a winter wind which, like the broom of Allah, sweeps southward from Algeria across the Sahara. While sculpting dunes, it chokes the air with a settling rouge. All night long, the Harmattan tattered us like torn sails. Our two-man ledges were repeatedly lifted and dropped, while suspended haulbags, heavy with water, were blown upward and dropped, smashing against us as we lay. In the morning, almost all of the maillon screw links securing the webbing to the portaledges had come unscrewed. When Ed's ashen face gazed out of his sleeping bag, he said, "Last night was absolutely bloody amazing. . . a Harmattan Rodeo!" He had just named our route.

The day's climbing progressed well. Toward evening, Scott danced up another crux pitch that ended on a boulder-strewn, guano-cushioned ledge on the lee side—a perfect wind-shadowed bivouac. Two days prior, Andy had punched a pencil-lead-sized hole in his shin. On the big ledge, his leg began to swell and throb. The next morning, he had chills and a titanic headache. A surly red streak took a poisoned path from his calf into his groin, but Andy insisted he was fit and keen to go higher.

The final two leads moved back onto the windy side of the tower. We climbed onto a windless summit, a dramatic and tiny island floating in an atmospheric sea of ocher dust. Feeling worse, Andy started down immediately, beginning the 1,400-foot rappel and the long slide down talus to Base Camp. Soon after, the rest of us began stripping the route of ropes and equipment. Then Peter, who was in the talus field, called us on the radio. While descending the talus, Andy passed out numerous times and Peter had carried him to camp. Andy was now unconscious.

We hired a Land Rover for the 1,000-mile, 20-hour drive to the nearest medical help in Mali's capital city, Bamako. Once in Bamako, Andy was treated at a French hospital with a massive regimen of antibiotic injections. His shin had developed a staph infection, causing phlebitis. The doctors told us that another day's delay would have cost Andy his leg and perhaps even his life.

While Ed and Andy recuperated in Bamako, we spent several days bouldering on Hueco Tanks-quality quartzite boulders in the Dogon country. There, we visited with a Dogon elder who told us to "climb with care; with the serene spirit of birds; and with an appreciation of the fellowship that climbing strengthens." The old man solemnly tapped his heart and said: "Understanding and brotherhood among all people is important above all other things."

LEFT: *The Hand of Fatima, Mali. Kaga Pamari is the 1,400-foot "little finger" of Fatima's hand.*
BOBBY MODEL

Later, as we prepared to fly home, we reminisced about our magnificent new climb. Andy and Ed proclaimed our 14-pitch route one of the finest and most difficult quartzite climbs in the world. We had been lucky to visit the African Sahel (the drought-beset region below the Sahara that includes Mali, Chad, Niger, Senegal, et al.; the exact line of Sahel/Sahara is constantly moving south) and to live for a time among the unique cultures of the region. We were going home safely and as stronger friends. We vowed always to climb with the serene spirit of birds.

PAUL PIANA, *unaffiliated*

# KENYA

*Point Peter, Northwest Face.* It was reported that on March 15, Ulf Carlsson, Nicolas Ganzin and Ian Howell made the first ascent of the Northwest Face of Point Peter (4757m), a sharp granite spire below the north face of Mt. Kenya. The team took a direct line to the summit via a series of cracks and corners roughly in the center of the face. Most of the climbing was moderate. The crux was the penultimate pitch, a strenuous and awkward corner that went at HVS 5a/b. This trio and others active in the area reported an alarming disappearance of ice in the north-facing couloirs and on the Diamond Glacier, which was reduced to almost half its size. (*High Mountain Sports* 197)

# MADAGASCAR

## Andringitra National Park

*Tsaranoro Atsimo, Never the Same, and Various Ascents.* In September, Italians Rolando Larcher, Marco Sterni, and Erik Svab established the 670-meter route *Never the Same* (V 5.13c/d A0) on the east face of Tsaranoro Atsimo. The 13 pitches of the route range from 35 to 60 meters each; 122 bolts were placed on the route, including 26 for the anchors. The team established the route and then worked it, freeing all the moves on the most difficult pitch (Pitch 8, 5.13c/d), which they climbed with one rest (but did not redpoint). On September 24, they made a one-day, eight-hour ascent of the route. Descent was made with double ropes. The route has obligatory moves of F7b (5.12b). Two other members of the team, Ermanno Francinelli and Mario Cavagnini, repeated five established routes on Tsaranoro, including *Gondwanaland* on Tsaranoro Be. A full report on *Never the Same* appears earlier in this journal.

*Tsaranoro Massif, Various Activity.* Last summer three different teams visited the Tsaranoro Massif in the Andringitra National Park. All the visiting teams, except Kurt Albert and Bernd Arnold, who had first visited the area some years before, used electric power drills to place bolts. All lines are bolted. Bolts are well-spaced and falls up to 20 meters are possible on most of the lines. All routes were opened ground up without previous rehearsal, except for *Tsac Tsac* (Gilles Gouthier and Alain Thiberghien), which was opened via rappel bolting. It's not described in this account.

In early April, Arnaud Petit and Stephanie Baudet (F) visited the area and made a repetition in two days (not one as claimed, since the second day was used to rappel 800 meters) of the longest route of the area, *Gondwanaland*. The route was climbed on-sight except the crux

*Little Karambony and Karambony. A: Fantasia (Pellizari-Piola). B: Rain Boto (Albert-Arnold).*
EMANUELE PELLIZARI

pitch. The overall grade (F7a+) was confirmed. Petit, with Gilles Gauthier, then made an attempt on the obvious dihedral of Tsaranoro Be, which joined the line of a previous attempt of Italians Campana et al after five pitches. The line up to there has difficulties of F6b/6c.

Later in the season, the team of Manlio Motto and Emanuele Pellizzari (I), Benoit Robert (F) and Michel Piola (Swiss) arrived for a one-month stay, during which they established seven new routes. From June 23 to 27, Pellizzari and Piola opened *Fantasia* (A3+ F6c), a predominantly aid route on the overhanging left corner on the left face of Karambony. It's opposite the first route of the area, *Rain Boto* (Kurt Albert and Bernd Arnold). The key pitch, a traverse right under a big roof, has potential for a dangerous (or fatal) fall. For the first 11 pitches, no bolts were placed apart from those at the belays. On pitches 11 and 13 (in the free climbing sections) there is fixed protection. It's impossible to retreat via rappel after the seventh pitch.

While the two were climbing *Fantasia*, Motto and Robert climbed the Normal Route (F5+ for ten meters) on Karambony, meeting Pellizzari and Piola on top. This is also the descent line for the formation.

Motto and Robert established the 250-meter route *Ebola* (F6b+) on the right slopes of Karambony. The four then joined forces to establish *Out Of Africa* (F7a, 14 pitches) from June 29 to July 2 on Tsaranoro Kely. It was repeated, again, by Pellizzari-Piola on July 3. As of today, this route can be considered the "normal" route to the summit of Tsaranoro Be. The line is on the right (lower) pillar of Tsaranoro.

Later on, the team split again, creating two new lines on Vatovarindy: *La Coix du Sud* (Piola-Robert) and *Veloma Madagasikara* (Motto-Pellizzari). *La Coix du Sud* takes the left

*Mitsin Joarivo, home to the ten-pitch* Le Crabe aux Pinces d'Or. EMANUELE PELLIZARI

ridge of the face and joins the center line of *Veloma Madagasikara* on the final belay. With *Veloma Madagasikara*, the Italians were looking for an easy line and got a reasonably diffi-cult one (F7a+), while the French, who were looking for a hard line, got an easy one with *La Coix du Sud*. At this point the team suffered from a shortage of bolts, not because they placed too many (never more than eight per pitch, with an average of six every 50 meters) but because they had climbed too much. On Mitsin Joarivo, a dome in between Vatovarindy and Tsaranoro, Piola and Robert then established *Le Crabe aux Pinces d'Or*, an overhanging line of ten pitches with maximum difficulties of F7b+.

Still not tired, the French-speaking team went to Le Dondy to open *Le Revoltes du Dondy*, a very exploratory 1600-meter line that gets to the summit of this very grassy mountain. The team reported overhanging turf, cow shit falling from above, and tropical grass.

All the routes except for *Fantasia* have been repeated. The rock is granite, and very solid. Most of the cracks are choked with tropical grass, which is very hard to remove; for the tal-ented, two ice axes and experience in dry tooling is enough to work out a nice line. All the face routes are bolted. Fall potential up to 20 meters is normal. *Fantasia* has bolts at the belays.

The valley and its inhabitants are not prepared for more than ten climbers/tourists at a time. They haven't food for themselves and too many people at once will ruin their culture. Water sources are poor. Hygiene is a delicate issue; climbers live higher than the locals, which means defecation up-stream will contaminate their water. Climbers will find nothing to buy in the villages. Do not buy the locals' food. If you do, they will use the money to buy ciga-rettes instead of food. Never give candy to the children, since they can't brush their teeth and you will forever ruin their smiles. They don't have shoes and don't need them. If you can, bring warm clothes for locals, which they do need. Don't carry pens or other typical Western gifts: give them food (they basically eat only rice), possibly proteins, especially for the children. With the equivalent of $50 you can buy them a few tons of beans—enough protein for a year. Don't leave any garbage, nor bury it: locals will recover it to see if they can find something useful and leave the rest to the wind to blow away.

Only really enviromentally conscious teams should consider an expedition to this area.

EMANUELE PELLIZARI, *Italy*

# ASIA

# INDIA

## UTTAR PRADESH

### CENTRAL GARHWAL

*Mukut Parvat East, First Ascent.* A Korean team made an important and difficult first ascent in July and August when Oksun Hong led an expedition to Mukut Parvat East (7130m). Two members of the team reached the summit. The team accessed the peak through the West Kamet Glacier. This was the last virgin 7000-meter peak in the Garhwal.

HARISH KAPADIA, *Honorary Editor, The Himalayan Journal*

*Badrinath to Kedarnath, Second Mortal Traverse, and Ascent of Pt. 5758.* The crossing of the Satopanth Col and across the Markanda Ganga valley involves a mixture of mountaineering and bushwhacking to negotiate three 15,000-foot ridges through some of the wildest bits of the Indian Himalaya. In 1934, after hearing the legend of a Hindu priest who had preached at both temples on the same day, Eric Shipton and Bill Tilman attempted what they thought would be a two-day crossing, and found themselves involved in a two-week epic hacking their way through dense forest and competing with bears for a diet of bamboo shoots when their food ran out. Two Bengalis who attempted to repeat the route in 1986 disappeared without a trace. In 1997, a team from Bombay led by Harish Kapadia attempted to repeat the route but via the Panpatia Valley. They were stopped lower in the valley and did not reach the Panpatia Col.

Between May 25 and June 7, an Indo-British team (Brede Arkless, John Harvey, Ben Lovett, Martin Moran, and Sobat Singh Rana) repeated the watershed crossing from the Badrinath to Kedarnath valleys which had remained unvisited since Shipton and Tilman's 1934 traverse. The route commenced at Badrinath, crossed the Inner Line at Mana village, then ascended the Satopanth Glacier to a col at its head at ca. 5450 meters. The icefall beneath the col was badly broken and objectively dangerous, so the team climbed a mixed face on the left, assisted by excellent pre-monsoon snow conditions. While camped at 5100 meters on the far side of the col, Arkless and Moran were able to ascend the unclimbed peak (Pt. 5758m) immediately south of the col, which they propose to name Shipton's Peak. The ascent (AD) was made by the south ridge and face, with descent down the north slope back to the col. The climb enabled a thorough inspection of the upper Panpatia Glacier, where there are numerous

*Gandharpongi Gad, "Shipton's Lost Valley," in the Garhwal Himalaya.* MARTIN MORAN

unclimbed summits between 5500 and 6000 meters, and of the big south wall of Chaukhamba. The south buttress of Chaukhamba II (7068m) looked most appealing, with some impressive granite walls in an extremely remote situation.

From the col, the team descended left of the icefall that had ensnared the 1934 party. With one traverse under a serac and two abseils, easy ground was gained and the descent continued to the Gandharpongi Gad, where the infamous bamboo valley, vividly described by Eric Shipton in his book *Nanda Devi*, commenced. The 1934 party was trapped in this valley for a week, fighting swollen monsoon rivers and competing with black bears for their diet. The 1998 party found evidence of occasional visits by trappers and root gatherers in the forest, and the crucial crossing of the big side stream at Pt. 2685m was bridged by a temporary log bridge. However, apart from the odd sawn branch, trails were non-existent and the party was fortunate that the main growing season for bamboo and brambles had only just begun.

From Pt. 2685m, the 1934 party had followed the Markanda Ganga Valley southward and eventually escaped at Kalimath. The 1998 team chose instead to strike directly uphill out of the jungle and over two days made a 1700-meter climb to cross the Dobri Khal ridge and reach Mandani. The Mandani Valley was similarly deserted and unspoiled, and trails marked on the map were overgrown. From Mandani, the party crossed the Simtoll ridge at 4500 meters, crossed the Kali Ganga Valley and finished direct at Kedarnath Temple on June 7, thus making the first proven direct crossing between the two Hindu shrines.

Eric Shipton's son, John, accompanied the expedition to 5150 meters on the Satopanth Glacier and then traveled around the south edge of the massif and trekked in from Kalimath to view the bamboo valley. As a child, he had often heard his father talk of his epic in the great valley.

MARTIN MORAN, *Alpine Climbing Group*

*Thalay Sagar, Attempts and Tragedy.* From August to October, a Japanese expedition led by Hiroshi Doke reached 6300 meters on the northeast ridge of Thalay Sagar (6904m). During the same time period, Hyung Jin Kim led a Korean expedition to the north face of the mountain. Korean teams had already made six attempts on Thalay Sagar via the popular East Pillar and West Ridge routes and on the technical north face. For the seventh attempt, again on the north face, the team left Delhi on August 23, made Base Camp on September 1 and established Camp I before making four bivouacs to reach a point 75 meters below the summit. Three members of the expedition, Hyung Jin Kim, Sung-Chul Choi, and Sang-Man Shin, died when a cornice near the summit broke and fell on them on September 28. A member of the expedition who was in communication with the team last heard from them at 5:30 p.m. that day. He then saw them falling through his binoculars.

Earlier, the team had decided to abandon its effort, as bad weather and continuous whiteout persisted for a number of days in the month of September, making progress difficult. On September 27, the weather had cleared, and the team had decided to make one last attempt. It is unclear how their line related to the 1997 Australian or the 1987 Hungarian routes on the north face.

*From reports by* Col. Ajit Dutt, *and* Harish Kapadia, *Honorary Editor, The Himalayan Journal*

*Chandra Parvat, Attempt.* In 1938, the first Austrian Himalaya Expedition made many ascents in the western Garhwal Himalaya, including the first ascent of Chandra Parvat (6728m), which was climbed via the west ridge by Leo Spannraft and Dr. W. Frauenberger. Spannraft was one of Austria's famous alpine pioneers and a decade-long member of the Mountain Rescue Association and the Alpenverein. He died at age 90 on a ski tour. In 1998, on the 60th anniversary of this first Austrian expedition, nine alpinists of Villach elected to attempt Chandra Parvat in memory of Leo Spannraft.

We started our expedition in Chitkul (3450m) in the Baspa Valley, crossed the 5282-meter Lampkhaga Pass to Harsil, and reached the Advanced Base Camp near the Suralya Glacier at 5100 meters on September 7. On the 8th, we established CI (5500m) near the southwest ridge and returned to ABC. On the 9th, the first team, along with the successful Indian climber Keendar Singh and the liaison officer Ganga Singh, started for CI. The next day, they established CII and continued climbing along the southwest ridge to 6600 meters where the west and the southwest ridges meet. They reached this point in six hours in bad weather but good snow conditions. The traverse to the 6728-meter main peak was impossible due to bad weather conditions (snow, fog, whiteout). The crew descended the same day to ABC. On September 12, in similarly poor conditions, the second team, including Mangal Singh, reached this west summit and descended in a snow storm to ABC.

DR. KARL PALLASMANN, *Austrian Alpenverein*

*Swachand, West Face, Attempt.* Malcolm Bass, Julian Clamp and Simon Yearsley (U.K.) attempted the west face of Swachand (6721m) during September and October. Swachand was first climbed by the Austrians Messner and Spannraft during the incredibly prolific 1938 Austrian expedition to the area. We ascended from the southeast via the Maiandi Glacier. The 1400-meter west face overlooks the Swachand Glacier and is steep and mixed. There have been no previous attempts.

Base Camp was established at Sundervan (4550m) below the southeast face of Shivling on September 8. Persistent rain and snow prevented ABC from being established until the 20th, when it was placed beneath the west face of Swachand at 5250 meters. Further heavy snowfall forced a retreat back to BC until September 27. On September 29, Clamp and I began up the face, reaching a bivouac ledge beneath a large overhang at 5850 meters as the sun hit the face at midday. Severe rock and icefall began and continued until evening, but we were safe beneath our roof.

In the early hours of the 30th, we hand-traversed left under the overhang, then followed a thin snow ledge across the wall until the angle above relented. We climbed steep mixed ground, including verglassed slabs (Scottish 6). The slabs led to a superb short ice gully (Scottish 4) and then to snow slopes above. We moved together up these, and reached the second major rockband on the face, where we dug a tent platform under a slight overhang (6070m). By midday, severe stone and icefall had begun again. On the morning of October 1, we climbed one mixed pitch above the bivy to gain access to an icy ramp cutting through the second rock band. It then became clear that the upper section of the face would be as exposed to stonefall as the lower. We decided to retreat from 6100 meters. We made a rapid abseil retreat in snowfall and reached ABC the same morning.

The quality of the climbing found on the lower sections suggests that the route would provide a magnificent mixed climb ideally suited to an alpine-style ascent. We don't know whether the levels of stonefall encountered are typical of this face, or a product of the very poor weather conditions. The unspoiled and remote ambience of the upper Gangotri and Swachand glaciers add to the experience of climbing here.

MALCOLM BASS, *United Kingdom*

*Bhagirathi I, West Ridge.* The participants were Michael Messner, Harald Riedl, Christian Zenz and me. It was our aim to climb the west ridge of Bhaghirathi I, which was first ascended alpine-style by a British expedition in 1983. After having completed the usual formalities, we arrived at Base Camp in Nandanvan on September 7 without any problems. We transported part of our equipment to the beginning of the ridge. Unfortunately, we were trapped in Base Camp until the end of September due to steady precipitation (snowfall to ca. 4000m). It was not until September 26 that we could start our first attempt, which we had to break off due to bad conditions.

On October 3, Christian Zenz and I started a further attempt and after four to five days of alpine-style climbing, we reached the top on October 7. The difficulties on the lower rocky ridge were UIAA III-IV, with some passages up to V and several easier sections. The steep rock pillar, which is ca. 300 meters high, was V-VI, with several longer passages at VI+. The mixed ground that followed was in good condition, as was the 800-meter ridge itself, after an initial 100 meters of deep snow. At ca. 6700 meters, the ridge is interrupted by a ca. 20-meter step of bad rock (IV-V). We reached the top at about 1 p.m. in beautiful weather and cold wind. Our descent was mainly done by abseiling the same route. Except for the abseil anchors, we left no other material or rubbish on the mountain.

JOSEF JOCHLER, *Austria*

*Bhagirathi III, West Face, New Route.* Alexander Odintsov, Igor Potankin, Yuri Koshelenko, Vladimir Kachkov, Andrey Lukin, Ivan Samoilenko, and Lioudmila Krestina (doctor) arrived at the Bhagirathi Base Camp in Nandanvan on August 25. The expedition took 12 weeks—one month more than they had planned. Six climbers started a route up the center of the west face; four summited. They spent 16 days climbing capsule style on their route and two more for the rappel. They experienced serious weather on the wall, including a storm on the descent that killed three Indian rangers in a neighboring valley and destroyed 25 kilometers of the road, which they later passed on foot. A full account of their route appears earlier in this journal.

*Bhagirathi III, South Face, Les Temps Sauvages, and Other Activity.* The expedition members had various goals. Alain Bruzy (leader), Christian Ravier, Frederic Salles, and Alain Miquel wanted to climb the Scottish Route, but altitude problems and dissension in the group prohibited them from doing so. Jerome Thinidres and Stephane Benoist wanted to put up a new route on the west face between the Slovenian and the Scottish routes. Instead, they climbed the Scottish Route from May 16 to 20, finding difficult mixed climbing.

Arnaud Guillaume and I wanted to climb the Spanish (Catalan) Route. On May 7, we were ready to start, but a big snow storm that lasted until the 11th deposited one meter of snow at Base Camp. When good weather returned on the 12th, we realized we didn't have enough time to climb the route. Furthermore, part of our gear had been lost when the Advanced Base Camp was destroyed by avalanches. We decided to have a look at the south face, which we thought would be drier, sunnier and quicker to climb.

We started climbing on May 15 at 1 a.m. up a 800-meter couloir (40°) before reaching a ridge that we followed for five pitches (V/V+). We installed our first bivy at 5400 meters. On the second day, we climbed a very nice, steep dihedral with beautiful wide cracks for five more pitches (V+/6a). The second bivouac was set up at 5260 meters.

The central pillar we climbed on day three was the nicest part of the route: long slabs with thin cracks protected by nuts and cams. We had to aid a few meters. The third bivouac was at 5900 meters. It snowed all night and we had to wait until noon before leaving. We then joined the Czech Route for five more pitches of wonderful granite, which led us to the summit snow slopes. It took us about four hours to climb them and we reached the summit at 9 p.m. on May 18. We had a hard time reaching the last bivouac in the dark, sometimes down climbing, sometimes rappelling. The next day, we rappelled the rest of the route to the access couloir.

Our route, *Les Temps Sauvages,* is a beautiful climb, not too hard on perfect granite. The sun reaches the face at 9 a.m. and stays until 7 p.m. To climb the route, you will need about two sets of cams, one set of nuts and 15 pitons. No equipment was left on the pitches. All rappels (45 to 50 meters) except for two are equipped with two pitons (the other two use a single bolt). From the second bivy, rappels are equipped straight down and don't follow the route. All bivouacs are comfortable on good ledges.

The weather was rather capricious. During our climb, mornings were sunny and afternoons cloudy with some snow. We departed Base Camp May 24.

REMI THIVEL, *France*

*Meru East Face, Attempt.* The original aim of the expedition was to make the first ascent of the north face of the highest summit in Himachel Pradesh, Reo Purgyil (6816m), which straddles the border between India and Tibet. Unfortunately, two days before the expedition was due to depart for India, permission was revoked by the Indian Government. This action came at the end of a week in which India conducted nuclear weapon tests. Despite the setback, we were still committed to flights and other arrangements, so the team traveled out to Delhi, and with the support of the IMF managed to obtain an alternative permit for Meru (6660m) in the Gangotri region.

The expedition was comprised of climbers Julie-Ann Clyma and Roger Payne. The new aim was to make an alpine-style ascent of the unclimbed east face of Meru. They were joined for the walk-in to Base Camp by Nicholas Clyma (N.Z.) and Tony Martin (U.S.).

The expedition set up Base Camp at Tapovan (4480m) on May 24. The weather in the pre-monsoon period was excellent at the end of May, but extremely unsettled during June. The first attempt on the mountain began on May 31, with Payne and Clyma reaching a highpoint of ca. 6300 meters on June 3. Progress was stopped here because of bad weather and avalanche danger. Two more attempts were made, but the poor conditions did not allow progress beyond 5100 meters. The expedition departed from Base Camp on June 14 and arrived back in Delhi two days later.

ROGER PAYNE, *British Mountaineering Council*


*Gorur Dome, First Ascent.* Prasanta Roy led an expedition that made the first ascent of an unnamed peak (known locally as Gorur Dome, 6268m) in May and June. The summit was reached on June 9 after about eight to nine hours of climbing from CII by Arnab Banerjee, Arka Ghosh, Avijit Das and HAP Surinder Singh Rawat.

HARISH KAPADIA, *Honorary Editor, The Himalayan Journal*


*Chaturangi Glacier, First Ascents.* From June to July, Amitabha Roy led a Rocks & Snow Expedition that succeeded in climbing two unnamed peaks in the Chaturangi Glacier area. Base Camp was established at 5030 meters on June 25, CI (5180m) on July 26, CII (5460m) July 27. The summit of a 6166-meter peak was reached by Mainak Das, Raghubir Singh and two HAPs, Balbir Singh and Lachman Singh, on July 29. The four then climbed an unnamed 6035-meter peak the same day.

HARISH KAPADIA, *Honorary Editor, The Himalayan Journal*


*Jaonli, Attempt, and Various Ascents.* A British expedition to Jaonli (6632m) failed to climb the peak due to a six-day spell of heavy rain from September 20 to 25. Deep fresh snow prevented any advance beyond 5400 meters on the normal Northwest Flank route. The team also had considerable difficulty in reaching Base Camp up the Lod Gad Valley. The route had not been visited for two years and has been abandoned by local shepherds. The Bhagirathi River was crossed by a wire bridge three kilometers north of Dabrani, then a difficult crossing was made of the Lod Gad side stream. From there, the first six kilometers of the route up the south bank of the Lod Gad was badly overgrown and took three days. For compensation, the team climbed three 5000-meter peaks on the south side of the Jaonli Glacier: Pt. 5447m by its northeast face (PD), Pt. 5349m by its north ridge (PD), and an unnamed peak two kilometers west of Pt. 5447, which was climbed by its west face and traversed (AD). This summit was reckoned to be ca. 5480 meters, making it the highest in this attractive group of training peaks. The name Trimulti has been suggested.

Three members also crossed a new col linking the Jaonli and Din Gad valleys at 5120 meters to the west of Pt. 5447. The route then crossed a small glacier at the head of the Kola

Gad to gain a broad saddle at 4800 meters on the Din Gad watershed. The grade of the traverse was PD+.

MARTIN MORAN, *Alpine Climbing Group*


WESTERN GARHWAL

*Banderpunch West, Ascent.* An Institute of Climbers and Explorers expedition led by Sudipta Mitra made an ascent of Banderpunch West (6302m) in September. The team reached Base Camp on August 31. Camps were placed as follows: CI at 5210 meters; CII at 5640 meters; and CIII at 5640 meters. The summit was reached by Taruneshwar Sinha, Ranjit Das and HAP Himalaya, and Gopi Chand Rawat on September 4.

HARISH KAPADIA, *Honorary Editor, The Himalayan Journal*


*Trisul I, West Face.* In August and September, a Korean expedition led by Yeon Soo Park made an ascent of Trisul I (7120m) via the seldom-climbed 1976 Yugoslavian West Face route. Two members, Hyung Yull Kim and Jong Young Park, reached the summit on August 29. Camp I was established at 5200 meters, Camp II at 5900 meters, Camp III at 6300 meters and the summit camp at 6500 meters.

HARISH KAPADIA, *Honorary Editor, The Himalayan Journal*


*Trisul I, Attempt.* Three years after a previous attempt, Iñaki Ruiz, Jesus Gómez and I returned to try Trisul I again. Our climbing style was simple: alpine-style, no fixed ropes, three high camps and two altitude tents for those three camps.

We arrived in Delhi on September 1, and reached Ghat on September 14. On September 19, we arrived at Sutol. After two rainy days, we pitched CI at 5000 meters, then returned to BC on September 22. After four more days of bad weather, we climbed up to CI on September 27. The next day we crossed the glacier through deep snow and after six hours we arrived at CII (5800m), 100 meters below the col. On October 2, we started for the final push from CI. On October 3, we reached CII in deep snow. The next day we climbed eight pitches (45-55°) from the col up to CIII (6300m). We set up camp in a narrow crevasse. The expedition was then called off due to bad weather.

On October 12 we departed for Ghat with 13 porters, arriving there two days later.

EDUARDO GÓMEZ TELLETXEA, *Basque Country, Spain*


*Changabang, North Face, The Lightning Route.* Carlos Buhler (U.S.) led a five-member team, four of whom (Andrei Volkov, Andrei Marei, Ivan Dusharin, Pavel Chabaline) were Russian, on a capsule-style ascent of the direct north face of the 6864-meter Changabang in the Indian Garhwal Himalaya between April 13 and June 6. The team spent 20 days working on the 1700-meter face, using eight 50-meter 9- and 10-mm static ropes and three dynamic 10-mm lead ropes. They spent four days fixing ten pitches of snow and ice slopes, ice-filled corners and steep ice-covered slabs, then moved onto the wall for 16 days, summiting on May 29 and returning to ABC late on the evening of May 31. On the wall proper, they climbed "Russian-style," with each member of the team taking one task (leading, belaying, hauling, etc.) for the duration of the climb. They called their climb, the line of which resembles a jagged bolt of lightning, the *Lightning Route*. An account of their climb appears earlier in this journal.

HIMACHAL PRADESH

*Leo Pargial, Ascent, and Medical Work.* Leo Pargial (6791m) in Hangrang (North Kinnaur) was first climbed on August 10, 1933, by a British team led by Marco Pallis via the west ridge. The first Indian ascent, led by D. K. Khullar, was also made via the west ridge on June 19, 1967. In June, 1998, it was climbed for the eighth time by a ten-member team from Calcutta 26 led by Milan Nag (leader) and Shyamal Sarkar (climbing leader).

An eight-member medical group accompanied them. Seven of them set up an eye camp at Rekong Peo, the headquarters of Kinnaur district, 220 kilometers north of Shimla. The camp ran from June 9-23 and treated 175 cases, of which ten were IOL operations.

HARISH KAPADIA, *Honorary Editor, The Himalayan Journal*

*Leo Pargial and Other Peaks, Various Ascents.* We (Arun Samant, leader; Aloke Surin, Anil Chavan and Ravi Wadaskar) went to the Chango Valley of the Kinnaur District in the Himachal Pradesh during July and August to attempt Leo Pargial (6791m), the third-highest peak of Himachal Pradesh, and other peaks encircling the Chango Glacier. We were established at Base Camp July 9. The unclimbed peak (6484m) seen prominently as one looks up from Base Camp lies close to Leo Pargial on the ridge above the right bank of the glacier. Ravi Wadaskar and Ramgopal Negi climbed the southwest face of the peak. A traverse led them to the steep, loose, rocky south ridge, which was followed to the summit. The summit, composed of an eight-meter boulder, was reached at 11 a.m. The descent to the summit camp required three hours. Anil and I then climbed Leo Pargial via the normal route, making a small variation to reach the West Col.

Ningmari (6173m) rises from the left bank of the glacier south of Base Camp. We attempted it, but the sun on the face made it a dangerous proposition in the afternoon and we had no alternative but to climb down immediately.

Aloke and Ravi were keen to attempt a few more peaks around Base Camp while some us returned to Chango. On July 28, Ravi and Aloke ferried loads toward a 6228-meter peak. Two days later, Chokdup, Ramgopal, Ravi and Aloke moved up to camp at 5700 meters. On August 1, they were up early for the summit attempt and soloed steep ice by headlamp, then worked their way up the icy northwest face. Finally they reached the summit ridge and proceeded to plod up to the snow summit. Wishing to leave nothing in doubt, they trudged across to the rocky summit at 11:15 a.m., which turned out to be slightly higher.

Team members also attempted Ningmari (6173m) and another unnamed peak (5900m). Three members of the team visited Ninjeri Col (6120m). After shifting to a new area opposite Rekong Peo, Khanej Peak on the Raldang Ridge was climbed by three members, who later crossed the Khanej Pass and descended to Sangla in the Baspa Valley.

ARUN SAMANT, *The Climbers, Mumbai, India*

LAHAUL

*Gephang Goh, Attempt.* A British expedition led by Ian Ford attempted Gephang Goh (5870m) in the Lahaul area in July-August, reaching 5500 meters. Progress was too slow due to difficult/dangerous crevasses.

HARISH KAPADIA, *Honorary Editor, The Himalayan Journal*

*Unnamed Peak, First Ascent.* A Polish expedition led by Andrej Zboinski made the first ascent of an unnamed 6130-meter peak in the Lahaul area in August-September. Two members, Richard Wrona and Kristofer Gardyna, reached the summit on August 21 via the northwest ridge.

HARISH KAPADIA, *Honorary Editor, The Himalayan Journal*

*Stok and Dhampu Peaks, Various Ascents.* It was reported that Alberto Urtasun and Patricia Viscarret made the first ascent of the northeast face of a peak they dubbed "Dhampu Peak" (5150m) in the Lahaul Valley via the route *Marsa* (30-80°, 400m). The team then climbed *The Tibetan Dream* (60-70°, 380m) on the north face of the Stok massif. (*Desnivel* 144)

LADAKH-RUPSHU

*Thugje, First Ascent.* A Chukyo Alpine Club (CAC) mountaineering party from Nagoya, Japan, made the first ascent of Thugje (6148m) in Rupshu, Ladakh, on August 14 and 15. Thugje is located northwest of Tso Moriri Lake in Rupshu in Ladakh. The average age of the 11 Japanese climbing members was 58. Base Camp (4600m) was established on August 8 on the right bank of a small stream, Pologongka Phu, about five kilometers west of Pologongka Pass (4940m). All luggage and foods were transported by vehicles up to the Base Camp from New Delhi via Leh, Upsi, Chumatang, Mahe and Sumdo.

Reconnaissance of the route to CI (5400m) was carried out through the southern slope of the main ridge, and CI was established on a moraine from the main ridge near a small stream. BC to CI was about four hours without gear. From C1, the route to the main ridge was via a huge rock slope (ca. 40-60°). About 100 meters of rope were fixed on the final part of the route to the main ridge. From the end of the fixed rope to the summit of Thugje, the climbing route followed a snow and rock ridge. Fortunately, it was not so steep and not so long. On August 14, at 11:45 a.m., six Japanese (Akira Ito, Masayuki Muto, Katsumi Hishidda, Tsutomu Nomura, Norio Hamada and Masato Oki), three Indians (the LO, Sorab Gandhi, and Guide Arun Roy Chowdhury), and two High-Altitude Porters (Lakpa Sanghe and Passang Tenzing) reached the summit. On August 15, four Japanese (Genichi Ozaki, Soji Harada, Susumu Takeda and Norio Hamada for a second time), A.R. Chowdhury (also for a second time) and two High-Altitude Porters climbed Thugje from CI by the same route.

On August 18, all luggage, unconsumed food and garbage was carried down from CI to BC. On August 21, all members started the return journey. During the climbing period, ten trekking members had enjoyed trekking around Leh, Tso Moriri Lake (4300m) and BC.

PROF. MASATO OKI, *Chukyo Alpine Club, Japan*

*Mentok I, Third Ascent.* A Japanese expedition led by Susumu Sasaki made the third ascent of Mentok I (6340m). S. Sasaki, M. Kimura, W. Ueno, and Sherpa Palden reached the summit via the east ridge on August 12.

HARISH KAPADIA, *Honorary Editor, The Himalayan Journal*

*Siachen Glacier, Exploration.* We (Harish Kapadia, leader; Vijay Kothari, Cyrus Shroff, Divyesh Muni, Vineeta Muni; Kaivan Mistry; and Captain Ashish Suhag, liaison officer) applied to climb on the Siachen Glacier in 1998. Permits were granted six months later. On July 3, with eight sherpas as support, we slowly moved up the glacier, using three camps over the next seven days. After the third day, we could see several groups of peaks in the northeast, including Afraj (6815m), and the massive Singhi Kangri (7702m), which justified its name (Singhi = difficult). To our immediate east rose the peaks at the edge of the Teram Shehr Plateau. Bullock-Workman had named one of the peaks Laxmi (wife of Vishnu and goddess of wealth). As Lord Vishnu is God of preservation, we chose to give the names of Vishnu to some of the peaks on the Teram Shehr Plateau. The name Teram Shehr is based on a Balti legend and means "destroyed city." We called the highest peak on the plateau Padmanabh (7030m). It is hoped that Vishnu will protect and prevent any further destruction.

A team was to reach Col Italia at the head of the Teram Shehr Glacier, but the prevailing war did not make it feasible to cross the glacier. Throughout our stay we were always aware that we were in a war zone. There were daily artillery firings across and above our route, helicopters were flying and we met soldiers on their way down, tired and haggard. It is a very different playground for the mountaineer.

After four further camps, we neared the head of the glacier. The stupendous walls of Sia Kangri I (7422m) and II (7092m) (formerly known as Hardinge) threatened avalanches, and all camps were placed carefully away from them. Our last camp on the glacier was a little above Bullock and Workman's 1912 "Ridge Camp." Turkestan La (East, 5810m) lay at the head of an eastern valley. On July 20, four of us plus a LO and sherpa left camp by 6:30 a.m. Winding our way through crevasses and up a gentle valley, we were at the la overlooking the Staghar Glacier in two hours. A deep notch in the ridge could be seen to the north. This was the Turkestan La (North) Col, the foot of which was reached by Francis Younghusband in 1889.

On July 22, we started at 6:30 a.m. and walked northward. After passing Faiz (6150m) ("one who is at the top"), a wide bowl opened in front of us. We were faced with the Indira Ridge and a vast panorama. To the north was the main Indira Col (West). After a walk of about two hours, Sherpa Pemba Tsering and I were at the pass and could look down the Urdok Glacier, which led northward to join the Shaksgam River. Several peaks were visible, though Gasherbrum I was unfortunately in clouds. To the north was Chinese Turkestan. We were standing on a major geographical as well as a political divide.

Another part of our team, Vijay Kothari, Kaivan Mistry, Vineeta Muni and Capt. Suhag, climbed toward the India Saddle. After a steep slope, they stood on the northern-most point of India and enjoyed similar historic moments. We all gathered at the camp by afternoon.

It had taken us 98 kilometers and 20 days to reach the Indira Col. The glacier rose from 3550 to 5840 meters over a distance of 72 kilometers. Our party returned to the base of the glacier eight days later. The climbing team had already left for Leh.

HARISH KAPADIA, *Honorary Editor, The Himalayan Journal*

*Bhujang, First Ascent.* When the main team of the Indian Siachen Glacier Expedition left for the Indira Col (see above), we descended to CIII to attempt a 6560-meter peak. From July 10 to 14, we established a Base Camp on the eastern bank of the main Siachen Glacier. On July 15, we climbed steeply over loose scree and mud slopes to the steep ridge coming down from the peak, reaching a suitable site for a camp at ca. 5570 meters.

From July 15 to 19, we had to wait as the weather was poor. Sherpas ferried loads one day and on the 18th we two also moved up. But again a day of poor weather intervened. On July 20, we started early and moved fast up the mountain. Cyrus Shroff and I front-pointed up the initial 500 meters of the climb to the point where the ropes and equipment had been left earlier. The sherpas moved up the rock route along the ridge. From this point we studied the route ahead and found a safe passage to traverse onto the col. The route from the col to the top was an easy-angled climb over snow with a few patches of ice in between. We were at the summit by 11:30 a.m. We started down by 12:15 p.m. On the return, we took a long time, carefully making our way down the loose rocky ridge back to the summit camp. We reached the camp by 4 p.m. with all our ropes and equipment. Two lengths of fixed ropes had to be left behind on the mountain.

This was the first ascent on the Siachen Glacier, and the first peak climbed on the Teram Shehr Plateau. As this peak rose like a serpent, we decided to christen it Bhujang, the legendary serpent associated with Lord Vishnu.

We moved down the mountain and reached the foot of the Siachen Glacier by July 24 and traveled to Leh. While waiting for the others to return, we climbed the ever-popular Stok Kangri on July 29.

DIVYESH MUNI, *India*

# NEPAL

*Changla, First Ascent.* In the autumn, the west summit of Changla in northwestern Nepal on the border with Tibet was successfully scaled for the first time. Changla had been attempted only once before, 15 years ago, by Japanese, who are believed to have tried to reach the south summit. Now a team of four Japanese and two Nepalese Sherpas (Satoshi Kimoto, Mamoru Taniguchi, Tamotsu Onishi, Ang Phurba Sherpa, and Chuldim Sherpa) climbed the north ridge to the west ridge to the top of Changla West Peak, which the climbing leader, Tamotsu Onishi, estimated was about 6150 meters high. It was an easy climb technically, he reported, but they had to use 550 meters of rope on soft snow that was about 30 centimeters deep. They had first tried to go to the main summit by its west face, but managed to get no higher than 5050 meters before they encountered a badly broken icefall they had no desire to climb.

ELIZABETH HAWLEY

*Saipal East, Attempt.* Bruno Baumann, a professional adventurer and writer who lives in Munich but is an Austrian citizen, gave up his hope of making the first ascent of a peak that he has decided isn't actually there. The peak is listed by Nepal's tourism ministry, which gives climbing permits, as Saipal East (6882m). He said before going to the far west of Nepal to make an historic climb that he had no information about this peak, but said he intended to make an attempt via its north face, if it had one. However when he got to Mt. Saipal, he was unable to find any eastern summit at all and concluded that it does not exist. Baumann writes, "At least we got on the foot of the mighty south face of Saipal, which I think has not been climbed yet. It's a fantastic amphitheater where the wall rises up with 3000 meters of vertical ice and rock. From my point of view it will be quite a tough task to climb it. I did some reconnaissance there, climbing up to 5500 meters. The wall rises from 4000 meters to the main summit, which is a little more than 7000 meters high. The valley is so isolated that it is one of the last paradises for rare wildlife, like snow leopards, bears (both kind of the big Himalayan bears) and blue sheep."

ELIZABETH HAWLEY

*Annapurna IV, Southwest Pillar, Attempt.* The Czech Mountaineering Federation and Sport Club—Mt. Blanc (Prague) set out in September for Annapurna IV. The expedition comprised climbers from the Czech Republic (Jiří Novak, leader; Martin Otta, substitute leader; Radek Lienert, Zdeněk Michalec, Václav Pátek, Tomáš Rinn and Ivo Wondráček) and from Slovakia (Ivan Krajčír and Henryk Zajac, doctor). Our expedition chose as its aim the pillar on the southwest face, which we accessed from the Seti Khola Valley. We experienced exploratory challenges similar to those faced by the first expeditions to enter Nepal in the 1950s. Our advance was complicated by unfavorable weather. Six days into the approach, with the passage of the 4500-meter saddle beneath Machapuchare and the following 1000-meter descent, the majority of the porters left us. Though we wanted to approach directly beneath Annapurna IV, we were caught in a blind valley at the very far end of the main valley. It was cloudy when we crossed the saddle, so we couldn't see what the upper part of the valley looked like and therefore didn't know how to get beneath the face. We had to detour via a glacier that wound beneath Annapurna III. It took us two more days to find a place to establish Base Camp (4700m). In that time we got acquainted with the quality of rock, which is catastrophically fractured. Because of the delays and the fractured rock, we realized that it wouldn't be possible to make an ascent via the pillar. After reaching an agreement with our liaison officer, we changed our goal to the southwest face and west ridge. After establishing CI on October 2 at 5500 meters, about 100 to 200 meters of the sharp west ridge was fixed due to many cornices. On October 14 and 15, two teams began their attempt at climbing the west ridge alpine-style to the top in three or four days. On October 15, Michalec, Otta, and Lienert reached 6200 meters. The next day the weather was worse. Lienert descended; the others waited to see what the weather would do, as did the second group (Krajčír, Patek) at a lower bivouac (6100m). Meanwhile, 50 centimeters of snow fell and all four decided to descend on October 17. On October 18 and 19, descent was made to 3500 meters, where the porters were gathering. An exacting march to Pokhara was made in three days.

JIŘÍ NOVAK, Czech Mountaineering Federation

*Dhaulagiri I, Attempt and Tragedy.* Chantal Mauduit and the Sherpa she often climbed with, one of several men named Ang Tshering (not a summiter of any 8000-meter mountain), were found lying in their second high-altitude camp at 6550 meters on Dhaulagiri I by Italians.

RIGHT: *Annapurna IV (pointy summit at left) and II (rounder summit at right). A is the southwest pillar; B is the west ridge.* JIŘÍ NOVAK

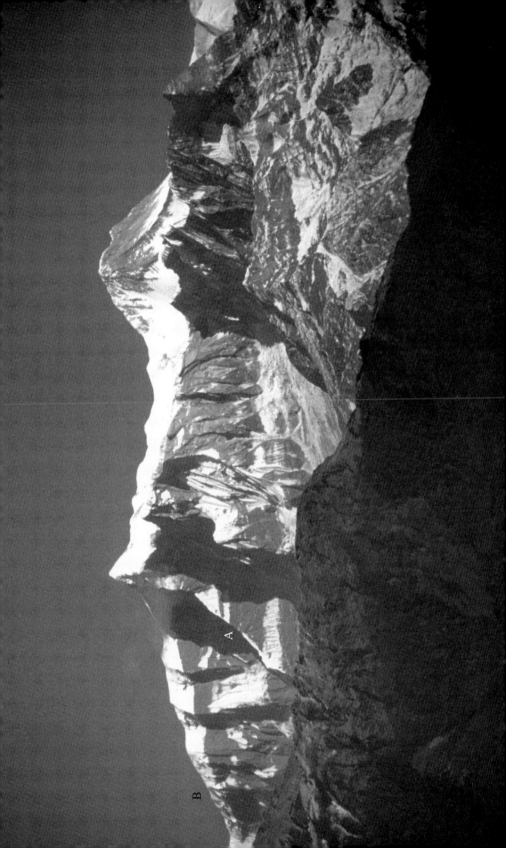

Miss Mauduit preferred to climb independently from other foreigners. She and Ang Tshering, a team of just two, went up to CII on May 7 at a time when others on the mountain didn't like the looks of the weather conditions and had already gone down to BC or did so the next day. The two remained there during the following days of snowfall and winds. She had already been as high as 7000 meters, where she had pitched her third high camp on about April 22 and from where a week later she had wanted to go for the 8167-meter summit, but strong winds had held her back.

Mauduit and Ang Tshering apparently never left CII. They arrived there at 4 p.m. on the 7th, a windy and snowy day; snow fell all that night, and next day it was very windy. Two Italians who were in their own CII slightly below descended to Base Camp that next day, leaving no one else in any other tents there. Other Dhaulagiri expeditions—there were also Spaniards, Slovenians, and a three-man team of New Zealand, American and Finnish climbers, as well as the Italians—never saw them move out of their camp, which had been pitched about 50 meters above those of the other teams.

Camp II was revisited by Italians on May 14, and one of them, Franco Brunello, went up to Mauduit's tent and found it almost entirely covered by the recent snowfall—not by avalanche debris, he said—with snow and pieces of ice pressing against one side of it. Brunello opened its zipper a little and found no sign of life. The next day his teammate, Celestino Toldo, took a shovel up to the tent and removed the snow so that he could open the zipper wider. He discovered two sleeping bags with bodies inside them.

Mauduit's expression was peaceful, but her jaw appeared to him to have been broken by a piece of ice on the outside of the tent. Brunello thinks that she was killed by ice striking her head and that she must have died "in a moment." But her jaw could have been broken after her death, and it is not clear to Brunello why Ang Tshering died, although he supposes the Sherpa suffocated. Indeed, both may have died of suffocation. However, her family in France, to where her body was flown from Nepal, are reported to have stated that vertebrae in her neck were broken, probably by the weight of the snow; they believe an avalanche jumped over a rock band, part of it crashed onto her tent, and this killed her.

ELIZABETH HAWLEY

*Dhaulagiri I, Northeast Ridge.* From April 12 to June 10, 14 members of the Slovenian Alpine Club (Tone Škarja, leader; Dr. Damijan Meško, Viktor Grošelj, Tadej Golob, Tomaž Jakofčič, Dušan Polenik, Rafael Vodišek, Davorin Karničar, Miha Marenče, Janko Meglič, Gregor Lačen, Andrej Markovič, Peter Mežnar, Blaž Stres) traveled to Dhaulagiri I (8167m). The chief goal of the expedition was to acquaint promising young Slovenian climbers with conditions at and above 8000 meters, and with the logistics of organizing a Himalayan expedition. The team was on the mountain from April 28 to May 27. On May 16, Italians climbers found Chantal Mauduit and a Sherpa at CII (6600m), who, with their tent buried in snow, had obviously died of suffocation. Seven of our climbers reached the summit: Gregor Lačen and Miha Marenče, on May 23; Tomaž Jakofčič and Peter Mežnar, on May 24; and Janko Meglič, Tadej Golob and Dušan Polenik, on May 26. As none of the seven had previously been higher than 7000 meters, the chief aim of the expedition is believed to have been reached.

TONE ŠKARJA, *Planinska zveza Slovenije*

*Manaslu, Northwest Face, Attempt.* On the great 8163-meter Manaslu, where six expeditions struggled unsuccessfully to scale the standard Northeast Face route this autumn, one pair of innovative Japanese mountaineers made the first attempt on its northwest face. After having spent nine days cutting through bamboo forest and constructing two small bridges to reach Base Camp, Yasushi Yamanoi and his wife Taeko were just at the early stage of their climb and had moved up the face to an altitude of 6200 meters with two bivouacs, when, on September 15, a large serac broke off above them and sent them rolling 100 meters down into deep snow, injuring both. "This route is dangerous," Yasushi Yamanoi said succinctly later. "There are many seracs. Maybe this route is not logical." They have no intention of returning to this face, despite the fact that it was not technically difficult.

ELIZABETH HAWLEY

*"Bhrikuti," Ascent.* Identifying mountains in remote parts of Nepal is not always easy, as a Spanish post-monsoon expedition to Bhrikuti (6364m) in north-central Nepal learned. The few maps of the area that exist have many mistakes, and the local people whom the Spaniards asked about Bhrikuti pointed to different peaks. So Jesus Gonzalez and his three teammates, Jose Alonso, Manuel Caballero, and Alvaro Roldan, climbed one of these mountains, all of which were about 6300 meters high, on October 17 via the northeast face, though they now wonder whether they actually scaled an unnamed virgin peak instead.

ELIZABETH HAWLEY

*Gyachung Kang, Attempts.* Two teams went to the 7952-meter Gyachung Kang, which stands on the Nepalese-Tibetan border between Cho Oyu and Everest, this autumn. It is very seldom attempted by climbers—probably partly because it is nearly 8000 meters high, but also because it is steep and difficult—and only three expeditions have ever gained the summit, all of them from its western slopes. This autumn's attempts by two parties of three Japanese and six Poles were made from the southeast, and they got no higher than 7000 meters. Like so many expeditions on the very high mountains in the post-monsoon, both were defeated by deep snow.

The Japanese, led by Takashi Shiro, aimed to go to the summit via the southeast ridge, but they stopped at 6700 meters, 100 meters below their final ridge, on October 11 while they were on a snow face of the south ridge, because they had run out of pickets. The Poles, under the leadership of Ludwik Wilczynski, managed to reach 7000 meters on a southeast pillar on October 3. They had climbed mostly at night because of the avalanching that warm daytime hours brought. But deep soft snow forced two members to spend 15 hours slowly plowing through it one day, and they were hit—but luckily not injured—by an avalanche. Their climb was abandoned after an important tent was covered by snow.

ELIZABETH HAWLEY

*All 14 8000-Meter Summits.* There were successes for three men approaching their goal of summiting all 14 8000-meter mountains, Fausto De Stefani and Hans Kammerlander of Italy on Kangchenjunga, and a Spanish Basque, Juanito Oiarzabal, on Dhaulagiri I.

Juanito Oiarzabal, a stickler for veracity amongst mountaineers who has blown the whistle on some errant ones, had a problem about the top of Dhaulagiri (8167m). On May 2, he came to an upright aluminium pole on the normal Northeast Ridge route very high on the mountain. He had been told that this point was considered to be the summit and that numerous earlier climbers had claimed success on the basis of having reached it.

But for him this was not the true summit but about 50 meters lower; one can see more peaks, including the true top, beyond it, he says. He made another summit push, but was turned back by high winds. Only on May 22 did he get beyond the pole's area by a different line above 8100 meters and satisfy himself that he had really summited Dhaulagiri I. He has now "conquered" his 12th 8000er without bottled oxygen. With him to the top on the 22nd went two Basque brothers, Alberto and Felix Iñurrategi, who have climbed all their 8000ers together (and also without bottled oxygen) and for whom Dhaulagiri was their ninth success.

An Italian who is getting close to summiting all the 8000ers is Hans Kammerlander. He was on Kangchenjunga this season and gained the summit of the 8586-meter giant on May 18 without artificial oxygen via the standard Southwest Face route with his teammate, Konrad Auer. But he said on his return to Kathmandu that he was not happy with this success, for the three weeks he spent on the mountain with three fixed camps along the route "is not my style. This is too slow." His toes became frostbitten while he waited for his companion to ascend his own first 8000er; "this [frostbite] is too high a price for a normal route." Now he was not able to go immediately to Manaslu, as he had planned, but had to have his toes cared for and wait until 1999 to scale this 8000er, when he hopes to climb K2 as well. That, he figures, will complete his "conquest" of all the 8000ers, although he has not reached the very highest peak of Shishapangma.

Fausto De Stefani, 46, now claims to have "conquered" all the 8000ers with his ascent of Kangchenjunga on May 15, despite the statement last autumn by his teammate on Lhotse that they did not actually reach that summit although they were "very, very near" it.

ELIZABETH HAWLEY

*Activity on the Nepalese 8000-ers in the Post-Monsoon.* This was a poor season on Nepal's 8000ers, even though all except one expedition attempted well-trodden routes. Seven expeditions went to Manaslu, four to Makalu, one each to Annapurna I and Kangchenjunga, and not one of them reached their summits. On Dhaulagiri I, there were seven teams and only one summited; nine teams went to Everest, but only two had success. On Lhotse's main summit Tibetans were the only climbers, and they did succeed. A Russian team put four members on the summit of Lhotse Shar. So only five of the 21 expeditions that attempted to scale any peaks over 8000 meters within Nepal's boundaries were successful; that made an 84% failure rate, which is unprecedented in recent years. Autumn seasons normally see less success on the 8000ers than springs, but not nearly this much less.

On Nepal's only other 8000er, Cho Oyu, there were no attempts from the Nepalese side but on the standard route from Tibet's side, there was striking success in notable contrast to the experience of teams on the 8000ers south of the border. Of the 22 Cho Oyu teams on what is probably the least difficult route on any 8000er, 19 put a total of 61 climbers on the top, 47 of them on just four days, the 24th, 26th and 27th of September and the 11th of October.

ELIZABETH HAWLEY

*Mount Everest, Activity in the Pre-Monsoon Season.* The pre-monsoon season saw more people reach the top of Everest than ever before in a single season, and the total number of ascents ever made has now passed the 1,000 mark. Altogether 118 people managed to get to the summit this spring, 73 from Tibet and 45 from Nepal. (Only two of them were women, Francys Arsentiev and an Uzbekistani, Mrs. Sventlana Baskakova, both from the north side.) It took 29 years for the first 118 summiters to get to the top. Now this spring the same number summited in just ten days, from May 18 to 27.

This spring's total is in striking contrast to no one at all atop Everest last autumn, and indeed is in notable contrast to the largest number of summiters in any previous season, 87 in the spring of 1993. It is clear that the terrible storm of the spring of 1996 did not drive people away from going for the summit of Everest.

This spring's 118 summiters included the first Native American (American Indian), Bernardo Guarachi, a tough 45-year-old Bolivia adventure travel agent from La Paz; the first amputee, Tom Whittaker, a British-born American from Prescott, Arizona; and the first Iranian ascent of the mountain. More than one-quarter of the summiters (34) had been there before. Most of these repeaters were Sherpas, but they also included two Russians, Serguei Arsentiev in his second ascent and Evgueni Vinogradski in his third; one New Zealander, Russell Brice, in his second ascent; and three Americans, Wally Berg in his fourth, Robert Sloezen in his third, and Jeffery Rhoads, who made his second trip to the top only a week after his first one, both times with a Sherpa named Tashi Tshering. So there is another record: one person, Babu Tshering Sherpa, had summited Everest twice before in the same season, but his two ascents in May 1995 were 12 days apart.

The net result of all these successes is that the total number of people who have ever gained Everest's summit now stands at 808 (43 of them women), and the total number of ascents they have made has reached 1,048. Furthermore, these numbers could have been even greater if more than 50 climbers who collected at the south summit on May 19 hadn't turned back because no rope had yet been fixed beyond that point; some of them returned later and got all the way to the top, but a number of them did not.

The mountain seems to be attracting older climbers in greater numbers. One Japanese group, the 1998 Showa Alpine Club Qomolangma Expedition led by Hitoshi Onondera, had a Young Men's Team and an Old Men's Team. All of the four "old men" were 60 to 64 years old; none reached the summit, but Masayasu Taruki, 64, is believed to be the oldest person ever to gain an altitude of at least 8,300 meters. (The oldest person to succeed in getting all the way to the top was a 60-year-old Spaniard living in Venezuela, Ramon Blanco, who summited in October, 1993.)

ELIZABETH HAWLEY

*Mt. Everest, North Ridge, Ascent and Tragedy.* On May 17, the husband-and-wife team of Serguei Arsentiev and Francys Distefano-Arsentiev started from ABC to the North Col with members of their Russian expedition. On May 18, Serguei, Francys and Boris Slepikovsky ascended to 7700 meters. On the 19th, Serguei and Francys ascended to 8200 meters. On May 20, they made an attempt to climb to the top, but turned back at the First Step (ca. 8600m). Anatoli Moshnikov, a member of their team, saw them from 8200 meters at about 3 p.m. descending from the ridge. When Serguei reached the couple's tent, he went to Moshnikov's tent and explained to him that because of dead headlamp batteries, they had started at 6:30 a.m., but that they would try again tomorrow. Moshnikov gave him an extra battery and offered to come with them. On May 21, Serguei and Francys tried to go up again but only managed 50-100 meters before returning to the tents.

Moshnikov returned from the summit at about 6 p.m. Serguei congratulated him on his success and again complained of dead batteries. Moshnikov tried to persuade Serguei to descend, but Serguei declined, telling him that they were fine.

On May 22, Serguei and Francys departed, perhaps as early as 2 or 3 a.m. Rustam Radgapov (a member of the Uzbekistan expedition) passed them on the steep snow slope below the summit ridge (8750 - 8800m) at about 3:30 or 4 p.m. Francys's pace was slow; she sat down very often. Radgapov was on the top at 4:45. About 5:45 p.m., on his descent, Radgapov met Serguei and Francys on the gentle slope near the rocks 100 meters from the top. Francys's pace was slower. Radgapov went with them for about 50 meters back toward the top, trying to persuade them to turn around because it was quite late. Serguei told him not to worry, that they felt good and had a cache down below between the First and Second Steps that included a bottle of oxygen, a tent and some warm clothing. Radgapov saw the cache at about 8630 meters on his descent, but though it included the bottle of oxygen, the backpack was otherwise nearly empty. Later the tent was found at 7700 meters.

Radgapov descended to 8200 meters at 8:30 p.m. The last time he saw them was at the Second Step (8750m) at 7:30 p.m. on their descent. It is assumed Serguei and Francys were on top at 6:15 p.m. They apparently descended to their cache at 8630 meters, where they spent the night without a tent.

On May 23, Oleg Grigoriev, Andrei Fedorov, Serguei Sokolov, Svetlana Baskakova and Marat Usaev, members of the Uzbekistan expedition, started up from 8200 meters at 6 a.m. They had ten bottles of oxygen with them. At about 9:35 a.m. at 8450 meters, they met Serguei, who asked them: "Where is my wife? Did she not come down?" They answered in the negative. Serguei started to descend to the tents without saying anything, and they continued their ascent.

At 10:40 a.m. the Uzbekistan climbers came to Francys above the First Step. She was half-conscious and leaned against the rock. There was no harness on her; the protection cord was clipped to the jacket zipper. After medical consultation with the doctors of the Czech and Slovak expeditions, they gave her a few tablets of trental and oxygen at four liters per minute (Fedorov gave her his mask), but she tore the mask off, mumbling something. Her feet were out of order, so she could not descend by herself. The examination results: dilated pupils, fixed look, frozen fingers. They made her sit down and massaged her legs and hands. At 11:40 a.m., Grigoriev decided that Sokolov, Baskakova and Usaev would continue the attempt, while he and Fedorov stayed with Francys. At 1 p.m., Fedorov also continued his attempt, leaving his mask and oxygen to Francys. Grigoriev went up for the summit at 1:30 p.m. Before going away, he secured Fedorov's oxygen mask to Francys and fixed her to the rope. One hundred meters higher, at 8630 meters, he found their cache, which included the empty sack, an empty oxygen bottle, a mask with regulator, a headlamp and water bottle. He took the mask and regulator for Fedorov. He found Francys's harness below the Second Step. Grigoriev passed Fedorov above the Second Step, gave him his half-used oxygen bottle and the mask with regulator that he had found at 8630 meters. When he met the three descending Uzbekistan climbers, he arranged that Usaev would give his half-used bottle to Fedorov. All three climbers were already using their second oxygen bottle.

Sokolov, Baskakova and Usaev were on the top at 2:30 p.m. On the descent, below the final ridge, Usaev gave his oxygen to Fedorov. Baskakova was the first to return to Francys, which she did at 3:50 p.m. She re-connected Francys's bottle with more oxygen. Sokolov, Baskakova

nd Usaev stayed with Francys until Grigoriev's return. Grigoriev was on the top at 4 p.m. At
:10, on his descent, he met Fedorov, who summited at 4:30. When Grigoriev reached Sokolov,
askakova and Usaev, he sent Sokolov and Usaev down. They descended to the tents at 8200
leters, where Sokolov told Serguei what was going on with Francys. Immediately Serguei
arted up without oxygen, but they persuaded him to take one bottle of oxygen, tea and medi-
ne with him. At 6:20 p.m., Grigoriev, with the help of Baskakova, started to bring Francys
own from the First Step. With two ropes, they managed to get her about 80 meters down and
len bring her 15 meters across to below a small rock. Fedorov descended to them at this point;
ls oxygen had finished at 8750 meters and he felt unwell. Francys started to convulse and
rigoriev sent Sokolova down. At 8:15 p.m., he fixed Fran, connected her to the last bottle of
xygen, set her gloves, hat and cowl straight and came down himself.

At 8 p.m., Grigoriev said by radio that he saw Serguei ascending. On the descent at 8:40
le two climbers met. To Serguei's question, "Is Fran here?" Grigoriev answered, "She is still
ive." Grigoriev reached the tents at 8200 meters at 11:15 p.m. Serguei did not return.

On May 24, Ilias Tukhvatullin, Andrei Zaikin and Alexei Dokukin of the Uzbekistan expe-
tion started from 8200 meters at 4:55 a.m. At 7:50 a.m., Tukhvatullin reached Francys, fol-
wed by Ian Woodall, Cathy O'Dowd, and four Sherpas from the South African expedition,
us the other members of the Uzbekistan team. Francys was still alive and connected to the
pe but could not recognize anybody. She cried repeatedly, "Help, help!" Her gloveless
inds were out of the jacket sleeves, her hat was off, her oxygen mask was off, and the oxy-
n bottle was disconnected. Serguei's ice ax and rope were 50 or 60 meters away. There was
other sign of him. The South Africans gave Francys tea and checked and massaged her
gs. They were certain that she could not move herself. Tukhvatullin offered to give her an
jection of adrenaline and even warmed the ampoule, but the South Africans declined. Then
l the South Africans, after conferring among themselves, canceled their attempt and went
wn without saying a word to the Uzbekistan climbers. Cathy O'Dowd cried.

At 9:15 a.m., after radio communication with Base Camp, the Uzbekistan climbers con-
ued up. They were overtaken by three Sherpas around half an hour later. They reached the
mmit, and, upon passing Francys at 6 p.m. on the descent, they found no signs of Serguei's
e ax. They saw jackdaws on Francys's body. Anatoli Shabanov, the leader of the Uzbekistan
pedition, told them by radio from Base Camp that the Sherpas had certified Francys's
ath, so they did not go to the body. They descended to 8200 meters at 6:30 p.m.

According to Shabanov, a Chinese communications officer in Base Camp came to him at 11
m. and told him that an American woman climber had died five minutes earlier in the hands
Sherpas. On May 29, the official report of the death of Francys Distefano-Arsentiev was sent
her family. Serguei Arsentiev is officially listed as missing, though he is presumed dead. The
-line publication RISK and The Mountaineering Federation of Russia wish to extend our con-
lences to all the friends and family of Francys Distefano-Arsentiev and Serguei Arsentiev.

THE MOUNTAINEERING FEDERATION OF RUSSIA

*erest, Scientific Expedition.* Wally Berg was on Everest with a special mission: to bolt to
drock as close as possible to the summit a GPS station from which signals can be sent to
tellites and thus reveal exactly where the summit is at any given time. This is of great inter-
t to scientists wanting to determine whether the mountain is actually drifting ever-so-slight-
to the northwest and also creeping upward.

Berg had been to the top in three previous years; he had no great ambition to stand again at the highest point on earth, but was there to do a job for the scientists. And he did it on May 20, getting his job done, and touching the top of the world once again.

ELIZABETH HAWLEY

*Everest, South Col/Southeast Ridge, Speed Ascent.* Speed ascents of Mount Everest have rarely been attempted. Now a well-known 35-year-old Sherpa named Kaji says he raced from Base Camp on the Nepalese side at 5350 meters to the South Col to the top of the world in the record-breaking time of 20 hours and 24 minutes on October 17, cutting two hours and five minutes off the previous record, which had been set ten years earlier via the same route by the French mountaineer, Marc Batard, when he was 36.

Kaji followed the same strategy Batard had pioneered by setting off from his base in the late afternoon, climbing all night except for brief stops at camps already established along the route, and making it to the summit early in the following afternoon. Batard, however, climbed the mountain without other teammates, although he employed Sherpas to help set up camps on the route, and climbers from two other teams had gone ahead of him on his summit day and made a good track that he followed to the top. Kaji, on the other hand, had five team members, two of whom accompanied him on the last leg of his ascent from the South Col at 7900 meters. Batard and his Sherpas used no artificial oxygen at any time, but two of Kaji's teammates, who climbed with him from the Col and broke trail for him, did use bottled oxygen, and he himself used it during a small part of his descent.

One of Kaji's men, Tashi Tshering Sherpa, summited a few minutes ahead of Kaji (the other had turned back at 8700 meters), and when Kaji became exhausted during their descent from the south summit and they wanted to press on with their retreat to their camp at the Col as quickly as possible, Tashi handed over his oxygen set to Kaji, who used it until they were back at camp.

ELIZABETH HAWLEY

*Everest, Ascents in the Post-Monsoon.* In addition to the summits by Kaji Sherpa and Tashi Tshering Sherpa (see above), Norichika Matsumoto led one of the few other teams who attempted Everest this season; his team failed to gain the summit via a route that diverged from the normal route Kaji had followed at about 6500 meters. A Spaniard, Carlos Pitarch who used bottled oxygen until his set froze, reported he had gone to the summit alone after others, Japanese and Sherpas, whom he was climbing with from the Col, had given up the battle against the terrible wind. These are the only Everest summit claims made this autumn. There were a total of four teams on the mountain's south side, but the others, two Japanese parties, made no such claims.

On the northern side in Tibet, there were five small teams and none of them went to the top. Deep snow in the early part of the season and very strong winds later were given as the reasons for failure by most. But a notable attempt to climb the mountain was made by one Japanese, Masafumi Todaka. He first attempted to scale the Japanese Couloir on the western side of the north face. Here he was defeated by hard ice. Then he changed the line of his ascent to the middle of the face to enter the Great (or Norton) Couloir, and here he made a valiant effort to gain the top.

Todaka had no Sherpas or artificial oxygen to help him: he was one man completely alone on the entire vast north face of Everest. He made a serious push for the summit from a camp at 5900 meters on the Rongbuk Glacier at the foot of the great face starting at 2:10 a.m. on September 14. With two bivouacs, one at the bottom of the Great Couloir that night and the next in the couloir on the 15th, he managed to surmount the couloir and reach 8500 meters on the morning October 16.

But now "my condition was not so good" because he had had no sleeping bag during the previous night, and he had become very sleepy. He spent 20 minutes considering his options and decided that he must save his remaining energy for a safe descent. "Ten years ago, I would probably have gone for the summit," said the 36-year-old mountain guide, but now he was more concerned about his safety. He descended without difficulty or frostbite, but he was very tired at the end.

ELIZABETH HAWLEY

*Lhotse Shar, Ascent.* On Lhotse Shar, the 8400-meter eastern summit of the Lhotse massif next to Everest, a team of 15 Russian climbers led by Vladimir Savkov sent four men (Alexandre Foigt, Evgueni Vinogradski, Gleb Sokolov, Sergei Timofeev) to the top on November 1. But they were forced to abandon what Vinogradski said was their "dream" of traversing from it to the middle summit of the massif. This middle peak (8410m) is the highest point on earth not yet touched by man.

The Russian team was not the first to scale Lhotse Shar with the intention of using it as a stepping stone to the middle summit, only to find when they were on the eastern summit that they were too tired and unprepared for the very difficult traverse at very high altitude, and none of them made an actual move to do so. The Russians this autumn looked at the horrifyingly difficult ridge they would have to move across and decided the better approach would be from Lhotse's main summit.

ELIZABETH HAWLEY

*Pumori, Southwest Ridge.* The Internet contributed this spring to a new type of awkward situation concerning membership of an expedition. A Swiss, Markus Sofer, saw that a Canadian team was listed for an attempt on Everest's neighbor Pumori, so he got in touch with them and signed up as a member. But when they met in Kathmandu, he announced that he would be entirely independent of them since he did not believe in expeditions. He did some climbing with the team, led by Tim Rippel, on its seldom-climbed southwest ridge, but most of the time he moved alone. He became the only one to go to the 7161-meter summit, which he reached on May 20.

ELIZABETH HAWLEY

*Ama Dablam in the Post-Monsoon.* As the season began, the Nepalese authorities expected 16 teams to come to Ama Dablam (6812m), but they continued to grant permits to everyone who asked for them, and by the time autumn ended, an all-time high number of 30 teams with a total of 201 climbers had been there from 18 nations. (The previous highest number of teams in the same season was 19 in the autumn of 1996.) Furthermore, all of this autumn's expeditions had chosen to climb the same route up the southwest ridge, which is quite narrow in some sections. At the busiest time, in mid-October, there were 17 teams at Base Camp or above. An American leader reported counting 130 tents pitched at Base Camp on one day. Some teams found themselves having to set up their base camps lower than they had planned because of the crowding. And more problems arose at times as climbers competed for space on the mountain. Queues sometimes formed at constricted spots on the ridge: a five-man Russian summit party had to wait in their descent from the top for one hour while others moved in the opposite direction (they were able reach their last camp only well after nightfall). A pair of American and Canadian climbers had to make an unexpected bivouac because of too many people on the route. Another American "got caught up in the traffic" while coming down from the summit and had to spend the night in someone else's completely empty tent while waiting for daybreak. Lack of space for camping at the site for CII at around 6000 meters forced several expeditions to skip pitching tents at that altitude and carry on somewhat higher to make their "CIII."

Many teams found their total climbing time was much shorter than they had expected since the route had been fixed with rope by the earliest expeditions from bottom to top. In fact, the multiplicity of ropes was actually a source of complaint; at one place there were nine ropes, and elsewhere "an unbelievable amount of useless rope," as one climber reported: thick ropes, thin ones, short ones, long ones, old ones and new ones, in a "mess." Nevertheless, despite the problems, the success rate was excellent. Twenty-nine teams sent a total of 160 people (including 13 women) to the summit.

On their return to Kathmandu, some leaders advised officials of the Nepalese tourism ministry, who give permission for expedition climbing, that there should be a limit on the number of permits issued for Ama Dablam in any one season. Ministry officials said they planned to seriously consider this suggestion, but there is room for doubt that the bureaucracy will actually put such a new rule into effect. Officials may intend to make recommendations to their superiors, but office-holders are changed so frequently that often nothing gets accomplished. Furthermore, ministers like to be able to reward relatives and hangers-on with money-earning posts, and since every team has to take with them and pay a government-appointed liaison officer, there is reluctance to reduce the number of these lucrative jobs.

ELIZABETH HAWLEY

*Kangtega, Northeast Face, New Route.* A seven-man French team (Erwan Le Lann, François Marsigny, Sebastien Montaz-Rosset, Francois Pallendre, Franck Plenier, Hervé Qualizza, Sebastien Schell) summited 6779-meter Kangtega in the Everest region southwest of Ama Dablam by what they believe was an unclimbed route on its northeast face. All seven members, led by Francois Pallendre, scaled their very technical route on extremely steep thin ice with two precariously placed bivouacs on the way up.

ELIZABETH HAWLEY

*Kasum Kanguru, Northwest Face.* It was reported that Yannick Graziani and Christian Tromsdörff established a new route, *Tendi*, on the northwest face of Kasum Kanguru. Further details are lacking. (*Klettern February '99*)

*Kasum Kanguru, East Face.* In April, Yasushi Yamanoi of Japan soloed a new route on the east face of Kasum Kaguru (6370m). He started from Base Camp at 4 a.m. on April 21 and

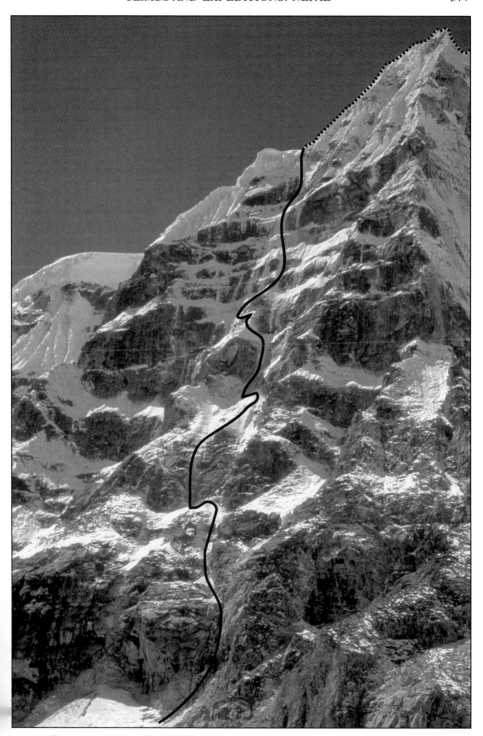

*The northeast face of Kangtega, showing the French line of ascent.* ERWAN LE LANN reached the summit 22 hours later. The first 600 meters of the route was steep rock, followed by 600 meters of steep snow. He named the route *Never-Ending Story* (VI 5.9 AI4, 1200m). A complete account of his climb appears earlier in this journal.

*Tarke Kang, Ski Descent.* A small four-member group of Czech mountaineers (Robin Baum, leader, Vladimír Smrž, Vladimir Prieložný, Josef Peterek) traveled to Tarke Kang (a.k.a. Glacier Dome, 7193m) with the goal of climbing the north face and then skiing it. They left Jomosom on September 21. After crossing Mesokantu La (5400m), they reached BC, which was placed close to a small lake near the main Tilicho Lake, three days later. They acclimatized by ferrying loads, which the mules had dropped four kilometers from BC. They established CI (5600m) near the base of the face, eight kilometers from BC.

On October 1, Baum and Smrž went to the face and set up CII at 6300 meters on a steep snow slope. Avalanche danger forced them down. When the weather improved, the second group, Prieložný and Peterek, started up the face. They couldn't find the tent, so they went on climbing.

On October 5, Baum and Smrž started up the left side of the north face. During their ascent, they watched as the second group descended on the right side of the face (the side of the first ascent). At 6300 meters, they set up the first bivouac on steep ground. The next day, they ascended ice slopes between seracs to 6700 meters. On the 8th, they advanced with skis only to the summit, which they reached at 12 o'clock. After one hour on top, they skied down toward the second bivouac. They packed their things and were at the base of the face by 3:30 p.m.

On the way to BC, they met Prieložný, who wanted to climb the right side of the north face overnight. During his ascent, he signaled every two hours with his headlamp to indicate everything was all right. At 8 a.m. he stood on the summit. For the descent, he chose a safer route to ski down and after five hours he was at the base of face and CI. On October 16, after 23 days on the mountain, the small expedition left BC.

JIří NOVAK, *Czech Republic*

GANESH HIMAL

*Paldor Peak Group, Attempts.* Sabine Krol and I were in the Ganesh Himal from February 12-March 6. Our goal was to make first ascents on mixed rock and ice faces on climbed and unclimbed peaks in the Paldor Peak group. Unfortunately, we had a lot of bad weather. We had blue sky and sun only in the mornings. By midday, clouds would arrive, and it would snow every afternoon and evening. Sometimes we had as much as one-and-a-half meters of new snow after four hours' snowfall.

We and our 12 porters needed four days for the 35-kilometer approach. After the second day, we walked in deep snow; it was very hard for the porters. Because of the bad weather, it was not possible for the porters to reach the main group of Paldor Peak (5928m). Our Base Camp was established at 4300 meters approximately three kilometers south of Paldor Peak. Near BC were some steep rock peaks between 5200 and 5400 meters high.

West of BC stands a 5250-meter rock peak with a long east ridge. A small rock pinnacle interrupts this east ridge. A 350- to 400-meter high rock pillar leads to the top of this rock pinnacle. We attempted this rock pillar on February 22, climbing 350- to 400 meters of mixed, with (sometimes friable) rock to UIAA V- and snow/ice to 50° with one section of 70°.

Approximately 50-80 meters below the summit of the rock pinnacle, we were stopped by heavy snowfall. We rappelled the route, leaving some pegs for rappelling.

Some days later, we attempted the unclimbed ca. 700-meter west ridge of a ca. 5380-meter rock peak east of Base Camp that looks like a pyramid. We reached the ridge via a small 300-meter north-facing couloir, encountering snow/ice from 50-65° and rock/mixed to IV-V. We climbed ca. 300 meters on the west ridge to a small rock pinnacle, where we were once more stopped by heavy snowfall. Difficulty on the ridge was up to V with some friable, loose rock. We tried the ridge two more times, but were stopped both times near the rock pinnacle by too much snow. We rappelled the west ridge and the north couloir, leaving some pegs behind.

After the last attempt on the west ridge, we left our Base Camp and walked back to the road in four days, then drove to Kathmandu. We removed our rubbish from the approach and BC and took it back to Kathmandu.

EDUARD BIRNBACHER, *Germany*

*Kangchenjunga, Ramtang, And Medical Research.* Base Camp was established at Pangpema at 5100 meters on the north side of Kangchenjunga. Chris Comerie and his seven-strong climbing team attempted to repeat the 1979 Boardman-Tasker-Scott route on Kangchenjunga via the North Col. They retreated from Camp IV due to persistent high winds. Research equipment (2800 kg) was flown in by helicopter to BC from Kathmandu via Ghunsa. The scientists resident at Base Camp studied 71 subjects as they passed through BC. Areas studied included: respiratory defense, migraine, changes in body weight and fat distribution, changes in lung fluid and the physiological control of breathing.

The Ramtang team shared the same Camp I as the Kangchenjunga team, which was established around October 10. We then avoided most of the icefall by scrambling up the lateral moraine to gain the upper glacier, where Camp II was pitched at 5900 meters. The serac band above Camp II was climbed more easily than anticipated. From here, it was an easy walk to the foot of the south face of Ramtang (6700m). Most of the face was threatened by a high band of seracs and a formidable cornice, so we elected to climb the shoulder leading to the eastern summit. This turned out to be an easy névé slope of around 55° (AD). Fixed ropes were put in place to safeguard descent. These were removed five days later. On reaching the eastern summit, we decided not to traverse to the main summit (which appeared only marginally higher) due to the presence of huge and dangerous double cornices.

Ascents were made as follows: October 18, Richard Weller, Ulrich Stiener, Nga Temba, Na Temba and Sange Saila Sherpa; October 19, Roger McMorrow and Nigel Hart; October 21, Sally Glynn, Simon Currin and Sange Saila Sherpa; October 22, Denzil Broadhurst, Chris Smith, Gerald Dubowitz, Nga Temba and Na Temba.

After early doubts about the difficulties and dangers of Ramtang, the route proved to be relatively easy, objectively fairly safe and most enjoyable. Ramtang is a fine vantage point for viewing the Kangchenjunga massif, and we had the great privilege of being the first team to receive a permit to climb this fine mountain.

SIMON CURRIN, *United Kingdom*

*Kangchenjunga, First Female Ascent.* My husband, Gary Pfisterer, and I led an international expedition to climb the north face of Kangchenjunga (8586m) in the spring. We were a small

team of three Americans (Gary, Chris Shaw, Tim Horvath), one Canadian (Paul Malo), and two British (Jonathan Pratt and myself). We left Kathmandu on March 21 and traveled for 20 hours to Basantapur before trekking for 13 days through a beautiful unspoiled region of Nepal to our Base Camp at Pang Pema (5000m). The team started work on the climb immediately, although Paul was forced to descend for a while due to serious altitude sickness. We climbed the Czech Route on the north face using a lightweight approach with no porters above Base Camp and no supplementary oxygen. We established fixed camps at 5800 meters and 6800 meters with a temporary acclimatization camp at 5400 meters. We dug a snow cave for Camp II at 6800 meters to avoid heavy spindrift avalanching off the Rock Band.

The main technical difficulties were the Ice Building at 6000 meters (150 meters of 40° blue ice) and the Rock Band (6800 - 7000m). We fixed both sections, but ropes on the Ice Building were frequently cut or buried by avalanche debris. The Rock Band was the crux of the climb with 50 meters of Grade 5 ice followed by rock pitches up to 5.9 in difficulty. It took five days to fix 400 meters of rope here.

Our first two summit attempts in late April and early May were thwarted by deep snow above the Rock Band (though we reached 7700m on the second attempt). It was frustrating to turn around with the summit in view, but our rate of ascent was too slow in such deep snow to realistically expect to reach the summit.

Paul returned home in early May, and the remaining five of us set out again in perfect weather on May 14. Our spirits plummeted when we arrived at Camp I to find that one tent had blown away, but we found it intact down a crevasse about 400 meters below camp. Conditions above the rock band were much improved, and we made good progress climbing alpine-style and pitching camps at 7400 meters and 7800 meters just beneath the Croissant rock.

Summit day dawned crisp and clear, and we left high camp between 4:30 and 5 a.m. We were distressed to pass the bodies of two Japanese climbers, who we later discovered had died on descent from the summit two days earlier. Conditions were good, but climbing at that altitude and the prior summit attempts had taken its toll on Gary, who was forced to turn around at 8450 meters. I continued on alone, passing Jonathan, Chris and Tim on their way down from the summit.

On the final summit ridge, I felt small and vulnerable knowing that one false move could send me hurtling down the south face. I reached the summit at 2:20 p.m. with mixed emotions: relief and elation at having finally made it, but disappointment not to be sharing this summit with Gary. Safely back at Base Camp, the reality of our success sunk in. Four of the team had reached the summit. Chris and Tim had climbed their first 8000er. Jonathan had now climbed the world's five highest mountains, and I'd made the first female ascent of Kangchenjunga, the last 8000-meter peak to be climbed by a woman.

GINETTE HARRISON, *United Kingdom*

*Jonsang, Attempt.* One of the few teams trying something innovative in Nepal last spring was the six-man Irish expedition led by Kieran O'Hara that planned to attempt the unclimbed southeast face of Jonsang, the 7483-meter summit of which forms the triple border point of

Nepal, Tibet and Sikkim. The Irish team were seriously delayed in Kathmandu due to the non-arrival of freighted gear, but finally established Base Camp during the second half of April at Pangpema next to the Kangchenjunga teams. The following two weeks were spent stocking an Advanced Camp at the start of the Ginsang Glacier and then attempting to find a safe site for CI close to the foot of the face. This proved impossible, so a site was eventually chosen at the foot of the Jongsang La which leads over into Sikkim. Hoping to climb the face in an alpine-style push, the Irish left on May 8 to acclimatize on the flanks of the 6954-meter Langpo Peak, which lies above the West Langpo Glacier southeast of the Jongsang La. They established two camps on this side of the mountain and reached an altitude of ca. 6800 meters before returning to Base Camp for a rest. On May 13, all six were at CI ready for an attempt on Jongsang the following day. At 12:30 a.m. on the 14th, Tomas Aylward, Seaghan Brogan, Garth Henry and Kieran O'Hara set off for the face with five days' food, leaving Robbie Fenlan and Malcolm McNaught to follow a day later. The four very soon found the climbing harder than anticipated and pitched sustained slopes of 55-65° on ice and mixed terrain (Scottish 3/4) for 20 hours before cutting out a bivouac site at 6500 meters. A sleepless night followed and the following morning Aylward and Brogan began to descend immediately. Henry and O'Hara continued to ca. 6600 meters but were soon engulfed in the bad weather that moved in on the 15th. They quickly realized that descent was the only realistic option. All four rappelled to the foot of the face, where they were met by the other two climbers. There was no time left for another attempt and the group could only strip their camps and return home.

LINDSAY GRIFFIN, *Alpine Climbing Group*


*Drohmo and Janak.* On April 13, a small Anglo-American-Nepalese expedition established Base Camp on the summer yak pastures of Lhonak (4650m), the site normally used for the penultimate overnight camp on the trek in to Kangchenjunga's North Side Base Camp at Pangpema. The main objective of this team was Janak (7035m), the unclimbed west summit of Jongsang, which lies on the border with Tibet. However, as a prelude the climbers wanted to make the first ascent of Drohmo (6850m), a complex mountain that stands opposite Wedge Peak overlooking the Kangchenjunga Glacier. As Jongsang is still unclimbed from Nepal, the expedition was required to have joint membership, so three climbing Sherpas made up part of the seven-man team.

After an initial period of reconnaissance and acclimatization, Julian Freeman-Attwood, Skip Novak and Doug Scott (who had initially contemplated Drohmo in 1979 while making the first ascent of the North Ridge of Kangchenjunga) established a camp on April 22 at ca. 5180 meters below the south side of Drohmo. The fourth member, Lindsay Griffin, was at this stage still at Base Camp attempting to recover from a stomach illness that had troubled him throughout the approach trek. On the 23rd, the three climbers made an inspection of the glacier below Drohmo and found that the steep south face of the mountain sported extensive serac structures, making any line leading to the main summit seriously threatened.

East of a deep notch, a sharp and corniced crest continued over a lower summit before eventually falling toward the Ginsang Glacier. With no safe route to the main (west) summit, the three decided on the central spur of the south face, which led to a point on the corniced crest well to the right of the lower (east) summit. Although just about any approach to the south face was not out of the firing line from a major avalanche or serac fall, the crest of the spur, once attained, appeared more or less safe.

On April 27, unforeseen circumstances forced Freeman-Attwood to leave the expedition. The 28th and 29th saw Griffin, Novak and Scott move up to camp on the upper glacier at ca. 5600 meters and on the next day ascend the glacier and climb five pitches of steep terrain in less than perfect condition to reach the crest of the central spur. Equipment was cached at a height of ca. 6000 meters before rappelling and descending to the glacier camp. The weather remained unsettled, and the combined effect of night-time snow fall, a reoccurrence of Griffin's illness and a general insufficient quantity of food left at the camp to await an improvement in both weather and Griffin sent the climbers down to Base. At this point, Scott decided to leave for home with his family, who had accompanied him to Base Camp, and Novak decided to go with him.

On May 4, Griffin, Novak and the three Sherpas removed all the equipment from the mountain, after which Griffin decided to remain with the Nepalese members, Nawang Karsang Sherpa, Norbu Zangbu Sherpa and Shera Zangbu Sherpa, in order to attempt the main objective. Unsettled weather kept the climbers at Base Camp till the 12th, when all four were able to move though the spectacular gorge that gives access to the lower Broken Glacier southwest of Jongsang. On the following day they established a camp at ca. 5800 meters below the upper south face of Janak. With the weather now good and everyone fit, May 14 was spent making a reconnaissance of possible lines free from objective danger. In the process of this, all four climbers made a traverse of a 6050-meter summit on the west ridge of Jongsang, which they christened The Wave. Snow conditions were found to be depressingly poor and the traverse along the unstable corniced crest more difficult than anticipated (AD+).

It snowed all day on May 15, but on the 16th the return of good weather, which marked the start of a relatively long settled spell, allowed Griffin, Nawang Karsang and Shera Zangbu to climb to a point at ca. 6250 meters on a south spur of Jongsang very close to the Long Ridge Pass. They were almost certainly the first climbers to visit both this and the upper Broken Glacier since the only previous visit by Dr. Alexander Kellas in 1910. The 1998 group, though not choosing the best route up the headwall to the Pass, climbed a short pitch of Scottish 3 (mixed). After this trial period on the hill with new companions, Griffin felt that it would be most unwise of him to continue without at least one other British climber on the team. No attempt was made on the proposed route, a committing but relatively safe mixed line of at least TD standard that led to the summit ridge of Janak, and on the 17th the climbers descended to Base Camp.

LINDSAY GRIFFIN, *Alpine Climbing Group*

*Drohmo, First Ascent.* Doug Scott and Roger Mear went to a 6855-meter mountain called Drohmo in far eastern Nepal north-northwest of Kangchenjunga. Drohmo was first attempted by Swiss in 1949, but they were unsuccessful, and few climbers have given it any notice since then till Scott had a good look last spring. Now he and Mear managed to scale the south pillar of the central summit, which Scott believes is probably the main summit. The climb up the pillar was partly on rock, which Scott said was good granite, but most of the surface was snow and ice, and he "was scared all the time" because of inadequate belay points, a condition that was "a bit unnerving." They needed three bivouacs while, with Mear leading much of the way, they struggled about 750 meters up to the top of the pillar, where they then climbed the ridge that led west to their summit. "Technically it was the hardest climb I've done since Shivling's east pillar in 1981. . . . This was a very satisfying trip." A full account of their climb appears earlier in this journal.

ELIZABETH HAWLEY

*Taple Shikhar, First Ascent.* Not far south-southwest of Drohmo is the 6341-meter mountain generally known as Cross Peak (its Nepalese name is Taple Shikhar). The mountain had been attempted only once before, by Japanese in 1963; it is not at the present time on the tourism ministry's list of peaks open to climbers. Nevertheless, a Japanese couple came to complete the effort of 35 years ago, and Mrs. Misako Miyazawa, who is not a highly experienced Himalayan climber, said she and three Nepalese (Pemba Lama, Gumba Sherpa, and Kancha Sunwar) managed to gain the summit in ten days' ascent of the south face to southeast ridge on October 8. "It was very difficult for me, but the Sherpas helped me, and thanks to them I got to the top. . . . I was very lucky—I was protected by God."

ELIZABETH HAWLEY

# PAKISTAN

*Pir Peak, Winter Ascent.* The Alpine Club of Pakistan launched its first winter mountaineering expedition to Pir Peak (6363m) in the Shimshal Valley, Hunza. The team left Rawalpindi on February 17, 1999, for a period of 20 days. This expedition, which comprised ten young climbers, was launched with a view to train young climbers in high-altitude mountaineering, especially in winter conditions. Muhammad Nasir Awan, an experienced and a very active member of Alpine Club of Pakistan, led the expedition. Accompanying him were Aman Khan, deputy leader; Muhammad Shahid Saleem, Naeem Shaukat, Umer bin Abdul Aziz, Wahab Ali Shah, Ghulam Amin, Ali Musa, Bakhatawar Shah, and Rahmat Ullah Baig.

The expedition reached Shimshal on February 21. Two more senior members were admitted to participate in the expedition: Rajab Shah, who had trained many of the young climbers, and Shambi Khan from Shimshal. Base Camp (4515m) was reached on the 23rd. The trek in was conducted through about three feet of deep snow. The weather was extremely bad due to continuous snowfall. The trail-breaking was very difficult. On the 24th, the first group (Aman Khan, Bakhtawar, Ali Musa and Shambi Khan) went in the early morning to establish CI at 4900 meters. The members cached equipment and food there and began breaking trail up to CII at 5420 meters, which took another three hours. After caching their loads, they returned to Base Camp in five hours. On the 25th, groups one and two (Umer bin Abdul Aziz, Shahid Saleem, Wahab Ali, Ghulam Amin and Rehmat Ullah Baig) started early in the morning for CII, which they reached in six hours. It was cloudy; after lunch at CII, two members from the first group and two members from the second group went for the summit, which they reached in five hours. Due to bad weather, they were not able to take proper photographs before returning to CII.

On February 26, groups one and two started climbing for the summit early in the morning in good weather. With the trail already broken, they reached the summit in four hours. After taking photos and resting on the summit, they came back to CII. After a light lunch at CII, they packed two tents and started back to BC. They left some food, equipment and one tent at CII for the third group (Muhammad Nasir Awan, Rajab Shah, and Naeeem

Shaukat). As the group started descending, an avalanche caught Rehmat Ullah Baig and Shambi Khan, who were behind the other members checking the sight of CII, and carried them down almost to BC. Luckily, the rest of the members remained safe from the avalanche. Aman Khan immediately informed BC about the accident. At BC, Muhammad Nasir Awan and Rajab Shah canceled their own program to come up at CII and rushed to rescue the injured. After ten minutes, Rehmat Ullah Baig contacted them by walkie-talkie and told them that he and Shambi Khan were OK. Nasir Awan and Rajab Shah soon reached Rehmat Ullah Baig and Shambi Khan and transported them slowly to BC. Shambi Khan was seriously injured and bleeding from his wounds. The rest of the team also reached the base safely, bringing with them the remaining equipment from CII. They took more than seven hours to descend because the avalanche had totally destroyed the climbing route. After this accident, the third group canceled their summit bid and the expedition was ended. All members of the expedition were in good health by the time they reached Islamabad on March 5.

MUHAMMAD NASIR AWAN, *Pakistan*

*Sani Pakush, Attempt.* It was reported that Andy Benson, Kenton Cool, Rich Cross and Al Powell attempted the ca. 2600-meter west buttress of Sani Pakush (6885m), the pyramidal peak north of Chalt on the watershed between the Kukuay and Batura glaciers north of Broad Peak. Three consecutive towers make up the lower section of the ridge. The team climbed and fixed the first tower in early August in 800 meters of mixed and rock climbing up to British HVS. After a return to BC in 16 rappels, the four began a continuous push on August 11, nearly getting hit by ibex-instigated rock fall en route. They ascended the second tower with one pitch of E1 5b and reached the bottom of the third tower on the third day. On the fourth day, they managed five mixed and rock pitches up to E3 5c before rockfall cut one of their ropes. Their high point of ca. 5600 meters was 400 meters short of where the buttress joins the south ridge, from where it is another 800 meters of 30° snow to the summit. *(High Mountain Sports* 196)

*Broad Peak, Attempt and Tragedy.* Eric Escoffier and Pascalle Bessières (F) were last seen on the summit ridge of Broad Peak (8047m) on July 29 by Poitr Putzelnik and Ryszard Pawlowski, members of a Polish expedition. The two were climbing up to a col at ca. 7800 meters when they saw Escoffier and Bessières moving slowly upward on the ridge above. "It was a snow storm and they had a long way to go for the final summit. They were on the ridge at approximately 8000 meters," said one of the Polish climbers. The search was abandoned when Pakistani Ashraf Aman returned from a futile attempt to locate the two French climbers. The third member of the French expedition, Jean-François Lassalle, managed to come down with the Polish team. The French shared a climbing permit for the normal route with Slovakian and Italian climbers.

ASEM MUSTAFA AWAN, *The Nation, Pakistan*

*Savoia Kangri, Attempt.* It was reported that Nick Bullock, Julian Cartwright, Jamie Fisher, Ewan and Ruaridh Pringle, Paul Schweizer and Alan Swann (U.K) attempted to make the first ascent of Savoia Kangri (7263m) via the southeast face in July. They deviated from the line taken by perhaps the only other attempt on the mountain, a 1982 Czechoslovakian group, by climbing the bow-shaped gully through the triangular buttress left of the 1982 line. On their first attempt, on July 15, Bullock, Cartwright, Fisher, and Schweizer reached a point about two-thirds of the way up the gully by dawn before rockfall forced them to bivy on a snow rib. A storm complicated departure the next morning, and when Fisher was hit by a rock at ca. 6000 meters, the four dumped their gear and descended.

The same climbers made another attempt on July 22, reaching the top of the gully in 12 hours of sustained Scottish 3/4 climbing. The next day, Fisher and Cartwright climbed the 700-meter ice face (55-60°) above in 11 hours to a bivy below a gendarme at ca. 6900 meters. A storm that dumped 60 centimeters of snow kept them pinned in their tents for two days. They then went for the summit, but deep unstable snow prohibited travel past ca. 7000 meters and they retreated again. One more attempt was made on August 5, reaching the top of the gully before more bad weather brought an end to the expedition. (*High Mountain Sports* 196)

*Gasherbrum I and II, Ascents, Attempts and Tragedy.* Our international expedition of 13, led by Peter Guggemos (Germany), successfully saw 11 summiting GII and one reaching the top of GI. The weather was persistently stormy and, aside from a week of fair skies at the beginning of July, afforded only isolated clear days. On July 31, having already summited GII, Toni Hinterplattner (Austria) and Guggemosset set out from CII at 6500 meters on Gasherbrum La for a fast and light summit bid on GI. A severe storm forced them to retreat only ca. 20 meters short of the summit. On the descent, a small avalanche threw Toni off balance. He fell ca. 200 meters, sustaining two broken ribs and a tib/fib fracture which, during his subsequent descent of over 1000 meters, turned into a compound fracture. After bivouacking with Peter in the storm at ca. 7400 meters, Toni descended to CII on his own, where a rescue party organized from BC (5100m) was able to reach him and transport him to BC for a helicopter ride out. Two members of a four-person Japanese expedition, last seen by Peter and Toni near the summit of GI, disappeared in this same storm. Their comrades went up in an attempt to find them and also disappeared.

HJORDIS RICKERT

*Latok I, North Ridge, Attempt, Harpoon, First Ascent, and Other Activity.* Our expedition consisted of Lyle Dean, John Bouchard, and myself. We established Base Camp at the head of Choctoi Glacier directly across from the north ridge and north east face of Latok I. In preparation, we first climbed the beautiful pyramid-shaped peak on the opposite side of the glacier from Latok (ca. 6000m). Lacking a name on any map, we dubbed the peak Harpoon.

Our ascent followed the obvious 2,500-foot couloir on the southwest face to the saddle on the south ridge. This was mostly snow climbing with some ice at the top to which we third classed, arriving at the saddle about noon. The following morning we climbed the remaining eight pitches of mostly rock and mixed up to 5.8 M4 along the south ridge to the summit. Although we did encounter some old retreat slings in the lower couloir, we found no evidence of previous climbing on the summit ridge. We reached the summit at approximately 1 p.m. on July 21 and descended that day to our high camp at the saddle and Base Camp the following day.

*Harpoon Peak, showing the line climbed in 1998 by Bouchard, Richey and Dean.* MARK RICHEY

HAR Pinnacle, showing the line climbed in 1997 by Richey and Bouchard on their Latok I expedition. This photo illustrates the note in the 1998 AAJ, pp. 319-20. MARK RICHEY

Over the next four weeks, bad weather and dangerous snow conditions prevented any attempt on Latok's north ridge. We did make one attempt on the Ogre's southwest pillar, only to have our ropes cut in half in serious rock fall in the couloir above the glacier. Also, John Bouchard and I made an attempt on Hanipispur (6047m), reaching the base of the most western summit block, a giant finger of granite. Oncoming bad weather and lack of time prevented us from getting the job done. The climbing to that point via the large south couloir to west ridge was excellent with several passages of rock up to 5.10 on the west ridge. The final vertical tower looked like if would involve three to four pitches of very difficult free climbing or aid.

MARK RICHEY

*Latok III, West Face, Attempt.* In July, Jay Smith, Kitty Calhoun, Steve Quinlan and Ken Sauls attempted an alpine-style ascent of the unclimbed west face of Latok III (6949m) just off the Biafo Glacier in Pakistan. The team made an initial carry of about 700 meters up the snow couloir at the base of the face to make a cache of food and evaluate conditions, but left no fixed rope. The climbing initially was quite moderate but hazardous due to substantial rock fall once the sun hit the face. After several days' rest, the team set off for the attempt, climbing as two rope teams of two and alternating leading and hauling. The climbing started as moderate snow couloirs and then turned to steeper mixed terrain with rock quality being less than optimal. Camps were quite difficult to establish as snow fields were very shallow and would barely allow ledges large enough for two small tents. Ten days were spent reaching a high point around 6000 meters, at which point the face turns into a large granite buttress for the remaining 1000 meters. The team was slowed in its progress at this point by several days of storms. during which they were tent bound. Upon reaching the vertical buttress at 6000 meters, the team was disappointed to find the wall devoid of continuous crack systems; it would apparently require a fair amount of aid climbing, although Jay was able to establish the initial portion via a mixed crack/chimney system. Several nights were spent at the base of the buttress while the team fixed ropes, waited out weather and evaluated a diminishing food supply. On the tenth day, with ropes fixed on the buttress, another storm moved in and, in light of limited supplies and the estimated length of time needed to reach the summit, the decision was made to retreat. On day 11, the team reached the base via some 30 60-meter rappels.

KEN SAULS, *unaffiliated*

*Shipton Spire, Inshallah.* In July, Steph Davis, Kennan Harvey, and Seth Shaw established a third route on Shipton Spire (a.k.a. Hainablak Central Tower), *Inshallah* (VII 5.12 A0, 4,300 feet). The trio spent 14 days on the wall and managed to free all but three moves of the climb. A full account of this impressive effort appears earlier in this journal.

*A Note on Names of Formations Rising from the Hainablak Glaciers.* Directed by Greg Child, Bernard Domenech (France) contacted the *AAJ* in the autumn of 1998 with a note on the naming of Shipton Spire. He wrote, "[In the 1936 expedition report], Ardito Desio gave the mountain [the name of Hainablak] because his porters, [who were from] the Baltic region, named it this way. [They]. . . remember that the remarkable wall opposite Brangsa, the last bivouac before the traverse [into China], always used to be called Hainablak. . . ."

Also in the autumn, we received an account from Thomas Tivadar on his team's 1997 attempt on Hainablak East Tower (see the cover of this volume, and pp. 207-8). When we inquired about the name, Tivadar sent photocopies from the Jan Kielkowski book, *Western Baltoro Mustagh*, which he had come upon in the German Alpine Club library while researching big wall objectives in the Karakoram. In addition to Hainablak East Tower, sketch maps in the Polish book refer to other formations rising from the Hainablak glaciers by the "Hainablak" designation as well. This includes the formation that has come in recent years to be known as Shipton Spire, which is labeled Hainablak Central Tower in its pages. The same formation is indicated as "Hainablak T." by the map *Karakoram*, published in 1991 by the Swiss Foundation for Alpine Research.

Hoping for local clarification, we contacted Greg Mortenson, a regular visitor to the area whose Central Asia Institute works closely with the Balti population (see pp. 184-5 in this volume). Mortenson sent runners into the local villages with copies of the sketch maps from *Western Baltoro Mustagh* with questions regarding the local names for the formations. Upon completion of his research, he wrote,

"The name Hainablak has been mentioned in older moutaineering literature by several explorers to the Baltoro-Trango region: 1. 1856, by German Baltoro glacier explorer Adolf Schlagintweit. 2. 1909, by Luigi Amedeo di Savoia (Duke of Abruzzi) and Vittorio Sella. 3. 1929, by the Geographical Expedition led by the Duke of Spoleto and Arditio Desio. [On page 292, this expedition book has a photo of 'Shipton Spire' designated as 'L'Ainablak nella valle del Tramgo.']

"I consulted with three elder Braldu Valley village chiefs, Haji Mousin of Pakhora village, Haji Ali of Korphe village and Hussein of Teste. Braldu Valley is the historic entrance to the Baltoro Glacier approach to K2. These villages have ancestral grazing rights to the Panmah-Choktoi glacier region [and the] Paiyu and Trango areas. All of them informed me that they have always known 'Shipton Spire' as 'Hainabrakk' ['brakk' in Balti is pronounced 'blakk,' which accounts for the discrepancy in spelling].

"Then, I requested additional information from Ghulam Parvi, director of Skardu-based Blue Sky Travel and local entrepreneur. Parvi referred me to a mutual Skardu friend, Mr. Husseinabadi, for clarification. Husseinabadi, a school headmaster, Islamic philosopher and linguist, is the foremost living scholar on Balti language. He was recently presented with a medal of honor by Pakistan's Prime Minister for his 15-year effort to translate the Koran into Balti. Here is Mr. Parvi's reply:"

January 7, 1999
Honorable Sirs and Madames,

Mr. Husseinabadi and myself consulted compiled Balti archives and dictionaries. We did not find any Balti word for the English word spelled as "Haina Blakk". But there is actually a Balti word pronounced "ainabrakk" ("aa-ee-na brakk," long aa, long ee and na). "Aina" means looking glass (mirror) and "brakk" means mountain.

When writing the actual Balti pronounciation in English, the letter "h" becomes silent (e.g, "honor"). If we keep the letter "h" silent in Haina, the actual pronounciation is "aina," or "looking glass."

The shape of Shipton Spire looks like a hard and smooth surface. When there is rain or the nearby water and snow give light, the reflection of the peak looks like a mirror.

The local Braldu valley people call Shipton Spire "(H)aina Brakk" (pronouced "aa-ee-na blakk"). I hope the name is now clear to you and honorable members of American Alpine Club.

Ghulam Parvi

Notes Mortenson, "If local Baltis take back their ancestral name for Shipton Spire, the British mountaineering clubs might demand a round of Scotch on the house compliments of the AAC." In addition to the individuals mentioned above, we wish to thank Jack Zektzer, Susanne Schenk, John Mudd, Mr. Aziz Ahmed, Hussein, Twaha, and Rose Ali for their help in this matter.

*Climbing above the Shoulder Camp on the second ascent of Eternal Flame.* JORGE CANALEJO

*Nameless Tower, Eternal Flame, Second Ascent.* In June and July, Alberto Sepulveda, Jorge Couceiro, Jose Maria Andrés and José Vicente Sáez completed the second ascent of the 1100-meter route *Eternal Flame* on Nameless Tower (6257m). The first three climbers, Alberto, Jorge and Josemari, fixed 700 meters of rope and spent 20 days on the wall. Base Camp was placed at 4000 meters on June 6, CI at 5100 meters on June 12, CII at 5500 meters on June 24 and CIII (portaledge camp) at 5900 meters on July 3. At this point, José Vicente was incorporated into the team, and we all finished the ascent on June 6 after 16 hours of activity. The descent was made the following day, stripping the route of the fixed ropes and the rest of the things and reaching Base Camp on

July 8 at night. The climbing was conducted amidst unstable weather; we found the first part of the wall very covered with snow and ice, with avalanches very often. This made going up to the shoulder, where we placed CII, more difficult. We used two 60-meter and one 10.5-meter ropes, one set of stoppers, two sets of microcams, four sets of Friends, 25 quickdraws, and 40 carabiners to overcome the perfect cracks of the steep wall.

JORGE COUCEIRO, *Spain*

*Drifika, Second Ascent.* It was reported that in July, Angelo Rusconi, Luciano Gimpa, Simone Rossetti, and Gino Hora (Italy) made the second recorded ascent of Drifika (6447m) via its north ridge. Hora stopped ca. 100 meters below the summit; the others carried on to the top on July 31. This was the route of first ascent as well. (*High Mountain Sports*196)

*Hushe Valley, Various Ascents.* Giuseppe Masdea, Maurizio Garota, Danilo Valsecchi, Corrado Valsecchi and I, all members of the Lecco Group of the Italian Alpine Club, arrived at Charakusa Base Camp July 19, after a very comfortable and easy approach. After a few days of reconnaissance in the vicinity of Base Camp, we realized the multiplicity of climbing opportunities the place offered. Within two hours' walk from camp, a beautiful pillar (the second of K7, ca. 4950m) split up the middle by an obvious crack attracted our attention. We made a first attempt to climb it via the southwest face and within the first few pitches realized that the granite is solid and very beautiful, but the cracks are horribly flaring. This made the climb more difficult than we had first anticipated.

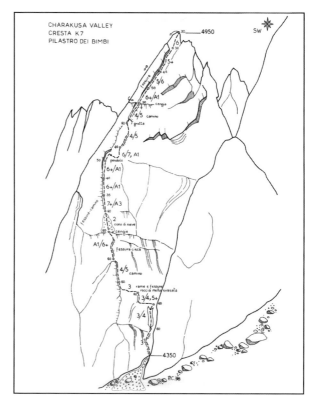

After climbing 300 meters, we came to a ledge that ran the entire length of the face, which allowed us to traverse to a couloir and then, with a series of double rappels, to descend easily to the base. After a day of rest we returned to the wall and, after 13 hours of climbing, we were able to reach the summit of the pillar via the beautiful crack, which had a very difficult section in the middle. We climbed the final pitches in a storm that impeded us more than a little. We propose the name *Pilastro dei Bimbi* ("Children's Pillar," VI 7+ A3, 650 meters) for the formation.

After a couple of days of rest at Base Camp, we decided to move our climbing gear to

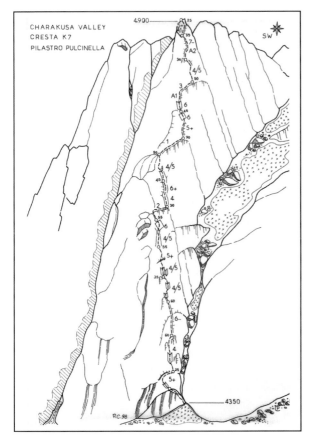

CHARAKUSA VALLEY
CRESTA K7
PILASTRO PULCINELLA

the base of another pillar (the fourth of K7, ca. 4900m) about three hours' walk from camp. By now we had been here for some time and the weather was always the same: the mornings would be good, at 2 p.m. there would be a little snow and after about three hours it would grow clear again.

This made us decide to fix the first few pitches on the southwest face to take better advantage of the good weather. The next day we climbed around 200 meters, fixing the route and then descending to camp. We went back up on the route the next day; the climb, *Pilastro Pulcinella* ("Punch's Pillar," VI 7 A2, 550 meters) was wonderful, with dihedrals, cracks and chimneys unfolding in a logical succession that spontaneously revealed the line of ascent. In the late afternoon, in the midst of the daily storm, we reached the top. We returned to Base Camp very satisfied with our climb and spent a few days enjoying the tranquility of the area.

We took an inventory of our remaining gear and realized (to the great delight of some) that we had only a little left and that therefore we could no longer aspire to any grand projects. However, above Base Camp was the beautiful pinnacle of The Dog's Knob (ca. 5400m), climbed by an English team some years before. Their route (V 6+A1, 250 meters) followed the crack that perfectly divides the mountain in two from base to summit. I don't think any alpinist could resist the temptation to climb such a beautiful wall. Thus we found ourselves struggling up the steep moraine that brought us to the base of the route. The team of Maurizio Garota, Danilo Valsecchi and Corrado Valsecchi climbed it on July 29; they were followed by Giuseppe Masdea and I on July 31. The climb was fantastic and extremely satisfying; in the middle of the daily dose of snowfall, we embraced one another on the summit, conscious of having had a fantastic vacation in this little-frequented valley.

We took the trouble to leave the valley as clean as we had found it in the hopes that others who come after us will be able to enjoy the beauty, emotions and joy that we savored and that we brought home with us after this experience.

DARIO SPREAFICO, *Italian Academic Alpine Club*

*Nangma Valley, Various Ascents.* A team of six climbers (Mike Turner, Steve Mayers, Elfyn Jones, Di Lampard, Louise Thomas and Libby Peter) from North Wales, U.K., visited the Nangma Valley in the Hushe region of the Karakoram from July 25 to August 30 and successfully climbed two new rock routes. The Nangma is a side valley off the main Hushe Valley. It has vast potential for alpine-scale rock and mixed routes on peaks up to about 6000 meters, but most of this is well hidden from view, hence it has received little attention.

The team set up a comfortable Base Camp two days' walk from Kande village. This was located at 4100 meters in a meadow (Sotulpa) and side valley above the Nangma Valley itself. The team operated from here as two separate groups climbing on opposite sides of the valley. Libby and Louise tackled the south face/pillar of Sotulpa Peak (4800m), ten minutes from Base Camp, resulting in *Ramchekor*, 600 meters of sustained 5.10 A2 climbing in cracks and grooves in 11 days between August 1-14. The route followed a natural line up the middle of the face heading for an obvious split pillar at half height. They fixed rope and reascended from base camp until they were close enough to go for the summit. The climbing combined free and aid climbing, relying on mainly natural protection with the addition of some pegs and a few bolts, where essential, at belays. The route finished just below the summit, which was barred by a ten-meter sheer featureless block. The pair descended the line of the route.

Sotulpa Peak has a rocky north ridge, which, on August 17, the two women climbed from base camp to the actual summit at an alpine grade of AD in a lovely day out that involved mostly dramatic scrambling with some rotten rock and exposed steps. Directly opposite Sotulpa Peak, the pair climbed the rocky Denbor Brakk (AD, 4700m) and explored the head of the valley, climbing in three days to a snowy col (PD, 5600m) that lies below and to the east of Drifica (6400m).

*Sotulpa Peak in the Nangma Valley, Hushe region, showing* Ramchekor. LIBBY PETER

*Armin and Nawaz Brakk, showing the 1998 British route.* LIBBY PETER

During the same period, the men's team started work on the imposing north face of Armin Peak (a.k.a. Amin Brakk, 5800m), previously attempted by a Spanish team. They were on the peak from August 2-6 before deciding that they did not have sufficient time to make a serious impression on the featureless granite nose. They then switched their efforts to a neighboring wall, Nawaz Brakk (5600m), where they established a new route that followed a 1000-meter line at 5.11 A3+. A portaledge camp was set up after 500 meters of initial slabs. From here the route followed a major corner system to the top of the wall, with some of the hardest climbing in the top few pitches. They were on and off it between August 8-23, with probably 13 days of climbing in total. They used fixed rope below and above the portaledge camp. The route gave the team a lot of free climbing on the lower half and mostly aid on the upper half.

LIBBY PETER, *United Kingdom*

*Changi Tower North Peak, First Ascent.* Changi Tower (ca. 5800m) (the actual height of Changi Tower was difficult to assess, firstly because of the poor-quality maps [all maps greater than 1:50,000 are classified as restricted military information], and secondly because the altimeter was lost) is located in the Nangma Valley, Baltistan, which is in the northern provinces of Pakistan. It is approximately an eight-hour walk from Khande village, which is six hours' drive from Skardu. Changi Tower is part of the larger Armin massif, an enormous granite block in the upper reaches of the Nangma Valley. The Armin massif includes Armin Peak, Changi Tower, and several other unclimbed spires. Most of the rock within Nangma Valley is either granite, gneiss, or schist; however, the predominant rock type is granite, and there is lots of it.

In August, Ned Norton (New Zealand) and I climbed *Just A Quickie* (VI 5.10+ A0) on Changi Tower North Peak, while Vera Wong, Nicola Woolford (New Zealand) and Abby Watkins (New Zealand) made the first ascent of *Excess Baggage* (VI 5.10+A2+) (see note below) on Changi Tower Main Peak (ca. 5820m). The routes head up the east face of Changi Tower, and both begin in a short couloir exposed to rock- and icefall from the "Off-White Spider," a classic spider-shaped snow patch midway up the east face. The couloir then doglegs left parallel to the face and the routes follow this to a small saddle and Camp I.

On *Just a Quickie*, from Camp I a short 100-meter traverse to the south intercepts a diagonal right-trending crack system that terminates two pitches short of the Spider. Climbing ranged from 5.7 to 5.10c with good bivy ledges located between the fifth and sixth pitches. This section took four days to climb and Camp II was established at the base of the Spider.

The route from Camp II took two days and proceeded directly up the center of the Spider before traversing right along a snow ledge to the prow of the North Buttress, where the high bivy was established. This section was prone to rockfall and cornice collapse, especially the central gully (these cornices were the same ones that hazarded Wong, Woolford and Watkins during their ascent of *Excess Baggage*). Climbing tended to be mixed rock and ice with one short waterfall section. The first pitch on the North Buttress was 5.10d and we pulled on pro to get through the crux. The remaining eight rock pitches ranged from 5.8 to 5.10c. The final pitch from the top of the buttress to the north summit was a snow ramp. We negotiated it in friction shoes, having left all our ice equipment two pitches below, and reached the summit at 7 p.m. The descent down in the dark took five hours to the high bivy. It then took another two days to return to Base Camp, ten days in total after departing.

PAUL WEBER, *Australia*

*Changi Tower Main Peak, Excess Baggage. Excess Baggage* starts directly above Camp I at the base of a four-pitch, left-facing corner. (Camp I is at the base of the bottom tier of Changi Tower. Changi is two-tiered on its east face, with the bottom tier being much slabbier than the top tier.) Nicola Woolford (New Zealand), Abby Watkins (Australia) and I climbed this in four 5.9-5.10 pitches; the second and fourth included short bursts of easy A1 aid climbing. The first three pitches of this route were first climbed free by Wong and Kynan Bazley in 1995. The corner joins Norton and Weber's route, which was then unknowingly climbed for the next eight pitches. *Excess Baggage* then branched left along the left-hand edge of the Off-White Spider, leading to two pitches, one of 5.9 and the other 5.10. This led to 100 meters of fourth-class ground and Camp II after three days' climbing. Camp II was located on the southern saddle between the upper and lower tiers of Changi Tower's east face.

The route continued up a prominent crack on the top headwall. This involved a 50-meter traverse on snow, followed by a short A1 overhanging aid section that led into the crack proper. It required two days to climb the flaring crack, with five pitches of 5.9 to 5.10+ free climbing interspersed with sections of A1 aid climbing. From the top of the crack, the route followed a rising traverse to the right along a moss-filled shallow seam. This was then followed by a pendulum into a parallel crack system, which led to a long sloping ledge threatened by cornices. The traverse pitch (A2+) was the crux of the route. On the left end of the ledge a 5.10 A2 pitch and a 5.9 A1 pitch led to the fifth and sixth nights' bivy. Day six of the climb was spent in a wet snow storm.

The final rock pitches took a 50-meter, boulder-filled, left-facing corner to a low-angled 400-meter snow ridge. The Main Summit of Changi Tower was reached at 11:15 a.m. on day seven and is approximately 20 meters higher than the North Summit. The descent followed the ascent route to the half-way saddle and continued down a southwest-facing scree- and snow-filled couloir. Four hours were needed to descend the low-angled couloir, with only one short five-meter abseil required. Base Camp was reached at 1:30 a.m. after a 20-hour day.

VERA WONG, *Australia*

*Charakusa Valley, Various Ascents.* Conrad Anker, Peter Croft, and Galen Rowell spent the month of July climbing five rock spires in the Charakusa Valley east of Masherbrum above Hushe. The longest climb of the expedition was Conrad and Peter's 23-hour round-trip on Spansar Brakk via a huge ridge traverse right from the Charakusa Glacier. The line is wholly visible from Saitcho Camp, one stage above Hushe, as the longest chunk of granite in front of K7 on the left side of the glacier. The route followed a knife-edge of granite for over 8,000 feet of ridge line. Doing Spansar in "normal" style with multiple ropes, sleeping bags, water, food, etc., would have taken the three of us at least three days, but Peter, who holds the El Cap speed record of four hours, 22 minutes, saw the possibility of doing it with one partner, one rope, one water bottle each, a few PowerBars, and no bivy gear. Peter calls the route "the biggest and best climb I've done—or seen—in my life." It was a 5.11a free climb with lots of simul-climbing for speed. From the first time Peter saw the continuous line of sharp ridge rising from the glacier to the summit, he was focused on it as his primary objective.

Before that climb, Conrad and Galen spent a day making the first ascent of Lucky Shinmo Spire (5.11b, 900'). This is the Balti name for index finger, referring to a set of three spires shaped like fingers on a hand in a side valley east of Spansar Brakk. From a camp in the same side valley, Galen soloed Nakpa Brakk (5.9, 1,200'), the third and final spire on the main

*Nayser Brakk (the "Luxor Pyramid") in the Charakusa Valley, Pakistan Karakoram, soloed by Galen Rowell via the 1,000-foot face to the left of the right skyline.* GALEN ROWELL

ridge of Spansar, and a couple of hundred feet lower than the main summit. He set off to explore the 17,500-foot spire for a later, roped ascent, but found an easy traverse ledge and decided to continue to the top in just a few hours.

While Peter and Conrad were preparing and resting up for Spansar, Galen decided to explore a possible route up the north arête of Nayser Brakk, an incredible dark granite spire shaped like the Luxor Pyramid between K7 Base Camp and Spansar on the north side of the Charakusa Glacier. He brought a rope and hardware for a safe self-belay and climbed a new 5.10b route up the 1,000-foot face to the left of the north arête, which we later learned had been climbed in 1988 by David Hamilton's British expedition using direct aid. At the time, Galen thought the summit to be unclimbed because he found no sign of passage above a rappel anchor 500 feet below the top, and the loose rocks on top had not been made into a cairn. An Italian party of Lecco Spiders camped below K7 said they knew of an attempt to climb a face route that failed well below the summit, where Galen's watch altimeter read only 16,500 feet. The report of Nayser's first ascent in the 1989 *AAJ* says that the spire, unnamed on maps, is 18,700 feet. Since our watches matched closely at other altitudes, but seemed low compared to maps, we would estimate that Nayser could be over 17,000 feet, but probably not over 18,000.

The day after Conrad and Peter's Spansar ascent, Galen teamed up with two Lecco Spiders, Villa Natale and Luca Maspes, to make the first ascent of Iqbal's Wall, a 1,100-foot dihedral of steep cracks up to 5.10d beneath the massive 6,000-foot granite wall of K7 (still off-limits to climbing because its other side borders a glacier linked to the ongoing Siachen Glacier war).

GALEN ROWELL

*Charakusa Valley, Various Ascents.* An Italian expedition comprising Maurizio Giordani, Luca "Rampikino" Maspes, Mattia Locatelli and Natale Villa were active in the Charakusa Valley in July, making a number of ascents, including the ascent mentioned above on Iqbal's Wall with Galen Rowell. A complete account of the Italians' expedition to the area appears in an article earlier in this journal.

*Brakk Zang, Ganyips.* From June 28 to July 5, Pep Masip and I put up a new route on the southeast face of a virgin mountain named Brakk Zang (4800m) in one of the secondary Hushe valleys of the Pakistan Karakoram. We called the route *Ganyips* (VI 6a A3, 540m), which is Catalan for a sort of dry fruit, like hazelnuts, almonds, peanuts. There is an offwidth on the third pitch. There are nine long pitches, one of them 75 meters. We spent nine days (eight bivies) on the wall, with some snowy days. We had fixed two pitches (110 meters) on June 25-26 before beginning.

There aren't any bolts on the new route, just pitons at some belays because we had to rap down the route. At first we thought we could descend by walking down the north side, but when we got the top we realized that it was too difficult.

SÍLVIA VIDAL, *Spain*

*Diran, Ascent.* Adrian Burgess and Rob Ziegler made the first American ascent of Diran (23,838') on July 10. The mountain was climbed in alpine-style over three days; we climbed the final 4,800 feet in eight hours to summit at midday. Base Camp was reached again at 10 a.m. on July 11. We were relying on information from the book *Himalaya Alpine-Style*; much of the information on the route in that book had been gleaned from Doug Scott's 1983 ascent. It should be noted that some of the structure of the face may have changed, as we found the face leading to the ridge extremely dangerous and at risk from collapsing seracs and wet snow slides. This forced us onto the ridge about two hours further west than the West Col, which accounts for the extra height on the last day. On the first two days, we actually climbed in the middle of the night.

ADRIAN BURGESS

*Nanga Parbat, Various Activity.* 1998 will be remembered by many for Nanga Parbat's (8125m) exceptional generosity. Of the six expeditions, that went after it, five—two Japanese, one Korean, one Australian, one Italian, one Spanish—(all expeditions this year attempted the Kinshofer Route) came back safely and successfully. Together with Rozi Ali, one of Pakistan's leading high-altitude porters, Andrew Lock reached the summit the same day the Korean, Park Young Seok, summited via the Kinshofer Route on July 21. Park has rushed up seven of the 14 8000ers in 13 months. He has only K2 and Broad Peak left in Pakistan. Of the two Japanese teams, the ascent by young Kitamura was the most difficult, as he was unescorted and broke his ribs in a fall during the descent. A politician, Senator Luis Fraga from Spain, made a solo climb to get away from some worries of public life. Beside him and myself, Fraga said there were probably two others in active politics who also happen to be mountaineers. What a foursome!

On July 20, an Italian couple, Nives Meroi and Romano Benet, were the second husband-and-wife team to summit Nanga Parbat, which they did in pretty bad weather conditions. The Italians were eight in number. Nives has climbed extensively with her husband in the Himalaya but without success on the 8000ers. Nanga Parbat was their first trophy. Among Pakistani climbers, a notable success was achieved by our well-known high porter, Rajab Shah, who summited Gasherbrum II on July 22, thus doing all the five 8000ers of the country.

Marred by the World Cup football and the nuclear blasts in India and Pakistan, 1998 was a bad year for tourism in general and mountaineering in particular. Most climbers and trekkers were shooed off by the over-cautious travel advisories of their governments. But those who ventured regardless had a nice time climbing and trekking. Tragically, a blot on the season and a great personal loss was the totally unnecessary murder of my friend Ned Gillette. Bereaved and herself injured in the attack, Ned's wife, Susie Patterson, displayed a courage and positive attitude that gave all of us heart. She was back in the mountains late last summer in Nepal, her love of nature, life and adventure undiminished.

NAZIR SABIR, *Pakistan*

*Nanga Parbat, Ascent.* Our summit day, July 21, saw a multi-national group from three different expeditions depart CIV at about 4 a.m. In one team were two Koreans, in the second were three Koreans and their high-altitude porter, Rosi Ali, and in the last group were Alan Hinkes and I. Rosi Ali and I shared the leads, alternating 50-meter pitches except where the route steepened or we moved into mixed ground, where I retained the lead. Disappointingly, no amount of cajoling, pleading or abuse was sufficient to motivate any of the other climbers to contribute. Very deep snow and a late afternoon blizzard contributed to Rosi's and my exhaustion; however, at about 4 p.m., I reached the base of the summit buttress around 7800 meters and was able to make better time. I led for the next hour or so until about 50 meters below the summit, where Rosi Ali overtook me and led through to the summit. Rosi reached the summit about 5:45 p.m. and I at 5:50 p.m. It took until 6:20 p.m. for all the other climbers to reach the summit and at 6:30 p.m. I commenced the descent. During the descent, Hinkes and I led most of the way until we reached the vicinity of CIV, which we were unable to locate. We separated and whilst I was searching, Hinkes was joined by some of the Koreans and together they located the camp. They did not call to me and I was not aware that the camp had been found. Around 2 a.m., I gave up and settled in for a bivouac. With sufficient light at 5 a.m., I moved off and found the camp a couple of hundred meters away, with the larger Korean team and Hinkes ensconced within. The other two Koreans had also bivied out.

ANDREW LOCK

# COMMONWEALTH OF INDEPENDENT STATES (C.I.S.)

CAUCASUS

*Mt. Dalar, North Face, and Traverse.* From August 9-13, a team led by V. Ivanov, together with I. Afanasiev, I. Bondarenko, and S. Egorin, all from the North Osetia Rescue Service Team, climbed M. Warburton's 1976 North Buttress route (6A) on the north face of Mt. Dalar (3979m), then continued to make a traverse along Dvoyniashka Peak (3843m) and the Zamok group (3930m). This route is the most difficult in the Uzuncol region: the north buttress of Dalar is a ca. 500-meter near-vertical rock pillar. To climb the route and then link it with the traverse of Dvoyniashka Peak and the Zamok group—rocky peaks and buttresses ca. one kilometer in length—was rather unusual.

VLADIMIR SHATAEV, *Russian Mountaineering Federation*

*Chegem Valley, Ice Climbing Exploration.* In February, an ice climbing expedition led by Alexander Kopylov made a reconnaissance of waterfall ice climbing possibilities in the Central Caucasus. It was the first time ice climbers had explored the Chegem Valley, which is one valley to the east from the popular and well-known Baksan Valley, which feeds into Mt. Elbrus from the south. Only a few icefalls were known about in the Caucasus, all in the Baksan Valley. Activity was concentrated on the Chegem waterfalls, a popular and well-known summertime venue. The rock face was discovered to have many routes in an area 200 meters long by 50 meters high. Only two other ice climbs in the Caucuses are known to exist of equal or greater length. The first ascent was made of the summertime waterfall Tyrniauz (90 meters of vertical ice), and Kopylov soloed a 50-meter route. An article and photos on the fruits of the exploration can be found at http://mountains.tos.ru/ice_foto.htm.

VLADIMIR SHATAEV, *Russian Mountaineering Federation*

*Mt. Donguz-Orun, North Face, Descent by Ski and Snowboard.* Mt. Donguz-Orun ("Mountain over the Lake of Pigs," 4468m), a spectacular massif southeast of Mt. Elbrus and with the Nakra-Tau (Cut Peak, 4431m) summit to the west, is covered with glaciers. The north face of Mt. Donguz-Orun is characterized by a unique glacier in the shape of an upside-down "7," the icefalls of which spill over the Baksanskoe Gorge. It is said that one mountaineer, after climbing up the normal route, was seen going down the glacier on his skis, but no one in Russia knows his name and today this sounds like a legend.

In the first part of July, Alexander Kopylov (ski) and Vladimir Kopylov (camera man), Vitalik Mikhaylov (snowboard) and Genadiy Melnikov (rescue team) climbed the north face of Mt. Donguz-Orun and then made ski and snowboard descents via the 1000-meter Semiorka ("Seven") Glacier, which reaches its steepest section of ca. 30° in the middle. The previous day, when the group was at ABC, a great ice fall and avalanche scoured the face, clearing it from danger. The upper part of the "seven" glacier was climbed by 11 a.m. and after 30 minutes' rest, the team made a descent with photo and video shoots. In the last moments, with only about 50 meters to go, a small avalanche passed near the group. The most difficult part of the descent was the icefalls and the crevasses.

VLADIMIR SHATAEV, *Russian Mountaineering Federation*

*Mt. Elbrus, Refuge of 11 Hut Fire.* The Refuge of 11—the famous high-altitude hut on Mount Elbrus—was completely destroyed by fire on August 16. This site for the hut was first used in 1909 when 11 Russian climbers spent a night here before climbing Elbrus. In 1929, a small hut was built in the same place, and during 1937-'39, the modern-day, all-metal Refuge of 11 was built. Now Bochki, which is situated at the end of the Karabashy chair lift at 3900 meters, is the last warm refuge on Elbrus's slopes.

VLADIMIR SHATAEV, *Russian Mountaineering Federation*

*Mt. Erydag, Northwest Face.* A team of the Dagestan Republic Rescue Service, led by V. Sogokon and comprising A. Goriaev and U. Slobodeniuk, climbed the right side of the north-west face of Mt. Erydag (3925m) via the 1982 Mikhalov route (6A) from September 15-19. Mt. Erydag is seldom visited, and the ascent of the ca. 800- to 1000-meter vertical rock face was a good effort for the Caucasus.

VLADIMIR SHATAEV, *Russian Mountaineering Federation*

# TADJIKISTAN

## FANSKIE MOUNTAINS

*Fanskie Mountains, Various Ascents.* A lot of famous mountains and good technical routes were climbed in August in the Fanskie Mountains of Tadjikistan during the Europe-Asia Association of Mountaineering and Rock Climbing Championships. All of the following routes are about 1000 meters high on very steep rock. First place was awarded to the team of A&C from Moscow (S. Schepachkov, leader, O. Milenin and I. Turchanski), which climbed the northwest face of Chapdara Peak (5050m) via the 1972 Solonnikov route (6B) from August 1-8. Second place went to the Alaudin, Russia, team led by S. Antonov, who, with D. Glaznev, U. Vlaznev and O. Kurova, climbed the left side of the west face of Bodkhona peak (5138m) via a variation to the 1987 Moshnikov route (6A) from August 14-19. S. Kosoturov (leader), D. Veretenin, A. Kustov and O. Pedenkoa of the Angarsk (Russia) Sport Team took third place when they climbed Peak Zamok (5070m) via the 1983 Tishchenko route (6A), which follows the central buttress on the north face. The team climbed the route from August 16-21. Fourth place went to the Krasnoyarsk City Region Team led by A. Savinich and comprising V. Alexandrov, A. Zakrepa, S. Fedorov and S. Cherezov, who climbed the northwest face of Chapdara Peak (5050m) via the 1972 Solonnikov route (6B) from August 7-12. Fifth place was awarded to the Krasnoyarsk City Travelers Center Team (D. Tsyganov, leader, I. Koriukin) who climbed the north face of Peak Adamtash (4700m) via the 1985 V. Grischenko route (5B) from August 1-4. The mountaineering club "Ushba" from Toliatty led by A. Abramov, together with V. Melnikov and P. Sokolov, took sixth place with their variation of the 1971 Zhitenev route (5B) on the left side of the west face of Peak Bodkhona (5138m), which they climbed from August 11-14.

VLADIMIR SHATAEV, *Russian Mountaineering Federation*

*Note on the Various Climbing Championships of the C.I.S.* The Russian Mountaineering Federation was established in 1982. Preceding and superseding that, the Soviet Mountaineering Federation was the governing body for climbing in the times of the U.S.S.R. At the time of the Soviet Union's disintegration, the leader of Soviet Mountaineering Federation was Eduard Myslovsky (who had to his credit first ascents of two of the most difficult faces in the former U.S.S.R., the Southwest Face of Peak Communism [1968] and the North Face of Khan-Tengri [1974], and who had, together with Vladimir Balyberdin, been the head climber of the 1982 Soviet Everest expedition). In the disintegration's wake, Myslovsky organized the Europe-Asia Association of Mountaineering and Rock Climbing to unite some of the former Soviet mountaineering federations (primarily the Ukranian and Kazakhstan federations).

Meanwhile, the leader of the Russian Mountaineering Federation at the time of the Soviet breakup was Anatoly Bychkov. Upon his death in 1993, the Russian Mountaineering Federation was headed up by Valery Putrin and Vladimir Shataev, who continue to serve as its leaders.

The system of championships is the same for both the Russian Mountaineering Federation and the Europe-Asia Association of Mountaineering and Rock Climbing. In the Russian Mountaineering Federation, there are a number of different climbing classes, such as the rock climbing class, technical climbing class, high-altitude climbing class, and winter climbing class. (An article by Vladimir Shataev that explains the Russian Mountaineering Federation and its championships can be found in the 1997 *AAJ*, pp. 108-111.) In 1998, the ascent of the west face of Bhagirathi III was awarded first place in high-altitude climbing class; the Russian-American ascent of the north face of Changabang took second, while the new route up the north face of Khan Tengri took third. The rock class climbing championship of Russia this year took place in Chamonix from June 28 to July 14. The two winning ascents were of the Petit Dru's north face via a new variation and the *No Siesta* route on the north face of the Grand Jorasses.

There were only two classes in the Europe-Asia Association of Mountaineering and Rock Climbing this year. In the high-altitude climbing class, all three entries were climbs of 8000 meter peaks. The technical class took place in the Fanskie mountains, and the results are listed below. As the Fanskie mountains are located in the Republic of Tadjikistan (which is currently politically unstable), the president of the Republic of Tadjikistan awarded his own prize to the youngest climbers to show the importance of this sports event in the time of the civil war. Our thanks to Vladimir Kopylov and Vladimir Shataev for their help in clarifying this matter.

*Muzkol Range, Various Ascents.* In 1996, an EWP expedition was the first West European climbing group in recent history to visit the Muzkol, a little-explored range in the southeastern Pamir of Tadjikistan. Several unclimbed summits were conquered and many more exciting future possibilities discovered. In 1997, EWP again visited the Muzkol. Base Camp was established on the Zartoshkol (Muzkol) River some 20 miles north of the 1996 camp. Several virgin 5000-meter summits were climbed, along with two 6000ers. In 1998, the 1997 Base Camp was again used on account of the easy vehicle access. The group was comprised of three American, nine English, two Welsh and three Russian climbers, together with a Russian cook, her son and a Russian doctor.

Part of the journey from Osh in Khyrgyzstan to the Muzkol follows the Chinese border, and it is also the main road leading to the sensitive Afghan border areas. For these reasons there is a high degree of security along the route with many checkpoints. Luckily, in 1998, one of the checkpoints (Kyzylart Pass, 4280m) was abolished, and our vehicles were not searched once. As a result, the journey in both directions went very smoothly.

After a rest day, a group set off to make the ascent of 5500.6m, a small peak located on the ridge system leading off northwest from Peak Muzkolski (first climbed in 1997). They camped the first night at Vanishing Lake (4300m), then at "Cwm Bivouac" (ca. 4900m) located about one-and-a-half kilometers northeast of point 5500.6m. On August 16, John Cederholm, John Clarke, Igor Gavrilov, Paul Hampson, Antony Hollinshead, Cerith Jones, Doug Jones, Harvey Jones, David Keaton, Chris Kinney, Valeri Rezhnik, Colin Sprange, Stephen Taylor, Kevin Turner, and Duncan Woods reached the summit of 5500.6m and called it "Four Nations Peak." The ascent took three hours of easy scrambling, scree and snow slopes. The climb was rated Russian 2b (Alpine II or PD). Cederholm, Keaton, Kinney and Clarke continued south for about one-and-a-half kilometers to take in two further points, which they named "Point Theresa" (ca. 5475m) and "Point Marina" (ca. 5500m) after their wives. The ridge provided excellent views of Zartosh East and West (the latter subsequently named "White Pyramid") together with the unclimbed and very impressive 5960-meter peak. During this period, Sergei Semiletkin, the Russian veteran of the Muzkol, and Andrew Wielochowski reconnoitered the access route to Zartosh. They found a beautiful glacier basin leading up to the north face of Zartosh, as well as a fine camp site one hours' walk from the face.

On the 19th, the group set off up into the Zartosh Glacier cirque. One night was spent at "Moraine Ridge Camp" (ca. 4500), a fine, west-facing, sheltered hollow offering good views of Peak Communism to the west. On August 20, "Glacier Camp" was established at 5050 meters and was used for the next few days as a base to explore and climb in the beautiful Zartosh cirque. On the 21st, "Leopard's Tooth" (ca. 5520m) was ascended by its elegant, snowy north ridge by Cederholm, Clarke, Hollinshead, C., D. and H. Jones, Keaton, Kinney, Sprange, Taylor, Turner, Woods and Wielochowski. This unique feature forms an "island peak" in the center of the cirque and is dominated by the surrounding giants. The ascent took three hours and was rated Russian 2b (Alpine II or PD). On the following day, Hampson and Clark attempted to reach a 5300-meter col that leads out of the cirque into the Bozbaital Valley to the southeast; steep snowy scree slopes and rotten rock put them off. At the same time, Hollinshead and Wielochowski ventured onto the superb 700-meter icy north face of Zartosh, confirming its great potential for some excellent ice routes.

On August 23, Cederholm, Clarke, Gavrilov, Hampson, Hollinshead, C., D. and H. Jones, Keaton, Kinney, Rezhnik, Taylor, Turner, Wielochowski, Woods plus Semiletkin, set off at 6

*Panorama, Zartosh and White Pyramid Peaks in the Muzkol Range, East Pamir, Tadjikistan.*
DAVID KEATON

a.m. for the first ascent of the White Pyramid (ca. 6060m). After one-and-a-half hours, they reached the end of the Zartosh Glacier. A 40° snow slope led to the snowy north ridge. This was followed over bulges to a broader section; several large crevasses were easily avoided and the col between Zartosh and the White Pyramid was reached soon after midday. An easy snow ridge led to the summit. The col and summit were estimated to be 6000 and 6060 meters high respectively. The ascent of the White Pyramid was rated Russian 3b (Alpine III or ADsup).

From the summit of the White Pyramid a possible route up Zartosh could be seen: an icy snow couloir led up from the col toward a rockier area, above which the angle appeared to ease. After descent to the col, several members of the group started up the couloir but turned back on account of deteriorating weather and lack of adequate equipment.

The original aim of the expedition was to climb the main peak of Zartosh. Instead, the White Pyramid, the west summit of Zartosh, was identified as an attractive and easier initial target that could be climbed with a minimum of equipment. After the successful ascent of this summit by all but one member of the team, little enthusiasm could be found in the last two days of the trip to reascend to the col from where Zartosh would be most easily tackled. The other very attractive way to tackle this magnificent 20,000-foot summit would be by one of the excellent-looking ice routes on the north face.

The weather in the Muzkol is normally very stable: in 1997 it rained only once at Base Camp, and that was only for half an hour in two and a half weeks. In 1998, the weather was unusual, with three days on which it rained for a few hours, and several days of partial cloud cover.

ANDREW WIELOCHOWSKI, *United Kingdom*

# KAZAKHSTAN

*Dzhungaria Ala-Tau, Various Ascents.* It was reported that British guide Nick Parks traveled to the rarely visited Dzhungaria (Dzhungarskiy) Ala-Tau, a range that straddles the Kazakhstan-Chinese border, in August with a group of school children. The team spent 15 days at or above Base Camp, in which time period they attempted 11 peaks, summiting on nine. All were first ascents. From August 8 to 21, members of the group climbed the following: Violetta (3800m) via the northeast face to the southwest ridge (F+); Natallia (3900m) via the north face and west ridge (PD); Olly's Point (ca. 3400m) via the south flank and west ridge (PD); Jumbula (4200m) via the north face (F+); Spudnick 4000m) via the east ridge (F) and west face (AD, 300m); the first summit northwest of Simonev Tien Shanski (4200m) via the southeast ridge (F+); Tara 3700m) via the west face. The team also attempted Simonev Tien Shanski via the northwest ridge, but retreated due to lack of time, and Chumsk (4400m) via the north buttress. Team members included Violetta Afuksenidi, Frances Cook, Adam, C.J. and Mark Edwards, Griff Freeman, Dominic Gill, Ollie Hickling, Miriam Manook, Nick Parks, Stas Petrovich, Dr. Barney Rosedale, James Torrance and John Turner. The team reports enormous scope for moderate climbs to the summits of virgin 4000-meter peaks. (*High Mountain Sports* 197)

# TIEN-SHAN

*Central Tien Shan, Overview.* The weather during the 1998 season in the Central Tien-Shan (Khan-Tengri/Pobeda region), typified by a lot of snow and storm, was extremely terrible. Peak Pobeda was climbed by only a few groups; one of them, from Japan, spent three days on the west summit plateau. One person from this group died before they were able to descend.

VLADIMIR SHATAEV, *Russian Mountaineering Federation*

*Development of the Anatoli Boukreev Memorial Fund, and Khan Tengri, Attempt.* Anatoli Boukreev was one of the great high-altitude climbers of modern times. His prolific career bridged the apex of Soviet mountaineering, its disintegration with the USSR's collapse, and the beginnings of its re-emergence in the latter part of this decade. It is fitting, then, that his passing has given the team that brought him to his potential, the Kazak Army Sports Club, some of the same opportunities that he experienced in its folds. After he died on Christmas Day, 1997, his American friend, Linda Wylie, began a plan to further his dreams of helping young Kazak mountaineers with their mountain apprenticeship. In August, some of Anatoli's closest friends created a non-profit organization to assist the Kazak Army Sports Club and create an exchange between that Club and climbers in the West.

In August, I joined Linda, Kevin Cooney and Alex Friedman (a representative of the National Outdoor Leadership School) in Almaty at the home of the Kazak Army Sports Club's coach, Rinat Khaibullin. Rinat had been part of the USSR national climbing team with Anatoli. In Almaty, we met with the heads of the National Sports Program, Messrs. Novicov and Illinski, to establish ties for the future exchange program that is now being conducted. Together with the young climbers of the Sports Club, and joined by Carlos Buhler, we traveled to Byancol and from there to the North Inylchek Glacier. Linda, Kevin, Alex and Carlos left after a brief stay, while Rinat, his team and I, joined by German climbing journalist Rollo Steffens and Alexander Ganovski and Susanne Kayatz, university students in Germany, attempted Khan Tengri (6995 or 7010m; estimates vary). It was a tremendous opportunity to experience a style of mountaineering quite different from the Western approach, and a lot of fun as well. Andrei Molotov and I reached a group high point of ca. 6550 meters on the normal route from the north side before turning around in tempestuous weather.

The board of the Boukreev Memorial Fund has now paid to fly two young men from the Sports Club to the U.S. this summer. They will take part in a NOLS mountaineering course in Wyoming, on scholarship provided by NOLS (one impetus for this is cultural exchange and to allow Kazak climbers to learn about environmental ethics in the wilderness). The Memorial Fund is also paying all expenses for one scholarship recipient, Stephan Graepel of Minnesota, to travel to Kazakhstan this summer and join Rinat and the Sports Club in climbing Khan Tengri and Pobeda. Jack Robbins, one of the board members, has been doing a series of fundraising slide shows in the Bay area, and other activities are planned.

It was an honor to climb in the memory of Anatoli Boukreev. The team is in the best of hands with Rinat, a kind and generous individual who has single-handedly insured the continuation of the Kazak Army Sports Club, and Anatoli's character is attested to by the commitment he continues to inspire in his many friends. Long may the Kazak Army Sports Club climb!

CHRISTIAN BECKWITH, *The Wayward Mountaineer*

*Khan Tengri, North Face, New Route.* There are 12 existing routes on Khan Tengri (7010m) that lead to the summit from the North Inylchek Glacier. Nine of these routes are on the north face. The giant buttress on the left is, between 6300 and 6400 meters, the steepest part of the face and was considered the last great problem. In August, a team of Russian mountaineers from Ekaterinburg (Alexander Mihailov, expedition leader and coach; Nicolai Zhilin, climbing leader; Yuri Yermachek, and Dmitri Pavlenko), joined by Sergei Borisov, Nicolai Shcabara, Vadim Popovich, Victor Shishmintsev and Alexander Korobkov at Base Camp climbed this line. Team members had worked as guides on the Northern Inylchek Glacier from 1994-'97 and thus knew the mountain well.

Base Camp (4000m) was organized at the base of the north face on July 1. After some acclimatization climbs, the team members climbed the normal route to the summit. On August 9, Zhilin, Yermachek and Pavlenko began fixing 12 ropes on the lower part of the route from the first bergschrund (50-70°). On August 12, the team started out. The first bivy was at 5100 meters. The next day they climbed 50 meters of frozen waterfall and several complicated ice and rock sections to approach the base of a 200-meter vertical rocky "nose" that was one of the key sections of the climb. They bivied at 5500 meters at its base. From 10 a.m. to 7 p.m. the next day, Zhilin and Pavlenko fixed two 50-meter ropes, then returned to the second bivy. On August 15, they finished climbing that part of the route by 6 p.m., the arranged a more-or-less comfortable place for the fourth bivy (5700m). On August 16, the climbed several ice-covered rock walls before making the fifth bivy at 5900 meters. In the evening they fixed two more pitches. The steepness of the next part of the route increased from 50-55° to 65-70°. On August 17, they climbed about 200 vertical meters, using aid some places, before bivying at 6100 meters. In the evening they worked on the route for an hour and a half. The next day they climbed the last meters of the buttress (the crux), which brought them to the eastern slopes of the summit at about 6300 meters. After that they move along a snowy/icy ridge to the base of the steep belt of red rock, where they bivied at ca. 6400 meters. On August 19, they climbed the red rocks of the presummit in three very complicated

*The 10,000-foot north face of Khan Tengri.* NIKOLAI CHTCHETCHNIKOV

pitches. After that, several labor-consuming pitches took them to the summit dome at 6900 meters, where they bivied again. The next day's climbing was not difficult. They left the camp at 10:30 a.m. and were at the summit at 12 p.m. They descended to Base Camp via the normal route the same day, reaching it at 8 p.m.

The route is 3950 meters long, with an altitude variation of 2710 meters. The team's climbing time, including evening and preliminary preparation of the route, was 89.5 hours. They used ice fifis 88 times, and rock hooks 78 times. They used gear such as stoppers and friends 147 times. The average steepness of the wall part of the route is 64 degrees from 5100 to 6300 meters, and of the whole route (from 4300-7010m) 52 degrees.This climb took third place in the high altitude mountaineering class in the Russian championships.

ALEXANDER MICHAILOV, *Russia*

# KYRGYZSTAN

## PAMIR-ALAI

*Laylak and Karavshin Regions, Clarification.* Vladimir Kopylov, co-author with Paola Sicouri of *Forbidden Mountains*, notes that C.I.S. climbers refer to the two famous climbing areas of the Pamir-Alai as the Laylak (or Laylak Ak-Su) Region, home to Ak-Su North Peak, Iskander, and Admiralteets, and the Karavshin (or Karavshin Asen-Usen) Region, which contains Slesova Peak (a.k.a. the Russian Tower), Peak 4810 (a.k.a. the Bastion), and Asen-Usen ("The Twins"). *The American Alpine Journal* will henceforth refer to the two regions as the Laylak and Karavshin Regions.

Ak-Su North Peak has been referred to in these pages as Rocky Ak-Su to differentiate it from the peak just to the south, which we referred to as Snowy Ak-Su. C.I.S. climbers refer to the latter as Ak-Su Main Peak. We will follow their lead in this matter as well.

### Laylak Region

*Ak-Su North Peak, North Face, Various Ascents.* The Laylak Ak-Su region is still one of the most attractive climbing regions in the C.I.S., with the most technically difficult peak being the north face of Ak-Su North Peak (5217m). From August 12-25, Pavel Chabaline (leader), A. Mochalov and I. Tukhvatullin of the Kirov (Russia) Sport Club Rodina climbed the 1986 V. Popov route (6B). The route was the first to ascend the central part of the north face more or less directly; the 1998 repeat, which was undertaken in bad conditions, was only its third ascent. The ascent was awarded first place in the technical difficulty climbing class of the 1998 Russian mountaineering championship season.

From August 12-18, a team from Magnitogorsk, Russia, led by B. Mineev and comprising A. Vashliaev and G. Kirievskiy, climbed the Cold Corner route (Antonov, 1997, 6A). The ascent was awarded third place in the technical difficulty climbing class.

VLADIMIR SHATAEV, *Russian Mountaineering Federation*

*Ak-Su North Peak, First Winter Ascents.* The winter season of 1998-'99 saw the first two winter ascents of the enormous north face of Ak-Su North Peak. Pavel Chabaline (Kirov) led the first team to summit; in typical Russian style, he led all the pitches on the route, *Cold Corner* (6A, 1860m), while the other two members, Alexander Abramov (Moscow) and Ilias Tukhvatulin (Tashkent, Uzbekistan), took other roles (belaying, hauling, etc.) for the duration of the climb. The team spent 11 days on the wall, topping out on the night of December 21-22.

The second team comprised two men from Ekaterinburg, Mikhail Pershin and Igor Nefyedov. After two days spent preparing the route, they started climbing the 1988 Chaplinsky route (6B, 1825m) on December 13. The two spent about seven of the 18 days they were on the route waiting for good weather. They made the top of the wall late on December 31 in a complete whiteout with terrible wind and reached the summit in time for the new year. Four rappels into the descent on January 1, they were stopped again by a terrible storm that forced them to wait another two days for "reasonably bad weather." An account of both ascents appears earlier in this journal.

VLADIMIR SHATAEV, *Russian Mountaineering Federation*

*Iskander, South Face, New Route.* A. Zhiltsov led a Tatarstan Republic team of N. Akifiev and A. Akhmadiev on a new route on the south face of Iskander (5120m) from July 20-25. The south face of Iskander is a ca. 800-meter granite buttress with overhanging sections and cornices on top. The new route ascended the center of the face between the 1983 Grischenko (6A) and 1983 Golubev (5B) routes.

VLADIMIR SHATAEV, *Russian Mountaineering Federation*

*Admiralteets, Bashkirov Route.* From July 27-30, M. Mikhaylov (leader), V. Akimov, A. Molotov, A. Puchinin and A. Chernov, all from the Kazak Army Sports Club (Almaty, Kazakhstan), climbed the pillar of Admiralteets peak (5090m) via the 1985 V. Bashkirov route (6A diff). The team reached the summit ridge and rappelled down the other side—a not-uncommon occurrence, as the top of the pillar is separated from the summit by a long rock ridge.

VLADIMIR SHATAEV, *Russian Mountaineering Federation*

*Ortochasma Valley, Exploration, and Ascents in the Karavshin.* On our latest climbing trips we have always tried to visit unpublished sites. This comes with the high risk of making a deep blunder. This year our attention was hooked by an unknown valley between the well-known Karavshin and Laylak regions of the Pamir Alai. We (Paolo Vitali, Sonja Brambati, and Eraldo Meraldi) had an excellent first contact with locals, hearty and expansive people who opened up their houses to us as they would to friends. With these good beginnings, we started our trip in the Laylak Valley, then crossed the Aktubek Pass (4300m) to reach our objective: the Ortochasma Valley. Unfortunately, we were unlucky—we found no granite there at all, only pudding-stones and loose rocks. After our initial disappointment, we had to make a demanding decision: go back? Do a trek only? What else could we do?

Consulting the Cyrillic map with Ranger, our best horse driver, we understood that with two additional long walking days we could reach the Karavshin region, where the granite is certain. After ten hours' walking for five days, we finally reached the nice grassy Karavshin Base Camp. Lots of great routes have already been climbed here by Russian and Western climbers, but still a lot remains to be done. For the second time in a few days we had to change our goals to meet the actual conditions: maybe because of El Niño, this year the weather of the range

*Paolo Vitali on* The Missing Mountain.
SONJA BRAMBATI

wasn't exactly the "clear blue sky" for which it's famous. The rain came every day. So, instead of new big wall routes, we spent our time climbing enjoyable shorter routes close to the Base Camp.

On the lower section of the Russian Tower, we followed a nice crack system that we christened *The Missing Mountain* (F6a/b, 580m), while on the lower section of the Central Pyramid we first climbed the slabby *A Better World* (F6a/b, with one pitch at F6c, 380m), and then the mixed *Take It Easy* (F7a, 360m). All of them are excellent free climbs on red granite with knobs and chickenheads; the difficulties are mostly obligatory.

We looked very carefully for any signs of preceding ascents during our climbs, but we found nothing. Regarding *The Missing Mountain*, we know of a route to the left of it, more in the center of the wall, just right of the white rockfall scar, that we joined in the penultimate pitch. We found one piton on that pitch, the only signs we could find.

We'll surely remember the ascents from this trip as much as the wonderful time spent with Artyk, our guide/cook, and our horsemen and their families, who gave us a great lesson in kindness and humanity.

PAOLO VITALI, *Italy*

## Karavshin Region

*Peak Gorniak, Third Ascent.* Peak Gorniak (5013m) is difficult to get to without a helicopter. It takes two days and entails crossing two passes from the Karavshin Base Camp in the Asan-Usen region. Only two routes have been established on it: one, the Lenivkovoy route (5B), ascends the northwest rib, and the second, the 1992 Sidorov route (6B), ascends the center of the north-northeast face. The latter took two attempts; it was a seriously organized expedition that used a helicopter and a lot of climbers.

The Altsport team from St. Petersburg of V. Shamalo, leader, and K. Korabelnikov made the third ascent of the mountain from July 31 to August 7 via a variation to the 1992 Sidorov route, which averages 78° and is 1100 meters high. They climbed the route without any help, without a helicopter or a base camp. They reached the face of Gorniak from Karavshin Base Camp and returned 19 days later. The route was awarded second place in technical difficulty climbing class for the 1998 Russian mountaineering championships.

VLADIMIR SHATAEV, *Russian Mountaineering Federation*

*Peak Gorniak, showing the variation to the 1992 Sidorov route taken by V. Shamalo, leader, and K. Korabelnikov.* RUSSIAN MOUNTAINEERING FEDERATION ARCHIVES

*Karavshin Region, Various Ascents.* We (Robert Lange, Bettina Boehmer, Mathias Engelien from Germany and Will Stites from the U.S.) hiked in from Bapyx to Base Camp in the Karavshin Ak-Su Valley on August 19. On August 23, I hooked up with the Canadian Guy Edwards (see below) to climb the Northeast Pillar (F6a, 1100m) of Pik 1,000 Years of

Russian Christianity (4507m), simulclimbing the route on-sight in about nine hours. We took 22 hours in total for the route, including approach and descent. Mathias and Will started on the route the same day, climbing it in the "usual" way, and reaching the bivy after the 25th pitch on the first day. On the second day, Will reached the top of the climb and dislodged a big rock while flipping the rope that hit Mathias on the back. He could neither stand nor walk, but he was able to rappel. They rappelled down to the bivy on the second day and on the third reached the base of the climb.

On August 25, Robert and Bettina climbed the first four pitches of a new route on the 300-meter lower walls of the Central Pyramid. On the 26th, we rescued Mathias from the base of the Northeast Pillar and brought him down to Base Camp. He was flown to Tashkent the next day by helicopter. On August 28, Robert and Bettina made the first ascent of the seven-pitch route *Für Mathias* (5.10d, 300m) on the lower wall of the Central Pyramid. One bolt was placed at the fourth belay. On August 29, Robert and Will made the second ascent and first red-point of the German Route (5.12a) on Pik du Pamir. The route had been put up by Rainer Pickel, Michaela and Dirk Groeger the week before. On September 1, Robert and Will climbed the Voie Francaise (5.12a, 700m) on the Central Pyramid (3895m) via the *Yellow Moon* variation in a day. The route has 19 pitches, with its greatest difficulties in the middle. We bivied near the summit, because the rappel was hard to find in the dark. Robert managed to on-sight the route—its first on-sight. We rappelled the route *Black Magic*, put up by Kennan Harvey and Topher Donahue the year before. On September 4, we prepared the first four pitches of the route *Der Kleine Prinz*, an eliminate line to *Für Mathias*. On September 6, Robert and Will made the second ascent of *Take It Easy* (5.11b) on the lower Central Pyramid.

On the 7th, Robert and Bettina started for Fishtower (ca. 3800m), the formation that stands between Pik 1,000 Years.... and Pik Kotin, with a haulbag and portaledge. We ascended the first three pitches (difficulties up to 5.11d), then bivied after the third pitch. The next day, we continued from the bivy through the right part of the wall. Robert climbed the second pitch on his second try after placing six bolts and estimated the difficulties to be 5.12c. The third pitch involves aid and free climbing up to 5.11b. Then it began to rain, and thunder and lightning started when it got dark, so we decided to finish our route to the top from the bivy by an easier line, which led us through the left and central part of the tower. We called the route *Vogelfrei* ("*Free Like a Bird*," 5.12c A1).

On September 9, we finished the first ascent of the route *Gül* (Kyrgyz for "sun," 5.10d) that we had started on the first day on the 400-meter high east face of Fishtower. The last four 60-meter pitches from the bivy to the top we equipped with one bolt at each belay.   Meanwhile, Will repeated *Für Mathias* rope-solo. He then left on the 11th to climb the 400-meter south face of Pik 4810 rope-solo, but retreated on the second day after the fifth pitch—the unexpected 13-hour approach took all his food. On the 12th, Robert and Bettina made the first ascent of Der Kleine Prinz (5.11b) on-sight. The route leads straight through the whole face and has six pitches with a bolt at each belay. On the 14th, a foot of snow forced us to leave Base Camp. We hiked down to Bapyx in three nice days.

ROBERT LANGE, *Germany*

*Karavshin Region, Various Ascents.* On August 5, Guy Edwards, Hermien Freriksen, Brian Webster, Kevin Christakos and I (Canada) flew from Bishkek, the capital of Kyrgyzstan, to Osh in the west, where our week-long epic approach to the mountains began. After intense border crossings, military bribes, food poisoning and heated dealings with the Tadjik donkey men, we finally arrived at Base Camp beneath the towering walls of the Ak-Su Valley. Already our three week trip to these stunning spires had been cut back to two due to the red tape "approach;" I then spent another week sprawled in my tent, delirious with a high fever and painful cough. This left just one week in alpine rock paradise!

While I was sick, Brian and Kevin climbed one of the smaller towers, Pyramid du Pamir, by its 300-meter west face (5.10-). Guy soloed a similar route to the right at the same time. Once I had recovered, Guy and I made a 27-hour round trip of the highest spire, Peak 4810, by its 750-meter south face (V 5.10+). We climbed 15 pitches of cracks and face on good granite to top out just below the summit at dusk, then spent all night descending back to camp for sunrise. During the same time, Brian and Kevin climbed the 1300-meter French route on the northeast buttress (V 5.10-) of Pik 1,000 Years of Russian Christianity in a little over two days up and down.

With only three days left, Guy and I started up our primary objective, the *Perestroika Crack* (VI 5.12, 900m) on the beautiful Russian Tower (Pik Slesova, 4250m). We climbed 12 pitches of 5.10 cracks on rock as good as Yosemite's finest while snow squalls blew through, soaking the stone, until the weather worsened and forced us into an early bivouac perched on top of a chockstone in a chimney. With the 5.11 and 5.12 pitches still to come and the rock plastered from the night's snow storm, we began rappelling with only half the route completed.

On the last day, Hermien and I climbed the Pyramid du Pamir by the line that Guy had soloed, eight pitches of 5.10-, just behind Brian and Kevin. Meanwhile, Guy hooked up with a German climber for a sub-24-hour round-trip of the French route on 1,000 Years of Russian Christianity. They climbed the 35-pitch route in ten simul-climbed pitches, then made 25 rappels through the night, arriving at Base Camp just in time to leave.

SEAN ISAAC, *Canada*
Supported by a grant from the Canadian Himalayan Foundation

*Akshirak and Pamir Alai Ranges, Various Ascents.* In July, Chris Seashore, Carol Petrelli, Blase Reardon and I went to the Akshirak Range in eastern Kyrgyzstan for ski mountaineering. The range is a day's drive (by old slow Russian army truck) due south of Lake Issykul. Base Camp was reached by driving about 20 kilometers up river from the small town of Kara Se to the end of the dirt track, then pushing another ten kilometers overland by truck, and finally walking about ten kilometers to the confluence of two large glaciated valleys that join to form the Kara Se River. The region is remote and untouched; we climbed and skied five unnamed and previously unskied peaks immediately surrounding the confluence. Peak heights ranged from 4500 to 4800 meters. The skiable terrain ranged from 350 to 500 meters of 35-45°. We judged anything steeper than 45° to be too dangerous because the thin layer of new snow was hanging on old blue ice. I would recommend skiing in the area earlier in the summer or late in the spring when there is more snow and colder temperatures.

After two weeks in the Akshirak Range, Chris Seashore and I traveled to the Pamir Alai where the peaks are higher. We skied three peaks near Peak Lenin. One, Ukana (5100m), is routinely climbed from the Peak Lenin Base Camp. The other two were approached by hiking straight up the valley as you trek from lower Base Camp toward Peak Lenin. (The path to Lenin turns left over a small pass). All the ski runs had pitches of consistent 45°, and all were, I believe, unskied. I ski-cut one oozing slide because we were too greedy and made a second run on one of the peaks late in the day. We also made two runs on the lower half of the standard route on Peak Lenin. Other possibilities abound, but we had some bad weather and ran out of time.

JON TURK

*Korzhenievskovo Valley, Various Ascents.* From July 2 to August 22, Rowland Barker, Steven Carter, Hamish Downer, Mark Stevenson and I visited the Korzhenievskovo Valley in southern Kyrgyzstan. We attempted ten peaks and reached the summit of seven. We climbed in lightweight alpine style, generally in pairs. The region is heavily glaciated and the peaks heavily eroded. The rock on the mountains was very broken and all major rock lines on relatively reasonable rock were threatened by serac fall. Snow conditions were generally firm, although deep soft snow was a problem at times.

There were rarely periods of good weather for more than half a week, and the bad weather usually lasted up to three days. There was often a weather pattern of the weather closing in during the late afternoon and rain, hail or snow in the evening. This would often clear by midnight and the morning would present good climbing conditions. However, this pattern could not be relied upon. We used very little protection, partly due to the climbs being less technical than expected and partly due to the lack of protection available. We never saw any rock we would trust to hold nuts or cams. The ice was generally not deep enough and too brittle to hold ice screws.

Most of the mountains have already been climbed and named by Russian climbers. However, we were not able to discover all of the names in our research, so we have simply referred to them by the height of the summit according to our maps. Ascents were as follows. The north face of 4810m, PD, July 20, Barker and Lassetter. The west face of 4931m, AD, July 25, Downer and Lassetter. The north ridge of 5015m, PD, Lassetter and Stevenson, August 19. The south ridge of 5525m, AD, Lassetter, solo, July 25, repeated by Barker and Stevenson the same day. The south summit (5845m) of 19th Party Conference Peak (5945m) via the south ridge, F, Downer and Stevenson, August 10. Pic Korzhenievskovo (6008m), PD/AD, Lassetter and Stevenson, July 28; repeated by Barker and Downer on July 30. Lassetter and Stevenson bivied just above the col (ca. 4600m) and took 17 hours to reach the summit from there and return. Barker and Downer bivied beyond most of the steep steps. The north ridge of Pic 6624, PD/AD, Lassetter and Stevenson, July 31. The east ridge of Pic Lenina (7134m), PD, Barker and Lassetter, August 9-11.

The group recommends the valleys in this area to those wanting solitude and the opportunity to experience exploratory mountaineering on high peaks of easy to moderate difficulty.

JAMES LASSETTER, *Cambridge University Mountaineering Club*

WEST KOKSHAAL-TAU

*Kizil Asker Area, Various Ascents.* In 1997, I traveled with an international team of five to the West Kokshaal-Tau range, the southwestern-most part of the Tien Shan mountains on the border with China (see 1998 *AAJ*, pp. 342-3). In 1998, supported by funding from a Mugs Stump grant, I returned with Carlos Buhler and Mark Price from the U.S. and Sean Isaac and Guy Edwards from Canada, traveling one valley to the west to the Kizil Asker

*Sean Isaac and peaks of the Kizil Asker region. A: "Peak Gronky" (Edwards-Isaac, 1998); B: "Peak Zuckerman" (Edwards, 1998); C: "Peak Unmarked Soldier" (Beckwith-Engelien-Green, 1997); D: Peak 4850 (Valiev et al, 1985); E: Panfilovsky Division (Valiev et al, 1985); F: Kizil Asker (main summit is hidden behind north ridge) (Valiev et al, 1985); G: "Peak Ljosha" (Isaac-Edwards, 1998).*
CHRISTIAN BECKWITH

region. Research indicates we were the second climbing team to visit this area, after Kazbek Valiev's team of 1984, which succeeded in making the first recorded ascent of Kizil Asker (5842m). (We have heard rumors of a 1960s ascent of the same mountain, but they remain unconfirmed.) Bad weather prevented us from achieving two of our objectives—the north ridge and east face of Kizil Asker—but we did manage to climb ten new routes on eight new mountains. Four of the routes and three of the mountains were climbed from the West Komorova Glacier, which we reached in half a day from our Base Camp. One of them was a pyramidal peak I had tried with teammates two times the year before. Carlos, Mark and I climbed the peak via the north face in 23 hours (V AI4, ca. 650m) while Guy soloed the mountain via the west ridge (ca. 650m), a route we used for descent. Guy reached the top first and named the peak "Butterfly Peak" (Pik Babuchka, ca. 5220m) for all the butterflies he found in the snow as he climbed. (All peak names are tentative. An account of the expedition has been submitted to the Russian Mountaineering Federation.) Guy then soloed a new route via the southeast ridge of "Peak Jerry Garcia" (ca. 5083m) before returning to ABC. Guy met us as we returned at 3 a.m. with water and clothes, then, after accompanying us back to ABC, soloed an ice couloir (AI4, 600m) on the east face of the Ocher Walls and traversed the tops of two peaks before descending a broader couloir roughly half a kilometer to the north. He was back in camp by mid-morning, and named the peaks "Zuckerman" (4750m) and "Carnovsky" (4700m) after the Philip Roth book, *Zuckerman Unbound*, he was reading.

*The virgin 2,000 to 2,500-foot "Great Walls of China" in the West Kokshaal-Tau.*
CHRISTIAN BECKWITH

After a return to Base Camp, on July 10, Sean, Guy, and I went to a peak across the valley from Kizil Asker. The west face was approximately 3,500 feet high; the bottom half was rock, while the upper half looked to be broken mixed climbing. We climbed nine pitches of rock up to 5.10+ A1, one of moderate mixed and two roped traverses/scrambles before finding a scree-covered ledge at 8 p.m., which we managed to even out just as a storm converged on us. A lightning-ridden night ensued. In the morning the storm continued, so we rapped down through waterfalls, reaching ABC in the early afternoon.

On July 14, all five of us were back in ABC. Sean and Guy began up the route again, while Carlos, Mark and I started up the north ridge of Kizil Asker. We climbed some 800 meters, including three pitches on the ridge proper (5.9 AI3), before we found a slanting ledge to bivy

*The unclimbed 1300-meter south and east faces of Kizil Asker.* CHRISTIAN BECKWITH

on. A storm moved in that night; when it showed no signs of letting up, we descended the next morning, leaving behind four days' worth of food. We reached ABC in the storm to find that Guy had taken a 25-foot fall onto a ledge, hurting his back. His rope had been nearly severed by rock fall. The two had managed to descend, but Guy spent the next two days on his back in the tent, unable to move.

By the 20th, he had recovered, and I joined him and Sean for another session at ABC. By now, we had grown accustomed to the very small windows of reasonably stable weather and decided to concentrate on some day routes. Guy soloed "Peak Bagger" (4600m) in an hour and a half on the evening of the 20th, noting what looked like a cairn on top. The next day, the three of us climbed "Peak Ecstasy" (ca. 4700m) and "Peak Yurnos" (ca. 4725m). The three pointy, picturesque mountains were not technical, but offered fun routes to the tops, from which the views undoubtedly would have been impressive had there been any.

The next day we were slated to climb a pointy mountain at the foot (north) of Kizil Asker.

I was sleeping at a camp half an hour from theirs, and when my alarm failed to go off, the two climbed "Peak Ljosha" (ca. 4600m, named for our cook) via the north face (III AI3/4 5.8, 600m), finding some steep ice and loose rock on their ascent.

After resting in BC for a day, we returned to ABC for a try at the north face of Kizil Asker. On the 25th we ascended to ca. 4800m via the glaciated slopes and bivied in a crevasse. The next morning we began climbing, encountering a 400-meter traverse on 50° snow that brought us to the col between the north ridge and the summit. White-out conditions forced us to wait in an ice cave and then later at the col for two hours. When visibility ceased altogether, we decided to descend, and continued down to ABC, arriving in the evening. That night, a storm deposited a foot and a half of snow. I returned to BC the next morning, followed by Sean a few hours later. The others remained at ABC.

The weather the next day was the calmest we had seen on the trip. I remained in BC with illness. Guy had started out to solo the west face of Panfilovski Division, but had felt ill as well and returned to his tent. (Bad mutton remains the suspect.) Carlos and Mark began up a mixed line on the west face of Peak Carnovsky. When Mark lost the bolt from the head of one of his tools, the pair, who had only three ice screws, began moving quite slowly, and endured an open bivy in a chimney on a small ledge. The next day they continued the one and a half pitches to easy terrain which they followed to the top of the ridge. On the descent, they rappelled near the line of ascent, getting their ropes stuck twice and reaching ABC at 8 p.m.

That same day, Sean and Guy climbed the peak we had tried at the beginning of the trip, reaching the top (ca. 5000m) via the west gully/north shoulder and naming the mountain Peak Gronky. They returned to BC that day, followed by Carlos and Mark the next morning. The truck had already arrived, and we loaded it for departure and left by 5 p.m.

CHRISTIAN BECKWITH, *The Wayward Mountaineers*

*Kokshaal-Tau, Various Ascents.* From July 18-August 26, the united team of Moscow district climbed in the West Kokshaal-Tau. The chief of the expedition was Boris Starostin; the trainers were Fedor Akhmatov, Valerii Boiko, Victor Efimov and Eugeny Monaenkov. The 25 members of the expedition traveled to Bishkek, the capital of Kyrgyzstan, by train. We then traveled to Lake Isykkul by bus, then drove to Base Camp over two days in two light passenger lorries. After the last military checkpoint, we traveled the final 25 kilometers in the wide valley along the Uzen-Gush River. This was only possible in the morning then the water was low. Due to the skillful navigation of our drivers, we were able to place our camp at ca. 3500 meters near the Grivoriev Glacier at the confluence of the Uzen-Gush River and the river from the Palgov Glacier.

We made first ascents on seven summits of this valley during the expedition. The team of F. Akhmatov made perhaps the first ascent (5B) of Peak Chon-Turasu (5780m, a.k.a. Dzholdash) and climbed Peak 5013m from the east. The team of E. Manaenko traversed Peak Kryl'ya Sovetov (5B, 5450m) Peaks 4758m (4A) and 5200m (4B); the only previous attempt was in 1938. The team of V. Efimov made ascents of Peaks 4530m (2A) and 4825m (5A). A new route (5B) to the summit of Dankova (5986m, the highest peak of the region) was made by a team led by V. Boiko. The two previous ascents were made in 1972. Boiko's team also climbed Peak 4730m.

On August 12, on the first ascent of Peak Cosmos (a.k.a. Schmidta, 5940m) via the north face, Igor Korsun was killed. All the group was covered by ice fall. All but Korsun incurred only bruises. Korsun suffered a fracture at the base of his skull. He did not regain consciousness and died two hours later. We lowered his body over two days to Base Camp. After this, the expedition was called off.

VIKTOR EFIMOV, *Russia*

*Chonturasu Glacier Area, Various Ascents.* In September, Pat Littlejohn followed up his 1997 guided expedition to the Chonturasu Glacier at the eastern end of the West Kokshaal-Tau with a second International School of Mountaineering trip, this time to the valley immediately east of the Komarova and visited briefly by his 1997 expedition. In contrast to the previous year, the weather was quite poor, with much heavy snowfall. The party climbed four easy snow peaks within striking distance of Base Camp before deciding to cut short their activities in the region.

LINDSAY GRIFFIN, *Alpine Climbing Group*

# TIBET

*Yebokangal Ri and Porong Ri, Ascents.* We were Reinier Zuidhoff, leader; Hans Van Der Meulen, Wilco Van Rooijen, Cas Van De Gevel (all Dutch), Thierry Schmitter (F) and Marko Prezelj (SLO). Schmitter and I planned to climb a new route on the south face of Shishapangma; the two rope teams of Zuidhoff and Van Der Meulen, and Van Rooijen and Van De Gevel wanted to repeat one of the established routes on the south face. We planned to act independently once we left Base Camp.

On April 8, we reached Nyalam, starting point for the three- to four-day trek to Shishapangma's south face BC. On April 9, we went with the local yak men to check the conditions in the approach valley. Deep snow made it impossible for the yaks to leave Nyalam. After asking for porters, the Chinese LO told us that we would need to pay 1000 yuan for insurance for each porter. That was not acceptable to us, so they offered us transportation to the north side of the mountain, site of BC for the normal route on Shishapangma. It was not a good substitute for the south face, as we had no information about the north side. Regardless, we accepted, and were first at BC on April 16.

Thierry and I decided to act as "alpine" as possible—that is, no troubling over mountain names and altitudes, just "see, go and climb." After a fast acclimatization on the north ridge from the glacier up to 6500 meters, we decided to climb the first mountain on the west side of Shishapangma. On April 20, we crossed the glacier below the east face of Porong Ri. The next morning, we left our tent and began our climb of the face. In six hours we climbed a new route on the east face to the northeast ridge, which we followed for the last 150 meters to the east summit of Porong Ri. I reached the east summit (7284m) in very strong wind; Thierry turned back 50 meters from the summit. We descended via the northeast ridge, where we found some fixed ropes (the ridge had been climbed in May, 1982, by a 14-member Japanese expedition that used three camps), then continued to our tent and on to BC the same day. The 1000-meter route has ice and snow with one short rock section. On the upper section, we found hard ice up to 60° covered with dry snow. The difficulty of the route is akin to the Austrian route on Les Courtes in the French Alps.

After six days of rest in unstable weather with strong winds, we left BC on April 28 for the next climb. This time we wanted to climb to the west summit (7332m) of Yebokangal Ri

*The east face of Porong Ri. The line of ascent is solid; the dotted line marks the descent.*
MARKO PREZELJ

(a.k.a. Jebo Kangri; the peak has two summits: the east summit is 7365m). Yebokangal Ri sits in front (north) of Shishapangma. If conditions were good, we wanted to continue up to the summit of Shishapangma.

We started at 6 a.m. from BC and after 13 hours we put up a tent at around 7000 meters below the ridge. The whole day was characterized by strong winds and drifting snow. We encountered one difficult section of powder snow over steep rock, but the rest was mostly snow and ice with short mixed sections, made more difficult by the powder snow over ice and rock and the constant wind.

On April 29, we climbed over the north ridge to the west summit (7332m), which we reached in strong winds at 2 p.m. We descended to the other side on the big plateau (7100m) where the normal route on Shishapangma goes. We put up the tent and decided to take one day's rest to dry our clothes and fuel our bodies with liquid and food for a fast ascent via the normal route the day after (the north face looked too icy with dry snow over it).

The rest day had almost no wind or clouds, so we expected similar weather the next day. But the next night was very windy and at 6 a.m. it began to snow a heavy, wet snow at 7100 meters. That forced us down the normal route, since we were afraid of deep snow on the normal route, which we knew nothing about. After two hours it stopped snowing and by 11 a.m. the sky was quite clear. By then we were already at CI, so we continued to BC.

After reaching BC, I caught a bad cold and was so weak I had no energy or motivation to attempt the normal (ski) route. On May 6, Zuidhoff and Van Der Meulen reached the central summit with one Spaniard and two South Tyroleans in one day of perfect weather from CIII via the normal route.

The weather was quite bad most of the time of my stay in BC. Hans, Reinier and I left BC on May 13. Wilco, Cas and Thierry stayed on for one more attempt on the normal route. The

*Yebokangal Ri (a.k.a. Jebo Kangri) showing the line of ascent and descent (ending in tracks in foreground). The northwest face of Shishapangma is in the background.* MARKO PREZELJ

weather become much better in the second part of May, and they, along with most of the members from many expeditions this season in BC, reached the summit.

Ours was the second ascent, via a new route, of Yebokangal Ri, and possibly the first ascent of the west summit and first traverse of the mountain. Our new route on Porong Ri was the third ascent of the mountain. Of the crowd of more than 100 "climbers" in Shishapangma BC this season, we were the only ones to do something other than the normal route. Some of the "conquerors" expressed surprise that we did not have a strong desire for the summit itself. Some of them didn't even know that there were mountains other than Shishapangma. That was a completely new experience for me. I think that the normal route on Shishapamgma is totally commercialized; you can buy entire altitude camps from the expeditions that are leaving BC.

MARKO PREZELJ, *Planinska zveza Slovenije*

NYANGLA QEN TANGLA SHAN RANGE

*Sepu Kunglha Karpo Massif, Various Activity.* The Nyangla Qen Tangla Shan in Eastern Tibet is topped by Sepu Kangri (6950m). After first seeing Sepu Kangri in 1982 from a plane while flying from Chengdu to Lhasa, I finally reached the area in 1996 and led another expedition to attempt the peak in 1997 (see 1998 *AAJ*, pp. 348-351). We returned in the autumn of 1998. Charles Clarke and Elliot Robertson set out three weeks before the rest of the team to find a route into the Sepu Kangri massif from the east. It was a particularly heavy monsoon and as a result they were unable to make their approach around the southern aspect of the Nyangla Qen Tangla Shan, but were forced to take the northern route through Nakchu and Chamdo. They reached Base Camp on August 30, two days after the main climbing party left the U.K. They crossed into the Yang Valley, to the west of Sepu Kangri, to get views of that aspect of the mountain before coming down to meet us at Khinda to make arrangements for our walk-in. We finally got away from the roadhead on September 10, having hauled all the expedition baggage across the river on a wire pulley. We established Base Camp on September 13, by which time the weather seemed to have settled. Our four-man climbing team consisted of Graham Little, Scott Muir, Victor Saunders and myself. In addition, we had a media team planning to film a fly-on-the-wall documentary of the expedition and also to send news reports back by satellite. We had had satellite communications the previous year, had run a web site from Base Camp and were planning to do the same in 1998. All of us had had mixed feelings about such instant communication, but the trip had been so expensive that sponsorship was essential and that meant television coverage. A web site is also attractive to sponsors. We ended up enjoying our communications, both as a means of keeping contact with home and also as a means of communication over which we had full creative control.

Victor and I both wanted to have a further look at "Fotheringham's Ridge and Corridor," which I had recce'ed the year before with Jim Fotheringham as a possible outflanking route. Whilst Graham and Scott made an unsuccessful attempt on Chomo Mangyal ("the Wife of Sepu"), Victor and I invited Elliot to join us on a recce. From a camp on the moraine just below the ridge, we reached the crest on September 20. It was a perfect day and we could see there was a straight-forward, relatively safe route up into the Western Cwm of Sepu Kangri and on to the summit. At the same time, Graham and Scott had discovered that snow conditions on steep ground were particularly dangerous, a strong disincentive against attempting their objective, the "Frendo Spur."

After a rest, we all set out on our first attempt. Victor and I invited Elliot to join us. The route through the seracs and crevasses of the Corridor proved fairly straight-forward and we camped at the edge of the Western Cwm at a height of 6150 meters. The Western Cwm was an easy walk and we decided to tackle the west ridge of the final summit mass, the northwest ridge leading down to Seamo Uylmitok showing signs of wind-slab avalanche. That night we camped at 6530 meters. We were within striking distance of the summit and needed just one more fine morning to make a successful bid. Once again we were out of luck. It started snowing that afternoon and kept on for the next three days. We retreated on the second day.

A week later we returned to the fray, but discovered that over a meter of snow had fallen. We only had three pairs of snow shoes between us and, as I was going slower than the others, we decided that Elliot and I should drop back to enable the other three to make a final attempt for the summit. They set out on October 10 from our second camp. It was a fine clear dawn. Graham was worried about the amount of snow and consequent risk of avalanche and therefore opted to turn back just short of our original top camp. Once on his own, his eyes were drawn to the back of Seamo Uylmitok, which beckoned from the other side of the Western Cwm, and he decided to snatch it before going down. It provided a straight-forward climb.

In the meantime, Scott and Victor reached the site of Camp III. Since it was still early and the weather was clear, they carried on up the mountain. The quality of the snow improved dramatically and they made good progress over a large bergschrund and up to the crest of the final summit ridge, reaching a height of 6830 meters, 150 meters below and about a quarter of a mile from the top. Visibility was down to a few meters and the wind was savage. On our radio call we had just given them an up-to-date forecast from the Met Office in England that the following morning was going to be fine. In view of this they decided to return to Camp III, hoping to make it to the summit early the next day. Once again we were out of luck. The weather

*Bonington, Saunders and Robertson on their way up the western cwm between camps II and III with Mount Sepu in the background.* CHRIS BONINGTON PICTURE LIBRARY

never recovered and after two nights they descended to Base Camp.

By then we had run out of time, but we had at least discovered a reasonable route to the summit. There are also a wealth of other climbs to be had in this fascinating area, both on the north and southern side of the mountain. The site of Base Camp is particularly attractive and our neighbors became good friends. It is an area I would strongly recommend to anyone attracted to exploratory climbing.

CHRIS BONINGTON, *Alpine Climbing Group*

# CHINA

*Mustagh Ata, Gasherbrum II, and Other Activity in the Chinese Karakoram.* Our expedition was co-led by Daniel Mazur and Jonathan Otto. On June 29, we set out from Kathmandu, Nepal, to Islamabad, Pakistan, across India by rail with 600 kilograms of mountaineering equipment. An in-progress war of nuclear detente was currently in full swing between India and Pakistan, which made the border crossings interesting. On July 20, our bus crossed from Pakistan into China via the Khunjerab Pass on the Karakoram Highway. On July 21, a four-hour, camel-supported trek from the highway into the Chinese Pamirs brought us to Mustagh Ata's clean, comfortable, grassy, well-organized, permanently established north side Base Camp at 4350 meters. On August 3, Ellen Miller led the way to the summit (7546m) in a wind-blown whiteout, with Angela McCormick and Daniel Mazur in tow. That afternoon, they tele-mark skied down from the summit and reached Base Camp.

By August 10, 11 of our team members (including Frank Pitula, Clint Rogers, Steven Ross, Patricia Peterson and Howard Yee) had reached the summit, either on foot, snowshoe, or ski. Richard Bothwell made a snowboard descent on August 9. Upon departure, we exchanged all

*Mike Sinclair at Camp II (5750m) on the north ridge of Gasherbrum II.* DAN MAZUR

of our in-place equipment, including ropes, fixing lines, snow, rock and ice anchors to a well-organized expedition we had met from Osaka, Japan. In this way, we tried to reduce the pollution of mountain environments that occurs with the unnecessary duplication of safety equipment on a well-traveled route.

On August 13, we began an attempt on the unclimbed south face of Mustagh Ata. After leaping initial time-consuming bureaucratic hurdles, including interesting visits to the police station, we entered the Mustagh Ata complex from the east side, crossing several technical 5000-meter ice and rock passes in the process. Our 80-kilometer mountaineering traverse was only possible because we carried lightweight, high-standard equipment. Weather and loss of time prevented us from making a bonafide attempt on Mustagh Ata's stunningly massive south face, but we did reconnoiter a very feasible route for the future.

During our travels across the Mustagh Ata complex, we made the first ascent of the 6100-meter Tokoruk Peak. Olivier Raimond and Richard Bothwell led the way on the semi-technical snow- and ice-covered west ridge, traversing several cornices and false summits before reaching the top, where we enjoyed a fine view of our entire eight-day traverse and of Mustagh Ata's classic south face itself.

On September 1, our team began the first attempt of the 8036-meter Gasherbrum II via its unclimbed north face. Eight of us made a rather pleasant trek, and a few exciting camel-assisted crossings of the snow-melt swollen river, through the desert-like Shaksgam River Valley. We established Advanced Base Camp I at 4650 meters and ABC II at 4800 meters on September 2. On September 11, in sunny warm weather, we finished fixing 700 meters of rope on the steep and icy 30-60° "Hilton Headwall." On September 13, we established CI at 5750 meters on safe flat ground at the edge of "Destruction Plateau" between the "Skyang Ice Cascade" and "Sinclair's Scepter." Our single-wall tents were deluged in snow and battered by winds from the Tibetan Plateau until October 1, when we fixed another 500 meters of line over three days. Our route of ascent was the "Wallis Traverse;" we reached a high point of 6400 meters. We found this to be a rather technical, but highly possible, route that stretched the limits of our equipment. On October 3, we turned back in raging winds, out of time, short on hot chocolate drink mix, and a tiny bit let-down, but wiser and 100% primed for a future ascent of this exciting, still unclimbed route.

On October 1, Ian Hatchett made the first ascent of the unclimbed summit of the 6061-meter Madame Butterfly via the east ridge. He climbed solo on 30-60° snow and ice, and his one-day, fast-and-light first ascent was particularly gratifying, as Andrew Dunn and Daniel Mazur had nearly reached the summit in 1996 via the west face.

On October 2, David Wallis and Andrew Hilton attempted to make the first ascent of 6850-meter Venus Rising. At 11 a.m., while climbing at 6400 meters on the east face, they were sucked into a mountain-wide, meter-deep slab avalanche. The two were tossed down the slope, somersaulting through fast-moving snow blocks. Andrew suffered a severely sprained ankle, and both climbers were stripped of ski poles, hats, goggles, and ice axes before coming to a halt at the edge of a rock precipice as the avalanche carried on and tumbled into a deep ice couloir.

On October 7, our entire team, assisted by the faithful Tadjik and Uighur people as camel caravaners, fled the Karakoram in stable, cold, windy weather and low-water river conditions. We carefully buried our biodegradable wastes, then burned and packed out every single scrap

*The unclimbed Urdok Hills, sub-7000m peaks at the confluence of Urdok Glacier and the Shaksgam River.* DAN MAZUR

of rubbish. During our 48-day expedition, we had encountered a few shepherd families and no other tourists. In fact, the mountaineering authorities told us that during the last two years, ours had been the only climbing expedition permitted to enter the Chinese Karakoram.

On October 10, at the end of the 100-kilometer camel trek out, while visiting Korul, a village of the seasonally-nomadic Kyrgyz people, a seven-year-old shepherd boy was hit by a flying piece of rock shrapnel thrown from a road builder's dynamite blast. Our expedition doctors Andrew Hilton, Mike Sinclair and Rob Allen amputated his shattered foot and nursed him through the night. We then transported him, his sister, and parents in our vehicles to the nearest hospital, where we pooled our resources to pay for an operation that his family would have been unable to afford. It was the first time any of them had ever ridden in a motor vehicle, or been to the nearest city. As a result of this mishap, we met with local government officials, and are currently joining together to create a health care system that will begin to fill the void for these people, who currently have nothing.

Finally, between October 15 and 27, we crossed Xinjiang Province and the nation of Tibet by rail, plane, and road with 300 kilograms of equipment, hosted along the way by regional mountaineering clubs. We were welcomed warmly, and were able to conduct extensive mountaineering research into high-altitude mountains in and around the Tibetan Plateau. As a result, we are planning expeditions and further explorations in Tibet and Xinjiang for the upcoming climbing season.

DAN MAZUR

*Mt. Kongur, Attempt.* Our group this year tried to climb Mt. Kongur (7719m) in the Kashgar Range. The extremely bad weather did not allow us to even approach the summit tower. The route (Bonington, 1981) is very long and indirect. We dug our last snow cave at 6800 meters. Due to avalanche-prone slopes (snow fell every day) and lack of visibility, we turned back.

OTTO CHKHETIANI, *Russia*

*Yunnan Province, Various Ascents.* In April, I traveled to northwest Yunnan province and made my way to the town of Dechin by public bus. From April 25-27, I recced the approach to Baima Shan, an unclimbed peak of around 5500 meters on the west side of the road between Zhongdian and Dechin. On the 28th, I climbed a small unnamed and unmarked 5300-meter peak on the east side of the road. I began climbing from my camp at around 4000 meters and reached the summit after three-and-a-half hours via the west ridge. Temperatures were -15°C on the summit at sunrise. I had great views over Sichuan and toward Tibet. The climbing was characterized by moderate snow and ice slopes plus two large gendarmes of rotten and loose rock that I was forced to climb over. I climbed by headlamp as there was no moon. The weather during my stay tended to be clear in the morning, hot in the afternoon, then stormy at night. Snow cover at this time of year was considerable, blocking the road from Zhongdian until mid-April, though I saw no signs of avalanches.

I returned to Lijiang, again by public bus. Then, on May 3-4, I approached Yulongxueshan, also known as Jade Dragon Snow Mountain (5590m), reaching 4200 meters on the south side. Bad weather and lack of food led me to descend and return to Lijiang.

DAMIEN GILDEA, *Australia*

## SICHUAN

### LOTUS FLOWERS MOUNTAIN RANGE

*Peak 5704m, First Ascent.* The 5704-meter main peak of the Lotus Flowers mountain range (a.k.a. Zharha Latse, Mt. Haitze) lies to the north of the Minya-Konka mountain area in Sichuan, China. It is about 20 kilometers north of Kangding and 350 kilometers west of Chengdu. The Japan Workers' Alpine Federation Trans-Mountain Expedition 1998 ascended this unclimbed peak via the southwest face in September and October. We were Hitoshi Yamaoka (leader), Yoshio Kondo, and Yoshitake Shirai. We reached Base Camp (3900m), a one-day walk from the nearest small village of Sutunba, on September 17. Though it was small, the glacier began at more than 5000 meters. Camp I was placed at 4900 meters on the moraine near the southwest face on September 23. It was easy walking from BC to CI. We made CII at 5400 meters on an unstable snow ridge on September 28 after climbing the southwest face in 15 50-meter pitches. The route followed the edge of the couloir and entailed snow, ice, and rotten rock between the south peak and the couloir itself (UIAA II-IV). On September 30, Yamaoka and Shirai climbed the mixed face of the main peak in nine 50-meter pitches, encountering unstable rock and snow (III-IV). Rainy weather had continued for 11 days after our arrival at BC. Fortunately, around the time we reached the summit, we had fine days. On October 6, Kondo and Shirai made the second ascent. Near here and in the north of Mt. Siguniang in Sichuan, there are some sharp peaks suitable for rock climbing.

HITOSHI YAMAOKA, *Japan Workers' Alpine Federation*

# Corrections

The 1996 *AAJ* (p. 245) reported the first ascent of Nyegi Kangsang (6983m), a high peak on the border of Arunachal Pradesh (India) and Tibet (China). A report of this climb was also published in the 1996 *Himalayan Journal*, Volume 52 (p. 9). According to Harish Kapadia, the summit of Nyegi Kangsang was, in fact, not reached by the Indian expedition led by Col. M. P. Yadav in 1995. The peak remains unclimbed. The Nyegi Kangsang expedition was organized by the Indian Mountaineering Foundation (IMF) in 1995. Col. M. P. Yadav, the then-Principal of Nehru Institute of Mountaineering, Uttarkashi, was appointed expedition leader. The expedition claimed to have made the first ascent of the peak on October 23, 1995. It submitted an article with a few photographs and a sketch map, which were published in good faith in the *HJ*. However, upon later studies, based on further availability of maps and photos, it was found that the team had reached a point about 600 meters below the main peak and about 1.25 kilometers away from the main summit on the northeast ridge. Mr. Jagdish Nanavati, President of the Himalayan Club, submitted a detailed study to the President of the IMF, Dr. M.S. Gill, who immediately appointed a Sub-Committee under Mr. Suman Dubey (Vice President) to study this. Leader Col. M.P. Yadav and two of the summiters appeared before the Committee. Faced with facts, the summiters admitted before the Committee that they had not actually reached the highest point of their "summit ridge" (see photo no. 2, opposite page 13, HJ Vol. 52). The Committee concluded that the expedition had failed to reach the main summit and had wrongly claimed an ascent. The findings were accepted unanimously by the Governing Council of the IMF.

In the 1997 *AAJ*, the account on page 262 of El Escudo, South Face, actually refers to a climb that took place in the Val di Mello, Italy.

In the 1998 volume, on the opening frontispiece photo of climbers approaching the summit of Latok II, the caption is mislabeled. In the photo are Alexander and Thomas Huber; the helmet and backpack of Conrad Anker are visible just behind Thomas. Toni Gutsch took the photo. On page 38, the photographer is Thomas Huber. Alex Huber is the climber in the photo. The photographer on page 39 is Thomas Huber. The caption for the photo on page 43 should read, "Thomas Huber on the day of the summit." Alexander Huber was the photographer.

Chris McNamara's name was spelled incorrectly throughout the book. On page 205, Marc Venery's name is spelled incorrectly. On page 235, the two photos of Mt. Ratz and Mt. Noel were miscaptioned. The correct captions are, "Above: Mt. Ratz, with the northeast face in shadow. The route climbed out of the cwm to the col and ascended the rock/ice juncture. Below: Mt. Noel. The West Face route ascends the central gully and rib." On page 262, the "we" in the Eduard Birnbacher account should include Stefan Wiebel. In the Cordillera Quimsa Cruz accounts in the same section, some Cordillera Occidental and Cordillera Real information was inadvertently included.

On page 263, we published a report of a first ascent of Nevado de las Vírgenes in the Cordillera de Quimza Cruz written by Javier Sanchez. According to Dakin Cook, the snowy massif pictured in his photo and identified as Nevado de las Vírgenes may or may not be Nevado de las Vírgenes. Wrote Cook, "Stan Shepardand I thought it was when we climbed it in 1992 (1993 *AAJ*, p. 174). The following year I began to have doubts as to whether this was, indeed, Nevado de las Vírgenes (I am still not sure). As a result, I wrote a correction in the

1995 *AAJ* (p. 201) saying that it was one of the peaks of the Kori Chuma group, but not Nevado de los Vírgenes. The original report of our ascent identified it as one of the peaks of the Kori Chuma group. The IGM map of this area labels this group of peaks Kori Chuma. Regardless of what it is named, in 1992 Stan Shepard, Mario Miranda and I climbed the snowy massif on the left shown in the Javier Sanchez photo (see 1998 *AAJ*, p. 263).

The photo on page 283 was incorrectly captioned. The caption should read, "Bruno Sourzac on the ice mushroom of *Exocet*, Cerro Stanhardt." On page 336, the photo of Asan is reversed. In the *In Memoriam* section, on page 405, the obituary for Joe Stettner included a note on his climb of Stettner Ledges on Longs Peak. The route was repeated three times in the next 15 years, not twice in the next 19 years as stated.

On page 326, a photo purports to show the west face of K2 and the line taken by the 1997 Tokai branch of the Japanese Alpine Club. Writes Jim Wickwire, "No portion of what is commonly referred to as K2's west face is visible in the photograph. In the *AAJ* account, expedition leader Osamu Tanabe mentions setting up Camp V on the 'shoulder of the West Ridge pinnacle area.' He then states that from the shoulder 'it was possible to descend onto the snow-covered west face in two pitches.'

"I am convinced that Tanabe's line on the photo is one face too far to the left (north). The West Ridge pinnacle he refers to is very prominent—it's the level platform on the right-hand skyline of the photo. The snow slopes are obvious and lead to the summit area. Nowhere did they reach the north ridge, except possibly right near the summit where all the ridges converge to the mountain's apex. With the proper line drawn, the photo does depict the new variation above 8000 meters. However, there have been other routes done along part of his dotted line." We are unable to elaborate upon Mr. Wickwire's notes as we go to press.

On page 69, the route line for the 1997 Australian route on the north face of Thalay Sagar is incorrect. The correct line is at left.

For these and any other errors that we have not caught, we offer our sincere apologies.

*The 1997 Australian route on the north face of Thalay Sagar.*
JAY SMITH

# Reviews

Edited by David Stevenson

IMAX *Everest.* Produced by MacGillivary Freeman Films. Mountain footage filmed and directed by David Breashears. Camera assistant, Robert Schauer. Screened at Edwards IMAX theater, Irvine, California. Price of admission: $7. Film time: 48 minutes.

*Everest*, the most popular large-format film of all time, features an ascent of the South Col route by Ed Viesturs, Jamling Norgay Sherpa (son of first ascender Tenzing Norgay), and Spanish climber Araceli Segarra. The cinematography and direction is by two award-winning filmmakers: Greg MacGillivary and accomplished climber David Breashears. Breashears, no stranger to Everest, made television history on one of his dozen expeditions to the world's highest mountain by sending the first live broadcast from the summit to televisions sets around the world. He has been dazzling audiences for 20 years, and this 70-mm film is no exception. Three months after Everest released, I went to see it on a Saturday morning—only to learn that all shows had sold out.

Part of the popularity, of course, is due to the public fascination with the May 10, 1996 tragedy that left five climbers dead and a sixth horribly frostbitten. The IMAX crew was on the mountain at that time, and with members like Breashears, Viesturs and Robert Schauer, their expedition was far and away the most respected and experienced. When disaster struck high on the mountain, Breashears was faced with a sticky decision: get involved with the rescue and risk the 5.5 million-dollar film project, or remain detached, preserve his group's resources and let the chips fall where they may. The story about how his crew dropped everything, offered up all their supplies and oxygen and marched up the hill to save lives is now history. They are remembered as heroes.

After the rescue, with supplies seriously compromised, the film crew exhausted, bodies of friends still frozen to various sections of the route, how does one inspire the team upward? I don't know how Breashears was able to keep focus, but against all odds, he made it happen. The pay-off is a nice long clip of Norgay Sherpa and Segarra climbing somewhere on the ridge between the Hillary Step and summit. This one shot is worth the price of admission.

But there are problems—"writing problems," as they say in the business. On summit day, Viesturs is nowhere to be found. Under strict orders from his wife, he sprinted ahead, tagged the summit and bailed. Thus, the conspicuous disclaimer: "parts of this film have been recreated." All the footage of Viesturs swimming through powder snow, presumably just outside a ski area somewhere, en route to the "summit," is a joke. The "summit" is a shocker, too: the camera angle is raked upward so as not to reveal higher summits in the background. Frederick Cook would have been embarrassed and any serious mountaineer will feel disappointed.

The story line suffers, too, though through no fault of the filmmakers. Most IMAX theaters (there are just under 200 worldwide) are connected to museums, and the museum directors often insist a scientific angle be woven into the script. But here it feels contrived and silly. I've seen this film twice and I still don't know what the story is supposed to be. Is this about Tenzing Norgay's son? About Viesturs? Why not just call it a travel log and let the images speak for themselves?

If you haven't seen it, *Everest* is well worth your time. If you have a choice of seats, go to the back row and sit dead center. The photography is outstanding, the soundtrack, with music from George Harrison, is inspiring, and once you realize the hell that this crew went through to bring back the footage, you'll leave with a lot of respect for the filmmakers.

MICHAEL GRABER

*World Mountaineering: The World's Great Mountains by the World's Great Mountaineers.* Audrey Salkeld, general editor. Forward by Christian Bonington. Mitchell Beazley: London, U.K. 1998. Numerous color and black-and-white photographs, maps, topos. 304 pages. $50.00

Poring over maps and thumbing through old references in search of new projects has consumed hours of my life. This is the dreaming, scheming phase of climbing that is nearly as pleasurable as the physical act itself. The pastime also serves to ground me in the humble realization that climbing remains a passionate and compelling journey—a journey that has been perpetuated by kindred spirits for many, many generations. Practitioners current and past are still searching for the same essence: personal confrontation in wild places where we have only the illusion of being in control. Thus Audrey Salkeld's definition of the intangible urge to climb is as on-the-money as any I have encountered to date: "This is what climbing is most about—taking back the responsibility for one's own existence."

*World Mountaineering* provides a wealth of geographical and practical climbing information for a fascinating diversity of mountains, laid out in a concise and effective format. Many areas that have little previous documentation are covered in impressive detail. An amazing amount of research went into this book, and it has produced a work that can be read as much for pleasure as for trip planning.

But more importantly, it provides a wonderfully complete feel for the history, spirit and personality of each mountain described. The book accomplishes this by enlisting the insights and anecdotes of an impressive list of climbers with the necessary credentials to reveal the essential intricacies of the mountain they characterize. The book goes straight to the source for the pithiest information. Who better to describe the Eiger than Victor Saunders and Anderl Heckmair, or Everest than Peter Athans and George Mallory II, or Gasherbrum IV than Stephen Venebles and Robert Schauer? It's these candid and personal accounts by the individuals most familiar with the important routes on each chosen mountain that make this book a real treasure.

Fifty-two peaks are described, beginning with a locator map that seems of limited value in many cases. The map of the Grand Teton, for instance, is relatively useless as a reference tool and serves merely as an artistic adornment to the chapter. For those interested in climbing a particular mountain, the maps referenced later will of course be essential. An introduction and informative overview of the various facets of each mountain is followed by a chronology of significant ascents that very effectively summarizes the essential climbing history. But by far the most practical feature for each selection is the black-and-white photo with routes clearly superimposed. Written route descriptions are minimal yet valuable in that they provide an objective appraisal of route quality, greatly aiding one in choosing between the myriad possibilities on any given mountain. Finally, a collection of practical information, including how to get there, available facilities, climbing season, recommended gear, maps and guides, local language, rescue and insurance considerations and a hint of the red tape you might encounter, provides the logistical kernel to facilitate more detailed trip planning.

The real hook, though, has to be the discussion of future climbing potential. Let's face it, this is what we all really want to get a handle on: what remains to be done? I'm always a little skeptical of these discussions because I have to wonder what the cognoscenti are not telling us. Are these local activists really going to divulge to the masses the last remaining unclimbed gems on their beloved home turf? Maybe, maybe not. In some instances this section merely discusses future styles of climbing appropriate to the particular mountain, but occasionally a real eye-popping new line is revealed.

I found this guarded readiness to reveal unexplored terrain interesting when read in conjunction with Bonington's excellent foreword. As one who should know, Bonington extols the pleasurable rewards of exploring unmapped wilderness while bemoaning the inexorable loss of this evanescent resource. Anyone fortunate enough to visit a corner of this earth before all others must struggle with the fact that the violated corner can never again be visited for the first time. Bonington deals with this dilemma in the obvious and predictable way: keep wild places as wild as possible by conducting ourselves humbly, responsibly and with regard for those who will inevitably follow. This is, of course, the only way to view our fragile and finite mountains. I detect a whimsical note of hyperbole in Bonington's statement, "There still are, and I believe always will be, obscure valleys and numerous mountain ranges off the beaten track, where climbers can find untouched faces and ridges, even unclimbed peaks." Let's face it, the day will certainly arrive when the last valley has finally been visited. But as Bonington implores, if we climb and explore with an eye to the future, the mountains will continue to reveal their pristine majesty to countless generations to come, and climbers will continue to redefine the limits of possibility. This book is a splendid celebration of majestic mountains and the ebullient human spirit of exploration that thrives within them.

ALEX LOWE


*Postcards from the Ledge: Collected Mountaineering Writings of Greg Child.* Greg Child. Mountaineers Books: Seattle, 1998. 25 black-and-white photos. 224 pages. $22.95.

Among the voices of the several climbers writing well about climbing today, Greg Child's seems to me unique. He has absorbed his influences and made them his own. Child has learned much from the self-deprecating Brits, from Tilman through Patey; has leavened their ironic understatement with a brash, unexpurgated candor, half Hunter Thompson, half native Aussie braggadocio; and has transfused his penchant for the satirical with an investigative reporter's passion for the truth.

*Postcards from the Ledge* finds Child at the height of his powers. Rare is the case of a climber still in the vanguard of ascent who achieves a balanced perspective on the glorious folly of mountaineering, and for good reason. Enthusiasm clouds detachment; only in golf do we trust the player to act as his own referee. It is no accident that Melville quit going to sea at 25, and only then began to write about it.

Pushing 40, Greg Child continues to tackle precipices as daunting as any being explored in the world today: witness his ascent last summer, with three companions, of Great Sail Peak in Baffin Island by its steepest wall, an exploit he narrated for National Geographic. Yet at the same time, some element of distance born perhaps of an innate skepticism about the excesses of alpine ego and pretension allows Child to make delightful fun of himself as well as of his mountaineering.

As in all gatherings of pieces originally written for magazines, some of the entries in *Postcards from the Ledge* survive the occasions that prompted them better than others.

Perusing Child's third (and finest) collection, I am struck anew by his versatility. He can blow a satiric riff in the vein of Patey or McNaught-Davis with the best of them; and he can also plumb the core of the comedic, as in his hilarious account of inviting his mother to watch him climb in hopes of allaying her fears. At the same time, he can bear clear-eyed and chilling witness, in "Soul on Ice," to the pointless tragedy of a French schoolgirl dying in a crevasse on the Mer de Glace.

And in two well-researched, closely reasoned accounts of climbers who may have lied about their accomplishments, Child marshals an impressive prosecutorial style. Before anyone had questioned Tomo Cesen's epochal solo on the south face of Lhotse, I had traveled to Slovenia to interview him. I found him so likable and genuine that when the Lhotse gossip began to circulate, I dismissed it as the sour grapes of rivals. Despite the fact that I had written a book about exploration hoaxes, it took Child's devastatingly logical presentation of the case to convince me that Cesen had faked his greatest climb.

Finally, one must pay tribute to Child's skill at that aspect of mountain writing that most eludes its authors: the delineation of character. In a few deft strokes, he captures Lynn Hill's cold efficiency, Alison Hargreaves's unaffected gaiety. But it is in his rueful recollections of two intense and troubled climbers, Bill Denz and a loner he calls Luke Skywalker, that Child's grasp of our beloved pastime at its weirdest and most unsettling comes to the fore. Reading these two unforgettable reminiscences, I found my thoughts drifting back to the kindred misfits I had crossed paths with in my own reckless years. Repeating an old mantra of gratitude to the gods of chance that had allowed me to survive the follies of youth, I added a coda for Greg, thanking the Fates for sparing him, so that he could write so well about what he has seen and done.

DAVID ROBERTS

*Fall of the Phantom Lord: Climbing and the Face of Fear.* Andrew Todhunter. Anchor Books/Doubleday: New York, 1998. 272 pages. $23.95.

What is it about risk-taking behavior that endlessly fascinates the human mind? And why is it that so-called "extreme" sports and vertical adventure—and books about such endeavors—have become the popular lenses for this spectacle? These are questions that plagued me as I read the tale of the late Dan Osman by *Atlantic Monthly* writer Andrew Todhunter. In fact, reading *Fall of the Phantom Lord* gave weight to my belief that risk-taking activities like climbing have become overwhelmingly glamorized by our culture for their "death-defying" sexiness, while the more subtle, perhaps more meaningful qualities of the sport—like grace of movement, or camaraderie with one's climbing partner—lay unexamined. For many climbers, the popular yet myopic view of climbing may miss the point of climbing altogether.

Published shortly before Osman's death, even the title of the book eerily foretells the seemingly inevitable fate of this theatrical and daring climber. Disappointingly, however, Todhunter focuses less on Osman's climbing accomplishments than he does on his more recent obsession with falling from great heights with the aid of climbing ropes. (It was during the pursuit of this activity that Osman lost his life in November.) On the heels of Osman's death, the pressing question now in my mind is this: will such a book serve not only to glamorize the Russian Roulette approach to the vertical world but also deify those who die in the process?

This is not to say that an exploration of risk and fear and facing the prospect of death are not part of the climbing experience, and Todhunter must be given credit for deftly describing the vertical world's seductive dance with risk, danger, and even death as an affirmation of life itself. The allure of this world is best captured in the chapter where he "meets the Phantom Lord" as he steps from a cliff for his first Osman-supervised "jump":

> In a mutation so swift as to be imperceptible, as if externally compelled, I pass irreversibly through Osman's moment of choice. In the attenuated heartbeats that fall between the moment of commitment and the moment of execution, the pooling fear distills, climaxes, and transmutes. The resistance of the will cracks and dissolves. My body, suddenly unbound, becomes weightless, soars in its position on the rock. My back straightens, my head instinctually rises to the sky. A deep, luxurious passivity imbues my limbs. The oxygen is rich, heavy. I have gained no deeper confidence in the equipment. I have in no way lost the visceral suspicion that I may soon lie mangled on the rocks below. I have simply been relieved of my command.

What seems to weigh down the otherwise elegantly told stories of both Osman and Todhunter is the inordinate amount of attention given by the author to the mechanics of climbing, ice climbing, and jumping, as well as the almost sycophantic references to who's who in the climbing world. Perhaps these details may be of interest to the general audience, or to a very enthusiastic beginner climber, but for most climbers, such excessive information seems wholly unnecessary. It also seems at odds with the Dan Osman minimalist philosophy the author wants to convey. For example, Todhunter recounts Osman's idea of a good top rope—one sling and a carabiner:

> For Osman, it appears, an anchor is either adequate or inadequate. This seems to be an issue of aesthetics rather than bravado. . . . In pursuit of mastery in any enterprise, one strives to attain or express a condition just so, and chasms of mediocrity—too much and not enough—yawn on either side. By this reasoning. . . superfluous gear on a top-rope anchor is not a harmless, sensible backup, but as regrettable—to borrow from another trad—as an overwritten phrase.

Aside from overwriting background information that is, like Osman's theory on anchor systems, superfluous to the story, Todhunter is an accomplished writer whose prose is lovely and compelling, if a bit self-conscious at times. But then, it is self-conscious terrain he has chosen to explore: throughout the strands of Osman's life that he's selected to showcase, the author has tied in the more compelling stories of his own evolving relationship with risk and danger. A climber and adventurer himself, Todhunter finds, in the two years that he is spectator to Osman's life, that the addition to his own life of a wife and child, seriously alters both his ability and his desire to take such risks. *Fall of the Phantom Lord*, told through Todhunter's keen and honest perceptions about his own experience, gives the book its soul—which is a far leap from anything popular culture has embraced about the vertical world.

AMY IRVINE

*Souvenirs from High Places, A History of Mountain Photography.* Joe Bensen. Mountaineers Books: Seattle. 151 color and black-and-white photos. 144 pages. $35.00.

*Souvenirs from High Places: A History of Mountain Photography* is a pleasing collection and celebration of photography from the world's mountains, yet it ultimately raises tough questions. I was delighted to see familiar classics, like the Bisson work from the Mt. Blanc region in the late 1800s, Byron Harmon's wanderings in the Canadian Rockies and the extraordinary archive produced by four generations of the Tairraz family. Bradford Washburn's sensuous Doldenhorn East Ridge is here, in an exquisite frame exposed as Washburn was flying toward the mountain, about to make his more familiar images of the ridge. We see Vitorrio Sella, too, though considering the author's kudos for him as "the greatest mountain photographer of all time," he is under-represented.

The real pleasure of this volume is in the surprises and arcana. Who cannot be seduced by the early 19th century etchings? Or by the German Alpine Club's quaint hand-colored postcards from the early 1900s? My favorite of all is a remarkable 1967 image by Czech photographer Vilem Heckel. With all the formal richness of a classic modernist photograph by Edward Weston or Arnold Newman, Heckel gives an intimate sense of a climber's fatigue on a broiling snow slog in Pakistan.

Once Heckel's show-stopper grabbed me, I realized how much this book was missing images that reached a similarly high level of artistry. Re-reading the author's introduction and musing on the title, it became clear that the book tries to cover too much terrain, that encompassing both "souvenir" and "history" leaves the book diluted and uneven. The book proposes to cover " . . . the highest state of the pictorial climbing art . . .[;] however, this is also the story of photographs taken over the years by the many thousands of ordinary citizen climbers . . . ." In the context of climbing photography, a souvenir is typically either a hero shot or a relatively casual snapshot of a person or place, like those seen here of a bivy hut on the Brouillard Pillar or a portrait of Reinhold Messner.

However much we may admire a place or person, the pictures themselves usually remain aesthetically inconsequential. On the other hand, "history" connotes a survey that intends to track creative change through time. In this vein, the book delivers fantastically artful images like Heckel's and Washburn's. But combining masterpieces with banal snapshots seems peculiar at best. This anthology would be much improved by focusing on one intention or the other: stay with snapshots and come up with a wry, wacky family album of the climbing fraternity, or focus entirely on the great art shots.

All of which raise a key question: how often has mountaineering photography actually entered the realm of fine art? This point could be argued ad nauseam by everyone from museum curators to the most museum-adverse climber. Since I have the remarkable privilege of writing this review and the opportunity to answer my own question, my response is: not terribly often. Most mountain photography, even by devoted, accomplished, and, in some cases, famous photographers, is fundamentally little more than hero shots or the by-product of being in the right place at the right time. It is usually not the result of the individual vision or soul. Photographers who can take us beyond passive description and into active visual creation, as Heckel and Washburn have, are exceedingly few and far between. The overall standard of climbing imagery has risen far in the past decade or so (witness the high quality of magazine covers and gallery displays in the climbing literature), yet too many images remain formulaic.

Those who take their photography seriously owe their art, their mountains, and their society much more. Transcendent images are floating around somewhere out in the ether, waiting to be born. I don't pretend to know how to bring them into this world, but I do know that their discovery will only be possible if we ask tougher questions of our art than most of us are currently asking. Like climbing 5.19, doing the impossible will result from someone pushing beyond the inherited forms and predictable ideas—and it will, no doubt, someday be done.

JAMES BALOG

*Eric Shipton: Everest & Beyond.* Peter Steele. The Mountaineers: Seattle, 1998. Black-and-white photographs. 280 pages. $24.95.

Fans and friends of Eric Shipton will be delighted and surprised at the appearance of this biography. For several years after his death in 1977, there were rumors (which turned out to be wrong) of various memorialists hard at work. As the years rolled by, it seemed a certainty that no summing up of Eric Shipton's life would appear. All the more reason, therefore, to celebrate Peter Steele's effort, and to commend him for persevering against the considerable obstacles involved. Four years after Shipton's death, his friend Steele traveled to the U.K. from his new home in the Yukon and conducted some 30 interviews, hoping to find enough material to justify a follow-up to Shipton's autobiography, *That Untravelled World.* Subsequently, Steele dropped the project for 20 years, then took it up again, did another 30 interviews (half of the 1981 interviewees had, by then, passed on), and convinced himself that there was enough material to "tell a story that Eric never told about himself."

Aside from interviews, the chief basis for this assertion are letters by and to Shipton from his wife Diana and successive paramours, lady friends, and mistresses. This epistolary data presents several difficulties for the author. One is that, like all biographers, he is caught in one of the traps of history: what accidentally comes out of the attic trunk shapes biographical reality. Two, Eric Shipton was neither a skilled writer (Steele believes him dyslexic) nor an avid reporter of ordinary life. Here is an example. In 1951, Shipton spent an overnight with the royal family at Sandringham. He writes Diana a five-sentence note on a socially "terrifying" evening, concluding, "When the Queen had gone to bed I got involved discussing religion with the Duke of Edinburgh, which went on till after one." Observe that he did not reveal the Duke's views, which might be of especial interest in the light of his carnal relations with the head of the Church of England. Could it be that the Duke in his cups said "religion was the opiate of the people?" We shall never know.

The third issue about these letters is that they lead Steele to present a highly sentimental picture of Shipton's amorous and sexual adventuring. On page 71, Steele writes about a collection of letters between Shipton and Pamela Freston. Shipton and Pamela were fortunate because the majority of the letters survived to cement their bond of love. So the usual military-style convoy lumbered through Tibet; and Shipton wrote to Pamela, "I should like to do a long journey through Tibet with just a rucksack and a pony." Undoubtedly he meant to add the words "and you." But he didn't. And this band-aid, and a thousand others, in language that echoes a gentlewoman's magazine, doesn't work.

Shipton rarely reciprocated the degree of affection that his Leslie Howard good looks and quiet charm inspired in women, to whom he was compulsively unfaithful. Phyllis Wint, the subject of the longest liaison (20 years), says Shipton "[a]lways wanted someone to be close to; all his life he was looking for something that wasn't there." To which Steele comments out of both sides of his mouth: Phyllis felt confident of his affection, despite his philandering track record, and her confidence was justified throughout their two decades.

I doubt the world gives a damn that Shipton lacked affect and emotional honesty with women. Misogynists like Tilman might actually think it a good thing, and that Eric's womanizing takes up too much of this book. The critical issue is the degree to which *Eric Shipton, Everest & Beyond* fills in the lacuna in our knowledge of him as explorer and mountaineer. The blanks that I'd have liked filled are the gossipy and pop-psychological stuff that Shipton carefully excluded from his own narratives. But Steele seems not to know much of this, though in private Shipton could be pretty candid. In the few hours I spent with him, he told me that both John Auden and Michael Spender, brothers of famous poets and who were with him in the Karakoram, hated one another; and that Smythe was a cold-blooded ego maniac.

Steele does offer fresh perspectives on Shipton's climbing career: the degree to which he had to live off his writings, his development as a self-taught surveyor, his absent-mindedness and lamentable organizing skills, his naïveté about those enemies in the Alpine Club and the Royal Geographical Society that sacked him from the leadership of the 1953 Everest expedition. Steele's chapter on this incident seems to reflect good research and reporting. In the appendix, Steele cites the names of over a dozen sources interviewed, including Hillary and Hunt (who checked the draft for accuracy). The conclusion Steele draws is that Eric brought this on himself more than he was ill done by others. This account should demolish whatever remains of the old rumor that he'd made enemies by cuckolding one of the climbing Establishment.

Thus far, my review has failed to convey the pleasure this book gave me. It is not a great evocation of the man, but an enjoyable reminder. The reader is left with a hundred fresh little details that would have dissolved in time and floated into the ether unless rescued by Steele. There is also a wonderful sprinkling of old photographs. The climbing community is lucky to have this presumably last look at the great explorer who defined the mountaineering ethics of a later generation.

JOHN THACKRAY


*Addicted to Danger: A Memoir about Affirming Life in the Face of Death.* Jim Wickwire and Dorothy Bullit. Pocket Books: New York, 1998. Black-and-white photos. 352 pages. $24.00.

On a grass field 100 yards long in the desert area of Central Washington State, a football star named Jim Wickwire ran beyond the goal posts to a career as a pioneer alpinist in world mountaineering. Jim Wickwire's memoirs, written with his friend Dorothy Bullit, are a collection of some of his expeditions that unfortunately involved tragedy—tragedy beyond talking about until this book.

In the introduction, Wickwire says his co-writer, Dorothy Bullit, "insisted I deal with issues I had never before faced, let alone published." Perhaps for most of us who have been close to tragedy in the mountains, dealing with the truth and circumstances of a death are hard enough to cope with on a personal level, let alone share and communicate to the public in a book.

The first chapter tells the tragic tale of young Chris Kerrebrock's death in a crevasse on the south face of Mt. McKinley. I don't believe any mountaineer—no matter how case hardened—cannot help but shed a tear upon reading this chapter. Next, Wickwire tells of his love of family and how he first started climbing. He recounts nail-biting adventures on the Willis Wall of Mt. Rainier and the failed attempt on K2 in 1975. His tenacious desire and drive would see him return to K2 and reach the summit, but on a training climb in Alaska, in preparation for his second attempt, his good friends Dusan Jagersky and Alan Givler would perish before his eyes while descending Peak 8440'. The tale of this accident and subsequent search for the bodies is emotionally described.

The fifth chapter recounts what Wickwire considers his greatest achievement: the first American ascent of K2. This adventure was a great expedition that showed true grit and brings out the usual in-house personality issues that had to be overcome to succeed. The following chapters go from "good times" to another high-altitude accident at 26,000 feet, this time on the north face of Everest, where Marty Hoey tragically falls to her death while climbing to high camp with Wickwire.

Unfortunately, Wickwire's association with death up close and personal does not end. One chapter tells of his futile attempt to find his missing friend, Japanese hero Naomi Uemura, on Mt. McKinley. Another relates the unbelievable circumstances of the senseless murders of his law partner, Chuck Golmark, his wife and two sons by a crazy man. Finally, climbing out of the "death zone," the reader relives happier times and expeditions as Wickwire tells of first ascents in South America and more attempts on Everest with his good friend John Roskelley.

Fate (fortunately!) also blessed Wickwire, giving him a wife as tough as himself. Mary Lou Wickwire, his wife of 37 years, is the heroine of the book, as he unabashedly admits.

I have not read a mountaineering book in a long time that held my attention so thoroughly as did this memoir. Its weakness is that if the reader is looking for a literary artwork, this book is not it. However, the truth of these tales and the candor of how they are told transcend the vertical world of white-knuckle adventure to a soul-bearing catharsis as a personal witness to tragedy. Jim Wickwire, on his long journey as a pioneering mountaineer, is a victim of circumstance. He chose to tread a razor's edge between the abyss of death and the ecstasy of life. Fate had him straddling that edge more often than he deserved.

CHRIS KOPCZYNSKI

*On Belay! The Life of Legendary Mountaineer Paul Petzoldt.* Raye C. Ringholz. Mountaineers Books: Seattle, 1998. 272 pages. $24.95.

Paul Petzoldt is a mountaineering icon who, at 91 years of age, represents a lifetime of achievement in exploration, alpinism, mountain guiding, outdoor education, and environmental awareness. In *On Belay! The Life of Legendary Mountaineer Paul Petzoldt*, Raye Ringholz takes the reader on a tour from the farm country of southern Idaho to the upper reaches of K2 in 1938, discussing these and many other facets of Paul Petzoldt's life. The book provides answers to questions that I have always had about this legendary climber, such as: what was the 1938 K2 expedition like from Paul Petzoldt's perspective? What really happened during his falling out with NOLS? Was Petzoldt really put on trial for murder in India?

Petzoldt's Teton years, the part of his life with which I am most familiar, are, for the most part, accurately portrayed. His Teton career is fascinating not only because he was, beginning with the fifth ascent of the Grand, one of the great pioneers of the range, but also by the fact that he is still very much alive today. Petzoldt is a living bridge between modern American climbing and its early beginnings, which were really not very long ago. Ringholz chronicles some of the great Paul Petzoldt/Glen Exum stories, such as their chivalrous defense of Jackson local Dorothy Redman one Saturday night. This good-old western barroom brawl ends with local villain John Emory being thrown across the porch and down the front steps of the old Jenny Lake dance hall by a well-placed Petzoldt punch.

Ringholz also provides, for the most part, accurate, well-researched historical detail concerning early Teton climbing history. A few errors are noticeable, such as the dialogue with an inquisitive Billy Owen over Petzoldt's ascent in 1924 of the Grand Teton with friend Ralph Herron. When asked what the youths had found on the summit, the plaque commemorating Owen's ascent is given as "proof" that the boys had made it to the top. They had actually seen the metal "Rocky Mountain Club" pennant that the Owen party had left up there; the plaque did not arrive until the dedication ceremony of Grand Teton National Park some five years later. Generally, however, the key role that Petzoldt played in making so much of the early Teton climbing history is handled well.

Ringholz provides an in-depth description of the 1938 American K2 expedition, a pioneering trip to the Himalaya on which Petzoldt demonstrated considerable strength, experience, and courage. Much of the author's research was based upon the expedition account, *Five Miles High*, by Robert H. Bates and other members. For me, the narration of the high-camp cooking ordeal, with Petzoldt and Charles Houston each taking turns striking the last of their matches in order to melt water, was fascinating. This episode is missing in the expeditionary account and provides a gripping tale of survival in 1938, the Stone Age in Himalayan mountaineering. I also enjoyed hearing of Petzoldt's secret purchase of extra pins as the expedition traveled through Paris, since, to his more-experienced rock technician's eye, K2 seemed like a rocky peak. This was during the time period where the use of such implements for mountaineering was eschewed by most, including Houston, who referred to pitons as "iron ware."

The post-expedition time period that Petzoldt spent in India is one of the gaps in his life about which I had heard rumors. Ringholz explores this strange interlude in Petzoldt's life in which he becomes employed by a retired American surgeon from California who, with his wife, had become a follower of a small religious sect in northern India. Petzoldt's wife, Bernice, who traveled to India from the States by boat after the expedition, joins Petzoldt there. Things gradually become quite strange as the Petzoldts become convinced that the doctor's wife is slowly poisoning Bernice. This conviction leads to a wrestling match with a loaded shotgun and an accidental collision with the doctor, who hits his head and shortly thereafter dies. All of this adds up to one heck of a way to end your first climbing trip to the Himalaya.

Ringholtz concludes with two chapters that outline Petzoldt's commitment to environmental awareness and outdoor education. From the beginnings of NOLS to the establishment of the Wilderness Education Association, Petzoldt's lasting legacy will certainly be his commitment to wilderness and to teaching people how to leave no trace of their enjoyment of it. I enjoyed reading *On Belay! The Life of Legendary Mountaineer Paul Petzoldt*.

RENNY JACKSON

*Facing the Extreme: One Woman's Story of True Courage, Death-Defying Survival and Her Quest for the Summit*. Ruth Ann Kocour with Michael Hodgson. St. Martin's: New York, 1998. 256 pages. $22.95.

*Facing the Extreme* does not merit inclusion in the *AAJ*, although the dust jacket and preface intentionally give the impression that the book is about a top woman mountaineer pushing the edge on Denali. The cover breathlessly promises "one woman's story of true courage, death-defying survival, and her quest for the summit" under a blurry photo of computer-generated hikers on an unidentifiable Alaskan ridge.

"I was pulled back to the lures of ascending in a vertical world by an invitation to climb Mount Kilimanjaro in 1986 with Peter Whitaker, a world-class alpinist from a legendary mountaineering family," Kocour (or rather, Michael Hodgson, who actually wrote the book) begins modestly. She goes on to talk of climbing Aconcagua, accompanied by Mark Tucker. Tucker happens to be a guide, but Kocour breezily mentions that he is there "training for an Everest attempt." On Denali, Kocour is "the most seasoned mountaineer [in the group] outside of Robert and Win [Whitaker]," who, by the way, are guides, too. Scattered, offhand details gradually clued me in to the fact that Kocour's self-described "shopping list of summits" consists of guided treks up the trade routes of moderate peaks, as opposed to self-directed ascents of new, difficult or dangerous routes as the cover led me to expect. A non-climbing reader would not pick up on this, and is evidently not intended to.

The first paragraph of the preface jumps right in and compares this story to the 1996 Everest disaster, although after reading the book I'm not exactly sure why. Interestingly, Kocour's "struggle" took place four years before that, and is only now being published. As it turns out, *Facing the Extreme* chronicles Kocour's harrowing achievement in being guided up the West Buttress of Denali (sometimes known as "the cattle route") with seven even less experienced clients. Coincidentally, while her group waits out storms in the social center camp at 14,000 feet, climbers whom Kocour has never met (such as Mugs Stump and Alex von Bergen) die in various accidents while climbing. When the weather improves, Kocour's guides herd the eight clients up and down the West Buttress, and they all go home.

For some reason, Kocour is convinced that she personally has "faced the extreme," and that her new-found familiarity with death puts her in the ranks of "mountaineers who would ascend to the lofty heights of world-class mountaineering." Despite Kocour's constant self-preening, jibes at other climbers, and lack of any real point, this book would not be truly objectionable but for the blatant misrepresentation of Kocour's role on her trips. The most interesting topic it offers is the question of why Hodgson and Kocour so deliberately obscure her role as a client. After all, one of the most charming collections of climbing essays is Jeremy Bernstein's *Mountain Passages* about being guided in Chamonix, a book that is engaging to guides, clients, and non-climbers alike. In Kocour's case, the obfuscation seems designed to plump her ego as her guides have done, and to fulfill her delusional sense that she is an "extreme" mountaineer. In Hodgson's and the publisher's case, the book is an even less excusable attempt to ride the Everest bandwagon and make some fast cash off someone else's tragedies. I, for one, will be relieved when that fad is over.

STEPH DAVIS

*Meeting the Mountains.* Harish Kapadia. Indus Publishing Company, New Delhi, 1998. 49 black-and-white photos. 30 maps. 398 pages. $27 (Order directly from <indus-intl.com>; reference IN 01019.)

W e mountaineers like to think of ourselves as individualists, but most of us are really herd animals, following slavishly where others have gone before, sticking to familiar trails and concentrating our efforts on a few well-known peaks. Now that mountaineering is ever more commercialized and virtualized, the herd instinct is, if anything, even more pernicious. So it is refreshing to see Harish Kapadia's new book packed full of defiantly unfashionable Himalayan peaks and obscure, forgotten trails.

In case you have not heard of Harish Kapadia, let me introduce him briefly. I first met him in 1985, when he led our Indo-British expedition to the Siachen war zone in the East Karakoram. His organization (bar one or two over-leathery chapatis) was exemplary, his historical research was meticulous and his exuberant sense of fun was an inspiration to us all. Most exciting of all was to head up the Terong Valley, knowing that only the Vissers' expedition had been there before, and that we were the first mountaineers to head this way for 56 years, attempting an unclimbed 7000er, Rimo, for which no detailed photographs were available. It was good old-fashioned exploring at its best, and Harish, a veteran of countless exploratory probings throughout the Indian Himalaya and Karakoram, was an old master at the game.

That Rimo expedition was included in Kapadia's previous compendium of climbs and expeditions from 1969 to 1997, *High Himalaya, Unknown Valleys*. He has also published a book specifically on Spiti, the Buddhist province on India's Tibetan border, just south of Ladakh.

His latest book is another wide-ranging collection, with accounts of some of his earliest (pre-1969) treks and the most recent journeys from 1992 to 1997. *Meeting the Mountains*, like *High Himalaya*, is mainly composed of previous articles from the *Himalayan Journal*, which Kapadia has edited for many years. To have that wealth of knowledge, complete with prolific photos and Arun Samant's excellent sketch maps, all contained in one volume, is truly valuable. If you want to find out about anywhere in the Indian Himalaya, from the desert wastes of Ladakh to the steamy jungles of Assam, Kapadia is your man. Unlike so many mountaineers, he is respectfully aware of his predecessors: although he has explored many new Himalayan corners, he is always the first to acknowledge that his explorations are usually variations or continuations of others' work.

Kapadia's real forte is high-level adventurous trekking, the sort of committed journeys over difficult passes at which Shipton and Tilman so excelled. Of course the journeys have included summits, some of them very fine peaks like Chiring We, in Garhwal, or Rangrik Rang, in Kinnaur, climbed with Chris Bonington; but you sense with Kapadia that it is the journey that really counts. He is passionate about wild mountain country, but also about the people who inhabit that country, for the Himalaya, paradoxically, is not true wilderness. The myths and legends of Bon, Buddhism or Hinduism are all part of the fun, as are his modern companions, fellow enthusiasts from Bombay, loyal retainers from Kumaon and, occasionally, lucky Europeans who get to tag along.

When Europeans are invited, they tend to be British, as Kapadia seems to have an indulgent weakness for his former colonial masters. *Meeting the Mountains* includes pieces on several British luminaries of the Himalayan Club such as Noel Odell, Jack Hawkins, Trevor Braham and John Auden, brother of the famous poet. The tone here borders on the reverential, but with their modern, less learned successors, Kapadia is altogether more jocular. He likes to poke fun gently at their British eccentricities, just as he ridicules the occasional bureaucratic idiocies of his own government. However, for all his anglophilia, he is a patriotic Indian to the core, brought up in the early days of independence and trained at the mountain schools established by Nehru in the wake of Tenzing's success on Everest. His enthusiasm for the Indian Himalaya seems boundless and his knowledge is probably unequaled. This book, in combination with *High Himalaya*, *Spiti: Adventures in the Trans-Himalaya*, and the recently republished *Exploring the Hidden Himalaya* must represent the most comprehensive source of information and inspiration for mountaineers on the Indian Himalaya. However, Kapadia's work is not finished. He still has many trips to plan and books to publish, for he is the first to concur with the old Hindu sage that, "in a hundred ages of the gods I could not tell thee of all the glories of Himachal where Shiva lived and where the Ganges falls from the foot of Vishnu like the slender thread of the lotus flower."

STEPHEN VENABLES

*To the Summit: Fifty Mountains that Lure, Inspire, Challenge.* Joseph Poindexter. Black Dog & Leventhal Publishing: New York, 1998. 300 color photos. 320 pages. $39.98.

The specter of mountain beauty and illusion dignifies this ambitious debut. This visually rich publication marshals 50 specific mountains (and some rock formations) scattered around the earth in an attempt to convey the essence and spirit of mountaineering. The creative format is extraordinary, with spellbinding images, beginning with the glittering cover of Paiyu Peak in the Karakoram. The sheer physical size is designed to overwhelm the reader with an immediate result. To glance at some of the irresistible 300 photographs is a powerful experience: sometimes images appear as a fictional landscape strewn with storm clouds dancing like ghosts. Some of the best of our mountain photographers have contributed to these images, the eight centerfold pages creating wide spreadsheets. However, a few of the results are grainy, meaningless, or overexposed. Two are inexcusably reversed (Mt. Kenya and Mt. Whitney, the latter unforgivable because this Sierra Nevada backdrop has appeared so often on calendars and in western films). Still, for the armchair traveler, perusing this publication is a luxurious way to grasp rock and ice. With a weighty seven pounds of paper, chemicals and ink, there is little danger of the book blowing away on a stormy day (it would make a good press for alpine flora).

*To the Summit* indeed captures the world's growing fascination with mountaineering, but it is not the only book that captures many aspects of what is stated as a national obsession. Nor is the format the most comprehensive work on mountains and mountaineering, as is purported on the cover jacket. Several recent atlas-sized books rise to this paradigm, notably the Stefano Ardito and Salkeld and Bonington creations. These authors, as well as Walt Unsworth, might rightfully disagree.

There is an expected symmetry between such recent books, but they do bring different pleasures. All of them contain lucid action pictures, vivid first-hand accounts, and in some fashion depict the story of mountaineering from the 15th century onward. Here, the 50 challenging and inspiring mountains chosen as subjects are nominally famous, ranging from Nanga Parbat to Yerupaja, Mt. Cook to Mt. Robson, Fuji to Devils Tower and El Capitan, and the Grand Teton to Mount Blanc. The preponderance of the subjects are the high alpine peaks, all arranged in regional sections and accompanied by helpful index locator maps. The author's text and historical research have a good sense of pacing, and he has managed to pin down the essential characterization of each chosen mountain. While the text is sometimes prosaic and uninformative, excerpts from a score of notable writings illuminate various aspects of the climbing experience from historic adventures to recent epics. Everesters from Mallory to Hornbein are quoted. There is a richness of insight (including epigraphs from Curran, Messner, Herzog), the best of which is from Mo Anthoine, who relates, "I don't think getting to the top is all that important. You can always have another go . . . . The nicest feeling is to know that you are relying on someone else and he is relying on you." This evaluation, together with the element of confrontational risk we generally fail to obtain in today's society, may well explain the appeal of alpinism better than Mallory's oft-cited explanation.

While the publication relates considerable mountaineering history, the writing is not scrupulously precise, and errors creep up unexpectedly. The author and his researchers have read many clippings, but loose editing makes this an inferior reference. Some of the factual breakdowns are date typos, a sprinkling of misspellings and inconsistency with accent marks, and the appearance of Wiessner as an Austrian. Once, Simpson and Yates appear as Yankees. The Grandes Jorasses is correctly identified in one picture caption and once not.

The book does present well-placed biographies of notable climbers from various nations. An analysis of equipment and technical rating systems, however, seems out of place in a coffee-table, armchair-reader publication. Flaws aside, however, this is a monumental and worthy publication overall.

FRED BECKEY

*Meditations on the Peaks: Mountain Climbing as a Metaphor for the Spiritual Quest.* Julius Evola, translated by Guido Stucco. Inner Traditions: Rochester, Vermont, 1998. 115 pages. $12.95.

At first glance, I thought *Meditations on the Peaks: Mountain Climbing as a Metaphor for the Spiritual Quest* was another of those climbing-as-self-discovery books that are proving so popular these days. Therefore, it was against all expectations that I found myself fascinated with this odd little book. Here are 20 short essays loosely arranged into three sections: "Experiences," "Doctrines," and "Appendices," of which there are five. The works were written between 1927 and 1942 and published for the first time as a collection in Italian in 1974, the year of Evola's death.

The Doctrine essays, which discuss how mountains have been used metaphorically in ancient religious literature, both Eastern and Western, were most fascinating to me. Evola tracks the mountain as metaphor from Valhalla to Olympus, from 11th century Tibetan ascetics to Tyrolean superstitions.

The essays collected in Experiences (and most of the Appendices) are extremely interesting as well. These are not run-of-the-mill stories and banal observations by professional climbing writers on heavily sponsored trips. These essays are comprised of Evola's observations garnered during his experiences in the 1920s and '30s in the Alps and filtered through his extensive background in comparative religions. In almost all the essays, the impact of mysticism is plain: "There are always moments . . . in which physical and metaphysical elements converge and the outer adheres to the inner." Most of the time this mysticism is of a clearly Eastern flavor, showing influences from Vedanta and Yoga: "When the mind, which is deluded by the apparition of the external world, has finally understood the teaching concerning phenomena, it experiences . . no difference between phenomena and emptiness."

Evola was not just content with mystical observation. He believed that the Eastern techniques of meditation could improve the mental discipline of the alpinist. The ability to dictate one's thoughts and not give into fear, the capacity for focus and concentration, the control of breath are all as important to meditation as they are to climbing.

This predilection for Eastern thought does not prevent Evola from writing insightfully about the Christian folk religion of the Tyrol, nor does it prevent him from lamenting its demise. His observations on the climbing culture of his day are particularly eye-opening. He says the 'new' generation of climbers

have turned athletic competition into a religion and appear to be unable to conceive anything beyond the excitement of training sessions, competitions and physical achievements; they have truly turned accomplishment in sports into an end in itself and even into an obsession rather than as a means to a higher end.

Sound familiar?

He also bemoans the advent of "extreme sports" and the "mania for that which is difficult and unusual for the sake of setting new records." These observations were made in about 1930, the generation of today's climbers' grandparents and great-grandparents.

Another strange kind of reverse déjà vu is Evola's dislike of crowds: "And thus in the mountains . . . there is no longer any room. It will be great luck if the best climbers are able to . . . find again in the mountains a really wholesome experience . . . ." He particularly disliked aerial tramways, calling them a "contamination."

However, if all this makes Evola sound like some kind of sanctimonious/vegetarian/holier-than-thou type, let me correct that impression. Although he carried a copy of the Bhagavad Gita on his climbs, he also carried a bottle of whiskey. I admire his life in both worlds: sacred and profane, transcendent and imminent. Even when he admits to the pleasures and diversions of this world, it is through a religious perspective. The best example of this is his tale of how he and his buddies get drunk one night in an alpine hut. In the middle of the night they walk out onto a nearby frozen lake in the dark. He theorizes that the lake must have been going through some temperature metamorphism, because it starts to crack and break up violently when they are out in the middle of it: "To feel all of a sudden under one's feet a roar that grows into a loud booming noise, which is then echoed by the mountain, is almost like hearing the voice of the earth itself." Very few could hear such an other-worldly noise and yet hear the voice of worldliness as well. This is what makes Evola unique.

DAVE HALE


*Distant Mountains.* John Cleare. Discovery Channel Books: New York, 1998. 160 color photos. 173 pages. $35.00.

❝What beautiful names the mountains and glaciers have in this region . . . ." said W.M. Conway of the Jungfrau region of Europe's Alps. These same words work to describe the contents of *Distant Mountains* by John Cleare. Not only has Cleare captured the descriptive prose of such mountain legends as Conway, Tilman, Murray, and others in his new book, he has once again captured for his readers a number of amazing mountain images as well.

John Cleare is one of the most respected mountain photographers in the history of mountain travel. In this book, as with his 15 previous titles, he has combined his art and abilities as a mountaineer, but here he has included too the inspiring words of some of his legendary predecessors and contemporaries to provide the reader with an amazing vicarious experience in some of the world's wildest and most beautiful mountain ranges. From the Highlands of Scotland to the Andes, from the Himalaya to the Rockies, *Distant Mountains* contains some 160 beautiful color photographs that serve to complement masterful essays. Nicholas Crane writes on the Pyrenees, W.M. Conway on the Alps, David Harris on the Canadian Rockies, Steve Roper on the mountains of the American Southwest, Mike Banks on the Andes, Kurt Diemberger on Pakistan Karakoram, Jim Perrin on the Garhwal Himalaya of India, Kev Reynolds on the Himalaya of Nepal, H.W. Tilman on the mountains of East Africa, and Cleare himself on Patagonia.

*Distant Mountains* is more than a large-format anthology. It also provides practical information for mountain travelers and armchair adventures alike by including in each chapter maps and tables, notes on the local geology, flora, and fauna, warnings regarding hazards specific to each mountain range, and suggestions on equipment. For instance, the chapter, "The Abode of the Gods" (Kev Reynolds), is followed by the very timely "The Nepal Himalaya 'Factfile,'" which provides a map and several paragraphs of information and advice under the subheadings Background, Access, and Climbing and Trekking. The information found here is clear and straight-forward. To wit, in Climbing and Trekking: "For climbers, the several hundred Permitted Peaks (none of which are virgin) offer plenty of new routes. Siege tactics, oxygen and big expeditions are, these days, considered inappropriate, and ideally climbs should be attempted alpine style. . . . Climbers and Trekkers alike should treat altitude . . . very seriously. AMS (Acute Mountain Sickness) regularly kills and there is no substitute for proper acclimatization." Important information and advice for anyone interested in visiting high, remote mountains, and well worth following.

Cleare's 40 years of climbing mountains and his commitment to providing a photographic record of his adventures, as well as his carefully selected essays, make this book an important edition to anyone's library who loves to escape into mountains either literally or via good writing and vivid photos.

The words of Tilman on the frontispiece of the chapter entitled "Snow on the Equator" captures the spirit of this volume: "On Kenya is to be found climbing at its best. There is no easy route up it, but much virtue may be got from a mountain without climbing it. For those who are not compelled to answer its challenge, let them camp near the solitudes of its glaciers, to gaze upon the fair face of the mountain in sunlight and shadows, to watch the ghostly mists writhing among the crags and pinnacles, and to draw strength from her ruggedness, repose from her aloofness."

There is "much virtue" to be found for both climber and non-climber between the covers of John Cleare's *Distant Mountains*.

MIKEL VAUSE

*The High Life: A History of High-Altitude Physiology and Medicine.* John B. West. Oxford University Press: London, 1998. $79.50.

In 1979, when I was in my pulmonary fellowship at the University of Washington, John West invited me to be a climber-scientist on the 1981 American Medical Research Expedition to Everest (AMREE). It was a pivotal event, both professionally and personally. My passion for the high mountains flourished with my growing interest in hypoxia and high-altitude physiology (strands of which have continued to weave intrigue into my day-to-day life as a pulmonary and critical care physician.) I had read about the high-altitude work in the Silver Hut in 1960-'61 that West, Jim Milledge, and Sukhamay Lahiri had done, and suddenly I was going to be mentored by them on this great adventure to Everest, at the end of an era when we were the only expedition there. My life as an academic physician was launched.

It was, therefore, with some trepidation that I accepted the invitation to write a review of John West's book, *The High Life: A History of High-Altitude Physiology and Medicine*. What if the book were flawed or overly biased? How could I publicly criticize someone who had been so supportive of me ever since AMREE? My fears soon dissolved as I was consumed by the lives and adventures of those men and women with whom I have shared a curiosity about high-altitude physiology. We have wanted to know how humans and animals "work" under such stresses, laced with the unknown and unidentifiable.

Years ago, in a lecture on the history of high-altitude research, I heard one of my professional heroes, Dr. Jack Reeves from the University of Colorado, say that we stand on the shoulders of giants who have gone before. This same recurrent theme emerges throughout the book by West. From the early experiences on trade routes at high altitude to the discovery of barometric pressure by Torricelli to the exploration of the possibilities of climbing the world's highest peaks, West spins a compelling story that is superbly and engrossingly written in a way that makes this book not only an excellent resource but also a compelling and suspenseful tale.

This task would normally be difficult for most writers, but as always, West writes in a style that carries the reader on a wave of anticipation. He takes joy in the human side of these explorers, scientists, and climbers as he recounts their histories and personal lives as well as their achievements. He conveys that he, too, stands on the shoulders of giants of old, while making us realize we stand on his and his contemporaries' shoulders, whom he generously lauds. For example, regarding Torricelli's discovery in 1644 that "we live submerged at the bottom of an ocean of air," West writes, "how simple and striking this is, shows astonishing perception and clarity." His adoration of bright and enterprising physiologists of the past and present is refreshing.

The volume is thoroughly documented and beautifully illustrated with old figures and photographs of historic events and people. I recognize many familiar, albeit younger, faces (Milledge with dark hair and ears!) in the photograph of the 1961 Haldane Symposium in Oxford. For instance, the photographs of the 1911 Pike's Peak team (Haldane, Fitzgerald, Schneider, Henderson, Douglas); Barcroft; and the 100-year-old Mabel Fitzgerald finally receiving her recognition and degree from Oxford in 1973 are marvelous to see and a product of West's typically thorough research. The dapper but gentle face of Ravenhill, who gave such poignant descriptions of altitude illness at the high mines of Chile in the early years, gives a prescient look into where the rest of his life as an artist after the trauma of WWI would take him. The nomadic but prodigiously talented Alexander Kellas, whose solo forays into the high Himalaya in the early 1900s provided precious speculation about the difficulties of extreme altitude climbing, is here as well. There are copies of original documents and graphs, all of which bring tangibility to the past. (They all look so much more serious and proper than I think many of us ever felt in the 1980s and '90s!)

*High Life* is not a climbing book per se, but for those who want foundation in their zeal for going to altitude, this is a climber's book. How can one not be inspired by the obsession of Kellar, who unfortunately died of a non-altitude related illness on one of his many forays to the unexplored Himalaya, by the ultimate quest, political and otherwise, of Everest in 1953 and the ascents of Everest by Messner, Habeler, and others without supplemented oxygen? (Remember that in the very early 1900s it was thought that human ascent above 21,000 feet or so was not possible.) The feats of the Duke of Abruzzi on K2 and the British Everest expeditions of the early 1920s astounded mountaineers and physiologists alike. One can't help but sense West's excitement about those early years.

I can not validly comment on the accuracy of the early history. It is all well documented, but the "modern era" (1950s to the present) is more familiar to me. The chronological unraveling of high-altitude pulmonary edema by the Peruvians, Hultgren, Houston, and others is a joy to read. The debate on limitation of performance at extreme altitude with particular emphasis on the field (AMREE) and chamber (Operations I, II) studies is appropriately given a lot of space, as the physiologists and climbers are still trying to find the mechanism (the joy of science!). All of this makes even the most rigid scientist marvel and wonder if there just isn't something unmeasurable that we'll never know.

If there is any room for comment on *High Life*, it would be in the proportioning of space and emphasis on the recent and ongoing projects, most of which have shifted out of the U.S.A. For instance, the Campana Margherita Hut on Monte Rosa seems to be short-changed. Over the past ten years, under the direction of Dr. Peter Bartsch of Heidleberg, this facility has been the most productive in research in the field of high-altitude illness. Others may want more space as well, and Messner probably remembers 1978, rather than 1990, as being the year he scaled Everest (page 407), but these are all minor points.

For me, this book is a treasure, both as a climber and as a scientist. Both appetites should be tantalized (whether they exist in the same person or separately). The human drive for achievement (in this case climbing), and the curiosity of how it can be achieved physiologically co-exist. *High Life* is a well-balanced diet that doesn't leave us wanting, but only wondering what the next chapter will bring.

ROBERT B. SCHOENE

*Rock Prints: A Collection of Rock Climbing Photographs.* Greg Epperson. Rock Prints Publishing: Bishop, CA. 1998. 81 black-and-white photographs. 96 pages. $35.00.

Greg Epperson, best known for his striking color shots of climbers in action, has produced a small but handsome volume containing black-and-white photographs of—you guessed it—climbers in action. Exquisitely printed on pricey paper, each of the 81 images contains much of interest, yet, oddly, the climbers themselves are often not the chief attraction. Rather, Epperson's composition skills and his infatuation with rock texture have combined to produce photos that sometimes reach that fabled realm called art.

It's not all photos here. Three mini-essays—by Peter Croft, John Long, and Pete Takeda—are thrown in for good measure, but these nice prose poems seem an unnecessary afterthought in such a book. Far more satisfying are the informative and witty captions (by Bob Van Belle) tucked into the back of the book so as not to interfere with the purity of the photograph—a nice decision, even though it makes for a lot of flipping back and forth.

We'll all choose favorite images, and here are four of mine. Page 7 shows a Joshua Tree climber on a dicey crossover move; dominating the left side of the photo is a colossal egg. The egg is a magically smooth boulder, the kind you want to lay hands on to see if it's real. Page 41 shows a spread-eagled climber on a route with cracks dropping toward the vanishing point. You don't need to flip to the caption to know there's only one possible locale for this one: Devils Tower. Page 60 has interest in every square inch: water streaks interlaced with rounded sills create a textured checkerboard. Finally, because it's so different, the Joshua Tree shot on page 70 appeals greatly to me. This is one of the very few images that puts the climb itself into the context of the climbing area. A tiny figure struggles up a classic-looking crack in a soulful landscape.

Although such images compelled me to return often to them, a certain sameness pervades the majority of the photos. To avoid the "butt shots" or "hair shots" we snapshoters are all too familiar with, Epperson took great pains to rig his ropes and scaffolding in just the right place. But too often he chooses the same point of view: 20 feet distant from his subject, looking downward at a 45° angle. Far too many images in this book follow this pattern, and far too many shots have climbers obviously coached by Epperson to grimace or to stretch unconvincingly for a hold. Another problem, perhaps unsolvable if one is to capture the feeling of exposure, is his overuse of wide-angle lenses. Thirty-foot routes, like *Pinched Rib* at Joshua Tree, appear to be three times as long and thus seem unnatural (after all, your eyes don't see it like this). Similarly, the legs of the climber in many photos look like withered appendages.

These are mild criticisms, and the book, like all works of art, is not meant to be looked at casually, or at one sitting. As mentioned, it's the texture and pattern of the rock that give these photographs their appeal. Give each image careful study and you'll discover yet again why we so much love to set fingers to stone.

STEVE ROPER

*Chomolungma Sings the Blues: Travels Around Everest.* Ed Douglas. Constable, England. 1997. 256 pages. $40.00.

In *Chomolungma Sings the Blues*, Ed Douglas, editor of *Climber*, a U.K. magazine, and *The* (British) *Alpine Journal*, recounts his experiences and observations on a trek through Nepal in 1995-'96. The main theme of this book (not always easy to decipher) is the degradation of Nepalese culture brought on by Western trekkers and climbers, of whom he does not have many nice things to say:

The megalomania of the climbers is matched only by the destructiveness of the culture that they bring with them, namely materialism and over-consumption. It is this westernizing influence that lies at the root of Nepal's many present-day ills.

Douglas believes this "destructiveness" of Western culture is what lies behind pollution and overpopulation in Kathmandu, garbage and deforestation in the Khumbu, and the exploitation of porters generally. This lack of respect for Nepalese culture and the egocentricity and smug patronizing of Westerners is exemplified for Douglas in the gesture of a young British trekker "sleek in his black jacket and sunglasses" who, after a quick perusal and a yawn, tosses a pamphlet on Sherpa culture onto a pile of magazines. This horrifies Douglas, because he wants Nepal to be "a haven in the distant corner of the world where life is simpler, purer, without the constant grind of money or position, where we can be free."

Despite Douglas's brave attempts to eschew his own Western outlook in favor of a more Nepalese/Buddhist one, there lingers the scent of contradiction by virtue of his own presence as a Westerner in Nepal. This leads to a bit of hand-wringing, especially when his wallet gets stolen. "My reaction to the theft had been typically Western . . . I took it personally . . . . I wanted retribution, revenge even . . . bad things to happen to a bad person in this world and not the next." Douglas reflects that his reaction was wrong, not by degree, but by cultural orientation: "For a Buddhist, the concept of merit lies at the heart of morality. . . . Sherpas don't appoint themselves moral authorities in this way."

Romanticizing about a more primitive culture has always been a big seller, and probably always will be. Literature as varied as *Paradise Lost* and *The Swiss Family Robinson*, as well as contemporary works like *The Snow Leopard* and *Black Elk Speaks*, not to mention films like Dances with Wolves, all imply that primitive societies are more harmonious and idyllic than ours. This search for a paradise lost is ingrained in our culture. Douglas's call for a "haven . . . where life is simpler, purer. . ." is yet another call to the Garden of Eden.

I want to make it plain that I applaud Douglas for his critique of arrogance, materialism, consumerism and the lot. And yes, no doubt, Western culture is partly to blame. But it is more complicated than that. All cultures teach good things and bad things. And often these are internally contradictory.

Douglas seems to put on a new culture with all of its attendant morality just like we would put on a new set of clothes, simply because there are parts of the old culture he finds morally questionable or wrong. It may work for him, but I don't think it will work for most of us. Attempts to adopt another culture usually come off as hackneyed as photographs of yourself spinning a prayer wheel in Nepal or bringing back prayer flags to hang over the backyard grill. Nepalese culture has no shortage of problems, its attitudes toward women and marriage among them (as Douglas alludes to in Chapter 10). We must pick and choose among good and bad in any culture. And therein lies the key to morality: choice, as opposed to cultural indoctrination, whether it be Nepalese or Western. Jerks are jerks, and we shouldn't let them off the hook by blaming their culture instead of them.

DAVE HALE

*The Quotable Climber: Literary, Humorous, Inspirational, and Fearful Moments in Climbing.* Edited by Jonathan Waterman. The Lyons Press: New York, 1998. 20 Photos. 253 pages. $20.00.

Put down the notebook you've been using to record your favorite quotes about climbing and go to your local outdoor retail shop or bookstore to purchase Jonathan Waterman's latest work. *The Quotable Climber*, a compilation of over 600 quotes, quips, and musings about the mountaineering experience, contains inspirational and thought-provoking pieces from authors as varied as the climbing community itself. Waterman has clearly done some digging while researching this book. Quotes appear from both well-known alpinists and rock aces as well as unknown or anonymous climbers. A pleasant surprise is the inclusion of several quotes about mountains and nature from more popular writers such as Camus, Hawthorne, Nietzsche, Thoreau, and the odd world leader like Churchill.

This small-format hardcover book is neatly divided into 19 chapters of different topics covering the full spectrum of thoughts, feelings, and emotions that climbing elicits. Chapters cover climbing accidents and epics, famous climbs, humor, and many other subjects. One chapter, titled "The Greatest Hill on Earth," is devoted entirely to thoughts about Mount Everest. Waterman provides, by way of a brief editor's introduction, historical anecdotes combined with his own personal experiences to convey the mood of an upcoming chapter. I found this organization to be practical and the historical commentary important to the book's allure. In lieu of an index, a final chapter provides a brief biographical sketch about each of the authors included. I found the absence of any reference to the page numbers of quotes included by a particular author a bit frustrating. This type of cross-reference would be helpful for those researching an individual climber or event. Also, the black-and-white photos that preface each chapter are appropriate, but some tend to be dark.

I had already spent time skimming through my personal copy of *The Quotable Climber* before I was asked to review it here. Minor complaints aside, my affection for this book has deepened after spending more time absorbing it. Whether you put a copy on your shelf or give it to a friend, its pages will undoubtedly see the light of day many times in years to come.

LEN ZANNI

*An Ice Ax, A Camera, and A Jar of Peanut Butter.* Ira Spring. The Mountaineers Books: Seattle, 1998. 283 photos. 240 pages. $24.95.

In 1930, the Eastman Kodak Company's Centennial Celebration gift to all 12-year-olds was a Kodak Box Brownie camera. Twins Ira and Bob Spring were born Christmas Eve, 1918, so they barely got in under the wire for claiming theirs at the corner drugstore. Inspired by a love of the outdoors gained through their parents, Ira and Bob were soon snapping black-and-white photos of local hills and valleys with these simple cardboard cameras. But upon reaching maturity with more sophisticated Speed Graphics that exposed 4" x 5" sheet film and film-pack, the twins embarked on photographic careers.

Ira Spring's numerous photo contributions to various newspaper *rotogravure* sections, travel and outdoor magazines, and hikers' guidebooks are well-known to Northwest hikers and travelers, but here is a well-illustrated document of his life of mountain photography and observations from travels around the globe. Richly presented is the essence of his life, from his childhood and youth in the timber community of Shelton, to his first photography with the Box Brownie, to graduation into military camera work in the Southwestern Pacific during World War II and subsequent professional career and world-wide travels with camera.

I first met Ira at Paradise Valley on Mount Rainier in the summer of 1941, when he ran the concessionaire's photo shop at Paradise Valley. There he got his exercise by racing ahead of my guided parties heading for the famed Paradise Glacier ice caves, setting up his camera along the way and at the cave entrances. He would then dash back to his darkroom, and by the time our parties returned, he had 8" x 10" glossies displayed—still dripping wet—for the tourists to order as mementos of their visit to the park.

After serving during World War II as photographer in the Southwestern Pacific in the Air Corps (today's Air Force), Ira joined his brother briefly in a studio business in Seattle that specialized in baby portraits. But their interests were in the mountains, and their expertise in alpine photography soon got them commissioned work with local newspapers and eventually national magazines. In time, Ira traveled widely throughout Europe with his family, taking photos for travel magazines and ads. For a while, they resided in a chalet in the shadow of Mont Blanc, where the kids attended the local schools and learned to ski.

*An Ice Ax, A Camera, and A Jar of Peanut Butter* covers Ira's adventures while photographing hikes and climbs throughout the Pacific Northwest, the Sierras and Rockies, Canadian Rockies, Alaska, the Alps, Iceland and Scandinavia, and Japan. In recent years he returned to visit some of the islanders he had photographed in the Southwestern Pacific during the war.

In subsequent years, Ira's photos illustrated hiking guidebooks, with text by various authorities in subjects ranging from local beach hikes, wildflowers and tree species, to hikes and climbs. Most frequent among his co-authors have been Northwest notables Harvey Manning, Ruth Kirk, Byron Fish, and E.M. Sterling. Ira's most stable income has been the royalties derived from 50 or more hiking guides to trails in the Pacific Northwest.

Ira's photographic travels and devotion to the beauties of the Northwest have helped inspire others to join the battle to preserve the area's scenic highlights, and his books have earned him awards during the annual Governor's Writers Day in Olympia. He has been among the activists fighting for preserving and enhancing the trail systems leading into these wild areas, and at his own expenses he has lobbied for such measures before legislative committees in Washington, D.C. In 1992, he was among 25 people nationwide to receive from President George Bush the Teddy Roosevelt Conservation Award.

It's good to have Ira finally tell in his own words his life of world-wide travels and photography.

DEE MOLENAAR

*Looking for Mo.* Daniel Duane. Farrar, Straus and Giroux: New York, 1998. 230 pages. $22.00.

Looking for Mo is Duane's first book of fiction and his second book in which climbing is the central action. His earlier book, *Lighting Out*, was an autobiographical memoir in which the person telling the story (ostensibly Duane himself) tries to balance climbing in Yosemite and the Sierra with his relationship with his girlfriend, a beautiful, troubled, new-age free spirit. *Mo* features a first person narrator who is in essence indistinguishable from the narrator of *Lighting Out*, both in his voice and interests. In fact, *Mo* reads very much like a sequel: it is mo' of the same, and even relies for one of its conflicts on an earlier book written by the narrator, a book very much like *Lighting Out* (but not exactly like *LO*, because that book is nonfiction and the earlier book referred to in this new book is fiction).

One of the funniest characters in *LO* is Aaron, who, in Duane's voice, tells hilarious stories, among the most memorable in *LO*, of being stoned in the desert and searching the wilderness for his dream woman. In *Mo*, Aaron has been changed to Mo, and Mo is upset with our new narrator for stealing his best stories and putting them down into a book form. Mo is also a very good climber (just like Aaron). The other sub-plot of *Mo* is the possibility of the narrator falling in love and developing a relationship with the lovely Fiona, but despite being enamored of her, he ignores her. Why? Climbing.

From page one, *Mo*'s narrator is obsessed with doing an El Cap big wall. One of the charms of *Lighting Out* is that both times the characters try the *Nose*, they bail, mostly out of simple intimidation. In this new story the narrator and Aaron/Mo try the *Salathé*. So if you've read the first book and are going on to the second, you can't help but read them as connected, and you can't help wondering how these guys went from two failures on the *Nose* to the *Salathé*, and you're wondering, is this why he calls it fiction? The book is about finishing unfinished business, but the reader can't really know whether the unfinished business is completing the story started in *LO* or completing the climbing in "real" life. Duane calls this story fiction—made-up—and yet if we've read the first, we "know" that some of it isn't made-up. Does he want it both ways? (Who doesn't?) What should it matter to readers?

The climb of the *Salathé* is the climax of the book and occupies close to a quarter of the whole (and it's not a very long novel) 230 rather small pages.The question for the reader is, how well does the writer succeed with his portrayal of the *Salathé*? For accuracy you might ask someone who's done the route (not me); but clearly Duane is aiming for more than a literal accuracy; he's trying to get the essence of the thing. As a piece of literary fiction, the portrayal is excellent.

Anyone writing about a climb—be it a climb they've done or one they imagine having done—faces the same problems outlined many years ago in David Roberts' "Slouching Toward Everest: a Critique of Expedition Narratives"(*Ascent,* 1980). A climb is a nearly linear ritual—a series of repeated problem-solving activities. Sure, there are variables, but they're the same variables: your partners, the weather, conditions of the route, and more recently, others on the route. The problem for the writer is how to keep any single account from sounding like any other account. Duane does quite well on this score: the tensions between the partners, the personal significance of doing the route for the narrator. In short, the human history that Duane creates on the page all work effectively with the familiar features of the route and nature of the climbing itself (these latter already known to readers who climb and know something of climbing in Yosemite). Even the thunderstorm that (surprise!) traps them in a soaking bivy for days works well because we know what the climb means to these characters, know that they are merely human and not possessed of god-like strength, skills, and courage.

While the climb itself receives a fully realized treatment, other aspects of the story, which seem to exist only as hurdles to be overcome before the climbing can begin, are in fact treated only briefly despite the great proportion of textual space they occupy. Romance and friendship are given short shrift, but I wasn't always sure if they were sacrificed intentionally to the climbing or unintentionally by the writing. A friend of the narrator's marries—the road not taken by the narrator. There's a Grateful Dead concert and a wild scene of performance art, both of which are interesting enough and help to fix the historical Californian moment, but neither of which seem particularly necessary to the real story (the climb).

I happened to read *Mo* during the only summer of the last seven or eight years that I didn't climb a single day in Yosemite, and in the shadow of Duane's prose I found myself dreaming of the Valley for weeks. His narrator's obsession is one we understand. Duane dedicates his novel to four people, "partners in an incomparable dream." The dedication, coupled with the climb the book describes, are a good reminder that for those who choose it: climbing *is* the incomparable dream.

DAVID STEVENSON

## IN BRIEF

A number of reviewers both here and elsewhere have noted that the phenomenal publishing success of *Into Thin Air* has spurred a rush of mountaineering books into print. Students of Everest 1996 will want to check out *Sheer Will: The Inspiring Life and Climbs of Michael Groom* by Michael Groom. Groom is a New Zealander who summitted on Rob Hall's expedition and has thus far succeeded on the world's four highest summits, all without oxygen. Matt Dickinson is a British cameraman who also summited Everest in May '96 from the north with Alan Hinkes. His *The Death Zone*, published in the U.K. in '97, is being reprinted this year in the U.S. as *The Other Side of Everest: Climbing the North Face through the Killer Storm*. *Within Reach: My Everest Story* is Mark Pfetzer's version, written with Jack Galvin. Pfetzer was 16 years old on his unsuccessful May '96 attempt. In addition, there are two South African books, one by team leader Ian Woodall (with Cathy O'Dowd), *Everest: Free to Decide*, and one by Ken Vernon, the team's newspaper correspondent, called *Ascent and Dissent: the South African Everest Expedition— Inside Story*. More Everest titles are appearing as we go to press, including books by David Breashears, Lene Gammelgaard, and Ed Webster.

While controversies surrounding Everest '96 continue, some historic ones may have been laid to rest. In 1997, Alan Lyall published (U.K.) *The First Descent of the Matterhorn*, a massive volume of research that examines "the day the rope broke" on Whymper's first ascent (descent).

Last year, *Cook and Peary: the Polar Controversy, Resolved*, by Robert M. Bryce, was reviewed in these pages. Another massive volume, this book is meticulously and exhaustively researched and should be of great interest to any reader of polar exploration. In his review, Jonathan Waterman implied a conclusion to Mr. Bryce's book that, in fact, Mr. Bryce did not reach. Although Mr. Waterman stands by his review, we wish to apologize to Mr. Bryce and to any of our readers who may have been influenced by this misrepresentation.

Readers of German and anyone under the spell of the Eiger will be interested in *Eiger Die Vertikale Arena* by Daniel Anker and published by AS Verlag of Zurich. Not quite traditional coffee-table sized, this is a lavish history with 260 illustrations, many finely printed in color with a detailed *bergmonographie*. It is one of the most beautifully published mountain books I've seen.

Finally, readers should know that The American Alpine Club Press is now associated with The Mountaineers Books of Seattle, a fact that in no way will affect our reviewing policies.

DAVID STEVENSON

# Club Activities, 1998

Edited by Fred Johnson

The American Alpine Club 96th Annual Meeting, Denver, Colorado, November 13-14, 1998. George Lowe was once overheard to remark, "I'm glad the Club is growing, but I miss the days when the Annual Meeting was only a few hundred people, all of whom were your friends." No chance of that now: the 96th Annual Meeting was a packed house on a sunny weekend in Colorado's Front Range, and if you did manage to find a friend or two in the festive crowds, it was wise for conversation's sake to hold tight to the hem of their fresh-from-the-mothballs attire. The late evenings were the only chance to sit down over a beer whilst the luminaries paraded past, and by then you would have earned it, for the days required more than a little endurance to watch every presentation by the star-studded cast.

And star-studded it was: from Steph Davis's self-deprecating narration of her ambitious outing on Shipton Spire with Kennan Harvey and Seth Shaw, to Kath Pyke's graceful journey through an invitation to Iran, a host of new routes in Rocky Mountain National Park, and a tantalizing tour of some of Britains' seacoast offerings, to Tom Frost's rich tribute to his 30-something years on Yosemite's walls, the breadth of climbing was on display in an inspirational line-up that pulled from the new while tipping its hat to the old. We have legends in our midst, and legends in the making: Nicholas B. Clinch, that far-flung emissary of American climbing, pulled a jewel from the vaults when he showed and narrated the film from the 1958 American first ascent of Hidden Peak, his characteristic wit and good cheer in ample supply. Steve House, überalpinist and the most inspirational figure on the American climbing scene today, set the audience back in their seats with glimpses of his stunning Alaskan ascents. Mark Twight warmed us up with a presentation of his Mt. Bradley climb with House and "Jonny Blitz," wearing a specially decorated jacket with a message intended to make everyone feel warm and fuzzy ("Talk - action = 0," read the line on the back).

And then there was Pete Takeda, sport climber turned big waller turned mixed aficionado turning Himalayan alpinist before our eyes; the bold, strong and gifted Jared Ogden; and Stevie Haston, reprobate, with an uncharacteristically subdued Saturday evening after-dinner presentation that was far more softly spoken than anyone expected. The reason: no fewer than three eminent leaders of the AAC took Haston aside before the show and cautioned him that he must not be drunk and must not be vulgar, thereby depriving the audience of any of his normal titillating narration.

If you get anything out of these gigs, one would hope it would be the sense of continuity in this mad pursuit—and of any time in climbing's history, today is the moment we need it. To see a connection between the stunning ascents of some of the young stars and the self-effacing exploits of a Nick Clinch is to understand that there is something worth fighting for here, and only at the annual meetings will you find such a connection. Yes, George, the tribe has grown, and the sea of unknown faces can leave one a bit giddy with the numbers, but the enthusiasm generated by the presentations leaves us aware the next time we slide our fingers into the recesses of a crack or feel the sharp sting of spindrift against the skin of our necks that we are continuing a tradition that has taught humility and greatness to those who have come before. We need such inspiration if we are to pass on the same to the future of American climbing.

CHRISTIAN BECKWITH


*AAC, Alaska Section.* The year began in February with an ice-climbing seminar in Eagle River Valley in which more than 35 climbers participated and AAC members provided on-site instruction and tips on how to master steep ice. The outing, organized by Steve Davis, provided a solid basis for climbers traveling to Valdez for the annual Ice Climber's Festival on Presidents' Day weekend.

Two Section meetings were held, both at the Alaska Rock Gym in Anchorage. At the first one, issues and projects were identified that included hosting a Swiss Alpine Club representative as part of an AAC and SAC exchange.

One particular project focuses on the potential loss of access to the rock cliffs along the Seward Highway south of Anchorage. This is a very popular rock and ice climbing area, and climbers could face future restrictions due to the public's (and government's) perceived opinion that climbing activities pose a threat to passing motorists. Those familiar with the cliffs know that the rock is typical "Chugach crud" and that natural rock fall is common. The highway passes very close to the base of the cliffs, and rock and ice debris often land on the road. The fear is that some day, when a stone or a piece of ice crashes through a windshield, any climbers seen in the immediate vicinity will be blamed. Another issue centers on climbing adjacent to the railroad tracks, which must be crossed to gain access to the cliffs. The Alaska Railroad has established a permit system wherein all ice climbers are required to register and acknowledge that they are familiar with both the trespassing laws and the fact that they may not loiter near the tracks. Climbers in the area remember a few years ago when one of the most popular rock formations was literally blown up by the Railroad after a number of instances in which climbers were observed belaying from the tracks.

To address both the rock fall and railroad issues, the Section has embarked on a proactive campaign. In coordination with the Mountaineering Club of Alaska, a trailhead-like sign has been designed listing a set of "common sense" rules. These rules are intended to remind climbers about the risks involved when climbing in the area. Efforts to minimize stone and ice fall and working as cooperatively as possible with the Railroad will reduce the chance that these popular areas might be closed to climbing. A grant to help support this project has been approved by the AAC's Domestic Conservation Committee.

In August, the Section welcomed Andre Reider of the Swiss Alpine Club. During a two-week visit, Andre met with Section members to exchange information on both clubs as well as to inform us about the climbing opportunities in Switzerland. The Section was fortunate to have Eliza Moran, AAC board member and Chair of the Club's Exchange Committee, in attendance during a part of the exchange. The objective of the Section was to provide Andre with a good overview of the climbing opportunities in south-central Alaska. During his visit, he sat in on a Congressional hearing on Denali Park rescues and spent several days with NPS climbing rangers in Anchorage, Talkeetna and Denali National Park reviewing current climbing management practices and rescue procedures. Section member Jay Hudson gave Andre a flight around Denali, Hunter, Foraker and the Ruth Gorge. Andre was then taken on a two-day trip into the Talkeetna Mountains. He also explored Girdwood Valley and climbed along the Seward Highway.

As mentioned above, a Congressional hearing was held in Anchorage by Senator Frank Murkowski (R-AK) to discuss the high costs of mountain rescues on Denali. The Section as well as the local NPS rangers share the opinion that current rescue costs are not excessive and actually are minor compared to the taxpayer's cost for other types of rescues in Alaska and elsewhere in the country. Still, there remains a public outcry whenever a high-altitude rescue is reported in the press. Detailed summaries of this hearing as well as an article supporting the climbing community's point of view have been provided to the Section web site.

RALPH TINGEY, *Chairman*

*AAC, Cascade Section.* A number of exciting things happened in 1998 with the goal of revitalizing the Cascade Section in 1999. We have a new web site that you can visit at www.alpineclub.org. As time goes by, we hope that our members will contribute articles and pictures for posting on the web page. We will post the Section newsletter and other pertinent local information on it as well. We also have a new newsletter and encourage members to submit articles for inclusion. We'd like it to be an informal way of keeping us informed about what everyone is doing.

We are also trying to start a committee to help with local access and conservation issues, and also one to plan Section activities. All of this work is possible due to a larger group of volunteers helping out. We are asking for even more volunteer help to keep the web site current and our newsletter full of interesting articles, increase Section activities and maintain meaningful participation in access and conservation issues.

STEVE SWENSON, *Chairman*

*AAC, Oregon Section.* A unique gathering of people interested in the many issues concerning mountaineering in Tibet occurred in Portland this year. American Alpine Club members Tom Bennett, Bob McGown, Jean Fitzgerald, Neale Creamer and Ian Wade, together with Barbara Brower and Christine LeDoux, took on the task of arranging the premiere Mazama Tibet Conference. Among the themes elaborated on were Ethics of Expeditions in an Occupied Tibet, Environmental Status of Tibet, and Present Mountaineering and Trekking Opportunities in Tibet. Special thanks go to Bill and June Hackett for hosting the conference reception, which turned out to be a great celebration and reunion.

At the pre-conference reception in the home of AAC and Mazama member Bill Hackett, conference speakers and Mazamas met and a lively exchange of information ensued. The highlight of the evening was the reunion of Lowell Thomas, Jr. and Khando Chazotang after 49 years. Khando, a niece of the Dalai Lama, was a four-year-old child living in Lhasa in 1949, and her photograph appears in Lowell's book *Out of This World*. Many of the presenters also enjoyed a summit climb of Mt. Hood. Since the conference, Tom Bennett has worked on a Mazama trek with Gary McCue to the Lhasa region; planning is underway.

In other section activity, there has been an accessibility crisis on a popular crag, the Madrone Wall, to which the Access Fund representative and Oregon section members have dedicated a considerable block of time. An excellent, air-vesicled red rock basalt quarry, the Madrone Wall is in danger of becoming a gravel pit. The climbing area, close to Portland, boasts approximately 150 south-facing sport and traditional climbing routes up to 150 feet in length. AAC members Lloyd Athearn, Jennafer Elias-Reed and Michael Lewis wrote significant letters to Clackamas County exhorting the value of the Madrone Wall as a park. Oregon section member Tom Thrall (AAC Conservation chairman and Mazamas access), Ian Caldwell (Access Fund Oregon chairman), Keith Daellenbach, Max

Davenport, Cris Carey (AAC), John Parssons, Susie McKim, Brian Walsh (webmaster), Mike Farrel, et al, have been actively meeting for the past year. We are presently awaiting a review of quarry data by mining engineer John Sprecker. Cris Carey and Kassem Ferris have been working closely with the Madrone Committee as legal counsel. Marty Groff and Dillon Wheeler put on a climbing fund raiser that brought in $900 for the committee's mailing expenses.

The largest gathering of K2 veterans ever assembled took place on the weekend of November 20-22 in Portland. The 1998 American K2 Reunion was sponsored by the Mazama youth climbing organization, Explorer Post 936. Organizers were Oregon AAC members Peter Green and John Youngman with Susan Barber, Mary Wolin, Josh Field and Jim Johnson. Originally billed as the 20th reunion of the first successful American ascent team of K2 in 1978, the 1998 American K2 Reunion grew into a two-day festival featuring 25 members of past expeditions to the world's second highest mountain. Climbers dating back to the 1938 expedition attended the festivities. This was the first time the 1978 team had assembled since their landmark ascent that put four climbers on the summit. Members of the 1978 team in attendance were Jim Whittaker, Dianne Roberts, Jim Wickwire, Craig Anderson, Bill Sumner, Skip Edmonds, Rick Ridgeway, Rob Schaller and John Roskelley. The entire seven-man membership of the 1953 expedition to K2—Charles Houston, Bob Bates, Pete Schoening, Bob Craig, George Bell, Dee Molenaar and Tony Streather—attended the banquet. Molenaar called it "the greatest gathering of mountaineers. . . (the) friendliest and most purposeful I've seen in many years." Houston and Bates were members of the first American K2 expedition in 1938.

The weekend began with a Friday night slide show by Greg Child that described his harrowing ascent of the north ridge of K2. Almost 1,100 people attended his show. The highlight of the weekend was a gala banquet held Saturday night and attended by 250 guests. Dr. Charles Houston presented a slide show and history of the American attempt on K2 in 1938. Jim Whittaker, leader of the successful 1978 expedition, shared his memories of the trip and then invited each team member to speak to the audience about his or her individual experiences. For many of the attendees, the weekend offered an extensive opportunity to visit with the climbers both before and after the banquet.

Planning is ongoing for the K2000 Climb of K2's North Ridge to celebrate the millennium and to start a clean-up plan for the Chinese side of the mountain. The team hopes to clean up and remove expedition debris from the route as well as from Base Camp to the camel drop. We feel that gathering the waste and packaging it will be relatively easy. If anyone has any ideas on how to get the CMA's cooperation in transporting the garbage loads out to the road, please share them with us. We are working with Brent Bishop and hope that this can be accomplished in a fashion that can be repeated for every trip to the north side of K2. Members of the team include: Paul Teare, Robert Anderson, Jeff Alzner, Wayne Wallace, Shawn O'Fallon, Zigfried Emme, Virginia Russel, Mike Bearzi, Charles Hsieh, Ivan Ramirez, Drew Hansen, and Fred Ziel. Please contact expedition leader Jeff Alzner (503-245-8501) or Bob McGown (503-244-0078) for details.

In climbing news, Jeff Alzner and Wayne Wallace ascended the West Buttress route on Denali in training for the K2 climb. Ed Godschalk, an active Oregon section member, actually ascended a WI2 waterfall in the Oregon coast range during an oceanic cold front.

William Atkinson of the New England section, Nobel prize recipient and former VP of the AAC Henry Kendall, Bob McGown and Lisa Randall met to discuss east coast climbing and AAC section activity. It was an enjoyable visit.

BOB MCGOWN, *with* PETER GREEN

*AAC, Sierra Nevada Section.* As we moved closer to the end of the 20th century, 1998 gave us some disconcerting glimpses of what climbers probably will encounter in the century to come. Facing the challenges of increasing commercialization of our national parks plus some misguided attempts by federal agencies to regulate bolting in Wilderness areas forced us to realize that being very organized, very vocal and politically savvy was our best defense. Section membership this year surpassed 500, taking AAC membership as a whole over the 5,000 mark with the enrollment of Jenny Lundberg of Palo Alto.

At the Club's Annual Meeting in Denver, three Sierra Nevadans (coincidentally, all from Berkeley) won top awards. Galen Rowell was made an Honorary Member, in acknowledgment of all the hard work and many contributions he has made throughout the years to the AAC, to other groups supporting good stewardship of Yosemite National Park and to the climbing community in general. Never one to rest on his laurels, Allen Steck amassed yet another this year, the Robert & Miriam Underhill Award for outstanding success in the various fields of mountaineering endeavor. The recipient of the David A. Sowles Award was Betsy White, for the valiant and successful rescue of her Makalu teammate, Mike Warburton, in 1980. In presenting this award, Jim Wickwire pointed out that it was Betsy's heroism in this rescue that inspired Andrew Kauffman to initiate the Sowles Award in 1981.

Two other Sierra Nevadans honored at the Annual Meeting were Greg Adair and Dick Duane, who, like Galen, have poured a tremendous amount of their time, energy and souls into the preservation of Camp 4 and the many issues affecting climbers in Yosemite National Park. Greg, a tireless activist, was instrumental in convincing the Sierra Club to file a parallel lawsuit against the National Park Service that has temporarily halted any new construction in the Swan Slab/Camp 4 area. Equally tireless is attorney Dick Duane, whose massive and cogent "Supplementary Application for Placement of Camp 4 on the National Historical Register" resulted in a favorable ruling that has granted Camp 4 consideration as a possible National Historic site.

In counterpoint to all the problems being dealt to the climbing community in Yosemite, George Gluck succeeded in forging trails, both physically and diplomatically, that now connect us in very favorable ways to our friends in the National Park Service in Yosemite. His Volunteers in Parks group completed ten monthly projects this year around the park, and in a remarkable gesture, the NPS has given George and his volunteers the green light to focus on the improvement of Camp 4, among other sites. George's VIP projects continue to offer climbers new ways to have a very positive impact on Yosemite.

On the international front, Eliza Moran is now the editor of a UIAA publication highlighting amateur climbers throughout the world. Her UIAA connections are also serving her well as the Chair of the Climbers' Exchange Committee. In May, she facilitated a highly productive exchange between the Alaska Section and the Swiss Alpine Club, and has several other exchanges in the works throughout the Club.

Another innovative idea by Eliza produced the AAC Authors' Night events in February and June. Keppler's Bookstore in Menlo Park was the venue for the February event, with local authors Galen Rowell, Chris Jones and John Hart featured. In June, Jim Wickwire joined local authors Steve Roper, Tom Holzel and Daniel Duane (son of Dick Duane) for the festivities, which were dramatically heightened by Tom's legendary "May Punch." Between these two events and in the depths of the year's terrible El Niño storms season, we enjoyed a sumptuous Annual Wine & Cheese Party at the home of Steve Russell in Atherton in March. The evening was punctuated by lively discussions and speeches by John Middendorf and Brock Wagstaff about the NPS's plans for Yosemite Valley. The ground swell of concern that surfaced at this event helped compel the AAC to eventually join the lawsuit filed by The Friends of Yosemite Valley.

As the year closed, our Section continued to closely monitor plans for Yosemite. Highway 140, which enters the park at the Arch Rock area and runs along the Merced River, will remain closed for many months. A massive project to widen and rebuild the roadbed, which was damaged heavily in the 1997 floods, has been initiated by the NPS. As a result, many of the most popular climbing cliffs in the Valley are temporarily closed, including The Cookie, Arch Rock, Elephant Rock, Pat and Jack, Cascade Falls and The Rostrum. The Reed's area on Highway 120 is slated for temporary closure as well.

By keeping abreast of future NPS plans and assessing their impact on climbers, our Section hopes to raise the political profile and collective voice of the world's climbing community as it continues to flock to "the granite crucible."

LINDA MCMILLAN, *Chair*


*AAC, Central Rockies Section.* This has been a progressive and prosperous year for the Central Rockies Section. The 1997 Section Banquet got our Section going financially and helped carry us into the new year. The Section also had several events to try to coalesce our membership and get folks out. A gear swap/wine & cheese party at the Boulder Rock Club started the year. The Section newsletter editor, Eric Wagg, continues with our quarterly publication, and a treasurer, Jennifer Shinn, has been added to our volunteer staff.

We became active this year with the Boulder Ice Climbers Coalition. This grassroots organization is working with several governmental agencies to explore options for manmade ice for climbing in Boulder Canyon. The Section has donated $600 to this non-profit organization and pledged continuing assistance. Other projects included Section T-shirts last winter and canvas shirts, with the AAC logo embroidered on them, this winter. The latter are available upon pre-paid orders (see web site). Another big step into the public eye is the creation of our web site by George Bell and Peter Hsi. Visit us at http:crs.alpineclub.org/.

The Second Annual Section Banquet, held at Trios Restaurant in Boulder, was by far the most enjoyable, social and well-attended event. It had an elegant feel, even though it was quite casual. The keynote slide show was provided by the legendary Tom Frost. His spectacular presentation, "In a Time Long Ago and Far Away," was a historic review from his first ascent of the *Salathé Wall* and the second ascent of the *Nose* of El Capitan in Yosemite Valley, set to the theme from *Star Wars*. This quality program was such a success that it was contracted for the AAC Annual Meeting in Denver in November.

Mike Houston gave the banquet's lead-in program, an account of his first ascent with Jed and Doug Workman of the east face of Mount Nevermore in the Kichatna Spires in Alaska. A silent auction for the benefit of the Section was also offered at the Banquet. The proceeds were due in part to the tremendous support of the outdoor equipment industry, including Black Diamond, Patagonia, 5.10, Trango, Backpacker Pantry, Cascade Designs, Red Feather, FILA, Clif Bar, Trails Illustrated and Madden Packs. They have provided our Section the opportunity to become a viable voice for the climbing community in Colorado, Wyoming and New Mexico.

Climber exchanges continue to be an interesting but complex way of creating interaction among both American and international communities. The CRS was deeply involved with the Slovenians early in the year. Christian Beckwith and Jeff Hollenbaugh put in many hours creating a tasty schedule for our guests. Unfortunately, the Slovenians had to cancel. Many of their members had spent long, grueling months on Dhaulagiri. They returned safely, but tired and broke. We are currently involved with our proposed CRS-NZAC exchange, slated for winter 1999-'00. We hope to receive the Kiwis in the summer of 2000. There are also irons in the fire for an exchange with the New York Section and the Russians in 2001.

GREG SIEVERS, *Chairman*

*AAC, South Central Section.* Texas rock climbers from Austin, San Antonio, Dallas and Houston climbing clubs have been working with the Central Texas Climbing Committee and park staff on a conservation project at Enchanted Rock State Natural Area. Volunteers (and even a few tourists) have moved many tons of rock by hand and wheel barrow on many weekends throughout the year. The project was designed to reduce the impact of foot traffic and to control erosion on the trails around Echo Canyon and Motor Boat Rock. The Granite Gripper Climbing Competition raised $825 toward the conservation effort. Natalie Merrill and Paul Majors raised another $2,000 with an environmental grant from Exxon. Although much has been done, it is a never ending project, one of which Texas climbers can be very proud.

Unfortunately, negotiations with the Texas Park and Wildlife Department (TPWD) over the Public Use Plan for Hueco Tanks State Historical Park in El Paso have come to a close. Despite significant climber input from numerous organizations, including the AAC, and many offers to help facilitate a reasonably liberal access policy that included capital improvements to the park, the TPWD has closed the major portion of Hueco Tanks to climbing. Only the North Mountain will offer climber access that is limited to the first 50 users (not necessarily climbers) who make advance reservations in the park. Overnight camping will no longer be allowed. Access to all other areas of Hueco Tanks will be limited to guided tours only. This is a devastating blow to climbing in Texas and an extremely unfriendly policy toward visiting climbers. Efforts are under way to solicit the assistance of the Governor and State legislators to reverse impacts of this plan.

The Section's annual meeting, hosted by Sun & Ski Sports, was held in Tulsa on October 3. Members bouldered in Chandler Park for two hours, then gathered for a short business meeting, the installation of officers, and a barbeque lunch, generously provided by Mike and Jean Doyle of Teocalli Consulting Group. The evening was topped off with slide presentations by Eddie Whitmore and Greg Child. Thanks to Jan Greenspan, Jim Donini and Leif Marquardt for donating gear to the raffle.

MARC ROSENTHAL, *Chairman*

*AAC, New York Section.* The year 1998 will be remembered for a number of significant events. In January, a group of 14 New York Section members and guests journeyed to New Zealand's South Island for two weeks of trekking, climbing and outdoor pursuits. Under the leadership of Robert and Kathleen Whitby and well-known Kiwi guide Guy Cotter, the group enjoyed superlative weather, excellent creature comforts and great camaraderie on the world-famous Milford Track, which lived up to its reputation as "the finest walk in the world." A smaller group of climbers then attempted Mount Cook. In threatening weather and hazardous conditions, Joe Di Saverio and Henry Hamlin succeeded in summitting this very serious objective. A few weeks later, in Chilean Patagonia, Ken Kleinberg succeeded on a guided ascent of the 2600-meter North Tower of the Torres del Paine, which involved a 22-hour summit day and climbing up to 5.10.

In addition to these significant group and individual efforts, the Section continued with its long-standing Adirondack Outings, both winter and summer, each attended by about 30 members and guests. This year's Winter Outing was marked by idyllic, almost short-sleeve weath-

THE AMERICAN ALPINE JOURNAL, 1999

er, while in June the persistent rains managed to hold off long enough so that the Spring Outing became one of the more successful in recent memory. The traditional after-dinner slide shows at the Outings were given by Ed Palen and Willits Sawyer.

In April, the Section sponsored Alpenfilm, the New York International Mountain Film Festival. Now in its ninth year and an annual get-together for the New York climbing community, Alpenfilm is a juried competition offering cash prizes to winning filmmakers. This year's top award for Best of Festival went to Lynn Hill's *Free Climbing the Nose*, while the prize for the Best Film on Climbing went to a New Zealand film, *The Fatal Game*. The People's Choice award went to Rick Ridgeway for a film on a spectacular first ascent in Antarctica. Before the screenings, members, guests, jury and filmmakers convened for a dinner and reception that benefited the Golden Clubhouse Fund.

In October, the Section hosted its 19th Annual Black Tie Dinner and Gala with famed British author/climber Joe Simpson as special guest speaker. A capacity audience of 140 members and guests listened in rapt attention to Joe's epic story of survival and courage in the Peruvian Andes related in the best seller *Touching the Void*. Before the main event, Section member William Rom told of his adventures on the China/Tibet border climbing Mount Gelandaintong, source of the Yangtze River. The evening benefitted the Library Computerization Fund. Later that month, the Section co-sponsored a slide show, cocktail reception and book signing by Rick Ridgeway at the Patagonia store in lower Manhattan.

Besides the above, a variety of informal hikes and other weekend events were organized in the spring and fall by members John Tiernan, John Palutis and Earlyn Church. Also worthy of note was a May New Zealand night at the Explorers Club where members of the 1998 Expedition mentioned above recounted their adventures, followed by a reception featuring an excellent assortment of New Zealand wines and cheeses graciously provided by the New Zealand Tourist Promotion Board.

Thanks to the efforts of the Sierra Nevada Section and our own web master, Vaclav (Vic) Benes, the Section now has its own web site, nys.alpineclub.org. We hope this will introduce the Section to prospective members as well as furnishing up-to-the-minute news of our activities to the local membership.

PHILIP ERARD, *Chairman*

*AAC, New England Section.* 1998 saw the beginning of a renewal of the Section as a more cohesive social entity and, perhaps in the future, a working entity as well. We have striven to gather the membership together more often than in the past and to field activities in more than one region of New England.

Our third Annual Dinner attracted 51 members and guests. Mark Synnott was guest speaker, and Henry Kendall assembled a remarkable exhibit of his "Climber's Camera" mountain photographs. Bill Atkinson was voted Section Chair, replacing Barry Rugo, and Nancy Savickas Vice-Chair.

In April, Al Stebbins, Eric Engberg and Fran Bennett went variously to Red Rocks (Nevada) and to Mount Lemmon, Queen Creek Canyon and side canyons of the Salt River-Cibeque Creek and Salome Jug (Arizona). Our June north country "Base Camp" attracted some 40 AAC and Appalachian Mountain Club climbers for an afternoon and evening at the North Conway grill and beer cooler of generous AAC board member Jim Ansara.

Mark Synnott joined a trip sponsored by the National Geographic Society to Baffin Island, where he took part in the first ascent of "Great Sail Peak" (see *National Geographic*, January 1999). Mark joined the NGS again in August to Iceland to explore volcanoes.

In the summer (after a crash healing regimen for Mark's injured arm), Mark Richey and John Bouchard flew off to the Karakoram. There they made another attempt on Latok II (7108m), encountering dangerous conditions yet again. However, they were able to make the first ascent of an unnamed 6100-meter summit which they chose to call Harpoon Peak. Paul Dale and Bill Atkinson returned to Chamonix, where they ran into Yuki Fujita on Les Grands Charmoz and Bob Clark on the Aiguille de l'Index at La Praz. Paul and Bill climbed Le Miroir d'Argentine at Villars in Switzerland, then traversed from Montenvers to the Torino hut via the Refuge du Requin with an attempt on the Dent du Geant. Yuki reports having climbed the Brenva Spur on Mont Blanc under heavy bombardment, as well as the Central Spur of the Aiguille du Midi, the Gervasutti Pillar on Mont Blanc du Tacul and the Grand Capucin by the Swiss route on the south face. In the fall, Rick Wilcox led a group into Nepal's Mustagh Kingdom, a remote and seldom-visited corner of the world. Finally, our November "Camp I," organized by Walt Hampton and Bob Clark in Connecticut, attracted a dozen or so climbers to top-rope and lead at Pinnacle Rock Ridge. Appropriately, since he discovered this crag years ago, Sam Streibert showed up to climb with Al Rubin, our New England climbing historian, for the first time in many a moon. We repaired at day's end to Steve Messina's Prime Climb gym in Wallingford for dinner and slides.

BILL ATKINSON, *Chair*

*The Mountaineers.* The Seattle Mountaineers climbing program, under the leadership of Barbara McCann, continued with expansion of its traditional alpine program by again offering courses and seminars in sport climbing, water ice climbing and other advanced climbing experiences. The traditional alpine courses remain as popular as ever, with a small number of people being turned away each year owing to the high level of interest in these programs. The Advanced Climbing Experiences (ACE) program, which was initiated during the 1995-'96 climbing season, continued to attract increasing interest. During 1997-'98 it offered a number of activities for more experienced Mountaineers. Most popular of these was an extensive series of Water Ice seminars, which included trips to Ouray, Colorado, and Banff, Alberta. Other ACE seminars addressed Aid Climbing, High-Altitude Travel, Denali Expedition Planning, and Leadership. Besides climbs in Washington's Cascades and Olympics, various destinations and climbs offered to club members included Yosemite Valley and Tuolumne Meadows, Iztaccihuatl (Mexico), Mount Shasta, Gannett Peak and the Grand Teton, and Icefields Parkway in Banff (Athabasca and Andromeda).

On an administrative level, climbers Steve Firebaugh and Peter Clitherow developed a web page for the club's climbing programs (www. eskimo.com/~pc22). The Northwest Environmental Issues Course is a popular class offered annually. It features a program of lectures and field instruction designed to empower participants to take actions that will protect the natural resources of the Northwest by expanding their awareness and knowledge of regional environmental issues. Students examined aspects of often conflicting interest—including population, lifestyle, forests, water, salmon, growth management, energy and transportation—through lectures by nationally recognized speakers and local environmental experts as well as group discussion and activities. Field trips were offered to engage the class actively in the issues they studied. Also, an ongoing theme of activism focused on ways to influence legislation, write persuasive letters, and determine the most effective forums to shape public policy.

New titles of note for Mountaineers Books were *On Belay! The Life of Legendary Mountaineer Paul Petzholdt*, Joe Simpson's *Dark Shadows Falling, Back Country Snowboarding (Dudes!)*, the full-color *l00 Classic Hikes in Washington* and the second edition of *GPS Made Easy.* Mountaineers Books received three international awards. *Eric Shipton: Everest and Beyond* by Peter Steele won the Boardman Tasker Award for Mountain Literature. Recognition at the Banff Mountain Books Festival included *Postcards from the Ledge*, which won the mountain literature category, and Charles Houston's *Going Higher: Oxygen, Man and Mountains*, which won the mountain exposition category.

DONNA PRICE, *Trustee*

*The Mazamas.* Problems with governmental agencies proliferated in 1998. The Oregon State Marine Board continued its vendetta to classify, regulate and tax the Mazamas as a commercial guide. The U.S. Forest Service took the same stance toward the Mazama Climbing Education Programs and caused the club to abandon the graduation climb as a part of Basic Climbing School. The USFS also began to sell season permits for parking at trailheads and stressed the size of parties in wilderness areas. Two Mazama climb leaders were fined for having a party of 13, one person over the limit, near the summit of Mount Hood. The fact that one of the leaders had picked up an unattached climber to provide for his safety gave no amelioration to the fine. The USFS declared a policy of not allowing climbing hardware, even rappel slings, in Wilderness areas. This presented mountaineers with an agonizing decision of whether to halt the use of prudent mountain safety practices in order to obey the law. Meanwhile, the USFS continued the policy of permitting unlimited expansion at Mount Hood Meadows Ski Area, which inflicts permanent damage on the wild east side of that peak. It would seem that dollars in the coffers of the government are the real issue, not the preservation of wilderness. The Access Committee of the Mazamas, originally considered an effort to solve temporary problems, is now being considered as a permanent committee necessary to cope with access in USFS lands.

Recipients in the Mazama Awards Program numbered: (8) Three Guardian Peaks (Hood, St. Helens, Adams), (1) Seven Oregon Cascades (Jefferson, Three-Fingered Jack, Washington, Three Sisters plus Three Guardian Peaks), (5) 16 Major Peaks (all of the above plus Olympus, Baker, Shuksan, Glacier, Stuart, Shasta), (1) 15-point Leadership Award.

The Outing Committee, chaired by Barbara Parker, conducted international trips to Belize, Peru, Tuscany, Ireland, the Dolomites, and Siberia's Lake Baikal. There were western trips to Crater Lake, a float trip of the Grand Canyon and hiking the Oregon coast. The committee annually presents its programs at the Festival of Outings as well as at the New Member Fair. They also present many Wednesday evening slide shows and lectures to inform the members of past activity.

The Trail Trips Committee, chaired by Richard Getgen, again increased its enthusiastic participation with 555 trips and a total of 5,253 participant-days. The trend of interest in weekday in-city hiking made the 1990s the decade of the "Street Rambles," which accounted for 33% participation of all Mazama hiking. The Trail Tenders subcommittee continued its program of weekend trail improvement with volunteer labor. Getgen, by the way, hiked his 10,000th mile in July along the north rim of the Grand Canyon of the Yellowstone.

The Expedition Committee, under the leadership of Shirley Welch, conducted two major activities. One was the Mazama Annual Decathlon at Vancouver Lake, which attracted 300 competitors on April 19. The second was the development of an Expedition Training Course for the winter and spring of 1999. This course plans a series of four lectures on trip organization and expedition ethics, three slide shows and panel discussions of potential areas of the world, and three weekend field sessions to practice expedition skills and procedures.

President Robert Hyslop retired from the Executive Council after two years as president. He was succeeded in October by Christine Mackert for the 1998-'99 fiscal year.

JACK GRAUER, *Historian*

*Arizona Mountaineering Club.* Membership and enthusiasm continue to grow as the Arizona Mountaineering Club enters its 35th year. The membership, now over 450, spans a wide range of interests and experience levels. In 1998, members trekked, hiked and climbed throughout Arizona, the country and the world. Monthly meetings in Phoenix were well attended, and nationally known speakers included Peter Croft and Jim Bridwell.

The club continues to be a strong supporter of the Access Fund. A membership drive conducted in conjunction with the Peter Croft slide show collected nearly $500. In response to appeals for help to fight the bolting ban, the club's Board of Directors donated $1,000 to the Access Fund. Locally, the club was active on various access issues, including Pinnacle Peak Park, McDowell Mountains and Baboquivari Peak.

Our three climbing schools (basic, advanced and lead) are offered twice each year. The classes, always filled, are highly regarded locally, largely due to the organizational and instructional skills of chief instructor Wayne Schroeter. In addition to the regular schools, a number of seminars were conducted on wilderness survival, orienteering, mountaineering skills, ice climbing and photography.

Other club activities included working with the National Park Service at the Grand Canyon, where we rappelled over the canyon rim to pick up trash. Many members assisted with the annual Phoenix Bouldering Contest, the largest outdoor climbing contest in the United States. Several Adopt-A-Highway cleanups were held throughout the year. Regular club outings frequented areas in and around Arizona and the Southwest. Trips to Indian Creek (Utah) continue to be popular, and the annual Thanksgiving outing at Joshua Tree National Park (California) attracted over 60 members.

TOM CONNER, *President*

*Dartmouth Mountaineering Club.* Dartmouth climbers pulled down harder than ever before in New England, out west and beyond this year. During off-terms in the winter, Matt Holmes climbed with the Los Alamos Climbing Club at White Rock, Penitente, Shelf Road, and Jack's Canyon, and Jon Waldman fared well during a month-long escapade at Red Rocks and Hueco. Back in Hanover, despite the warm weather, Thad Law led the *Black Dike* on Cannon Cliff. Brian Staveley and Ben Fuller tied for first place at Middlebury's climbing competition, but a month later Middlebury's Matt Wilder prevailed at Dartmouth's fourth annual intercollegiate climbing competition. The DMC also made a fabulous showing at Hampshire College's comp, with Ben Fuller winning the men's division and Ann DeBord winning the women's division. Our annual spring break pilgrimage out west, this year to Hueco, was again a wonderful success due to steep rock, cheap bread and warm sun. While some of us worked the beta on classics including *Moonshine Roof* and *Sex After Death*, Gus Moore and Thad Law made a nude ascent of *Indecent Exposure*, providing an unparalleled view for everyone below at the *Mushroom Boulder*.

As the weather warmed up and club members returned to local crags, Bobby Hardage began a meticulous and productive search for undiscovered boulders in the area after returning from a nine-month road trip. Ben Fuller spent almost every weekend bouldering at the

Gunks and snagged the fifth ascent of the difficult *Illustrious Buddha*. DMCers also confirmed their reputation on campus by hosting a fabulous party centered around a giant pool of blue jello.

During the summer, ten of us met up at Kentucky's Red River Gorge, and found the long steep sandstone a welcome contrast to New Hampshire's granite slabs. Pat Leslie and Rich Harvell spent two months trekking and adventuring in Greenland, and Luke Cudney, Kevin Tompsett and Jon Waldman made a quick trip out to Wyoming's Cirque of the Towers and climbed the classic Pingora. Thad Law and Rusty Talbot climbed many of the Cascades' snowy volcanoes, completing an impressive 50-mile technical traverse with 50-pound packs in 50 hours.

Fall was the most active term for the DMC. We were happy to have many new and experienced freshmen join the club, including Freddie Wilkinson and Bart Paull, who during their first weeks here made a quick ascent of Cannon's *VMC Direct Direct*. We visited Cannon, the Gunks, Rumney and Cathedral, and a few students gave up a weekend to partake in an AMGA instructors course. Former DMCer Andy Tuthill talked about some of the amazing climbs he did during his years with the club long ago, and Bobbi Bensman came to town, inspiring us with her slide show. She also taught a clinic in our climbing gym, which is soon to be doubled in size, thanks to the dedication of John Joline and Brad Molyneaux and a donation from Judith Drake in memory of Charles Drake and Josh Hane. As the term came to a close and the snow began to fall, Chris Reidy and Chris Leander began planning an upcoming expedition to Nepal, and Thad, Freddie and Rusty prepared for a winter trip to Katahdin. Eight lucky club members drove out to Vegas immediately after exams, and if all went well, Cheryl Shannon became Dartmouth's first woman to climb 5.12.

JON WALDMAN, *club member*

# In Memoriam

Edited by David Harrah and Angus Thuermer, Jr.

## HARRY C. MCDADE, M.D.
### 1924-1997

*Harry McDade holding the Nathan Smith Distinguished Service Award, received from the New England Surgical Society in 1996.* COURTESY OF THE CALEDONIAN RECORD

In last year's *In Memoriam*, Bill Putnam tells well of Harry McDade's honors from surgery, his remarkable mountain rescue work and his AAC Sowles Award. During his 33 years as a club member, Harry climbed or piloted his plane when medical work permitted. He climbed often with H. Adams Carter, making first ascents of Paccharaju and Paccharaju Sur in Peru and helping to make a new route on Mt. Foraker. In 1966, Harry was with Eric Shipton, Adams Carter and me on Mt. Russell. We expected to finish a new route the next morning, but a long, continuous storm dumped eight to ten feet of snow on us, making location of our lower camp with its food doubtful but essential.

Harry also reached Phoksamdo Tal in the Kanjirobi Himal, Nepal—the second Westerner to get there. In separate years, he flew his plane to Point Barrow, Baffin Island and Greenland, Victoria Island and Teslin Lake in the Yukon. For these and many other reasons, our club can be proud of him.

ROBERT H. BATES

## ICHIRO YOSHIZAWA
### 1903-1998

Ichiro Yoshizawa, a member of The American Alpine Club and one of Japan's most distinguished mountaineers and mountain scholars, died at the age of 95 in September. Mr. Yoshizawa led the first Japanese expedition to the Andes in 1961 that made the first ascent of Pucahirca Norte, one of the last unclimbed 6000-meter peaks in Peru, as well as various first ascents in the Cordillera Apolobamba. In 1977, Mr. Yoshizawa was the leader of the successful Japanese expedition to K2.

*Ichiro Yoshizawa.* NICK CLINCH

His writings and translations were prodigious. Besides writing several books about his climbs in the Japanese Alps and the Japanese K2 expeditions, he edited *Encyclopedia of Mountaineering* and the monumental two-volume work, *Mountaineering Maps of the World.* He introduced Japanese climbers to many important English-language mountaineering books through his translations. Among the books he translated were Smythe's biography of Edward Whymper, Shipton's *Upon that Mountain,* and Tilman's *Snow on the Equator.*

He joined the Japanese Alpine Club in 1925, served on its board and later became vice president in 1972, and was elected an honorary member in 1977. He conducted a vast correspondence all over the world, and for many years furnished information on Japanese mountaineering to Ad Carter, editor of the *AAJ.* Mr. Yoshizawa was a member of various other foreign alpine clubs, including The Alpine Club (London).

He had a long-standing friendship with American mountaineers that began in 1961 when I realized that there were four and not just three 6000-meter peaks in the Pucahirca group, and that two of them were unclimbed. When I told him that there were two "North Pucahircas" and not just one, his expedition was able to make the first ascent of the unclimbed one. Years later, in 1969, when I was president of the AAC, he was visiting the United States and accompanied me on a trip to visit the western sections. He loved the opportunity to meet members of the Club.

Mr. Yoshizawa's warm courtesy had no seeming limit. In 1963, my plane from India to the United States stopped briefly at the Tokyo airport to refuel at three in the morning. Mr. Yoshizawa drove for more than an hour through a rainy wind-swept night to spend 15 minutes with me in the transient lounge before returning home. We have lost a friend.

NICHOLAS B. CLINCH

## BERNARD PIERRE
### 1920-1997

Bernard Pierre was born in Chelles, France, became a doctor of law and a graduate of the School of Political Science, and became head of the family textile business. From his earliest years, he devoted his leisure time to mountaineering and to writing.

With Gaston Rebuffat, he made several classic ascents in the Alps, including the North Face of the Drus, the Northwest Face of La Civetta, the second ascent of the Northeast Face of Piz Badille, and the second ascent of the Black Needle de Penterey. In addition, he shared leads on the first ascents of the North Arête of the Aiguille des Aigles and the face of the Aiguille de la Brenva. In 1951, he visited the Hoggar in North Africa and made several first ascents there. In 1952, he and three French colleagues joined four AAC members in Peru and made the first ascent of Salcantay (6271m).

In 1953, he led an expedition to Nun Kun, the second-highest peak in Kashmir (7135m), on which Pierre Vittoz and Claude Kogan reached the summit. In 1954, he led a Franco-Iranian expedition to Iran to make the first ascent of Demavend. He led expeditions to the Mountains of the Moon in Ruwenzori (1955-'56,) the Caucasus (1958), and Hoggar (1961). Pierre's career as a writer was extraordinary. His first book, on synthetic textiles, was honored by the Institute de France. His mountaineering writings include books about his own expeditions (*Escalades au Hoggar*; *Salcantay, Geant des Andes*; *Une Montagne Nomee Nun Kun*; *Une Victoire sur l'Himalaya*; *Montagnes de la Lune*; *Mes Galons d'Alpiniste*; *Une Victorie sur les Andes*; and *Ils ont Conquis l'Himalaya*), books written in collaboration with others (*Face a l'Everest*, with Eric Shipton; *Escalades et Randonees au Hoggar*, with Claude Aulard), and several books for young readers. In addition, he produced some lovingly written books about the great rivers of the world (*Le Roman du Nil*; *Le Roman du Mississippi*; *...Danube*; *...Gange*; *...Loire*). He received a number of literary prizes, and his books have often been translated into other languages.

Pierre became a member of the Groupe de la Haute Montagne in 1949. He became a member of the AAC in 1953, and Honorary Member in 1991.

GEORGE I. BELL, SR., W.V. GRAHAM MATTHEWS, *and* DAVID HARRAH

## HARRY HOYT
## 1924-1997

Harry Hoyt was born June 20, 1924, in Grinnell, Iowa. Since he suffered from asthma, he was sent as a teenager to the YMCA Camp Chief Ouray near Granby, Colorado, where he became a counselor and developed his love of the mountains. While there, he made his first of many ascents of Longs Peak in 1941. He then went to the University of Colorado, where he obtained his undergraduate degree in physics and remained for a further year as a teaching assistant. During these summers, he served as an instructor and guide for the university's Mountain Recreation Department. His ascents during that time included many climbs of Longs Peak, including Alexander's Chimney and Stettners' Ledges and many others in the Colorado Rockies and the Tetons.

Harry received his Ph.D. in physics from the California Institute of Technology in 1953 and immediately accepted a position as staff member in the Theoretical Division at the Los Alamos Scientific Laboratory in the Jemez Mountains of New Mexico. Harry remained active at the Laboratory until shortly before his death. He displayed a talent for devising computer programs to solve difficult technical problems, ranging from the propagation of shock waves though layered media to the detection of fraud in the patterns of Medicare billing. He was also greatly respected as a mentor of less-experienced colleagues. For this role, he developed a somewhat curmudgeonly manner, and used it to good advantage to help his colleagues distinguish hype and speculation from knowledge.

Harry was one of the founders and prime movers of the Los Alamos Mountaineers, organizing and leading instructional courses and technical climbs for the club. He also participated in some of the summer outings organized by the Alpine Club of Canada and there met the Swiss guide, Eddie Petrig. Subsequently, Harry did a number of long classic Zermatt climbs with Eddie, including the Marinelli Couloir on Monte Rosa and the West Ridge of the Taeschorn.

One of Harry's favorite activities was climbing in the San Juan Mountains of Southwestern Colorado in the spring, often over Memorial Day. Many of these mountains have poor rock, so we liked to go there early in the season when there was plenty of snow on which to make the climbs. We would drive as far as possible, then backpack, perhaps a few miles, to camp in some neat place like Yankee Boy Basin or Silver Pick Basin— often among the ruins of old mines or mills. Around daybreak, Harry was always among the first up to light a fire and start breakfast cooking. Since his asthma continued to bother him, he would also use an inhaler at this early hour and cough and snort to clear his lungs for the day's climb. Then we would set off to climb some little-known peak such as Teakettle, or Gilpin, or Vermillion.

On one of these trips, after two days of wonderful climbing, we spent the night in a campground just north of Ouray, Colorado, before heading back to work. As usual, Harry was up early, starting a fire and clearing his lungs. After the rest of us had emerged from our sleeping bags and were eating breakfast, some other campers came over and expressed concern. They asked if we had heard the bear in the campground. They had heard the bear around dawn, coughing and snorting something awful; they thought he sounded old and cross and they worried that he might come back again....

We miss you, old bear.

GEORGE I. BELL

## HENRY CECIL JOHN HUNT
### 1910-1999

Lord Hunt, who led the successful British expedition that made the first ascent of Everest, and who was an honorary member of The American Alpine Club, died on November 8, 1998. He was 89.

Some men do things right. John Hunt was one of them. More than 45 years after the event, it is easy to forget what the circumstances were regarding Everest in 1953. The British had made innumerable attempts on the mountain. All had failed. The Nepalese opened the mountain to other countries and in 1952 the Swiss attempted Everest twice from the south side and almost succeeded. The British had permission for the following year and after that, permission had been granted to other countries. It was apparent that Everest would be climbed. The only question was, by whom? More than 30 years of effort was coming down to one last throw of the dice.

At this critical moment, the Everest Committee decided to switch the leadership of the expedition from Eric Shipton, a very popular mountaineer who was one of Britain's finest Himalayan mountaineers and had made five expeditions to Everest, but who basically ran his trips off the back of an envelope, to John Hunt, an army officer with great organizing ability. The decision was correct, but it was handled badly. Years later, Hunt, who had nothing to do with the decision, was still embarrassed by it.

*Henry Cecil J. Hunt.* GEORGE BAND

Handicapped by the manner of his selection, facing monumental difficulties of logistics, obtaining oxygen apparatus, selecting personnel and getting them to work as a team, and under intense public scrutiny, John Hunt brought it off. As always, it required a break in the weather, but Hillary and Tenzing, after a tremendous effort, reached the summit on May 29, 1953. The news of the success reached England on June 2, the day of the Coronation of Queen Elizabeth II.

John Hunt was more than a military organizer. He was a mountaineer. He began climbing in the Alps as a young man. Later, while serving in the army in India, he went on various Himalayan expeditions, including an attempt on Saltoro Kangri (a 25,400-foot avalanche trap in the Karakoram) and a reconnaissance of the Kangchenjunga massif. After the Everest expedition, he regularly went to the Alps to climb and ski. He also led British parties to the Caucasus in 1958 and to the Pamirs in 1962.

Hunt was born in Simla, India, on June 22, 1910, the son of an army officer. He was educated at Marlborough College, where he was first in his class, and then at Sandhurst Military Academy, where he was again first in his class, and was awarded the King's Gold Medal and the Anson Memorial Sword. After service in the King's Royal Rifle Corps in India, he returned to England in 1940, where he was appointed chief instructor in the Commando Mountain and Snow Warfare School. Later, he was given command of the 11th Indian Infantry Brigade and was with them until the end of World War II.

He left the Army in 1956 to run the Duke of Edinburgh's Award Scheme for British youth, during the course of which he led a youth expedition to East Greenland. In addition, he was Chairman of the Parole Board for England and Wales, President of the Council for Volunteers Overseas, and involved with numerous other organizations and commissions. He was Knighted in 1953, and made a Life Peer in 1966. For his dedicated public service, the Queen made him one of 24 Knights of the Garter in 1979.

Hunt also remained active in mountaineering and exploration matters. He was president of The Alpine Club, the Climbers' Club, the British Mountaineering Council, the National Ski Federation, and the Royal Geographical Society.

But hidden behind this incredible record of accomplishment (and at times a diffident appearance to strangers) was an extremely warm and generous man. A caring husband to his wife, Joy, and father to their four daughters, John Hunt was kind to everyone, and especially to his friends. His life and character is best summed up by the word this proper English gentleman scribbled over the printed greetings contained in his last Christmas card: "Love."

NICHOLAS B. CLINCH

## LUTHER GERALD JERSTAD
### 1936-1998

Lute Jerstad possessed a magical quality born of the mountains that affected all those around him. He was a good friend of my father's and, as a young boy in Washington, D.C., I remember getting excited when hearing that Lute would be coming to visit. Lute and my father would stay up late drinking, laughing, and telling stories about far-off places that captivated a young boy's imagination. Lute's tremendous laugh and presence filled a room. It's hard to imagine that a persona as powerful as Lute's won't be joining us for another round.

Lute was born in Minnesota in 1936 on his parent's farm: weighing only slightly more than three pounds, he was incubated in a shoe box and fed with an eye dropper. At 12, Lute and his family moved to Gig Harbor, Washington, where he attended high school and was introduced to the mountains of the Northwest. An exceptional athlete, Lute lettered in football, basketball, and baseball at Peninsula High School. Lute attended Pacific Lutheran University where he played basketball, making two trips to the NAIA tournament in Kansas City. He was voted the Inspirational Award his senior year.

During high school and college, Lute spent a great deal of time climbing throughout the Northwest. He climbed most of the major peaks in the Cascades. Lute began guiding on Mt. Rainier during the summers, logging more than 40 ascents of the mountain. Lute's climbing travels then took him to the top of Mt. McKinley. Norman Dyhrenfurth, the expedition leader of the 1963 American Everest Expedition, was impressed with Lute's climbing resume and invited him to join the team. He was only 26 years old.

On May 22, 1963, Lute and his climbing partner, Barry Bishop, stood on the summit of Everest as members of the first American team on the mountain. Not only did Lute summit Everest, but he carried a motion picture camera to the roof of the world and recorded the first motion pictures from the summit of that mountain. Even more remarkable, Lute and Barry joined Tom Hornbien and Willie Unsold after their successful ascent of the West Ridge that afternoon, and the four descended to the South Col together. They did not make it to Lute and Barry's high camp and were forced to spend the night out at 28,000 feet before reaching the safety of camp the next morning. This bivouac was an extraordinary feat, but the public had no real awareness of its significance.

Following his success on Everest, Lute obtained a master's degree from Washington State University, and a doctorate from the University of Oregon. He taught at Franklin Pierce High School in Tacoma, Washington, Lewis and Clark College in Portland, Oregon, and The University of Oregon in Eugene, Oregon. He started Lute Jerstad Adventures in Oregon, and offered river rafting, mountaineering and outdoor experiences in the United States and Asia. One of his greatest joys was teaching and leading people to reach heights of success they would not have thought possible. He introduced deaf children, blind adults, the mentally retarded, and the physically disabled to the rigors of outdoor adventure.

Lute's love of the Himalaya and his desire to explore saw his return in later years to champion environmental causes. He worked with various business partners in India and Nepal to conserve wildlife parks and forests so that endangered species might survive, and at the same time provided a once-in-a-lifetime experience for those visitors who traveled with him.

Impressive as Lute's accomplishments are, it was his personality that made the real mark in the world. He was opinionated, outspoken, and as politically incorrect as they come. He made no apologies for his beliefs or actions; it was the world according to Lute. Lute loved his cigarettes, scotch, and the poems of Robert Service, and was never wanting for a candid opinion: he had a way of crashing through life with integrity that is not found easily in this day and age. Gil Roberts, a member of the 1963 Everest expedition, tells of Lute, "He could occasionally be his own worst enemy, he got mad about stuff, but he was a loyal friend who always wondered what he could do for other people. He'd give you his down jacket or his last 50 bucks if he though you were cold or broke."

Lute was extremely humble, never basking in his accomplishments on Everest, always downplaying them. He wrote to me after I climbed Everest in '94 with the following advice: "Accomplishing such a feat isn't much in and of itself, but in the long run it provides a mortal with a new, fresh and satisfying view of the world below. Now you erase the word can't from your vocabulary." It was with this attitude that Lute approached the world, accomplished so much, and touched so many people.

His final trip to Nepal was a trek to Everest Base Camp with his grandson and some close friends. They stopped to visit the chortans of Jake Breitenbach and Barry Bishop, fellow '63 Everest team members, on the ridge at Thangboche monastery. Lute allowed as to how he wouldn't mind ending up there by and by. Two days later, he dropped of a sudden coronary at Dugla. He is out on the ridge now. The view up valley to Everest is pretty special. If you get there, go out and share a beer with Lute, his friends, and the goraks.

BRENT BISHOP, *with input from* STEW MORTON *and* GIL ROBERTS

## NED GILLETTE
### 1945-1998

"Ned left me and a lot of us with the courage, passion and imagination to
push on, to go and live our dreams."
—Susie Patterson Gillette

Ned Gillette, 53, was killed by two bandits on August 5, 1998, in the Haramosh Valley of northern Pakistan in an apparent failed robbery attempt. He was at the end of a Himalayan trek with his wife, Susie Patterson, when two assailants blindly shot into their tent during the middle of the night, fatally wounding Ned. Susie, in serious condition, survived and was evacuated to Gilgit with the help of shepherds and police.

Ned lived an extraordinary and energetic life, remarkable for the variety of adventures he created, the skills he mastered to complete them and the colorful way he engaged a wide audience with accounts of his experiences. He defined his outlook in a piece called "The Meaning of Life," in which he said, "If life is to have any meaning, it's essential to carve out your own niche, to become special. Special things happen to special people. Climbing, skiing, and ocean voyages to remote corners of the world are often so gnarly and so scary that you wish you'd never left home. But eventually the sun shines again. You must be an optimist."

Ned grew up in Barre, Vermont. He began skiing at age five, and spent summers sailing New England's coastal waters. From Holderness School in New Hampshire, he went on to Dartmouth, where he was captain of the ski team. He was NCAA cross-country ski champion in 1967, the year he graduated, and became a member of the 1968 Olympic team. In 1970, he helped establish the cross country ski program at the Yosemite Mountaineering School under director Wayne Merry, which he ran for several winters. He then returned to Vermont to head the Trapp Family Lodge's Ski Touring Center in Stowe.

His first expedition was a 1972 ski traverse of the Brooks Range in Alaska. Along with three teammates, he covered 300 miles of the proposed oil pipeline. He then began dreaming up his own adventures, usually carried out with three companions.

*Ned Gillette climbing Haramosh Pass, northern Pakistan, in 1998.* S. PATTERSON GILLETTE

In 1977, Ned led an expedition that skied over 500 miles up Canada's Robson Channel and around Ellesmere Island, pioneering the use of specialized sleds that enabled self-supported expeditionary travel. In 1978, Ned and Galen Rowell circumnavigated Mt. McKinley; the two later completed the first one-day ascent of the peak, climbing and descending over 10,000 vertical feet in 19 hours. In 1979, he completed a ski traverse of New Zealand's Southern Alps.

In 1980, Ned led a 285-mile winter ski crossing of the Karakoram Mountains, a venture that he often cited as the most physically demanding of his expeditions. Also in 1980, Ned completed the first ski descent of the 24,757-foot Muztagata in China. In 1981-'82, Ned organized the Everest Grand Circle Expedition, which circumnavigated Mt. Everest, and completed the first American winter ascent of Mt. Pumori (23,422').

In 1988, after designing and supervising the construction of a 28-foot rowboat, Ned rowed with three companions over 600 miles in 13 days across the Drake Passage from Cape Horn to Antarctica through some of the world's "most mad seas," an adventure that Ned documented in a feature article for National Geographic.

These accomplishments required not only extraordinary athletic ability, endurance, discipline and mental toughness, but also vision and optimism. His deep-set hazel eyes sparkled with intense delight and energy with each fresh idea for traveling the world's wild places. Ned's brilliance was to approach the world in creative ways, bringing the excitement of discovery to familiar arenas. Resourceful and self-reliant, he meticulously prepared for each foray, anticipating known hazards and minimizing the risks of capricious nature.

Following their marriage in 1990, Ned and Susie Patterson, a U.S. slalom and downhill champion, and also a former Olympic skier, took up residence near Sun Valley, Idaho. Two years later, they walked 5,000 miles of the historic Silk Route across China and other Central Asian countries in authentic "caravan style," with six camels.

Ned chronicled these experiences in his captivating writing and photography, focusing on skiing, mountaineering, sailing, and outdoor photography. He contributed adventure travel articles and photographs to numerous publications, including *National Geographic*, *Outside*, and *Outdoor Photographer*. He authored two books: *Everest Grand Circle*, with Jan Reynolds, and *Cross Country Skiing*, with John Dostal.

Ned was a generously warm and insightful person who used humor to keep life in perspective. Certainly, he will be remembered for his imaginative exploration of wild and remote regions. But more satisfying to him, and more enduring, was his ability to energize and inspire each of us to push beyond our self-imposed limits, and to live life with vitality and commitment, determined to excel in whatever venture we've chosen. His family and his friends will always love, remember, and miss him.

DEBORAH GILLETTE LAW *and members of Ned's family*

## FRANCYS DISTEFANO-ARSENTIEV
## 1958-1998
## SERGUEI ANATOLIEVICH ARSENTIEV
## 1958-1998

About five years ago, Francys Distefano, a long-time member of the Telluride community and a rapidly improving high-altitude climber, arrived home with Serguei, her guide on a Russian climbing expedition. Serg, a native of St. Petersburg, had a long resume that included many years of difficult climbing on high Soviet peaks and 8000-meter summits in the Himalaya with Russian teams. Almost as interesting, he boasted a list of careers that included electrical engineer, rocket scientist, logger, and steeplejack. Serg started working with us as a carpenter and took a whirlwind tour of the American Dream: Coca Cola, an old Chevy pick-up truck, Carhartts, a motorcycle, new teeth, and an Audi. He quickly learned English and, eventually, our measuring system. Serg was the carpenter everyone relied on to handle tough jobs. Single-handedly, with only some help from Fran, Serg built a beautiful home in Norwood, Colorado. They also took annual expeditions to Russia or Alaska. When Fran asked me about refinancing their house to go on an Everest climb, I realized that living the American Dream wasn't going to totally contain their intellect—not with the Himalaya beckoning.

I should have extracted more stories from Serg when I could, instead of planning to talk more when we were both 80, lounging in our rockers at the old folks' home. I keep expecting to see him arrive at a construction site and to tell him, "Serg, cut the sentimental bullshit and get your nail-belt on."

CHUCK KROGER

Serguei and Francys Arsentiev died on Mount Everest last spring. The Arsentievs are the only husband-and-wife team to attain Everest without the use of supplemental oxygen.

Sergei, one of the foremost Russian alpinists of this century, will be remembered perhaps more for his gentle, unassuming demeanor. In St. Petersburg, Serguei studied at the Leningrad Electrotechnical Institute and later worked in a factory that manufactured spy satellites, "looking on the U.S.," he once explained amusedly. He came up with the concept of using magnetism at the Earth's poles to keep satellites from spinning in orbit so that they could focus continuously on America.

Besides being a rocket scientist, Serguei proved his physical mettle in climbing. A man of remarkable focus, intelligence, and strength, with a natural ability to acclimatize quickly, Serguei completed more than 100 routes in the Caucasus and the former Soviet ranges, Tien Shan and the Pamirs. To his credit are the first winter ascents of Peak Korzhenevskaya (7105m) and Peak Lenin (7134m), and a 20-hour round-trip climb of Khan Tengri Peak (6995m). "One would have to go back to that era to understand the stature of these achievements," said

Serguei's friend, Antoine Savelli. "Serguei's nonchalance disguised his greatness."

Serguei earned the honorary name of Snow Leopard for climbing the five highest mountains in the Soviet Union. At the age of 30, he was awarded Master of Sport with Honors. As such, Serguei was an important team member in some of the most lauded Soviet expeditions, like the 1989 Kangchenjunga traverse when he summited all "Three Tops." On May 7, 1990, Serguei became the first Russian to climb Everest without bottled oxygen. The achievement came on the Everest Peace Climb, a joint U.S.-Chinese-Russian expedition conceived and led by American Jim Whittaker. For this, Serguei was presented the National Friendship Medal by President Gorbachev and became a national hero.

In 1991, Serguei met Francys Distefano in the Himalaya. Fran, an American and young mother from Telluride, Colorado, had grown up skiing in the U.S. and Switzerland and had recently taken to mountaineering. As the story goes, she went to Nepal with a boyfriend and summited the 6000-meter Loboche, Island, Pokalde and Mera peaks, then crossed the Khumbu Glacier to Serguei's tent. That fall, she accompanied Serguei on a Russian expedition to Annapurna I and climbed as far as Camp II. Serguei and a Russian partner made short work of the 8000-meter peak, ascending the north face with light packs and no oxygen in typical Russian style. A year later, Fran and Serguei registered their marriage in the Soviet Consulate of Kathmandu, and the couple went on to climb Elbrus's east and west tops. Fran skied from the West Top to the foot of Elbrus, becoming the first American woman to do so.

In the summer of 1992, Fran brought Serguei to Telluride (after Serguei convinced the Politburo that he would not divulge Russia's spy satellite secrets in the United States). While I was working for a Telluride newspaper, Serguei and Fran asked me to write an article about their mountain-guiding business, Trek Around the World. Describing his achievements to me (Serguei was just learning English), Fran was in awe of Serguei, her blue eyes gleaming in rapture.

Serguei was shy, enigmatic and instantly a friend. That winter, Serguei and I, both illegal aliens, landed jobs shoveling snow for cash. We waved our shovels in greeting on many dark mornings as we cleared sidewalks on opposite sides of Main Street.

Trek Around the World never matured as a business, but Serguei and Fran returned to Russia each year to climb Korzhenevskaya, Lenin, Communism (7495m), Vorobyov (5691m), and Peak of Four (6299m). In 1994, they made a first ascent of Peak 5800m, which they named Peak Goodwill, located in the remote Muzkol Range of the East Pamirs, and also summited Chottukay Peak (5823m). In 1995, they successfully summited Denali via the West Buttress. Serguei, meanwhile, had become a proficient carpenter, working for a Telluride construction company owned by climber Chuck Kroger and his wife, Kathy Green, and had built a house for himself and Fran in Norwood, a neighboring mesa town. He was known by his co-workers as "the gentle giant." Despite her passion for mountaineering adventures, Fran was devoted to her son, Paul, from a previous marriage.

Kroger recalled first meeting Fran in 1984 when she was new to Telluride and to climbing; even then she expressed a desire to climb Everest. As testimony to her determination, Fran is the first American woman and the second woman in the world to verifiably summit Everest without the use of supplemental oxygen. Why she and Serguei kept climbing for the summit after they had fallen way behind the mid-day turn-around that Everest mandates, we confound ourselves asking. To borrow from Reinhold Messner, "...the same questions are unanswered as yesterday, and as in the beginning. And every answer is a new question for those who are left behind."

Serguei is survived by his teen-aged daughter, Alevtina, who lives in Russia. Fran is survived by Paul Distefano, who lives with his father in Telluride.

RHONDA L. CLARIDGE

# Appendices

## Appendix A: Expedition Regulations and Permits

Regulations and information for obtaining expedition permits to the countries listed below are available on request from the agencies noted.

ANTARCTICA
> National Science Foundation
> Office of Polar Programs
> Room 755
> 4201 Wilson Boulevard
> Arlington, VA 22230

BAFFIN ISLAND
> Superintendent of Auyuittuq National Park Reserve
> Parks Canada
> Eastern Arctic District
> P.O. Box 353 E.
> Pangnirtung, Northwest Territories
> XOA ORO
> CANADA

BHUTAN
> Trekking and Mountaineering Manager
> Bhutan Tourism Corporation
> P.O. Box 159
> Thimphu
> Bhutan

CHINA
> The Mountaineering Association of China
> Number 9 Tiyuguan Road
> Beijing
> The People's Republic of China

> The Mountaineering Association of Tibet, China
> Number 8 East Linkhor Road
> Lhasa
> Tibet, China

> The Mountaineering Association of Xinjiang, China
> Number 1 Renmin Road
> Urumqi, Xinjiang
> China

INDIA
> Indian Mountaineering Foundation
> Benito Juarex Road
> Anand Niketan
> New Delhi 100 021
> India

NEPAL
    HMG Ministry of Tourism and Civil Aviation
    Mountaineering Division
    Kathmandu
    Nepal

(Trekking Peaks In Nepal:)
    Nepal Mountaineering Association
    P.O. Box 1435
    Kathmandu
    Nepal

PAKISTAN
    Government of Pakistan
    Ministry of Culture and Tourism
    Tourism Division
    Islamabad
    Pakistan

C.I.S.
    Georgia
        Mountaineering and Climbing Association of Georgia
        MCAG
        P.O. Box 160
        380008 Tbilisi
        Georgia

    Kyrgyzstan
        Federation of Alpinism and Rock Climbing of the Republic of Kyrgyzstan
        105 Panfilov Street
        CIS-720035 Bishkek
        Kyrgyzstan

    Ukraine
        Ukrainian Mountaineering Federation
        Eksplanadna 42
        252023 Kiev
        Ukraine

C.I.S.: Other organizations
    Euro-Asian Association of Mountaineering and Climbing
    Sokolnicheskaya pl. 9-1-134
    107014 Moscow
    Russia

## Appendix B: Meters to Feet

| meters | feet | meters | feet | meters | feet | meters | feet |
|--------|------|--------|------|--------|------|--------|------|
| 3300 | 10,827 | 4700 | 15,420 | 6100 | 20,013 | 7500 | 24,607 |
| 3400 | 11,155 | 4800 | 15,748 | 6200 | 20,342 | 7600 | 24,935 |
| 3500 | 11,483 | 4900 | 16,076 | 6300 | 20,670 | 7700 | 25,263 |
| 3600 | 11,811 | 5000 | 16,404 | 6400 | 20,998 | 7800 | 25,591 |
| 3700 | 12,139 | 5100 | 16,733 | 6500 | 21,326 | 7900 | 25,919 |
| 3800 | 12,467 | 4200 | 17,061 | 6600 | 21,654 | 8000 | 26,247 |
| 3900 | 12,795 | 5300 | 17,389 | 6700 | 21,982 | 8100 | 26,575 |
| 4000 | 13,124 | 5400 | 17,717 | 6800 | 22,310 | 8200 | 26,903 |
| 4100 | 13,452 | 5500 | 18,045 | 6900 | 22,638 | 8300 | 27,231 |
| 4200 | 13,780 | 5600 | 18,373 | 7000 | 22,966 | 8400 | 27,560 |
| 4300 | 14,108 | 5700 | 18,701 | 7100 | 23,294 | 8500 | 27,888 |
| 4400 | 14,436 | 5800 | 19,029 | 7200 | 23,622 | 8600 | 28,216 |
| 4500 | 14,764 | 5900 | 19,357 | 7300 | 23,951 | 8700 | 28,544 |
| 4600 | 15,092 | 6000 | 19,685 | 7400 | 24,279 | 8800 | 28,872 |

## Appendix C: Ratings

To help our readers in their research and to further the use of the *AAJ* as a reference tool, we offer the following explanations of the various systems of the world. Where appropriate (i.e., rock climbing grades), we compare the various systems. For snow, ice, mountaineering and aid, we describe the systems according to their individual merits.

SNOW AND ICE GRADES

There are currently four major systems used to grade the severity of snow and ice climbs: Scottish Winter Grades, New England Ice Rating System, Canadian Ice Grading, and the Water Ice (WI) system developed by Jeff Lowe. Each is described below.

SCOTTISH WINTER GRADES

The two-tier system gives an overall grade based on an extended version of the previous I to V system. The overall difficulty is expressed by the Roman numeral. Technical grades apply to the hardest move or a short technical section of the route and are expressed by an Arabic numeral. It is the combination of the two that makes the system work.

The Scottish ethic is for ground-up leads in winter conditions. Pre-placed gear as employed in American mixed climbing is not considered good style. The defining characteristic of Scottish winter climbing is the weather—the humidity tends to produce hoar frost or rime on the rock, which makes progress more complex than movement over pure rock or pure ice.

Grade I: Climbs for which only one axe is required (e.g., snow gullies around 45° or easy ridges).
Grade II: Axe and hammer are required because of steep snow, a difficult cornice, or a short ice pitch. Difficulties are usually short. The ridges are more difficult but usually still scrambles in summer.
Grade III: Similarly technical but more sustained than Grade II. Sometimes short and technical, particularly for mixed ascents of moderate rock climbs.
Grade IV: Steep ice from short vertical steps to long pitches of 60-70° that requires some arm strength. The mixed climbs require more advanced techniques such as torquing.
Grade V: Sustained steep ice (70-80°) or mixed climbs that require linking hard moves.
Grade VI: Vertical ice; mixed routes, either long and sustained, or, if short, sufficiently technical to

| YDS | UIAA | FR | AUS | GER | CIS | SCA | BRA | UK | |
|------|------|-----|-----|-------|------|-----|--------|-----|-----|
| 5.2 | I | 1 | 10 | | III | 3 | | | D |
| 5.3 | II | 2 | 11 | | III+ | 3+ | | | |
| 5.4 | III | 3 | 12 | | IV- | 4 | | | VD |
| 5.5 | IV | 4 | 13 | | IV | 4+ | | | S |
| 5.6 | V- | | 14 | | IV+ | 5- | | 4a | HS |
| 5.7 | V | 5a | 15 | VIIa | | 5 | | 4b | VS |
| 5.8 | V+ / VI- | 5b | 16 | VIIb | V- | 5+ | 4  4+ | 4c | HVS |
| 5.9 | VI | 5c | 17 | VIIc | | 6- | 5  5+ | 5a | E1 |
| 5.10a | VI+ | 6a | 18 | VIIIa | V | 6 | 6a | 5b | |
| 5.10b | VII- | | 19 | VIIIb | | | 6b | | E2 |
| 5.10c | | 6b | 20 | VIIIc | | 6+ | | | |
| 5.10d | VII | | 21 | | V+ | 7- | 6c | | E3 |
| 5.11a | VII+ | 6c | 22 | IXa | | | 7a | 5c | |
| 5.11b | | | 23 | IXb | | 7 | | | |
| 5.11c | VIII- | 7a | 24 | | VI- | 7+ | 7b | | E4 |
| 5.11d | VIII | | 25 | IXc | | | 7c | 6a | |
| 5.12a | VIII+ | 7b | | | | 8- | 8a | | E5 |
| 5.12b | IX- | 7b+ | 26 | Xa | VI | 8 | 8b | | |
| 5.12c | IX | | 27 | | | | 8c | | |
| 5.12d | IX+ | 7c | | Xb | | 8+ | 9a | 6b | E6 |
| 5.13a | | 7c+ | 28 | Xc | | 9- | 9b | | |
| 5.13b | X- | 8a | 29 | | | | 9c | | |
| 5.13c | X | 8a+ | 30 | XIa | | 9 | 10a | 6c | E7 |
| 5.13d | | 8b | 31 | | VI+ | | 10b | | |
| 5.14a | X+ | 8b+ | 32 | XIb | | | 10c | 7a | E8 |
| 5.14b | | 8c | | | | 9+ | | | |
| 5.14c | XI- | 8c+ | 33 | XIc | | | | 7b | E9 |
| 5.14d | XI | 9a | 34 | | | | | | |

YDS=Yosemite Decimal System; UIAA=Union Internationale des Associations D'Alpinisme; Fr=France; Aus=Austria; Ger=German (Saxon); CIS=Commonwealth of Independent States; Bra=Brazil; UK=United Kingdom

require careful calculation.

Grade VII: Multi-pitch routes with long sections of vertical or thin ice. Mixed routes requiring fitness and experience to link many technical moves.

Grade VIII: At present, the hardest few routes in Scotland.

Technical grades on ice:
As a rough guideline, 3=60°, 4=70°, 5=80° or vertical steps, 6=vertical. It should be noted that the Scottish Grading System extends to 8.

CANADIAN SYSTEM

The following description of the Canadian System is presented by Joe Josephson. He notes that all grades stated in this description are arrived at by comparisons between routes in the Rockies. Little or no thought is given to routes outside the range.

In the Canadian System, the grade of a route is the combination of its length, commitment required, technical difficulty and seriousness. Most people seem to focus solely upon the Technical Grade; however, ice climbing in the Rockies involves a number of variables, many of which are unique to the area.

*Commitment Grade* (Roman numerals I to VII): Also called Engagement Grade. The key factors here are the length and difficulty of approach and descent, length of the climb itself, the sustained nature of the climbing, and the objective hazard. The present modern routes are progressively thinner and on more fragile features. In some climbing areas, these qualities are included in the overall Commitment Grade. However, due to the added factor of severe remoteness of many Rockies routes, this notion is hard to include in a Rockies Commitment Grade. Thus, this system adds a Seriousness Grade (to be discussed later). Commitment Grades given here are specific for frozen waterfalls and alpine routes that are considered as waterfall ice routes.

I. A very short and easy climb within minutes of the car with no avalanche hazard and easy descent by fixed anchors or walking off. Very little commitment.

II. A route of one or two pitches within easy reach of a vehicle or emergency facilities, and little or no objective hazard. A quick descent by rappel or walk off.

III. A multi-pitch route at low elevation or a one-pitch route with an involved approach (one hour or more and/or no trail) on foot or ski demanding good winter travel skills. The route may take from several hours to most of a day to complete. The approach and/or the climb are subject to occasional winter hazards including avalanche. Descent is usually by rappelling and may require you to make your own anchors.

IV. A multi-pitch route at higher elevations or remote regions and thus more subject to weather patterns and objective (primarily avalanche) hazards. May require several hours of approach on foot or ski with a greater knowledge of mountain travel and hazards. Descents may be over hazardous terrain and/or require construction of your own anchors.

V. A long climb that requires a full day to complete by a competent party. Usually on a high mountain face or gully ending above treeline. Subject to sustained climbing and/or avalanche hazards with a long involved approach on foot or ski. A high level of climbing experience and winter travel skills are needed to climb safely. Descent involves multiple rappels from your own anchors.

VI. A long waterfall with all the characteristics of a large alpine route. The climbing will be very sustained for its given technical grade. Only the best climbers will complete it in a day. Often requires a ski and/or glacier approach with a difficult and tiring descent. Objective hazards will be high, and may include: avalanche, falling seracs, high altitude, whiteout, crevasses and/or remoteness. An extraordinary degree of fitness and experience is required.

VII. A route that has every characteristic of a Grade VI but considerably longer and harder, both physically and emotionally. The climbing will be technically very difficult for many pitches and may take days to approach and climb. Objective hazards, such as large avalanche bowls and/or active seracs, will be very high. A 50-50 chance of getting the chop.

*Technical Grade* (Degree 1 to 8): This part accounts for the pure nature of the climbing on the single most sustained technical feature of a route. The predominant features contributing to this Technical

Grade are length of a pitch, its overall steepness and the usual characteristics of the ice, which may include blue or plastic ice, chandelier mushrooms, thin plates, and/or overhanging bulges. In this description, it is designated by the acronym WI ("Water Ice"). In order to distinguish it from its Engagement Grade, the Technical Grade can also be summarized as the Degree of a route.

WI1: A frozen lake or stream bed. No one has had the audacity to yet claim a first ascent of a WI1.

WI2: A pitch with short sections up to 80°. Good possibilities for protection and anchors.

WI3: Sustained ice up to 80°. Requires that parties be adept at placing protection and establishing belays. May have short sections of steeper ice but will have good resting places and the ice is usually good.

WI4: A sustained full pitch of off-vertical or a shorter length (10-25m) of vertical ice. The ice may have some technical features like chandeliers and may have long runouts between resting places.

WI5: A long strenuous pitch. May be a full ropelength of 88-90° on good ice with few if any resting places, or a shorter (20-40m) pitch on bad featureless ice. Adequate protection will require excellent technique.

WI6: A full 50-meter pitch of dead-vertical ice or a shorter length of nasty proportions. Few if any resting sites. Protection will be put in while standing on frontpoints or in awkward situations. The ice quality is variable and the climbing is technical. Technique and efficiency are at a premium.

WI7: A full pitch of near-vertical or vertical ice that is very thin, or a long overhanging technical column of dubious adhesion. Requires diverse and creative techniques to climb and find protection. A very physically and emotionally draining pitch.

WI8. These routes do exist. We should never say that we have reached the pinnacle of technical possibility. All we need is the proper vision to see the lines and an adequate sense of the requirements needed, both technically and in terms of the hazards involved. Some time will be needed to establish and understand the WI8 grade and for people to learn how "to see" routes of such insane difficulty.

*Seriousness Grade*: R: Reserved for very thin routes, this is similar to the "runout" designation given in many rock climbing areas. Depending upon the season and the time of year, particularly early season, many routes may fall into this category and then fill out to a safer thickness later in the year. The "R" designation should be reserved for routes that are traditionally very thin even in the best of years. On these routes, a party will be faced with long runouts with difficulty and/or creativity required to find adequate protection from the ice and/or the rock. Mixed routes may fall into this category.

X: These are very fragile routes that stand a possible chance of collapse while climbing them. By definition, these routes are usually runout as well. Therefore all the caution reserved for an "R" climb should be noted here. Again, an early season ascent can place a steep pillar into this category and then later in the year it may fill out to be quite solid.

*Rock Grades*: When a pitch is given a rock grading, this means the climbing is mostly on rock but may have sections of verglas, moss or snow. Rock climbing is graded on the YDS system from 5.0 to 5.10 and up. However, these pitches usually involve crampons, so direct translation is very sticky indeed. The rock grade is generally how difficult the pitch "feels." With rock shoes and a chalk bag in the sun it will undoubtedly be easier, but it still means you must be competent at the stated grade.

*Length (in meters)*: Understanding the length of climb is important in estimating its overall difficulty and your ability to safely complete the route. Length means the total vertical gain from the bottom of the route to the top.

NEW ENGLAND ICE RATING SYSTEM

This system was first described by Rick Wilcox in the early 1970s. It is used extensively in New England and was developed for the water ice found there. This system applies to a normal winter ascent of a route in moderate weather conditions. The system also incorporates a Commitment Rating, which indicates the time and logistical requirements of a climb.

NEI 1: Low-angle water ice of 40-50°, or long, moderate snow climbs requiring a basic level of technical expertise for safety.

NEI 2: Low-angle water ice routes with short bulges up to 60°.

NEI 3: Steeper water ice of 50-60° with 70-80° bulges.

NEI 4: Short, vertical columns, interspersed with rests on 50-60° ice; fairly sustained climbing.

NEI 5: Generally, multi-pitch ice climbs with sustained difficulties and/or strenuous vertical columns with little rest possible.

NEI 5+: Multi-pitch routes with a heightened degree of seriousness, long vertical sections, and extremely sustained difficulties.

*Commitment Rating*

I: Up to several hours.

II: About half a day.

III: A full day (up to seven or eight hours).

IV: A substantial undertaking; a very long day, possibly including a bivouac.

V: A big wall climb of one-and-a-half to two days. Could be done in a single day by a very fit team.

VI: Multi-day big wall climbs requiring more than two days.

VII: Big wall ascents in remote alpine situations.

WATER ICE, ALPINE ICE, AND MIXED GRADES

Jeff Lowe began developing a system in the late 1970s for grading the technical difficulties of ice routes. It was meant to be used in conjunction with the Commitment Rating of the New England System. The type of ice to be found on a climb is designated by the letters AI, indicating alpine ice, or WI, indicating water ice, preceding the technical classification. When the primary difficulties of a climb are on mixed rock and ice climbed in crampons, the classification is proceeded by an M.

| Ice Classification (AI, WI, or M) | Rock Classification |
|---|---|
| 1: Up to 50° snow or 35° ice | 1st to 3rd class |
| 2: Up to 60° snow or 40° ice | 4th class |
| 3: Up to 80° snow or 75° ice | 5.0-5.7 |
| 4: Up to vertical snow or 85° ice | 5.8-5.9 |
| 5: Overhanging cornices or 90° ice | 5.10 |
| 6: Very thin or technical 90°-plus ice | 5.11 |
| 7: 95° ice or overhanging mixed | 5.11 |
| 8: Technical or overhanging mixed | 5.12 |
| 9: Technical overhanging mixed | 5.1 |
| 10: Sustained overhanging mixed | 5.14 |

MOUNTAINEERING GRADES

There are currently four major systems used to grade the difficulty of mountaineering objectives. The French system pioneered the concept of grading. It has stood the test of time and is still in use. The National Climbing Classification System (NCCS), developed largely by Leigh Ortenburger in the United States, denotes grades for alpine objectives. The Russian system with its three-fold class structure is very applicable to high elevations. The Alaskan Grade, developed by Jonathan Waterman, is based on a 1966 Boyd J. Everett, Jr. paper, "The organization of an Alaskan Expedition." The quality and consistency of the routes used as standards in this system have led to its rapid acceptance. As with the ice ratings, each system is best described according to its own particular merits.

FRENCH SYSTEM

The overall seriousness of the climb is assessed as a whole (based on normal conditions but taking into account altitude, length, objective dangers, problems of retreat, difficulty of route finding, quality of rock), then combined with the technical standard of individual rock pitches, which are described by French rock grades. Overall standards are described as:

| Facile | (F) |
|---|---|
| Peu difficile | (PD) |
| Assez difficile | (AD) |
| Difficile | (D) |
| Tres Difficile | (TD) |
| Extrement Difficile | (ED1, ED2) |
| Abominable | (ABO) |

RUSSIAN

The Russian system is comprised of three different systems (Categories, Grades, and Classes) that, when combined, represent an accurate portrayal of a route.

*Grades.* There are 11 grades and sub-grades of difficulty in the Russian system. These range from 1B through 6A/B. These grades do not denote whether a route is ice or rock or at a high or low altitude. Grades only take into account the ascent and not approaches and descents; they reflect the overall experience and knowledge necessary for a climber to adequately ascend a route. Thus an ascent of Shiprock and the West Buttress of Denali could both be classified as 3B. A route on the Eiger and on El Capitan could both be classified as 5A. The classification of 6B is reserved for the extraordinarily hard, top-level routes.

UIAA ratings are used to describe the difficulty of individual pitches on a route. These range from I to IV, with sub-grades of + and - between II and VI. A1-A4 are used to describe the difficulty of aid pitches. A lower case "e" is used to indicate if bolts were placed on the pitch.

1B: You may encounter rocks, with elements of II climbing on rocks, ice or snow. There is no need to use any gear to set up belay points or anchors.

2A: Contains one to two pitches of II+ category climbing. The rest (up to ten pitches) will be easy II category climbing that may require use of a rope but does not require anchors or belay points.

2B: Normally contains one to two pitches of II+ category climbing with elements of III category climbing. The rest, up to ten piches, can be II climbing.

3A: Contains one or one-and-a-half pitches of III or III+ climbing. Could be a rock, mixed or ice/snow route.

3B: A 3B route would have one to two crux pitches of III+ climbing with elements of IV category climbing. It normally takes six to 12 hours to complete the route, or it can be longer depending on the area and conditions.

4A: IV climbing routes normally contain two to three pitches of IVto IV+ climbing. The rest (up to ten pitches or more) is III to III+ climbing. Normally, it takes one-half to one day to complete the route. It can be a rock, mixed or ice/snow route.

4B: Contains two to three pitches of IV+ climbing with elements of V (crux moves or overhangs) climbing. Total number of pitches is about five to 12. The rest of climbing is IV to IV. It would take one-half to two days to complete the route, depending on the area.

5A: Contains two to three pitches of V climbing. The rest of the pitches (up to ten or more) are IV to IV+ climbing. There are rock, mixed and ice/snow 5A routes. It takes one to three days to complete the route, depending on the region of location.

5B: Significantly harder than 5A. Normally a two (or more) day route. It should contain at least two or three pitches of V climbing with elements of VI climbing. Normally, these routes are about ten to 12 pitches long, so the rest of climbing is IV+ to V climbing. Can be either rock or mixed routes.

6A and 6B: The harder routes. They should include several pitches of VI climbing. They are normally about 20 or more pitch routes where the rest of climbing is V climbing.

*Classes*: Classes were developed under the old Soviet system of competition mountaineering. Of the eight classes, four would be chosen for a given competition.

High Altitude: Peaks above 6500 meters

High Altitude—Technical: Peaks between 5201 meters and 6500 meters

Technical: Peaks between 4200 meters and 5200 meters. Big walls usually fall into this class.

Rock: Peaks less than 4200 meters.

Ice-Snow: This class was implemented to raise the technical ice climbing skills of Soviet climbers, which were lacking due to inferior equipment.

Traverse: The linking of two or more mountains, climbed one after another, with descent by a different route.

Winter: This class relies entirely on the temporal aspect of the season. Ascents must fall within certain dates in each region.

NCCS GRADES

The National Climbing Classification System (NCCS) describes the overall difficulty of a multi-pitch alpine climb in terms of time and technical rock difficulty. It takes the following factors into account: length of the climb, number of hard pitches, average pitch difficulty, difficulty of the hardest pitch, commitment, route-finding problems, ascent time, rockfall, icefall, weather problems, approach, and remoteness of an area. It should be emphasized that an increase in grade mandates an increasing level of psychological preparation and commitment.

Grade I: Normally requires only several hours to do the technical portion; can be of any technical difficulty.

Grade II: Normally requires half a day for the technical portion; can be of any technical difficulty.

Grade III: Normally requires a full day for the technical portion; can be of any technical difficulty.

Grade IV: Expected to take one long hard day of technical climbing (longer on the first ascent); the hardest pitch is usually no less than 5.7.

Grade V: Expected to take an average of one-and-a-half days; the hardest pitch is rarely less than 5.8.

Grade VI: Usually takes two or more days; generally includes considerably difficult free climbing and/or aid climbing.

Grade VII: Big walls in very remote locations that are climbed in an alpine style. These are long climbs that are exposed to severe weather with complex approaches.

ALASKA GRADE

A grading system unique to Alaska is needed because of the severe storms, the cold, the altitude, and the extensive cornicing. Each ascending grade has all the elements of the previous grade.

Grade 1: An easy glacier route.

Grade 2: Moderate, with no technical difficulties aside from knife-edges, high altitude, and weather problems.

Grade 3: Moderate to hard; a mildly technical climb with occasional cornicing and short steep sections.

Grade 4: Hard to difficult; involves more sustained climbing.

Grade 5: Difficult, with sustained technical climbing requiring a high level of commitment. Scant bivouac sites.

Grade 6: Severe, with poor retreat options (generally long, corniced ridges), hanging bivouacs subjected to spindrift avalanches, or offering the highest standards of sustained technical climbing for over 4,000 feet.

AID CLIMBING

(The following explanation of the A1 to A5 grading system for aid climbing pitches is given by John Middendorf.) Climbing sections of rock that are impassable free but accept gear to allow progress is considered aid climbing. Aid climbing's greatest value is that it allows climbers to ascend the long awesome rock walls and faces in the world's wild places that would otherwise be unclimbable. Special techniques, skills, and equipment are required. Aid climbing, though more cumbersome and complex than free climbing, is an essential technique for a climber's ability to ascend the vertical and overhanging milieu of his or her pursuit.

The scope of this description is to define the A1 to A5 system of grading individual aid pitches. First a note on the overall grading system of a particular big-wall climb. A climb rated Grade VI 5.10 A4 indicates the length (Grade VI indicates a greater than two-day climb), the maximum free difficulty (5.10), and the hardest aid pitch (A4). The overall grading system, however, never tells the full story. The same Grade VI 5.10 A4 rating could apply to an eight-pitch, three-day route with only one pitch of A4 and a short, well-protected section of 5.10, or it could represent a horrendous 30-pitch, ten-day nail-up, with multiple horror-show A4 pitches and bold unprotected pitches of 5.10. Big-wall climbing is such, however, that the general difficulty of a route becomes apparent once you see the climb in question, and the intimidation that one feels when looking up at a massive chunk of stone is roughly proportional to the effort and skill that will be required to climb it.

*Ratings*

A0: Also known as "French-free." Uses gear to make progress, but generally no aiders required. Examples: Half Dome Regular Route, sections of the *Nose* route on El Cap, the first two pitches of the West Face (either a quick 5.10 A0 with three points of aid, or tricky 5.11c).

A1: Easy aid. Placements are straightforward and solid. No risk of any piece pulling out. Aiders generally required. Fast and simple for C1, the hammerless corresponding grade, but not necessarily fast and simple for nailing pitches. Examples (clean): the non-5.12 version of the *Salathé* Headwall, *Prodigal Son* on Angel's Landing and *Touchstone Wall* in Zion.

A2: Moderate aid. Placements generally solid but possibly awkward and strenuous to place. Maybe a tenuous placement or two above good pro with no fall danger. Examples: the right side of El Cap Tower (nailing), *Moonlight Buttress* and *Space Shot* in Zion (clean).

A2+: Like A2, but with possibly several tenuous placements above good pro. Twenty- to 30-foot fall potential but with little danger of hitting anything. Route finding abilities may be required. Examples: the new-wave grades of *Mescalito* and the *Shield* on El Cap, the Kor route on the Titan in the Fisher Towers area.

A3: Hard aid. Testing methods required. Involves many tenuous placements in a row. Generally, solid placements that could hold a fall found within a pitch. Long fall potential up to 50 feet (six to eight placements ripping), but generally safe from serious danger. Usually requires several hours to complete a pitch due to complexity of placements. Examples: The *Pacific Ocean Wall* lower crux pitches (30 feet between original bolts on manky fixed copperheads), Standing Rock in the desert (the crux being a traverse on the first pitch with very marginal gear and 30-foot swing potential into a corner).

A3+: Like A3, but with dangerous fall potential. Tenuous placements (such as marginal tied-off pins or a hook on a fractured edge) after long stretches of body-weight pieces (here body-weight placements are considered for all practical purposes as any piece of gear not solid enough to hold a fall). Potential to get hurt if good judgement is not exercised. Time required generally exceeds three hours for experienced aid climbers. Example: Pitch three of *Days of No Future* on Angel's Landing in Zion, with a crux of 50 feet of birdbeaks and tied-off blades in soft sandstone followed by a blind, marginal Friend placement in loose rock that is hard to test properly, all above a ledge.

A4: Serious aid. Lots of danger. Sixty- to 100-foot fall potentials common, with uncertain landings far below. Examples: pitches on the *Kaliyuga* on Half Dome and the *Radiator* on Abraham in Zion.

A4+: More serious than A4. These leads generally take many hours to complete and require the climber to endure long periods of uncertainty and fear, often requiring a ballet-like efficiency of movement in order not to upset the tenuous integrity of marginal placements. Examples: the "Welcome to Wyoming" pitch (formerly the "Psycho Killer" pitch) on the *Wyoming Sheep Ranch* on El Cap, which requires 50 feet of climbing through a loose, broken, and rotten diorite roof with very marginal, scary placements like stoppers wedged in between two loose, shifting, rope-slicing slivers of rock, all over a big jagged loose ledge that would surely break bones and maim the climber. The pitch is then followed by 100 feet of hooking interspersed with a few rivets to the belay.

A5: Extreme aid. Nothing really trustworthy of catching a fall for the entire pitch. Rating should be reserved only for pitches with no bolts or rivets (holes) for the entire pitch. Examples: pitches on the *Jolly Roger* and the *Wyoming Sheep Ranch* on El Cap, Jim Beyer routes in Arches National Park and the Fisher Towers.

A6: A theoretical grade. A5 climbing with marginal belays that would not hold a fall.

# Contributors' Guidelines

*The American Alpine Journal* records the significant climbing accomplishments of the world in an annual volume. We encourage climbers to submit brief (250-500 words), factual accounts of their climbs and expeditions. While we welcome submissions in a variety of forms, contributors are encouraged to follow certain guidelines when submitting materials. Accounts should be submitted by e-mail. Alternatively, submit accounts by regular post both as a hard copy and on disk; both Mac and PC disks are acceptable. When submitting an account on disk, please save it as a text file. Please include your club affiliation when submitting accounts.

Deadlines for all accounts are February 1 for the preceding calendar year of January 1 to December 31. For Patagonian climbs, the deadline is extended to February 15.

We encourage contributors to submit relevant photographs; we accept both black-and-white and color slides and prints. When submitting an image to show a route line, we ask that you submit the image along with a photo- or laser-copy and draw the lines in on the copy. Alternatively, submit two copies of the same image (a virgin copy and a copy with the route line drawn in), or draw the line of the route on a vellum or similar tracing paper overlay. Please do not draw directly on the photograph.

We prefer original slides and artwork in all instances. Duplicates should be reproduction quality. Please send all images via registered mail. *The American Alpine Journal* is not responsible for images lost or damaged in the mail. Topos and maps are also encouraged; camera-ready original copies are necessary for quality reproduction.

We do not pay for accounts or lead articles. Those accounts from which we publish a photograph will receive a complimentary copy of the *Journal*. Authors of lead articles and the photographer of the cover photo will receive a one-year complimentary membership to The American Alpine Club.

Please address all correspondences to:

The American Alpine Journal
710 Tenth Street, Suite 140
Golden, Colorado 80401
Tel.: (303) 384 0110
Fax: (303) 384 0111
E-mail:aaj@americanalpineclub.org
http://www.americanalpineclub.org

# Index

Compiled by Jessica Kany